Britain's
MOTOR INDUSTRY

As part of our ongoing market research, we are always pleased to receive comments about our books, suggestions for new titles, or requests for catalogues. Please write to: The Editorial Director, G. T. Foulis & Co., Sparkford, Near Yeovil, Somerset BA22 7JJ.

Britain's MOTOR INDUSTRY

THE FIRST HUNDRED YEARS

The fluctuating fortunes of Britain's car manufacturers, from Queen Victoria's time to the present day

Nick Georgano, Nick Baldwin, Anders Clausager and Jonathan Wood
Edited by Nick Georgano. Foreword by HRH Prince Michael of Kent.

G.T. Foulis & Company

First published in 1995

British Library Cataloguing-in-Publication Data:
A catalogue record for this book is available from the British Library.

ISBN 0-85429-923-8

Library of Congress catalog card no. 95-78121

G. T. Foulis & Company is an imprint of Haynes Publishing, Sparkford, Nr. Yeovil, Somerset, BA22 7JJ.

Printed in Great Britain by BPC Hazell Books Limited.

Contents

Acknowledgements

The Editor and Publisher would like to acknowledge the assistance of the following organisations, without which the publication of the book would not have been possible:
The British Motor Centenary Trust
The Michael Sedgwick Memorial Trust
The Museum of British Road Transport, Coventry
The Society of Motor Manufacturers & Traders

The Editor and Authors would like to thank the following for their great help in the preparation of the book.

Tony Benn for granting an interview and permission to use unpublished excerpts from his diaries, as well as published material; Ron Lucas for a lengthy interview; David Burgess-Wise, Mircc Decet, Brian Demaus, Bryan Goodman, Derek Grossmark, Brian Heath (Editor, *The Automobile*), Ferdy Hediger, Peter Hull, Malcolm Jeal, Ivan Mahy, Keith Marvin, Kevin Morley, Philip Porter, Alan Sutton and Michael Ware (Curator, National Motor Museum). Also Annice Collett and Marie Tieche of the National Motor Museum Library for their unstinting help; Lynda Springate and Jonathan Day of the National Motor Museum Photographic Library; Karam Ram of the British Motor Industry Heritage Trust; and Elaine English of the Hulton Deutsch Collection.

Henrietta Georgano gave invaluable last-minute help with indexing and collating the manuscript.

Key to acknowledgements abbreviations: BMIHT: British Motor Industry Heritage Trust; NB: Nick Baldwin Collection; NMM: National Motor Museum, Beaulieu.

Conversion Chart

Measurements appearing in the text have been largely left in the forms used during the period to which they refer. The following is designed to assist the reader in converting these to metric equivalents.

Weights
1 lb = 0.453 kg
1 kg = 1.208 lb

Dimensions
1 in = 2.54 cm
1 ft = 0.305 m
1 mile = 1,609 km
1 acre = 0.405 hectares
1 m − 3.281 ft
1 cm = 0.394 in
1 km = 0.621 miles
1 hectare = 2.471 acres

Money
1d (penny) = 0.417p
12d = 1s (shilling)
1s = 5p
20s = £1
1p − 2.4d

Foreword by
HRH Prince Michael of Kent

A centenary is always worth celebrating, particularly when the hundred years cover such a rich history as does Britain's Motor Industry. It is an astonishing story of high hopes, achievement, abject failure and, on occasion, downright knavery. In the industry's infant years characters abounded such as Harry Lawson, who was more interested in floating companies than in making cars, and Edward Joel Pennington, whose claims for his machines bordered on the fantastic.

Given the prejudice of the public and the hostile legislation of Parliament, combined with the charla-tans' activities, it is surprising that the industry survived at all. But it did, and in 1913 Britain turned out 34,000 motor vehicles, of which 25,000 were passenger cars.

In the 1920s our industry surged ahead to overtake France as the leading European car maker, second only to the United States. The star players were now industrialists like Herbert Austin and William Morris, ably backed up by W.O. Bentley, Cecil Kimber of MG and, later, William Lyons of Jaguar. All these men, and many others, are described in this book through the eyes of four of our leading motor historians. Though complex matters are covered, such as the labour problems in the post-war era, and Britain's decline as a producer and exporter, the story is always readable as well as informative.

We now have a motor industry in Britain, as opposed to a British motor industry. The overseas investment in our manufacturing base reflects great credit on the British workforce and the way it has adapted to the challenges of a world industry. We can be proud of our history, and look forward with con-fidence to a successful future as we continue to satisfy an ever more demanding consumer.

Here's to the next hundred years!

The Pioneers

Nick Georgano

The beginnings of the motor car are not the same as the beginnings of the motor industry. Among important industry figures one would think of Herbert Austin, William Morris and Frederick Henry Royce; but who, apart from dedicated historians, has heard of Edward Butler, Frederick Bremer, John Henry Knight or the Santler brothers? Only the Santlers built more than one car each, yet all were the true pioneers of the British motor car, even if they had little to do with the industry itself.

The origins of the British passenger car can be traced back to the middle of the nineteenth century. It is often forgotten that at least 50 steam carriages had been built before 1850, and that some of these operated regular services in London, particularly on the Stratford to Paddington via the Bank route, which Walter Hancock worked with his 22-passenger steam bus, *The Automaton*, in 1836. Hancock concerned himself mainly with buses, which are outside the scope of this book, but his last vehicle could certainly be considered as Britain's first passenger car. It was built in 1838, and was a four-seater machine variously called a gig or phaeton. He drove it mostly around his home village of Stratford, but on occasions ventured 'up west' to Hyde Park where he joined the fashionable carriage folk, parading round for three or four hours, making little noise and causing no alarm to horses. A correspondent to *The Mechanic's Magazine* observed that it manoeuvred well and attracted the favourable attention of British and foreign nobility, including the Prussian ambassador, Prince Puttbuss.

On the other hand, George Dacre, clerk to the trustees of the Middlesex & Essex Trusts, wrote that 'a person of the name of Hancock travels about continuously by locomotive engines on the road, and with smaller ones which he calls gigs . . . and they frighten the horses to such an extent that I have often been requested to interfere on the subject . . . I see him every day; he first alters one part of his machinery, then another . . . it is merely an experiment.'

'Merely an experiment' described most of the subsequent machines up to the 1890s, but one engineer did go so far as to offer his carriages for sale. He was Thomas Rickett, manager and chief engineer of the Castle Foundry at Buckingham. This small works went in for agricultural engineering, making ploughs and seed drills, and in 1857 added steam engines to their range. A year later Rickett built a steam plough which was demonstrated at a number of agricultural shows. It was probably at one of these that Rickett came to the attention of the Marquess of Stafford

The Earl of Caithness's steam carriage on the occasion of its epic journey from Inverness to Barrogill Castle in August 1860. The Earl is at the tiller; next to him are the Countess and the Revd. William Ross of Kintore. Thomas Rickett is seated at the rear, where he would have been busy stoking for much of the journey. (NMM)

who was very interested in steam cultivation, and later, as the Duke of Sutherland, was to spend £250,000 on the reclamation of Scottish moorland for agriculture, using the Fowler two-engine ploughing system. Possibly the Marquess suggested the idea of a steam road carriage, or perhaps Rickett had thought of it already. Anyway, it was ready by the end of 1858. It was a three-wheeler powered by a two-cylinder engine with a bore and stroke of 3 x 9 in, which drove the offside rear wheel by chain. The boiler pressure was 110 psi. There was a bench seat at the front for three passengers, one of whom was responsible for the steering tiller and had under his control the regulator, reversing lever and brake lever. At the rear of the carriage sat, or rather crouched, the stoker, and beside him was the coal bunker.

The Marquess's car was typical in that it was built purely for pleasure and interest, with no commercial use in mind. However, another customer soon appeared in the person of the Earl of Caithness; the machine which Rickett built for him differed from the first in having a shorter stroke (3½ x 7 in), a 150 psi boiler, and spur gear drive in place of the chain. The seating arrangements were the same. A top speed of nearly 20 mph was claimed on level ground, though with a full load 10 mph was a more realistic figure.

The Caithness carriage became more famous than its predecessor, owing to a 146-mile drive over very hilly terrain, from Inverness to the Earl's seat at Barrogill Castle, near Thurso. This has now resumed its older name, the Castle of Mey, and is the home of Queen Elizabeth the Queen Mother. The Earl set out on 3 August 1860, accompanied by his wife and the Rev William Ross of Kintore, with Thomas Rickett occupying the stoker's place at the rear. The most daunting part of the journey was the ascent of the Ord of Caithness, a climb of nearly 900 ft in five miles. The crowd was so great that the passengers could hardly dismount from the car,

but not all the spectators were enthusiastic. 'The Earll will ne'er get o'er the Ord,' muttered the fishermen of Helmsdale gloomily, but undeterred he set his little carriage at the hill, which rises straight out of the town, with gradients of 1:7 in places. 'Winding up the precipitous route,' reported *The Illustrated London News*, 'the deep, strong but regular beat of the engine told that, though severely taxed, the task was not more than it could manage, and without once stopping or flagging it reached the summit.'[1]

The Earl was subsequently made an honorary Burgess of Wick, and at the presentation his wife made a rousing speech: 'This is one of the proudest and happiest days of my life, to see my husband made a Burgess of Wick, and to think that he, a Caithness man, has taught the people in the South that it is possible to cross the Ord in a steam carriage, which many thought an impossibility. [Loud cheers.] I am sure that as long as Caithness can boast of a steam carriage on its common roads, it has no cause to be ashamed, and may claim to itself what the Americans would style the character of a go-ahead county.'[2]

Parkyns was found guilty of riding at 5 mph, and fined one shilling

---

For how long the carriage ran on the roads of Caithness we do not know, but the Earl was sufficiently pleased to write enthusiastically about it in *The Engineer*. This encouraged Rickett to place an advertisement in the same magazine in November 1860, quoting a price of £180 to £200 each. Equivalent to about £9,000 today, it does not seem an unreasonable figure, and was less than a first-class horse-drawn carriage from a London coachbuilder such as Barker or Hooper. However, the market did not exist; with the exception of wealthy enthusiasts like the Marquess of Stafford and the Earl of Caithness, those who were interested in steam cars preferred to build their own rather

than buy a ready-made product from someone else.

1865 saw the passing of the second Locomotives Act which, among other things, restricted speeds to 4 mph in open country and 2 mph in towns and villages. (The 1861 Act had been more generous, the limits being 10 and 5 mph.) It also stipulated that at least three persons should be in charge of each vehicle, one of them to precede the locomotive at a distance of 60 yd, and to carry a red flag. Referring mainly to agricultural traction engines, which were far more numerous than private carriages, it has been blamed for discouraging the development of the car, particularly as it was not repealed until 1896, when the petrol-engined car was becoming well-established on the Continent. This is probably truer of would-be manufacturers than of private constructors, who regarded legal restrictions as a challenge. One who hoped in 1862 to begin a trade in 'quick-speed locomotives', Richard Tangye, blamed the Act for Britain's lagging behind other nations many years later. Writing in 1905, he said 'But for the action of a bovine Parliament, the manufacture of motor cars would have taken root in England forty years ago, and the foreign nations would have been customers instead of pioneers followed at a distance by ourselves.'[3]

Despite their discouragements, at least twenty engineers built light steam cars between 1860 and 1880. None got anywhere near commercial production. In 1881 A. H. Bateman & Co, cycle makers of East Greenwich, built a steam tricycle designed by Sir Thomas Parkyns of Beckenham, Kent. It was fired not by coal or coke, but by liquid fuel, at first methylated spirit, then petrol, and apart from a box at one side of the rider's legs resembled a pedal tricycle. Unfortunately Parkyns was found guilty of the heinous crime of riding at 5 mph in a built-up area, and was fined one shilling on each of five counts. He appealed to the High Court but lost. This put paid to the plans that Bateman and Parkyns had for manufacture. The famous pioneer motorist Sir David Salomons cancelled his order for a steam tricycle, though he later bought Parkyns' machine. It appeared at exhibitions in 1889 and 1895.

Britain's first passenger car to be exported was an electrically-powered four-seater dogcart made by Magnus Volk, who had designed the electric sea front railway at Brighton. In 1887 he began testing his machine, which had a 0.5 hp motor made by the Acme & Immisch Electric Works of London, and a walnut wood body with *dos-a-dos* seating, built by Job Pack of the Sussex Coach Works in Brighton. On a smooth level surface it could reach 9 mph, but any loose surface brought the speed down to 4 mph, and it could not cope with a gradient of more than 1:30.

Volk's car was written up not only in the British papers, but in the *Leipzig Zeitung*, which somehow came to the attention of the Sultan of Turkey, Abdul Hamid II, known as Abdul the Red. He was so taken with the sound of Volk's dogcart that he ordered his chamberlain to send a telegram to Brighton: 'Seen in the Leipzig illustrated newspaper description of your electric dogcart. Please give me details of its price, and where to get one.' Two days later, before Volk had time to reply, the impatient Sultan sent another telegram: 'Please send speedily to my address one electric carriage. The price mentioned in your dispatch will be paid by myself to the Ottoman Bank first.' Worried by the delay, and doubtless used to getting what he wanted instantly, he sent a third telegram: 'No need for discussing price. Send dogcart earliest possible.'

Preparing the royal machine took some months. It used the same combination of Immisch motor, though now with double the power at 1 hp, and body by Mr Pack which was upholstered with the Turkish Imperial Crest. On test at Camden Town skating rink (conveniently near Immisch's works), it reached a giddy 10 mph. Unlike the original which was a three-wheeler, the second car had four wheels, with the front pair set close

Magnus Volk on his first electric three-wheeler of 1887. It had a 0.5 hp electric motor, and two speeds, 3½ and 7 mph. Next to him is his sister-in-law and on the dos-a-dos *seat is his son, Bert. (NMM)*

together, and centre pivot steering. Even so, it was reported that the Sultan's slaves had to manhandle the vehicle around the narrow paths of the Palace.

The Sultan was sufficiently impressed to order a second carriage, which had a body by the famous London firm of Thrupp & Maberly. One or two more electric cars were made by Volk, and possibly by Acme & Immisch on their own, but there was insufficient demand to justify anything which one could call production. This was the great problem for all the pioneers; the technology was there, and some respectable revenue would have enabled it to be improved more quickly than it was, but public awareness was too small. Even Carl Benz might never have started production without orders from his French agent Emile Roger.

Although it eventually became the dominant motive power, internal combustion fared no better than steam or electricity as far as pioneers were concerned. Only six known such vehi-

cles were made in England before the production year of 1896, of which the first was the 'Petrol-Cycle' three wheeler completed by Edward Butler in 1888. Butler was a London engineer who had served his apprenticeship with Brown & May, traction engine builders of Devizes, Wiltshire. In 1884 he applied for a patent for 'the mechanical propulsion of cycles', and drawings were shown at the Stanley Cycle Club Show and the International Inventions Exhibition, both of 1885. It was another three years before Butler's car was completed; as he had no suitable workshop, it was built by Charles T. Crowden at the Greenwich factory of steam fire-engine makers Merryweather & Sons. Crowden later became chief engineer of the Humber Cycle Co and works manager of the Great Horseless Carriage Co of Coventry.

Butler's Petrol-Cycle was in some ways an advanced machine; the single wheel was at the rear, and it had something of the appearance of the later French-designed Leon Bollées, which were the first passenger vehicles to go into production in England. The two-cylinder engine was originally a two-stroke with dimensions of 2¼ x 8 in giving a capacity of 1,041 cc, but it was redesigned as a four-stroke with a stroke reduced to 5 in. Capacity was then 650 cc. Among advanced features were Ackermann steering of the front wheels, mechanically operated inlet valves, and a spray carburettor five years before Wilhelm Maybach made his. There was no clutch or gearbox, and starting was effected by raising the driving wheel from the ground on small rollers, and starting the engine by compressed air, in the manner of some stationary engines.

Before the tricycle had been completed, Butler planned his Patent Petrol Cycle Syndicate to manufacture his machine, but he seems to have got cold feet very rapidly, and even before the tricycle took to the road he abandoned plans to make any replicas, 'because of the current state of highway law'. According to an article in *The Autocar*[4] quoting Charles Crowden, 'the machine was got to work, and worked fairly satisfactorily, but as they were unable to run it in this

country, the syndicate who found the money for it would not go any further with it.' After the Locomotives on Highways Act of 1896 raised the speed limit to a more reasonable 12 mph, Butler took his tricycle out again, and then sold the design to the British Motor Syndicate. This was one of H. J. Lawson's enterprises, and bought up many patents which it did not exploit.

While Butler was testing his machine at Erith in Kent, on the other side of the country another car was taking shape. The Santler brothers, Charles and Walter, were general engineers and cycle makers and repairers in Malvern, Worcestershire. According to their own claims they built a four-wheeler powered by a high pressure, vertical compound expansion, marine-type steam engine in 1889. In about 1891 a gas engine powered by a cylinder of compressed coal gas replaced the steam engine, and was subsequently replaced by a petrol engine in 1894. There has been much controversy about the date of the original car; it still exists in its final, Benz-like, form, and has been dated 1894 by the Veteran Car Club, though its engine is now a Benz as the original

petrol unit had disappeared. The brothers claimed the date 1889 on an advertising postcard issued in 1907, and in support of this Dr R. A. Sutton, the present owner, has done a great deal of research which was published in 1987 by the Michael Sedgwick Memorial Trust. He points out that the Santlers had nothing to gain by falsifying the date, and that there were many employees and others who would soon have exposed the deception, had there been one.

The Santler, or Malvernia as it is often called, can certainly be claimed as Britain's first four-wheeled car. A second car was built by the Santlers in 1897, though it had no immediate descendants. A small number of Santler cars were built between 1901 and 1922, but they owed nothing in design to the original Malvernia.

The next car was a light two-seater built by Frederick William Bremer (1872–1941) of Walthamstow, London. Completed in 1894, it had a water-cooled, single-cylinder petrol engine. This was mounted horizontally at the rear, with belt primary and chain final drive. An original feature was a wick carburettor with float feed and hot water heating to help vaporization. Bremer had little money and no workshop but plenty of ingenuity; for a flywheel he used a grindstone, and a clay pipe stem served as insulation for the sparking plug.

Bremer's car did not cover many miles before its inventor tired of it. He did make a few trips into Epping Forest (as had Hancock sixty years earlier), but they had to be conducted very early on Sunday mornings to escape the attentions of the police. The car survived to be an exhibit in the first motor museum, opened by the proprietor of *The Motor*, Edmund Dangerfield, in Oxford Street in 1912. It then spent many years in the Walthamstow Museum before emerging to take part in the Brighton Run in 1964 and 1965.

Another pioneer car which has survived to the present day is that made by John Henry Knight

The Santler, or Malvernia car laid up in a blacksmith's yard at Malvern. Photo taken between 1900 and 1907. (Courtesy Dr R. A. Sutton)

(1847–1917) of Farnham, Surrey. He was no stranger to road vehicles, having made a steam car in 1868, and by the 1890s he was in business making stationary oil engines. His three-wheeled car, powered by a single horizontal cylinder and with hot tube ignition and chain final drive, was tested during July 1895. In April 1896 he converted it to a four-wheeler. His aim in building it, he said, was 'chiefly to bring to public notice the restrictions which have hitherto prevented the use of motor carriages in England.'[5] However, by 1896 he said that he was looking for someone to take up manufacture. He never found a manufacturer, and after covering about 500 miles he retired the car in 1898 when he bought a 3½ hp Benz.[6] The Knight is now in the National Motor Museum at Beaulieu.

By the end of 1895 two British companies were offering to build cars, though neither delivered any. Atkinson & Philipson were partners in an old-established coachbuilding firm, the Northumberland Coach Factory of Newcastle upon Tyne, which had been in business since 1774, and had made railway carriages for George Stephenson. Their 'car' was a crude-looking steam brake with iron-shod wheels which they continued to advertise into 1896, though apparently without finding any buyers. Ultimately more successful was James D. Roots of London, who advertised his Roots Petrocar or Petroleum Motor Carriage in November 1895, at a price of £180. Even the three-wheeled prototype was probably not running until early 1896, but by 1897, trading as Roots & Venables, he was selling light four-wheelers. They had oil engines, like all his products which were marketed up to 1904. From 1902 they were made for Roots & Venables by Armstrong-Whitworth.

Several other companies had cars on the road by the end of 1895. They included Petter of Yeovil, whose car was also oil-engined, and George Johnston of Glasgow, whose designs were later made as Arrol-Johnstons.

The Bremer car after finishing the 1964 Brighton Run on a Walthamstow Corporation lorry. It was also entered in 1965, and completed the 54-mile journey in 7 hours, 55 minutes. (Nick Georgano)

Despite all this activity, no British-built car was available to a purchaser until the latter part of 1896.

Matters were progressing much more encouragingly on the Continent. Carl Benz built and sold his first four-wheeler in 1892, and by the end of 1894 he had sold 136 cars. In France, Panhard and Peugeot were in production with several different models, powered by Daimler-designed V-twin engines, by 1894. That year saw the first motor competition to attract more than two entries; the Paris magazine, *Le Petit Journal*, organized a trial (not a race) over the 73 miles between the capital and Rouen. By the end of April, no fewer than 102 vehicles had been entered; many existed only in the minds of their inventors, and several strange forms of motive power were listed, including 'multiple system of levers', 'system of pendulums', and 'weight of passengers'. M. Rousillot of Paris described his motive power as 'gravity', which must have presented problems on hills, and Messrs Garnier and Delannoy relied on a 'combination of animate and mechanical motor'. [7]

However, when the 21 entrants appeared for the eliminating trials on 19 July the only motive powers repre-

sented were steam and petrol. Among the latter were five Peugeots and four Panhards. The winner of the actual contest was a De Dion Bouton steam tractor pulling a horse-type carriage, but as it needed two men to operate it, it was relegated to second place, and the prize went jointly to a Peugeot and a Panhard. The main purpose of the Paris–Rouen Trial was to boost the circulation of *Le Petit Journal*, but it had the much more important side-effect of triggering a widespread interest in motor cars. Within a year Continental cars were running on British soil, and having a much greater influence than the isolated efforts of Bremer or the Santlers ever did.

As one might expect, there have been claims and counter claims about the first car to arrive in Britain. For many years it was thought to have been a Benz which London tea broker Henry Hewetson claimed he had ordered in Mannheim in August 1894, and which arrived in England on 30 November. However, a study of Benz numbers shows that this particular car (No. 309) would have left Mannheim in December 1895 or January 1896[8]. Clearly Mr Hewetson, who later held the London Benz agency, had made a false claim, though it is interesting that he did not do so in his literature of 1899, but only two years later, when sales of Benz cars were beginning to fall.

The first documented import was that of a Panhard which the Hon Evelyn Ellis bought in Paris in June 1895, and transported via Le Havre to Southampton in July. Ellis was the sixth son of Lord Howard de Walden, and was the second-largest shareholder in the Daimler Motor Syndicate which at that time was selling only engines, not complete cars. Ellis kept a man-hauled fire engine whose pump was driven by a Daimler engine at his Thames-side estate at Datchet, and also had four Daimler-powered river launches. He drove the Panhard from Micheldever to Datchet, having presumably taken it by train from Southampton to Micheldever. The 56-mile journey was written up by Ellis's partner in the Daimler Syndicate, F. R. Simms, in *The Saturday Review* of 20 July. Interestingly he refers to the Panhard as 'one of our Daimler motor carriages' on the strength of its Daimler-designed engine. The early Coventry-built Daimlers owed much more to Panhard design than to the German Daimlers.

The success and freedom from prosecution of Ellis's trip encouraged at least one sale. T. R. B. Eliot of Kelso had seen a Panhard in Paris in May, but had been put off buying one from fear that he would be prevented from using it; now he felt more confident and ordered one through Simms's Syndicate. He took delivery in December, being the first to import a car into Scotland, and also the first to buy a car through the trade rather than directly from the makers.

However, the first car on British soil, though not an import, came to the Channel Island of Guernsey a year earlier. Guernsey-born Major A. Thom was a Salvation Army officer based in Switzerland, and in the summer of 1894 he visited the island in his Peugeot *vis-a-vis* to see family and

friends and to distribute Salvation Army periodicals. It is likely that the Peugeot was not his own property but that of the Salvation Army (was it the first company car?). In November 1895 Sir David Salomons mentioned 'as an illustration of the lasting qualities and practicality of the vehicle . . . one of the Daimler-driven carriages used by the French Salvation Army, and read a letter showing that it had been in use over 7,000 miles without mishap, both on the Continent and in the Channel Islands'.[9] Major Thom stayed for several weeks, giving rides to many people and racing the local electric trams.[10] Speeds of up to 20 mph were spoken of, and these would presumably not have attracted the attention of the police, for, being semi-autonomous in government, the Channel Islands had never accepted or implemented the Locomotives on Highways Acts.

In October 1895 Sir David Salomons organized a motor exhibition at the South Eastern Counties Agricultural Show ground at Tunbridge Wells. As this was private land, the participants

had no fear of police interference. Four vehicles were shown, Salomons's own Peugeot, Ellis's Panhard, a De Dion Bouton tricycle ridden by Georges Bouton himself, and a De Dion Bouton steam tractor pulling a barouche whose front wheels had been removed, making a similar vehicle to the one which had set fastest time in the Paris–Rouen Trial. In charge of this was the Count de Dion. The vehicles were demonstrated for two hours, after which Salomons led them out onto the road into Tunbridge Wells, though they stopped short of the built-up area. The demonstration attracted much more attention than solitary journeys such as that of Ellis and Simms; national papers including *The Times* and the *Daily Telegraph* covered the event and spoke out against the legal restrictions on cars.[11]

By the end of 1895 there were perhaps two dozen motor vehicles on British roads, mostly petrol driven. The stage was set for the great expansion of the following year, when a native industry was at last to be set up.

John Henry Knight's car in its original three-wheeler form of 1895. On its conversion to four wheels in 1896 the wire-spoked rear wheels gave way to wood-spoked artilleries, and a third coil spring supplemented the two visible in this photograph. Seated on the car is Knight's foreman George Parfitt, who did most of the work on the car. (NMM)

CHAPTER ONE

The Background

Nick Baldwin

Steam power was a major force at sea, in industry, and on our rails even before Queen Victoria came to the throne in 1837. By then the first tentative steps had taken place to put steam on the common highway. The Victorian age was full of new mechanical marvels and even powered flight seemed to be within the grasp of the inventor. The development of the internal combustion engine on the Continent in the 1880s was studied with fascination by the far-sighted and ambitious and it was hardly surprising that many dreamed of making motor vehicles in Britain. After all, the Industrial Revolution had created immense manufacturing confidence, a skilled labour force, and vast wealth for a larger number of families than had even been encompassed by the traditional land owning hierarchy.

The story of the arrival of the motor vehicle in Britain follows several clearly defined paths. Firstly there were the traditional ironworking and engineering industries which looked on Continental developments as a possible direction for future business. Then there were the new light engineering concerns typified by the sewing machine and bicycle makers of Coventry and elsewhere. They were usually situated a long way from historic industrial sites or sea transport and needed to make high value items from the least possible weight of raw materials. Thirdly came the importers and business entrepreneurs who were anxious to obtain a slice of what might prove to be a lucrative business. They sought engineers in Britain who could copy or originate designs and then used their expertise to lure investors and shareholders. Finally there were the firms already involved in land or waterborne transport who became involved in the motor car business either to hedge their bets or else from a sincere belief that the future might lie with personal transport. Into this group fall surprisingly few of the railway vested-interests but instead several marine engineers like Vauxhall, Thornycroft, Maudslay and Thames.

One might also have expected traditional carriage makers and coachbuilders to have become important in the new infant industry as they did in America. However, in Britain they were less adventurous, even if Bartles and Angus Sanderson did eventually make cars. Their reluctance to make complete motor cars was in a way no more surprising than the myriad small suppliers of metal components to manufacturing industry in London and Birmingham. They wanted to see if the autocar would be a nine days' wonder before committing themselves. When some of them eventually took the plunge it was usually

The Birmingham firm of Alldays & Onions had the longest history of any British car maker, with Onions having been founded in 1650. Quadricycles were made from 1898 and light cars from 1903. This is a 7 hp two-seater entered in the Automobile Club's 1904 Light Car Trials. (NB)

with an assembled product heavily dependent on overseas ideas or materials, an example being Brown Brothers Ltd (founded 1888), whose Brown and Albruna cars were available in the 1901–12 period. Another example was Seabrook Brothers, whose Seabrooks of 1911 onwards were based on a successful cycle components factoring business founded in 1895. There was also the Marlborough, made from

1906 of French components by André & Co, a firm that was to become an important supplier of specialized parts to the motor industry. Gamages was another retail business that entered the car field, though in this case it was to supply a projected sales requirement with foreign products badged with its familiar name. The traditional engineering firms proved to be a much more conservative group who were

generally slow to put their industrial might behind the new invention. No doubt it was more difficult for a long established company with a history of careful decision-making and gradual evolution to be swept into new crazes like bicycling and automobilism.

Vickers Ltd (or Vickers Son and Maxim Ltd, as it was then called), as a relative newcomer founded in 1867, might have been expected to make a contribution, but it preferred to do so at arm's length after several years of development when it acquired Wolseley's Autocar department (run by Herbert Austin) from the Wolseley Sheep Shearing Machine Co in February 1901. Sir W. G. Armstrong Whitworth & Co, established in 1847 and with vast experience of heavy engineering as well as precision repetition work (as Vickers had with Hiram Maxim's machine-gun), was a little more adventurous. Sir Joseph Whitworth, pioneer of the standard steel thread, had merged his business interests with those of William Armstrong in 1897 and a motor components division followed soon afterwards. However, the manufacture of complete vehicles did not take place until established manufacturers could be acquired, initially Roots and Venables in 1902. This business had been making oil motors and self-propelled machines in London since 1896. Then in 1904 Armstrong Whitworth took the London built Wilson-Pilcher car under its wing and in 1919 the Siddeley Deasy, from which grew Amstrong Siddeley. Mention of Roots and Venables reminds one that components for this early pioneer came from BSA, itself an engineering concern that had grown from the late seventeenth-century Birmingham gun trade. It would become important in the car and motor cycling field and ultimately acquire Coventry Daimler in 1910.

A business with roots going back even further into Birmingham's industrial past was Alldays (1720) and

Before Starley's Safety Bicycle was available, those not sufficiently adventurous to ride a highwheeler preferred three wheels. Here is Thomas Humber on one of his company's 'Cripper' Automatic Steerer Tricycles, c.1886. (Brian Demaus/E. Chorley).

An 1892 Humber bicycle with, third from left, John Davenport Siddeley, who worked for both Humber and Rover before starting his car activities. These were to involve Siddeley, Siddeley-Deasy and Armstrong Siddeley. In 1937 he was created Baron Kenilworth. (NB)

Onions (1650), which became Onions Pneumatic Engineering Co Ltd in 1889. It made equipment for blacksmiths, such as blowers and hearths, and then added stamping machines and pneumatically-operated machinery. To these were added bicycles, and then from 1898 motor quadricycles followed by cars. In 1908 Alldays & Onions acquired the Enfield Autocar Co Ltd, a car manufacturer sharing common origins with the Royal Enfield motor cycle concern, both of which had grown from a mid-Victorian needle manufacturer named George Townsend of Hunt End, near

Redditch. His company had become the Eadie Manufacturing Co, a bicycle maker where Alexander Govan of Argyll car fame was originally employed. The Enfield Cycle Co Ltd and Eadie Manufacturing were run as separate businesses and the latter was taken over by BSA in 1907.

Clearly the motor car industry preceded that of aviation, though many car firms would later become involved in aero engines and complete aircraft. One that had equal interests in both from its virtual outset in 1905 was Iris, where Ivon de Havilland was designer. He made the first engines there for his

brother Geoffrey's burgeoning empire.

Lest the impression given is that all these great engineering firms were in England, spare a thought for the traditional heavy engineers of Scotland's Clydeside. Steam firms like Alley & Maclellan, established in 1875, eschewed the pleasure car market and made Sentinel steam wagons from 1906. The mighty Beardmore concern grew from William Beardmore's partnership at the Parkhead Forge in 1861. Famous for ships and steel, the firm also had links with steam lorry makers Duncan Stewart and J. I. Thornycroft. William Beardmore Jr was also the largest shareholder in car maker Arrol Johnston from 1902. Beardmore supplied components to many other vehicle firms before putting its own cars into production at the end of the First World War. Cars bearing the Arrol-Johnston name were built from 1896, with initial financial backing from Forth Bridge consulting engineer Sir William Arrol. The Mo-Car Syndicate, of which he was Chairman, employed George Johnston and also N. O. Fulton and T. Blackwood Murray, the latter two leaving to create the Albion Motor Car Co in 1899. Blackwood Murray had previously worked for electrical engineers Mavor & Coulson, where one of his tasks had been to perfect an electric ignition system for the Coventry Daimler. Interestingly, George Johnston of Arrol-Johnston, like Henry Royce, had received his early engineering training in a steam locomotive works.

Major steam firms with an interest in transport seemed reluctant to take the plunge into steam cars, let alone internal combustion-engined ones. Beyer, Peacock of Gorton were typical of dozens of railway locomotive builders who remained aloof, as did Ransomes Sims & Jefferies, major agricultural engineers who had built a traction engine as early as 1842. Their sometime associates, Ruston Proctor, entered the car field, but not before its merger with Richard Hornsby in 1918. Another famous agricultural steam engineer, Fodens Ltd, became important for steam lorries at the end of the Victorian era but never made cars. However, yet another agricultural firm, Bentalls in Essex, which had introduced a patent plough in 1797, most certainly did. Following a whole range of farm machinery it added internal combustion engines in about 1900. Its cars were a natural succession from 1905 but only about 100 were built before production ended in 1912.

Arnold's engineering and milling machinery business in East Peckham, outside London, was the unlikely home of the Benz in Britain after Walter Arnold imported one in 1895 and then made several replicas and developments. Another agricultural engineer to build for local requirements was the Cutlers Green Ironworks near Bristol, whose Mendip was typical of small regional producers. Not far away was Petters of Nautilus Works, Yeovil, which was famous for grates and stoves before experimenting with cars in the 1895–8 period. However, it was its Petter engines that were to gain major significance, followed later by its Westland aircraft. Another to make engines was Jowett in Yorkshire, which had produced gas engines, whilst the next generation, Bill and William Jowett, tinkered with bicycles. It was to be a relatively short step from stationary engines for the brothers to sell engines to the makers of Scott motor cycles and then to add complete Jowett cars.

The mention of Scott reminds us of another familiar motor cycle name. Douglas, like Jowett, favoured flat twin engines and made a small number of cars with this feature. It is remembered in its home city of Bristol for its cast iron manhole covers. These were also a speciality of Cutlers Green and of another ironfounder, named James Bartle, in London, whose company also made coachwork and was behind the Windsor car of the 1920s.

Royce's dynamos and electric cranes built up a loyal following

Dorman and Tylor were both respected Victorian ironworking firms who were to achieve fame as builders of proprietary engines for cars. Tylor, like its rival Gwynne, was famous for London-built pumps (Tylor was also a sanitary engineers) but, unlike Gwynne, it did not attempt to make complete vehicles (except when involved in an abortive 1920s attempt to keep the Angus Sanderson alive).

Steam engineers which did make a successful transition to petrol-engined motor cars included Peter Brotherhood Ltd, established in 1867, though in its case with a bought-in design from Percy Richardson, ex Daimler. Its Brotherhood-Crocker car later evolved into the Sheffield Simplex. Then there was S. Straker & Squire Ltd, which bought its initial internal combustion-engined car designs from France. Another long established engineering company, Thomas Turner & Co of Wolverhampton, dating from 1800, also bought in a Continental design, in its case a steamer from Miesse of Belgium, before embarking on its own petrol cars in 1906. Another steam engineering firm to gain later fame was that founded by Henry Spurrier at a little blacksmithy in Leyland, Lancashire. In this case most efforts were to be directed towards commercial transport apart from a handful of luxury cars in the 1920s.

If most heavy engineers and iron founders failed to make the grade or else never attempted car manufacture, then electrical engineers generally fared little better, even if some – like the previously mentioned Mavor & Coulson – employed figures who were to become important in their own right. Another electrical breeding ground was New & Mayne in London, which trained one of the 1901 co-founders of the James & Browne Ltd motor car business. The enormous Brush Electrical Engineering Co Ltd made petrol cars for only a couple of years before concentrating on commercials and bodywork. An exception to the rule was Henry Royce, a Great Northern Railway Locomotive Works apprentice, who started a small workshop in Manchester in 1884. His dynamos and electric cranes built up a loyal following and his cars would ultimately set the standard for the industry.

If all these ironworking enterprises had been introduced to the motor vehicle by events happening outside their direct field of experience then the next category, the light engineers of Coventry and elsewhere, were the partial cause of the whole revolution. Coventry was in the unusual position of having developed a highly skilled pool of labour that was familiar with the intricacies of specialized cloth-making machinery. Special equipment for woven pictures made famous as Stevengraphs, and indeed Cash's woven name tapes, were examples of the work that could be undertaken. As noted earlier, Coventry was not blessed with the raw materials of the typical heavy industrial area, although it did have a coalfield to the north of the city. Being about as far from the sea as it was possible to be in Britain made transport of raw materials and finished goods uncompetitively costly unless of especially high value and low weight. Nearby Birmingham had a similar problem and its jewellery quarter and gun-making industry were amongst the ways in which it had overcome its geographic disadvantages.

From Coventry's speciality in mid-Victorian times, of intricately made clocks and cloth machinery, grew its important sewing machine industry. The first successful perpendicular action machine was the work of Isaac Merritt Singer (unconnected with the Singer car) in America in 1851, and from it were developed hundreds of thousands of machines suitable for lightweight domestic use. Machines were then devised in America that incorporated virtually all the features of today and when the patents were pooled with those of Singer in 1856 it looked as if European development would be stifled. There were half a million machines in use in America by 1860 and Singer opened a factory in Glasgow in 1868 to try to tap the potential before the joint patent expired in 1877. Singer helped to establish a vast demand in Victorian households that soon was met in part by Coventry-made machines. Interestingly the first English machines came not from Coventry but from another cloth-working town, Oldham in Lancashire, where Bradbury & Company built examples from 1852 (and later became a motor cycle manufacturer). A rival making cloth machinery parts in Oldham was

Rothwell & Hough (later the Eclipse Machine Co Ltd), which made a fortune from sewing machines and phonograph parts before adding Rothwell cars in 1901.

The Coventry Sewing Machine Company was founded in 1861 and as the Coventry Machinists Company from 1869 it became one of the major names in the new industry. With the firm from 1861 was James Starley, who designed several domestic and industrial sewing machines. The Paris agent for the company was Rowley Turner, who in 1868 introduced a Michaux velocipede to the Coventry management. A year later works manager James Starley started to make the Michaux under licence and in 1870 formed a partnership with William Hillman to make Ariel bicycles. In 1874 Starley patented the tangent spoked wheel, followed in 1876 by a lever tricycle and then by one with a differential in 1877. Following his death in 1881 James Starley was commemorated as 'the father of the cycle industry', but there were several other Starleys following in his footsteps. The most famous was John Kemp Starley, born 1855, whose diamond-frame safety bicycle of 1885 revolutionized the whole industry. His Rover tricycle

of a few years earlier introduced a name that would become famous on cars in the twentieth century. The mention of Hillman and Starley shows that there were other names in the sewing machine, bicycle and allied businesses that would become famous in the infant motor industry. Notable ones were Riley, Lea and Francis, Rudge, George Singer, Calcott, West (Progress), and Bayliss & Thomas. The Coventry Machinists Co itself became the Swift Cycle Co in 1896, makers of motor vehicles from 1898.

William Pilkington made weldless tubes for the cycle industry and was founder of the Rex Motor Manufacturing Co Ltd. However, in a wider context, far more significant was the consortium he helped to form that became Tube Investments Ltd. Another famous tube firm was Accles & Pollock, whose founder James George Accles (an Australian of Irish stock) had learned about precision manufacture working on Colt firearms in America. He made Accles-Turrell cars in Birmingham from 1900–2 and then concentrated on Accles & Pollock Ltd. Yet another famous name in the cycle and then motor business was that of Thomas Humber, whose machines were initially made in Nottingham

An 1896 Rover 'Royal' Ladies' Safety Bicycle, which cost £20. (Brian Demaus/P. A. Saunders)

(home also of Raleigh cycles) but which had a Coventry branch from 1887. One of the employees there in the 1890s was champion cyclist J. D. Siddeley, who was later to run Wolseley for Vickers (after Austin's departure) and then joined Deasy. Wolseley's origins have already been touched upon briefly but it was the metallurgical skills of its Birmingham work-force that made the mechanical sheep-shears developed in Australia a production possibility. The little known La Plata car also came from a firm that made sheep-shears (no doubt, with a name like that, for the wool trade of South America).

Birmingham was also the place where Frederick Lanchester found employment before and whilst developing his revolutionary car in the mid-1890s. It was at T. B. Barker's Forward gas engine works that he invented many of his internal combustion ideas and where he was works manager from 1889. His pendulum governor earned him royalties and Forward was also the UK pioneer of tube ignition. His young brother George's premium apprenticeship was paid for at Forward by Frederick until George was old enough to replace him in the engine factory.

The satisfactory acceptance of the bicycle, and indeed of Lanchester's car, was in part made possible by the invention of J. B. Dunlop's pneumatic tyre, though interestingly a forerunner, Thompson's pneumatic belt, had been available on the Ariel wheel for horse-drawn vehicles as early as 1847. Components Ltd used Ariel as its trade name and after making roller skates added all manner of items for the infant motor industry.

Whilst the Coventry bicycle industry takes precedence there were many other bicycle firms in other locations who joined the motoring elite. Amongst them were the Dennis brothers from Devon, who set up the Universal Athletics Store in Guildford in 1895 after John Dennis had gained experience with an ironmonger in the town and also with component suppli-

ers Brown Brothers. Having made Dennis bicycles, he added motorized machines in 1899. Other firms with bicycling antecedents included the Belsize works of Walter Radermacher in Manchester and J. van Hooydonk's Phoenix factory in London and then at the new Garden City of Letchworth. Both men were enthusiast cyclists turned manufacturers, as was Dan Albone who named his cycles and then his cars and tractors after the River Ivel, near his works.

Cycle component firms Chater Lea and Perry (the engineering firm Harper Bean used the Perry car as the basis for its popular 1920s Beans) ultimately became involved in complete vehicles. Yet another bicycle exponent turned car-maker in Birmingham was George W. Hands, later responsible for the Calthorpe and then Hands cars. To the west of the city, in Wolverhampton, a japanner (a metal painting process) named John Marston opened the Sunbeamland cycle factory in 1887, whilst his relative Charles Marston started component firm turned engine-maker Villiers Engineering nearby. From 1901 Sunbeam cars and then motor cycles quickly became more famous than those of another neighbour, the Star Cycle Co Ltd, which as the Star Motor Co Ltd added cars in 1898.

Several clockmakers turned to the motor instrument trade

Once a bicycle component industry existed it was possible for bicycles to be made near any railway station or carrier's depot and there were few towns that did not boast at least one. Many of these were quite prepared to assemble a car from proprietary parts, though few made the grade to series manufacture. If bicycles and sewing machine parts were intricate, then even more so were the products of the Burden family in Salisbury, who were clockmakers before starting the Scout Motor Works. Of course several other

clockmakers turned to the motor instrument trade, notably S. Smith in London and Rotherhams in Coventry. Likewise it was a relatively small step for Joseph Lucas, born in 1834, and his son Harry to add motor lamps and other accessories to its King Of The Road bicycle range. Later the New Hudson Cycle Co, also in Birmingham, was to attain fame as a maker of brakes for the motor industry, culminating in its use of Captain A. H. Girling's system in the 1920s. A unique background to motor manufacture, however, was enjoyed by the Wilkinson Sword Co Ltd which, as its name implied, made swords as well as razors and other blades. Though its 1903 car was of Belgian origin its metallurgical skills soon became useful when manufacture was undertaken in London.

As makers of nuts and bolts, Guest Keen & Nettlefolds were soon involved as suppliers to vehicle factories and many other GKN motor products were soon added. Over the years numerous businesses were absorbed, including parts of Bean and the Hardy Spicer propeller shaft and Salisbury axle factories. Sankey, from the Milnes tramworks in Hadley, Shropshire, made chassis frames, wheels and other essentials. John Thompson of Bilston was a famous boiler maker which also made chassis frames (and later its TB cyclecars). A near neighbour was Rubery Owen, that also made chassis and many other vehicle parts, including axle casings, steel channels, studs, and nuts and bolts.

As we have seen, the younger and more flexible industries made the transition to the motor car more successfully than the traditional heavy engineers. In the latter category even the exponents of steam proved to be rather dilatory in their response to the new mode of transport, though there were exceptions, notably amongst the makers of the lighter types of high speed steam engines for marine use, such as that founded by Henry Maudslay (born 1771), perfector of the micrometer, screw-cutting lathe, and slide rest, and one of the architects of Britain's position as workshop of the world. His great-great-grandsons Cyril and Reginald Maudslay were motor industry pioneers, establishing an internal combustion marine engine factory in Coventry in 1899. In 1901 this grew into the Maudslay Motor Co and soon afterwards Reginald created the Standard Motor Co, the name signifying an early example in the motor industry of standardization and thus interchangeability of components. Henry Maudslay's workshop had been on the banks of the Thames, and other London area neighbours to move from boat engineering to vehicles included Thames, Thornycroft and Vauxhall. The Thames Ironworks, Shipbuilding & Engineering Co (founded 1857) had first experimented with vehicles at the turn of the century. Thornycroft made steam wagons from 1896, followed by internal combustion-engined cars in 1903 from its new factory in Basingstoke. Vauxhall grew from a naval engineering business founded in 1857 by Scotsman Alexander Wilson. It began to experiment with internal combustion engines around 1898 and offered cars from 1903. The Lifu car, likewise developed in London, was unusual in coming from a marine firm that actually retained a steam engine, albeit liquid fuelled (hence its name). It lasted only from 1899 to 1902. As an aside it may also be worth mentioning that Lionel Martin's partner in the Aston Martin car project, Robert Bamford, had been engineer to Hess & Savory's Teddington Launch works.

It was internal combustion engines for stationary and potential marine purposes that inspired William Crossley. Honeymooning in Germany, he met Nikolaus A. Otto, inventor of the four-stroke cycle of engine operation and, in 1869, after consultation with his engineer brother Frank Crossley, he acquired major sales and manufacturing rights. He was thus typical of the entrepreneurs who make up a large part of the early growth of the motor industry in Britain. Often they found designs on the Continent

and then raised money to turn them into reality in British factories. Talbot was just such a British flotation to rely initially on Continental designs, as were Aster and the original Peugeot-based Siddeleys. From America came Wilbur Gunn, who established the successful Lagonda concern, and Edward Joel Pennington, whose Pennington vehicles were a disaster but who was nevertheless able to attract vast sums of money from would-be investors, manufacturers and hopeful customers. He was a friend of Harry Lawson (who was ultimately gaoled for one of his money-raising schemes) and of Ernest Terah Hooley, another speculator in the acquisition of funding for the infant industry.

Companies were often fronted by peers to inspire confidence

Nottingham stockbroker Hooley (1859–1947) was typical of the company promoters of the 1890s, who made vast sums from buying up under-capitalized companies and refloating them with vague and glowing prospectuses to a trusting and unsophisticated public. Hooley and his kind pocketed the difference, and the public were left with over-valued shares from which no dividends were ever paid. His companies were often fronted by peers who allowed their names to be used for a consideration (the agricultural depression had left many land-owning aristocrats in need of funds) and the new group of lower-middle class investors were very susceptible to the appeal of a lord on the board of directors. Hooley openly admitted that he had a tariff for noble directors to inspire confidence in a prospectus; £25,000 for a duke, £15,000 for an earl and a mere £5,000 for a baronet. For the Dunlop flotation in 1896, Hooley secured the names of the Duke of Somerset, Earl de la Warr, and the Earl of Albemarle.[1] There was always the risk, however, that if the companies collapsed the noble peers

suffered public humiliation. This has been given as an explanation for the relatively small number of aristocrats to invest in the motor industry.[2]

Not all Hooley's companies were fraudulent. Among household names which he floated were Bovril, Schweppes, and Boots the Chemists, and in the cycle field he brought to the market Humber, Raleigh, Singer, and Swift. His most successful flotation was that of the Dunlop Pneumatic Tyre Company, from which he allegedly netted £2 million (about £100 million in today's money). His partner in Dunlop, and also in Humber and Swift, was Harry John Lawson (1852–1925), who had entered business in a small way in the cycle trade in Brighton. In 1876 he patented a low bicycle with wheels of nearly equal size. A few examples were made, but it was an imperfect design, and in no way comparable with John Kemp Starley's Rover Safety Bicycle of 1885, despite Lawson's later claim to have invented the safety cycle.

Lawson is thought of as a company promoter with little or no interest in the vehicles themselves, and this is largely true of his involvement in the motor industry. However, in his early cycling years he did design and patent a number of ideas before the lure of large profits took him away from the practical field. Between 1888 and 1896 he promoted at least 22 companies, some of them banks with high-sounding titles such as the Issue Bank of England and Wales, and the London & Scottish Trustee and Investment Company. He also floated in 1891 the Beeston Pneumatic Tyre Company, which was liquidated two years later, and, in partnership with Hooley, Humber & Co Ltd in 1895. This and several offshoot Humber companies in the USA, Russia, Portugal, Denmark, and Sweden provided Lawson and Hooley with substantial fortunes. Some of this went to Lawson's purchase of the Daimler patents and formation of the British Motor Syndicate. Lawson may have brought the fledgling motor industry into disrepute later, but it was his own finance which he put into the first companies to offer cars for sale in Britain.

If a dark cloud followed this group then a happier image was portrayed by Harvey du Cros, an important investor in the French and British bicycle and motor industries. His fortune derived from his holding of the Dunlop pneumatic tyre patents. He was instrumental in the success of Panhard in London and backed Swift, Napier and Austin, the latter firm actually making a model originating from his French-owned Gladiator business.

There were plenty of engineers with Continental experience or background in the early factories, a prime example being Louis Coatalen, who went to Sunbeam from Hillman and Humber. There were even more who believed that an Anglicized version of a Continental car could make their fortune (indeed Sunbeam had used a Berliet design prior to Coatalen's arrival). Dozens involved nothing more than a foreign vehicle with an English name and prominent sales premises, though as already recounted there were lots who adopted Continental designs and then gradually evolved their own. One figure who tried most aspects of the business, and whose career helps to sum up the cut and thrust nature of those early years, is Henry George Burford, born in Somerset in 1867. After a six-year apprenticeship with a typically rural millwright and general engineer he moved to various engineering companies, including Lifu's marine division, before joining the Electric Motive Power Co in London in 1896, makers of electric vehicles. He then obtained rights to produce the Belgian Vivinus car, which from 1900 in Britain was known as the New Orleans. In 1901/2 Burford left this business to join tram-car maker G. F. Milnes, which was embarking on motor bus manufacture utilizing chassis from German Daimler. As a result of this connection he became involved in British Mercedes Ltd, importers of Mercedes

cars. For three years from 1909 he was general manager of Humber and then part owner of the makers of Riley-powered Lotis light vans (a firm in which the Editor of *The Cyclist* and then *The Autocar*, Henry Sturmey, had been involved – he had also been a director of Daimler through his friendship with

Lawson and had been behind the famous Sturmey Archer bicycle hub gear of 1903). Burford soon found greater profit in lorries and tractors imported from America and badged here with his by then familiar surname. Ultimately he produced them in Britain in the 1920s and 1930s.

A military cyclist with the Rover 'New Popular' of 1897. This had 30-in front, and 28-in rear wheels. (Brian Demaus/D. Irvine)

CHAPTER TWO

An Industry Gets Under Way

Nick Georgano

1896 was a catalyst year, bringing together two vital elements for the foundation of an industry. The first was the existence of large amounts of money looking for a new home; and the second was a burgeoning technology that only needed finance to be set on its way. The money and the initiative were largely provided by H. J. Lawson. The technology came from the Continent.

The Daimler Motor Syndicate had been founded in 1893 by F. R. Simms, taking over his own firm Simms & Co. This owned the British rights to Daimler high-speed petrol engines, and Simms enjoyed a good trade in fitting these to boats. As we have seen, Evelyn Ellis owned four Daimler-powered boats, and also used an engine in a manually-pulled fire engine. A Daimler engine was used in a Pembrokeshire lifeboat, and they powered launches in the Isle of Wight and Suffolk, among other places. Some of these survived in use for more than 30 years. They were also advertised for powering tramcars and light locomotives. Daimler cars were operating in small numbers in Germany, but there was no question of the Daimler Motor Syndicate making cars in England. All the engines were imported, as Simms had no factory.

In October 1895 Lawson made an offer of £35,000 for the Daimler Motor Syndicate, which was accepted, and the following month he refloated it for £150,000 as the British Motor Syndicate. The stated aim of this was to buy patents and to 'manufacture, sell, let on hire or otherwise deal in motors, cycles, carts, wagons, vehicles, ships, boats, flying machines, and carriages of all kinds.'[1] This seemed pretty comprehensive, but such vehicles were not much use if they could not be operated at sensible speeds, so another stated aim of the Syndicate was to 'procure all Parliamentary powers to enable the carrying of these objects into effect.'

Though he was to be instrumental in setting up Britain's first two 'makes' of car, Coventry Bollée and Daimler, Lawson did not see himself as a manufacturer of cars in the autumn of 1895. The purpose of his Syndicate was to acquire patents and sell them on at a profit once cars had been freed from their legal restrictions. He was confident that this freedom would not be long in coming, for in June 1895 the Locomotives on Highways Bill was introduced into Parliament. Its sponsor was George Shaw-Lefevre, Liberal MP for Bradford Central, whose uncle Charles Shaw-Lefevre (later Viscount Eversley), had been a friend of steam in the 1830s. George had long been a supporter of the traction engine lobby and it seems that he became aware of passenger cars during a visit to Paris early in 1895. He visited a factory (probably Panhard et Levassor) and saw that the numerous cars in the streets did not alarm the horses. The main purpose of his Bill was that vehicles under two tons in overall weight should not be subject to the same speed restrictions as heavier machines.

Matters did not proceed as quickly as Shaw-Lefevre, Lawson and others had hoped, for although the Bill passed its first reading on 17 June, the Liberal Government fell four days later, and was replaced by a Conservative administration under Lord Salisbury. It was March 1896 before another Locomotives on Highways Bill was presented, this time in the House of Lords by Lord Harris. After many vicissitudes, including arguments about the maximum weight of a 'light locomotive' (the makers of an electric bus claimed that they could not meet the two ton limit), the Bill passed through the Commons and became law as the Locomotives on Highways Act, on 14 November 1896.

There were many clauses but the most important was that light locomotives (under three tons unladen weight) would be regarded in law as carriages and subject to a maximum speed limit of 14 mph, or less if Local Government Boards demanded it. They did, in fact, reduce it to 12 mph, and lower still for vehicles weighing more than one and a half tons. There were stipulations about lights and 'audible warning of approach'. Two regulations were very vague; the vehicles must be in the charge of a competent driver, and must be in a safe condition. These were a nod to Paris police regulations which contained similar requirements. In fact there was to be no formal testing of drivers' competence until 1935, and no overall testing of vehicle condition until 1961, though the police always had the power to stop a vehicle which they had reasonable grounds to think unsafe.

Lawson and his partners were the main beneficiaries of the new Act, and to celebrate he organized a grand tour of motor cars from London to Brighton, retrospectively called the Emancipation Run, or Brighton Run. Under the auspices of the Motor Car Club which he had founded, he attracted 58 entries for his event, which he had been planning since July. Only 33 turned up for the start, but even so, this was far more than had ever been gathered together in Britain before, and represented between a third and a half of all the motor vehicles in the country. Resplendent in the pseudo-nautical uniform of the club (described by *The Engineer* as 'not exactly the garb of a German band, and not exactly the dress of an excursion steamer steward, but something between the two only more pretentious'), Lawson rode in the leading car, the Panhard which had won the 1895 Paris–Bordeaux race. There were 23 other petrol cars, including the Panhard of Evelyn Ellis, seven electrics and two steamers. Statistics of the first Brighton Run are contradictory; some of the entrants never intended to complete the route, only to make an appearance, and five did not get as far as Streatham, five miles from the start in Northumberland Avenue. Thirteen cars were declared official finishers, and the driver of an American Duryea claimed that he had arrived first. Lawson was not interested in this claim as he did not number Duryea among his numerous patents. *The Autocar*[2] and *Automotor Journal*[3] reports gave first and second places to Leon Bollées.

To get an idea of Lawson's importance to the infant industry, one has to go back at least a year before the Brighton Run. In November 1895 he acquired the patents of two electric car makers, Walter Bersey, who later operated a fleet of electric cabs in London, and Garrard & Blumfield of Coventry, ex-cycle makers who had built a pneumatic-tyred electric car in 1894. To these he added an unwise purchase, that of the Kane-Pennington patents. Edward Joel Pennington (1858–1911) was an American company promoter and inventor. He was no engineer, and his inventive talents played a poor second to his persuasiveness and imagination. He was involved in at least five different companies on both sides of the Atlantic, yet no more than 15 cars were made, some barely ran and none was sold to a private buyer. The patent which Lawson acquired referred to a strange three-wheeler with a parallel twin engine of very long stroke (62.5 x 305 mm) and a capacity of 1.9 litres. An advertisement showed it laden with nine passengers, though even Pennington did not suggest that it actually ran with such a burden. The tubular frame was made by Humber, which was also involved with Lawson's more successful project to build Leon Bollée three-wheelers in Coventry.

It is a tribute to Pennington's silver tongue that the normally hard-headed Lawson parted with £100,000 for the Pennington patents, and that he

The modest premises of the Daimler Motor Syndicate, Arch No. 71 by Putney Bridge railway station, which F. R. Simms rented from the Metropolitan Railway, and from which he sold Daimler engines from 1893 onwards. (NMM)

bought them personally, with his partner Martin Rucker, rather than in the name of the British Motor Syndicate. He never made a penny from them, and although another Pennington design, the raft four-wheeler, featured in BMS advertising for a while, this did not survive beyond 1897.

In May 1896 Lawson organized an International Horseless Carriage Exhibition at London's Imperial Institute, which was opened by the Prince of Wales. Lawson was very astute in involving the Imperial Institute which had as its patron the Queen, and as its president the Prince of Wales. 'With this mark of approbation and the influence and backing of the Institute, the horseless carriage movement should be largely benefited,' said *The Autocar* (25 January 1896). Much of the day-to-day work of organization fell to Claude Johnson, the Institute's principal clerk, who was to become the invaluable partner of Rolls and Royce.

Lawson secured 11 vehicles for the exhibition, including a De Dion Bouton tricycle demonstrated by the Count himself, a Duncan & Suberbie motor bicycle, a Bersey electric, and a Serpollet steamer. On the eve of the opening he gave a dinner for several press barons including Sir George Newnes of *Tit Bits*, and T. P. O'Connor, proprietor of *The Sun* and *The Star*. The exhibition remained open until July, by which time a Britannia electric car had joined the throng. It undoubtedly helped Lawson's image as well as that of the horseless carriage, the two being virtually identical at that time. Salomons had organized a smaller exhibition at the Crystal Palace two weeks before Lawson's, but it had attracted less publicity, and the cars did not perform well.

During the Imperial Institute exhibition, Lawson announced the formation of the Great Horseless Carriage Company, floated for £700,000. It is hard to define its actual role, but it was described as a parent company, controlling all the Lawson enterprises, apart from the Pennington and De Dion licences which Lawson himself held. Its premises were the Motor Mills in Sandy Lane, Coventry, a disused mid-19th century factory which

Mr and Mrs H. J. Lawson, he wearing the uniform of the Motor Car Club, at the start of the Emancipation Run, 14 November 1896. (NMM)

A German built Cannstatt-Daimler landau at the start of the Emancipation Run. It was called Present Times *as it had run in the Lord Mayor's Show the previous week in company with a horse-drawn stage coach,* Old Times. *At the wheel is F. R. Simms and in the rear seat, on the left, Gottlieb Daimler.* (NMM)

had belonged to the Coventry Cotton Spinning & Weaving Company and, at the time of Lawson's purchase, just happened to belong to his business associate Ernest Hooley. In fact the Motor Mills were bought in the name of the Daimler Motor Company in April 1896, and almost immediately the Great Horseless Carriage Company offered to buy half the premises. This more than compensated the Daimler Company for their outlay on the whole 13-acre site, and was an ingenious transfer of funds from a richer Lawson company to a poorer one. This was the first time that Lawson had actually mentioned manufacture. Nothing happened at the Motor Mills until the autumn of 1896, after which Leon Bollées were made in the GHCC part of the factory and Daimlers in their own part. From the summer of 1897 Daimler-like cars were made in the GHCC part under the name MMC (Motor Manufacturing Company).

Of the two foreign licences that Lawson acquired, only the Leon Bollée saw fruit in actual vehicles. The Count de Dion distrusted Lawson, who had offered shares in the British Motor Syndicate in part payment for the licence. Bollée was not very happy either, as the greater part of his payment was in promissory notes which Lawson had omitted to sign. Eventually this was put right, and Lawson had the rights to manufacture the Bollée three-wheeler.

This was a remarkable machine, the fastest of its day, for although its 640 cc engine gave only 3 bhp, its weight was no more than 353 lbs (160 kg) and it could reach about 40 mph (64 km/h). On the debit side, it was very noisy, temperamental, and the driver and passenger sat so low that they were engulfed in dust in summer and spattered with mud in winter. The driver sat just ahead of the single rear wheel, with his passenger in front of him. Leon Bollée is credited with the first use of the word 'voiturette' but although he tried to confine it to his own machine, it soon became widespread for any small car. Few were made by Bollée himself, for French production was sub-contracted to sewing machine maker Diligeon et Cie.

In May 1896 Bollée brought the first car he had made to Coventry, 'where he created immense excitement among the inhabitants by dashing wildly through the crowded streets in every direction'.[4] The car was part of the Imperial Institute exhibition a week later, and it was there that Lawson decided to buy the British rights. He planned to have it made in the works of the Humber Cycle Company, but on 17 July, the Humber premises burnt down, consuming the Bollée prototype. Lawson's partner Herbert Osbaldiston Duncan was hastily dispatched to Le Mans where Bollée fortunately had another machine completed. This and a new set of drawings were the basis of the cars which were made by Humber at the Motor Mills.

It is difficult to establish exactly when manufacture began. *The Autocar* of 12 September 1896 reported 'Mr Crowden hopes to have his first British-built Bollée on the road this week.' Hopes are not the same as certainties, but by November *The Autocar* was able to report that nine Coventry Motettes were shown at the Stanley Cycle Show in London. The names Coventry Motette and Coventry Bollée were both applied to these vehicles, though Motette was generally adopted after manufacture had passed out of Lawson's hands. This took place at the end of 1896 when Lawson's secretary Charles McRobie Turrell founded another factory at Parkside, Coventry, and resigned his position to run the new works. The Coventry Motor Company, which made the Motettes, was established in October 1896, as a wholly-owned subsidiary of the British Motor Syndicate, so some Motettes may have been made at the Motor Mills. It has been suggested that only four of these machines were made at the Motor Mills,[5] but this is contradicted by the presence of nine at the Stanley Show in November, before

Turrell's Parkside works had got under way.

How many were made by the end of 1896 is not certain, but even if there were no more than the nine seen at the Show, one could say that manufacture began that year. In January 1897 *The Autocar*, reporting on the shareholders' meeting of the British Motor Syndicate, said that the streets of Coventry teemed with Daimler carriages, Bollée tandems and New Beeston motor cycles.[6]

By far the most important of Lawson's company flotations was the Daimler Motor Company, whose prospectus was issued in January 1896. The purpose was to exploit the patents held by the British Motor Syndicate (itself a successor to the Daimler Motor Syndicate), the significant difference being that the Daimler Syndicate was concerned with marketing imported engines, while the Motor Company was to manufacture complete vehicles. The directors included several famous names: Lawson, of course, as Chairman[7]; Evelyn Ellis; Henry Sturmey, first editor of *The Autocar*; J. H. Mace, a long-time Lawson associate; and Gottlieb Daimler. F. R. Simms was consulting engineer. The company was Lawson's first complete promotional success, with all the £100,000 worth of £10 shares being taken up, and indeed over subscribed. Most were bought by small investors, only two having more than £1,000 worth.

Among the claims of the prospectus were that the Daimler patents were the most valuable in existence (true, as far as engines were concerned), and that production of cars could be started in two months. The latter was quite wide of the mark, though the use of 'could' rather than 'would' shows a rare degree of caution from the usually optimistic Lawson. He had acquired an option to purchase the premises that would become the Motor Mills in November 1895, though he did not exercise the option until April 1896. The factory was still full of disused cotton spinning machinery which had

to be broken up and removed before new machinery could be installed. This took a long time to be delivered. The Daimler premises consisted of a double line of ground floor workshops which surrounded on two sides the main four-storey mill building.

It was July before any activity was recorded; *The Autocar* announced 'the fitting up of the works has been progressing rapidly of late, and the laying out and arrangement of the plant has been so far completed that on Monday last the works commenced running for the actual manufacture of motors . . . everything points to the production of the completed article ready for the public in five or six weeks from now'. [6] There is some confusion because a few Daimler cars were running in Britain in the summer of 1896, but these were German-built rear-engined designs, though at least one had a British body. This was owned by John T. Clark, an Aberdeen coachbuilder who had made carriages for the Queen, and who fitted one of his bodies to a Cannstatt-Daimler. In August he was invited to demonstrate this before the Royal Family at Balmoral, though it seems that only the housekeeper volunteered for a ride.

Over the next few months conflicting reports appeared about the Motor Mills. In September it was said that the Great Horseless Carriage Company had only just got around to ordering its machine tools. A month later Lord Winchelsea reported that three of the four floors were in use, Humber making Leon Bollées on the ground floor, while above them Pennington was 'busy on his odd creations'.[9] *The Autocar* noted during a visit early in 1897 that the approach to Pennington's floor was via an outside stairway, whereas the shops under Mr Crowden's management had an interior staircase. They were very flattering about Pennington, praising his originality and inventiveness, and also the tidiness of the factory which was shared by the men working there. 'Mr Pennington believes that good work can only be obtained when the men responsible for it are neat and cleanly in themselves.'[10]

The Daimler Motor Company was said to have premises in the Mills, though Lord Winchelsea said nothing about manufacture. In fact, Daimler occupied a separate single-storey building, as we have seen. Then, in mid-November, the Great Horseless

Like a triton among minnows, a Panhard-Levassor makes its way to Brighton surrounded by cyclists. 'Wheelmen and wheelwomen' far outnumbered the competing cars; press estimates of their numbers varied from 'hundreds, perhaps more than a thousand' (Morning Post) to 'over ten thousand' (Brighton Herald). (NMM)

One of many advertisements placed by Pennington in The Autocar *during 1897, this shows his three-wheeler laden with nine passengers, though the text says it was made to carry four people. The engine had a primitive needle valve which dribbled raw fuel into the air intake, hence the boasted absence of a carburettor, and a 'long-mingling spark' which Pennington never explained properly.* (NMM)

Carriage Company announced in an advertisement[11] that they had 'nearly completed the organization of their immense new works at Coventry', and that orders could be taken for some of the following makes: Daimler, Kane-Pennington, Leon Bollée, and Bersey. Of these, we have seen that only 15 Penningtons were ever made, the Bollée soon migrated to another factory and the Berseys were mostly electric cabs, a fleet of which was put on the streets of the capital by the London Electrical Cab Co Ltd.[12] This was another Lawson enterprise.

This left Daimler as the sole representative of the petrol-engined passenger car, and chassis did indeed emerge from the Mills before the end of the year. They were taken on railway wagons to Northampton, where bodies would be mounted by Mulliners. While not directly linked to Lawson, Mulliners had shared interests with the Coventry promoter. Herbert H. Mulliner was on the board of the British Motor Syndicate and the Great Horseless Carriage Company, and became Chairman of the London Electrical Cab Company, while his cousin Henry Jervis Mulliner also joined the board of the latter. In 1900 he formed H. J. Mulliner Ltd in London, the first coachbuilder to specialize in motor car bodies. Mulliners continued at Northampton, but their products were not in the first rank, as were H. J. Mulliner's.

Daimler production in the first half of 1897 is difficult to establish. The Daimler carriages with which the streets of Coventry were said to be teeming in January 1897 may have been German-made cars. With editor Henry Sturmey being a director of Lawson's companies, one would not expect *The Autocar* to be too scrupulous about the nationality of the cars. The cars which went to Mulliners are not recorded as having been sold during the first seven months of 1897. Even Lawson himself did not claim that a complete Daimler car had run before 2 March 1897, two days before shareholders were invited to the Motor Mills to see progress. However, at least one chassis was supplied to a Scottish coachbuilder, J. & C. Stirling of Hamilton, North Berwick, in January 1897.[13] By April Stirling was taking orders and by October more than a dozen Stirling-Daimlers were said to have been sold.

In March the Daimler company loaned a wagonette to the Brighton Motor & Cycle Co, which gave sixpenny rides from the Brighton

Aquarium to the Devil's Dyke and back, while on 20 April Ernest Estcourt took delivery of a car from the Motor Mills and drove it home to Hampstead in London. His journey took 10½ hrs, including stops for meals, fuel and water. Estcourt would seem to be the first private purchaser of a Daimler car, though *The Autocar* accorded this honour to Major General Montgomery of Winchester who did not collect his Daimler until August. In fact, the car had been earmarked by Henry Sturmey for a drive from John O'Groats to Land's End. He gave it up to the Major General as the company was so behind with deliveries, and postponed his journey to October. However, the company claimed that 20 had been completed and sold by July, and that 200 men were turning out three cars per week. By November the weekly number was said to be up to four, still a very limited output. *The Autocar's* Midland correspondent understood that they could increase this to six per week, but for their inability to get sufficient material. 'This is, of course, by no means for want of funds – a commodity with which the company is happily well blessed and it seems difficult to attribute a reason for this paucity of material.'[14] On the same page he notes a rumour that Daimler's fellow occupant of the Motor Mills, the Great Horseless Carriage Company, was getting on very badly. 'It is to be hoped that this company, which started under such brilliant auspices and seemed to promise so well, will see a brighter day. Personally, I regret that one hears so little from the directors to counteract these rumours.' They were said to be making Daimler-type cars, with engines, gearboxes and frames coming from next door to be mated with GHCC-built bodies. These were sold under the name MMC, but this business did not really get under way until 1898 when it was renamed the Motor Manufacturing Company, with new designs by George Iden, formerly with the London, Brighton & South Coast Railway.

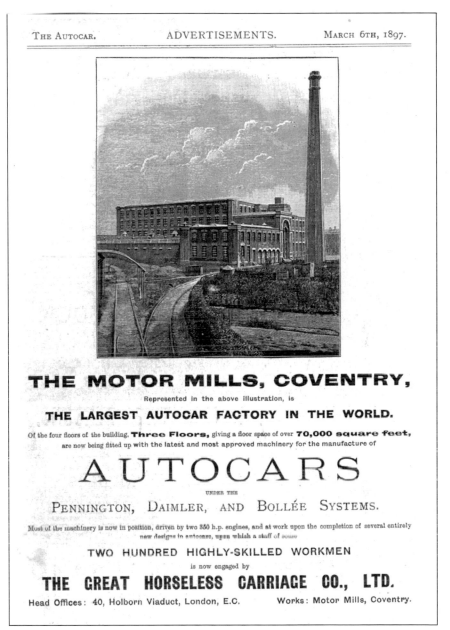

The Motor Mills in Sandy Lane, Coventry, in early 1897. The outer single and two-storey buildings belonged to Daimler, while the main four-storey building belonged to the Great Horseless Carriage Co, and was used at various times for making Leon Bollées, Penningtons, and MMC cars. Most of the buildings were destroyed by enemy action in 1941. (NMM)

These broke completely with the Daimler layout, having rear-mounted horizontal two-cylinder engines. They were not apparently very successful; A. C. Brown, who joined the company as an apprentice fitter in 1897, observed 'I worked on most of George Iden's "Flight of Fancy" designs. Some did not go at all and some went a bit, and most of them were flops.'[15]

The 1897 Daimlers were cars of Panhard type,[16] with front-mounted vertical-twin engines, automatic inlet valves and tube

By March 1897 Leon Bollée production had migrated from the Motor Mills to Parkside, where they were made by Charles McRobie Turrell and sold under the name Coventry Motette. (NMM)

ignition, a sliding gearbox with four forward speeds and a reverse, chain drive, and solid tyres. Prices ranged from £368 for a phaeton to £418 for a private omnibus. Bodies were made initially by Mulliners, and each model had a different name according to the type of body fitted, the Grafton, the Rougemeont, the Universal,

the Wyley, and the Jaunting Car.

Lawson had been replaced as Chairman of the Daimler Motor Company by Henry Sturmey in June 1897. By October he had left the board, and thereafter he really contributed nothing to the growth of the motor car in Britain. The electric car companies he sponsored, Britannia

and New & Mayne, were both bankrupt by the end of the year, and over the next few years he tried to enforce his patents without success. An example of his ineffectiveness was his prosecution of C. S. Rolls for running his Peugeot without a Lawson licence. Rolls retorted that he had tried to obtain his car through the British Motor Syndicate, but had failed. He therefore bought it directly from the manufacturers, rendering Lawson's claims ridiculous. Rolls did, in fact, pay £15 for a licence fee, hardly a fat sum even then, but in his suit against Roots & Venables, Lawson failed to get a penny.

From then on, it was all downhill. The value of Great Horseless Carriage Co shares slumped during the year 1897, and cycle shares fared even worse. He continued to promote various companies for the next seven years. In 1900 he travelled to America where he met a man after his own heart, Colonel Albert Augustus Pope (1843–1909). The Colonel, a Civil War veteran, had a virtual monopoly of the American cycle industry, and was trying to obtain another monopoly with electric cars. Lawson sold him the idea of a very simple two-seater car powered by a single front wheel. It was manufactured under the name Tri-Moto by the Western Wheel Works of Chicago. Production was 'significant' according to historian Beverly Rae Kimes.[17] While in America, Lawson passed himself off as Sir Harry Lawson. In 1904, with his old partner Ernest Hooley, he promoted the Electric Tramways Construction & Maintenance Company, but they were prosecuted for conspiracy to defraud the company's shareholders. It must have been a dramatic trial, with two of the leading barristers of the day, Sir Edward Carson for the prosecution and Rufus Isaacs, later Marquess of Reading, for the defence. The latter's efforts were to no avail, and Lawson was sentenced to 12 months hard labour. He was still writing letters to *The Autocar* in the early 1920s, and died in 1925.

Throughout his career Lawson was less interested in the motor car than in making money, but he undoubtedly did a great deal for the movement. His self confidence, publicity and sheer energy made the public aware of the new machine, and without his efforts it is unlikely that Parliament would have passed the Locomotives on Highways Act as early as it did.

During 1897 the choice for the patriotic Briton who wanted to buy a native product widened, though the majority of the cars sold that year were still imported. One of the participants in the Emancipation Run was an Arnold, a modified Benz built by a firm of agricultural engineers at East Peckham, Kent. The company had in fact entered five cars and a van in the Run, but only one was British-made, and that was assembled from German components. Nevertheless the interest generated by the Run prompted Walter Arnold, who was then 77 years old and had witnessed the Paris–Rouen Trials, to offer cars for sale. He quoted a waiting list of six weeks in the autumn of 1896, but it is likely that only the prototype was made that year. In the following two years 11 cars were turned out, all basically Benz but with an Arnold-made engine which had different cylinder dimensions and bronze castings instead of iron. As often happens, the 'production' Arnolds have all disappeared, but the 1896 prototype survives to this day.

It was bought from the makers by electrical engineer H. J. Dowsing, who fitted the world's first electric starter. This was a dynamotor coupled to the flywheel which was supposed to assist the car up hills as well as start it.

In Scotland, Stirling of Hamilton sold a number of Daimlers with their own coachwork, possibly as many as 20. T. R. B. Elliot, who had brought the first car into Scotland in December 1895, sold it to George Johnston and bought a Stirling, which he fitted with rubber tyres as he found the vibration caused by iron tyres to be unacceptable. In December Stirling's Motor Carriages Ltd was floated for £100,000, and the company became the first in Britain to pay a dividend.

Coventry Motettes in production at the Parkside works, c.1897. A variant with side by side seating was made from 1899, under the name Motor Sociable. (NMM)

Shareholders received five per cent per annum until at least 1900.[18]

Scotland's other pioneer manufacturer was Arrol-Johnston. Locomotive engineer George Johnston was reported to be driving around Glasgow in a 3hp dogcart in November 1895. It was described by the *Glasgow Weekly Herald* as a phaeton and by *The Autocar* as a dogcart. Unfortunately neither journal mentioned its mechanism. If it resembled the first production Arrol-Johnston it would have had an opposed-piston two-cylinder engine. Within a year Johnston had bought Elliot's

Panhard, and was also said to have experimented with electric traction, but production cars showed little Panhard influence, apart from chain final drive which was common anyway. Johnston's design was taken up by Sir William Arrol, a well-known consulting engineer and architect of the Forth Bridge, and additional finance came from textile manufacturer Archibald Coats. They formed the Mo-Car Syndicate Ltd, and production began in a small factory at Bluevale, Camlachie. They remained there until 1901 when they moved to part of the

Engine erecting shop at the Motor Mills, 1897. At least 11 of the vertical twin engines are visible. There is no electricity supply; each bench is illuminated by a gas flare. (NMM)

Coats thread mill at Underwood, Paisley. There they stayed until 1913 when a pioneering factory was built on a greenfield site near Dumfries. (See Chapter Three.)

The Arrol-Johnston gave birth to another Scottish make. In December 1899 two members of the Mo-Car Syndicate, Dr T. Blackwood Murray and Normal Fulton, left to set up their own company in Glasgow, which they called the Albion Motor Company. Their first car of 1900 was on Arrol-Johnston lines, with a similar opposed-piston engine, chain drive and dogcart body. While George Johnston had used a steering wheel from the start, very unusual in 1897, the Albions remained tiller steered until 1902. Neither of the Scottish pioneers were large businesses at this time. Exact production figures are not known, but it is unlikely that either was making more than 100 a year up to 1902.

Large they may not have been, but Albion and Arrol-Johnston were certainly of native design. This could not be said of most of the rest of the British motor industry up to the end of the nineteenth century. It is perhaps understandable that capitalists preferred to devote their money to designs which had been proven on the Continent, as long as they did not have to pay too much in royalties. As well as Arnold, two more substantial companies entered the motor industry via the Benz design; they were Star of Wolverhampton and Marshall of Manchester, whose cars were better known under the name Belsize.

A very early Daimler, possibly made in 1896 with Panhard components, before the familiar rounded bonnet was adopted. The spoon brake on the leading edge of the rear wheel was soon relocated on the trailing edge. Works manager J. S. Critchley is at the tiller. (NMM)

Star had a typical background in the cycle trade. As Sharratt & Lisle they had started in business in 1883, changing their name to the Star Cycle Co in 1896, when capital was £120,000. Their first venture into motor cars was to make the running gear for a curious electric three-wheeler called the Bushbury Electric Cart. Steered by reins rather than tiller or wheel, this vehicle was 'highly commended' at the electric vehicle trials held at the Crystal Palace in May 1897, but nothing more was heard of it. When Edward Lisle decided to enter the motor trade, later in 1897, he chose the 3½ hp Benz Velo as a model. Local content was high from the start, and it does not seem that any components were imported from Germany. By 1900 the Star Motor Company, which had been founded as a separate concern from the cycle business, could boast that all components except the Clipper tyres and Brampton roller chains, were made in the works. The first car to be imported into New Zealand, in 1898, was a Star, and by 1899 the company claimed that they could make a car from scratch in seven days. They went on to become a leading manufacturer in Wolverhampton, of cars and commercial vehicles. After Sunbeam they were the most important vehicle firm in the town up to 1914, though eclipsed after the war by the rapid rise of Clyno and the growing importance of commercial vehicle makers Guy. Star was eventually absorbed by Guy, and the last cars were made in 1932.

Marshall & Company built their first car in 1897, using as their pattern a French-built Hurtu which was itself a copy of the Benz Velo. The works covered one acre and employed 90 workers. Marshall merged in 1901 with bicycle makers Walter Radermacher whose Belsize Works were to give a new name to the cars. This was possibly to avoid confusion with the well-known Lincolnshire agricultural engineers, Marshall of Gainsborough. Having served their apprenticeship with Benz, Marshall,

like Star, soon progressed to more individual designs. The 1901 Belsize had a vertical twin engine made by the French company, Buchet, and they were soon making their own engines. By 1914 the work-force had risen to 1,500, and during the First World War 50 vehicles a week were being made, as well as shells and aero engines. Vehicle

production lasted until 1925 when competition from mass producers and imports led to liabilities of more than £500,000.

Other less important ventures to seek inspiration from the Benz were William Lea of Liverpool who made a few 3½ and 6 hp Liver cars in 1900–1, and Anglo-French. The impressively

Daimler and Daimler-derived Stirling as advertised in The Autocar *for 3 July 1897. The Daimler ad speaks of 'our newest English-made motor vehicles', dispelling the prevalent (and originally correct) belief that foreign components were used.* (NMM)

named Anglo–French Motor Carriage Company was floated in August 1896 to acquire Emile Roger of Paris, who held the Benz rights for France. It promised manufacture at Digbeth, Birmingham, and Maidstone, of 'Lorries, Vans, Broughams, Cabs, Victorias, Coaches, Dogcarts and Char-a-bancs'. Four vehicles were entered by the company in the Emancipation Run in November, but as the factory was not even equipped until the spring of 1897 they were clearly imported Roger-Benzes. They were said to be in business by April 1897 and making vehicles, but quite how many were turned out at Digbeth is uncertain. *The Autocar* visited the factory in July and saw in the body shop barouches, charabancs and a brewer's dray, but these could have

been imported from France and bodied in Birmingham.[19] The company was not mentioned after November 1897, when *The Autocar*'s Midland correspondent observed 'I hear that as excellent as are the prospects of the Anglo-French Motor Co of Digbeth, they are not at the moment doing much in the way of manufacturing; but for this they have doubtless good and sufficient reason.'[20]

Two British companies who made cars to their own design were Roots & Venables of London and Petter of Yeovil. Both employed heavy oil engines which had been made by their respective companies before car manufacture was thought of. James Dennis Roots is said to have installed an oil engine in a boat in 1890, and a year or two later he was making such engines

for H. E. Vosper who was later associated with Thornycroft in boat building. In 1896 he built a three-wheeled car with tandem seating as in the Bollée and a 1½ hp single-cylinder engine. By the spring of 1897, now in partnership with Cuthbert Venables, he was advertising four other designs as well as the three-wheeler, two- and four-seater four-wheelers and delivery vans with three or four wheels. He was keen to point out that his were the only cars to use oil motors, all other so-called oil motors using benzoline spirit. He used any kerosene or paraffin with flash point of 73°–150°F. 'The oil motor is the only safe motor; benzoline spirit is dangerous'. The Roots Oil Motor & Motor Car Co Ltd was capitalized at £30,000 in 1897, though the company name Roots & Venables was

1900 Daimler belonging to Percy Richardson, Daimler's London manager, at Sheen House, Richmond. Behind it is an earlier model, of c.1898. (NB)

A travel-stained Arnold dogcart at the start of the 1896 Emancipation Run. At the controls is Walter Arnold's partner, Benz agent Henry Hewetson. The Arnold was closely based on the Benz Velo. Two other Arnold vehicles on the Run were in fact imported Benzes. (NMM)

also used. They had premises in Lambeth, but many components were made for them by BSA, and from October 1902 the cars were made complete by Armstrong-Whitworth in Newcastle upon Tyne. Production ended in 1904.

Roots & Venables were never significant makers of motor vehicles, but their output was certainly greater than that of Petter. Percival Petter designed a gas engine inspired by an article in *The Boy's Own Paper*, and fitted it to a carriage made by a local firm, Hill & Boll. When he decided to go into production he abandoned gas in favour of heavy oil, using a horizontal two-cylinder engine, with double chain final drive. In November 1896 Petter combined with Hill & Boll to form the Yeovil Motor Car & Cycle Company. *The Autocar* reported that the vehicles which had been delivered had proved very satisfactory, and that a new and commodious factory for their production was well in hand and would be ready for occupation early in January.

'By the time that spring is well advanced Yeovil autocars will be coming through the factory in regular supplies for West of England wants.' Alas, no more than 12 were made, some with electric motors, though Petters later became well-known suppliers of stationary oil engines, and had 500 employees by 1912.

A limited number of electric cars were made in England up to 1900. The Volk designs made by Acme & Immisch have already been referred to, and two coachbuilders, Thrupp & Maberly and Offord, made a few. The Britannia Electric Carriage Syndicate of Colchester, Essex, was a Lawson enterprise which made a small number of landaus and barouches on horse-drawn lines. In London Carl Oppermann of Clerkenwell was advertising in May 1897 that he would supply complete electric cars of any description, or motors and gearing only. He had certainly completed one by that date, a two-seater with centre pivot steering, and went on to make a

variety of electric vehicles up to 1907.

Demand for motor vehicles was really very small in the years 1897 to 1899, and once the euphoria generated by the Locomotives on Highways Act and Brighton Run had evaporated, public interest dropped for several years. As the pioneer motorist Charles Jarrott observed: 'Before the Run horses were to be superseded forthwith and only the marvellous motor vehicles about which they had read so much in the papers for months previously would be seen upon the road'; afterwards 'everybody, including even horse dealers and saddlers, relapsed into placid contentment, and felt secure that the good old-fashioned animal used by our forefathers was in no danger of being displaced.'[21]

There is no doubt that Lawson, who had attracted so much attention to the movement, harmed it in the end. The company promoter was a mistrusted figure in the 1890s, and the taint of the speculator attached to all would-be car makers. In December 1896 *The Automotor Journal* observed that shares in all motor companies were almost unsaleable on the Stock Exchange.[22] Shares were advertised privately; in January 1897 *The Autocar* carried the following notice: 'FOR SALE Five Daimler motor shares, fully paid up, genuine offer. Apply to A. Ganniclifft, hairdresser, Clevedon, Somerset.'

There was also the fact that, as with passengers for the steam coaches of the 1830s, there were not enough people adventurous enough to try a motor car in preference to a horse. They were difficult to drive and notoriously unreliable. Several years later, an American car advertisement listed as one of its virtues 'Goes and Comes Back', hinting that many of its rivals failed to make the return journey. A horse never failed in this respect, so why reject it for a noisy, smelly, vibrating creation which might well leave you stranded with no convenient garages or knowledgeable passers-by to give assistance? The most tangible asset of the motor

This Arrol-Johnston dates from 1905, but it is similar in appearance and design to the original models of 1897. Intended for military work in the Sudan, it had a searchlight on the trailer, and non-standard disc wheels. (NMM)

car, and one frequently proclaimed by its proponents, was that it did not need feeding when not in use, but this was not enough to persuade many.

Exact figures for the number of cars in use in the years 1896 to 1900 are hard to come by. There was no registration or licensing of cars until 1904, and the excise duty returns were only concerned with vehicles of between one and three tons. Some of the heavier passenger cars such as the Panhard and Daimler just exceeded the one ton lower limit, but most cars were below it. The Benz Victoria weighed about 15 cwt and the Velo, probably the most widespread car in Britain, 6 cwt; the Leon Bollée weighed less than 4 cwt. The figures for one to three tonners paying excise duty at the end of each March, were: 1897 16; 1898 75; 1899 61; 1900 230; 1901 198; 1902 334.[23] One should multiply these figures by at least five to get an idea of all passenger cars in use. Even then, the 1897–9 figures are very low. At the end of 1897 the Hon John Scott-Montagu estimated that there were 650 motor cars and motor cycles in use in Britain.[24] He was close to all aspects of the motoring scene, and his estimate is likely to be pretty close to the mark.

CHAPTER THREE

Growing Pains

Nick Georgano

If the Emancipation Run had little impact on the British public at large and, as Charles Jarrott said, was followed by a period of indifference to the motor car, the next major event in Britain was very different. This is because the cars were seen by a much wider public, and the four years that had elapsed had witnessed a growing acceptance of new ideas. Called the Thousand Miles Trial, it was organized by the Automobile Club of Great Britain & Ireland (Royal Automobile Club from 1907) as a demonstration of the motor car's abilities, to prove that it could be a serious form of transport for long journeys. Inevitably a lot of the country had to be covered by the route, and this had the additional advantage of demonstrating motors to many people who had never seen one.

At the beginning of 1900 the ACGBI was low in funds, having lost £1,600 in organizing a motor show in Richmond Park the previous June, and with dwindling support from members. It was probably the club secretary Claude Johnson who dreamt up the idea of a nationwide trial, but it would not have been possible without the backing of newspaper owner Alfred Harmsworth, who guaranteed the club against any losses arising from the Trial, and put up £452 for a prize fund. As well as demonstrating the viability of the motor car, the purpose of the Thousand Miles Trial was to test the cars to the limits, by a series of hill climbs in remote areas such as Shap Fell. They would have raced, too, had it not been illegal on British public

roads. At the time there was no consensus on how a car should be powered or driven, whether by steam, internal combustion or electricity, by belts, chains or propeller shaft, and whether the engine should be at the front or rear of the frame. The Trial was therefore a test of these systems, though in fact it was the build quality rather than the design which enabled the best performers to win honours. Only two steam cars took part, both American-made, and, hardly surprisingly, there were no electric vehicles.

A series of hill climbs would test the cars to the limit

From a start at Hyde Park Corner, the route ran through Reading to Bristol, and then to Birmingham, Manchester, Carlisle, and Edinburgh, 556 miles from London and the most northerly point of the Trial. The 50-odd survivors of the 65 starters returned via Newcastle, Leeds, Sheffield and Nottingham. Only 35 reached London. The Gold Medal for 'the most meritorious vehicle to be accompanied throughout by its owner, and driven by him or her for at least half the distance of the Trial' went to the Hon C. S. Rolls on his 12 hp Panhard.

The cars were exhibited in eight centres, and took part in four obligatory hill climbs (Shap was optional) and two level speed trials in private estates. The last hill, Bunny

Hill, near Nottingham, was a surprise, as well as being the steepest of the obligatory hills. Several passengers had to dismount, in order to push or at least lighten the load; these included the crew of the Hon John Scott Montagu's Daimler, which nevertheless won a Bronze Medal in the final classification. Scott-Montagu, father of the present Lord Montagu of Beaulieu, was the only Member of Parliament taking part in the Trial. One cannot always rely on the reporting, though. Among the cars listed in *The Autocar* (26 May, 1900) as 'stuck' on Bunny Hill was a Star voiturette. The following week, Edward Lisle of the Star Cycle Company wrote in protest: 'I most emphatically state that the Star car did not stick on this hill, or any other hill throughout the run'.[1]

Of the 65 cars and tricycles which took part in the Trial, 33 were of British manufacture. Of these, only Daimler, MMC and Star were in any way significant producers, and none of the three was of British design. Lanchester, Napier, and Wolseley were entered, but were not yet in quantity production. However, the next four years were to see an increase in the proportion of British-made cars on the road, though they would not exceed those of imports until about 1910. During the first five years of the new century, several household names appeared, among them, Humber, Lanchester, Riley, Rover, Standard, Sunbeam, Swift, Vauxhall, and Wolseley. Apart from Sunbeam at Wolverhampton and Vauxhall at

Competitors in the Thousand Miles Trial at the Edinburgh stop. At the front of the column is the 12 hp four-cylinder Daimler of the Hon John Scott-Montagu, followed by J. S. Critchley's 6 hp two-cylinder Daimler, a de Dion Bouton voiturette and a Marshall. As the latter two were trade entries, their drivers' names were not listed in the programme. Scott-Montagu's private status is indicated by black letters on white (did the A stand for amateur?). The 'works' Daimlers were all 6 hp twins, the three 12 hp fours being all privately owned. (NMM)

Luton, all were in the Coventry or Birmingham area, the two cradles of the British motor industry. It is worth examining the reasons for concentration of manufacture in these cities, particularly Coventry.

By the middle of the nineteenth century, Coventry already had a pool of labour skilled in detailed mechanical work, particularly engaged in weaving, ribbon making, sewing machine manufacture and watch making. The 1860s saw a decline in these industries, sewing machines and watch making in particular suffering from cheaper imports from America. Providentially, in 1869 James Starley set up his Coventry Machinists Company, to manufacture bicycles to the designs of the Frenchman Ernest Michaux. Weavers, watchmakers and others down on their luck soon found employment in the cycle shops.[2] By 1881 there were 16 cycle makers in Coventry and by 1898 about 75, though this number soon dwindled as the larger firms took trade from the artisan-manufacturers.

Birmingham also had a long tradition of industry. As early as 1448 the town was mentioned in a deed as 'containing many wholesale merchants known as ironmongers'. In 1538 the traveller John Leland wrote of a visit to Birmingham, and 'a street called Dirty. In it dwell smiths and cutlers'. Alldays & Onions, who made cars from 1898 to 1918, grew out of two Birmingham engineering companies making blacksmiths' equipment, of which Onions was founded in 1650.

The cycle industry was very important in providing a labour force skilled in the kind of work needed for making small cars, which in some cases grew out of motor cycle or tricycle designs. An example is the Riley. The Riley Cycle Co built their first powered vehicles, a tricycle and a quadricycle, in 1899. Between 1903 and 1907 the tricycles gradually took on the appearance of light cars, the saddles giving way to seats, though still in tandem, and the handlebars being replaced by a steering wheel. In 1907 they made their first four-wheeled car, and tricars were dropped in 1908.

Though Humber cars were mainly associated with Coventry, the firm had another factory at Beeston, near Nottingham. Like James Starley, Thomas Humber (1841–1910) based his first machines on the Michaux velocipedes which his friend William Campion had seen at the 1867 Paris Exhibition. His first six cycles, made in a shed behind his house in Nottingham, were copies of the Michaux, but he then made improvements, including a larger front wheel. This became the high-wheeler or Ordinary type, nicknamed the Penny Farthing (though this name was never used at the time). After several different addresses in Nottingham, Humber, Marriott & Cooper, as the company was now called, moved out to Beeston in 1878. In that year tricycles were added to the range, and 1887 saw the first of the new safety bicycles, with chain drive to the rear wheel. This took the bicycle from the realms of the sporting enthusiast to those of a mass public, including ladies, and over the next few years demand for cycles boomed. Humbers were made at Coventry and Wolverhampton, though the latter were built for Thomas Humber's ex-partners Marriott and Cooper by Dan Rudge. In the early 1890s Humber came under the influence of E. T. Hooley who energetically promoted the company, with subsidiaries in the United States (in a factory later used for the manufacture of Locomobile steam cars), Portugal, Denmark, Sweden, and Russia. Hooley's disgrace and bankruptcy in 1898 had an adverse effect on Humber's reputation, and it was fortunate that a new factory in Coventry had just been completed, to replace the one burnt down in July 1896, which destroyed the first Leon Bollée. The foreign factories all had to be sold.

Humber's start in the motor industry was hesitant and difficult to chart. One car was made at the Wolverhampton cycle works in 1896.

It was designed by Christopher Shacklock, and was not called a Humber. The Coventry Bollées and side-by-side Humber Motor Sociables were made up to 1899, when a light two-seater, four-wheeler was made, with front-mounted engine and belt drive to the rear axle. It was listed in 3, 3½ and 5 hp sizes, but it is not known if all were made, or indeed if any cars were sold. In November 1899 Humber exhibited at the Stanley Show a curious machine called the MD quad. This had a single cylinder engine driving the front wheels, while steering was by the rear wheels. Starting was effected by giving a sharp turn to the steering wheel, which gave the crankshaft about three revolutions, via a system of bevels, cross-shafts and chains. Although *The Autocar* said that the MD 'is meeting with a very favourable reception'[3] it is not thought that it went into production. Motor cycles were made from 1902, also tricars which gradually became more car-like, in the same way as the Riley. Bicycles were continued until the early 1920s, so Humber were among the few firms (Rover and Sunbeam were others) to make pedal cycles, motor cycles and cars at the same time for a considerable number of years.

Small cars with 4½ hp De Dion Bouton engines were made in 1901, but car manufacture did not really get going until the arrival of Louis Herve Coatalen (1880–1962), a French-born engineer who designed a 12 hp four-cylinder car and, more importantly, a light two-seater with 5 hp single-cylinder De Dion engine, called the Humberette. This was the car that established Humber's reputation as a serious maker of four-wheelers. It was the first car to be made at both the Coventry and Beeston factories, establishing a tradition that the Beeston cars were better equipped and in a higher price bracket. It was reliable for its day, and reasonably priced at £125 for the Coventry-built model, and £150 for the better-equipped cars from Beeston. These had bucket seats instead of a bench, and small doors. Between June and December 1903 the Coventry factory made 310 Humberettes and the Beeston factory 190.

1904 Humberettes, known as

The 8 hp Napier driven by S. F. Edge in the Thousand Miles Trial, at the Calcot Park (Reading) stop. Edge is at the wheel, next to him is the future historian St. John Nixon, and standing beside the car is owner Edward Kennard. (NMM)

The first car made in a Humber factory was completed in 1896 at the Wolverhampton bicycle works. It was designed and built by works manager Christopher Shacklock, who had been transferred to Wolverhampton from Beeston. The car had a two-cylinder horizontal engine driving through a two-speed epicyclic transmission. Shacklock is at the tiller, with his wife Frances next to him, and in the rear seats her parents Joseph and Julia Bilton. (Courtesy Mrs P. A. Wood)

Royals, had slightly larger engines of 6½ hp. They were made up to the end of the 1905 season, by which time single-cylinder cars were thought to be obsolete, and the company concentrated on fours, a 10/12 hp from Coventry and a 16/20 hp from Beeston. 1906 production reached about a thousand cars, making Humber Britain's largest car maker. Profits that year were £106,559, and in 1907 reached £154, 537. Optimism led to the erection in 1908 of a vast new factory at Folly Lane (later renamed Humber Road) in the Stoke district of Coventry. At about 22.5 acres, it was the largest car factory in England, and remained so until the opening of the Ford plant at Trafford Park in 1911. All production was concentrated in the new works, the car factory at Beeston and the bicycle works at Wolverhampton being both closed. The Stoke plant survived Humber's merger into the Rootes Group, and subsequent ownership by Chrysler and Peugeot-Talbot. One block was used for Hillman Imp components in the 1960s, and another made precision tools for other factories in Peugeot-Talbot.[4]

The new factory brought a need for more working capital, and a new share issue was made in 1908; however, this was a slump year for the motor industry, and only 39,174 of the 100,000 30-shilling shares were taken up. Early in 1909 the company was facing bankruptcy, and was only saved by a wealthy shareholder, Earl Russell, leading a reconstruction plan. A short-lived scheme to make aeroplanes was not fruitful, and was discontinued after two years. Smaller cars were made from 1909 onwards, though the range included cars up to 28 hp, and in 1913 the Humberette name was revived for a V-twin cyclecar. A profit of £5,045 was registered for the 19 month period up to the end of 1910, and in 1912 profits were up to £25,670. Output in 1913 was about 2,500 cars, putting Humber in third place in the British industry, after Ford

The Humberette was the first car made by Humber in serious numbers. Both the Beeston and Coventry factories made them, the former being more expensive and of higher quality. This is a Beeston-built 6½ hp Royal Humberette, entered in the Automobile Club's 1904 Small Car Trials. (NB)

(6,139) and Wolseley (about 3,000).[5]

Rover were almost as important as Humber in the cycle trade, but waited until 1904 before essaying car manufacture. It was John Kemp Starley's Safety bicycle that started the boom, for the number of people brave enough to ride highwheelers was inevitably limited. Starley's company grew out of the Coventry Machinists Company, which also gave birth to Ariel, Hillman, Lea-Francis, Singer, and Swift. The first vehicle to carry the name Rover, signifying that it could rove around the countryside, was a Starley tricycle of 1884, and the Rover Cycle Company was formed in 1896, with capital of £150,000 together with £50,000 in five per cent debentures. 11,000 bicycles were made in 1896, and 15,000 in 1901, the year in which John Kemp Starley died at the early age of 46. His son, also christened John Kemp, and known as Jack to distinguish him from his father, would eventually become managing director, but control of the company was in the hands of general manager Harry Smith. It was he who decided to venture into motor cycles in 1902 and cars two years later.

The first Rover car was designed by Edmund Lewis, who Smith had 'poached' from Daimler. It was a light two-seater, of the same overall size as the Humberette, though more powerful with a 1,327 cc engine rated at 8 hp. It cost £200. The most unusual feature of its design was the tubular backbone frame, quite different from anything Lewis had known at Daimler, but the idea was not followed on subsequent Rovers, probably because the tube had a tendency to break where it was bolted to the back axle assembly. Lewis's 6 hp of 1905 had a conventional wood and flitchplate chassis and cost only 100 guineas (£105). In November 1905 the company name was changed from the Rover Cycle Co to the Rover Company Ltd, indicating a downgrading of bicycles, though these were in fact made up to 1924. Motor cycles were also phased out in 1924, with 10,401

At £105 the 6 hp Rover was good value, and very reliable according to the Hon Leopold Canning, owner of this example. 'Not only have we been on the rough Exmoor tracks, but we have steeple chased over them. She and I have leapt ridges and water courses together, and come down goodness knows where. I have often thought how horrified the makers would be if they saw these performances, but I have not succeeded in breaking anything yet', he wrote in The Autocar *in 1906. (NMM)*

having been made. Bicycle production totalled 426,530. Lewis left Rover for Deasy in 1905 and there was a lack of direction in the design department for several years. Cars with single- and two-cylinder sleeve-valve engines were made in 1911 and 1912, but were not a success, probably because the sleeve valve design was not suitable for so few cylinders.

In September 1910 Owen Clegg joined Rover, having previously worked with Wolseley and Vickers. He designed a 2.2-litre 12 hp car with cylinders cast en bloc, an innovation for the industry. The blocks were cast for Rover by Willans & Robinson of Rugby, one example of the importance of the component manufacturer, which will be considered further later in this chapter. Clegg's Twelve was an immediate success, and helped sales to grow from 400 cars in 1911 to 1,300 in 1912, 1,600 in 1913, and 2,000 in 1914. In 1913 shareholders received a dividend of 40 per cent, the highest in the industry. The Twelve was made up to 1924, though Clegg left Rover in 1912 to design a generally similar car for Darracq.

The third major cycle maker to diversify into cars was Sunbeam,

located at Wolverhampton. Unlike Humber and Rover they did not make highwheelers or tricycles, but entered the industry just as the safety bicycle boom was beginning. John Marston (1836–1918) made tinplate and japanned metal ware at Bilston, and in 1887 he bought the Jeddo Works in Wolverhampton, also tinware manufacturers, where he had been apprenticed. He changed the name to the Sunbeamland Cycle Factory. Here he turned out a high quality cycle, known for its chain which ran in an oil bath. His most promising assistant was Thomas Cureton, so Marston was not unresponsive when Cureton suggested a move into motor cars. Cureton built a prototype in 1899, and the following year submitted a memo to the directors, having gained Marston's approval first. It is worth reproducing Cureton's memo in full:

For several months past I have been watching the Motor Car industry, and have been reading up the subject in various papers and making enquiries from both buyers and makers. The result points to the fact – to put it shortly – that I believe there is a good trade to be done with a good car. As a go-ahead firm I think we should not let a subject so important pass without giving same our serious consideration.

I mentioned the matter to Mr. Marston some weeks ago, and with his approval have taken steps in order to be in a position to bring the matter forward in a definite form. I am of the opinion that it would be to our advantage to make Motor Cars, the following being a few of my reasons.

1. Nearly everyone you meet thinks the Motor Car has a large future.

2. Cars have been largely used in France for years [*a little exaggeration here – Ed.*] and an enormous capital is invested in this industry.

3. If we are to believe reports, all English Makers are busy, but unfortunately like most of the Cycle Companies they are heavily over-capitalised, and like the Cycle Co's again there is wanting that personal attention on the part of the Principals which is so necessary for the success of any business.

These are general facts: now to bring the subject more into focus.

1. We have a good reputation for our Cycles and if we make a Car as good there should be a ready sale for it.

2. We are well known to many good cycle agents who have confidence in us as a firm, and for this reason would take up our Cars, knowing that we would not put one on the market unless it was reliable.

3. We have a building adjoining the Villers Cycle Co.'s which is most convenient in every way for making Cars on a small scale at first, at very little dead expense, this place is empty and not made use of at the present time, motive power can be carried from the next factory at a small cost, and there is a paved way some sixty yards long admirably adapted for trying Cars without being open to public curiosity.

4. Many of the various parts of a Car can be made on our Auto Machinery (which is not being used to its fullest extent by any means – either here or at Villiers C.C. Co.

5. Should this branch of the

business prove a greater success than we at present anticipate, there is ample room for extension on the property at Blakenhall.

6. I have drafted a specification of a Car which should meet the reasonable requirements of the market and which will show a good profit at the selling price of about £140.

7. I have reason to believe that the first Car would cost about £200, after which they should be produced at something like £70; of course these are only rough estimates.

8. A Chain case on a Car would be a special item which is not at present made, and which I think we could undertake to produce.

9. I have a man whom I believe to be a first class Mechanic who is ready to make Cars from start to finish, supplying all the drawings required, in fact produce the car *in toto*.[6]

The man Cureton referred to was named Dimsdale, and with an apprentice, Harry Wood, he made the first Sunbeam almost entirely himself. The parts were cast locally, and even sparking plugs were specially made, as was the radiator. This took the name Marston radiator, and from these early beginnings sprang the Marston Radiator Company, which became one of the biggest suppliers to the industry. The car was assembled in the disused coach house mentioned by Cureton. As he forecast, this building grew into the Sunbeam car works, and was supplemented in 1907 by the Moorfield Works, much larger premises on the other side of Upper Villiers Street. This was Sunbeam's home until after car production ceased in 1935. It was used for trolley-bus manufacture until 1953 when Guy Motors, who then owned the factory, transferred production to Fallings Park.

The two cars that Cureton designed never saw production. The first had a vertical single-cylinder engine, the second a horizontal engine. *The*

Owen Clegg's 12 hp Rover with monobloc four-cylinder engine saved the company and boosted sales from 400 in 1911 to 2,000 three years later. This tourer, bereft of lights in this photograph, is shown with a young chauffeur, though the Twelve was an ideal owner-driver car. (NMM)

Autocar described the latter in some detail, but the most significant words were in the final paragraph: 'The firm are also engaged in producing a voiturette of a special design to sell at a very popular figure, but details of this are not yet available for publication'.[7] Cureton's cars were one-offs, but the 'voiturette of special design' was produced for three years. It was the work of an outsider, Mr Mabberley-Smith, and was a most ingenious design. The four wheels were arranged in diamond pattern, one at the front, two in the centre and one at the rear. A 2¾ hp De Dion Bouton single cylinder engine drove the centre wheels by two-speed belts, and steering was by the front and rear wheels. The driver sat over the rear wheel and the two passengers sat in front, facing crosswise. Nothing like it has been seen before or since, yet this curious device was listed up to 1904. One of its attractions was the low price of £130 (interestingly close to Cureton's forecast for a quite different design). At a time when there was less consensus about how a car should look or be designed, it probably did not seem so eccentric as it does to us. Anyway, it kept the Sunbeam motor department going until the arrival of a conventional four cylinder car based on the French Berliet and designed by Thomas Pullinger, who had worked for the French Darracq and Teste et Moret companies. Mabberley-Smith, who received a royalty for each voiturette made, disappeared after 1904, and the following year Cureton left to join Humber at Beeston.

Pullinger's crypto-Berliets were followed by a native 16/20 hp four from Angus Shaw, but Sunbeam's fortunes really rose with the arrival of Louis Coatalen who had left Humber in 1907, and designed the first Hillman on his way to Sunbeam, where he arrived in 1909. His 12/16 hp Sunbeam was described as 'one of the great commercial successes of the pre-war era'.[8] Profits rose from £5,395 in 1909 to £40,998 in 1910/11 and £93,409 in 1913, when 1,700 cars were

made. The 1912 figure, and Sunbeam's pre-war peak, was 2,350. These figures are all the more remarkable as Sunbeams were by no mean cheap cars. A 12/16 tourer cost £390 and a 25/30 £670, compared with £331 for a Rover Twelve, and £125 for a Model T Ford.

However, not all car makers had cycle links. Daimler had no previous industrial background, using at first imported engines in a wagon-like chassis with coachwork built away from the car factory, at Mulliners in Northampton. Vauxhall's London origin was in steam marine engines (as was Maudslay's in Coventry), though when they moved to Luton in 1905 production was largely concentrated on cars. Interestingly Vauxhall, like Lanchester, tested their petrol engine in a launch before trying it in a car. Other non-cycle backgrounds of well-known companies included electric cranes (Royce & Co, Manchester), sheep-shearing machinery (Wolseley, Birmingham) and armaments (Armstrong-Whitworth, Newcastle upon Tyne).

For a native industry to grow, three factors were essential – capital, a suitably skilled labour force, and greater public acceptance. All these were in evidence by 1905. Capital came from a wide variety of sources. The larger companies raised it through public issues, such as Daimler's £100,000 in 1896, Argyll's £230,000 in 1905, and Darracq, a French make but capitalized in England, which in 1905 issued £375,000 in ordinary shares and £150,000 in debentures.[9] Rover went to the market several times to raise capital, in 1896 when the Rover Cycle Co was capitalized at £150,000, in 1906 when the Rover Co Ltd was formed with £100,000 capital, and in 1908 when capital was increased to £200,000. More interesting was the way in which personal contacts often provided capital. The Standard Motor Co Ltd was set up in 1903 by Reginald Maudslay, a 32-year old engineer who was working for the Tower Bridge

The unconventional Sunbeam-Mabley was the first production car to bear the Sunbeam name. Although a few prototypes with diamond-pattern wheel layout were later made in America, the Mabley was the only one to be made in any numbers. This survivor, running on trade plates, was photographed in about 1930. (Bryan Goodman Collection).

An Argyll advertisement of c.1914 showing the famous marble halls at Alexandria, together with a Flying Fifteen tourer. In 1914 Argyll went bankrupt, and the factory was sold to the Admiralty. (NMM)

designer Sir John Wolfe Barry. When he confided his ambition to build motor cars, Barry agreed to invest £3,000 in the business; the balance of £2,000 came from two fellow pupils of Barry's, Rastat Blake and Alexander Gibb.[10] Autocars & Accessories Ltd of West Norwood, London, grew out of the association between a clever engineer, John Weller, who had designed an advanced car but had no funds, and a prosperous owner of a chain of butcher's shops, John Portwine. The latter invested the modest sum of £200 to enable Weller to build a prototype. Although only one was made under the Weller name, the association led to the formation in 1904 of Autocars & Accessories which made a three-wheeled trade carrier, the passenger version of which was called the AC and led to a famous make which, with many changes of ownership, still survives in 1995.[11]

The butcher Portwine was somewhat unusual as a provider of capital in that he had no connection with motors or engineering. But then West Norwood was far removed from

the centres of the cycle or motor trade. More often, finance would come from local sources in the Midlands, business contacts who were part of the network of component firms on which the cycle and motor trades depended. The chief shareholder in the Rex Motor Company was William Pilkington, formerly a Birmingham tube manufacturer whose company Tubes Ltd, later became the present day Tube Investments Ltd. The other main shareholders were also members of his family, a manufacturer from

Birmingham and an engineer from Coventry. The early capital for White & Poppe, who supplied engines to so many car makers, came from the White family, who were in the watchmaking business.

A less familiar source of capital to set up the Ryknield Engine Company in 1902 came from the brewing industry. Located in Burton on Trent, a leading centre of British brewing then and now, Ryknield's cars, lorries and buses were designed by Ernest Edwin Baguley, an engineer formerly with Bagnalls of Stafford; but the chairman and organizer of the £30,000 initial capital was A. Clay, a director of Bass. In the long run, commercial vehicles were a more important part of the business than cars, and orders from firms such as Bass and Truman, Hanbury & Buxton, kept them going.[12]

Then as now, companies both large and small relied on the banks for advances and overdraft facilities. Lack

Arrol-Johnstons were very old-fashioned up to 1905, in which year they brought out a range of more conventional cars with horizontal-twin engines under the bonnet. This tourer dates from 1905 to 1907. (NMM)

of such support (probably well-founded from the bank's point of view) resulted in the downfall of several small firms. For example, the Clarendon Motor Car & Bicycle Co Ltd of Earlsdon, Coventry, was founded in 1902 to make a light two-seater car with single-cylinder engine. By 1904 it had debts of £2,500, and could not obtain an overdraft from either Lloyds or the Midland Bank. Liquidation inevitably followed.[13] 27 years later a much more distinguished firm suffered from lack of bank confidence, when the Lanchester company's £38,000 overdraft was called in, forcing them into a merger with Daimler. Larger companies fared better; in 1908 Daimler obtained a £10,000 loan from the London & Westminster Bank for the purchase of tyres, though their main account was with the Midland.[14]

Individual wealthy backers were less common, perhaps because several had burnt their fingers through lending their names to the enterprises of Lawson and Hooley. However the Hon Evelyn Ellis invested £10,000 in Daimler debenture shares in 1897 and a further £3,000 in 1900, helping substantially towards saving the company. In 1902 the Earl of Shrewsbury & Talbot invested in the Clement-Talbot company, originally formed to import French-built Clement cars into England, but subsequently a sizeable manufacturer. Three years later the Earl of Macclesfield, an Oxford undergraduate, was involved in a collision with bicycle maker William Morris. The two became friends, and in 1912 the Earl invested £4,000 in preference shares in WRM Motors Ltd, without which Morris would never have been able to set himself up as a car maker. Macclesfield became president of the company, and in 1919, when it was reorganized as Morris Motors Ltd, he took a further £25,000 of seven per cent preference shares.[15] Three years later Morris bought out the Earl's holdings, and had no further business dealings with him. Some links

One of the smaller Daimlers of the immediate pre-war period, probably a 15 hp. By this time all Daimlers had sleeve valve engines and shaft drive. This car, photographed in France, has a French number plate, 830-R3, in addition to its Lincolnshire plate, DO 872. (NMM)

remained, however, for the Earl used a 1931 Morris Minor fire engine on his Shirburn Castle estate in Oxfordshire, rumoured to be still there in the 1980s.[16]

Rolls-Royce was in a slightly different position in that it grew out of C. S. Rolls & Co, a car agency set up in 1902 by Lord Llangattock for his son to run. When it was formed in 1906, Rolls-Royce Ltd was a public company capitalized at £60,000. Rolls put no capital of his own into the new company, and wrote to a friend: 'It is principally a matter of bargaining for the best price we can get for CSR & Co's business and goodwill'.[17] In fact

the issue was not fully subscribed, but the shortfall of £10,000 was made up by Arthur Briggs, a wealthy Yorkshire businessman who had been a major shareholder in C. S. Rolls & Co.[18]

Sheffield-Simplex, a short-lived make but well respected in its day, was financed largely by Earl Fitzwilliam, a very rich coal magnate whose Yorkshire seat, Wentworth Woodhouse, was said to be the biggest private house in Britain. A large factory was erected in Sheffield in 1906, at the Earl's expense, and at its peak turned out 25 chassis a month. However, the company seldom made a profit, and by the mid-1920s Earl

Fitzwilliam found he had lost around £250,000. He ended car production, though Ner-a-Car motor cycles were made in another factory at Kingston-on-Thames. In the 1930s Fitzwilliam took over the stock of the Invicta Car Company and assembled a few cars from parts in hand.

Attitudes to the motor car in Britain changed rapidly in the first ten years of the century. In the early 1900s car owners were regarded with suspicion if not outright hostility at both ends of the social spectrum. The aristocracy, wedded to the horse and suspicious of change, saw the car as 'the most potent symbol of the irresponsible and corrosive plutocracy by which the patricians felt themselves threatened from the 1880s onwards.'[19] The car threatened the settled country existence which they had enjoyed for centuries, it frightened horses, and its smell put foxhounds off the scent. It was seen as the toy of the *nouveaux riches*, who were thought always to be restlessly seeking a new thrill. The rapid conversion of Mr Toad, the ultimate *nouveau riche*, from caravanning to motoring, and then to flying, summed up the feeling. *The Times* shared these sentiments. 'The number of owners and drivers of motor cars who are not gentlemen would seem to be unduly large. There is no turning a cad into a gentleman, but there is such a thing as making even cads fear the law'.[20] In 1903 Lord Wemyss, speaking in the House of Lords, described motorists as 'going about in goggles and a ghastly sort of headgear too horrible to behold. It was clear that when they put on that dress they meant to break the law.'[21] In the Commons a Mr Redmond suggested imprisonment for a second speeding offence. 'I believe it would do some of these flying millionaires all the good in the world'.[22]

The poor suffered more directly, as their houses were close to the road, and motorists sent clouds of dust into open windows, as well as killing chickens and domestic animals. Their feelings were expressed in the ballad *Stone Cracker John*:

'The rich go by in their wildcat machinery,
And they kicks up a dust and they spoils all the greenery.
So, whack, fol-di-riddle-oh, if I had my way,
I'd whack 'em and crack 'em, if I had my way.'[23]

Not that the rural poor were all that familiar with cars for some time. Laurie Lee observed that hardly a car was seen in his remote Gloucestershire valley until the early 1920s.[24] But gradually everyone came to terms with the motor car, even if they did not love it. Aristocractic enthusiasts like the Hon Evelyn Ellis and the Hon John Scott-Montagu (from 1905 Lord Montagu of Beaulieu) were joined by others who found the car indispensable for an extended social life. Among middle-class professionals, the best customers for the car were doctors. If pleased with their choice they were very useful salesmen, as patients contemplating car purchase would be likely to take their doctor's advice.

Motor shows were another effective way of spreading the gospel, acting like magnets to manufacturers and customers alike. Sir David Salomons's working display at Tunbridge Wells in 1895 attracted only four participants, while the ACGBI's Richmond Show four years later saw about 75 cars and commercial vehicles. It was impossible to give an exact figure, as vehicles came and went from one day to the next. In 1902 the Society of Motor Manufacturers and Traders (SMMT) was formed, with the purpose of 'the encouragement, promotion and protection in the United Kingdom and abroad of the motor trade (including the trade of manufacturers of, and traders in, motors and motor cars, motor cycles and vehicles of every description, constructed so as to progress by means of any kind of mechanical or other power, and also of aircraft, and manufacturers of, and traders in, all components parts thereof, and all accessories thereto

respectively, and all ancillary and allied trades and every branch of any such trade.'[25] The SMMT organized their first motor show at the Crystal Palace in February 1903. There were more than 180 exhibitors; with an area of 87,000 square feet it was the largest motor show in the world.[26] The SMMT show moved to Olympia in 1905, when there were two shows, in spring and autumn, and thence to Earls Court in 1937.

Indifference or hostility to the car, serious problems to manufacturers in 1900, were virtually non-existent by 1910. Incidentally, this was the first year that motor cabs exceeded the horse-drawn variety on London's streets.[27]

The growing number of important manufacturers in the Midlands drew more and more labour to these regions, so that by 1910 the majority of Britain's cars were made in Coventry, Birmingham, Wolverhampton and the districts in between. Notable exceptions were Vauxhall in Luton, Napier and Talbot in London, Straker-Squire in Bristol, Crossley in Manchester, Vulcan in Southport, and Rolls-Royce in Derby, with the main Scottish makes being Argyll at Alexandria-by-Glasgow and Arrol-Johnston at Paisley. Two very important exceptions were soon to appear, the Ford assembly plant at Trafford Park, Manchester, and Morris at the Oxford suburb of Cowley. Both of these firms are dealt with in Chapter Four. In fact car making was very widely distributed, though there were no important manufacturers outside the places mentioned. Among unlikely locations were Bath (Horstmann), Salisbury (Scout), Chewton Mendip (Mendip), Lowestoft (Brooke), and Cockermouth (Cumbria). Among the few English counties which never made a car are Huntingdonshire and Cornwall, though the latter was home to two commercial vehicle builders.

Though not the province of this book, it is interesting to note that commercial vehicles were much more widely distributed, because they were not so linked to the light industry of the Midlands. The leading makers of steam wagons – Foden, Sentinel, and Thornycroft – were located at Sandbach (Cheshire), Glasgow (then Shrewsbury from 1917), and Basingstoke respectively, while in the petrol field, Dennis were made at Guildford, and Leylands in the Lancashire town from which they obtained their name.

While Wales has never had any motor industry to speak of, apart from Ford's components and engine plants at Swansea and Bridgend (only set up in 1965 and 1980 respectively), Scotland was home to more than 50 makers of cars, motor cycles and commercial vehicles. At least four concerns were already established by the turn of the century – Albion, Arrol-Johnston, Stirling (see Chapter Two), and Argyll. Unlike their heavy compatriots, the first Argylls were light cars on Renault lines, with a tubular steel chassis, cycle-type wheels and a tiny MMC-De Dion engine of only 258 cc. In 1900 the Hozier Engineering Co of Glasgow was formed to manufacture them, backed by W. A. Smith of the National Telephone Co, with initial capital of £15,000. Over the next few years Argylls increased in size, and production grew encouragingly; in the second quarter of 1904 they built 156 cars, which managing director Alexander Govan considered a record for the British industry.[28] This optimism led to one of the classic cases of over-expansion, the building of a new and extravagant factory at Alexandria-by-Glasgow, on a 25-acre site in the Vale of Leven.

Opened by Lord Montagu of Beaulieu on 26 June 1906, the factory's office block had a road frontage of 760 ft, the central tower contained a clock surmounted by an egg-shaped dome clad in copper, and above that, a lantern. The main hall contained a marble staircase leading to the director's offices, Georgian in style for the managing director and Elizabethan for the board. The southern wing contained a dining hall and a lecture theatre large enough to hold orchestral concerts.[29] The comfort of the workers was on a lavish scale also (see Chapter Eight, p188). An admirer, Fred Gillett, was moved to verse:

'Motor Mary of Argyll,
In thy home among the Highlands
In the new ancestral halls,
Where the staircase can outmarble
Even Pall Mall clubhouse walls,
I have gazed upon thy workshops,
And thy silent golden domes.'[30]

The marble halls cost at least £220,000 (Napier's new factory at Acton cost only £32,000) and never justified their lavishness. As Lord Montagu (son of the man who opened the works) said: 'Alexandria was never more than half full, and the firm's press photographs of the works in action are a dreadful give-away, showing misty, echoing halls, with the odd chassis conveniently posed in the foreground.'[31]

Govan died suddenly in May 1907, which robbed the firm of direction, but even without this loss, prospects were not good. 1908 saw a slump in the British motor industry, and in August Argyll went into liquidation. It was reconstituted and production continued until bankruptcy in 1914, with debts of £80,000; ten shilling shares were worth no more than 7½d.[32] The marble halls were sold to the Admiralty, becoming the Royal Naval Torpedo Factory, and continuing as such until the factory was sold to Plessey Ltd in the 1970s. The Argyll name did not disappear immediately, though, as cars were made in small numbers at the original Glasgow factory until 1928. Fewer than 300 cars were made post-war, but total Argyll production amounted to about 6,000. Among Argyll apprentices who became celebrated in later years were tractor maker Harry Ferguson and television pioneer John Logie Baird.

Arrol-Johnston, meanwhile, continued with their opposed-piston cars, mostly with very old-fashioned looking dogcart bodies, up to 1905, when a new design was introduced, also with a horizontal twin engine but now mounted in the conventional position under a bonnet. At the same time, the company was reorganized under the name New Arrol-Johnston Car Co Ltd. The backer and chairman was Sir William Beardmore, later Lord Invernairn, who controlled several companies, one of which made cars in the 1920s. The horizontal twin was dropped after the 1909 season, replaced by a range of four-cylinder cars designed by T. C. Pullinger. Their only unusual feature was a dashboard radiator and coal-scuttle bonnet, à la Renault.

The Paisley factory was insufficient for Pullinger's ambitious plans, and in 1913 Arrol Johnston moved to a greenfield site on the outskirts of Dumfries. Here an advanced factory was built, designed by the Trussed Concrete Steel Company and built on the principles of Albert Kahn, the American architect who had been responsible for the Ford plant at Highland Park, and after the war would design the GAZ plant at Gorky in the Soviet Union. The main features of Kahn's design were concrete framing, multi-storey layout and curtain walls of glass, making for a much lighter interior. It was the most advanced car factory in Britain, but few cars were made before the outbreak of the First World War. Military production included Beardmore aero engines and airframes. Arrol-Johnston sales were disappointing in the 1920s, and after a merger with the Aster company, Arrol-Aster cars were made up to 1928. Arrol-Johnston production was always smaller than Argyll's, not more than 300–400 per year, compared with a peak of 700 from Alexandria. The third of Scotland's 'Three As', Albion, made even fewer cars, as commercial vehicles assumed increasing priority in the years up to 1914 and took over completely after the war.

Up to 1914 there were four leading makes in the luxury car class: Daimler,

An early Napier, a 16 hp Type H 70 as made from the second part of 1900 and into 1901. Although it developed 24 hp, the maker's designation was 16 hp. The forward/reverse gearshift changed crown wheels, giving as many speeds in reverse as forward. This car was exhibited at the Automobile Club show in May 1901. (Bryan Goodman Collection).

Lanchester, Napier, and Rolls-Royce. Not far behind were Sheffield-Simplex, and the top models of Sunbeam, Vauxhall, and Wolseley. These competed with imports such as Panhard, Delaunay-Belleville, Benz, Mercedes, and Fiat. While imported cars continued to be sold, the improved quality of the domestic product meant that the proportion of foreign cars dropped substantially between 1900 and 1914.

Of the four top makes, Daimler had the soundest reputation, due to its status as the pioneer British car maker and also because it was the choice of the Royal Family. The press ignored the fact that King Edward VII really preferred his Mercedes, as he said the chain drive was quieter than the Daimler's bevel gears. For public appearances in Britain Daimlers were always used, and after the accession of George V in 1910 the Mercedes disappeared from the royal fleet. Despite the sound reputation of its cars, the Daimler company had some rough passages at the beginning of the decade. In 1898 most of the original board members resigned in protest at the election as Chairman of Richard Bannister who, by his own admission, knew nothing about cars. Those who resigned included Evelyn Ellis and Gottlieb Daimler, though Daimler was given the title of honorary president of the company. A committee was set up to represent the shareholders' interests, and their report was highly critical of the board. Among other things the report said that the board had been appointed by the British Motor Syndicate, holders of the Daimler patents, and that they were likely to put the interests of the Syndicate before those of the Daimler Company. In particular it was said that the price of £40,000 paid by the Company to the Syndicate for the patents was too high.[33] The report also accused the board of lacking the necessary technical expertise to run a motor company, and of taking too much remuneration from the company, whose finances were nowhere near as rosy as the optimistic report of October 1897 led the shareholders to believe. The report caused a sharp fall in the value of the company's shares, and at a meeting in January 1899 there was a move to wind it up. This was defeated, and a new board was elected with E. H. Bayley as chairman. Henry

Sturmey resigned in May as he no longer had any influence in the company, and it was thought that to be a director of Britain's leading car maker and editor of the leading motor journal (*The Autocar*) might represent a conflict of interests.

New models were introduced in 1903, which finally broke away from the old Panhard-inspired designs. The work of Percy Martin, they had longer chassis, though stand-by tube ignition was retained, just in case the magneto failed. Further improvements came in 1904, when the famous fluted radiator was adopted, and larger models of 18/22 and 28/36 hp were launched. 1904 also saw another reorganization of the company, now called The Daimler Motor Co (1904) Ltd. The Motor Manufacturing Company, which still made MMC cars, went into liquidation, and its premises in the Motor Mills which had been leased to

the Great Horseless Carriage Co were purchased by the new Daimler Company for £14,500. This gave a 75 per cent increase in floor space. The number of men employed in September 1905 had risen by 137 per cent over the figure in the same month of 1901, and cars ordered by 140 per cent.[34]

Though Daimler was on a stronger footing after 1904, helped by a successful £200,000 share issue, they were in trouble again three years later. The apprentice Sammy Davis recalled that, in order to show a healthier balance sheet at the time of the annual audit, completed chassis were dismantled and the parts stored. This was because the book value of the components was greater than that of complete cars.[35] A £49,286 loss was recorded for 1908, and finances were not helped by Daimler's taking up the Knight sleeve-valve patents. All 1909

models had sleeve-valve engines, but a lot of money was spent on developing them for production (in which Frederick Lanchester was deeply involved), and by the end of 1909 Daimler was once again faced with bankruptcy.

It was saved by an amalgamation with the Birmingham Small Arms Co, familiarly known as BSA. Birmingham had been a centre of gun making since the end of the seventeenth century, and in 1861 a group of small manufacturers merged to form the Birmingham Small Arms Company. They added bicycles to their range in 1880 when a period of peace meant a slump in demand for arms, and in 1908 they made their first car, followed by a motor cycle a year later. They were a very much richer company than Daimler, as the following figures, from the close of the financial year 1908–9, show:[36]

	Share capital issued		Debits & Loans	Ordinary Dividend	Reserves carried forward
	Preferred	Ordinary			
BSA	£203,150	£517,225	Nil	10%	£175,600
Daimler	£80,880	£200,000	£51,000	Nil	£253,330

A fine example of a Silver Ghost with relatively light body, in this case a 1912 tourer by Barker. This is the kind of car which might have used the long-stroke engine that Royce experimented with. It was noisier than the standard engine, and Royce said 'the duchesses, perhaps, won't have it. They would call it a racing car, and you know what that means.' The duchess trade was vital to the business, so the long-stroke engine never went into production for the Ghost, though some of its points appeared in the design of the Phantom 1. (NMM)

The Financial Times said of the merger: 'The combination is one of the most important ever effected in the motor industry'.[37] In that it preserved the Daimler car for posterity this was certainly true. The new board consisted of directors from both companies; among the BSA men was F. Dudley Docker, whose son Sir Bernard Docker was to be Chairman of BSA from 1940 to 1956 (see Chapter Six). A long-standing chairman of BSA had been Herbert Chamberlain, and in 1913 the board was joined by his nephew, Neville Chamberlain, Prime Minister from 1937 to 1940. Another board member was Colonel H. C. L. Holden who had been in charge of the design of Brooklands Motor Course.

In 1912 Daimler opened a new factory known as the Radford Works, also in Coventry. The Motor Mills continued in use until 1937, and were destroyed by enemy action in 1941, which also left 70 per cent of the Radford Works in ruins. Radford built bus chassis between the wars, and today serves as an assembly plant for Jaguar XJ6 and V12 engines, also for front axle milling and machining.[38] In 1911, Daimler sanctioned production of 1,153 cars in six models, four fours and two sixes, from a 1.7-litre 12 hp selling for £375 complete to a 6.2-litre 38 hp six at a chassis price of £700. An 8.5-litre 57 hp six was also listed at £900 for the chassis, but not sanctioned for production, so presumably the engines had been completed the previous year and put into stock. King George V took delivery of three of these 57 hp cars, one of which had been ordered by his father but never used. In 1923 he ordered two more with the 57 hp engine, and it is possible that a few were available to private citizens. All had Knight sleeve-valve engines, as did every Daimler until 1933.

The second-largest company in the luxury field was Napier. Like Daimler, but unlike Rolls-Royce and Lanchester, Napier built a variety of models, from quite reasonable cars to very expensive ones, and also made commercial vehicles. Although the London area has been home to more than 400 car makers very few have been famous, apart from Talbot and Napier. The parent company had been set up in Soho in 1808 by Scots-born David Napier, who moved to Lambeth in the 1830s. Among the varied products of the company were steam-powered gun-finishing and bullet-making machinery, followed in 1854 by machines for minting coins and printing stamps and banknotes. All these tasks demanded a high degree of precision, ideal for making quality cars, but Napier declined in the latter half of the nineteenth century, and on the death of David's son James in 1895 only seven men were employed at Lambeth.

She answers to the speed lever as does a hunter to a spur

James's son Montague was a keen cyclist, and his hobby inadvertently led to a revival of the company. One of his rivals was Selwyn Francis Edge (1865–1940), the Australian-born manager of the Dunlop Tyre Company's London branch. Edge's first car was an 1896 two-cylinder Panhard which he bought for a high price from H. J. Lawson. When it failed to live up to expectations he asked Montague Napier to make improvements. These included replacing the tiller with a steering wheel, adding a radiator and modifying the engine to use coil ignition in place of hot tube. Edge was sufficiently impressed with this car to form a company, the Motor Power Co, for which he promised to buy Napier's cars so long as he had the exclusive rights. The arrangement was similar to that reached between Rolls and Royce a few years later.

The first Napier car was made in 1900, using an engine similar to the replacement unit in the Panhard. Edge drove it in the Thousand Miles Trial, winning a Bronze Medal. It was no more than an improved Panhard, but no worse for that as the French company was still the leader in design. They had been making four-cylinder engines since 1896, and Napier built his first four in 1900, a car which Edge entered in the Paris–Toulouse race. Though the Hon John Scott-Montagu had driven a Daimler in the touring class of the 1899 Paris–Ostend Race, the Napier was the first entry of a British racing car in a Continental event. It did not complete the course but Napier and Edge were to redeem themselves two years later when a 30 hp car won the Gordon Bennett Cup. Sales to the public began in 1900 and hire purchase facilities were available from November 1901. Among early Napier customers were Prime Minister Arthur Balfour and Mrs Edward Kennard, wife of the owner of the Thousand Miles Trial car, who enthused over the 1902 model: 'She answers to the change speed lever as does a high-mettled hunter to the touch of a spur'.[39]

Growing demand for Napier cars made the old premises at Vine Street, Lambeth, inadequate, and in the summer of 1903 car production was moved to a new factory built on a four-acre site at Acton in West London. In October they announced a six-cylinder car, which Edge proclaimed as the first of its kind in the world. Counter claims have been made on behalf of the Dutch Spyker (which also had four-wheel drive), but this was a one-off competition special, whereas the 30 hp Napier went into production and gave rise to an all-six-cylinder range within a few years. So linked to the six was Napier's image that when they built three four-cylinder cars for the 1908 Tourist Trophy Race they were entered under the name Hutton.

Napier expanded their works in 1904 and again in 1906. The following year they employed 1,200 men, but only turned out two cars per week[40]. These were the Forty and Sixty, the latter costing £1,200 for a chassis, making it the most expensive British-built car. The years 1906 to 1911 saw

Napier's reputation at its peak – more than 160 members of the aristocracy, army and church were listed as customers in the 1910 catalogue, and the make was particularly popular with Indian rulers. The 14½-litre Ninety was built largely for the sub-continent, some nearly 20 feet long and with three or even four rows of seats. Some were also made for competition, including the two survivors.

In July 1907 Edge reorganized his company as S. F. Edge (1907) Ltd, with an agreement not to handle any other make of car so long as Napier provided him with at least £160,000 worth of cars each year. This worked for a while, but in 1911 Edge complained that the cars were old-fashioned and of poorer quality than before. In 1912 Edge issued a writ against Napier for providing unsatisfactory cars, and the upshot was that Edge's company was bought by Napier for £152,000. Edge agreed not to engage in the motor trade for seven years, later becoming involved with AC.

In fact the years 1909–13 saw the peak of Napier's production, with about 600–750 cars per year made, compared with only 100 in 1907. The all-six policy had been well and truly abandoned, with small two- and four-cylinder chassis being offered, though the former were mostly intended for taxi-cab work. London had over 600 Napier cabs in 1912, and cab production exceeded that of cars in 1910, by 556 to 366. In 1912 the figures were reversed, deliveries being 574 passenger cars, 122 cabs and 95 commercial vehicles.[41] A good 30–35 hp six was made from 1909 to 1915, as well as four-cylinder Colonial models with higher ground clearance, available in 'Colonial' and 'Extra-Strong Colonial' forms. No more than 300 cars were made in 1914.

Napier's decline coincided with the rising popularity of the Rolls-Royce, which even S. F. Edge grudgingly admitted was 'certainly quite a nice car'.[42] The success of the Rolls was surprising in that from 1908 it was made in only one model, the expensive 40/50, with no back-up from smaller cars and commercial vehicles or, as in its later years, aero engines. Not all Rolls-Royces had been winners; the original 10 hp twin was a well-made little car, much smoother than its contemporaries, but it did not stand out particularly among its many rivals and in any case only 16 were made. The four-cylinder Twenty had some sporting successes, including victory in the 1906 Tourist Trophy and sold 40 examples, but the first six, the 30/40 suffered – like many of its kind from torsional vibration of the crankshaft. Then with the 40/50 everything came right. The credit must go largely to Henry Royce, who completely redesigned the engine; the 30/40 was essentially three blocks of the 10 hp twin, an early example of standardization which simplified production. However, the journals and pins designed for a twin now had to do duty for a crankshaft three times as long. In the new engine Royce used two blocks of three cylinders, and the pins and journals were nearly twice the diameter of those in the 30/40. He also replaced the inlet-over-exhaust valves, which all previous Royce designs had used, with side valves.

There is no engine as far as sensation goes, nor are one's auditory nerves troubled

---

The new car was introduced at the Olympia Show in November 1906, and by April 1907 13 chassis had been built. Number 12 achieved lasting fame; a Barker bodied tourer with silver paint and silver-plated fittings ordered by Claude Johnson, it carried a plate with its name, *The Silver Ghost*. It was not unusual for cars to carry individual names, other 40/50s being called *The Silent Rogue* and *The Dragon Fly*. As the 40/50 was the only model after 1908, there was no need for any name, and it was usually called simply the Rolls-Royce. However, when the New Phantom, also a 40/50, arrived in 1925, people who wanted to refer to the previous 40/50 models called them Silver Ghosts, and the name has been used ever since.

The original *Silver Ghost* was tested by *The Autocar* in April 1907, and was pronounced to be of remarkable silence. 'At whatever speed the car is being driven on its direct third, there is no engine as far as sensation goes nor are one's auditory nerves troubled . . . by a fuller sound than emanates from an eight-day clock. There is *no* realisation of driving propulsion; the feeling as the passenger sits either at the front or back of the vehicle is one of being wafted through the landscape'.[13] It is interesting that the subject of the clock, used in American RR advertising in the 1950s, should have originated so long ago.

Claude Johnson, who master-minded the marketing of Rolls-Royces, would not allow a car to reach the public until thorough testing had taken place. This included driving the *Silver Ghost* continuously from London to Glasgow until 15,000 miles had been clocked up. This was considered to be the equivalent of three years normal use. A hiatus between showing a car and delivering examples to customers can be fatal – one thinks of the Cord 810 and Chrysler Airflow in America – but in the case of the Rolls-Royce public curiosity was whetted, and when the car went on sale in September 1907 demand was high. The 30/40 was obviously dropped, and the Twenty followed soon afterwards, although the decision to concentrate on a one-model policy was not taken until March 1908. By then the move to a new factory was well under way. The original premises in Cooke Street, Manchester, where car making was shared with that of electric cranes, were too cramped. A search for new premises was made, and after considering another location in Manchester, and also sites in Macclesfield and Nottingham, they had almost settled on Leicester when Derby Council made an offer of reduced rates on premises at

Nightingale Road.[44] The decision to move to Derby was taken in December 1906, and it was not until July 1908 that the factory was opened by Lord Montagu of Beaulieu. The success of his magazine *The Car Illustrated* had made him much in demand for ceremonies like this. Soon production at Derby was averaging seven chassis per week (350 per annum) and remained at this level for several years, reaching 600 per annum by 1913.

The 40/50 was a car of contrasting character, depending on the coachwork and chassis length. On the one hand were the landaulettes and limousines, the cars for the 'duchess trade' on which the company depended for their bread and butter. On the other hand sporting models, such as the London–Edinburgh and Alpine Eagle, offered driving enjoyment such as could never be obtained from any Daimler or Napier. Alan Clark wrote of his two-seater: 'On a fine evening there are very few pleasures comparable to driving a light, open Ghost on country roads . . . There are 27 separate actions, all of them involving beautifully crafted mechanical linkages, from turning on the gravity petrol feed to actually cranking the starting handle. And after they have been completed in the correct sequence it will – infallibly – fire on the first compression.'[45]

The title 'the best car in the world' was used for the Rolls-Royce by the *Pall Mall Gazette* in November 1911, though Rolls-Royce themselves called the 40/50 'the best six-cylinder car in the world' as early as March 1907. 'The best car' title was adopted by the company in their advertising. While later Rollses basked in the compliment, it was earned by the 40/50.

The fourth leading British make was Lanchester, the most idiosyncratic of all, and the product of a brilliant engineer who worked from first principles rather than following other people. Frederick William Lanchester (1868–1946) worked for the Forward Gas Engine Company in Birmingham before going solo to build a motor boat

in 1894 and his first car a year later. This was gradually put together during 1895, and made its first road run in February or March 1896.[46] It was a remarkable design, owing practically nothing to the ideas of Daimler or Panhard. The engine had a single horizontal cylinder with two overhanging balanced cranks, each with its own flywheel and connecting rod. The cranks revolved in opposite directions giving a smoothness of running unknown in any contemporary car. The gearchange was epicyclic, the frame tubular, and the body was a full-width four-seater of varnished walnut.

Fred Lanchester and his brothers George and Frank were in no hurry to put a car on the market until it had been thoroughly tested. A second car with two-cylinder engine was built in 1897, and it was another two years before the Lanchester Engine Company was formed, in December 1899. Authorized capital was £60,000, but only £42,525 was paid up, and of that only £25,000 was in cash, the rest being represented by the patents,

machinery and other assets of the syndicate the brothers had already formed. A factory had to be bought and fitted (in Sparkbrook, Birmingham), and after that there was very little cash left for developing new models.

Only six cars were made in 1901, all going to directors, so there was no income for the company. The cars were similar to the second model of 1897, with centrally-mounted horizontally-opposed two-cylinder engines, three-speed epicyclic transmissions, and worm-driven rear axles. Steering was by side tiller, or lever as the Lanchesters preferred to call it. This was continued until 1911, long after all other car makers had gone over to wheel steering. Up to 1904 only two-cylinder cars were made, mostly of 10 or 12 hp. The engine capacity was the same, but the 10 was air-cooled; it was reckoned that the fans absorbed 2 hp at maximum speed, hence the difference in quoted power.

In 1904 the first four-cylinder Lanchester appeared, a 20 hp of 2,470 cc, now mounted vertically and

Silver Ghost chassis, in parallel and tapered bonnet form, on the build line in Number 1 Shop at Derby, c.1912. Tyres were not fitted to the chassis until they were complete, and even then they were only slave tyres, used to move the chassis around the factory. (NMM)

at the front. It was located between the driver and passenger, continuing the 'bonnetless' look of the mid-engined cars. Up to 1914 all Lanchesters had very short bonnets due to their engine position. Also in 1904 the company was reorganized and Fred Lanchester was demoted from general manager to 'designer and consultant', with a drop in salary of nearly 30 per cent. This reinforced his distrust of businessmen, and increasingly bad feeling between him and the directors eventually led to his resignation in 1913.

The 20 hp four was joined by a 28 hp six in 1906, and with enlarged capacity these were the sole Lanchester models up to 1914. By then the four was a 25 hp 3.2-litre, and the six a 38 hp of 4.8 litres. In 1913 they cost £800 and £1,110 respectively, for a complete closed car. Since 1903 Lanchester had their own coach-building department, and although a separate chassis was quoted, very few were supplied to outside coach-builders. Comparable prices for their rivals were £1,175 for a 45 hp Daimler, £1,045 for a 45 hp Napier and £1,145 for a 40/50 hp Rolls-Royce.[47] The 38 hp Lanchesters were thus among the top-price cars, though of smaller engine capacity. Their owners were a relatively small band (1913 production was 200 cars, less than a third of Rolls-Royce and a fifth of Daimler output), but very loyal. Among the most loyal was Prince Ranjitsinhji, the Jam Sahib of Nawanagar, better known as Ranji the cricketer. He bought his first Lanchester in 1902; by 1912 he was on his tenth, and his final purchase was in 1947. However, the last was a Lanchester in name only, for it was in fact a Daimler DE27 fitted, at the Prince's request, with a Lanchester radiator.

Wolseley, like Lanchester, was a pioneer make which took some years between first prototype and a production car. Although it bore the name of Frederick York Wolseley (1837–99), he played no part in any designs. These were the work of Herbert Austin (1866–1941), followed after 1905 by John Davenport Siddeley (1866–1953). In the 1890s Austin was the general manager of the Wolseley Sheep Shearing Co, which had been founded by Frederick Wolseley in Australia in 1887. Finding the quality of the Australian-made machines unsatisfactory, Wolseley relocated in Birmingham. As it was the heart of British engineering, one might have expected better results, but much of the work was sub-contracted to small firms whose quality was indifferent. The company's reputation had sunk to a low ebb by 1894, but Austin persuaded the directors that all manufacture should be under one roof, and that new products such as machine tools and bicycle components should be added to the range. In the autumn of 1895 he visited Paris where he saw the Léon Bollée three-wheeler. During the winter of 1895/6 he built a car of basically similar layout, though he used his own design of engine which was, to say the least, unorthodox. It had two horizontal cylinders, with a single combustion chamber mounted above the crankcase. In the words of the inimitable Anthony Bird, instead of acting directly on the pistons 'the expanding gases had to find their way into the cylinders down two long exposed tubes and round several corners by which time, one opines, they had lost most of their initial energy'.[48]

It has been suggested that Austin did not proceed with this car because he feared legal action from H. J. Lawson, who acquired the British rights to the Bollée patents in May 1896. However, the completely different engine design, and the fact that the Bollée seated two in tandem, with the driver behind, while on the Wolseley the seats were back to back, means that they were not really all that alike. It is just as probable that Austin found the first car did not work satisfactorily, and in 1897 he built another. Apart from the fact that it also had three wheels, it could not have been more different. The single wheel was now at the front, steered by a long tiller like that of a Bath chair, the engine was a more conventional horizontal twin, and the transmission was a two-speed epicyclic in place of the belts and sliding gearbox of the first car. Evidently this was not satisfactory either, for later in 1897 the twin was replaced by a single-cylinder engine and the gearbox became a Benz-type belt-and-pulley system. Whereas Austin had built the first car more or less in secret, the second was approved by the directors, and a catalogue was issued for the 'Wolseley Autocar Number 1' quoting a price of £110 for a two-seater, or £150 for a four-seater. The latter was never built, and only one of the two-seaters was made.

Wolseley could engage in any business except making cars

In 1899 Austin progressed to a four-wheeler, with a horizontal single-cylinder engine, chain drive, and a large radiator which wrapped around the short bonnet, all features which found their way onto the production cars of 1901. The first four-wheeler was entered in the Thousand Miles Trial, being joined at Birmingham by a second car with a two-cylinder engine which did not complete many miles. The first, however, driven by Herbert Austin, was awarded first prize in Class B.

Few if any cars were sold in 1900, and in February 1901 the car manufacturing side of the business was bought by the big engineering and armaments concern, Vickers, Son & Maxim Ltd, for £12,400 in cash plus 67 five per cent second debentures of £100 each to the Wolseley Company, and 33 of these debentures to Herbert Austin.[49] The Wolseley company was free to engage in any business except that of car manufacture. It continued with its traditional products, later adding horse-clipping machines and cream separators. Vickers bought a factory at Adderley

Park, Birmingham. New models were announced on 1 May 1901, being a single-cylinder 5 hp and a 10 hp twin, similar to the 1899 car apart from having wheel steering and artillery wheels in place of the tiller and wire wheels of the prototype. They sold well, 383 being delivered during the remaining eight months of 1901.

A 20 hp four was introduced for 1902, and this was made up to the end of 1904, latterly being called a 24 hp. Exports took the cars as far afield as India, Africa, Malaya, and Australia, but sales slowed as the horizontal engine went out of fashion. Profits up to 1903 gave way to losses in the next two years, but Austin stubbornly refused to consider a new type of engine. Meanwhile J. D. Siddeley had

been making small cars with vertical engines (actually close copies of the Peugeot) at another Vickers-owned factory, at Crayford in Kent. These outsold the Wolseleys, and Siddeley was invited to become sales manager for Wolseley. Herbert Austin saw this as a snub, and resigned as General Manager early in 1905. Ironically he left Wolseley over an apparent devotion to the horizontal engine, yet when he began to make cars under his own name a year later, they all had vertical engines.

Though the Austin-designed singles and twins were sold through 1906, there was soon a new range of Siddeley-designed Wolseleys, sometimes called Wolseley-Siddeleys, on the market. These took Wolseley into a

higher price bracket, for the 1907 range ran from a 10 hp twin to a 45 hp six costing £975 complete. Wolseley was the only British car maker apart from Daimler to receive the Royal Warrant. Queen Alexandra took delivery of a 24 hp landaulette in 1904 and a 50 hp limousine in 1910, while in 1906 King Edward VII ordered an 18 hp to be delivered to the convalescent home for officers at Osborne House on the Isle of Wight.

Siddeley was thought to be too high and mighty by Wolseley's directors, who resented the prominence he gave to his own name, telling a group of dealers that the cars would not, for the moment, carry the Wolseley name. Growing animosity led to his departure in 1909, when he joined the Deasy company to make the Siddeley-Deasy. This became Armstrong-Siddeley after the First World War. J. D. Siddeley had a very successful career with this company, being knighted in 1933 and created Baron Kenilworth in 1937. Design at Wolseley had meanwhile passed to Alfred Remmington who continued the vertical engine theme with a wide variety of models. In 1910, when more than 1,000 cars were made, there were eight models from a 2.2-litre 12/16 to a 9.9-litre 60 hp. In 1910 Wolseley expanded their Adderley Park premises into the factory vacated by the Metropolitan Railway Carriage & Waggon Co, also owned by Vickers. This company later merged with the wagon-building division of shipbuilders Cammell Laird, and then with Weymann, to form Metropolitan Cammell Weymann, maker of the Metrobus in the 1980s.

The additional premises allowed Wolseley production to grow, so that by 1913 they were making about 3,000 cars a year, as well as 1,500 of the smaller Stellite at a separate factory.

A factory shot of Lanchesters, c.1908. Both lever and wheel steered models are visible, and most have very light test bodies with neither doors nor hoods. (NMM)

They also made several hundred commercial vehicles. This put them in second place behind Ford, and therefore the leading British car manufacturer. Their 21-acre site was said to be the largest factory in Europe devoted solely to the manufacture of motor vehicles. The factory had electric lifts, one per block, each of which could carry a completed car.[50]

Wolseley were unusual in making practically all of their cars apart from tyres and ignition coils. Their steel came from Vickers's works at Sheffield. Rolls-Royce were also almost completely self-sufficient apart from tyres, making their own electrical equipment, carburettors, and fuel pumps. Not until the 1930s would they start to buy in such components. For many other firms, though, especially the smaller ones, a reliable supply of components was essential. The larger manufacturers liked to boast that their engines and chassis at least were of their own manufacture, but even here one needs to be wary of the words 'own manufacture'. Rover's monobloc casting on their Twelve was made for them by Willans & Robinson, while Austin turned to Sankey or Rubery Owen for frames and wheels if seasonal demand was too great for their own factory.[51]

There were two reasons for a firm buying its engines from an outside source; their own premises might be too small to allow for the casting of a cylinder block, or they might not want to invest the necessary capital in expensive machinery, preferring to be assemblers. The best-known example of the latter was William Morris who bought practically everything in to start with, and only became a 'manufacturer' in the 1920s by buying up his component suppliers, such as Hotchkiss engines, Wrigley gearboxes, SU carburettors, and Hollick & Pratt bodies. The main suppliers of engines in the pre-1914 era were De Dion Bouton and Aster, the latter a French company with an English factory at Wembley, and two Coventry concerns, White & Poppe and Johnston, Hurley

A Herbert Austin-designed horizontal-engined Wolseley 10 hp tonneau, with a 22 hp Daimler, taking part in the Automobile Club Thousand Miles Trial in 1903. The Daimler was one of only four cars which came through the road trials with a clean sheet. (NMM)

& Martin, who marketed their engines under the name Alpha. During the cyclecar boom of 1912–14, makers of single- and two-cylinder engines catering to the cyclecar trade included Anzani, Coventry-Simplex, J. A. Prestwich (JAP), and Precision.[52]

Of the Coventry companies, White & Poppe was the largest. Founded in 1899 they made shell fuses during the Boer War and engines for motor cycles from 1903. Their first large order for car engines came from Swift in 1905, and at the Olympia Motor Show in November 1906 no fewer than 15 car makers exhibited White & Poppe-powered products. These included Calthorpe, Clyde, Dennis, and Singer. Among foreign manufacturers to buy from White & Poppe were Thrige in Denmark and Tarrant in Australia. Their first engines were made to a standardized design, with T-head valve layout and dimensions of 80 x 90 mm in one-, two-, three- and four-cylinder models at first, joined by a six in 1906. Relatively few sixes were made, but customers included Calthorpe, Climax, Heron, Horbick, and West.[53] An important buyer of W&P engines was Siddeley-Deasy,

which took several hundred of the 80 x 130 mm 2.6-litre fours between 1911 and 1915. W&P's best known customer was William Morris, who ordered a 1,018 cc four-cylinder engine for his first Oxford. W&P also supplied the gearbox, clutch and carburettor for these cars. The connection with Morris might have lasted longer had not White & Poppe been bought up by Dennis in 1919. This assured the Guildford firm a supply of engines for their lorries and buses. P. A. Poppe became a director of Dennis up to 1924, after which he joined Rover as chief engineer, designing their 14/45 model. From 1906 W&P made carburettors, selling some 20,000 over the next six years. Among users of W&P carburettors was Vauxhall.

Other components for which the industry depended heavily on outside suppliers were radiators, electrical equipment, and tyres. The Motor Radiator Manufacturing Company of Coventry included among their customers Argyll, Crossley, Lanchester, Rover, Star, Swift, Vauxhall, and Wolseley. In 1912 their output was 4,000 to 5,000 per year, accounting for about 20 per cent of the total needs of the industry.[54] Morris bought his radiators from Doherty Motor Components Ltd and in the 1920s bought the company.

Electrical equipment was a specialized field and apart from Rolls-Royce few companies made their own. Almost all magnetos came from the Simms Manufacturing Company of Willesden, London. F. R. Simms had developed the magneto with Robert Bosch, and made them under Bosch licence. He also branched out into car and lorry manufacture from 1901 to 1908, but this venture was not successful, and in 1907 Bosch bought up the magneto department, hence forth supplying magnetos from Germany. This naturally ceased at the outbreak of war in 1914, but fortunately an American factory had been set up in 1910, and this supplied British needs until production re-started at Willesden. Large numbers of magnetos were made there for aircraft engines in the Second World War, and the company survives today as part of Lucas Industries plc.

Lucas was another well-known name in the motor and cycle trade. Joseph Lucas (1834–1902) had started in business in 1860, making buckets, shovels and galvanized chamber pots. In 1873 he began to market the Tom Bowling ship's lamp, and three years

later he manufactured it. Oil lamps for bicycles, named 'King of the Road', were introduced in 1878. With his son Harry he formed Joseph Lucas & Son in 1892, which became Joseph Lucas Ltd in 1897. He called his cycle equipment 'Cyclealities' and registered the name 'Motoralities' in 1901. They were first offered in the Lucas catalogue for 1902, but were put at the back, in secondary position to all the cycle lamps. The first Motoralities consisted of an oil light, a 'King of the Road' acetylene light, a bugle-type horn, and garage equipment such as pump, girder wrench, grease injector, and tyre repair outfits.[55] From 1907 cars were obliged to carry lights at night (it is surprising that this did not become law earlier). Car makers did not generally supply lights as standard equipment, so Lucas's trade grew dramatically. Motoralities overtook Cyclealities in importance. In 1910 Harry Lucas registered the name Electricalities to cover electric lighting systems. Electric side and tail-lights first appeared in the Lucas catalogue in 1909, and the first 'King of the Road' battery and electric horn in 1911. Until 1912 Lucas systems relied entirely on batteries, but in that year the 'King of the Road' Dynamo Lighting System was introduced. In 1915 William Morris ordered for his new Cowley

model a Lucas system consisting of a 6-volt dynamo (driven by a flat belt from the fan pulley) and a set of three lights, two combined head and side lights and a tail-light.[56]

Another industry which grew to prominence through the bicycle boom was that of the pneumatic tyre. The first air-filled tyre was patented by Robert William Thomson (1822–73) in 1846, but there were no suitable light vehicles to make use of the invention. A horse-drawn brougham was demonstrated in Regents' Park in 1846, but the matter went no further. The pneumatic was re-invented by a Scottish-born veterinary surgeon working in Belfast, John Boyd Dunlop (1840–1921), in 1888. Initially he had no plans to manufacture his idea, which he developed as a means of giving his ten-year old son a more comfortable bicycle ride on the cobbled streets of Belfast. However, a year after he patented the design he began to make bicycles equipped with his tyres. The Dunlop name might have been restricted to Belfast had he not met racing cyclist Arthur du Cros, son of William Harvey du Cros, a successful Dublin businessman of Huguenot stock.

Using Dunlop's patent, Harvey du Cros founded the Pneumatic Tyre & Booth's Cycle Agency in Dublin in November 1889, the name changing to the Pneumatic Tyre Co and then, in 1896, to the Dunlop Pneumatic Tyre Co Ltd. By then the cycle boom had provided a vast market for pneumatic tyres. Du Cros cemented his position by buying patents for detachable tyres and valves. Dunlop himself resigned from the company in December 1894, even before his name went onto the tyres, where it has remained ever since. Du Cros moved his factory from Dublin to Coventry in 1895, and also

One of the largest Edwardian Wolseleys, a 50 hp open-drive landaulette, photographed at the Rolls-Royce works in Nightingale Road, Derby. 1913 was the last year for these 8.6-litre monsters. (Bryan Goodman Collection)

sct up manufacturing bases in the United States and Australia. In 1896 the company was bought by Ernest Hooley, who floated it on the Stock Exchange for £5 million. Four years later Dunlop moved from its relatively small Coventry premises, where tyres were still hand-made, to a mill in Birmingham. In 1902 further premises were acquired at Aston Cross, Birmingham, and in 1916 a new factory was opened on a 400-acre site and christened Fort Dunlop.[57]

The use of Dunlop tyres on S. F. Edge's Napier which was victorious in the 1902 Gordon Bennett race gave a great boost to the company's links with the motor trade. As the manufacture of rubber tyres was so different from any of the other processes connected with car making, which largely employed metal or, in the case of bodywork, wood, no manufacturer, not even Rolls-Royce, made their own. Dunlop were the major providers to the British industry, though foreign companies such as Michelin (France), Englebert (Belgium) and Continental (Germany) provided strong competition. By the end of the First World War Dunlop was the largest rubber company in Europe.[58]

Wheels were made by several specialists of which Sankey and Rudge-Whitworth were probably the best known, the former for pressed steel artillery wheels, the latter for wire wheels. The Riley Cycle Company made detachable wire wheels said to have been supplied to 183 car makers. These included foreign firms such as Hispano-Suiza, Mercedes, Panhard, and Renault, and in England Napier and, rather surprisingly, Rolls-Royce.[59] Joseph Sankey & Sons of Bilston were important suppliers to the motor industry, for as well as wheels they made pressed steel mudguards, metal body shells for wooden frames and, from 1908, all-steel bodies. The demand for wheels grew so large that they set up a separate factory at Wellington which was making 30,000 wheels a year by 1913.[60]

The chief supplier of chassis frames was Rubery Owen of Darlaston, who began with rolled steel channel and tubular frames in 1896. Four years later they installed heavy hot presses which involved making templates, marking out sheets, hand cutting, heating, straightening, and sand blasting. The American method, used among others by the Dodge brothers who supplied frames to Henry Ford, was a cold press which simplified the process but was expensive to make in the first place. Thus it was only cost-effective if there was a long run of identical frames, something hard to come by in Britain, where small runs of different designs were the norm. Such manufacturers stipulated that their design should not be made for any other firm, yet would not order in a sizeable quantity. This is thought to be a major reason for the delay in mass production in the British industry

The industry was already an important employer of labour

Rubery Owen did turn to cold presses, and indeed their pressed steel pattern of axle casing was taken up by American firms.[61] Rubery Owen supplied most of the well-known British manufacturers, including Daimler, Rover, and Austin, though the car makers were not always happy to acknowledge this. The stigma of being mere assemblers making 'component cars' was something shunned by respectable firms. Yet to a large extent that is what most car makers have always been; they may design their components but much of the finished product is made by specialists. In the 1960s, components for the Jaguar Mark X came from 15 towns as far afield as Plymouth, Chelmsford, and Blackpool.[62] Today components for the British-made Toyota Carina are sourced from no fewer than ten different European countries, as well as the UK. These include seat belts from Austria, door handles from Monaco, and electrical

components from Portugal and Ireland.[63]

In 1913, the last full year of peace, the British motor industry built about 25,000 cars and 9,000 commercial vehicles. This put them in third place in the international production league, well behind the United States' 461,500 (cars only), and somewhat behind France's 45,000 cars.[64] Ford's assembly plant at Trafford Park turned out the most cars, 6,139, while of the native firms, Wolseley was the leader with about 3,000, followed by Humber (2,500), Sunbeam (1,700), Rover (1,600), and Austin (1,500). There were only a few others which reached four figures, among them Arrol-Johnston, Belsize, Daimler, Singer, and Star.[65] These figures include taxi-cabs, which were usually built on car chassis at this date, but not goods vehicles. Morris, which was to be such an important part of the industry within a few years, had barely started, and built only about 300 cars.

The industry was already an important employer of labour, with an estimated 50,000 people working in actual car manufacture and also in component firms such as Sankey and Rubery Owen. Daimler had about 5,000 workers, Wolseley 4,000, and Humber and Sunbeam about 2,500–3,000 each. Productivity was low compared with America; no British firm achieved one car per man per year before the 1920s, whereas Henry Ford made 1,700 cars with 300 men as early as 1903.[66]

The cars made varied greatly, from crude cyclecars at under £100 to luxury cars like the 45 hp Daimler which cost £1,175 with a standard body. Even so, the differential was less than it is today, when a basic Mini at £5,675 is compared to a Rolls-Royce Silver Spur at £119,428, let alone the stratospheric prices of supercars such as the McLaren F1 at £634,500.[67] Yet income differentials after tax were much greater in 1913 than in 1995, meaning that far fewer people were in a position to buy a car than today. The light car, of which some good examples

More car-like than some cyclecars, the Adamson had a 2-cylinder Alpha engine and final drive by belts. This one is climbing South Harting hill in Hampshire, c.1913. (NB)

were available in 1913 – such as the Singer Ten at £185 and the Standard 9.5 hp at £175 – were aimed at the professional man of modest income, or at the sons and daughters of wealthier families, not at the working man. Henry Ford might boast in 1914 that his cars were cheap enough for the men who made them to buy, but this was far from the case in Britain.

The cyclecar was a short-lived phenomenon, an attempt to use motor cycle technology in a three- or four-wheeled car, selling at a price below that of any conventional car. It began in Britain and France almost simultaneously in 1910, with the French Bedelia and the British GN. The latter used a V-twin engine by JAP or Peugeot in an ash frame, with final drive by belts, and steering by wire and bobbin. It was the work of two young engineers, Archie Frazer Nash and H. R. Godfrey, who had worked at Willans & Robinson in Rugby. Youth was a characteristic of many cyclecar makers and owners; Frazer Nash and Godfrey were 21 and 23 respectively when they built their first GN. Henri Borbeau and Robert Devaux, makers of the Bedelia were both 18. GN 'production' began in the stables of the

Frazer Nash family home, 'The Elms' in Hendon, moving shortly afterwards to The Burroughs in Hendon, a series of sheds occupied by a number of small businesses, the equivalent of today's industrial park. They gradually introduced improvements such as their own engine, still a V-twin but with inlet over exhaust valves, and chain drive. In 1913 the two-seater GN cost £99 15s. It was one of the best-known and most respected of the cyclecars, yet production never rose above two per week.

In 1911 the GN and the Morgan three-wheeler were the only British-made cyclecars on the market, yet by November 1912 37 makers exhibited at the Motor Cycle Show at Olympia. The new magazine *The Cyclecar* launched by the publishers of *The Motor* to cater for what was seen as a separate market, sold 80,000 copies of its first issue and a further run of 20,000 was ordered before the Show ended. An article in that issue by 'the well-known statistician and Member of Parliament Mr L. G. Chiozza Money' predicted a market of 350,000 possible cyclecarists, based on the number of houses in annual rental bands between £20 and £100. Between £41 and £100 there were 336,000 households, the heads of which were assumed to have incomes between £400 and £2,000 a year. In the £20 to £41 band there were 1,088,000 households, of which Mr Money estimated that 100,000 could afford to buy and run a cyclecar. The latter figure seems on the optimistic side, given that this band represented mainly urban terraced houses, ie working-class dwellings

A good example of the quality light car made in Britain on the eve of the First World War was the 9.5 hp Standard. This is a Ranalagh coupé of 1912 with very good weather-proofing for a small and comparatively cheap car. (NB)

where the breadwinner is unlikely to have brought in more than £3 a week. There was also the problem, which Mr Money admitted, of accommodating even a motor cycle in a terraced property with no garage or even access to 'what is euphemistically termed the "garden" '.[68]

However, the downfall of the cyclecar was not brought about by lack of a garage but simply by the poor quality of many of the machines on offer, which was evident even when they were in pristine condition at the Show. Both in design and construction, many of the cyclecars were sub-standard and below that of the two-wheelers whose components many of them used. It is significant that practically none of the makers of full-size cars went in for cyclecars, with the exception of Humber and Swift, and their offerings were at the upper end of the market. Many of the cyclecar companies were started and run on a shoestring. Six years earlier *The Motor* had harsh words for those who operated under-capitalized companies: 'We constantly see firms starting to manufacture cars with a capital of £5,000 or £10,000. Such a sum is a mere drop in the ocean, and is almost bound to be totally lost. Not only that but the industry suffers through a firm coming into it with inadequate capital, making a few cars at a loss, dying out and then leaving the users with cars for which spares are unobtainable'.[69] This applied with even greater force to the cyclecar industry, which had some parallels with the kit car business in the 1980s. In March 1913 *The Cyclecar* listed 82 makes of cyclecar, though some, like the Calthorpe, Wilton, and Morris Oxford, were light cars. Prices ran from a very low £55 for the 4 hp Dew monocar to £175 for the Wilton and Morris.[70] The boom was already waning by the outbreak of war, though there was a brief revival in the early 1920s, before the breed was wiped out for good by the advent of the Austin Seven in 1922. *The Cyclecar* became *The Light Car & Cyclecar* in October 1913, later becoming simply *The Light Car* and surviving as such until 1956.

Apart from the Model T Ford – which was in a class of its own, being quite large at 2.8 litres and 1,500 lb in weight, yet very reasonably priced at £125 – the cars built in the largest numbers were the four-cylinder tourers and two-seaters in the 2- to 3-litre class, such as the Austin Ten (£325), Humber Eleven (£310), Rover Twelve (£350), Star 10/12 (£305), and Wolseley 16/20 (£475). Though a breakdown of production by models is not available, it is likely that these cars formed the bulk of their respective company's output. Their makers were among the larger in the industry in 1913 (all were in four figures), and were on a sound financial basis (though all were to experience problems in the post-war years, Humber and Star losing their independence and Wolseley being sold by Vickers to William Morris). Other firms which catered to the middle-class market included Argyll, Arrol-Johnston, Belsize, Enfield, Palladium, Phoenix, Sunbeam, Swift and Talbot. The total number of car manufacturers in Britain in 1913 has been quoted at 113.[71] However *The Autocar* listed 91 manufacturers in its Buyers' Guide in November 1913, only some of which overlapped with *The Cyclecar's* list of 82 in March that year. Some very small regional firms such as Mendip never made it into *The Autocar* list, so it would be safe to say that about 140 manufacturers catered to the 25,000 car buyers of 1913. To these must be added 112 imported makes listed by *The Autocar*.

Almost every British-made car was petrol-powered. Unlike America, where the electric car was at its peak in the years 1910–15, Britain made no electrics, and sold very few imported ones. There had been a plan for Arrol-Johnston to make a slightly modified Detroit Electric under licence. The announcement of 1913 spoke of a preliminary run of 50, but it is unlikely that more than one was made.[72] Electromobile survived as a maker of taxis only, though in 1919 they showed at Olympia a limousine called the Elmo, for which the exorbitant sum of £1,050 was asked, plus £250 for batteries and £42 for tyres.[73] Steam was no more popular; only one British firm was offering steam cars in 1913, Pearson-Cox of Shortlands, Kent, and their output was very small.

An Austin tourer, c.1914, typical of the medium-sized four-cylinder car which made up the bulk of production from many British firms. The men holding up the white sheet behind the car were a familiar part of many car photographs. The sheet would mask out any inappropriate background and aid reproduction of the photo in cut-out form, as was often used in magazines of the time. (NB)

CHAPTER FOUR

Moves Towards Mass Production

Nick Baldwin

The Industrial Revolution had turned Britain into the workshop of the world by early Victorian times. Steam ships and boats, steam railways, and then steam traction on the land, were all by-products of the original steam pumping engines for mines. It was these mines that had produced the raw materials to fuel the boom and many entrepreneurs and engineers had become rich on the proceeds.

Whilst Birmingham, Coventry and the Black Country had their fair share of the natural resources they lacked the water transport facilities that had allowed, say, Manchester to blossom in the cotton trade or the great shipbuilding ports to flourish. To compensate for this the Midlands had to concentrate on light-weight, compact goods containing a disproportionate input of added design, engineering and labour. Birmingham was traditionally famous for its manufacturing jewellers and metalworkers, and the Black Country to its west made all manner of boilers, chains and other specialized goods. To the south was Redditch, famous for its needles, fish-hooks and springs – soon Terrys valve springs would be amongst the best-known in the motor industry, along with those of Salter's, traditionally weighing-machine makers in West Bromwich.

Meanwhile, in Wolverhampton in 1859, sheet-metal worker John Marston acquired a metal lacquering, or japanning, factory. This process was invaluable in the bicycle industry, in which his Sunbeamland factory of 1887 became an important cog. From this grew the Sunbeam car of 1901,

which by 1910 was being made at the rate of around ten per week. In the Black Country at Bilston, Thompson Brothers, boiler makers, was adding motor components (and later complete TB cyclecars) to its range. Its rival Rubery Owen (or Rubery & Co as it was then called) in Darlaston had 13 basic motor car chassis and three for omnibuses in 1907, and within a decade listed 148 different chassis sidemakers. The Austin car of 1905 was one of the first to use a Rubery frame.

He tested compounds on a brake powered by a water wheel in his garden

---

As was noted in Chapter One, it was Coventry that became the most important home of the bicycle, though Birmingham could lay claim to supplying many of the components. Indeed, its Components Ltd (associated with Ariel) was a massive supplier of everything from cotter pins and bearings to pedal cranks. Another key name in this field was Birmingham Small Arms, where Bernard Docker was later to work. His father was a director of BSA and had learned about rolling-stock mass production at the Metropolitan Carriage & Waggon Works. In 1910 BSA, by then itself a car maker, acquired Daimler and thus began the long Docker association with Coventry. In 1912 BSA became one of the first to offer all-steel body-work, which it found reduced costs.

Manchester, where the Belsize car

was to grow from a bicycle maker, was home to the immensely important Renolds chain works. Hans Renolds had come to Britain from Switzerland in 1873 and in 1895 invented the silent inverted tooth chain that was to revolutionize power transmission. His principal competitors were Brampton Brothers Ltd and the Coventry Chain Company. The three companies played an important role in the emerging motor business and were ultimately to merge in 1930. From Manchester too came Herbert Frood, a manufacturing agent who married the daughter of the owner of Rossendale Belting and noticed that offcuts of this material were used as brake blocks by the local carters. From these small beginnings grew his mighty Ferodo brake shoe business at Chapel-en-le-Frith after he had tested various different compounds on a brake powered by a water wheel in his garden.

As we have seen, Coventry had come to the bicycle via textiles and sewing machines. It was also an important watch-making centre that gave it a pool of precision tool makers and operators. Whilst many of these moved into the motor component field it was left to S. Smith & Sons (Motor Accessories) Ltd to become a household name in the motor instrument field. Though founded as a watch-maker in 1851, the firm was not known under this title in London until 1914, by when it had made 50,000 speedometers, with Humber and Crossley amongst its important customers. Smith's Cricklewood factory employed 400 men in 1915 and in 1919 became sole agent for the products of KLG before taking over the firm in 1927. It also acquired ML Magnetos and the AT Speedometer Co as part of a specialization that was to sweep the motor industry in the 1920s. KLG was, incidentally, named after racing driver Kenelm Lee Guinness, who designed a high-performance spark plug that was made from 1912 in a little factory adjoining the racing headquarters in the Bald Faced Stag hostelry on the A3. As Robinhood Engineering, it grew from 30 workers in 1915 to 600 by 1929 and included Louis Coatalen amongst its early directors (he had been involved with the original Humber cars, then Hillman, and was to be chief engineer of the Sunbeam Talbot Darracq combine).

So, little by little, a precision components industry was developing. But what of the cars? By 1900 a few handmade cars were emerging from factories and workshops, notably in the industrial Midlands. Amongst the earliest and most important had been the well capitalized Daimler from the Motor Mills in 1896. Frederick Simms had met Gottlieb Daimler in Germany and acquired British rights to his designs. Simms was also a friend of Robert Bosch and their joint development of Simms-Bosch Magnetos was to have far reaching consequences. This was not least because it helped to make Britain independent of the almost universal German supplies of this strategic component as war clouds gathered. The other key supplier was Thomson-Bennet, which was snapped up promptly by Lucas in 1914 for the same reason.

Productivity figures from this era make interesting comparison with what was to happen in the future. In 1903 Vauxhall, for example, employed approximately 150 men to make 43 cars. The figures for 1909 were 195 cars from 350 men and for 1913 387 from 575. Thus 0.3 cars per person per year had improved to 0.67 in ten years. Austin calculated it another way, saying that one car was a week's work for

A batch of Model T Fords nearing completion at Trafford Park, c.1913. At that time about 20 cars were leaving the factory every day, so each row of cars represents one day's output. (NMM)

104 people in 1910. It was a week's work for only 16 in 1926 (and for four in 1958). Plainly a revolution had taken place, but how exactly had it been achieved? To begin with manufacturers had simply increased their work-force to meet growing demand. Thus traditional methods persisted, for example in specifying rough castings and solid forgings that were handled by machine only to the extent of 'roughing out'. After that it was down to skilled men with hacksaw and chisel followed by file and scraper. The marker off was a key man, because it was his skill that interpreted the designer's drawings onto the actual metal. He could make the most of an inferior casting, or have it reduced to scrap after hours of machining and hand-work when an imperfection could not be removed from a critical area. To show that the machinist had not erred, the marking off dot would always be left split precisely in half to show that it was not his fault.

For the first 20 to 30 years all engine bearings were made of white metal

which, in its molten state, was poured into position and then scraped to make the perfect fit. And by perfect fit it had to be neither too tight nor too loose. If the crankshaft could be turned by a lever less than, say, two feet long it was too slack for running-in purposes and the bearings had to be replaced. This was bad enough with a two or three bearing engine but imagine the skill required to set up a five or seven bearing unit. One of the most complex items in the car, then as now, was the crankshaft. It became a specialized item from outside suppliers but was often produced in-house in the early days. Sunbeam made its own from solid billets weighing up to 410 lb (185 kg) and hundreds of hours thus went into each engine, which was then tested on the bench for 18 hours before dismantling and checking. No wonder that veteran cars were so expensive in terms of labour and materials.

It was in an effort to reduce the individual nature of each hand-built car that Reginald Maudslay established his Standard Motor Co Ltd in Coventry

Four Model Ts at Brooklands. The two-seater, called the Runabout, cost £125, the tourers £135, and the landaulette – which carried the American-sounding name 'Town Car' – £180. All these prices were exceptionally low compared with European equivalents. The Town Car cost no more than a basic two-seater Morris Oxford. (NB)

in 1903. Standard was picked as a name not to denote something dreary, as in sub-standard, but to show that it was not some sort of one-off blacksmith's contraption, but made of parts that were 'tried and tested and accepted as reliable standards'. Thus, in theory at least, if a part broke, a telegraph to the factory would produce another piece that fitted, instead of one that had to be fettled for hours.

The whole subject of how cars were made is too vast to go into in detail. Suffice to say that in the early stages, the car was built onto its chassis in a fixed location within the assembly bay. Components would come from workshops and machine shops around the factory and literally be bolted to the chassis, which rested on trestles. Holes were reamed for a perfect tight fit, often by hand, and virtually no welding was employed until the 1920s. Allen Liversidge had perfected an oxyacetylene system by about 1913, but distortion was a problem that kept bolts and rivets to the fore in the vintage period. Electric welding began to

be employed in car factories in the 1920s and was to replace most other fastening methods in the 1930s. Most artillery wheels of the vintage period were electrically welded by such firms as Sankey and Rubery Owen.

Until moving tracks and conveyor belts made car assembly a more precise science at the time of the First World War a motor factory actually needed to be very little different from any other engineering premises, normally including a railway siding to bring in raw materials and the few finished items or forgings and castings that could not be made on the premises. Items like glass, tyres, magnetos, carburettors, and wooden spoked wheels probably arrived by road transport. As we have seen, a multi-storey textile mill made an adequate early home for Daimler, and existing premises were adopted by most other fledgling manufacturers. Herbert Austin made use of a former tin printing and box manufacturing plant when he left Wolseley and set up on his own at Longbridge in 1905. The first purpose-built car fac-

tory in Britain was that for the production of the electrically-propelled Madelvic at Granton, Edinburgh, in 1898. This was followed soon after by Dennis, which had outgrown its sports shop and bicycle sheds and consequently built a factory at Guildford. Happily both are preserved, as is a large part of the spectacular Talbot works established in Barlby Road, North Kensington, in 1903. Dennis was one of many firms to keep prices down by buying cheap, mass-produced engines from De Dion-Bouton in France, whilst Talbot also relied on French design expertise in its earliest years. There were myriad early motor firms, many of whom succumbed to a slump in Edwardian times that left only a few dozen significant manufacturers.

In 1910 total UK vehicle production (including commercial types) was 10,500, a figure that climbed dramatically to 34,000 in 1913. A major contributor to this state of affairs was Ford, which by 1914 could produce about 8,000 vehicles a year at Trafford

Park, Manchester. As Wolseley came second in the league with only 3,000 chassis one can obtain a clear idea of the relatively small scale of even the more important of the other protagonists at this stage.

Ford was an archetypal example of the very different way in which motor manufacture had been tackled on the other side of the Atlantic. There it had been recognized from an early stage that there was only a very limited market for expensive, hand-built cars. As here, much had been learned of mass production in the weapons, clock, typewriter, and bicycle industries, to which should be added the Chicago Stockyards: Henry Ford was proud of his farming ancestry and it is said that the scientific way in which cattle were reduced to so many joints, chops, and bones encouraged him to reverse the process in his motor business. The key was to have the cheapest and strongest parts available in the right place at the right time. The labour-intensive, hand preparation of components was not for him and his American rivals at the cheap end of the car market. He laid down expensive dies and tools that could mass produce parts to exact tolerance. The cost of this equipment had to be amortised as quickly as possible and to this end production had to be massive. Cars sold readily if they were cheap enough, and Ford and the other great American firms had the advantage of a large and relatively wealthy market. Because their production methods could use high tensile pressed vanadium steel to do the same jobs as heavy and expensive iron or non-ferrous castings did in the typical British factory, further savings were made in materials and manpower.

Late in 1911 the British Ford operation moved into the former Dick Kerr electrical equipment factory (which had produced tramcar motors amongst other things) on Westinghouse Road, Trafford Park, Manchester. The site was chosen because of its proximity to the railway and the Manchester Ship Canal for components arriving from the USA. (The packing crates were

While Ford made 20 cars per day, Morris took a week to turn out the same number. Here is a week's output of Oxfords outside the factory, a former military academy at Cowley at which, when it was Hurst's Grammar School, William Morris's father had been educated. (NB)

recycled, to manufacture wooden items for the cars). One of the keys to Ford's success in England was in employing handymen rather than tradesmen, thus avoiding some of the union involvement and demarcation problems that were to bedevil the industry. Despite the fact that less skill was required to assemble more accurate components, the handymen were actually paid better than other tradesmen in the area and received 8½d to 1s 3d per hour (later a flat rate of 1s 3d in 1914). Only the skilled toolmakers did better, earning up to 4s per hour.

From an early stage the sheet metal was sourced locally and the adjoining firm of Scott Bros was acquired for jig-building the bodywork. Elsewhere on the Trafford Park Industrial Estate were several other suppliers to Ford, including windscreen makers Hodgsons. Bodies were installed on the chassis in 22½ minutes and spray painting saved hours when compared with the traditional multi-coat hand processes with labour intensive rubbing down

between stages and lacquering at the end.

1913 marked the arrival of the first moving track assembly operation at Ford in Detroit. A few months later a similar system was installed at Trafford Park. It was the first of its sort in Europe and was 114 ft long. It was set to run at three different speeds, taking 90 minutes to complete its course at the slowest and 50 minutes at the fastest. Components were fed in from overhead conveyors and up to 21 complete chassis per hour could be completed. By then the British content included virtually everything but engines and axles. Petrol tanks and radiators were made on the premises by highly automated machines and the wooden wheels were spun in a bath of paint for complete protection. The Ford idea worked well and local suppliers, like the pub where some of the work-force retired at lunch, learned from the system – it lined up the pints ready for the first influx! When the workers first arrived at the factory in the morning they placed their over-

The Austin Seven was the oustanding British light car of the 1920s, restoring prosperity to the company and, by its quality and price, forcing cyclecars off the market. This is an early model Chummy with its owner, E. J. Vardon, at the Kent home of William Rootes, father of the brothers William and Reginald Rootes. (NMM)

A. Harper Sons & Bean hoped to lead the British motor industry, with an output of 50,000 cars a year. Their best month, July 1920, saw 505 cars delivered, so even if this rate had been maintained, output would barely have exceeded 6,000. In fact the original company collapsed, and a revived Harper Bean Ltd made no more than 100 cars a week, at best. This is an 11.9 hp coupé, c.1920. (NB)

coats on racks that were hoisted up to the roof at the start of the shift – woe betide the custodians of any vacant hangars! An account by a group of visitors to Trafford Park in 1915 noted rather snootily that 'although we are by no means suggesting that this car sets a standard of automobile engineering we are accustomed to in England, yet the low figure at which it is produced, and the service it is rendering, make it an engineering proposition by no means to be despised.' It was explained that if imported complete the Model T would still undercut other vehicles on the market. However, vast savings in shipping costs came with packing the parts for many cars into the smallest possible space. Even the wheels came without hubs so that they would pack flat and the chassis rails came unriveted together.

Each semi-skilled man would stand beside the moving track and walk alongside it until his allotted task was completed, before returning to the following chassis. Our visitors stated: 'There is no doubt that the organisation and assembly processes are very complete. In these processes, at any rate, no skilled labour is required. We noticed particularly that the fitters who were employed upon the job carried nothing but a few spanners, and that all the parts went together without a hitch.'

Compare this with an account of the Daimler factory in 1913,[1] where electrically-heated rivets and mechanical presses for assembling chassis had recently trebled efficiency compared with the former hand methods of heating the rivets in a hearth and then hammering them home and burring their ends. Less work was also required in 'truing' the chassis after it had been made by the new method. An electric crane then moved the chassis onto four pedestals where dumbrions were fitted. These were now correctly proportioned compared with the rough castings that had previously been fitted and then hand finished to suit each individual spring (a process that could take hours with hammer and chisel and

still, in 1913, involved reaming out the spring eye on the factory floor instead of it being made to a standard size at the spring works). As often as not the holes in the axle spring table had to be slotted to align correctly with u-bolts and springs, though this was said to be a less frequent chore now that better jigs were used. However, more time was lost due to the recent adoption of underslung springs at the rear, which made it a much more difficult operation to fit the heavy axle by crane. The steering gear had in earlier years been forced to mesh easily by filing and grinding in a vice adjoining the assembly position. The box and chassis then had to be drilled, whilst 1913 practice was to supply a ready tested box which, however, still had to have its top flange filed before it would rest comfortably on the chassis and align with the holes already drilled in the latter.

Each man walked along the moving track until his job was done

---

The motor arrived complete from the engine shop but then had to be partially dismantled to fit the frame. Aligning engine and gearbox was a highly skilled task and holes could only be ratchet-drilled *in situ* because of variations in the outrigger castings and holes. At that stage Daimler was one of the few firms using archaic ratchet drills instead of the new electric drills, but the workmen claimed that the job was far easier than fitting the old chain gearboxes. An added problem then was that the holes in the sprockets and brake drums seldom lined up. The leather cone clutch now arrived ready for installation instead of requiring its gunmetal bush to be reamed to fit the crankshaft spigot. The pedals seldom had the correct 'set', because of problems with pinning the clutch fork boss, and had to be forced into position with a 'twisting wrench'. The actual gear positions had to be established by filing and fitting the change quadrant with great skill, though this operation had

been eased thanks to better initial machining. Another improvement was that the carpenters, who had previously got in the way at this stage, to make and fit the scuttle or dash plate, had become redundant because a cast aluminium scuttle had been substituted. In addition the radiator had been simplified so that 20 minutes was no longer wasted in trying to fit nuts to hidden bolts. Also the tubes had, formerly, been frequently bent to allow the starting handle to pass through.

Our contemporary critic visiting Daimler was dismayed at the number of different models being built and at the amount of hand fettling and the frequent need for rectification required afterwards. He was also puzzled as to why the advance/retard control was routed down the column to the steering box, then forward to the radiator, then across the frame and back to the magneto, when far simpler linkage was feasible that would have saved time, complexity and materials. However, compared with building similar cars in 1906 he estimated that something like 14 hours of assembly time had been saved and that many more hours were waiting to be released if work study procedures were adopted.

In 1921 the Institution of Production Engineers was formed, the vast majority of its members being drawn from the motor industry and machine tool makers. At Daimler, meanwhile, the First World War had brought many changes. Afterwards the arrival of L. H. Pomeroy as chief engineer brought new working practices resulting from American experience. He was joined as works manager by E. W. Hancock from Vauxhall. Hancock had also spent time in America, learning from General Motors how to boost output at Luton, and what he learned was applied in the late 1920s to Daimler's progressive assembly line. This was still not powered but at least chassis were now rolled from station to station instead of staying in one spot.

During the First World War no less than 30,000 Model T Fords were built for essential services – by far the largest output in the industry. However, others had learned from it, and the Associated Equipment Company (AEC), makers of London's buses, also used a moving track to produce over 10,000 three-tonners for war service. Interestingly it too bought in as many components from America as was feasible, though the disruption to shipping caused it, like Morris, to switch to local suppliers.

We will look at Morris's activities in the 1920s in some detail, but suffice to say at this stage that it had arrived on the scene in 1912, when an Oxford entrepreneur named William Morris made arrangements to mass-produce a light car based on the best components that he could buy-in cheaply. White & Poppe of Coventry made the engines and gearboxes whilst E. G. Wrigley of Soho, Birmingham, was responsible for axles and steering gear. Interestingly Wrigleys was on the site of the old Matthew Boulton & Watt's steam engine works which had originally helped to mechanize the early mining, textile and engineering industry. When later Morris began to buy up his suppliers, Wrigleys became home to the Morris-Commercial in 1924.

Morris production reached nearly a thousand in a former military college at Cowley in 1914 and in an effort to cut costs still further William Morris went on a buying spree to America. He discovered that an equivalent to White & Poppe's engine built under the efficient American system could be bought from Continental of Detroit for a mere £18 (well under half the price of the Coventry engine). Likewise gearboxes, axles, and steering gear from the Detroit Gear & Machine Co cost less than £25. However, shipping losses to enemy action put an end to this project when fewer than 3,000 sets of components materialized at Cowley. Another way in which Morris attempted to save money was in joint development costs, as when it shared the dies for Sankey wheels with the Perry car.

The First World War had a profound effect on both the industry and the public. The former had learned about the latest American production methods and the latter about driving, often by courtesy of His Majesty's Government. Lots of individuals, their horizons stretched by the first experience of travel, foresaw that cheap cars – epitomized by the Model T Ford – would revolutionize the nation's

transport. However, the future of the Model T was limited by the imposition of horsepower tax in 1921. Being rated at 20 RAC hp it had to pay £20 per year compared with only a few pounds for smaller cars.

The Austin Twenty, meanwhile, was supposed to be Longbridge's own answer to a one-model policy, but it was rapidly discovered that this model was out of step with public thinking. In 1921 the company went into receivership after two years of heavy losses. Something was urgently needed to save the 'largest motor factory in the Empire' (58-acres of floor space) and the answer proved to be smaller horsepower cars like the Twelve of 1921 and then the Seven of the following year. The latter clocked up its 100,000th sale in 1929, the year in which Austin overall had captured 37 per cent of the British market. In 1924 Morris had become the first to outsell Ford and several other firms like Standard, Singer, and Jowett were snapping at its heels.

Until the arrival of the Austin Seven the dreams of all the little businesses making frugal cyclecars seemed assured. However, the public was not impressed by tiny cars with minimal weather equipment and dubious specifications. A few like the GN and GWK sold in thousands, but none was a lasting success. Even the firms with satisfactory designs for substantial family cars soon found the going to be tough. Lots of them – like Angus Sanderson, Cubitt, Ruston-Hornsby, Bean, and Clyno – failed to make the grade and some, like the ambitious Whitehead-Thanet and Hammond, barely made it off the drawing board.

The Bean must have seemed the most likely of all to succeed as it

Another firm whose ambitions exceeded reality was Angus-Sanderson. Larger than the Bean, with a 2.3-litre engine, it was intended to compete with American imports. Not more than 3,000 cars were made, between 1919 and 1927. The attractive radiator was designed by Cecil Kimber, later of MG fame. (NMM)

emanated from a respected large-scale supplier of motor components that was said to supply some 50 per cent of the industry. It had been founded in 1901 in the Black Country to carry on a stamping, casting and forging business established in the previous century. As noted earlier, the Bean car was based on the soundly-engineered Perry, which was re-engineered by an expert from Willys-Overland to suit mass production methods. A prospectus was issued in November 1919 capitalizing the new A. Harper Sons & Bean Ltd at £6 million. The share issue was over-subscribed. However, when the time came to pay for the applications, nearly half the capital was not forthcoming.

What money the new firm had was used to buy in to numerous suppliers like Gallay Radiators, Harvey Frost, Jigs Ltd, The Regent Carriage Co, Rushmores (lamps), Birmingham Aluminium, Ransome & Marles Bearings, Marles Steering, Coopers Mechanical Joints, and the British Motor Trading Corp (supposed to be a large-scale sales organization). Also bought were 50 per cent shares in the Swift motor vehicle business in Coventry, 60 per cent of Vulcan's car and commercial vehicle factory at Crossens, Southport, and 44 per cent of ABC Motors Ltd (car, motor cycle and engine makers). All of this was supposed to make the Bean car virtu-

ally self-supporting up to the planned output of 50,000 cars per year. This would have made it by far the most prolific British car, but still a shadow of some of the vast American operations. To this end it laid out three 450 ft moving tracks in a former projectile factory in Dudley and used boys on roller skates to convey messages to section leaders.

Bean was not alone in miscalculating the scale of demand in inter-war Britain and the Empire. Even if the demand had been there it seems extremely unlikely that the fragmented purchasing and manufacturing sections could have kept pace with the grandiose plans. As it was, output

Interior of the former munitions factory at Aylesbury, Bucks, with Cubitt chassis ready for bodying. Their best output was about 20 cars per day, and total production over six years was about 3,000. The parent company, Holland, Hannen & Cubitt, was a descendant of the building company founded by Thomas Cubitt in 1815, which was largely responsible for the development of the Belgravia district of London. (NMM)

A CAR BODY SIDE AT ONE STROKE.

Impression of the giant press at Cowley, which, in one operation,
stamps from sheet steel a complete side
for an Isis saloon.

Drawing by H. Radcliffe Wilson.

The 1,600-ton Hamilton press at the Pressed Steel works at Cowley which rose 28ft above floor level. It could stamp out a complete side for a Morris saloon. (NB) reached 100 cars in the month of January 1920 and 505 in the following July. This was to mark the peak of the original business, which collapsed soon afterwards with piles of unsold cars and unbalanced stock, and all manner of financial difficulties. Colonel Sir Thomas A. Polson KBE CMG MP was brought in to sort out the mess and a new company named Harper Bean Ltd was formed. The minutes of its first AGM on 25 July 1921 make salutary reading and consist mainly of the arrangements made to dispose of its many associated companies (amongst them Vulcan went on to an unhappy relationship with Lea-Francis). In the end Bean was placed on a relatively sound footing and managed to make, and more importantly sell, up to 100 cars in a good week. This still made it one of Britain's most important suppliers, but that was not enough for continued success. It abandoned car production in 1929, by when it had been acquired by Hadfields of Sheffield, its steel supplier. After a couple of years of concentrating on commercial vehicles it threw in the towel and became once more a major supplier of forgings, castings and stamps to its former rivals. (Ironically, after Reliant went out of business in October 1990 Bean, which had supplied engines for the three-wheelers, took over the project and became a manufacturer of complete vehicles once more.)

There were many other wildly ambitious plans formulated at the end of the First World War. Whilst the Bean had started as an 11.9 hp car the Angus-Sanderson from Birtley, Co Durham, was a larger car designed to compete head-on with American types at home and in Britain's traditional export markets. It too was made in a former armaments factory and employed some of the Belgian labour that had fled there during the war. Unlike the Bean it was largely an assembled job, though the attractive coachwork was made on the premises (Sir William Angus, Sanderson & Co Ltd had formerly been coachbuilders),

utilizing specialized woodworking machinery, panel presses, and paint sprayers. By January 1920 the project was already in trouble and a prospectus was issued to create a £4 million combine consisting of Angus, Sanderson, Smethwick Iron Foundry & Stamping Co, NUT (motor cycles), E. G. Wrigley (axles and gearboxes), and J. Tylor & Sons Ltd. This last firm had been an old-established London sanitary engineer that had made proprietary engines on a small scale before the war but had become one of the major suppliers to AEC army lorries during the conflict. A rival in its sanitary and pump business was Gwynne which, incidentally, was endeavouring at this time to break into the car field and was soon to add another London made car, the Albert. Angus Sanderson (1921) Ltd moved to the Grahame-White Aviation factory at Hendon (where the manufacture of cyclecars and furniture was also tried in the absence of aircraft orders). Angus Sanderson itself died in the mid-1920s after only a few thousand cars had been sold.

Mention of E. G. Wrigley reminds us that not all was doom and gloom in the new-found enthusiasm for mass production. As noted earlier, Wrigley, instead of sinking with Angus Sanderson, became a cornerstone of the Morris empire. Its principal gearbox rival in Birmingham was the Moss Gear Co, founded in 1910, which in 1928 moved to spacious modern premises in the rural suburbs of Tyburn, Erdington. We noted that its Continental engine undercut the pre-war White & Poppe units. In 1919 White & Poppe was acquired by Dennis Brothers of Guildford, which by now had abandoned cars to concentrate on commercial vehicles, and Morris looked around for another supplier. The French Hotchkiss car and armaments business had established a gun factory in Coventry which was looking for work. It began to supply a copy of the Continental engine to the reconstituted Morris Motors Ltd (capitalized to £150,000) in mid-1919. Morris Motors lost £8,000 in its first year of trading and stocks of unsold cars were mounting. Although costs were still rising William Morris took a decision in 1921 that was to have far-

A rotating tumbril at the Morris factory, 1927, which turned the chassis over while it received its initial coat of black paint, sprayed on under pressure. (NB)

MG was the first British company to make sports cars in reasonable numbers and at a low price. This view of the production line at Abingdon in 1931 in fact shows a relatively rare model of Midget, the C-type, of which 44 were made. (NMM)

reaching consequences. He slashed the price of his already cheap Cowley and more up-market Oxford 'Bullnose' models and saw sales of 68 in January leap to 377 in March. By the end of the year 3,077 cars had been sold. Ford was overtaken and in 1925 sales reached 54,151.

This had been made possible by a spate of acquisitions. Hotchkiss for £350,000 became the Morris Motors Engines Branch; Wrigley, as noted earlier, the home of the light trucks; Hollick & Pratt in Coventry the main body works; and Doherty (later Osberton) Radiators was moved to a former skating rink in Coventry; Fisher & Ludlow became the group's pressings division; and in 1926 the SU Carburettor business was acquired for £100,000. In that year the various Morris factories added up to a ground area of 42.25 acres. Chassis frames, which had originally arrived from Belgium, were soon sourced locally and were drilled from both sides simultaneously on Wilkins & Mitchell machines on arrival at Cowley.

The most important of all William

Morris' steps towards mass production followed his visit to America in 1925. There he visited the Edward G. Budd Manufacturing Co of Philadelphia and arranged for a partnership between this pioneer of pressed steel bodies to join Morris Motors and a merchant bank in the creation of the Pressed Steel Company of Great Britain Ltd. This was set up at an initial cost to Morris of £410,000 and started production in 1927. A set of dies for the first American-designed bodies cost £120,000 and soon several Morris models, as well as those of newly acquired Wolseley, had Pressed Steel bodywork. Providing the production runs were big enough this produced an enormous saving when compared with traditional wood and metal methods of body production. The snag was that Morris and Wolseley could not absorb all the potential output of the giant presses. The biggest was a 1,600 ton Hamilton press that shook the ground for hundreds of feet around. It weighed 245 tons and was 28 ft above floor level and 16 ft below. In all 1,000 men were employed making 100 bodies

daily on the 11-acre site by late 1927. They fitted panels into jigs that were then arc welded. The welding was semi-automated in 1931.

Morris found it very difficult to obtain outside business because rivals were not happy at two members of the Pressed Steel board being Morris directors who might be tempted to pass on plans for future models. The sister British Paint & Lacquer Co, with joint American ownership, was in the same boat and was converted into an independent company after about six years. Its sprayed Bripal oven-dried cellulose was standard on all Morris cars from late in 1928. Budd retained its controlling interest in Pressed Steel until 1936 but Morris had greatly reduced its own involvement in 1930 so that other car companies could help it to share the colossal costs involved. As well as Wolseley, Morris now had another brand under its control, that of the MG sports car. By using cheap mass-produced components from the family cars this was able to open up a whole new market for fun motoring. Traditionally sports cars had been low production and therefore expensive items, but the first MG Midget of 1929 was to change all that. It soon earned a factory in its own right in part of the Pavlova Leather Co premises at Abingdon.

Before leaving this most successful of the early British attempts to mass produce cars, we should pay a visit to the Morris Motors Engines Branch in Gosford Street, Coventry, for it was here that chief engineer Herbert Taylor and director and general manager F. G. Woollard put mass and flow production most successfully to work following the factory's acquisition from Hotchkiss in 1923. Woollard had been educated at Goldsmiths and Birkbeck Colleges, and after involvement in the design of the Clarkson steam omnibus and some consulting work he had joined Wrigleys on the Morris contract. During the First World War he had been recommended for the MBE by Winston Churchill for his work on the production of 'land ship' (tank) engines at Wrigleys and had joined the Engines Branch in 1923. There he put his 'Eighteen Basic Principles for Mass and Flow Production' into practice in a transfer machine for the production of cylinder blocks. It was 181 ft long, weighed 300 tons, and employed 81 electric motors and 21 men. From rough casting to finished article took 224 minutes. It was followed in 1924 by an Archdale automatic transfer machine for gearboxes and then an Asquith machine for the mass production of flywheels. Output leapt by 66 per cent and even Ford's Detroit chief production engineer was impressed. Woollard's great friend was chief experimental designer A. G. Pendrell, who was responsible for many of the later 1920s engines, including the overhead camshaft 2½ litre types.

In 1931 Woollard left to become managing director of Rudge Whitworth (well known for bicycles, motor cycles, wire wheels) and soon joined the board of Birmingham Aluminium Castings, a rival to the aptly named Birmingham Repetition Castings. In 1934 his important book *The Principles of Mass and Flow Production* was published to widespread industrial acclaim. A glimpse into the newly extended Engines Branch in 1930, shortly before he left Morris, showed gravity rollers to take castings to the pickling vats. After neutralizing the acid in soda the blocks were taken by chain conveyor to the various machining positions. The blocks were located in jigs where milling cutters and multiple drills completed several operations. Visitors noted that the operations involved little manpower and were

The 'all-British Overland' wasn't quite that, for the chassis components came from Canada. The use of a 14/28 hp Morris Oxford engine was an attempt to beat the horsepower tax. The same car with a 2.7-litre American-type engine paid £19 annually, while the use of the 1.8-litre Morris engine brought the tax down to £14. (NB)

plainly the shape of things to come.

Whilst the activities of Morris were a constant source of fascination to the motoring press, several other factories were making equally impressive strides towards efficiency. Vauxhall was acquired for £300,000 by General Motors in October 1925 and quickly moved from being a small producer of quality cars to one of the principal exponents of cheap, mass produced family cars. Its sales in 1926 were 1,513 cars, of which 292 were exported. Whilst new models were prepared

there was little change for the next three years but then, in 1930, output leapt to 8,930, out of which 217 were exported. For most of the rest of the 1930s exports accounted for around a third of production, which reached 16,329 (including the new Bedford commercials) in 1932 and 40,456 in 1934. The figure for 1937 was a staggering 59,746, or roughly 40 times the total of only ten years before.

Cars in use on British roads overall shows what enormous strides took place from 1904, when only 8,465 were

registered. The figure exceeded 100,000 for the first time in 1913 and reached 141,621 in 1916. It then dropped due to the First World War, but reached 186,801 in 1920. After that there was no stopping it, with virtually half a million reached in 1924 and one million in 1929. One and a half million was attained in 1935. In May 1939 Morris at Cowley became the first British factory to have produced one million cars, many of which had gone for export.

Austin's 58-acres of factory buildings had been reorganized for mass production in 1919, with the machine shops dovetailed into the approximate positions in the production lines where their products would be needed with minimal transport. This, and the new spray-painting facilities, allowed 14,000 cars to be built in 1927 (production in 1922 had been only 2,500), at a time when about 10,000 people were employed.

Though some firms were therefore rising to the challenges of mass production, many more of the traditional ones were falling by the wayside. Really the Wall Street Crash of 1929 and the Depression that followed marked a watershed for these firms. It marked the end of the hand-built regional makers like Hampton in Stroud, Gloucestershire, and the second rank of largish producers like Swift in Coventry, or Star in Wolverhampton. Those that attempted to take on the big battalions without sufficient resources also paid the price. Amongst these was Clyno, which had started by making motor cycles but which in the period 1922 to 1930 tried to shadow the exploits of Morris. However, it did not buy its suppliers but instead used the promise of large orders to secure optimum discounts. Output of 5,000 cars in 1925 grew to 12,000 in 1926, but then came the mistake of expansion into a new, four-acre factory where, in the first year, a profit of only £24,000 was earned on a turnover of £1.25 million. An attempt to introduce a spartan-looking £100 car met with little success and princi-

pal suppliers like Coventry-Climax engines, Dunlop, and Lucas helped to bring production to a close when they realized that they were unlikely to be paid. The 1920s marked the virtual end of the proprietary engine industry for cars (but not commercials) although a few makers like Morgan and Frazer Nash made cars that sportsmen wanted, but in such small numbers that bought-in engines had to be employed.

Humber cars were better priced than other Coventry marques

When Clyno was first making the transition from motor cycles it employed Henry Meadows as its works manager. He left to start the proprietary engine and gearbox firm bearing his name in Wolverhampton. It soon had at least two dozen regular car customers, the most important of which became Lea-Francis. Meadows's main rival was Dorman of Stafford, which allegedly made 1,000 engines per month in 1920 but rapidly lost the majority of its car, rather than commercial vehicle, customers. In the 1930s Invicta, Lagonda, and Frazer Nash were Meadows's staple customers along with former car-turned-truck makers like Guy. Sidney Guy had been works manager at Sunbeam before starting the Guy Motors business in 1914.

Sunbeam itself in 1919 joined Talbot, French Darracq, commercial vehicle maker W. & G. du Cros, and components firms Jonas Woodhead and Heenan & Froude, in the £3.3-million capitalized STD Motors Ltd. An Anglo-French enterprise was an ambitious move, but one that failed to take advantage of the savings that could be achieved from rationalization. True, a Darracq design became the basis of the small 8/18 Talbot and there was a limited amount of cross-fertilization between Talbot in London and Sunbeam in Wolverhampton, but regrettably most of these efforts went

into unsuccessful models. Sunbeam sailed on its very traditional and labour-intensive way and failed to harness the publicity it gained from racing and land speed record successes into products that would appeal to its admirers. In a last-ditch attempt Georges Roesch, the chief engineer at Talbot, came up with the 14/45, of which 7,000 had been made by the end of the decade. It was the first of an impressive range of competitively priced, high performance, six-cylinder models that would probably have saved Talbot if other constituents of the Group had not been failing. In the end the Rootes brothers took over Sunbeam and Talbot in 1935 whilst the other constituents went their separate ways.

The Rootes brothers were successful garage owners from Maidstone in Kent who had done well from distributing several marques, including Clyno. They considered saving that firm but had already become involved with Humber, in which they ultimately acquired a 60 per cent stake by 1931. Humber had bought commercial vehicle maker Commer in 1925 and had then added its Coventry neighbour Hillman in 1928. Humber made good quality cars that were rather more competitively priced than other Coventry marques like Armstrong-Siddeley and Daimler. Rover at that stage had not started its move up-market that followed the Wilks family (ex Hillman) involvement of the 1930s. Indeed, with its little Eight in the early 1920s it had a 17,000 best-seller (which had been made not in Coventry but in a former munitions factory in Tyseley, Birmingham). Rover made between 4,000 and 6,000 cars a year through much of the decade, or probably rather more than Humber. Hillman, on the other hand, had a larger production of cheaper cars and was the perfect vehicle with which Rootes could attack the mass-market with its new Minx of late 1931. This was to account for 152,000 sales up to the Second World War. Rootes was to add Singer to its stable after that war, but in the meantime that particular Coventry, then Birmingham, factory was by 1930 the fourth-biggest producer in the land. At that stage it was capitalized at £2 million, and had 8,000 employees and 44 acres of factory producing roughly 8,000 cars per year. Like many of its competitors it had embarked on an expansion programme in the early 1920s that added Coventry Premier, Coventry Repetition, Sparkbrook Manufacturing, Calcott, Aster (to be its London service depot) and, most importantly of all, a new six-storey factory in Small Heath, Birmingham, in 1927. This had been surplus to BSA-Daimler's requirements and, like the ferro-concrete structures of Arrol Johnston at Dumfries and its Scottish sister Galloway at Tongland, it was modelled on modern American work practices. Despite the obvious advantages of working on one floor it had been found that, in addition to savings in land cost, the construction costs were 20 per cent cheaper per square foot of floor space using structural steel and even less using pre-stressed concrete. Building Singer chassis and bodies on different floors may have seemed quaint, but thanks to large capacity lifts it was surprisingly efficient.

Incidentally, both the aforementioned Scottish factories still stand as memorials to a once proud industry that never quite made it into the successful world of mass-production. The Galloway was made by a largely female work-force under female management but sadly not enough young ladies in the early 1920s supported their sex by buying the product. As ever, this was because cars like the Austin Seven and Morris Cowley were cheaper and, arguably, just as good. The large ship-building and engineering group Beardmore had little luck with cars either, though its taxis became popular, and Argyll staggered through the 1920s without ever living up to its early promise.

By the mid-1920s the industry had new techniques to speed production, like quick-drying nitro-cellulose paint.

AC was possibly the first to make use of its properties, though by then its endeavours to become one of the larger makers had failed. Before 1920 it had made over 2,000 economical three-wheelers. It was controlled from 1921 by S. F. Edge, originally connected with Napier, who also became managing director of the firm making the Cubitt car in Aylesbury. This well-funded project made a large 'colonial' type of car in 1920–5 in the idiom of Angus Sanderson and Ruston-Hornsby. With ten acres of factory and £600,000 at its disposal (some from building firm Holland, Hannen & Cubitt Ltd) it looked to be a reasonable proposition. However, as all but a few were to find, the market for such cars was well catered for by mass-produced American imports that were usually cheaper, even after the imposition of tax (known as McKenna Duties). Many of these motor firms, both old and new, were brought to their knees by the moulders strike that followed the Armistice.

Citroën produced a car every ten minutes in 1927

The Ruston-Hornsby was again a well-funded inter-war project from the Lincoln-based engineering firm of the same name that had grown from the 1918 merger of Ruston Proctor and Richard Hornsby. Traction engines, threshing machines, excavators, and latterly aircraft had been its specialities and the skilled carpenters from the aero department were put to work on the car bodies. Sales were entrusted to the British Motor Trading Co, which had a brief and unhappy liaison with several firms, especially after its Bean involvement. Like the Cubitt, the Ruston-Hornsby was dead by the mid–1920s, showing that adequate supplies of finance, a sound product, and ample factory backing were not in themselves enough to woo the public. Plainly an established dealer network and a familiar name were more important requisites.

We have already noted the arrival of Ford and General Motors on these shores. Dodge was also present here and became more important after its American parent was acquired by Chrysler in 1928. Another of the large transatlantic motor firms, Willys-Overland, struck up a deal with Crossley of Manchester in 1919 which saw them share a former aircraft factory at Heaton Chapel, Stockport. The Overland car achieved some success, as did its sleeve valve sisters with Knight-licensed engines once agreement had been reached with Daimler, who held British rights to the Knight patents. One model of Overland actually went so far as to be 'all British', thanks to the adoption of a Morris engine and running gear. Peak output of all types may have been as high as 250 per week (350 including commercials) but the Great Depression soon wiped out Willys-Overland-Crossley and drove the British partner out of the car business soon afterwards.

A few other foreign companies became involved in British assembly, but by far the most ambitious after the American 'big four' was Citroën. Its fellow countrymen Berliet had two acres of former skating rink at Twickenham, but this was small beer compared with what happened on the 60 acre site of a former munitions factory at nearby Slough. The great Slough Trading Estate had been the brain-child of Sir Percival Perry, who had formerly controlled Ford's Trafford Park operations. As we shall see, he was later called back to help Ford at Dagenham. Citroën appeared in France after the First World War and borrowed heavily from American mass-production expertise. Its Slough factory was said to be the largest motor plant under one roof in Britain when it opened in 1926. It produced a car every ten minutes during 1927, many of which – like Morris – had pressed steel bodywork produced under Budd licence. Citroën continued to make right-hand drive cars at Slough until 1965.

In the 1920s Jowett was the most regional of Britain's medium-sized companies. With an output of 85 cars a week by 1929, sales were higher in the Northern Counties. This is a 1926 Short Two which sold for £150. (NB)

Another French firm to take a serious interest in the British market was Michelin, which established an important tyre factory at Stoke-on-Trent in 1927. The American giants Goodyear and Firestone also became major producers here, as did Pirelli from Italy and Englebert and Bergougnan from Belgium. The famous pioneering Dunlop firm meanwhile acquired the Mackintosh and India business. Takeovers were also happening in other areas of the components industry. Lucas, which in 1880 had employed 58 men, had 3,000 in 1920, 8,000 in 1930, and 20,000 in 1939. As already mentioned, it had acquired the makers of Thomson-Bennet magnetos in 1914 and in 1924 added the Brolt lamp and electrical accessories business. This had been set up in about 1911 by Messrs Brooks and Holt, formerly with C. A. Vandervell (CAV). Vandervell, born in 1871, had started business at the age of 21 and had expanded to Acton, near the works of Napier, in 1904. CAV had the Clyno,

Austin, and Lea-Francis contracts and was a useful addition to the Lucas portfolio in 1926. In that same year it acquired Rotax, which had started in about 1905 and in the 1920s supplied Belsize, Crossley, Daimler, Riley, Singer, Sunbeam, and Talbot. Lucas lost £17,000 with the collapse of Clyno but at least held on to both the Austin and Morris business. These two rivals were not very happy about the situa-

tion, especially as Morris regularly placed orders of double the value of those received from Austin. Not that Lucas had a complete monopoly, as Autolite and Delco Remy from America both opened factories here.

In 1929 Lucas added two more electrical firms. One was Rists, which made batteries and cables and had won the Ford Model T flywheel magneto contract in 1919. The other was Powell & Hanmer, whose Birmingham factory became home to Rotax. Lucas also took an interest in non-electrical components. The Bowden brake and bodywork firm in Tyseley, Birmingham, was acquired. Here Stromberg carburettors were made under licence along with Bendix starter drives and Bendix-Perrot braking systems. Stromberg was eventually sold to Zenith in London and Bendix acquired its own factories and bought the Douglas

The first Ford aimed specifically at the European market, the 8 hp Model Y, at its launch at the Albert Hall in February 1932. This is one of 14 American-built prototypes. Production models from Dagenham had more of a point at the bottom of the radiator grille, and a dip in the middle of the bumper. (NB)

motor cycle (and former car) factory in Bristol in the 1950s. Lucas owned two thirds of the brake company in 1932 and gained outright control shortly before the Second World War. Lucas also took over the Girling brake interests in 1943. Girling had been a subsidiary of the New Hudson bicycle firm which had acquired Captain Girling's ideas after Rubery Owen and Ross Steering in America had turned them down. With four-wheel brakes virtually universal from the mid-1920s the Girling system of wedge and roller actuation with low friction linkage and rods under tension proved attractive to Riley, Rover, and then Austin and Ford.

The rival Lockheed hydraulic system was used from 1924 by several manufacturers. Malcolm Loughead (he simplified his name for the brakes) was of British extraction but American nationality. He made a fortune when Chrysler adopted his brakes, and the even stopping power of one of these cars so impressed one of the founders of Automotive Products of Leamington Spa that his company acquired world rights outside America. The Zephyr Carburettor Co in Leamington Spa began to produce the Lockheed brakes in 1928 and Wolseley became one of its first customers. In 1931 Automotive Products added another important American invention to its line, the dry plate Borg & Beck clutch. A large factory was built in Tachbrook Road, Leamington Spa, in 1931–2 where 138 people were employed to make the aforementioned items, to which were soon added Purolator filters and Thompson steering and suspension joints. The millionth Lockheed hydraulic brake set outside America left the factory in March 1939. Automotive Products had been created in 1920 and this was the same year that another well-known group was formed – that of Turner & Newall, which was to acquire the previously mentioned Ferodo brake and clutch linings business in 1925.

Ransome & Marles bearings were touched on in connection with Bean but there were, of course, several other well-known bearing makers. The major Swedish maker SKF established a factory at Luton in 1911, where the work-force of 150 initially made 180 Skefco bearings a day from charcoal crucible cast steel produced in Sweden. From 1918 all-British bearings were made and 775 employees made 24,000 per month. Bentley, Rover, and many others adopted Skefco bearings and by 1936, when Skefco was floated publicly on the London stock exchange, it had 2,000 employees. Another to choose Luton was the Adamant Engineering Co, makers of Marles Weller steering gears, 'fitted to the best, and nearly all the rest'. A famous area for straw hats, Luton had been well placed within easy reach of London to attract the new growth industries.

90% of the UK workforce was unionised compared with 10% in the US

These stories of expansion show that despite the loss of many of the smaller British car firms, output from the successful ones was booming. From 71,396 cars in 1923 it reached 182,347 in 1929 and, though it subsequently fell back a little during The Depression, it had reached over a quarter of a million in 1934 and 353,713 in 1936. Even firms that had not gone over to full mass-production had tried to streamline their manufacturing processes. In 1922 Vauxhall had found that to make three types of vehicle at the rate of 26 per week involved 1,200 people from ten distinct crafts (90 per cent were said to be unionized in the British industry compared with ten per cent in the US, where production was deliberately laid out for less skilled operatives). The 26 cars contained 39,000 parts involving 162,000 operations in their assembly. Even before General Motors came on the scene a flowline system was being adopted at Luton.

In Coventry, apart from the many firms already mentioned, Riley was preparing for its own mass model, the technically advanced and competitively priced Nine of 1926, made at the rate of about 2,000 per year. Daimler and Armstrong-Siddeley made cars by traditional and therefore highly labour intensive methods. Daimler's output is uncertain, as its records were lost in the Blitz, but it is known that between 1919 (when it adopted aspects of the Marmon design from America) and 1930 Armstrong-Siddeley made about 30,000 cars, including a small number of its only real concession to a mass-produced economy car, the Stoneleigh. This was little more than a four-wheeled motor cycle, a type also tackled by Ariel, BSA, Matchless, New Hudson, and other motor cycle firms (which at this stage still included Rover). AJS left the field alone until too late (its car was adopted by the ailing Willys-Overland-Crossley factory) and Triumph's first sortie into the car market in the 1920s was not with a motor cycle-inspired machine but with relatively up-market types.

There were many other economy cars on the market but few enjoyed the commercial success of either the Jowett or the Trojan. Jowett was unusual in being situated well away from the traditional motor industry, at Bradford in Yorkshire. Its frugal little two-cylinder vehicles had lots of torque and ideal gearing for the local hills. Jowett became one of the few examples of regional makes that were to last beyond the 1920s (indeed to 1953). Its 1920s output of about 17,000 cars was virtually the same as that of Trojan at Kingston upon Thames and then Purley, Croydon. However, there the similarity ended as the Jowett was relatively conventional (at least it was until two cylinders became highly unusual in the next decade). The Trojan, on the other hand, was one of the most bizarre designs ever to see series production. To save money, Leslie Hounsfield's design used solid tyres and soft suspension to avoid the cost and unreliability of pneumatic tyres. It had an easy-change epicyclic gearbox like a Model T Ford and a two-stroke four-cylinder engine under the seat. The engine had two working cylinders and two others parallel with them and sharing common combustion chambers that were principally for scavenging. There was a sheet metal punt underframe instead of a conventional chassis, and chain drive to one of the rear wheels. Quite why the mighty Leyland commercial vehicle firm adopted something so unconventional is uncertain – especially as its own foray into the car market in 1920 had centred on the ultra-luxurious and expensive Leyland Eight. In any event, Leyland plainly believed that private motoring was here to stay and, as it had a redundant aircraft factory outside London, it seemed a good way to utilize it, once ex-military lorry refurbishment had been exhausted. At the end of 1927 rights to the Trojan reverted to Hounsfield, who moved the business to Purley Way. Non-mainstream cars were by then on the wane, though he eked out many more years from the design in the form of vans for such firms as Brooke Bond Tea (who ultimately bought more than 5,000 Trojans).

Whilst little is known of Trojan's manufacturing methods, we have a first-hand account of an engineer's visit to the Jowett factory in 1930.[2] He was told that the firm had acquired new premises at Idle at the beginning of the 1920s and that these had been gradually expanded to reach 2½ acres of covered space and 600 employees in 1927. Output was then 100 cars per week and, because of the piecemeal expansion, the single storey factory was not particularly well organized. There was overhead line shafting powered by a diesel-electric installation. The stores, which had gradually expanded back in a narrow line from the frontage, supplied raw materials to the machine shops, and then the completed items to the assembly sections via either overhead runways or platform trucks. Possibly the latter were the newly introduced Reliance trucks from nearby Heckmondwike.

Everything in Jowett's stores was gauge or jig measured and Brinell tested for hardness where necessary. Somewhat ominous was the provision of a straightening press for items that were out of true. There were several Potter & Johnston automatic machines set up for specific tasks in the machine shop. Before the 1920s it was usual for manually-operated machines to do several different jobs, thus wasting time in resetting. A Cincinatti centreless grinder took care of axle ends and Jowett proudly pointed out that this expensive machine had been bought cheaply and reconditioned in the works and that it made its own milling cutters. Jowett also used Herbert lathes and milling machines, Gisholt turret lathes, Natco multi-spindle drilling machines, Lapointe broaching tools, and much other modern equipment. Some interesting and specialized machines rolled out and wired the edges of the mudguards, which were then hung up to receive poured-on rather than brushed or sprayed enamel. These were then placed in a stove for an hour and a half before rubbing down and being finished in cycle enamel for a further two hours 'stoving' at 360° Fahrenheit.

The carpenters' shop adjoined the open-air wood seasoning yard and drying sheds and contained Wadkin planers and a Crossley machine for making tenon joints. Body framing was shaped to match wooden templates. The most modern part of the plant was the bodyshop, where 'handwork has been reduced to a minimum'. Panel, as opposed to fabric, bodies were spray-painted and baked in a gas oven in a continuous process. Adjoining the body shop were assembly benches where batches of 100 components from the stores were pieced together. They then went by overhead runway to the chassis line. Engine cylinders were tested for combustion chamber capacity by filling them via the plug holes with a previously measured amount of oil. This might sound rather hit and miss, but presumably any slight variation could be equalized

by pairing identical cylinders on each side of the 'little engine with the big pull'. Batches of engines were run up on belts from the line-shafting and then run under their own power for an hour at 1,000 rpm followed by a shorter burst at 2,750 rpm. During these periods the engines were actually helping to run the factory line-shafting, which in turn was used for running-in the gearboxes. After this, one in every 50 engines was tested on a dynamometer to check power output. As a final test completed chassis were made to run against a test axle and wheels on a sort of rolling road. A hand-wheel brake varied the resistance of the axle, and the car had to be able to exceed a specific number of ft/lb in each gear.

Where Jowett scored over most of its rivals was in having a one-model policy that enabled reasonable economies of scale to be maintained. Although there was one basic chassis and engine, the firm was able to ring the changes with a wide assortment of bodywork from van, via open and closed four-seaters, to sporty little two-seaters.

Rather late in the day the somewhat similar Seaton-Petter arrived in Yeovil, made in the works of the well-known Petter engine firm in 1926. It had a twin-cylinder two-stroke unit and briefly cost only £100, which proved to be of little attraction to a public by now used to 'proper' cars. Brocklebank & Richards, operating from some wartime aero engine sheds adjoining the Wolseley works in Birmingham, tried another approach at about the same time. They made a clone of an American Hudson, which had proved to be the sort of large robust car that sold well in countries like Australia and South Africa. To make a saloon that cost only £395 would have required highly efficient mass production on a grand scale. The Brocklebank lacked such facilities but bought in components that had the advantages of scale – in other words, mostly from America. As only 600 Brocklebanks found customers, this form of assembly turned out to be doomed in the face of imports and reliable cars like the Austin Twelve and Twenty (the latter model, interestingly, also having been inspired by Hudson – as indeed, to a lesser extent, had been Rolls-Royce's first owner-driven model, its Twenty).

Talking of American ideas brings us conveniently back to Ford, which, after building over 15 million Model Ts around the world by 1927 (about 310,000 of them at Trafford Park, Manchester), badly needed a new design. Not that there was anything wrong with the Model T; it had simply, after 15 years, become 'old hat'. Ford had been led at Trafford Park by various different managers after Sir Percival Perry resigned in 1919 (he had been knighted for industrial service during the First World War). Ford had the problem of trying to make and sell a product that had become the butt of music hall jokes and an amusing prop in silent films. From accounting for 41 per cent of all the vehicles on British roads in 1919 and reaching its highest production total in 1920 (46,362, including 7,000 vans) the Model T was finally toppled from number one sales position by Morris in 1924. In America Ford felt that England should be the springboard for the whole of its European operations and decided to create a version of the self-sufficient River Rouge plant. Instead of looking west from Manchester the new factory would face Europe and provide even better access to shipping. In 1924 Ernest C. Kanzler, Edsel Ford's brother-in-law, selected a 300-acre area of marshland at Dagenham, Essex, and London County Council agreed to build rented housing for 25,000 families.

Whilst the marshland was being filled with refuse from the capital, Trafford Park and Ford's Cork plant in recently divided Ireland began to prepare for the new Model A. In many ways this was a far more conventional car than the Model T, with sliding

The Ford assembly line at Dagenham in 1939. The second car is a 10 hp Prefect, while the others are 8 hp Model 7Ys. Unlike the American-designed Model Y, these were styled by Ford of Britain. They were continued after the war, the Prefect little changed, the 8 hp renamed Anglia and with a different front end. A small number of Anglias were made from 1939 to 1941. (NMM)

mesh 'crash' gearbox in place of the old epicyclic system. Ford reasoned that enough people had learned how to change gear, with the aid of double de-clutching, for the complexities of its old ideas to be abandoned. Whilst the Model A that appeared around the world in 1928 was usually powered by a 24 hp four-cylinder engine, most of those for Britain and Ireland were AF models rated at a more tax-efficient 14.9 hp. Roughly 3,500 men worked at Trafford Park during the period that about 14,000 Model As were produced, up to its closure in 1932.

Construction work had begun on Ford's 71-acre premises at Dagenham in 1929, with Sir Percival Perry back at the helm at the express wishes of Henry Ford. Adjoining the Ford factory was to be an industrial estate housing several essential suppliers, the first to arrive being the American body building firm, Briggs Manufacturing Co. Whilst the rest of the motor industry reeled from the aftermath of the Wall Street Crash, Ford continued to sail forward, to the admiration of one journalist in particular: 'It's an example of heroic pluck, the rearing of this hive of industry, which stands like a lighthouse of hope in a storm-tossed sea of industry'. This industry had to sink or swim, as it has been estimated that in Britain in 1930 each motor firm employee was responsible for just one and a half cars per year, as against eight in America.

Behind the scenes Ford was extremely worried, as sales were falling and £5 million was an enormous price to pay for a potentially massive output from Dagenham. This, the first totally integrated plant in Europe opened on 1 October 1931 (a couple of weeks after the first of 1,500 workers transferred there from Trafford Park by train). First off the line was a Model AA truck, followed by many more in the coming months as the production facilities came on stream. As at the Ford plant in America, Dagenham had its own blast furnace, foundry, power station, and dock and was the largest motor factory in Europe at that time. The blast furnace was first used in 1934 and was a unique feature for a British car factory. Its raw materials arrived by sea and river, and indeed many completed vehicles departed by the same route. Interestingly, one of its by-products was benzol, which was used for fuelling completed cars. The power station ran from 1935 and burned an assortment of fuels including coal and up to 300 tons per day of processed rubbish. Ironically the site was also built on rubbish, though by then resting on a mat of steel reinforced concrete on top of 22,000 piles driven deep into terra firma underlying the marshland. The production buildings had a roof area of 14 acres, much of which was glazed to give 'daylight working' conditions.

Only five cars were amongst the first three months' production at Dagenham, partly because demand was at a low level. Sir Percival Perry saw that a car with an even smaller engine was desperately needed, and thus was born the 8 hp Model Y that was created in a record-breaking ten months and represented 60 per cent of Dagenham's output by the end of 1933 (and 15 per cent of total British output). Initially costing £120, this figure was reduced in a price-war (against Morris in particular) to an extraordinary £100 – the first and last time that this was achieved on a 'proper' four-seat saloon. Admittedly at the showrooms the salesmen did all they could to steer purchasers away from the basic model to something with a few more frills and therefore profits. By the time it was replaced by a new Eight in 1937, 157,660 examples of the Model Y had left Dagenham.

Morris responded to all the new machine tools and labour-saving ideas at Ford with a new system of five parallel tracks at Cowley in 1934 (Standard adopted similar ideas in the same year). Those at Morris were fed by 12 miles of conveyors bringing in parts made on the premises and by suppliers (122 of whom were acquired by Morris during the 1920s and 1930s). In 1936 Austin initiated four new tracks and by then 90 per cent of British cars were made by just a handful of firms. Mass-production was here to stay.

CHAPTER FIVE

The Specialist Car

Anders Ditlev Clausager

Even to this day, Britain is notable for the variety offered by her smaller motor manufacturers. In the 1990s, apart from the 'big seven' mainstream producers operating in the UK – Ford, Honda, Nissan, Peugeot, Rover, Toyota, and Vauxhall – there were almost 20 small independent manufacturers: a number which, incidentally, was comparable with that of the 1940s, and not a disastrous reduction even from the immediate pre-Second World War period when some 25–30 such makers were active. In terms of size there were great differences between the specialists of the 1990s, annual production figures ranging from less than 100 cars to perhaps 2–3,000 in a good year. In addition there was one example of an intermediate-sized specialized manufacturer – Jaguar – as well as examples of specialist cars made in-house by the big manufacturers, notably the MG but also other Rover Group products. With a combined output of typically around 5,000 cars per year, the independent small specialists contributed less than 0.5 per cent of the motor industry's total annual output; even Jaguar built only two per cent of all cars in Britain. In numerical and commercial terms, these small manufacturers were therefore wholly insignificant; yet among them were some of the most famous names in the industry world-wide; Rolls-Royce, Bentley, Aston Martin, Lotus, and Morgan, apart from Jaguar. There is no doubt that the continued prestige of these marques contributed measurably to the international standing of the

British industry, as well as of Britain as a nation.

No other car manufacturing nation in the world could muster a comparable list. In the USA, the depression of the early 1930s killed off many specialist car makers, and most of the survivors later succumbed to commercial pressure from the 'big three'. In France and Germany, the Second World War and its aftermath put paid to virtually all of the specialized car makers, only a few newcomers appearing in later years, while in Italy the tendency to rationalize the industry went hand in hand with the inexorable rise of Fiat – which ended up taking over most of the surviving specialists. In Japan the motor industry blossomed late but explosively; this, coupled with the impoverished state of early post-war Japan, meant that specialist car manufacturers would never have stood a chance, even if they had emerged in the first place.

It was different in Britain. One fundamental reason why more specialist car makers have survived for longer in Britain is undoubtedly that British car buyers have always craved greater choice and variety than their opposite numbers in most other countries. Car makers which would never have been started up, much less flourished elsewhere, have almost perversely thrived – at least for a time – in Britain. There is also a national predilection for the eccentric, even downright oddball, which at times finds odd historical echoes: what was the 1990s Rocket other than a modern incarnation of the AV Monocar of some 70 years before?

The side-effect of the British desire for variety is that, particularly since 1970, Britain has become an importer's Mecca, with more different foreign cars being available than in most other countries, and more imported cars being sold than British-built ones.

There are also historical reasons why Britain's specialized car makers have collectively led a more charmed life than similar groups in other countries. The 1930s depression did not affect the motor industry in Britain nearly as much as it did in the USA, while in the immediate post-war period many British specialist car makers flourished because of government policies encouraging exports, other car making nations being unable to meet the demand, and the British home market being closed to imports. Those specialist car makers who were prepared to tackle export markets stood to make immense short-term gains. The best-known and most important phenomenon was the love-affair of the American public with the British sports car, and suddenly almost 'everything' was available with left-hand drive and metric instruments, even Armstrong-Siddeleys, Rovers and the other "true Brits[1]".

Then, the rationalization of the British motor industry proceeded more slowly and in a different manner to that in other countries. When a respected maker of specialist cars got into trouble, rather than go to the wall it was often 'rescued' by being taken over by another manufacturer, either a competitor, or even a mass-producer wishing to spread its market coverage.

The 1929 Lanchester straight-eight (above) *and the Fourteen saloon of ten years later* (below) *could both be described as specialist cars, but of very different kinds. The straight-eight was a high-quality car from an individual maker, and one of the most expensive British cars on the market at a chassis price of £1,325. Here George Lanchester stands proudly by a cup-winning saloon at the 1929 Southport Rally. By contrast the 1939 Fourteen is a Daimler DB18 with a Lanchester radiator and Bendix brakes in place of Girlings. At £525 it was £75 cheaper than the DB18.* (Both NMM)

Thus Wolseley and Riley were taken under the wings of Morris, Triumph fell to Standard, while Sunbeam, Talbot and Singer ended up in the Rootes Group; further down the scale, Lanchester was taken over by Daimler which in turn was taken over by Jaguar, and Bentley was absorbed by Rolls-Royce. In at least two cases a new specialist car make was created on the back of a strong mass-producer – MG in the 1920s, Austin-Healey in the 1950s.

Very often such take-overs led to a fundamental alteration of the weaker party's product and market position – with almost immediate effect in the cases of Lanchester, Bentley, and Sunbeam-Talbot – though all of these remained specialist car makers. On the other hand, some specialists flourished in their originally chosen field after being taken over, such as Wolseley in the 1930s, or notably Triumph after the war. This inevitably had much to do with the financial stability which came by being allied to a larger company. By contrast, financial difficulties have often bedevilled the small manufacturer wishing to stay independent, a notorious example of which is the tortured history of Aston Martin. The problems of undercapitalization and inadequate sales revenue have in more recent times become almost insurmountable as the cost of developing a new product has escalated. Not surprisingly, for a long time the majority of small independent manufacturers have relied on the big battalions for the supply at least of mechanical components.

Regrettably, most of the taken-over specialists were ultimately degraded into mere badge-engineered luxury or sporting versions of commonplace family cars, and often a once-prestigious historic brand name was left woefully under-exploited or even abused by a new owner: witness the Riley Elf or the Humber Sceptre. When the British motor industry belatedly initiated drastic rationalization from 1968 onwards, most of these subsidiary badges were discontinued as being uneconomic – not surprisingly so, when poor product policies had led to the erosion of a once loyal customer base. Previous to this, however, the existence of specialist brands within the big manufacturing groups had put an uncomfortable amount of pressure on the small independents where there was direct competition. A classic case is that of Lea-Francis, a small independent maker of sports saloons which failed to keep costs and thus prices down to the level of their then closest competitors, the Nuffield-owned Riley brand. In consequence Lea-Francis failed, while Riley prospered for a few more years.

The other factor which put many

specialist car makers under threat from the 1930s through to the 1960s was the emergence from within their own ranks of two dominant manufacturers which each, while still independent – if for very different reasons – grew to become in effect intermediate-size manufacturers with a strong degree of popular appeal: Jaguar and Rover. In their chosen fields these two makes successfully challenged and overcame competition from group-owned specialists (Humber, Riley, Wolseley) and also effectively saw off several of the smaller independents (Allard, Armstrong-Siddeley, and the Daimler-Lanchester combine).

What was really interesting, and where Britain differed markedly from all other car manufacturing nations, was that for almost every small specialist which disappeared, a new make would spring up. Almost every decade has seen new additions to the ranks of specialist car makers, and around half of today's makes are post-war creations. Many of these started life as kit car manufacturers, a surprisingly fertile field from where we may yet see further new names added to the established industry, type approval and other legislation always permitting. The rapid transformation of Lotus in the 1950s, from a backyard maker of Austin Seven-based specials to a world-leading racing car constructor, must be considered an industrial miracle. Others have followed similar paths, though none so spectacularly.

Up until the early 1970s, it was arguably internal motor industry pressures – whether competition, take-overs, badge engineering or rationalization – which were mostly responsible for the demise of specialists. Then came the 1973 oil crisis, high inflation, and a general recession, which in very short order proved that even the apparently most well-established specialists were not immune from disaster. Jensen was the most prominent of the 1970s casualties, while both AC and Aston Martin suffered upheavals, and Jaguar was barely protected by being under the BL umbrella which was

itself under threat. Since then, further fluctuations in the general economic climate world-wide have contributed to the changing fortunes of Britain's small car makers. Rolls-Royce saw wildly fluctuating sales figures from year to year in the 1980s and 1990s. Jaguar was still to a large extent dependent on US sales and therefore suffered under the periodic cyclical slumps in this market which was more mature and more saturated than any other. They were also influenced by the extreme and often rapid shifts in the value of the Pound and the exchange rate which made it difficult to ensure medium-to-long term price stability – and thus profitability – in the crucial export market.

Not surprisingly, the fact that Britain harboured a relatively large number of surviving specialist manufacturers with a proud heritage and a world-wide reputation, eventually attracted the interest of foreign car manufacturers wishing to broaden their portfolio. The American Ford company was particularly active, taking over the Aston Martin-Lagonda company in 1987 and Jaguar-Daimler in 1989, as well as controlling AC

between 1987 and 1992. General Motors bought Lotus in 1986 but in 1993 sold it on to the new Italian Bugatti company. There were continued rumours of Rolls-Royce and Bentley also being sold to a foreign company, with BMW, Ford, Mercedes-Benz, and Toyota all being mentioned as possible suitors. Interestingly, while the Rover Group in terms of production figures and model range was still mostly a mainstream mass-producer, their relative contraction and their increasing reliance on niche models while drawing away from full-scale confrontation in the popular market, more and more earned this company the description 'leading specialist manufacturer' even before their surprise take-over by BMW in 1994. Curiously their new masters seemed to be more aware of the potential value of old-established respected brand names; while at least the re-introduction of the MG sports car had been set in motion well before the take-over, there was now much speculation that BMW might initiate a rebirth also of makes such as Austin-Healey, Riley or Triumph.

The particular example of the mod-

Lea-Francis could not keep their costs down to those of Riley. This is the Fourteen Saloon, described by Michael Sedgwick as having Riley performance if not Riley looks. Unfortunately, at £1,100 it cost £425 more than the 2½-litre Riley RM. Only 252 were made between 1949 and 1953, of which only 90 had the 2½-litre engine. (NMM)

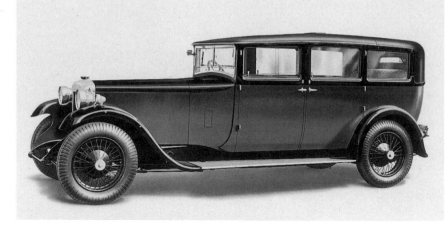

The Daimler was the most dignified quality car of the inter-war years, favoured by royalty and the staider aristocracy and gentry. This is one of the smaller models, a 20/25 hp with seven-seater Mann Egerton enclosed landaulette body. Interior trim included upholstery in light fawn cloth, green furniture hide for the front seat, and cabinet work of highly polished mahogany burr. It sold for £1,300 complete. (NB)

crn Rover Group supports the hypothesis that the definition of a specialist car maker is not dependent solely on the company's size or the annual output, but just as much on the type or types of vehicle manufactured. Historically, however, few specialist car makers in Britain have yet exceeded an annual production of 50,000 cars: MG did so in the early 1970s, Jaguar at the end of the 1980s, but with changing market conditions neither could sustain such prodigious activity for any length of time. Turning to the consideration of what is a specialist car, some categories are comparatively easily defined – such as the luxury car or the sports car, these being the two types of specialist car that have existed for longest. Other categories are more fluid or elusive, but especially in a British context it is worth highlighting the continued existence for much of the industry's history of the upper-middle class quality car, catering to the sector of the market that Sedgwick famously summarized as 'Betjeman-Land . . . the world of tennis and bridge'.[2] Modern market researchers

might prefer to define this type of vehicle as the 'executive car' – a description which defies logical analysis, yet has become remarkably well understood.

Another problem which arises when trying to chart the history of individual makers, is that many have changed course – sometimes dramatically, sometimes almost imperceptibly – over a period of time. Singer, for instance, was by any standards a mass-producer in the 1920s, yet 30 years later had become an insignificant specialist whose staple product had come to differ but little from popular cars except in terms of the price asked for it. Market pressure leading to financial difficulties forced Standard-Triumph to adopt a radically changed role in the 1960s, virtually abandoning the popular mass market in favour of a diverse range of more specialized cars. It has

been much more difficult for a specialist manufacturer to move into a wider market – arguably no British manufacturer has done so since the 1920s, and those who have tried have usually come to grief.

By and large, however, the business of making specialized cars has continued to thrive. The early-to-mid 1990s saw Britain's specialist car makers proceed with undiminished vigour. Although at this time at least one category of car became extinct – both the Rolls-Royce Phantom VI and the Daimler DS420 limousine went out of production – a host of new models, from the independents as well as from those companies which were part of bigger conglomerates, gave the lie to the often asserted theory that car design was stifling under the impact of legislation, and that all cars were becoming the same.

At the start of the motor industry, every car was in a sense a specialized product. The emergence of specialist cars which could be clearly defined and

'A very excellent vehicle of somewhat uninteresting American type' was the opinion of writer and former racing driver J. T. C. Moore-Brabazon on the Rolls-Royce Twenty. Among its American features were coil ignition and a central gear lever. This is a two-seater with dickey by Joseph Cockshoot of Manchester. (NMM)

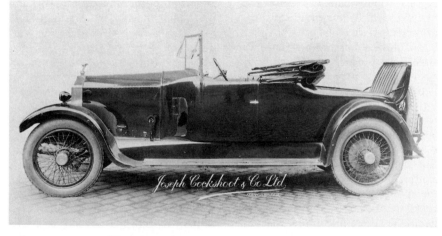

Joseph Cockshoot & Co Ltd

categorized as such had to wait until the industry had matured and settled down. Nor was there initially a great deal of demarcation between different types of car – a sports or even racing model might simply be a light two-seater body on an ordinary chassis. Of the handful of car makers starting up in Britain before 1901 only Daimler achieved any significant production, and while this company and most of the other early contenders usually implemented some form of recognizable standardization as far as chassis, engine and other mechanical components were concerned, the detailed specification, especially in the matter of bodywork, could show extreme variation due to the requirements and wishes of individual clients.

For the first ten years or so of the British motor industry, the car remained largely a plaything for the affluent eccentric sportsman. Hardly any of the British manufacturers had as yet perceived the wider opportunities for making, marketing and selling motor cars, nor had they attempted to put the car on the map as an essential necessity and accepted part of everyday life. There is little doubt that the way in which the British motor industry developed in the early years of the century contributed more to the later relative predominance of specialist cars, than it did to the development of mass-produced popular cars; yet it was only with the advent of mass-production, and the development of certain types of popular family or touring cars, that the specialist car emerged with its own clearly defined identity in a number of different categories. Crucial to later developments was the fact that the idea of mass-production only took hold in Britain at a fairly late stage, and then it was imported from the USA.

At the turn of the century, the USA was relatively less industrialized than the leading European countries, and had a far greater and more widely scattered rural population. Many of the American car pioneers had rural backgrounds, and from the start it was natural for them to consider the auto-

The Vauxhall Prince Henry tourer was a fine example of a pre-war fast tourer, capable of around 75 mph. It was one of the first cars to combine docility with power. Early models had doorless four-seater bodies, but this 1914 example has small doors for both front and rear passengers. The chassis price was £515, and the body illustrated cost £120, including hood and a CAV 12-volt dynamo lighting set with head, side, and tail lamps. (NB)

mobile as a convenient replacement for the farmer's horse and buggy. Helped by the existence of a sophisticated machine tool industry, and by the experience gained in other branches of industry of the mass-production of identical articles such as firearms from precisely machined standardized components, companies such as Oldsmobile, Cadillac and, most notably, Ford almost from their individual beginnings set out to mass-produce popular cars. (For a detailed study, see J. J. Flink *The Automobile Age*, 1988.)

As early as 1904 the USA had overtaken France to become the world's largest producer of motor cars (Britain was a poor third). The Ford Model T was introduced in 1908, the same year that Ford began the first experiments with a moving assembly line, and by 1913 Ford's Highland Park factory in Detroit was fully fitted out with powered moving assembly lines.

By then Ford had also started operations in Britain. The Trafford Park factory in Manchester was opened in October 1911, and in the summer of 1914 moving assembly lines were installed in the British factory.[3] The right-hand drive Model Ts made here, at first assembled from kits of parts

shipped over from the USA, gradually came to include more and more British-made parts, although it took Ford much longer to gain recognition as a 'British' manufacturer. Nevertheless, they quickly became the largest producer in Britain, their 1914 output of 6,000 cars being more than twice the number of any indigenous manufacturer – and Ford cars sold for £125–£135, prices that no British maker could hope to match. Mass-production had arrived.

The response of the British companies to Ford's challenge in the 1912–14 period was the introduction of some of the first examples of what later became known as 'light cars'. Unlike the flimsy motor cycle-engined cyclecars, light cars were proper cars with four-cylinder engines of less than 1.5 litres; typically they only had two-seater bodywork, and they cost between £175 and £200. Standard and Singer entered this field together with many others, the most famous of the breed in the long term being the Morris. While still not able to challenge Ford, the relative success of these practical small cars proved that the market demand existed. However, proper mass-production of British cars did not start in earnest until after the First World War when the McKenna duties and the horsepower tax combined to diminish the threat of continued large-scale importation of American cars, and to thwart for the time being the market dominance achieved by Ford. It is only with the coming of the Ford Model T and the British light cars just before the First World War that we can begin to detect a pattern, and see the gradual differentiation between the popular car and the specialist car.

The point will become clearer if we refer briefly to some of the leading British manufacturers of the pre-1914 period. Austin, Daimler, and Wolseley were at this time three of the most important companies. Broadly speaking, they often made cars of comparable type, size and price, catering to the upper-middle class as well as the carriage trade proper. Neither had much of an interest in the untested market for popular small cars, although Austin catalogued a 10 hp model. The original 1.1-litre model was replaced by a beefier 1.6-litre in 1912; this car was actually rated at 15 RAC hp and cost £260 in chassis form. Daimler's smallest contender was a 1.7-litre 12 on a commodious wheelbase of 8 ft 10½ in which cost £375 complete and was only offered for the 1911 season. Smallest of the Wolseleys was the 12/16 with a 2.2-litre engine – interestingly enough of monobloc design – current from 1910 to 1912,

but it was always outsold by the same maker's 16/20 hp model, an altogether more imposing 3-litre machine. The unenthusiastic reception granted to these small-car efforts was unencouraging to their makers, of whom only Wolseley showed any interest in the light car market – and then, perhaps wisely, sold the resulting design under the name of Stellite.

By contrast, these three companies were to follow widely divergent paths after 1918. Austin quickly embraced the ideal of mass-production of a single type of car, and eventually broadened their product range and moved downwards in the market-place, to become one of Britain's biggest producers of popular cars. Daimler divorced itself completely from the popular mass market, became a leading maker of luxury cars and also for a time played the field in the market for medium-sized quality cars. Wolseley suffered from poor management and a lack of direction, failing in both the popular and luxury markets; attempts at concentrating efforts in the semi-specialist quality market came too late to prevent bankruptcy but when they were revived under Morris's ownership from 1927, they became notably successful in precisely that market sector.

Similar themes were played – with variations – elsewhere in the British motor industry in the years before and after the First World War. There is,

however, one major exception to the general rule that specialist cars only established themselves in the years from 1918 onwards. This was Rolls-Royce, which within an incredibly short time-span became the virtually undisputed leader of the luxury class. (See Chapter Three). Before 1914 only Lanchester followed the Rolls-Royce example of building a limited range mainly for the luxury market, from 1911 to 1914 offering only the 25 hp four-cylinder and the 38 hp six-cylinder model, costing in complete form between £800 and £1,200.

It was mainly due to the activities of Rolls-Royce that the concept of the luxury car, and more particularly of the luxury car manufacturer, had become well established by 1914. A fair number of manufacturers joined – or tried to join – this select group in the immediate post-1918 period. Lanchester's post-war offering was the 40 hp model, by no means as adventurous as some of the company's early products which had been designed by its founder, Frederick William Lanchester – Dr Fred was never an engineer to let convention stand in the way of his undoubted genius, even if some of his notions were eccentric and many of his solutions overly complicated. The 1919 Lanchester Forty nevertheless had some features of merit such as an overhead camshaft for its 6.2-litre six-cylinder engine. Like Lanchester, Napier also chose to concentrate their post-war efforts on but a single luxury car, the 40/50 hp T75, with cylinder dimensions similar to the Lanchester and also an overhead camshaft engine. Whereas Rolls-Royce at this time still only supplied cars in chassis form, both Lanchester and Napier would supply complete cars with 'standard'

A Vauxhall 30/98 with the maker's own Velox tourer body. This is an E-type with 4½-litre side valve engine and brakes on rear wheels and transmission only. 270 of these were made between 1919 and 1922, followed by 313 of the OE-type up to 1927. Three out of every five 30/98 chassis were sold in Australia. (NB)

In contrast to later open Bentleys which mostly had four-seater bodies, this is Chassis #2, made in 1919, with a light two-seater body by J. H. Easter & Sons which was fitted in 1921. After a successful racing career including 11 first placings, #2 was sold in 1923 to J. E. Foden of the steam waggon company, and survives today, though much modified and without her original engine. (NB)

bodywork, typically costing between £2,500 and £3,000 – as did most Silver Ghosts by then. Daimler also supplied complete cars. At the top of their characteristically wide range were 30 hp 5-litre and 45 hp 7.4-litre sixes, fitted, like all Daimler cars since 1910, with Knight-type double-sleeve valve engines.

A newcomer to the car market was the well-established Lancashire truck manufacturer Leyland, whose Eight was a sensation of the 1920 Motor Show. This was Britain's first car with an in-line eight cylinder engine, again with an overhead camshaft, and a capacity of 7 litres. The price was over £3,000 for a complete car (a figure which, like other 1918–39 car prices, may be multiplied by 50 to give an approximation of 1990s' values) and there were few takers, with total production amounting to not more than 18 units. The Leyland Eight bristled with ingenious features and had considerable performance potential, as evidenced by the special racing versions developed by its designer Parry Thomas which gave up to 200 bhp and set several speed records.

There were a few other luxury car makers who attempted to compete with Rolls-Royce in the early 1920s, but the remainder were exceedingly obscure and short-lived. Of those mentioned above, Napier ceased car manufacture in 1924 and concentrated

on aero engines, while Leyland soon returned to the relative safety of commercial vehicle manufacture. Lanchester was taken over by Daimler (already owned by the BSA group) in 1931 and only the name survived, on a range of cut-price Daimlers, for another 25 years. Daimler themselves continued to prosper in the luxury car market, their unique possession of the Royal Warrant giving them a cachet that other makers lacked. In any case

they were bolstered by belonging to the then still considerable BSA group, and had a useful second string in the form of commercial vehicle manufacture (especially buses), their name also being found on a range of smaller middle-class quality cars.

Their prestige was further enhanced when the company introduced Britain's first V12, the Double-Six model of 1927, while the adoption of the fluid flywheel and pre-selector

The Aldington brothers, H. J. (left) and W. H. with the road test demonstrator Frazer Nash, probably in August 1925. New in June 1925, PE 3339 had a 1½-litre Anzani engine and a three-seater body. (NB)

A Riley Nine Monaco saloon at the start of a Midland rally, c.1929. Beside the car is Mr Bury, deputy Mayor of Leamington, and next to him Mr Howell, the local RAC manager. (NB)

gearbox in 1930 was not only a boon to the inexperienced motorist in the days before the universal adoption of synchromesh, but also made Daimlers the perfect choice for processional motoring. During the 1930s some admirable straight-eights continued the Daimler tradition at the top end of the market, while similar engines in lighter chassis offered competition for the new breed of fast touring car typified by the post-1931 Bentley.

Daimler sold well to a traditionally-minded clientele, headed by the Royal family. Rolls-Royce cars in the 1920s had a much 'faster' image, and were as yet eschewed by the staider members of the aristocracy. This attitude was summed up by a chauffeur whose memories dated back to the early 1920s. 'The real people', by which he meant the aristocracy and gentry, preferred Daimlers; Rolls-Royces, he said, 'were for people who had made their money from jam and pickles and things like that'.[4] Only gradually did Rolls-Royces acquire the respectability which later came to be associated with the marque, while at the same time largely shedding their original reputation for high performance, founded on

the TT victory in 1906 and reinforced by the early Silver Ghosts. Their quality and refinement was never in doubt, not even when in 1922 the well-established 40/50 hp model was supplemented by a smaller 3.1-litre 20 hp car, available as a complete car for as little as £1,600 and originally criticized as being 'of American type', with its centrally-mounted ball-type gearchange and coil ignition. For the remainder of the inter-war period, Rolls-Royce always had two models in their catalogue. However, more important to the continued prosperity of the company at this time was the increasing aero engine business, their true second string which in time would come to dominate – and then break – the original Rolls-Royce company. The main factors which made the reputation of their cars were their silence and refinement, coupled with the exquisite care which went into their manufacture – qualities rigorously enforced by F. H. Royce and unswervingly adhered to by his successors.

Originally, all cars were to a degree sporting implements. Only when the motor car became an established form of daily transport did specialized cars

of overtly sporting type begin to appear, appealing to drivers who sought greater performance and better handling but who were prepared to sacrifice carrying capacity and comfort. Some such cars had begun to appear already before 1914. In Britain, sports car development (as opposed to the development of proper racing cars, which largely remained a Continental preserve) was spurred on by the nature of the nation's greatest motor race, the Tourist Trophy held in the Isle of Man annually from 1905 to 1908 (and briefly revived in its original location in 1914). As indicated by its name, this race was intended for cars of touring type, and the regulations went some way to ensure that too-specialized racing machinery was excluded. Some of the contestants appear, in fact, to have been stuck with particularly unsuitable vehicles. This race regularly attracted a wide entry of British cars, and contributed much to the development of lighter, faster and more sporting versions of the typical touring cars of the time.

On the Continent, the fashion was for supervised road trials of touring cars, events where endurance and regularity were as important as performance. In Germany, the Prince Henry trials were held from 1908 to 1910, then the Austrian Alpine Trial took over as the premier European touring car contest until 1913. The Austrian event especially attracted British participation. Like the Tourist Trophy, these events influenced touring car design, and contributed to the development of sleeker, more streamlined body styles. It is no coincidence that two, at least, of early sporting British cars took their names directly from these Continental events: the Vauxhall 'Prince Henry' and the Rolls-Royce Silver Ghost 'Alpine' model. It is also significant that against the British background, these cars were strictly speaking fast tourers, derived from touring models rather than pure racing cars; despite the availability of Brooklands, one of the few purpose-built motor racing tracks of the pre-

Armstrong Siddeley catered to the upper-middle class market with cars which were generally staid and un-sporting. However, this 17 hp coupé is being exercised in the 1937 Hastings Rally by Miss V. M. Wilby. A lady driver is appropriate as this body style, also available on the 12 hp chassis, was termed by the makers 'for the daughters of gentlemen'. (NMM)

1914 period, few British manufacturers took racing seriously. Napier, Sunbeam, Talbot, and Vauxhall were exceptions, but despite the encouraging results achieved by some of these in international competitions, it was only in the 1920s that British cars really began to create an impression in international motor sport, and then at first in sports car events, such as the Le Mans 24-hour race. On the whole, however, such motor sport as took place in Britain before 1914 tended to be parochial and of a type confined to the island.

The sportsman's ideal was therefore the fast touring car. Most such cars carried the four-seater bodywork for which they had been designed and which, in any case, was required for most touring car contests, whether in Britain or abroad. (While proper racing cars were at this time two-seaters, a convention imposed by the need to carry the obligatory mechanic, as far as road cars were concerned, two-seaters were associated mostly with small,

After varied fortunes in the 1920s, Rover had a very successful decade in the 'thirties, production rising from 5,000 to 11,000 between 1933 and 1939. The distinctive wing line was introduced for 1937; most Rovers from then until 1940 were saloons, the four-light sports saloon illustrated, or a six-light version, although a few dropheads were made. They were available in 10 hp (saloon only), 12 hp, 14 hp, 16 hp and 20 hp models. This 16 hp is taking part in the 1937 Welsh Rally. (NMM)

Best-selling Wolseley in the late 1930s was the Series II 14/56, of which 17,839 were sold, out of a total for the six-cylinder Series IIs of 23,776. Like other Series IIs, it shared bodies with Morris, whose equivalent was the Fourteen. For an extra £40, Wolseley buyers got overhead valves, Easi-Clean wheels, three-toned colour paint schemes, and more sumptuous interior woodwork. (NMM)

cheap cars which had neither the dimensions nor the power to cope with four-seater bodywork. The two-seater sports car was largely an invention of the later 1920s.)

In the early 1920s, the fast tourer/sports car was logically developed from its 1914 forebears. Some manufacturers – such as Austin and Wolseley – briefly catalogued 'sporting' models which were largely their ordinary touring car chassis fitted with lightweight four-seater touring bodies and skimpy wings. There was even at one stage a similar derivative of the Bullnosed Morris Cowley. At the other end of the scale, Rolls-Royce pulled out of the sporting market altogether, and Lanchester also abandoned their short-lived 1914 'Sporting Forty' in order to devote their efforts to the carriage trade. Far more important was the Vauxhall 30-98 which was a direct successor to the Prince Henry, built in small numbers already in 1914.[5] This explained the fact that the car employed an unashamedly Edwardian engine, with four cylinders dimensioned at 98 x 150 mm for a capacity of some 4.5 litres. Nor did the side-by-side valves surprise, in spite of Vauxhall's advanced twin ohc GP car of 1914, while the five-bearing crankshaft held the promise of robustness. The quoted maximum power of 90 bhp was in deference to the lengthy stroke developed at a leisurely 3,000

rpm. The 98 bhp suggested by the car's title was probably the preserve of specially developed racing versions. The model was guaranteed to attain 100 mph when stripped for racing.

The 30-98 represented the most important link between the Edwardian fast tourer and the Vintage sports car proper. Although its actual competition career was negligible, it attracted and retains a devoted following as a road car, and has always been considered as the main rival to the slightly more sophisticated Bentley. For 1923, an overhead valve engine of 4.2 litres was fitted, with a slightly shorter stroke and power improved to a maximum of 120 bhp at 3,500 rpm, while later models even had hydraulic brakes, on the front wheels and transmission. The most commonly seen bodies were Vauxhall's own Velox and Wensum styles, the latter more rakish, with no doors, a V-shaped windscreen and a short boat-tail. By the time the great 30-98 was discontinued in 1927, Vauxhall was owned by General Motors and would soon concentrate its efforts on a very different type of car.

A post-1918 newcomer was Bentley. The company's founder and chief designer, Walter Owen Bentley (1888–1971) has, almost alone of the industry's founders, left behind him a considerable body of published works which make it simpler to trace the history of his cars and company. In his

youth a railway apprentice, this experience may have left a lasting legacy in the dimensions and weight of his cars, which, however, contributed greatly to their robustness and thus success in endurance events. Others, like Ettore Bugatti, dismissed Bentleys as 'the fastest lorries'. Bentley entered the car business as importer of the French DFP in 1912, greatly improved its performance by fitting aluminium pistons, and brought one of these cars to the finish of the 1914 TT race. During the First World War he designed a rotary aero engine. In 1919 he set up a modest establishment in London and began to build his own first car, the Bentley 3-litre. If its long-stroke four-cylinder engine betrayed an Edwardian heritage, the overhead camshaft was the product of the new era, and four valves per cylinder were still extremely unusual. Rough and noisy the early Bentleys were, but they were also robust and reliable, and, in short chassis speed model form, capable of 100mph. The young company quickly made its mark in competition, was the first British make to compete in the Le Mans 24-hour race (inaugurated in 1923) and, in the following year, scored the first of five victories in this prestigious event.

Almost from the start, Bentley attempted to cover two markets – luxury as well as sports. The standard chassis had a wheelbase of 130 in, and could therefore accommodate a variety of closed touring bodies, Bentley offering complete cars which cost anything up to £1,450. More enduringly famous was the 117 in wheelbase Speed Model with a tuned engine; the classic Vanden Plas open sports tourer, similar to the Le Mans winning car, cost £1,125, while the 100 mph model on a 108 in wheelbase with two-seater bodywork cost £1,050. The original 3-litre model was later replaced by an even bigger four of 4.5-litre capacity, of which the limited production supercharged model is, in popular imagination, the greatest Bentley of them all; in fact it had a rather mixed career in racing, with dubious reliability, its most famous result being second place in the French Grand Prix of 1930. Bentley's own instinct was to enter the field for six-cylinder luxury cars, which he did with the 6.5-litre model in 1925. This was more suitable for the carriage trade but was still an effective sports car, winning twice at Le Mans, in Speed Six form with lightweight body. The grandest of all was the 8-litre of 1930, an enlarged six-cylinder car which was credited with a top speed of over 100 mph, even in limousine form.

By then Bentley's perennial financial difficulties had caught up with them. In 1926 the company had been rescued by an injection of capital by the South African motor racing millionaire Woolf Barnato (who won Le Mans three times for Bentley). His investment carried the company through to the summer of 1931 when, under the influence of the depression, Barnato – who claimed to have lost £90,000 on the Bentley venture – decided not to pay out a further £65,000 in settlement of two outstanding mortgages, and the company went into receivership. [6] An initial proposal to merge with Napier, with the intention of producing a Napier-Bentley car, was frustrated when Napier was outbid by Rolls-Royce. For a time, W. O. himself continued under the new regime although he was not involved in the design of the new cars sometimes

A classic four-light sports saloon, the prototype Continental Rolls-Royce Phantom II with coachwork by Barker. Henry Royce is said to have asked Ivan Evernden to design a body in the spirit of the Riley Nine Monaco saloon. (NMM)

referred to as Rolls-Bentleys, but he left the firm in 1935 – still only 47 years old, he had yet to produce perhaps his most outstanding car design in the shape of the Lagonda V12. While the original Bentley company failed, after having produced some 3,000 cars, it left behind one of the most long-lived legends in the British motor industry; and while the Rolls-Royce-built cars from 1933 onwards were of a distinctly different type, they were still fine cars, worthy of their epithet 'the silent sports car'.

Few of the Bentley's contemporary competitors demonstrated the same single-minded pursuit of success in motor sport. The Sunbeam company of Wolverhampton came perhaps closest – their victory in the French Grand Prix of 1923 marking a high point in their career – even if the car leant heavily on the same designer's Fiat GP car. Afterwards, Sunbeam was more active and more successful in their pursuit of the land speed record, which they raised regularly from 1922 to 1927. Their production range was dominated by fairly commonplace touring cars, but the Three-Litre, made from 1924 to 1930, was a different breed altogether. Its highly sophisticated twin ohc six-cylinder engine was directly derived from the 1923 GP car. It was fast as well as flexible, but acquired a reputation for tricky high-

speed handling, and was not as robust as the Bentley (the second-placed Sunbeam Three-Litre in the 1925 Le Mans had a broken chassis at the end of the race).

Of the multitude of small sports car manufacturers which suddenly emerged in the 1920s, only a half dozen or so have acquired lasting fame. Alvis of Coventry started making cars in 1920. The 10/30 was a refined (and fairly costly) quality light car, advertised as the 'light car de-luxe', but it quickly distinguished itself with a better than average performance. In 1923 the overhead valve 12/50 model followed, winning the 200-mile race at Brooklands the same year. Increasing demand for Alvis cars stretched the company's modest resources, debts mounted, and in 1924 the receiver was called in. Happily the major creditors agreed to a scheme of reconstruction, based on a debenture issue. [7] Remarkably, from 1925 onwards Alvis built a range of front-wheel drive cars, initially for racing but later also, in limited numbers, as road cars, the first British front-wheel drive production cars. Most ambitious was a supercharged 1.5-litre straight-eight GP car. As road cars they had many of the shortcomings associated with early front-wheel drive and were also noisy, especially in saloon form. With prices ranging from £600 to £750 they were

also expensive for a 1.5-litre four-cylinder car. Alvis nevertheless survived, went back to rear-wheel drive, brought out a six-cylinder car, and widened their product range considerably during the 1930s, jettisoning their smaller sports models in the process.

Aston Martin was even more troubled by financial problems than Alvis. While they stuck to making sports cars, and only increased their original 1.5-litre to a 2-litre in 1936, like the front-drive Alvis they were exceedingly expensive, costing from £550 to £675 in 1928. Production was inevitably on a tiny scale; it has been estimated that the total number of Aston Martins made in the vintage period was less than 100, and the best individual pre-war year was 1933 with 105 cars. The original car was conceived in partnership between Lionel Martin and Robert Bamford, the so-called 'prototype' of 1913–14 consisting of a Coventry-Simplex engine in an Isotta-Fraschini chassis. By the time the production model emerged in 1921–2 Bamford had left and Martin gave the car his own name, coupled with the Aston Clinton hillclimb which had been an early success. Most of the early cars had side-valve 1.5-litre engines, though single and twin ohc engines were found in some racing models. Some 60 to 70 cars were sold before the original company was wound up at the end of 1925. In 1926, however, A. C. Bertelli and W. S. Renwick took over the moribund firm, moving operations from London to Feltham in Middlesex, and by 1927 had started small-scale production of a new model which was fitted with a Bertelli-designed ohc 1.5-litre four, and which later became the famous International.

The new model marked the true start of Aston Martin's rise to fame, if not fortune. While the cars were extremely successful in racing and, for instance, became consistent class winners at Le Mans, by 1932 further financial problems led the company to form a short-lived alliance with Frazer Nash. The company next came under the control of R. G. Sutherland, under whose regime some cost-cutting became evident but the price was brought down to £500 for the cheapest model. The 2-litre of 1936 was always reckoned to be 'softer' and did not attract quite the same following but stayed in production until the outbreak of war in 1939. By then a few cars with aerodynamic bodywork had been built and experiments were taking place with the still-born Atom saloon. Sutherland retained control until after the war, when Aston Martin was taken over by David Brown.

Like Aston Martin, the Frazer Nash was very much a car for the die-hard sports car enthusiast – although a few such cars were built, the idea of a saloon-bodied Frazer Nash was anathema. Its origins lay in the sporting GN cyclecar, a joint product of H. R. Godfrey and Archie Frazer Nash. When the partnership split up, Frazer Nash began to build cars under his own name in 1924. The hallmark of his cars was the transmission which featured a dog-clutch gearbox and final drive by chains, one for each gear, to a solid rear axle. Engines were a variety of proprietary units. Although the cars had a devoted following, financial

security was absent as usual, and in 1929 the faltering company was taken over by the Aldington brothers. Production of the chain-drive cars continued through most of the 1930s but was supplemented and later all but ousted when the Aldingtons began to import German BMW cars, sometimes fitted with British coachwork, and sold under the Frazer Nash-BMW badge.

The Lagonda company had been established since the early days of the industry, but production had never amounted to much until a light car with an 11 hp engine and – remarkably for its day – unitary construction of body and chassis was introduced in 1913. Its successor was replaced in 1925 by the first sporting Lagonda, a 2-litre four. The engine featured two high-mounted camshafts activating overhead valves in a 90° V-formation in hemispherical combustion chambers, foreshadowing the better known Riley engine. The 14/60 proved capable of considerable development and was soon supplemented by a range of six-cylinder cars. The shape of the radiator and the sports bodies often fitted to Lagondas gave them more than a passing resemblance to Bentleys. A charming but unprofitable smaller sports model with an 1,100 cc engine was launched for 1934 under the Rapier name. By then the company's biggest model was the 4.5-litre which confounded many observers by winning the Le Mans 24-hour race in 1935. Sadly, by then the money had run out, and in the week following the Le Mans victory the Lagonda company was auctioned off. The buyer was Alan Good who promptly engaged the services of W. O. Bentley as chief designer; in due course the result was the magnificent Lagonda V12.

While the name of Lea-Francis goes back to 1904 and the company exists to this day, it has the unique distinction of having been dormant for longer than it has actually made cars. The early production period lasted only from 1904 until 1906, while the period from 1920 until 1935 was to be the

An early photograph of William Lyons in pre-SS days, astride a Harley-Davidson motorcycle. (NB)

The first four-door saloon from the SS stable, and the first car to carry the Jaguar name. The 2.7-litre engine had the bottom end of the Standard Twenty with overhead valves by Harry Weslake and Bill Heynes. The attractive saloon body, not unlike that of a Bentley costing four times as much, went onto 1½- and 3½-litre chassis as well, and lasted into the post-war years. (NMM)

most prolific in its history. The early 1920s cars were moderately undistinguished light cars with proprietary engines, but the L-type 12/40 of 1925 with a Meadows 4ED engine marked the start of Lea-Francis's career as a sports car manufacturer. Variations on this theme predominated for ten years, with rather less successful six-cylinder cars being offered alongside from time to time. The first supercharged model with the famous sloping radiator followed in 1926, and the Hyper Sports won a notable victory in the 1928 TT race. At around the £500 mark, the car was cheaper than either the Aston Martin or the front-wheel drive Alvis. It was to little avail; Lea-Francis went into receivership in 1930 and the company was only sold four years later. Car production on a small scale had continued throughout but ceased altogether in 1935. The name was revived by a

new company in 1937 but the Lea-Francis cars made until 1953 were of a less sporting nature, falling into the sports saloon category which developed during the 1930s.

Together with Alvis and Lea-Francis, Riley was a small Coventry firm which came to prominence as a maker of sports and sporting cars in the 1920s and 1930s. It had the interesting distinction of being family-owned and operated until 1938. The first Riley car was made as early as 1898. Their post-1918 model was a

quality light car with a copybook side-valve 11.9 hp engine, of which the most sporting derivative was the Redwing, featuring a polished aluminium two-seater body in a style similar to the Alvis 12/50 and often as not with wings painted red. The Riley Nine of 1927 introduced the famous 'PR' cylinder head, named after its designer Percy Riley, with overhead valves in a 90° V-formation and hemispherical combustion chambers, the valves being operated by short push-rods from two side-mounted camshafts high in the cylinder block. The most famous original Nine was the Monaco fabric-bodied saloon, of four-light design and with a small built-out boot, which set the style for a new generation of sports saloons.

The promise of the Nine's advanced engine was fulfilled when Thomson and Taylor at Brooklands developed the low-slung Brooklands racing model. Like so many other British

An interesting shot of the production line at the Rolls-Royce factory at Derby c.1934, showing a 20/25 followed by two 3½-litre Bentleys, proof, if any were needed, of the close links between the two models. Among differences were the Bentley's higher compression ratio, twin carburettors and improved cylinder head design. (NMM)

sports car makers, Riley became a *habitué* of the Le Mans 24-hour race, with a Biennial Cup win to their credit. They also introduced a 14 hp six-cylinder car with a similar engine design, from which was developed the MPH sports model, and which inspired the ERA racing car engine. Several other Riley engines perpetuated the same valve arrangement. The best was probably the 12 hp 1.5-litre four, while an 18 hp V8 was relatively unsuccessful, and the 16 hp 2.4-litre Big Four only really made its mark in the post-war period, when Riley had come under different ownership, the Nuffield Organisation having bought the company in 1938. Previous to this, the MPH had been followed up by other sports cars such as the 9 hp Imp and 12 hp Sprite, and some of the Riley body styles, such as the fast-back Kestrel sports saloon, were of surpassing elegance. The company was also notable for making wide use of the Wilson pre-selector gearbox.

Another devotee of the Wilson box was the London-based Talbot company. This company had a distinguished career in the sport before 1914 – a Talbot was the first car to cover 100 miles in an hour – but their 1920s products were light cars or touring models. They were allied with the Sunbeam company, as partners in the Anglo-French Sunbeam-Talbot-Darracq combine. In 1926 Talbot brought out the excellent 14/45 touring car designed by Georges Roesch

with an extremely efficient ohv push-rod six-cylinder engine which proved capable of amazing development. The heyday of the sports Talbot was from 1930 to 1934. The original 2.3-litre racing model was soon replaced by a 3-litre which was unbeatable in its class. An outstanding range of road cars with engines up to 3.5 litres was developed, but not all Talbots were of sporting mien; long wheelbase chassis were fitted not only with limousine coachwork but were often used for ambulance work. The short and meteoric career of the Talbot sports car came to an abrupt end in 1935 when the Rootes Group took over the company together with Sunbeam, and soon initiated a range of badge-engineered Hillman/Humber cars which eventually became known as Sunbeam-Talbot.

These were the most famous of the sports car names which appeared during the 1920s; even so, we have yet to consider the longest-lived and most famous of all sports cars – the MG, which is so important in its own right that it merits a more detailed analysis, given in a following section. There were many others which emerged sometimes literally out of nowhere in the period from 1925 to 1935, some fizzling out before they got properly under way, others having their short moment of glory, and some being the surprising by-products of concerns otherwise mainly occupied in the manufacture of more mundane vehicles.

However, from 1930 onwards there were relatively fewer newcomers in the sports car field, and by 1939 only a handful of makers still persisted with the out-and-out sports car. This paralleled developments in other European countries where, by the late 1930s, there were very few sports or even sporting cars available, and hardly any at the lower end of the price bracket. While a dearth of small sports cars persisted in Germany, Italy and France after 1945, in Britain the genre was unexpectedly rejuvenated by post-war demands from export markets, notably the USA. Certainly the sports car continued to exist throughout the 1930s, in greater numbers in Britain than anywhere else, but generally most of the efforts of specialist car makers in the last pre-war years were concentrated on the upper-middle class semi-specialist quality car which only sometimes had sporting overtones. Their development will be considered next.

The most striking development of the British motor industry during the 1930s was the emergence of the group of six big mass producers which came to dominate the market. By 1939 it was estimated that between them they accounted for 90 per cent of cars produced or sold in Britain. The original pioneers in the popular market were Austin and Morris; they were now joined by a resurgent Ford company, the General Motors-owned Vauxhall, the Rootes Group formed by the merger of Hillman and Humber, and Standard. Most of these offered wide ranges of family cars in the popular classes, typically from 8 to 16 hp (broadly speaking, between 1- and 2-litre capacity). Yet alongside these many specialist car makers continued to flourish. As ever the most famous specialists were the small makers of luxury or sports cars, but the bulk of

Lagonda sports saloon of 1938–9. This might be a six-cylinder LG6 or a V12. Distinguishing features were the horns, exposed on the LG6 and concealed on the V12, but they are not visible in this side view. (NMM)

specialized car production came from makers selling what might at first glance seem fairly ordinary family or touring cars. Some of these sold in considerable numbers, if never quite enough for their makers to qualify as mass-producers.

Whereas in the 1930s an ordinary 10 hp or 12 hp family saloon from a mass-producer could typically be bought for around £200, a similarly-sized vehicle from a specialist could cost £250–£300 or even more. Such cars were not truly bespoke but their limited production gave them some claim to exclusivity. They were generally considered to be of higher quality. They frequently had better-finished coachwork or some luxury touches. They might be more stylish than ordinary family cars but did not necessarily have any better performance, although some of them were of a sporting nature. Their technical specification differed little from cheaper cars although engine design was usually a little more advanced while by 1939 only two (Morris and Vauxhall) of the 'big six' had made the change from side valves to overhead valves, almost without exception these better-class cars employed ohv, or more rarely ohc, engines.

What such cars did offer was considerable snob value. Here lies perhaps the real reason for their relative success in Britain during the 1930s. While it was still largely only the middle or upper classes who could afford to buy and keep cars – which, incidentally, helped to keep the British motor industry busy throughout the depression – car ownership was finding a slowly widening base, and popular cars had become cheaper over the years. One way that the more affluent car buyer, with £300 to £800 to spend,

could mark the distinction was to choose a Humber rather than a Hillman, a Wolseley rather than a Morris, or pick one of the more unusual makes such as Armstrong-Siddeley or Lanchester. Much the same argument applies in the 1990s, except that most of the better-class British makes have been replaced by foreign alternatives in what is now called the executive car class.

The sector for such slightly up market, semi-specialist quality cars became firmly established in the 1930s. A look at the history of Rover between the wars will serve to illustrate how they developed. In 1919, Rover's staple product had been a development of their pre-war 12 hp car, now called the Fourteen and getting a little old-fashioned; it was joined by the air-cooled flat-twin Eight which was little more than a cyclecar, if quite the best of the breed. Deservedly popular, the Eight was eventually ousted by the Austin Seven. Rover then decided to abandon the popular class altogether, but their initial attempts at moving up-market were not particularly successful. The smallest 9/20 and 10/25 models were undistinguished, the technically complex 14/45 was expensive and heavy, with poor performance, and some of the early six-cylinder models were quite nasty. The renaissance of the marque was initiated when the broth-

ers Spencer and Maurice Wilks took charge. The Pilot of 1932, with a 1.4-litre 12 hp six cylinder engine, was developed into the rather better Fourteen, supplemented by 10 and 12 hp fours, and bigger sixes rated at 16 and 20 hp. Apart from the fact that the Wilks brothers had the good fortune to launch this product range at exactly the point in time when demand for such cars rose, the 1930s Rovers had many admirable qualities. They were conservatively engineered but with great attention to detail. They were of sound construction, and had rather elegant coachwork. Their ohv engines gave them good performance but they were largely without any sporting pretensions; a triple-carburettor Speed Fourteen model was hastily dropped as it did not quite fit the emerging Rover image. Rover's production from 1933 to 1939 rose from 5,000 to 11,000 cars and even then hardly kept pace with demand. The company was also highly profitable.[8] The product fully lived up to Rover's new motto, 'one of Britain's fine cars'.

Even better-selling at the time was Wolseley, since 1927 owned by Morris. Like Rover they for a time floundered, although notable commercial success had come with the introduction of the Hornet in 1930, first of the pint-sized sixes (it had a 1.3-litre engine) which for a time had a following in Britain.

Two approaches to sports car design, on the left a Jensen powered by a 3½-litre Ford V8 engine in a British chassis, and on the right an SS100 with 2.7-litre ohv six-cylinder engine derived from the Standard. They are seen at the end of the 1937 Welsh Rally. (NMM)

Cecil Kimber with the MG Magic Midget on Pendine Sands in 1932. (Courtesy Mrs Jean Cook)

Especially in its sporting versions, the Hornet became a controversial car, although its ohc engine was also used by some MG models. Paradoxically Wolseley only became established as the market leader in its sector from 1935 onwards when the marque's traditional ohc engines were replaced by ohv engines derived from basic Morris designs, while at the same time rather Morris-like body styling was introduced. Their best-seller was a 1.8-litre 14/56, smallest in a range of six-cylinder cars which came in three wheelbase lengths and with five different engine sizes up to a 3.5-litre 25 hp. Like Rover, they also kept a brace of fours – a 10/40 and a 12/48 – in their catalogue, and would even have introduced an Eight had war not intervened in 1939. Annual production topped 17,000 cars in 1937–8, which meant that Wolseley on their own had a market share of almost five per cent.

Humber was in a similar position to Wolseley, being a member of a bigger combine, in this case the Rootes Group. Unlike Rover and Wolseley, they largely eschewed the sector below 2 litres, a 1.7-litre 12 hp car being discontinued in 1937 after only 8,500 had been made over a period of four years. They concentrated on six-cylinder cars from 2.3 up to 4 litres and pro-

duction in the late 1930s is unlikely to have exceeded 3–4,000 cars per year. While on the one hand their side-valve engines were a little old-fashioned for the quality market, on the other hand Humber was early in adopting independent front suspension. Their bodywork was handsome but showed some influence from contemporary American styles. The final pre-war model was the Super Snipe, a compact saloon fitted with the largest size engine, offering 85 mph performance for £398.

These three marques were the leading contenders in the non-sporting sector of the quality car market. Similar products – if typically at higher prices and generally aimed a little further up in the market – were offered by Armstrong-Siddeley, the less sporting versions of Alvis, and the Daimler-Lanchester range. A 15 hp Daimler introduced in 1933 had grown into the DB18 model of 1938 with independent front suspension; this chassis attracted some pretty body styles such as the Ritz sports saloon and the Dolphin sports tourer. Like all Daimlers, these cars were fitted with the fluid flywheel transmission and a pre-selector gearbox. The first new Lanchester after the Daimler takeover had been a 15–18 hp model whose

main claim to fame is that it won the first RAC Rally in 1932. This was followed by the Lanchester Ten of 1934, also available with a side-valve engine and a BSA badge, and a 1.4-litre six-cylinder model which for a season or two was offered under both names without attracting many customers in either form. After this the BSA name was reserved for the front-wheel drive three-wheelers and four-wheeled Scout sports car, and the Lanchester Roadrider with a choice of four or six-cylinder engines was introduced, proving a better car than its immediate predecessors but failing to make much impact against similarly-sized Rovers and Wolseleys before war broke out.

Alongside these strictly non-sporting contenders, a new breed emerged in the 1930s: the sports saloon. First of the breed had been the previously-mentioned Riley Nine Monaco of 1927, its styling attracting countless imitators over the next few years. While the better and more interesting sports saloons were built on genuine sporting chassis with high performance engines, some makers exploited the vogue a little cynically: in the case of Rover, for instance, the sole difference between the sports saloon and the ordinary body style was that the 'sports' saloon was a four-light style, lacking rear quarterlights, and had slightly less generous rear seat accommodation. The four-light style became a hallmark of sports saloons and was even executed on such exalted chassis as the Continental version of the Rolls-Royce Phantom II. The alternative description of 'close-coupled saloon' was a discreet way of indicating that rear seats were often cramped. Some mass-producers offered similar styles, such as the Austin Kempton and Greyhound models, while Standard later called their variation Touring Saloon, and Morris preferred two-door versions which they called Special Coupés or Sports Coupés. Eventually the four-light style was adopted also for non-sporting saloons, starting with the 22 hp Ford V8 and the Vauxhall Ten in 1937, and universally so in the post-war era.

Riley was one of the leading manufacturers in the sports saloon field, offering a wide variety of styles. A similar model range was offered by Triumph. From a modest start with the small Super Seven model of the late vintage period this company launched the first of the Gloria range in 1933. Touted as 'the smartest cars in the land', the original 10 hp engine was later replaced by 1.5- and 1.8-litre units and the inevitable six-cylinder models were added, though none exceeded the 2-litre threshold. Under the influence of Donald Healey, Triumph also developed sports tourers and the occasional real sports car, though the amazing straight-eight Dolomite of 1934, with a twin ohc supercharged 2-litre engine based on the Alfa Romeo design, remained stillborn. The Dolomite name was later applied to an upgraded saloon range with the distinctive if ugly fencer's mask radiator grille. The financial ups-and-downs of Triumph's car manufacture were cushioned by the company's healthy motor cycle business, but when this was sold in 1936 the writing was on the wall. Three years later Triumph went into receivership, having lasted only a little longer than arch-rival Riley. The name only was resurrected after Standard took over in 1944.

Partly responsible for the failure of both Riley and Triumph was a new make which appeared in the 1930s. This was the SS, later SS Jaguar, brainchild of William Lyons (1901–85). His original Swallow side-car business had branched out into coachbuilding, moving from Blackpool to Coventry in the process, and in 1931 Lyons was ready to launch his first complete car, the SSI. This was a low-slung six-cylinder machine with an immensely long bonnet and a claustrophobically short coupé body, looking at first almost like a caricature of itself. The mechanical components were supplied by the Standard company and were, frankly, pedestrian. The instant appeal of the car came from its dramatic styling – billed as the '£1,000 look'

– coupled to the actual sales price of £310. With side-valve engines of 2 or 2.5 litres, performance was not its strongest point. The SSII was the same thing with four-cylinder engines and a shorter bonnet, and remained largely unloved.

By 1935 Lyons had added an open two-seater sports model on a shorter chassis and, while it still had the side-valve engine, somewhat improved performance – enough to justify the SS90 label, supposedly indicative of top speed. He also had a new range of cars in preparation, with a new overhead valve engine, a 2.7-litre six made to his specification by Standard. Launched to tremendous acclaim in the 1935 Motor Show, the new car for the first time bore the Jaguar name. For the first time also a four-door saloon body was fitted, this and a handsome new radiator flanked by Lucas P.100 headlamps lending the car a passing resemblance to a Bentley which would cost three or four times as much. The SS Jaguar sold for £385, and the top speed was near the 90 mph mark. It was accompanied by the SS100, broadly

speaking the SS90 with the new ohv engine. For 1938, Jaguar led the specialist car makers by introducing all-steel bodywork for the saloon model, at the cost of prolonged teething troubles which cost the company much in lost production. There was now also a 1.8-litre four-cylinder ohv model, while the bigger saloon and the SS100 could both be obtained with a 3.5-litre engine, guaranteeing the sports car a 100 mph top speed and costing £445. Production for the 1939 season was over 5,000 cars. Even if Jaguars still had a rather dubious reputation, the formula proved a great success in the market-place, apart from adding considerably to their competitors' problems.

The final important group of specialist cars in the 1930s bridged the gap between the sports and luxury markets. Before 1914 there had been a considerable degree of overlap between the luxury car and the high-performance car, and some of the first sporting machines were derived from luxury models, the sports versions of the Rolls-Royce Silver Ghost being a case in point.

Cecil Kimber (front row, second from left) with senior MG staff in October 1939. First left is general manager George Propert, and on Kimber's left are sales manager T. W. Slingsby and publicity manager George Tuck. (NB)

However, in the 1920s British luxury car makers in general avoided the sporting market: there was at first no British equivalent of the Hispano-Suiza, the Duesenberg, or the supercharged Mercedes-Benz. Only with the emergence of the six-cylinder Bentleys (previously discussed) did a British car combine the ultimate in luxury with outstanding performance. In 1931 Rolls-Royce made their first serious concession to the demand for a higher-performance car with the introduction of the Phantom II Continental. This was followed in 1933 by the more significant Bentley 3½-litre, the first car to be built by Rolls-Royce under the newly-acquired Bentley name. While it disappointed devotees of the 'real' Bentley, it was a refined high-speed touring car, capable of 90 mph – nearly as much as the Phantom II Continental, despite the Bentley having an engine of half the size. The Bentley was advertised as 'the silent sports car'. It was in effect a rediscovery of the fast touring car of some 10–20 years before. The new Bentley was quickly followed by a number of imitators, some of them, like the SS Jaguar, at a fraction of its price.

Among those which deserved to be taken seriously as Bentley challengers were the Alvis Speed 20 and Speed 25 models. The original 1931 Speed 20 was a straight forward 2.5-litre six-cylinder sports tourer in the mould of the vintage Bentley, with excellent performance due to its low build and weight. It later acquired independent front suspension and an all-synchro-mesh gearbox. A 3.5-litre version for heavier coachwork followed in 1936. In 1937 this became the Speed 25, and Alvis also launched the ultimate development of the theme: the 4.3-litre, which in short chassis sports tourer form would easily better 100 mph and also cost a lot less than the Bentley, at just under £1,000. Almost as fast and equally desirable was the final flowering of the Roesch-designed Talbot, the 3.4-litre 110, which was short-lived in consequence of the Rootes take-over.

W. O. Bentley himself had left Rolls-Royce in 1935 and accepted the job of chief designer at Lagonda. Here he set about effecting fundamental improvements to the rough-and-ready 4.5-litre six-cylinder sports tourer, and also began the design of an alternative engine of similar capacity: a short-stroke high-revving V12 with a single overhead camshaft per bank, developing 180 bhp. The new engine was fitted in a much-modified chassis with independent torsion bar front suspension, also used for the later six-cylinder cars. The Lagonda V12 was not intended as a sports car but as the comfortable fast tourer par excellence, and its ability to maintain cruising speeds of over 100 mph in saloon form was all but unheard of at the time. Two light-weight sports versions ran like clockwork in the 1939 Le Mans race, finishing third and fourth. These cars were easily capable of 120 mph but were never fully developed; nor, sadly, was the great V12 brought back after the Second World War.

MGs are worshipped with a devotion bordering on fanaticism

The Lagonda was the most serious challenge to the Rolls-Royce-built Bentley car, which in turn emerged with an enlarged 4.25-litre engine and an overdrive gearbox, expressly installed to ensure trouble-free high-speed running on the new motorways in Germany. The ultimate expression of the pre-war Bentley was the stream-lined car built by French coachbuilder Paulin for the Greek shipping magnate Embiricos. The top speed was over 115 mph and this particular car finished sixth in the 1949 Le Mans race – when it was ten years old. In 1939–40 Rolls-Royce built a prototype of a similar high-performance car, the Bentley Corniche, while a few examples of the Mark V model with independent front suspension were built in 1940.

Almost able to match the best fast tourers on performance, if not on refinement or quality, were those odd cars which have become known as 'the Anglo-American sports bastards'. These followed a standard formula of a large American engine (and sometimes chassis) adapted with British-built coachwork, sometimes in the form of stark sports cars, more often luxurious sports saloons or drophead coupés. Because of the low cost of standardized American components these cars could be sold at much lower prices than the Bentleys, Alvises, or Lagondas. First and most famous of the breed was the Railton, based on the Hudson-Terraplane, appearing in 1933. The 4-litre straight-eight gave it a top speed of nearly 90 mph coupled with extreme flexibility, and originally the price was just under £500. Later cars were mostly heavier, and also more expensive. Similar recipes were offered, with less success, by Brough Superior and Lammas-Graham, while even Captain George Eyston of MG and Thunderbolt record car fame lent his name to a special-bodied Chrysler derivative. Sidney Allard built his first cars just before the war, using the Ford V8 or Lincoln Zephyr V12 engine. More notable were the early Jensens, products of a coachbuilding firm at West Bromwich. The first cars were little more than special-bodied Ford V8s but the bodies were handsome and by 1939 they had progressed to a 4.3-litre car using a Nash straight-eight engine. Railton made a brief post-war appearance but cost was by then prohibitive, and in any case it was far from easy to get hold of American engines in post-war Britain. Jensen found an alternative indigenous power unit in the shape of the 4-litre Austin, while Allard managed to make do with British-made Ford V8s. The rest did not attempt a come-back.

There were fewer new recruits to the sports car sector during the 1930s. Apart from the occasional Triumph and the SS100 described above, two makes made the transition from three wheels to four: the front-wheel drive BSA Scout and the Morgan, whose first 4/4 came out in 1936, with a Coventry-Climax engine of 1,122 cc.

Others included the HRG – made by H. R. Godfrey, erstwhile partner of Archie Frazer Nash in the GN – and short-lived makes such as the Atalanta and the exotic Squire. AC, maker of a fine ohc 2-litre six-cylinder engine since 1919, gradually introduced more sporting models including the first Ace of 1933. Then there was Singer. In the 1920s this company had been one of Britain's largest motor manufacturers, with substantial factories in Coventry and Birmingham. However, they lacked a true best-seller and instead built too large a range of fairly uninspired cars, the more interesting of which had ohc engines but little else could be said in their favour. Their first proper sports car was based on the ohc-engined Nine of 1933, and the Le Mans model which developed from it was an effective rival for the contemporary MGs. They had a following on the Continent and did well in their class at Le Mans. A parallel range of six-cylinder cars was less notable. Probably unwisely, in 1936 Singer chose to concentrate on the Bantam which was a carbon-copy of the Morris Eight, if with an ohc engine; sports cars were dropped, except for a 1939 9 hp sports tourer based on the Bantam. This continued after the war, together with a pair of uninspired 10 and 12 hp saloons. Singer's lack of direction in the 1930s would lead directly to the firm's loss of independence but their decline was a protracted affair, drawn out over 25 years until they were taken over by Rootes in 1955.

As ever, the most prestigious make of car in Britain was Rolls-Royce. The ageing Silver Ghost gave way to the first of the Phantoms in 1924, while the smaller model was gradually uprated with larger engines. By the early 1930s sharply rising standards in refinement, especially among American luxury cars, led Rolls-Royce to undertake a radical redesign of their largest model. The result was the Phantom III, introduced in 1935. This was the first Rolls-Royce with independent front suspension, while the engine was an all-new V12 of 7.3 litres,

developing an estimated 165 bhp. This enabled a 2½-ton limousine to cruise at 90 mph; with lighter bodies 100 mph was not unrealistic. This marvel of engineering complexity was in many ways the finest Rolls-Royce ever, but like its contemporary, the Lagonda V12, was never fully developed – nor did it come back in production after the Second World War.

At almost 75 years of age, MG is Britain's most successful, most famous and most enduring sports car, with a name that is instantly recognized throughout most of the world. Total production of all MG cars has comfortably exceeded one million. They are worshipped by enthusiasts with a devotion bordering on fanaticism. Not that there is anything particularly special about most MG cars – they have usually been good, but rarely great cars. They owe their success to the fact that they have mostly been small cars, always reasonably priced and therefore within reach of a wider clientele. This product policy has only been possible because MG has always been allied to, or part of, a larger mass-production car manufacturing firm. This has also mostly ensured the marque the sort of

financial support that was denied many other promising sports car makers, apart from giving them access to the mechanical components they needed to make a car at the right price. It is quite true that the humble origin of many of their engines has usually prevented MGs from possessing outstanding performance, even for their size and at the time, but on the plus side they have mostly been less temperamental and more easily maintained than other, more highly strung sports cars.

It is an extraordinary fact that, to a degree, the MG legend still rests on the competition successes they achieved in one period of only five years early in the marque's history. Their career in motor sport was intermittent and patchy after 1935 and the last works-supported racers ran in 1968 (if we disregard the 6R4 rally car of the 1980s). Their greatest commercial success came, by and large, only after they stopped racing. While the MG story proves that racing does improve the breed, it also suggests that sporting success does not necessarily lead to increased sales.

MG was the concept and creation

MG production lines at Abingdon, c.1930, with 18/80s in the foreground and M-type Midgets behind them. (NB)

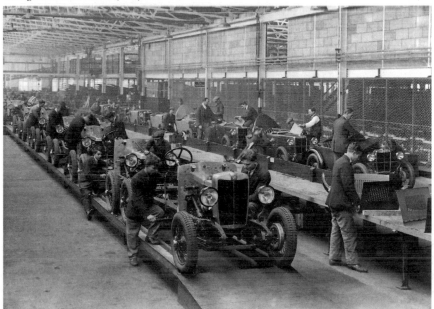

largely of one man, Cecil Kimber (1888–1945). His philosophy was best expressed in a paper entitled 'Making modest production pay in motor-car manufacture' read to The Institution of Automobile Engineers in March 1934 and subsequently published.[9] Here he expressed his conviction 'that if a firm could offer the public a product only ten per cent better than anyone else's, that firm could command a 50 per cent better price.' This may have sounded a little cynical but fits the early Morris-based MG cars perfectly. Kimber faced up to the fact that if limited production has to be profitable, the product would inevitably be more expensive. He attributed his success to 'the intense individualism of the Anglo-Saxon race. Mixed up with this is a certain amount of innate snobbery. Without it, all efforts would be hopeless. To this end a motor car must be designed and built that is a little different from and a little better than the product of the big quantity manufacturer.' This, broadly speaking, amounts to a blueprint for the activities of almost any specialist car manufacturer before or since, and perfectly expresses their common aspiration. Unlike many would-be competitors, Kimber was also a realist: 'In selling a speciality car it has always to be remembered that there is only a definite size of market for it, and it is merely foolish to be unduly optimistic.' Also: 'In our case we have found our racing and competition successes of a certain definite value, but chiefly because our product is a sports car, and any such successes have a direct bearing on the prestige of that car.' Yet, he continued, 'with regard to racing, our policy has always been to let other people do this for us'.

The MG Car Company Limited was formally set up in 1930 after MG cars had already been in production for some years. Until 1935, the company was in the personal ownership of Sir William Morris (Lord Nuffield) who, through his personal holding company Morris Industries Limited, invested £18,995 in the venture, five remaining £1 shares being held individually by Morris personally; Kimber; and Morris's secretary, solicitor and accountant respectively. All of the initial capital was expended by the new company buying the existing MG business from Morris Garages Limited. Working capital was then provided by loans totalling £30,000 from Morris Industries Limited.[10]

MG's best export market of the late 1930s was Germany

In 1935, Lord Nuffield sold the MG company to Morris Motors Limited, receiving, it seems, only the same £1 per share that had been the issue price in 1930; but because the purchase was paid for by the issue of new £1 shares in Morris Motors Limited it is possible to estimate the value of the MG company at this time by the stock-market valuation of Morris, which in late 1936 was just over £8 for each £1 share – in other words, by 1935–6 MG was effectively worth eight times £19,000 or over £150,000. Key figures of the 1930s MG annual accounts are reproduced in table form in this chapter. Also of interest is the table giving the specific figures for MG's expenditure for competitions compared to their total PR budget throughout the period.

Kimber also stated in 1934 that 'I was fortunate in having Lord Nuffield behind me, who did not draw profits out of the business. Practically the whole of our expansion has been out of profits.'[11] In most years during the 1930s, the MG business was in fact profitable, and indeed no money was taken out until the payment of a £25,500 dividend in 1938. However, the running of the operation continued to be financed by advances from Morris Motors Limited which by 1940 had reached nearly £125,000, including a sum of almost £25,000 advanced in 1939 for MG to buy freehold the factory at Abingdon (which had previously been leased from the Pavlova leatherworks).

Post-war MG became a wholly owned subsidiary of BMC and later British Leyland, although the use of the name 'The MG Car Company Limited' was continued until around 1972 – by then merely a polite fiction undoubtedly intended to assuage owners and enthusiasts. The war-time accounts of the company also exist, and while they show the dramatic increase in turnover caused by war production, they are of little interest in charting MG's development in car manufacture. Post-war accounts are less detailed and incomplete, reflecting MG's loss of independence as an accounting unit.

In production terms, substantial progress had been made in the early years, from 200 cars in 1925 to almost 1,000 in 1929. Following the move to the new factory at Abingdon in 1930, production shot up and reached a peak of 2,400 in 1932. There was then a setback – also reflected in the income from sales in the accounts – to less than 1,300 cars in 1935, while the new TA sports car and the SA and VA sports saloons were responsible for the best pre-war figure of 2,901 cars in 1937. In the same year, incidentally, 433 MG cars were exported, amounting to 15 per cent of production. The best export market of the late 1930s was surprisingly Germany, followed by Australia and other more traditional Empire markets.

While enthusiasts bemoaned the lack of design independence of the MGs after the 1935 take-over by Morris, clearly the new models were commercially more successful, and while no more racing cars were built, the MG name was kept in front of sports enthusiasts by works-supported trials teams as well as exploits with record cars. Perhaps there were sound commercial and publicity reasons for Goldie Gardner taking the MG EX.135 record car to Germany in 1938, apart from the convenient availability of Autobahnen. Kimber quickly adapted to the new paymasters of 1935 and occupied himself by returning to his original love of coachwork design, undoubtedly contributing to the elegance of the SVW-range of models. Sadly he was dismissed from the company in 1941, having clashed with Morris's managing director Miles Thomas over MG's war-time effort, and was killed in a railway accident in 1945.

The total of MG cars made until 1939 was around 22,500 and few had been exported. That an essentially pre-war product should so quickly catch on in the post-war American market must have been a surprise, if a welcome one, to the parent company. Subsequent MG sports cars were mostly exported to the USA, and this market came to influence the design of the product, especially after the US safety regulations came into force in 1968. Most new models broke production records – 10,000 TCs were followed by 30,000 TDs, 101,000 MGAs and over half a million MGBs. In the early 1970s, MG for a short while produced more than 50,000 cars per year. Only when starved of investment in the 1970s in favour of other British Leyland products did MG's lustre slowly begin to fade. By the time the last MGB was made in October 1980, both this and the Abingdon factory were old-fashioned and out-of-date.

Most MGs of the post-war period were sports cars, but from 1947 to 1972 there were always saloon models in the catalogue, selling in respectable numbers at least in the home market (an attempt at selling the BMC 1100 derived MG 'Sportsedan' in the USA in the 1960s met with little response). However, the original saloon range ultimately degraded into mere badge-engineering. When for a time there were no more MG sports cars in the 1980s, the Austin Rover Group deemed the MG badge and reputation too valuable to consign to the scrap-heap together with Morris, Riley and Wolseley, and the MG name re-appeared on a new range of badge-engineered Austin-based sports saloons, made from 1982 to 1991.

With the SA/VA/WA range of saloons and drophead coupés, MG moved into Jaguar territory in 1936. They had elegant coach-work, but drew on the Nuffield parts bin for components. The 2-litre SA illustrated used a modified Wolseley 18/80 engine, the 1½-litre VA a Wolseley 12, and the 2.6-litre WA, a bored out version of the SA's unit. Only 369 WAs were made. (NB)

By then the Rover Group had a new master, British Aerospace, who according to their 1991 report intended 'to exploit the profit potential inherent in the Rover Group's portfolio of brand names . . . The "MG" marque is believed to have further potential' (a sentiment that Cecil Kimber would surely have applauded). Despite the good intention, the 1992 MG RV8 was only partly successful in meeting the stated objective. Only in 1995 did MG make a real come-back, with a small and reasonably priced open two-seater sports car. Despite a specification that was radical by almost any previous MG standards, the fact that the new model was based largely on components from mass-production Rover saloon cars, and the fact that it offered affordable fun motoring (if not outstanding performance) meant that it was very much a car in the tradition of the 1929 M-type Midget and most other MGs between then and the present day.

The MG story amply demonstrates both the advantages and disadvantages to the specialist manufacturer of being allied to a larger mass-producer. In favour must count the financial support, availability of components, access to a dealer network, and a general sharing of overheads, against are the risks of badge-engineering, of misdirected product policy, of being starved of investment, and of being dragged down if things go wrong for the parent company. Yet the fact that MG has survived, and despite the occasional hiatus has thrived for more than 70 years where others with a similar product have failed, must prove something. The secret perhaps lies in being able to pursue just the right course of independence – to preserve that vital little difference from the product of the quantity manufacturer, or rather the quantity product from the same manufacturer. To that end, the Kimber formula is likely still to prove successful.

Table 1a: Key figures from the accounts of The MG Car Company Limited, 1930–5

		Year ending 31.12.1930	Year ending 31.12.1931	Year ending 31.12.1932	Year ending 31.12.1933	Year ending 31.12.1934	Eight months to 31.08.1935
Total sales		£394,772	£289,844	£452,960	£446,339	£452,448	£175,571
Plus:	Value of stock, at end of period	£75,123	£67,756	£58,822	£62,368	£84,693	£67,144
Total:		£469,895	£357,600	£511,783	£508,707	£537,142	£242,715
Less:	Value of stock, at beginning of period	£74,620	£75,123	£67,756	£58,822	£62,368	£84,693
Less:	Productive purchases	£293,589	£209,721	£317,057	£330,257	£349,876	£121,094
Less:	Productive wages	£21,883	£22,006	£26,290	£31,839	£20,915	£8,961
Less:	Tool charges by suppliers	–	–	£710	–	–	–
Less:	Spares reserve	–	–	–	–	£1,000	–
Equals:	Gross profit	£79,804	£50,750	£99,970	£87,789	£102,984	£27,967
Plus:	Other sundry income	£1,125	£1,369	£2,264	£2,859	£2,655	£1,092
Total:	Profit plus sundry income	£80,929	£52,118	£102,234	£90,648	£105,640	£29,059
Less:	Overheads	£63,165	£65,165	£77,321	£95,834	£84,780	£57,215
Equals:	Net profit (loss)	£17,763	(£13,046)	£24,914	(£5,186)	£20,859	(£28,156)
Plus:	Balance carried forward, from end of previous period	–	£17,318	£335	£23,900	£14,122	£30,666
Less:	Income tax	£445	£3,937	£1,348	£4,592	£1,375	£2,092
Less:	Bonus paid	–	–	–	–	£2,941	–
Equals:	Balance to be brought forward	£17,318	£335	£23,900	£14,122	£30,666	£418
Total of assets/liabilities (from balance sheet)		£115,518	£110,380	£116,221	£106,127	£121,569	£106,832

Note: All figures are quoted to the nearest whole £.

Table 1b: Key figures from the accounts of The MG Car Company Limited, 1935–9.

		Year ending 31.08.1936	Four months to 31.12.1936	Year ending 31.12.1937	Year ending 31.12.1938	Year ending 31.12.1939
Total sales		£391,150	£225,293	£695,590	£613,305	£424,450
Plus:	Value of stock, at end of period	£62,534	£65,956	£89,855	£109,930	£77,089
Plus:	Tool charges unexpired, at end of period	£7,714	£6,292	£6,337	£7,543	£3,932
Total:		£461,398	£297,541	£791,782	£730,778	£505,472
Less:	Value of stock and tool charges at beginning of period	£67,144	£70,248	£72,248	£96,193	£116,538*
Less:	Productive purchases	£301,563	£176,556	£559,493	£501,990	£281,906
Less:	Productive wages	£12,024	£5,914	£16,698	£14,690	£11,425
Less:	Tool charges by suppliers	£9,769	£870	£7,493	£6,359	£81
Equals:	Gross profit	£70,899	£43,953	£135,851	£111,547	£95,522
Plus:	Other sundry items	£2,819	£1,074	£3,171	£3,075	£2,563
Plus:	Rebate from Morris Motors Limited	–	£8,500	–		
Total:	Profit plus sundry income	£73,718	£53,527	£139,021	£114,621	£98,085
Less:	Overheads	£90,158	£37,494	£113,585	£108,933	£94,358
Equals:	Net profit (loss)	(£16,440)	£16,033	£25,436	£5,688	£3,727
Plus:	Balance carried forward, from end of previous period	£418**	(£12,102)	£7,887	£33,258	£8,031
Less:	Income tax	£3,118	–		£5,347	£3,451
Less:	National defence contribution	–	–	£1,000	£68	£264
Plus:	Income tax recovered	–	£3,956	£935	–	–
Plus:	Transferred from Morris Motors Ltd advance account	£7,039**	–	–	–	–
Less:	Dividend	–	–	–	£25,500	£574
Less:	Transferred to capital reserve account	–	–	–	–	£7,457**
Equals:	Balance to be brought forward	(£12,102)	£7,887	£33,258	£8,031	£13(?)
Total of assets/liabilities (from balance sheet)	£137,420	£138,111	£174,199	£171,546	£175,120

* Except £936 worth of consumable stores transferred to the expense account.
** These two amounts equal the transfer to the capital reserve account in 1939.
Note: All figures are quoted to the nearest whole £.

Table 2: MG competitions and trials expenses 1930-1939

Competitions/ Period	Total PR trials expense	% competition expense	of total PR
1 Jan to 31 Dec 1930	£1,011	£9,153	11.05%
1 Jan to 31 Dec 1931	£4,902	£15,177	32.30%
1 Jan to 31 Dec 1932	£2,789	£12,261	22.75%
1 Jan to 31 Dec 1933	£5,863	£19,119	30.67%
1 Jan to 31 Dec 1934	£3,505	£17,122	20.47%
1 Jan to 31 Aug 1935	£4,406	£12,801*	34.42%
1 Sep 1935 to 31 Aug 1936	£1,915	£24,544	7.53%
1 Sep to 31 Dec 1936	£1,317	£11,237**	11.72%
1 Jan to 31 Dec 1937	£3,671	£32,658	11.24%
1 Jan to 31 Dec 1938	£4,243	£27,529	15.41%
1 Jan to 31 Dec 1939	£1,364	£19,518	6.99%

* First eight months so no motor show expense in PR budget.
** Four months only.
(Source: Annual Accounts of The MG Car Company Limited, owned by Rover Group, held in British Motor Industry Heritage Trust deposit in Modern Records Centre, Warwick University Library.)

CHAPTER SIX

Export or Die

Jonathan Wood

In the 100 years of the British motor industry's existence, a single decade stands out as one of tragically missed opportunity. This was the ten years which followed the ending of the Second World War in 1945, from which the industry emerged relatively unscathed. By contrast, the car factories of Germany, Italy and Japan had been devastated by the conflict and the world was desperate for wheeled transport. America, the traditional provider, was preoccupied with satisfying the needs of its home market and the void could have been filled, in the long term, by Britain, had the Government intervened to promote the sort of strategy that was so devastatingly effective, from the 1950s onwards, by the Japanese Ministry of International Trade and Industry.

But the chance was missed. Instead the British Government relied on cajolery and 'advice' to encourage manufacturers to produce the right type of vehicle for the post-war world, although its pleas went mostly unheeded. Too many manufacturers continued to inefficiently produce too many different models and, when the Government did encroach into the industry's preserve in the crucial 1945–51 era, it was to direct the car makers to export their products to a car hungry world, though only *after* they had produced mostly unsuitable vehicles. Having said that, a handful of models did have considerable export potential; the Land-Rover and Ferguson tractor were cases in point, and so was the Morris Minor. It had been produced in the face of opposi-

tion from Lord Nuffield, despite Alec Issigonis having designed the finest small car in the world. But an introspective, myopic management failed to recognize its worth. It was starved of development, and, although the first British car to reach a million units, it was discontinued in 1971 with its potential unrealized, leaving that massive sector of the world market to the growing might of Volkswagen and its Beetle.

> ### The roles of government and industry were ever more closely entwined

Nevertheless, those cars that were sold abroad did, in the short term, find grateful buyers. Britain became the world's leading exporter of cars in 1949, and these sales brought valuable foreign exchange to a hard-pressed economy. The export drive also stimulated the revival of the British sports car, which dominated the world market until it was overtaken by the Japanese in the 1970s. A further benefit of this emphasis on exports was that the reviled and protectionist 'horsepower tax', which had been in force since 1921 and favoured small capacity, long-stroke engines was, in 1948, replaced by a flat rate system. This meant that manufacturers would not be penalised for producing cars with big-bored engines which were more suitable for overseas markets. Despite this, and perhaps wisely, few did.

The roles of government and industry were becoming ever more closely

entwined. The first step had been taken before the war, when Stanley Baldwin's administration introduced the Shadow Factories scheme, which recognized that a conflict with Germany was inevitable. From 1936 new plants were built and equipped at the tax-payers' expense and run by the motor industry, initially to mass produce Bristol aero engines. After the war, these spacious new works could be used by the motor manufacturers for burgeoning car production. However, on a less happy note, cars were subjected to purchase tax for the first time, which had been introduced in 1940 (although, inevitably, it had little impact during the war years). Also the 1950s are remembered as the 'stop-go years', when the industry became a lever of governmental economic regulation with tax and higher purchase conditions being variously tightened and relaxed to prevent the economy from overheating.

Despite these strictures and the shortages and regulations of the early post-war period, demand ensured that motor manufacturing output soared between 1945 and 1960. Britain's pre-war output had peaked in 1937 at 397,310 cars, but this total was surpassed in 1949 and production doubled in the years between 1950 and 1958, when the million barrier was broken for the first time. These figures paint a picture of an outwardly confident, successful industry, but the unpalatable truth is that it was producing cars in a seller's market in which an unconcerned clientele was clamouring for four-wheeled transport. The effects of overseas competition were first felt on the export market when, in 1956, Britain was overtaken by Germany as the world's largest exporter of motor vehicles. In the previous year that country had also overtaken the United Kingdom as Europe's largest car maker, a position it had held since 1932.

During this period imports were minimal, the French Citroën and Renault companies excepted as they had assembled their products in Britain since the 1920s. But all other imports were banned until 1953 and were then only permitted on a quota system which was not relaxed until 1959. In any event, they had jumped nearly threefold from 10,940 cars in 1959 to 27,066 in the following year, when Renault emerged as Britain's most popular foreign make.

It was not until 1952 that the structure of the industry changed for the first time since the 1930s. The 'big six' became the 'big five' when, after over 30 years of rivalry, the Austin and Morris companies merged to form the British Motor Corporation, which was the country's largest car manufacturer with around 39 per cent of production, and was the fourth largest car maker in the world outside the 'big three' of America. So it was in terms of output too, though Britain was still a long way behind – in 1951, Austin and Morris had built 243,211 cars when Chrysler, the smallest of the US giants, produced 1.2 million. Neither did BMC head the European car makers for long, being overtaken by Volkswagen in 1956. Rootes also grew modestly by acquisition when, in 1955, it purchased the ailing Singer company, while the American-owned sector consisted, as before, of Ford and Vauxhall.

There were also some new recruits. Monte Carlo Rally veteran Donald Healey introduced his 100 mph Warwick-built car in 1946 and it was transformed into BMC's Austin-Healey in 1952. The German BMW-inspired grand touring Bristol followed in 1947 and, in 1953, the

Two contemporaries but with very different construction methods. The Jensen PW saloon (above) had a separate chassis and a bodyframe which was partly steel and partly ash, clad in aluminium panelling. Only 15 PWs were made. In contrast is a 1947 Hillman Minx, (left) with unitary construction and pressed steel body, of which about 25,000 were made between 1940 and 1947. This example was the first car owned by Lord Montagu. (above NB) (left NMM)

ranks of Britain's sports car makers were joined by 25-year old Colin Chapman's Lotus.

If there were new arrivals, some old friends disappeared. No more BSA cars were built after the war and the old established Lanchester make, which had been part of the BSA stable since 1931, breathed its last in 1956. Another casualty of the post-war years was the Jowett company, which had been building cars in Idle, Yorkshire, since 1910. It had courageously chosen to join the mass-producers with the advanced Javelin saloon but, as we shall see, over-reached itself and there were no more Jowetts after 1954. Perhaps less surprisingly, Lea-Francis, which had experienced a financially turbulent 1930s, closed its doors in 1953 although intermittent attempts were subsequently made to revive it.

The means of building cars were also changing. Pressed steel body panels were well established by the 1930s, though the specialist manufacturers still relied on coachbuilders which produced attractive hand-crafted bodies. But the Vauxhall 10/4 of 1937 heralded the arrival of monocoque construction. These units were built in a special in-house facility, known at Luton as 'The Million Pound Shop'. Morris followed suit with its 10 hp car of 1939 and the Hillman Minx of 1940 had a unitary hull. Ford introduced monocoque bodies with its Consul and Zephyr models of 1951 and the first chassis-less Austin was the A30 of 1952. The arrival of the Standard Eight saw the process extended to Canley's products in 1953.

The move to unitary hulls and the increasing demand for cars at home and abroad meant that there was a considerable incentive for the motor manufacturers to control their own facilities and follow the lead given by General Motors to its Vauxhall subsidiary. In 1953 came such a take-over, when Ford purchased Briggs Motor Bodies, which had been building its bodies at Dagenham since the car company had opened its plant there in 1931. The newly created British Motor Corporation followed Ford's example later the same year, when it bought body manufacturer Fisher and Ludlow of Birmingham. This immediately caused problems for the smaller Standard company, which relied on Fisher and Ludlow for the majority of its own body building requirements. As a result, in 1954, it forged closer links with its other, though secondary, supplier, Mulliners Ltd of Birmingham, which was the largest of the smaller body builders. Standard

obtained the exclusive output of Mulliners's bodies and this association culminated in its take-over of the firm in 1958.

Standard's closer alliance with Mulliners in turn nearly spelt the end of Alvis car production because it relied on the Bordesley Green company for its bodies. Although some were built, in 1955–8, by Willowbrook of Loughborough, it was not until the latter year that output gained a renewed momentum when Park Ward took over their manufacture. Daimler, which was also a customer of Mulliners, was in a similar predicament, so its BSA parent snapped up the Coventry-based Carbodies. For the same reason, David Brown, who owned Aston Martin, bought Tickford of Newport Pagnell, Buckinghamshire,

at the end of 1954 and, from 1957, car production was transferred there from Feltham, Middlesex, its home since 1926. These take-overs meant that, by the end of the decade, Pressed Steel was the only major body builder not allied to one of the car makers.

Inevitably, the end of the separate chassis meant that the specialist coach-builders were operating on borrowed time. Prospects further deteriorated when their traditional customers, Rolls-Royce and Bentley, although retaining separate chassis, adopted standardized Pressed Steel bodywork in an essential move to increase output. The first of these, the Bentley Mark VI, appeared in 1946 and was followed in 1955 by the Rolls-Royce Silver Cloud and Bentley S Series, which were externally identical, apart from their radiators. In 1938 Rolls-Royce had bought the Park Ward coachbuilding company and similarly, in 1959, H. J. Mulliner of London was also drawn into the corporate fold. Soon afterwards, in 1961, the company's specialist coachbuilding division was united under the Mulliner, Park Ward name. Other firms were less lucky and, by 1959, such old-established names as Barker (bought by Daimler in 1938), Freestone and Webb, Gurney Nutting, Lancefield, and Windovers had all disappeared from the British motoring scene.

A new cheaper material, fibreglass, which required less skill to work, was beginning to replace the traditional ash, aluminium and steel. It first appeared in Britain on the open Singer SM of 1953 and was similarly employed on Jowett's last gasp, the R4

Although Sir Stafford Cripps was often portrayed as an austere socialist, he numbered among his admirers George Farmer of Rover and Sir Miles Thomas of Nuffield. He is seen here, in September 1949, with a very young looking Harold Wilson (President of the Board of Trade), addressing a meeting of industrialists and TUC officials about the importance of car exports to the USA. (Hulton Deutsch Collection Ltd)

sports car of the same year, although only four were built. The material subsequently appeared on a number of specials, many of which were of dubious quality, but Lotus hit the headlines in 1957 with the world's first fibreglass monocoque. Despite the car's impressive appearance, with performance up to the expected Chapman standards, the Elite proved to be excessively noisy and a loss maker for its manufacturer. The experiment was not repeated.

Technically, British cars followed – like their American counterparts – the theme laid down before the First World War of a front-mounted water-cooled engine which drove the rear wheels, via an open propeller shaft. However, all this was to change with the arrival, in 1959, of Alec Issigonis's front-wheel drive, transverse-engined Mini, the most technically significant car in the British industry's history. It was destined to change the course of car design throughout the world but failed to make BMC, its manufacturers, any profits and was a contributory factor in the Corporation's demise in the 1960s. That being said, during this period British cars – with a few notable exceptions – tended to be less technically adventurous than their counterparts in Continental Europe. There, by 1939, one car in four was driven by its front wheels and, after the war, rear-mounted power units, air-cooling, diesel engines, and aerodynamically influenced bodywork were frequently encountered.

The demand for cars in the post-war era brought another problem for the car makers. Previously, the motor industry had been a seasonal employer which paid good wages though only guaranteed work in the autumn, winter and spring with lay-offs occurring in the summer months as manufacturers prepared their new models for the October motor show. Trade union recognition had been the price exacted by the Transport and General Workers Union's Ernest Bevin, for his acceptance of the post of Minister of Labour in Churchill's war-time coalition, and all the car

factories were unionized by 1945.

These problems were in the future when, on 27 July 1945, the Labour party was returned to power with a massive majority of 154 seats over the opposition parties. Clement Attlee's new government was pledged to pursue a policy of full employment, a wide-ranging programme of nationalization, and the creation of a National Health Service. It also presided over a country which had been bankrupted by war and, because of this, exports became a prime weapon in the Government armoury to obtain valuable overseas currency. In the first instance this was concentrated on such old-established outlets as cotton and ship-building. The motor industry was initially overlooked because it had sold so little abroad before the war. In the peak inter-war year of 1937, Britain exported 53,655 cars worth £6.4 million, which was the equivalent of 14 per cent of production. In the same year, Germany exported 20 per cent of its output, a figure that rose to 23 per cent in 1938, representing 65,069 cars.

Those British cars sold abroad went, almost exclusively, to Empire markets, where they benefited from Imperial Preference tariff concessions. The majority were destined for Australia, which in 1937 took nearly 38 per cent of output, and most of the balance went to New Zealand, South Africa, India, Malaya and Ceylon. European sales were usually confined to Denmark and Sweden. American manufacturers, by contrast, had a very real advantage because their value-for-money products were as suitable in their native country as they were in the Australian or South African bush. Unlike their numerous transatlantic counterparts, they benefited from larger home and also overseas sales, which meant that manufacturing costs could be accordingly spread over a larger number of vehicles, reducing unit costs. Despite this American dominance of Empire markets there was, nevertheless, a small though regular overseas trade in those cars at which Britain

excelled: namely, luxury saloons and sports cars.

When war broke out in 1939, a record two million cars were in use in Britain, which was approximately double the 1930 figure, and there was no shortage of models to choose from. In 1938, *The Economist* pointed out that the 'big six' produced 'no less than 40 different types of engine and even a larger number of chassis and body types. In the United States, however, the three largest manufacturers (General Motors, Ford and Chrysler) accounted last year for about 90 per cent of a total output of no fewer than 3,915,000 units, but actually had *fewer models* [my italics] in production than the six British manufacturers.'[1] The writer went on to point out that, in the previous year, '26 out of 40 models achieved sales of less than 5,000 units. And such an output is uneconomic.' This state of affairs was not solely the fault of the car makers: 'the industry may claim, indeed with some justice, that the Government cannot escape responsibility for the present state of affairs. Its horsepower tax has split the British market in an inordinate number of sub divisions.'

All these multifarious activities came to a halt during the war, although a handful of cars were produced for service use throughout the hostilities. In addition, from 1943 the Society of Motor Manufacturers and Traders (SMMT) obtained governmental approval for the car makers to proceed with new designs for the post-war years and, by October 1944, no less than 56 firms had been permitted to start experimental and preparatory work.

As the prospects for peace improved, the war-time administration set up what was titled a reconstruction committee, charged with examining 'industrial problems.' It met for the first time in January 1945, and commissioned a series of secret reports on the states of various British industries and their respective export potentials. That undertaken on the motor industry, as the extracts indicate, is of great relevance because so many of the findings are strikingly similar to those made, exactly 30 years later, by the central policy review staff and published, following the British Leyland collapse, as *The Future of the British Car Industry*. Taken together, these two documents show that the indigenous motor industry had, by and large, failed to respond to the opportunities and markets of the post-war years.

The reconstruction committee received its document, entitled *Post-War Resettlement of the Motor Industry*[2] in April 1945. Four months later, Labour overwhelmingly won the general election. Predictably, the new Government was more interventionist than its predecessors and made attempts to direct the industry to mend its ways but shied away from a policy of direct confrontation. So, apart from some perceptive governmental tinkering in the form of exhortations by Sir Stafford Cripps, the motor industry's structure remained essentially unchanged. Its future was left for market forces to determine, with the result that its triumphs in export markets were achieved in a competitive vacuum and were soon successfully challenged by the revived European and then the Japanese industries. The Government and the tax-payer were left to pick up the pieces when the British-owned sector finally collapsed at the end of 1974.

So the opportunity was missed in 1945. This was because, as Corelli Barnett argues, 'the war-time British Establishment's whole approach to the question of industrial strategy was rooted in a Victorian mercantile conception of a myriad of firms competing in a market place – industry was still often referred to as 'trade' – . . . The Establishment – politicians, civil servants, hired economists – had not yet grasped the twentieth century concept, pioneered by the great American and German corporations, of the massive technology led operation that conquers its own market almost on the

analogy of a great military offensive.'[3]

Ironically, it was a Conservative government in the following decade that did exercise an essential policy of rationalization on a major British industry when, in 1958, the Macmillan administration initiated the creation of the British Aircraft Corporation. However, its trump card was the close contacts it maintained with the aeronautical community, in the shape of lucrative defence contracts, and this made the task somewhat easier. There were echoes with the motor manufacturers in that, at the end of the Second World War, the British aircraft industry consisted of an unwieldy 27 airframe design companies and eight aero engine manufacturers. Interestingly, BAC's British Aerospace successor was to end up owning what was left of the British-owned automotive sector when it purchased the Rover Group from the Government in 1988.

But, in 1945, exports were the order of the day and it was the President of the Board of Trade's task to exhort car makers to abandon the practice of a lifetime by turning their collective backs on the home market and producing cars for the world. Attlee had given this vital portfolio to Sir Stafford Cripps. It is difficult to think of a greater contrast to the motor industry magnates than this eccentric, Winchester-educated, intellectual, vegetarian socialist, who neither drank nor smoked. Yet Cripps, unlike many politicians, had direct experience of industry. A brilliant chemist, he had, however, followed his father to the bar in 1913. Medically unfit for the army, in the early part of the First World War he drove lorries for the Red Cross in France but, in 1915, was appointed assistant superintendent of the Queensferry explosives factory which, through his efforts, became the most efficient of all munitions plants. After the war, Cripps returned to his legal practice and, in 1927, he was the country's youngest King's Counsel. Soon afterwards he joined the Labour party.

Cripps's 1945 appointment was

probably the result of his term as Minister of Aircraft Production during the Second World War, which took effect from 1942. This, in turn, was because of the reputation he had attained at Queensferry and, over the following three years, 'he produced order, though also a slower rate of production, after the chaos which Beaverbrook had left.'[4] This brought him into close contact with motor manufacturers, many of which were engaged in MAP work. It was for all these reasons that Cripps had a grasp of the industry's ills and was also well aware of the limitations of its pre-war products.

The Government's task was made somewhat easier by the fact that wartime steel regulations were still in force when it took office, for steel allocation would be geared to export performance. Four months after Labour had won the election, in November 1945, Cripps spelt out not only the need for the export effort but also, unprecedentedly, the type of car that the Government wanted to see its car makers produce. The occasion was the annual dinner of the SMMT, and Sir Stafford informed his audience, drawn from the industry's leaders, that: 'We must provide a cheap, tough, good looking car of decent size – not the sort of car we have hitherto produced for the smooth roads and short journeys of this country – and we must produce them in sufficient quantities to get the benefits of mass production.'[5] With, no doubt, the large variety of models built by the industry before the war in mind, Cripps told the car makers: 'We cannot succeed in getting the volume of exports we must have if we disperse our efforts over numberless types and makes.' As far as the export quota was concerned, he said that the lowest possible figure to be considered was 50 per cent, which evoked reactions of 'No' and 'Tripe!', to which Cripps snapped back: 'I have often wondered whether you thought that Great Britain was here to support the motor industry, or the industry was here to support Great Britain. I gather from your cries that you think it is the former.'

There could, however, be no argument that, prior to 1945, and for all the reasons already cited, the British motor industry had not been producing suitable cars for export. In the early post-war years the correspondence columns of *The Autocar* were peppered with pleas from overseas readers for the industry to design cars geared to world markets. In its issue of 8 June 1945, the magazine published one such communication from K. G. Johnson who, writing from Sydney, Australia, declared that: 'I would prefer to buy a British car, but unless design and quality are changed I shall be forced to purchase another American car when available.' He identified such necessities as cooling systems designed for extremes of temperature, a higher ground clearance than hitherto, and better headlamps. Efficient dust-proofing was another essential prerequisite.

On 19 October 1945, REME Major J. R. A. Green, based in the Middle East, bluntly told the car makers: 'The small high revving engine is useless under colonial conditions . . . With any overseas market one must give after-sales service, and this is where we are hopelessly behind.' His experience was of South Africa and East Africa, where the 'only British cars which, before the war, might have challenged the American market were the Super Snipe Humber and 3½-litre Jaguar'. The South African viewpoint was later underscored by J. Van Heerde from Cape Town, who signed off a detailed article on that country's requirements by stating: 'Unless British manufacturers are going to build cars entirely suited to overseas conditions and

Though British manufacturers were generally not geared to exports before the war, Hillman at least demonstrated a Minx tourer 'in colonial conditions' in 1934. Despite the Coventry numberplate, this picture was taken in genuine colonial territory, probably South or East Africa. (NB)

requirements, their future in this country will be a repetition of the comparatively unsuccessful past.'[6] Particular problems were 'washboard' road surfaces, mud in the winter, and the enduring problem of dust.

Some of the motor manufacturers did attempt to grapple with these problems, but it was some time before their efforts had any effect. Maurice Platt, formerly technical editor of *The Motor*, who joined Vauxhall in 1937 and, after the war, became its chief engineer, has recalled that 'the unhappy results of exporting unsuitable vehicles had already shown how necessary it was to test prototype cars and trucks under severe, yet controlled, conditions.'[7] The outcome, in 1946, was the creation of the Motor Industry Research Association (MIRA), jointly funded by the SMMT and the Government, in the form of a grant from the Department of Scientific and Industrial Research.

In 1948 MIRA established a test circuit on a former war-time airfield at Lindley, Warwickshire, where a priority requirement was the creation of a

washboard track to reproduce the conditions that British cars were likely to encounter on the roads of under-developed countries. Their vulnerability was soon exposed. Dr Albert Fogg, who was MIRA's first director, recounted that when cars started using the facility, not one vehicle 'was able to complete the half-mile track without losing something or breaking something. Before long we lengthened the track to one and a half miles. It taught us valuable lessons and the reliability of British cars gradually improved.'[8]

Nevertheless, there can be little doubt that the Government's insistence that manufacturers sell their essentially pre-war products on a world market for which they had never been designed, particularly in the 1945–8 era, took the industry a long time to live down. Fogg later reflected on 'the hammering' the cars received 'on appallingly rough roads in many of their export markets. So they acquired a reputation for unreliability that persisted for years.' Yet there was one product of Britain's car makers which the world enthusiastically welcomed.

A 1956 Hillman Minx in a mud trough at the Motor Industry Research Association's proving ground. Despite such tests, British cars were still criticized abroad for poor quality proofing against water and dust. (NB)

This was the cheap, light-weight Ferguson tractor, and the Government, in the form of Sir Stafford Cripps, played a key role in it being manufactured in Coventry by the Standard Motor Company.

In 1933 Harry Ferguson, a silver-tongued Ulsterman, created a tractor which incorporated what he called the Ferguson System, whereby its implements were raised and lowered by hydraulic power and not human effort as hitherto had been the case. Ferguson did not possess manufacturing facilities and he was thus dependent on others to produce the vehicle which his organization would then purchase and market. In 1938 production was begun by David Brown at Huddersfield, but Ferguson soon fell out with Brown and manufacture ceased the same year. The inventor subsequently crossed the Atlantic and interested Henry Ford in the design with the result that, from 1939, the Ferguson-Ford tractor was built in small, loss-making quantities throughout the Second World War. In a tangled affair, the Ford liaison was subsequently dissolved following a lawsuit that was settled in the Ulsterman's favour.

After the war, Harry Ferguson had hoped that a British manufacturer would take up his invention and, in 1945, he established himself at Claridge's hotel with his chauffeur-driven Rolls-Royce on hand to whisk him to meet any potential suitor. These were noticeably absent. One of those who turned Ferguson down was Lord Nuffield, who visited him in London. To the dismay of his managing director, Sir Miles Thomas, following the meeting the Morris Motors supremo told him that he had 'heard enough of this wild Irishman's ideas.'[9] For his part, Thomas believed that a great opportunity had been missed.

In view of his lack of success, Ferguson took his case to Sir Stafford Cripps, with the persuasive argument that his tractor 'would be a big dollar earner, pointing out too that more home produced food would cut down on costly imports. Thus it was in the nation's interests to sanction steel supplies for the production of tractors and implements'.[10] Cripps was at this stage non-committal but he subsequently attended a successful demonstration of the tractor which was witnessed by, amongst others, Standard's managing director, Sir John Black. Ferguson then returned to the Board of Trade, where he applied for

sufficient materials to produce 200 tractors a day. Cripps granted the request but he also 'instructed the Standard Motor Company to take on the production.' This, says Ferguson's biographer, 'was not quite such a case of state interference in private enterprise as it might appear at first sight, for the Banner Lane factory belonged to the Government and was only on lease to the company.'[11]

The plant in question was a million square foot shadow factory managed by Standard during the war, which was an addition to a similar, smaller facility adjoining its plant in the Canley district of Coventry, which was likewise annexed. As will have been apparent, Sir John Black was already familiar with the Ferguson and had also received a visit from its creator, but he had been unable to commit himself because of steel shortages. This was despite the fact that Standard was looking to expansion in the postwar years and, to these ends, in 1944 had bought the moribund Triumph company for £77,000.

But finding a use for Banner Lane was a priority and, coincidentally, Sir John had been thinking of diversifying into the production of a light agricultural vehicle which Standard prophesied would be as 'useful for running about the farm as driving for market.' It never entered production because the firm agreed to Cripps's initiative. Standard was also in the process of developing a new car, which emerged as the Vanguard, and, sensibly, its engine would also be used to power the Ferguson. But before this unit was ready, precious dollars would be required to import Continental engines, as a stop-gap measure, from America.

The decision to proceed with the Ferguson project was reported to the Standard board on 28 August 1945, but there was still the matter of dollars to be resolved and, at the end of September, a meeting was held between Black, Ferguson and the Treasury's Sir Wilfred Eady. Black and Ferguson requested half a million dollars for machine tools, five million for Continental engines and three million for implement parts. The request went to the Cabinet where it was approved with the minimum of discussion though Eady, writing to Ferguson of the decision, warned him that in 'any public statement on this new project there must be no mention to the amount of preliminary dollar expenditure involved without prior reference to us.'[12]

Ferguson tractor production began at Banner Lane in 1946, and in 1947–8 Standard briefly built more tractors than cars, accounting for 47,209 and 37,023 vehicles respectively. In 1947 the last of 25,000 Continental engines was fitted to the Ferguson, and was replaced by Standard's own wet-liner four-cylinder which also appeared, from 1948, in its Vanguard car. The arrangement was that Standard would build the tractors and they would then be sold by the Coventry-based Harry Ferguson Ltd. Standard therefore had no marketing costs, Ferguson paid promptly and, in 1951, this contract contributed over 60 per cent of Standard's pre-tax profits. These stood at a record of £2.2 million but were still the smallest in the industry.

By 1953 annual tractor production was averaging 60,000 units and accounted for no less than 70 per cent of Standard's £1.6 million surplus, but that year Ferguson sold out to the Canadian Massey-Harris company. An enraged Black threatened to scrap the agreement but, by December of that year, had committed Standard to a 12-year manufacturing agreement with what was to become Massey-Ferguson. This ensured Standard's survival in a decade which saw its share of British car production fall from 11.6 per cent in 1946 to 8 per cent in 1960.

This decline was, in part, due to the failure of the Vanguard to sell on the world markets for which it had been specifically designed. After the war the company, like many of its contemporaries, had reintroduced its pre-war range, in this instance the Eight, Twelve and Fourteen. Such a variety

was an anathaema to Stafford Cripps, though motoring journalist Dudley Noble probably spoke for many of his contemporaries when he wrote that the President of the Board of Trade was 'inflicting pet Socialist theories on the country . . . One amongst the motor manufacturers who was influenced by Cripps was John Black.'[13] In 1948 the Standard range was scrapped and replaced by a single model, the Vanguard, which, the firm said, was 'made in Britain – designed for the world.'[14]

This was a completely new car with no carry-overs from previous models. It had been sanctioned early in 1945, and was announced by Sir John at a press reception at the Dorchester in July 1947. *The Motor* was positively ecstatic when it wrote that the car represented 'a turning point in the history of the motor industry.' According to the company, Black's brief to his designers was for them to produce 'the car for the world. It must seat six in comfort . . . It must be not merely up to date but a little ahead of its time in looks and in equipment. It must be noticeably economical to run and low in price.'[15] The stubby, fast-back lines were uncompromisingly

American and Standard's stylist, Walter Belgrove, had spent hours outside the American embassy sketching visiting cars, in particular Chrysler's low cost Plymouth. The robust shell was mounted on a cruci-form chassis and the Vanguard's engine was an economical 2-litre four-cylinder overhead valve wet-liner unit. The gearbox was a three-speed affair with column gear change, and synchromesh on bottom gear was a unique feature on a car of this price. It sold for £544. Handling, perhaps predictably, was 'bad American with violent tyre howl on corners.'[16]

The Vanguard did, in the first instance, find plenty of buyers in a car-starved world and around 185,000 examples were built of the Phase I car, which endured until 1952. But from there on, a slow decline set in. The Phase II model of the 1953–5 era, with notchback styling, found 81,074 buyers, but only 37,194 examples of the restyled unitary construction Vanguard III were produced in the two years following its 1956 arrival. The line finally petered out in 1963, powered by a much needed six-cylinder engine, of 2-litre capacity, which had belatedly appeared in 1961.

'A turning point in the history of the motor industry.' The Standard Vanguard with its American-inspired styling and new 2-litre ohv engine was intended to be a 'world car', but it was not suited to Belgian roads, let alone those of Africa. This is a Phase One Vanguard, the best-selling model, in the 1952 London Rally. (NMM)

Standard's one model policy had come to an end somewhat earlier, when the Vanguard was joined in 1953 by the Eight which, curiously, perpetuated the pre-war tradition of identifying a car by the RAC horsepower rating of its engine.

So what went wrong? There can be little doubt that the Vanguard reflected Standard's naivety, at this time, of the type of conditions the car was likely to encounter overseas. Thirty six years after its announcement, Alick Dick – who had joined the company in 1934 and, at the time of the model's launch, was John Black's personal assistant – spoke candidly[17] of the background to the model's conception: 'The Vanguard was, of course, supposed to take care of world conditions. But none of our engineers, and none of our senior sales force, had really been round the world to see what the conditions were. So we were only surmising from what we had been told by dealers that we had appointed.'

Because time was of the essence, the prototype Vanguards were 'taken to the steep hills and rough roads of Wales to try it under something approaching overseas conditions.'[18]

Maurice Wilks, Rover's Technical Director from the mid-thirties and 'father of the Land-Rover'. He conceived it because he needed a light 4x4 for his farm, and gave the vehicle its name. (NB)

These, unfortunately, did not begin to replicate conditions that the car would experience even across the English Channel. It was soon after the Vanguard had been on sale in Belgium that Freddie Troop, the company's service manager in Scotland, was informed by his boss that the car was not behaving well on the Belgian *pave.* He was recruited to look into the problem because he was the only man in the department who possessed a passport. 'When I got there I found they really had problems, particularly with the chassis and suspension. The fractures in the chassis had to be seen to be believed. The shock absorbers were weak after a few thousand miles.' The Belgians had tried to resolve the problem by filling them with thicker oil but 'that made them go solid when they hit a bump. It used to fracture the bolts to the chassis and used to come up and over and straight through the wing.'[19]

It was much the same story much further afield in the potentially valuable South African market. When Alick Dick was in Cape Town, he was delighted to see a Vanguard with an attractive young girl at the wheel. But, on enquiry, he found she was a far from satisfied customer because 'she'd driven from Johannesburg to Cape Town over dust roads and corrugations. And in the back was her mink coat, on the floor, and it had got dust on it, and then it had rained, and it was set in mud.[20]

Sir John Black was not the only British motor industry executive to have pondered what to do with a million square foot shadow factory. In 1945, and 20 or so miles to the west at Solihull, a similar problem had been preoccupying Spencer Wilks, managing director of Rover. The eventual outcome was a vehicle similar in spirit to the Ferguson tractor, but one that was of the company's own making and, thankfully, as the world famous Land-Rover survives there to this day.

Wilks was a former colleague of Black's when both had shared the running of Hillman in the 1920s. He had joined the near bankrupt

Coventry-based Rover company in 1929, and played a key role in revitalizing the concern with a range of well-equipped and engineered cars for the professional middle classes. Wilks became managing director in 1933, while his brother, Maurice, was responsible for engineering policy. By 1939, when it built over 11,000 cars, Rover was making profits of £200,000 a year. The company participated in the shadow factory scheme in 1936 although, unlike Standard, there was no room for the shadow on its Helen Street site, so it was built at Acocks Green, Birmingham. This became operational in 1937, but it soon became apparent that a further facility would be required. So a second shadow plant, for which Rover was also responsible, was built in 1939 on a 65-acre site at Solihull. Prudently, the company purchased a further 200 acres of adjoining farmland from which it would reap benefits in the expansionist post-war years.

Rover got involved in jet, then tank, engines during WW2

During the Second World War, in addition to producing aero engine parts Rover became involved, from 1940, with the development of Frank Whittle's pioneering jet engine. However, late in 1942 it ceded this work to Rolls-Royce and, in compensation, the company received the manufacturing rights of the Merlin-related V12 Meteor tank engine which would keep its Acocks Green factory busy for many years after the war.

With the outbreak of peace, Rover decided to dispense with its cramped and, by then, bomb-damaged Coventry factory, to concentrate car production at the massive Solihull plant. This meant, in the first instance, the pre-war four-cylinder Ten and Twelve, and the six-cylinder Fourteen and Sixteen, though a low production 20 hp did not survive the war. Despite the apparent multiplicity of models, there was considerable interchange-ability be-tween them, and the over-head valve engines shared a related 100 mm stroke. Maurice Wilks, Rover's technical supremo, had learnt the necessity for rationalized engineering during his apprenticeship at General Motors in America in 1926–8. The factory was officially opened on 2 February 1946 by Sir Stafford Cripps and, perhaps to anticipate a speech on the need for a one model policy, Rover produced a special display to show how many common parts were used in its current range. However, in his more conciliatory address, Cripps revealed that he had learnt to drive in a single-cylinder Rover . . .

Cars had begun leaving Solihull at the end of 1945 but they only absorbed a small part of the factory and A. B. Smith, at the time Rover buyer and stores controller, recalled 'Spencer . . . saying in despair to his brother "We shall never be able to use a million square feet in all our lives! We shall have to let it out."'[21] There were thoughts of making a small car, but the 699 cc M1, of which prototypes were built, was scrapped in 1946 on grounds of expense and its lack of export poten-tial. But in 1948 all these problems were swept aside with the arrival of the Land-Rover, which was precisely the type of vehicle required in those car hungry, export-orientated years.

It is now one of the legends of British motoring history that what became the Land-Rover was born on Maurice Wilks' 250-acre farm on the Isle of Anglesey. The story does, nevertheless, deserve retelling for no other reason than that it serves as a reminder that not all good ideas emanate from inside a car factory.

After the war Wilks was tidying up the estate and was using, in the first instance, a Ford V8-powered half-track. It proved too unwieldy for his requirements so he bought one of the many war-surplus Jeeps then on the market and its optional four-wheel drive facility soon proved its worth. Unfortunately, it was far from reliable and was being regularly returned to Solihull for repair. Then, early in 1947, Spencer Wilks was visiting his brother on Anglesey, and he asked him what he intended to do when the Jeep finally expired. "Buy another one, I suppose," answered Maurice, "*There isn't anything else.*"[22]

So the idea for the Land-Rover, as Maurice Wilks, promptly named it, was born. In the spring of 1947, he assigned the project to chief engineer Robert Boyle and he, in turn, deputed it to five section leaders. Wilks had written that the requirement was 'to design a vehicle rather similar to a Jeep . . . even more useful to the farmer . . . a proper farm machine, not just another Jeep . . . Much more versatile, much more use as a power source . . . able to drive things, to have power take-offs *everywhere* . . . to be able to be used as a tractor at times . . . to be able to do everything . . .'[23]

A Jeep-based prototype was built by the summer and, on 4 September 1947, the Rover board sanctioned the production of 'an all purpose vehicle on the lines of the Willys Overland Jeep.' As a result, it was agreed to build 25 pilot vehicles for evaluation, though this was later extended to 50. Because steel was still in such short supply, the Land-Rover's body was made of more expensive aluminium which also had the virtue of being easier to work by hand. It was then that the President of the Board of Trade became involved, as Sir George Farmer – later Rover chairman but, at the time, company secretary – has recalled: 'We were particularly fortunate in that Sir Stafford Cripps . . . was a very far-seeing and a brilliant chap. He . . . expressed a wish to come down to the works and see what we were doing. Fortunately, at that stage, we had just made a batch of these vehicles which used extensively non-rationed materi-als, particularly aluminium. He accepted the recommendations that we made to him that here was something new for the British motor industry which had a future, not only in exports, but for agriculture. He gave it his full support and, indeed, when he became Chancellor of the Exchequer (in November 1947) he specifically exempted the Land-Rover from purchase tax. So we were able to do

The first prototype Land-Rover used a Jeep frame, Rover Ten engine, and rear axle and springs from the Rover car range. It was built in the summer of 1947, and the design was sanctioned for production on 4 September. Production models differed considerably; the central steering wheel was abandoned, the spare wheel moved to the bonnet top, and a larger 1.6-litre engine was used (2 litres from 1951). (NMM)

Like Standard, Rover adopted a one-model policy with their radically-styled 2.1-litre six-cylinder 75 saloon introduced in September 1949. The first of the 'Auntie' Rovers, it later lost its cyclops headlight and gained a wider range of engines, from a 2-litre four to a 2.6-litre six. (NMM)

what the Japanese and Germans did, and what any manufacturer who wants to export successfully does, we were able to build at least a modicum for the home market from which he could then go out into the world and export. So that when I finished in 1973, we were exporting to no less than 176 different countries.'[24]

Appropriately announced abroad, at the Amsterdam Motor Show of 1948, and initially priced at £450, the vehicle's functional lines, sound engineering and go-anywhere specifications, coupled with optional four-wheel drive, meant that it was in immediate demand the world over and, since then, over 70 per cent of output has been exported. Originally a 1.6-litre overhead inlet/side exhaust four-cylinder engine was employed, as used in the Rover 60 car, but from 1951 this

was enlarged to 2 litres and from 1957 there was a diesel option, the first of many variations. Output soared. The 100,000th Land-Rover was built in 1954 and the million barrier was breached in 1976.

Ironically, the vehicle's success began to cause Rover problems, as the facilities provided by the million square foot shadow factory were, by the early 1950s, beginning to be absorbed. Government policy prevented the company expanding its Solihull plant so there was no alternative but to create less efficient smaller satellite plants in the Birmingham area. In 1952 a works was established at Perry Barr, and another in Percy Road in 1954. This was a reflection that, since 1949, Solihull had built more Land-Rovers than cars; Maurice Wilks' doughty work-horse

had ensured Rover's survival.

Unlike the Land-Rover, in the 1950s most Rover cars stayed at home after export sales had peaked in 1951, when 60 per cent of output was dispatched overseas. The essentially pre-war car range had been replaced, in 1948, by the stop-gap 60 and 75 of 1.6 and 2.1 litres respectively. Outwardly similar to their predecessors, they were respectively powered by new four- and six-cylinder overhead inlet/side exhaust engines but, in September 1949, Rover responded to Cripps's creed by replacing them with a single model, the 75, which employed the new six. This was the first of the famous P4 'Auntie' Rovers, and the 75 was also to be the most popular model of the ensuing range with 43,677 examples built between then and 1959.

The model encapsulated the

company's successful formula of mechanical longevity, combined with sound engineering and a comfortable, finely trimmed leather and wood interior. The result was a quiet (Rover led the British industry on sound deadening techniques), reliable, 80 mph car which was good value at £1,106 and appealed to customers who could not afford £4,038 for a Bentley Mark VI and would never have contemplated buying a Jaguar. The range would ultimately endure for 15 years with the last of 130,342 examples built in 1964; demand did not peak until 1954, when 13,486 cars were produced. The 75 remained the sole P4 until the 1954 model year, when it was joined by the four-cylinder 60, which used the 2-litre engine developed for the Land-Rover, and there was the more powerful 2.6-litre 90. For a year this overlapped the 75, although the latter was revised for 1955 and its engine enlarged to 2.2 litres. The range was further extended for 1957, with the arrival of the supplementary 105S and 105R, powered by twin carburettored versions of the 90 engine and the latter's Roverdrive system employed an elaborate, semi-automatic transmission. In both instances few were built, accounting for 3,499 and 7,201 units respectively. The 60 and 75 continued essentially unchanged until the range was slimmed down for 1960.

The largest capacity P4 was the 2.6-litre 90 but, for 1959, the company introduced a new model in the shape of the 3-litre luxury saloon, which was powered by a 2,995 cc version of the P4 engine. The P5, as it was internally designated, was also significant for being Solihull's first monocoque though, such was the 'belt and braces' approach to its design, the car ended up over 1 cwt heavier than the six-cylinder P4. The 3-litre's lines were also notable because they were the first to be executed by the company's own stylist. Prior to the arrival, late in 1953, of 26-year-old David Bache, formerly of Austin, this all-important task had been the responsibility of Maurice Wilks. Like so many of Rover's

appointments, Bache proved to be an inspired choice and he was to emerge as one of Britain's outstanding stylists of the post-war years.

During the 1950s, Rover not only consolidated its pre-war stature but also widened and enhanced it. Profits continued to grow and the £1 million figure was exceeded for the first time in 1960. In 1956 Maurice Wilks had joined his brother as joint managing director and Spencer took over as Rover's chairman in 1957, a position he held until his retirement in 1962. The Wilks brothers had made Rover one of Britain's best run car companies and it is a tribute to their stewardship that the name survives today, while many of its contemporaries have disappeared. By the 1950s the company had a competent and experienced engineering team while a new generation of the family arrived in the shape of the Wilks's nephews, Spencer King and Peter Wilks. Any charge of nepotism should be instantly dismissed: King was closely involved in the development of Rover's experimental JET 1 of 1950, the world's first gas turbine powered car, and would provide the company with the concept of the Range Rover, which has proved to be as enduring as its Land-Rover forebear; while Peter Wilks was closely involved in the creation of the highly regarded 2000 saloon of 1963 and became a worthy successor to his uncle as Rover's technical director. Indeed, had the British motor industry possessed more individuals of the quality to be found at Solihull, its fate might have been very different.

If the Land-Rover represented an export triumph for Rover, and Britain, down to the south in Cowley, by 1945, Morris Motors possessed – in what was to become the Minor – arguably the world's finest small car, which could have made an enormous impact on overseas markets. But, unlike the Land-Rover, it had been produced in the face of indifference and the downright opposition of the company's chairman, the 68-year-old Lord Nuffield.

Before the Second World War, Morris had been Britain's largest car maker, with around a quarter of the market and, from 1946, had reintroduced its established Eight and Ten which continued to sell strongly. Both typified the concept of the small British saloon although, when the physically formidable Ernest Bevin found himself allotted a Morris Ten as his ministerial car in 1940, he later complained that he was travelling 'with his knees in his mouth.'[25] During hostilities, Sir Miles Thomas, vice-chairman of the Nuffield Organisation (of which Morris was the principal component), had encouraged Alec Issigonis to create what would have been the first of a new generation of Morris cars, which was coded the Mosquito. Issigonis had arrived at Cowley as a suspension specialist in 1938, and his small design team consisted of two draughtsmen, Jack Daniels and Reg Job, who were retained to interpret his free-hand sketches. Unusually, Issigonis was responsible for the design of the entire car and he later immodestly described himself as 'the last of the Bugattis'. Its lines were finalized, right down to the door handles, by 1942, and although the Minor's appearance did, in fact, reflect some current American thinking, Issigonis succeeded in endowing the two-door unitary construction saloon with its own utterly distinctive persona.

Below the surface the car was appropriately advanced, with Issigonis having specified torsion bar independent front suspension and rack and pinion steering. These, coupled with a deliberate strategy of making the car nose heavy, endowed the Minor with superb handling. In addition, its creator also specified 14-in wheels at a time when 17-in ones were the norm. As originally conceived, the Minor was to have been fitted with an 1,100 cc flat four side valve, water-cooled engine. A prototype car was built in 1943 but, after the war and to the exasperation of Miles Thomas, his chairman was reluctant to sanction its production.

'Lord Nuffield was in no mood for changes. His argument was that we had more orders for the Morris Eight than we could cope with, so what was the point of putting the . . . Morris Minor on the market . . . I pleaded that the Morris Eight was rapidly becoming out of date, the Morris Minor would give us a commanding lead. He was adamant. The frustration left a sour taste in my mouth.'[26]

Nuffield was not alone in his dislike of the car. Issigonis himself has remembered that 'none of the directors were very keen, from Donald Harrison, the sales director, downwards. "This thing" that Issigonis is doing, they would say. It was because it didn't look like any other car.' And to Lord Nuffield, the Minor's creator was 'Issywassi's, what's his bloody name', while the car looked like 'a poached egg'.[27]

Sir Miles had met Sir Stafford Cripps during the war and had 'developed a great admiration' for his 'energy and single mindedness'. The President of the Board of Trade's oft

Sir Miles Thomas, who championed the Morris Minor against opposition from Lord Nuffield and Sales Director Donald Harrison. Frustration over the Minor led to his resignation in November 1947. Nuffield's loss was BOAC's gain, when he joined the nationalized concern in 1949. (NMM)

repeated message therefore fell on responsive ears, and by 1947 Thomas 'was trying to rationalise the range of cars we made, avoiding a near duplication of models . . . I failed to see the point of selling what is practically the same car under different names, as denoted mainly by the radiator badge.'[28]

Matters came to a head in November 1947, when Sir Miles – who was, unquestionably, the company's most able executive – resigned from his £20,000 a year post. Soon afterwards, in 1949, he became chairman of the nationalized British Overseas Airways Corporation and, later, pursued a distinguished business career which included the chairmanship of the British division of the multinational Monsanto Chemicals corporation. He was made a life peer in 1971. His place as Nuffield's deputy was taken by Reginald Hanks, who had joined Morris in 1922 and, fortunately, knew Issigonis well and was a great believer in the Minor. It was he who sanctioned the car's production although, perhaps fortuitously, its original compact though unconventional engine was sidelined and it appeared powered by the pre-war 918 cc Eight side valve unit.

This was at the 1948 Motor Show, and the car was in almost immediate demand; an impressive 176,000 examples of the primary Series MM were produced by 1953. Such was the unhappy background to the car's birth but, as Paul Skilleter has pointed out in his perceptive study of the Minor,[29] a factor in the company's resistance was that 'the sales people . . . were afraid of the Morris Minor because it was too different; they preferred to sell something which was familiar to the customer. There was also a general feeling at Cowley – and in other sections of the motor industry, to be fair – that a small car was wrong for the times, and that as export was the priority, and that export markets traditionally seemed to want larger cars, all efforts should be concentrated on cars like the Minor's "bigger sisters".'

These were the simultaneously announced Morris Oxford MO and Six, and in-house Wolseley 4/50, on which the Minor's lines were unhappily scaled up. But they attracted few buyers, the Oxford excepted, and that was discontinued in 1954.

So the Minor entered production against Lord Nuffield's wishes and, initially, he refused to be photographed with it for publicity purposes or even to drive it. Issigonis later remembered that 'I only met him twice in my life. The second time was . . . when we'd made a million Morris Minors. Then he had the grace to thank me.'[30] Despite the apprehensions of the Nuffield export department, of the 29,000 or so Minors produced in the first year of production, 75 per cent were exported. The figure rose to 80 per cent in 1950 and hit a high in 1951 when 90 per cent of output was sent overseas. From there on, this allocation rapidly declined as production was diverted to the needs of the British motorist. In common with many other cars, Australia became the Minor's principal overseas market, followed by America, Eire, South Africa, and New Zealand. Of them all, America represented the greatest sales potential for the Minor even though, at this time, it had no tradition for buying small cars. In view of this, it comes as no surprise to find that the number of Minors sent there were relatively small. In 1949 a mere 974 were exported to the US, though dispatches briefly peaked at 2,126 in 1952, of which 1,118 were saloons and 1,008 tourers. But in 1954 and 1955 American imports dropped, to 706 and 463 respectively, at precisely the time that the market for imported cars was expanding.

Incredibly, the habits of the American car buying public were changing. Since the war, and to a great extent exacerbated by a seller's market, the proportion of imported cars had risen, though it represented less than one per cent on the whole. Then, in what was to be the watershed year of 1955, foreign car sales soared by 80 per cent, although their penetration remained at under one per cent of a much inflated total. It was a year in which the American motor industry built a record 7.9 million befinned, gas-guzzling monsters. However, in the wake of this huge output, domestic demand dropped in 1956, as did the industry's output by a substantial two million units, and this triggered a downturn in the economy. As a result, 'by the second half of 1957 . . . consumers began to look for smaller, cheaper, more manoeuvrable cars . . . Small inexpensive European cars looked like what the new American market wanted.'[31] And the vehicle they bought, which accounted for 31 per cent of imports in 1957, was the 1,192 cc Volkswagen Beetle, of which 64,803 were sold. Although the Minor did benefit from this upturn (45,128 found American buyers between 1957 and 1961) demand peaked at 14,991 in 1959, in which year Americans bought 120,442 Beetles. Imports had broken the 10 per cent barrier.

The reasons for VW's phenomenal success have been well documented. From the American standpoint, it has been summarized as Volkswagen applying the slogan of ' "service first, sales second" . . . accompanied by rigid requirements for spare parts stocks, mechanic training, and even size and appearance of service bays.'[32] Considerable anti-German feeling, and the fact that the VW was a completely new make with no established reputation, make Volkswagen's achievement all the more remarkable. But the well-built and, to American eyes, unconventional car, aided by a subtle advertising campaign ('I don't want an imported car. I want a Volkswagen.') ensured success.

British cars, by contrast, were encountering increasing sales resistance, due largely to unreliability. The main culprit was lack of preparation for totally different conditions; Kjell Qvale, the most successful West Coast importer of British cars, told journalist Tony Hogg that 'there are people in England designing cars especially for

The Morris Minor prototypes were named Mosquito and had flat-four engines. This one dates from 1945 and has headlamps concealed behind the grille. (BMIHT)

the US market who have never set foot in the US.' Hogg also observed: 'The motoring conditions in England, generally, are so totally different from what they are almost anywhere else in the world; and I'm talking about *all* conditions. Until the motorways went in there weren't any roads as we over here know them . . . The climate is another thing; there's no great variation as there is here, between winter and summer, one place and another, and so on. No extreme altitudes. The average Englishman has absolutely no conception of motoring under any conditions than his own. They're a very, very Island race, the English.'[33]

If the cars were unreliable, so were deliveries. 'I sold imported cars in the '50s for Russ Sceli in Hartford, Connecticut. I could never predict to my customers when they would get delivery of their British car unless it was on the water or in the country. If there wasn't a wildcat strike at the factory, the dock workers would walk off. In a moment of inattention I sold a person a Hillman Husky. Twenty years later I ran into that same individual. He still hasn't forgiven me.'[34]

Nevertheless, compared with VW, Morris Motors had a positive advantage because the in house MG marque had, from 1947, established a foothold in the American market and both makes were usually sold by the same retail outlets. Initially the TC sports car, with its uncompromising pre-war lines, attracted relatively few buyers, but it paved the way for such best-selling lines as the MGA and MGB from the same stable and the Jaguars, Austin Healeys, and Triumphs, that would dominate the world's sports car market for the next 20 years, long after British saloons were forgotten.

The TC was little more than a mildly updated version of the TB which had appeared in 1939. Power came from a 1,250 cc four-cylinder overhead valve Morris 10-related engine, and top speed was a rather breathless 70 mph or so. Production began in 1945 and exports started the following year. In 1947 just six of the 1,656 cars sold abroad went to America; once again, it was Australia that got the most but, eventually, 2,001 of the 10,000 built crossed the Atlantic. Despite these small numbers, the TC's impact was considerable. This was a fact readily acknowledged at the time by John R. Bond, founder of the respected *Road & Track* magazine, who wrote in 1954 that 'the TC . . . formed the backbone of the revival of sport cars and road racing in this country.'[35]

By contrast, the model's TD successor sold in much larger numbers. Built between 1950 and 1953, of the 29,664 produced no less than 23,488, or 80 per cent of output, found American buyers. Outwardly similar to the TC, it was, nevertheless, updated with a new chassis and independent front suspension, courtesy of its Y type contemporary. That was the only other MG in production at this time, related to the Morris 10 and built, mostly in saloon form, in the 1947–53 period. Perhaps less desirably, the TD also inherited the Y's distinctly unsporting disc wheels. Fortunately, wires were once again available as an option on the TF, which succeeded the TD in 1953, but an increase in capacity to 1,500 cc in 1954 could not aid sales of a by then rapidly ageing concept. Only 9,600 examples of the TF were built, of which the Americans took 6,272.

Journalist Keith Marvin gives an American view of the MG: 'I saw my first TC in 1947. These cars were, to me, everything typical of British design and I even ordered one to be delivered early in 1949. The price was around $2,200 and I would have gotten the car except for about this time, the Willys-Overland Jeepster lowered its price tremendously as a promotional gimmick to increase sales and, at $1,679, I couldn't see the value of a two passenger car at a much higher price. I never regretted my decision. The Jeepster was one of the best cars I ever owned. And then the TD MG supplanted the TC and I realized how much more comfortable it was. Yet, I felt the TC has classic lines and the TD was a "nothing" car. However, they were enormously popular even if their Y series open models were not. By this time Jack Inskip had taken over

MG too, and he didn't like the Y any more than I did. Thus, he ordered about a dozen TDs, lengthened the chassis and added a rear seat. I thought they were terrific but I understand the MG people did not and when those were sold there weren't any more made. MG was always popular. I think that the TF was a handsome car, too, not as exciting in design as the TC but certainly a big improvement on the plain Jane TD. I especially liked the sweep of the front wings which gave the car a rangy look.'[36]

'We could pick the sort of man we wanted to own a Riley'

Since 1929 MGs had been manufactured at Abingdon, near Oxford, and in 1949 the Nuffield Organisation transferred the production of Riley cars there from Coventry. The move came in the wake of a mild reorganization of its manufacturing facilities which followed Reginald Hanks's appointment as vice-chairman. He had little illusion that he was running a group which was crying out for rationalization and where the managers of the separate businesses tended to go their own ways. As a result, board meetings spent too much time on trivia – 'we talked about bands and awards to firemen'[37] – and he bluntly told Lord Nuffield: 'Rome is burning.' Hanks requested that no less than nine directors resign, which, despite his chairman's protestations, they did at the end of 1947. One was Victor Riley, who later summed up the seller's market of the early post-war years thus: 'It was not a case of a man choosing one of our Rileys, we were in a position to pick the sort of man we wanted to own a Riley.'

Because the firm's Coventry factory had been badly bombed during the war, Riley had the opportunity of creating one of a handful of new British designs to appear immediately after the war. This consisted of a duo of saloons, with distinctive fabric roofs,

which possessed the traditional Riley good looks, though, less desirably, the cars incorporated an amalgam of old and new influences. The lines were BMW inspired while the independent front suspension and rack and pinion steering were concepts borrowed from the *Traction Avant* Citroën. But the body was wood framed and hand-built and, as such, the cars retained a separate chassis. Also the potent but expensive and weighty Riley engines, in 1.5-litre RMA and 2.5-litre RMB forms, were retained. Later, in 1948, came the curious 2.5-litre RMC roadster with three-abreast seating and 20-gallon fuel tank, intended for the American market. Just 501 found buyers.

Initially, these good-looking cars were in strong demand and 10,504 examples of the 1.5-litre were produced between 1945 and 1952. The 2.5-litre was capable of 90 mph but weighed 1.5 tons and sold 6,900 over a similar period. But thereafter demand slipped away; only 3,446 more of the smaller capacity model were made before production ceased in 1955, while just 1,050 units of the 2.5-litre RF (an RMB derivative) were built by 1953. Thereafter the marque settled into a slow decline.

As these RM series cars were still identifiably Rileys they shared no components with other Nuffield products. Wolseley, which built well-equipped cars – some of them on the Morris theme – reintroduced its 1930s range virtually intact after the war. In consequence, there can be no other make which more encapsulates Sir Stafford Cripps's criticisms of the British motor industry than the cars from Ward End, Birmingham; for between 1945 and 1948 Wolseley was producing no less than six different models and, even in these car-hungry post-war years, the top-selling 18/85 – which is fondly remembered for its police car role – accounted for a mere 8,213 units. The production records of the other models make similarly dismal reading: there were 5,344 Eights and about half that number of Tens, while 12/48 sales amounted to 5,602 cars. A similar number of 14/60s were built and there were just 75 examples of the commodious 25 limousine.

Like Riley, in 1949 Wolseley was moved from its Midlands factory, car production being transferred to Cowley. But the story did not improve much thereafter. The range was slimmed down to just two models, the 1.5-litre four-cylinder 4/50, and the 6/80 which was a 2.2-litre six. Like the Morris MS, the Wolseleys' lines were those of a scaled-up Morris Minor but with its traditional radiator grille, complete with illuminated badge, uneasily grafted on to the unitary hull as a sop to Lord Nuffield. Both models were powered by single overhead camshaft engines. However, only 8,955 examples of the smaller model were built by 1953 while the 8/80, surviving for a further year, found 24,886 buyers. Had it not been for the success of the later 1500 model, originally conceived as a Morris Minor replacement and of which over 100,000 were built in the 1957–65 era, the marque would have surely disappeared earlier. As it was, Wolseley lingered on until 1975.

Yet despite the relative failure of Riley and Wolseley, and the operational inefficiencies of running no less than 16 factories, the Nuffield Organisation was, throughout most of the early post-war years, the British-owned sector's most profitable car company. The pre-tax surplus stood at £2.9 million in 1946 and rose, thanks largely to the success of the Morris Minor, to £7.6 million in 1950, which was the second highest in the industry behind Ford's £9.7 million. Nuffield had also wasted little time in establishing an Australian subsidiary in 1945, even though it had a protracted birth, while, in India, the Birla brothers were building the Morris 10 from 1946 under the Hindusthan name. Today this Calcutta-based operation still manufactures what is essentially the Morris Oxford of 1954 vintage.

Lord Nuffield was in his 74th year in 1951. He had no heir and it clearly made sense for the Organisation to merge with Austin, its largest competi-

tor. Regrettably, what should have taken place in 1945 or 1948 did not occur until 1952, by which time the two firms had expended much money and effort in fruitless competition.

In 1945 Austin was still selling its essentially 1930s line of Eight, Ten and Twelve models. Longbridge had played second fiddle to Morris throughout most of the inter-war years with its well-built, reliable, though slightly old-fashioned cars, and the 16 of 1945 was the first overhead valve Austin. The big Sheerline of 1947, and the strangely duplicated Princess of 1948, were the first instances of Austin products possessing independent front suspension. The latter had its body built by Vanden Plas of Kingsbury, North London, which Austin bought in 1946, the company's first satellite plant. In 1948 Austin unveiled its first truly modern design of the post-war years, the A40, powered by a new 1.2-litre four-cylinder overhead valve engine, which survived, in essence, in BMC B Series form until 1980. Styling was 1941 Chevrolet, a chassis was retained and, even if handling lacked precision, the model was Britain's best-seller of its day with a formidable 354,000 Devon and Dorset saloons built before production ceased in 1952. As befitted the times, the majority of these were exported and went mostly to the Antipodes and America. Later in 1948 came the 2.1-litre A70, and the bigger bored 2.6-litre A90 Atlantic convertible followed in 1949.

The 'Lords' of Cowley and Longbridge had not spoken since 1936

Like the Riley Roadster, this was a naive attempt by a British manufacturer to gauge what the American public required. The car was, accordingly, endowed with what the English Midlands considered to be Detroit styling, and a power-operated hood, and was capable of an alarming 90 mph. Despite a batch of stock car

records falling to an A90 at Indianapolis, the $2,460 for which the four-cylinder Atlantic sold could have bought a home-produced V8 with automatic transmission and an acceptable ride. Not surprisingly, the Americans were unimpressed and, despite a swingeing $1,000 price cut, only 350 Atlantics were sold there. Australia and Sweden were the top two overseas markets but took only 821 and 429 cars respectively.

Leonard Lord complained: 'We went to Indianapolis to prove what the British car could stand up to, and I think we proved it. Now the question is – what benefit have we got in sales in America? I am afraid the answer is none. The response to the A90 has been disappointing.'[39] A hardtop followed the open car in 1950 though it was discontinued in 1952 after 7,981 Atlantics had been built, of which 45 per cent were exported. Ironically, its engine was later to power BMC's Austin-Healey sports car that became a firm favourite with American customers.

By 1949 Austin was offering the largest model range of any European manufacturer. In doing so, Lord was proffering the Labour government in general, and Sir Stafford Cripps in particular, a metaphorical V sign that was not intended as a victory salute. But to Austin's chairman the real prize was an alliance with Morris and since the war he had made a number of overtures to Lord Nuffield, both indirect and direct, with a view to getting him to agree to such an association. The sticking point, as in so many instances in the British motor industry's convolute history, was a clash of personalities. The 'Lords of Cowley and Longbridge' had not spoken since they had clashed in 1936 and Leonard Lord had slammed out of Morris Motors, threatening to tear the place apart 'brick by bloody brick.'

Both firms publicly agreed to co-operate in 1948 to 'effect maximum standardisation' but the dialogue was stillborn and Austin then proceeded to develop the A30, its Morris Minor

A late Morris Minor convertible, dating from 1967. By this time about 1.4 million Minors had been made. The last convertible was made in June 1969 and the last Minor of all, a Traveller, in April 1971. However, one car was assembled from spares at a customer's request, and delivered in October 1974. (NMM)

challenger, which, in many respects, encapsulated the need for a merger. It entered production in 1952 and was Longbridge's first unitary construction car which was, initially, badged Austin seven in memory of its famous forebear. The A30 was a stubby, economical saloon which, although it lacked the flair of Issigonis's Minor, was destined to survive in A35 form until 1959, by which time some 480,000 had been built. Under the A30's bonnet was an excellent 803 cc overhead valve four-cylinder engine which was destined to assume apparent immortality as the BMC A Series unit which essentially survives in the evergreen Mini.

Lord spent lavishly in the post-war years to update Longbridge's manufacturing facilities, which culminated in the opening of the new Car Assembly Building in 1951, which was fed, via underground tunnels, with components supplied from other parts of the complex. These improvements gave Austin the most modern factory in the country, capable of producing 100,000 cars a year.

Following the breakdown of merger talks after the tentative 1948 alliance,

Lord nevertheless continued to make overtures to Nuffield and they were finally rewarded in November 1951, when news broke that Austin and Morris were to merge. However, the resultant British Motor Corporation, which came into existence in February 1952, was destined for a difficult and protracted birth.

If Leonard Lord was initially to preside over a multiplicity of factories and models, to a great extent the reverse applied to the Rootes Group. In the post-war world, production was almost exclusively concentrated on a single plant and, while the range consisted of the Hillman, Humber, and Sunbeam-Talbot marques, they did benefit from a higher degree of component rationalization than the products of the Nuffield Organisation. The Group also differed from its contemporaries in owning its retail outlets, Rootes having grown from the country's largest car distributor of the 1920s into a mainstream motor manufacturer. It was also the only member of the 'big six' to be run by a single family and was, accordingly, Britain's only motoring dynasty. Its chairman was Sir William (Billy) Rootes,

knighted in 1942, whose long-running deputy was his brother Reginald, similarly ennobled in 1946. After the war, the younger generation was beginning to take a more active role in the firm's affairs. Billy's son, Geoffrey, became managing director of Humber in 1949 and deputy chairman of the Group in 1955. Brian, his younger brother, was responsible for establishing Rootes Motors Inc in New York and later became chairman of the retail arm of Rootes Ltd.

The Group was yet another beneficiary of the shadow factories scheme – indeed, it was Billy Rootes's favourable response to the original idea, first voiced in 1936, that had ensured its success. Rootes's first shadow had been built adjoining the Hillman and Humber works at Stoke Aldermoor, Coventry. Work began on the project in 1937 and it was a year in which the Rootes mainstay, the Hillman Minx – which had arrived in 1931 – broke the 100,000 barrier and production continued, at a much reduced rate, throughout the war. Work also soon began on a second shadow factory for which the Group was responsible, built four miles south-east of the city at Ryton on Dunsmore, and opened in 1940.

After the war, Stoke was relegated to the role of a machining and engine/gearbox and transmission production facility, with vehicle assembly concentrated on the massive shadow plant at Ryton. In a further rationalization, in 1946 the former Talbot factory in West London, where Sunbeam-Talbots had been built since 1938, was closed and became a service facility. However, the Group's British Light Steel Pressings plant at Acton was maintained along with the nearby Thrupp and Maberly works at Cricklewood, which continued to build the coachwork for the big Humber Pullman and undertook completion work on other models.

Rootes and Standard were the 'small two' of the 'big six' and, as such, were particularly vulnerable. Standard did not break the 100,000 cars a year barrier until 1959, and even though Rootes had achieved this figure in 1955 it was still not large enough to achieve the economies of scale for truly cost effective production. At this time, the Group's products tended to be strikingly non-innovative from an engineering standpoint and Rootes was not able to respond as quickly to technical refinements as its competitors.

Despite the fact that a seller's market was operating during this period, Rootes's share of British car production remained essentially static, having stood at 10.7 per cent in 1946 and being marginally down to 10.5 per cent in 1960. While the group remained profitable throughout this time, its first significant loss (of £600,000) came in 1956–7, which was a poor year for the industry but a pointer to troubles ahead.

Rootes would require no lessons from Sir Stafford Cripps as far as exports and a one model policy was concerned. Billy Rootes had been a firm advocate of overseas sales, had even established a sales outpost in far-away Argentina in 1931 and, since then, had made many trips to America which gave his speech a transatlantic twang. After the war, Rootes had wasted little time in creating departments for service and supply at Long Island, Chicago, and Los Angeles. On the other side of the world, Rootes (Australia) was established in 1946.

The business's volume producer was Hillman which built, no doubt to the President of the Board of Trade's delight, just one model: the 1.2-litre Minx. This unitary construction car had entered production in 1940 and was as mechanically uncomplicated as its predecessors, being powered by a side valve four while suspension relied on all round half elliptic springs. For 1949, at long last, came independent front suspension and the Phase III had well executed American-inspired lines, with input from the Raymond Loewy organization; Rootes had secured a contract with the London office of the US-based industrial designer in 1938. The majority of the 90,832 produced

were sold abroad. Not until 1955, and the Phase VIII Minx, did the model finally acquire much-needed overhead valves.

Rootes had created Sunbeam-Talbot in 1938 from a union of the well-known names that the company had acquired earlier in the decade. These cars can be considered as up market variations on the Minx theme, with the Ten and 2-litre reintroduced immediately after the war. In 1948 they were impressively restyled by Rootes's Edward (Ted) White and Loewy with the 1.1- and 2-litre engines now fitted with overhead valves for the 80 and 90 respectively. As they retained a separate chassis, the 80 tended to be underpowered, though the 2-litre 90 was a livelier 75 mph sports saloon which retained a beam front axle until 1951. That year came the Mark II with an enlarged 2.2-litre power unit, courtesy of the in-house Humber Hawk but employing overhead valves. The IIA 90 of 1952 was the best-selling model of the range, with 6,381 built, and 1953 saw the arrival of the open two-seater

Sunbeam Alpine derivative aimed for the overseas market, which was built until 1955. The same year the Sunbeam-Talbot name was dropped and the Mark III saloon became a Sunbeam. The final version of this handsome, but by then outdated, heavy car was produced in 1957.

Humber was top of the Rootes price-range although there was the inevitable cross-pollination from other in-house makes. The Hawk of the 1945–8 era was Hillman 14-based and this was competitively revised as the Hawk III, which was a larger car than its predecessor; 10,040 were built. Its full width styling once again reflected the White/Loewy alliance but, while independent front suspension was welcome, the old 1.9-litre side valve four was retained. Performance was marginally improved when capacity was upped to 2.2 litres in 1951 and overhead valves finally arrived with the 70 bhp Hawk VI of 1954–7.

Next came the Super Snipe, which was a 4-litre six which retained side valves until 1953 when the Mark VI

The MG TC was described as 'the backbone of the revival of sports cars in America', despite the fact that only 20 per cent of TCs were sold in the US. The TD's penetration of the market was much higher, with around 80 per cent being sold there. This TC is taking part in the Waterford Gymkhana at Detroit in 1961. In the background is a Chevrolet Corvette whose sales benefited from the initial boost given to sports cars by the MG. (NMM)

acquired a 4.1-litre overhead valve unit, borrowed from the in-house Commer truck range. Demand was modest and only 5,286 examples of the Mark IV were built by 1956. The model had been fitted with Rootes's unyielding transverse leaf spring independent front suspension until 1952, when coils and wishbones took over.

Top of the Humber line and, indeed, the flagship of the Rootes fleet, was the commodious Pullman limousine, produced between 1945 and 1954. This was a peace-time version of Humber's war-time staff car and, throughout its manufacturing life was powered by the six-cylinder side valve engine initially used in the Super Snipe. The Mark II of 1948 anticipated that model's body revisions of the same year and sold surprisingly well, accounting for 2,200 cars, but the by then ageing model ceased production in 1954, after only 414 of the final Mark IV version had been made.

With the Minx firmly established as a strong seller in the medium-sized car market, Rootes chose not to produce a small model and did not do so until the arrival of the 875 cc Hillman Imp in 1963. A small car line was similarly ignored in the 1950s by Vauxhall, which since 1925 had been owned by the American General Motors Corporation. Like Rootes it only possessed one factory, at Luton, but also enjoyed the luxury of its own body manufacturing plant. During the 1930s Vauxhall had achieved spectacular growth, in 1929 accounting for a mere 1.1 per cent of British car production but by 1939 and despite being the smallest member of the 'big six' – claiming 10.4 per cent of output. This figure was again attained in 1947, when 30,376 Vauxhalls were built.

The Riley RMC roadster was intended for the American market, though few were sold there. Four overriders and flashes on the wings were concessions to supposed American taste. Early models had steering column gearchange, later ones for the home market had floor change. (Nick Georgano)

Nevertheless the post-war period cannot be regarded as a particularly auspicious one for the firm. Although production had risen to 145,142 cars by 1960 this only represented a marginally improved 11 per cent of British automobile production.

Compared with Ford, Britain's other American-owned car maker, Vauxhall's performance was indeed sluggish. This can, in part, be put down to Ford enjoying a far higher degree of autonomy than Vauxhall, and Luton did not benefit from the continuity of management enjoyed at Dagenham. When Vauxhall's managing director since 1929, Sir Charles Bartlett, retired in 1953 he was replaced by the English-born, American-educated Walter Hill. He remained at Luton for only two years and his place was then taken by Philip Copelin, who had run GM's Belgian subsidiary, and he held the post until 1961. During this period came the calamitous corrosion problems of the F series Victor of 1957–9 which played havoc with the firm's reputation and took many years to live down.

The post-war Vauxhall range consisted of three models introduced in the late 1930s: a 1.8-litre 14, a 10 of 1.2 litres, and a related, bigger-bored 1.4-litre 12. These all featured Vauxhall's characteristic overhead valves, independent front suspension and unitary construction. The 10 was dropped in 1947 and the other models endured until 1948. All were replaced for 1949 by the L type, fashionably a single model, with a common body/chassis structure: how Stafford Cripps must have approved! It was, in fact, a cleverly repackaged 12 with new front and rear ends and was, ingeniously, available with four- and six-cylinder engines, the cars being respectively titled Wyvern and Velox. They were replaced in 1951 by Vauxhall's first truly new post-war model in the shape of the roomy E series cars, inspired by GM's Holden from Australia.

The theme of four- and six-cylinder engines in a similar hull was perpetuated, as were the Wyvern and Velox names and their engines. These power units were replaced, in the spring of 1952, by oversquare 79 x 76 mm engines which, curiously, shared identical dimensions with Ford's newly-introduced Consul and Zephyr models. Later, in 1955, came Vauxhall's response to the Ford Zodiac in the shape of the better-equipped six-cylinder Cresta. The E series was Luton's first big-seller of the decade and a total of 512,388 of all types was built between 1951 and 1957. Little wonder that, in 1956, Vauxhall's £80

per vehicle profits were the highest in the industry, compared with Ford's £45, BMC's £35 and Standard's £30.[40]

The successful E series range was replaced by two models: the 1.5-litre F Series Victor, which was a four, and the six-cylinder 2.2-litre PA Cresta. Resembling a scaled-down Chevrolet, the Victor, with its innovative panoramic windscreen, was – for Britain – an audacious concept, and the lines were the work of Vauxhall's talented chief stylist, David Jones. It was approved in 1954 by corporation president Harlow Curtice, on his first visit to Luton, when he announced a £36 million three-year expansion plan at Luton. But, disastrously, the Victor's announcement date was later brought forward by six months, from the autumn of 1957 to February.[41]

With such a radical design there were production problems, the door seals proving to be imperfect: the cars leaked and later rusted badly. Nevertheless the Victor survived until 1961, by which time a respectable 390,747 had been built. Some 31,000 were exported to America and Canada where they were sold through Pontiac dealers. It was also dispatched, in CKD form, to GM plants in Commonwealth and Benelux countries which had more experience of assembling tricky body structures than Luton. The company made successful efforts to ensure that the same problems did not plague the less radical, though still overtly transatlantic PA Cresta of 1958, which was built until 1963. Vauxhall's production and market share was to rise modestly during this decade but the reality was that, at this time, Britain was the only major country where General Motors products were outsold by Ford.

Like Vauxhall, Ford's share of British car production had risen dramatically before the war, although the arrival of the horsepower tax in 1921 had toppled the Model T from its unrivalled position as the country's best-selling car. Ford had opened its new and sole British plant at Dagenham, Essex, in 1931, and the arrival the following year of the purpose designed 8 hp Model Y gave the company a renewed grip on the market which it maintains to this day.

The Y had been speedily designed by the parent company in Detroit and Ford Britain was charged no less than $210,000 for its services. Thus, when the Y was due for a facelift, the bodywork of the revised 8 and 10 hp cars of 1937 was designed, much against America's wishes, in Britain. It was left to Dagenham's purchasing manager, Patrick Hennessy, who had already established a good rapport with Henry Ford, to accompany the prototypes to the US. Thankfully, Hennessy and his Irish brogue won the day and it says much for the standing he enjoyed in America that Sir Patrick, as he had become, was made managing director of Ford's British operations in 1948, a position he held until his retirement as chairman in 1968.

'If we do not obey the Government, we do not get the materials'

The cars that Ford manufactured in the early post-war years were unashamedly pre-war products and spiritual heirs to the legendary Model T. The range consisted of the 8 hp Anglia and the more popular mechanically related 10 hp Prefect. In 1947 came the V8 Pilot, a combination of the pre-war 22 hp chassis and 3.6-litre V8 engine, but there were few takers; only 22,189 were built by the time that it ceased production in 1950. All shared the same basic specifications of a robust side valve engine, transverse leaf suspension, and mechanical brakes. Many owners would curse the vacuum-operated windscreen wipers that ceased to operate when the cars were being driven uphill.

The Pilot excepted, these tough, low-cost vehicles were in strong demand after the war and, by the time that the Prefect and Anglia were discontinued in 1953, their combined production totalled an impressive 546,203 units. The theme was then perpetuated with the seemingly indestructible Popular, a combination of the 10 hp engine in the two-door Anglia body which survived, incredibly, until 1959. Selling for £390 on its introduction, it was the cheapest car on the British market.

In 1946, the first full year of production after the war, Ford built 31,974 cars, a figure which rose to 93,499 in 1952. This was second only to the newly-created British Motor Corporation that, with 235,777 cars to its credit, achieved well over twice Dagenham's output. Yet in 1959 Ford manufactured a record 314,793 cars and BMC 431,247. Not only was the production gap narrowing but Ford's £32.2 million profits, compared with BMC's £21.4, were the highest in the industry. It was a pointer to further troubles ahead for the Corporation.

No other major car company in Britain was to improve its financial and market position in the 1950s as dramatically as Ford. Its sure-footed growth was geared to the fact that it recognized not only that the market would expand, but that it would grow more prosperous. From a starting point of the 'sit up and beg' models of the late 1940s, there was only one way to go, and that was up. However, like so many of Britain's car makers in the early post-war years, Ford chafed at what it perceived as unnecessary government interference in its affairs. The company's deputy chairman, Sir Rowland Smith, probably spoke for most of his contemporaries when he complained in 1948 that when the firm reduced its prices, it had to inform the Chancellor of the Exchequer, the President of the Board of Trade, the Minister of Supply, and the Minister of Agriculture and Fisheries. In June of that year, Sir Patrick Hennessy complained in a similar vein when he informed a Detroit management group that 'they (government officials) tell us what to do, what to make, when to make it, what to do with it when we have made it . . . If we do not do what they want, we do not get the material.[42] The latter reference related to steel supplies, which were geared to export performance.

This market was to dramatically change. In accordance with Ford's '1928 Plan', in addition to Britain, Dagenham would produce cars for sale in Europe, Turkey, the Middle East, and Africa north of Rhodesia. Significantly, the British plant would not export its cars to America, which was regarded as Detroit's own. This policy endured until 1948 when, in February, Henry Ford II drove off the assembly line the 250,000th car built at Dagenham and took the opportunity of announcing that the vehicle, a Prefect, was the first of a large consignment to be sent to America. This was the first occasion that a British-built Ford had officially crossed the Atlantic, but by 1957 it was the industry's largest exporter to the US, dispatching 17,062 cars there (some 3,000 ahead of BMC's MG marque). Dagenham was also encouraged to sell its products throughout the world, something that Henry Ford had assiduously prevented.

His grandson, Henry Ford II, had in 1945 inherited an ailing business, the legacy of a generation of management by inspiration, hunch and prejudice. The younger Ford, aided by Ernest Breech – who had been recruited from General Motors – introduced much-needed management reforms of the sort initiated by the latter Corporation in the 1920s. Following input from the high-flying 'whizz kids', Ford America would more confidently face the post-war years, and management reforms were soon to be felt likewise at Dagenham. There, in 1948, a policy of graduate recruitment was introduced, an initiative rarely practised within the British motor industry, which retained a deep-rooted, emotional attachment to the engineering apprenticeship and the practical skills which went with it. The British Motor Corporation's management, for instance, was almost exclusively 'home-grown'.

Ford, however, began to look to an entirely different type of recruit and it was for this reason that Terence (Terry) Beckett, an engineer *and* economist, joined the company. Destined to be a future Ford of Britain chairman, he is forever identified for his role in the creation of the highly successful, and profitable, Cortina range in 1962. Beckett has recalled: 'when I'm asked, "Why did I join Ford," I'm a bit like the girl who married a chap and, when people wondered why, she responded, "Well, nobody else asked me." '[43] The appointment of Beckett and his university-educated contemporaries – initially there was only a handful of them – was a reflection of the fact that Ford's British operation was to enjoy a greater degree of independence from Detroit than it had previously experienced. It will be recalled that the well-received Model Y had been American-designed, and although its successors were Dagenham developed, this flew in the face of corporate diktat.

In that pivotal year of 1948, when so much changed at Ford Britain, the parent company recognized the need for it to develop its own cars, although the US would still have the last word. This represented a considerable endorsement of Hennessy and his all-British management. In the course of a meeting, held with Henry Ford II and Graeme K. Howard, head of the international division, it was decided that: 'The introduction of a Chief Engineer is required as well as a Body and Styling Engineer . . . Action is necessary.'[44] But it would be a gradual process, and it was only when Ford America found itself overburdened with engineering work that Mr Ford informed Hennessy: 'Look here, Pat, you'd better take care of your own problems.'[45] This shift in emphasis did not, however, influence the design of the next generation of British Fords, in the shape of the American-designed Consul and Zephyr models introduced for 1951, and it would not be felt until the arrival of the 105E Anglia in 1959.

From 1952 onwards Ford also enjoyed a considerable logistical advantage over its rival BMC, which was operating from a variety of factories that had sprung up in piecemeal fashion over the previous 50 years, spread over a roughly triangular area bounded by the cities of Oxford, Birmingham and Coventry, with all the inefficiencies that this entailed. By contrast, until the opening in 1963 of Halewood on Merseyside, Dagenham was Ford's only major assembly plant; indeed, it had closed almost all the satellites it had operated during the war. However, in 1948, Ford did purchase a factory at Langley, Buckinghamshire, for commercial vehicle manufacture, but most of Ford's remaining post-war expansion took place on its Dagenham doorstep. In 1947 the firm bought the Kelsey Hayes wheel company, but its greatest prize was the purchase, in 1953, of the American-owned Briggs Motor Bodies' British subsidiary, which had been opened to service the needs of the Dagenham complex.

What had preoccupied Hennessy, in particular, was what would happen when Walter O. Briggs, the firm's founder, died. Across the Atlantic, Briggs's largest customer was Chrysler, and Hennessy feared that it would buy the company and then control Ford Britain's body supply. He therefore began to make strenuous efforts, from 1951 onwards, to buy Briggs and, early in 1953, finally succeeded. The agreed price, for 62 per cent of the shares owned by the parent in its Essex-based operations, amounted to almost $9 million, which was the equivalent of £3.2 million. Hennessy then had to worry about the dollars because, at the time, there were rigid governmental controls in place to prevent the export of such a valuable currency. However, the new Conservative administration gave its approval and the purchase went ahead. It gave Ford autonomy in the body building field, for which a shortage of capacity would be a constant feature of the 1950s and 1960s. Hennessy later spoke of his initiative as 'one of the most important events in Ford-England's post-war history.'[46] As a result, Ford inherited a further three

The Austin A40 was one of the industry's greatest export successes. Here are some of a cargo of 420 cars ready to be loaded on the Pacific Stronghold *at Manchester Docks, bound for the West Coast of America and Canada in March 1948. The car in the foreground is a two-door Dorset, much rarer than the four-door Devon.* (NMM)

Briggs-owned plants at Romford, Doncaster, and Southampton.

Despite Briggs having Ford as its principal customer, it did welcome contracts from other car makers and, in these early post-war years, the most significant came from Bradford-based Jowett Cars. Since late in 1947 Briggs's Doncaster plant had built body shells for Jowett's advanced and respected Javelin saloon, but the under-capitalized company had overreached itself in developing such a design. It soon found itself in trouble and, for an eight-month period in 1948–9, owed its body builder £100,000. Subsequently Javelin sales picked up and in 1951, the peak year of production, Briggs built 5,769 Javelin bodies.[47]

Thereafter sales slumped, caused in part by an overall decline in the car market in 1952 but coupled, alas, with the model's growing reputation for unreliability. It followed the company's ill-fated decision, taken as a cost-cutting measure, to manufacture its own gearbox rather than buying it, as hitherto, from Henry Meadows. Jowett's own J gearbox was introduced in the autumn of 1951. Problems soon manifested themselves, and of the first 1,000 cars to be so equipped 78 resulted in warranty claims, which were running at the rate of about nine a week.[48] Although these gradually declined, the damage had been done. In addition, the Javelin's horizontally-opposed flat-four engine began to suffer from crankshaft breakages, which proved to be less common than the gearbox maladies but further tarnished the car's image.

Like some latter-day sorcerer's apprentice, Briggs continued to produce Javelin bodies for which there was no market and these began to pile up in and around Bradford; even the town's football ground was pressed into service to accommodate them.[49] In December 1952, Jowett had no option but to order Briggs to cease body production, some two months, it should be noted, before Ford's successful bid. Production never restarted and Jowett, which had been in the car business since 1910, ceased to be so in 1954. Yet details of the crisis year of 1952 were little known outside Jowett's native Bradford and there was a general belief amongst the public that Ford's purchase of Briggs had been responsible for the company's demise; in fact it had been a victim of its own ambitions.

Ironically, its money-spinning product of the post-war years had been the no-nonsense Bradford introduced in 1945, a sort of poor man's Land-Rover of which some 38,000 had been built. Archaically, it was powered by a 1-litre horizontally-opposed two-cylinder engine which dated back, in essence, to 1910 when the Jowett brothers began their venture into motor car manufacture.

It is difficult to think of a greater contrast than that between the utilitarian Bradford and the costly, exclusive Rolls-Royces and Bentleys which provided transport for so many of the rich and well-to-do during the inter-war years. Up until the outbreak of the Second World War, these were produced at the Derby factory where the world-famous Rolls-Royce aero engines were also built. With hostilities looming, in 1939 the Air Ministry recognized the need to substantially increase Merlin aero engine production and, in the first instance, it established two further plants for its manufacture, one at Glasgow and the other at Crewe, both of which Rolls-Royce administered.

Despite the company concentrating its formidable expertise on the war effort, the future of its Car Division was being addressed by chief experimental engineer William Robotham. Up until 1939 almost every Rolls-Royce and Bentley was different on account of the fact that the firm only built its cars in chassis form. They were then bodied by a specialist coachbuilder, a practice that dated back to the dawn of motoring. This inheritance, coupled with the time-consuming, meticulous approach to manufacturing its cars bequeathed by the perfectionist Henry Royce, meant that since the mid-1930s the business had been reliant on the substantial revenues generated by its aero engines. In 1935, the year of the Merlin's introduction, Rolls-Royce had recorded a gross profit of £1.2 million, of which some £320,000 or 27 per cent, was contributed by chassis sales. By 1938 this latter figure had declined to £64,000, or a mere five per cent of the total.[50]

However, Robotham recognized that if Rolls-Royce was to survive the postwar years as a car maker, it would have to radically alter the way in which it built its products. The answer, he believed, was for the firm to dispense with the coachbuilt body and adopt pressed steel shells of the type that had been employed by Britain's 'big six' car makers since the early 1930s. In January 1944 Robotham therefore approached the Pressed Steel company with a view to it producing such a saloon body, and was horrified to find that the tooling would cost at least £250,000.[51] He had been thinking of production rising to around 2,000 cars a year but was informed that 'we should have to sell at least 5,000 bodies to exactly the same design if we were to get the potential cost reductions.' This flew in the face of the Rolls-Royce formula for exclusivity, but the nettle had to be grasped. As Robotham subsequently reflected, 'I felt that we had no alternative but to buy these tools or go out of the automobile business – and I had a secret hope that spending this amount on tooling might force the company to go to 10,000 cars a year.'[52] This was, he calculated, the minimum number on which the firm could make a reasonable return on its capital.

Interestingly, since 1945 Rolls-Royce car production has never begun to approach the 5,000 figure, let alone 10,000. So up until 1968, when the Car Division made its first surplus (albeit a modest £59,000 one), it lost money, and by the 1960s the deficit was running at around £300,000 per annum.[53] Hitherto, corporate profits had been exclusively contributed by the buoyancy of its aero engine sales.

Following the war, car manufacture was concentrated on the former Merlin aero engine plant at Crewe and, as for actual as opposed to projected production, it was running at below the 1,500 a year figure throughout the 1950s. Production did, however, begin to rise from 1965 onwards, following the appearance of the Silver Shadow, destined to be the best-selling Rolls-Royce since the Silver Ghost. During the 1970s it never dropped below the 2,000 mark, and broke the 3,000 barrier for the first time in 1975, when pre-tax profits reached £3.4 million (although by this time the Car Division was separated from its parent, following the firm's 1971 bankruptcy). Output peaked in 1978, at 3,347 cars, a figure which has never been exceeded but is still some 1,500 units below Robotham's original anticipated figure.

The company's performance in the late 1940s and 1950s should been seen in the context of the fact that civil and military aviation was in the ascendancy and such considerations as a profitable car division were not uppermost in the thoughts of Lord Hives, ennobled thus in 1950, the year in which he became Rolls-Royce's chairman. During the war, in 1942, he had secured a masterly deal with Rover whereby the car company swapped its pioneering gas turbine work, undertaken for Frank Whittle's Power Jets, for the manufacture of the Meteor tank engine. This gave Rolls-Royce a world lead in jet engine technology, which was reflected in the business's pre-tax profits which rose seven fold, between 1946 and 1959 from £677,000 to £4.8 million.

The Car Division meanwhile continued its loss making pre-war performance, but even here the adoption of a pressed steel body, so assiduously championed by Robotham, represented a move in the right direction. Hives, as director and general manager, had approved Robotham's recommendation, and the pressed steel body was adopted, despite a fierce rearguard action fought by Sir Arthur Sidgreaves, Rolls-Royce's managing director since 1928. He, however, retired in March 1946, having been replaced by Hives at the beginning of the year. But it was Bentley rather than Rolls-Royce which was the first recipient of the new bodywork and its Standard Steel Mark VI saloon was announced in May 1946. It could, nevertheless, still be specified with bespoke coachwork.

As expected, it was to sell better than any of the company's pre-war cars and, of the 7,521 examples of the Mark VI and its R-type successor built until 1955, some 6,219 or 83 per cent were of the uniform body design.[54] By contrast, the model's Rolls-Royce equivalent, the Silver Wraith, was only available with coachbuilt bodywork. Then, in 1949, came the Silver Dawn which was, in effect, a Mark VI Bentley saloon with a Rolls-Royce radiator, introduced so that the model might appeal more in America where the Rolls-Royce name was known and Bentley was not. Only 168 examples of the Mark VI/R-type were sold there; in an era geared to exports, most Bentleys stayed at home. Australia, the largest market (the US came next), imported just 294 cars.[55]

Under the Mark VI's bonnet was a 4.2-litre six-cylinder overhead inlet/side exhaust engine, which represented the fulfilment of a rationalization process begun by William Robotham in 1937. At the time there was little relationship between the power units of Rolls-Royce's Phantom range and its smaller models, and the outcome was the B Series engine family. These shared common pistons, connecting rods, and valves, and were produced in four-, six- and eight-cylinder forms, respectively designated B40, B60 and B80. Despite Rolls-Royce not listing a four-cylinder car, the B40 found plenty of military applications, most notably in the cross-country Austin Champ announced in 1952. The B60 powered the vast majority of Rolls-Royce and Bentley

Right: *William Rootes, with elbow on the bonnet, drove a prototype Hillman Minx for thousands of miles in Europe and North Africa. Here he is at the Swiss-Italian border in May 1931. (NB)*

Below: *Colonel A. T. Goldie Gardner (centre, with pipe) stands between an A40 Devon and an A90 Atlantic on the occasion of record attempts at Indianapolis. Next to him is Austin's PRO, Alan Hess. (NMM)*

cars until 1959. Similarly, the B80 had military and industrial applications but it was also used for the majestic Phantom IV of 1950 and Britain's last straight-eight car, which remained in production until 1956. As it was only available for monarchs and heads of state, a mere 16 were built.

By contrast, the Mark VI Bentley

Two Hillman Minxes outside Peter Satori's Continental Car Co in San Francisco in 1954. The front car is an older model, dating from 1949–50. Keith Marvin described the Minx as probably the most popular British import, along with the Austin A40. (NB)

was a mass-produced model. It still retained a separate chassis, and despite the standardized bodywork the car's interior was reassuringly furnished in the best pre-war traditions, with comfortable, leather-upholstered seats, and the dashboard and door fillets finished in fine walnut veneers. There were few major changes to the specification, apart from the engine being enlarged to 4.6 litres in 1951 and the saloon being uprated in bigger booted R-type form in 1952. It survived until 1955.

The Mark VI Bentley was capable of approximately 95 mph, but in 1952 Rolls-Royce unveiled a model which reflected the marque's impressive sporting pedigree. The 115 mph R-type Continental, created in the spirit of the pre-war Grand Routiers, was distinguished by its handsome two-door fastback body, designed by Rolls-Royce and executed by H. J. Mulliner. On announcement, it had the distinction of being the fastest four-seater production car in the world but, at £4,890 and initially only available for export, it was also one of the most expensive. It could be specified with bespoke coachwork to the owner's preference, but this only applied to 15 chassis of the 208 built. In 1955 came the outwardly similar S-type version of which 221 of the 388 total were Mulliner coupés. This ceased produc-

tion in 1959 but the Continental name continued to describe a variety of coachbuilt S-types until 1965.

In retrospect, 1959 can be seen as the beginning of a decline in the fortunes of the Bentley marque and a corresponding ascendancy of Rolls-Royce. In the 13 years from 1946 until 1959, production of Bentley chassis outnumbered that of its legendary stable-mate by more than two to one for, during this period, Crewe built 11,266 Bentleys compared with 4,911 Rolls-Royces. This was a recognition of customer acceptance of the pressed steel body which, once it was extended, in 1955, to Rolls-Royce, relegated the Bentley to the role of clone, with the cars being distinguished only by a model letter rather than a name. It would not be until 1990 that Bentley production would, once again, outnumber that of Rolls-Royce.

This closer alliance of the two makes was encapsulated with the arrival, in 1955, of the Rolls-Royce Silver Cloud and its Bentley S1 equivalent. These shared a new Pressed Steel saloon body, there was a new chassis, and the six was enlarged for a final time to 4.9 litres, a revised unit which had first appeared in the R-type Continental of 1954. Automatic transmission was standardized. Both models survived, in essence, until 1965, and they could be specified in coachbuilt form. Despite this, the overwhelming majority – no less than 98 per cent of the total – were bought 'off the peg'. In the first instance, the Bentley saloon was considerably more popular than the Rolls-Royce, accounting for 3,107 and 2,231 cars respectively.

This trend was reversed from 1958, when the long running six was replaced by a 6.2-litre V8, an engine which, in its essentials, remains in production at the time of writing

(1994). The outwardly similar Silver Cloud II sold 2,417 examples and the Bentley S2 nearly 500 less at 1,932, and this trend was maintained with the arrival of the 1962 Silver Cloud III/S3 generation (distinguished by twin horizontally located headlamps) that endured until 1965. It was a year in which the Car Division made an unprecedented loss of £919,000 on account of the impending arrival of the Silver Shadow, but this was offset by corporate pre-tax profits reaching a record £6.9 million. There was, it seemed, still plenty of money to be made in the aviation business.

Rolls-Royce was not the only company to underpin its car line by the production of aero engines. Another was Coventry-based Armstrong-Siddeley, which had also begun their manufacture during the First World War. The first cars to carry the name were built in 1919 but they were overshadowed by a generation of air-cooled radials which enjoyed great popularity until the mid-1920s, when the firm's lead in that sector was decisively overhauled by Bristol. Nevertheless, Armstrong-Siddeley continued to be a significant force within the British aero engine industry, and in 1935 the firm merged with the Hawker Aircraft Company and was to form the nucleus of the Hawker Siddeley Group.

During the Second World War, the Group produced some of the most famous aircraft of the conflict, namely the Hurricane fighter, the Whitley bomber, and its Lancaster successor. It was therefore appropriate that Armstrong-Siddeley's first cars of the post-war years reflected these famous names. The Lancaster, rooted in the pre-war 16 hp, was a six-light saloon, powered by a 2-litre six-cylinder overhead valve engine, enlarged to 2.3 litres in 1948. Manual transmission could be specified but a pre-selector gearbox, which the make had employed since 1929, was the more popular choice. In addition to the Lancaster saloon, there was the Hurricane drophead coupé and the Typhoon two-door close-coupled saloon. In 1950 the six-light

Lancaster was replaced by the Whitley four-light saloon. These cars perpetuated the marque's pre-war theme of uninspired, if well-built, reliable transport pitched somewhere between Daimler and Rover in the upper-middle class sector. This first generation of cars was to sell reasonably well and accounted for a grand total of 12,570 examples built; but they were currently, it should be remembered, in a seller's market.

In 1952 the firm announced its all-new model, the Sapphire, which was destined to be the most popular Armstrong-Siddeley of the post-war years. Under its bonnet was a new 3.4-litre engine with, unusually, inclined valves operating in a hemispherical cylinder head activated by pushrods from a high mounted camshaft. There was the usual choice of transmissions – manual or pre-selector units – although the latter now enjoyed electrical activation. The model named after the company's successful Sapphire jet engine – was a commodious, well-appointed, though conservatively-styled saloon which could reach

100 mph in twin carburettored form. But at £1,728 it was a significant £241 more than Rover's 75. After 7,207 examples had been built, in 1959 the big saloon was revised in enhanced 4-litre Star Sapphire form, which would account for a further 980 cars.

The Sapphire was the sole Armstrong-Siddeley model until 1956, when the firm introduced the smaller and visually unhappy Sapphire 234/236 range, destined to be one of the most memorable commercial flops by a mainstream British car manufacturer in the post-war years. Both were uncompetitively priced and the more expensive six retailed at £1,657, which was over £300 more than Jaguar's sleek 2.4-litre saloon. The 234 was powered by the Sapphire's unit in four-cylinder form, and sales did not reach four figures: just 803 cars found owners. The 236 was a six, powered by the Whitley's old 2.3 litre engine, but this was even less popular than the four and sold just 603 examples. Production of both models came to an abrupt halt in 1958.

It was against this bleak background

The Hillman Hawk III was new in its styling and coil independent front suspension, but had the same unexciting 1.9-litre side valve engine and four-speed column gearchange. Behind this chassis is a complete car, and across the aisle at the 1948 Earls Court Show is one of its rivals, the Rover 75. (NB)

that Armstrong-Siddeley cars were overtaken by events. At the Government's behest, the aircraft industry was being streamlined and the number of airframe and engine manufacturers was being drastically reduced, an initiative that culminated in the creation of the British Aircraft Corporation in 1960. As a prelude, in April 1959 Armstrong-Siddeley Motors merged with Bristol Aero Engines to form Bristol Siddeley Aero Engines.

The car line was by then reduced to the low volume Star Sapphire and, clearly, there was no place for a much depleted loss making automobile business in this newly allied company In March 1960, it was therefore decided to discontinue car manufacture by 31 July and the final Armstrong-Siddeley, an example of the Sapphire's rare long-wheelbase Limousine, was dispatched to Ghana on 6 September.[56] There was one final twist to the story because, in 1968, Rolls-Royce, which had already purchased the Bristol Aeroplane Company, bought the shares in Bristol Siddeley held by the Hawker Siddeley Group and so gained control of the firm.

Soon after the First World War, Armstrong-Siddeley had produced a new 14-cylinder two row radial aero engine and, when it came to naming it, the firm decided to perpetuate the animal theme of its war-time Puma unit. The new engine, which was destined for a long and successful manufacturing life, was named Jaguar. During 1935, two miles from Armstrong-Siddeley's Parkside works in the Foleshill district of Coventry, the chairman of SS Cars, William Lyons, was pondering on what to call his new 1936 range of overhead valve models. He had asked his London-based Nelson advertising agency to compile a list of animal names and 'pounced on *Jaguar* for it had an exciting sound to me, and brought back some memories told to me, towards the end of the 1914–18 war, by an old school friend (Arthur Breakell) . . . who had joined the Royal Flying Corps . . . He was

stationed at Farnborough and he used to tell me of his work as a mechanic on the Armstrong-Siddeley Jaguar engine. Since that time the word *Jaguar* has always had a particular significance to me.'[57]

'For every £10 on the price of a car, you lost so many customers'

Armstrong-Siddeley's permission was sought and willingly given for SS to adopt the name, which became known to an even wider public after the Second World War when Lyons was obliged to change the name of his company from SS, with its Nazi taint, to Jaguar Cars Ltd – which, prudently, he had registered in 1937. Jaguar was to enjoy an era of spectacular growth; in 1946 it had built a mere 1,132 examples of its stylish, value for money saloons powered by Standard-based engines, and had made a pre-tax profit of £22,852. In 1959 this surplus soared to £1.6 million and Jaguar's output rose to 20,876. The cars were now powered by the company's own purpose-designed engine which, flying in the face of convention, employed twin overhead camshafts, a design that had hitherto been associated with temperamental low production sports cars of the pre-war era. Not only did this XK six-cylinder engine prove its worth under the bonnets of Jaguar saloons, but it was of sufficient potency to power the sports racers which gave Jaguar no less than five wins in the famous Le Mans 24 hour race.

Little wonder that, by the 1960s, William Lyons (knighted 1956) was the highest paid executive in the British motor industry with a salary of £100,000 a year. He was a man of multifarious talents who not only styled practically all his own cars but also had a flair for choosing talented subordinates. He was canny, financially sagacious and autocratic. Chief engineer William Heynes, the most powerful man in the company after Lyons, who became a director in 1946, later

recalled that the Jaguar board meetings were 'a real joke. He (Lyons) just said what he wanted to do and everyone agreed with him, except,' said Heynes, 'me'.[58] Having joined SS in 1935, Heynes had plenty of opportunity to study Lyons at first hand and recognized that, in addition to his formidable stylistic skills, he was 'also a true economist; every penny that could be saved without affecting quality was saved, and the economy passed on to the customer. His argument was that for every £10 on the price of a car you lost so many customers.'[59]

After the war Jaguar was still based in the factory which, as SS Cars, it had occupied since 1931. Lyons briefly contemplated buying the moribund Triumph company, which had been located next door, but decided against it. Whereupon Triumph was, in 1944, snapped up by Standard's Sir John Black, who viewed Lyons with a mixture of fear and respect, and ambitiously believed that he could use Triumph to challenge Jaguar.

Like so many of his contemporaries, William Lyons was running a company which, for the first time, had to look to overseas sales: he later reflected that SS 'had only enjoyed a limited export market before the war, because we had always been able to sell every car on the home market that we could make'.[60] Car makers needed steel and, with its post-war allocation dependent on exports the firm produced a lavishly illustrated brochure to display its model range, which also listed the countries for which the cars were intended. The Jaguar chairman then delivered this document 'personally to Sir George Turner . . . Permanent Secretary at the Ministry of Supply, and I elaborated verbally on our plans and obtained his promise of support. Within two weeks we received a permit for the full quota of steel for which we had asked.'[61] Lyons was the first to recognize that he was selling his products in a car-starved international community and 'we went flat out to establish selling outlets throughout the world.'

Unlike so many British car companies which only benefited from a buoyant export trade in a seller's market, Jaguar's strategy was a long term one and is a policy that endures to this day. In the years between 1946 and 1959 the firm always exported more cars than it built for the home market. This peaked in 1952 when, of the 8,979 cars produced, no less than 7,978, or 88 per cent, found overseas buyers. Export strategy was applied particularly to America where Jaguar, along with MG, began to open up the market for British sports cars. However, while MG built considerably more sports cars than saloons, the reverse has always been true of SS and Jaguar, whose memorable low-production open two-seaters have always played second fiddle to the more popular, and profitable, cars for the family.

After the war Jaguar did not revive its lovely SS100 sports car but in 1948 unveiled the sensational Super Sports model, that was soon renamed the XK120 to reflect its top speed. Based on a shortened version of Jaguar's newly introduced Mark V saloon, its roadster bodywork was inspired by a special bodied BMW 328 which had run in the 1940 Mille Miglia race. Jaguar, along with many other British car companies, had borrowed the car for evaluation after the war and Lyons wasted little time in transferring the lines to the 120, which was expressly created for the export market. It was powered by the legendary 3.4-litre twin overhead camshaft XK engine that had been conceived during the war under the overall direction of William Heynes, assisted by development engineer Walter Hassan and, in a more junior capacity, Claude Baily (who in 1948 was promoted to the post of chief designer).

This high performance unit had, ironically, not been conceived for sports car use but had been designed to propel at 100 mph a luxury saloon that Lyons had conceived for the post-war years. It was fortunate that the six so ably lent itself to a pure performance application, and it was destined to

power every Jaguar model until 1971 and the in-house Daimler limousine until its demise in 1992.

No less than 92 per cent of XK120s were exported and, in turn, this led to the XK140 of 1955, to be followed in 1957 by the XK150, also available in 3.8-litre form, that survived until 1961. The entire XK series amounted to a total of 30,537 cars which, over 13 years, represented just 18 per cent of output.

It was, however, the saloon line that so preoccupied Lyons and up until 1948 this consisted of three models, all introduced in 1938, production of which had been interrupted by the war. There was a 1,776 cc four-cylinder '1½-litre' and two sixes of 2½- and 3½-litres capacity, respectively based on the contemporary 14 and pre-war 20 hp Standard units but with Weslake designed overhead valve cylinder heads. After the war Lyons had succeeded in buying their tooling from the mercurial John Black and Jaguar was thus no longer dependent on Standard for the supply of all-important cylinder blocks. The range was

refined for 1949 in Mark V form, which was a stop-gap model. This used a new chassis with independent front suspension. The low production four was discontinued and the two larger capacity models survived until 1951, when they were replaced by the model for which the XK engine had been originally conceived.

This was the Mark VII (Mark VI being skipped because Rolls-Royce was using it for the Bentley saloon). Based on the V's chassis, it was the first closed Jaguar to be powered by the XK engine and, accordingly, was a 100 mph car, designed with the American market much in mind. There its roomy interior and long-legged performance – the power of the twin cam six was a match for most of the indigenous V8s – made it plenty of friends, who were little concerned that the big car's fuel consumption was around 16 mpg. Successfully launched in the autumn of 1950 in London and America, by November $30 million-worth of Mark VIIs had been reserved by dealers. Later in 1955 came the more powerful VIIM, which was succeeded by the

As an arm of General Motors, Vauxhall benefited in export markets from having a well-established and widespread dealer network. Ahmet Buldanlioglu's Turkish agency, with premises in Izmir and Istanbul, handled Bedfords and Vauxhalls, quite possibly Chevrolets as well, and also Ruston stationary engines. Here are a Bedford O-type 5-tonner and Vauxhall L-type Velox, both c 1949 (NMM)

mechanically as it got older, being impressively revised in Mark II form for 1960 when an additional race-bred 3.8-litre engine became available that proved to be the most popular version in the range. Production lasted until 1968, by which time 83,800 Mark IIs had been built which compared with 36,700 examples of the original version. As Lyons later reflected: 'This range of models accounted for a substantial increase, not only in our volume of production, but also in our profits, which rose five-fold between 1955 (£218,085) and 1968 (£1 million)'.[63]

Jaguar's burgeoning sales in the 1950s were undoubtedly aided by the triumphs of its sports racing cars which had been designed with the express purpose of winning the Le Mans 24 hours event. The firm had first entered a car – a mildly modified XK120 – in 1950, and followed this with the space-framed C-type which won, first time out, in 1951 and again in 1953. The C, in turn, led to the famous D-type which was victorious at the Sarthe circuit in 1955, 1956 and 1957, though for Lyons the greatest prize was the world-wide publicity that these successes generated. As Andrew Whyte has perceptively emphasised, 'what were these victories for, if not to win confidence in the Jaguar name and more sales for *series* production models?'[64]

By the end of the decade, Jaguar's upwardly spiralling output ensured that the business, to use Sir William's phrase, was once again 'bursting at the seams.' Still unable to expand in

refined Mark VIII of 1957, whilst the last of the line was the 3.8-litre Mark IX, with all round disc brakes and power assisted steering.

Jaguar's carefully nurtured post-war growth began to present the firm with problems because, as output rose, it was rapidly outstripping the confines of the Foleshill factory. By 1951 Lyons found that 'the need for expansion was vital to our continued progress, but we were faced with a particularly difficult position because, although I went to the highest level, we were unable to obtain permission to extend our factory; there was a complete embargo on building in Coventry.[62] It then came to the firm's notice that a former shadow factory in Browns Lane at Allesley on the outskirts of the city,

which had been managed by Daimler during the war, was 'falling into disuse.' Like all such plants, the shadow was still in the Government's ownership, but Jaguar was able to buy, rather than rent, the premises on condition that it take on the manufacture of the Rolls-Royce Meteor tank engine. The move was effected by November 1952, with the minimum of disruption to production.

In 1955 Jaguar announced its really big seller of the day. This was the medium-sized 2.4-litre saloon which represented the car company's first excursion into unitary body construction. Competitively priced at £1,343, it was offered from 1957 with a supplementary 3.4-litre engine. Perversely, the model improved both visually and

Coventry, and equally not wishing to move away from its industrial heart-land, in 1960 Lyons was able to double Jaguar's factory floor-space by the purchase of Daimler, which had been building cars in the city since 1896.

If Jaguar represented the success story in the specialist sector in these early post-war years, then Daimler, located in the Radford district of Coventry, encapsulated the other extreme. Shielded from commercial reality by its membership of the BSA arms and motor cycle group, it contin-ued to 'muddle through', much as it had done during the inter-war years. In 1927 the firm had listed 23 different models and by 1955 it was still produc-ing no less than ten in an era when rationalization of its model range was a prime requirement for any car company's survival. Not only that, but some of the models were built in penny numbers and the cars overlapped one another. However, in the main they were well engineered. A distinctive feature of the vast majority was the fitment of a pre-selector gearbox used in conjunction with a fluid flywheel. This combination had been introduced in 1931 and the result was a semi-auto-matic transmission although, on the debit side, fuel consumption was heavy and, ultimately, servicing costs high. Yet another shortcoming related to the cars' visual appearance for, by the 1950s, what had once been elegant, traditionalist styling simply made many of these post-war Daimlers look old-fashioned.

Directing the company's affairs during this crucial period was Sir Bernard Docker, son of Dudley Docker, who had been instrumental in

The 1950 Ford Consuls and Zephyrs broke new ground with their McPherson strut independent front suspension, over-square engines, unitary bodies and slab-sided styling. The second generation, such as this 1956 Consul II, had longer wheelbases and larger engines, but continued the general theme. Bodies included saloons, convertibles and estate cars. (Nick Georgano)

the BSA group's creation. The younger Docker became BSA's chair-man in 1940 and the following year took over the same position at Daimler. Later, in 1944, in a further blatant piece of nepotism, Docker's dying father also appointed him to the post of BSA's managing director. It had also been in 1940 that Daimler had absorbed the old-established London-based Hooper company, which had bodied so many of its products and had, for its own part, purchased the respected Barker concern in 1938.

Daimler's smallest capacity post-war model was essentially carried over from 1939. The well-regarded DB18 of 1946 was powered by a 2,522 cc six-cylinder engine and, still retain-ing a separate chassis, it was made in saloon form by Mulliners of Birmingham, and there was a drop-head coupé by Tickford. They accounted for a respectable 3,365 cars sold in these car-hungry years. The model was discontinued in 1950 and replaced by the updated DB18 Consort saloon, which was more popular than its predecessor and accounted for 4,250 examples built by 1953. Then there was the Barker-bodied DB18 Sports Special three-seater drophead coupé of 1949; despite a price of £2,560, no less than 608 found buyers.

The Daimler heavy brigade, also announced in 1946, consisted of a newly-introduced big six and the inevitable straight-eight, the firm having introduced such a model in 1934. The 4-litre six-cylinder DE27 resembled a slightly smaller version of the eight and, also produced in sombre long-wheelbase DH27 form, was built until 1951 and accounted for 255 examples. The DE36 was Britain's penultimate straight-eight, the Rolls-Royce Phantom IV being the last version of the breed. Daimler's car featured a 5.5-litre unit with a detach-able cylinder head, the pre-war model having, anachronistically, retained a fixed one. This monster weighed nearly three tons, was capable, if neces-sary, of an effortless 80 mph and was surprisingly manoeuvrable. Since 1902 Daimler had supplied cars to the British monarchy and King George VI maintained this tradition by taking delivery of no less than four laun-delettes although, more ominously for the Coventry firm, in 1950 the future Queen bought the first Phantom IV. Nevertheless, no less than seven royal families around the world ordered this Daimler and 205 examples were deliv-ered between 1946 and 1953. Numerically less successful was the Regency, powered by a new 3 litre six-cylinder engine related to that of the

in-house Lanchester 14. Just 51 had been built by 1954 when it was replaced by the 3½-litre Regency II, of which only 219 were produced in 1955 and 1956; an increase in capacity to 4.6 litres did little to aid sales.

More popular was the DB18's replacement which appeared in 1953, named the Conquest because it cost £1,066, less purchase tax (full price to the UK buyer was £1,511). Destined to be the best-selling Daimler of the decade with over 9,000 built, its origins were rooted in the Lanchester Leda, which had begun life as the 14 hp in 1951. The Conquest shared its chassis whilst the new 2.4-litre engine was also related to that of the Leda's four. The model proved to be an 80 mph performer, coupled with the usual Daimler flexibility. There was also the supplementary Conquest Century of 1954 with alloy cylinder head, twin carburettors and a possible 90 mph. It even enjoyed a brief career in saloon car racing. The last traditional Daimler appeared in 1955 in the form of the 4.6-litre DK400 Regina Limousine. Still with separate chassis, it was built for the ensuing five years.

And then, of course, there were the Docker Daimlers, which represented a combination of the talents of Hooper's accomplished chief stylist, Osmond Rivers, and Sir Bernard's wife, Norah, whom he had married in 1949. Docker was impressed by her interest in his business; he made her a director of Hooper and installed a drawing board in their Mayfair home. 'I was ashamed to discover, both at home and abroad, the superb Daimler was in danger of becoming a relic,' she later recalled.[65] The outcome was 'The Gold Car' – created specially for the Dockers – which appeared at the 1951 Motor Show. It was based on the straight-eight Hooper Touring Limousine, but dramatically finished in black with its side panels speckled with gold stars, whilst everything that had hitherto been chromed was gold plated. That this car and its four successors provided Daimler with considerable publicity is indisputable; whether it

was the right type of advertising for a royal warrant holder is more open to debate. Nevertheless, these visually arresting cars continued to enliven London motor shows until 1955.

In due course, Sir Bernard Docker found himself the butt of criticism from his fellow directors for his lack of communication and the ostentatious, publicity-filled life-style that he and his wife seemed to court. He thought little, for example, of flying Star Dust and Golden Zebra, the 1954 and 1955 extravagances, at a cost to the company of £2,140, for his wife to attend the wedding of Prince Rainier.[66] In 1956 motor cycle sales were booming, and BSA recorded a £1.6 million profit, but Daimler cars were a consistent loss maker. Matters came to a head in May 1956, when Sir Bernard, imitating his late father's approach to BSA appointments, proposed making his wife's brother-in-law, R. E. Smith (at the time Daimler's general manager), a BSA director. Docker used his casting vote and the appointment was ratified. However, this proved to be a Pyrrhic victory and, in August, he was ousted from the BSA chairmanship, whereupon he and his wife each bought themselves Rolls-Royces.

He advertised in The Times *offering a car company for sale*

Docker's place as chairman was taken by John Young 'Jack' Sangster, who had joined the board when BSA bought the Triumph motor cycle business for £2.4 million in 1951. Sangster recruited Edward Turner, Triumph's talented but dictatorial managing director, who continued this role and also took charge of BSA's newly-created automotive division. By this time it was reduced to one make, that of Daimler, the last Lanchester car having been produced in 1956. The new management clearly meant business because it was soon offering Borg-Warner automatic transmission as an option on the improved Regency, the

3.4-litre One-O-Four of 1956, as an alternative to the long-running fluid flywheel/preselector gearbox. But the public stayed away: only 459 were built.

The last Conquest Century was built in 1958 but the Majestic, which replaced the One-O-Four in 1958, was a 3.7-litre car with 100 mph performance and all round disc brakes, a first for a British car. It cost a not unreasonable £2,495, but only 940 found buyers. With its demise, there was no 'small' car in Radford's portfolio until the 1959 New York Motor Show, where the very un-Daimler like 120 mph Dart sports car was unveiled. This soon adopted its factory SP250 coding, following protests from Dodge, which owned the Dart name. It had cost-conscious, chunky, fibreglass bodywork, a fine Turner-designed 2½-litre V8 engine, and a TR3-inspired chassis. Although aimed at the American market, more right-hand drive cars than left were eventually built and accounted for 1,445 examples compared with 1,200, making a total of 2,645 by the time of the model's demise in 1964.

In 1960 BSA achieved record profits of £3.6 million, but the sands were rapidly running out for its car business. In 1959 the Majestic received a new 4½-litre V8 engine to become the Majestic Major. However, soon after it entered production Sangster received an offer from Sir William Lyons for the company, which Jaguar purchased for £3.4 million in May 1960. Under this new ownership, the already slimmed-down range was rationalized. Although Turner's V8s remained in production until 1969, from then on Daimlers were powered by the XK engine.

Jaguar had not been the only car company to have developed a twin overhead camshaft six-cylinder engine for saloon car application during the war years. Down in the south, at Staines in Middlesex, Lagonda, with W. O. Bentley as its technical director, had also created such a unit, of 2.6-litre capacity, to power an advanced vehicle with a cruciform chassis and all independent suspension. The engine was running by 1945, well ahead of Jaguar's, and prototype cars were built. Unwisely, however, the firm wanted to call the new model the Lagonda-Bentley. Rolls-Royce had owned the Bentley name since 1931 and, late in 1946, sued Lagonda for trade mark infringement. Rolls-Royce won and the decision cost Lagonda £10,000, a goodly sum in those days. This, combined with attendant steel shortages, resulted in Alan Good, who headed the consortium which owned the business, to put it up for sale. Lagonda was eventually bought by industrialist David Brown, at his second attempt, for £52,500. The news broke in September 1947 and the saloon finally entered production in 1948. But demand for this heavy, overly complicated, expensive car, with its dated bodywork, was limited and when it ceased production in 1958 it was not immediately replaced. Much more significant was the fact that when David Brown bought Lagonda, he was already the owner of Aston Martin, having purchased the moribund concern for £20,500 earlier in the year. The result was that the Lagonda-Bentley's engine, designated the LB6, would have a far wider application than its creator had ever envisaged.

Sports car maker Aston Martin, based at nearby Feltham since 1927, had effectively ceased car production in 1937 to concentrate its resources developing a new generation of cars, created by chief engineer Claude Hill. This was represented by a single prototype saloon with a chassis of rectangular section tubing and independent front suspension, coded Atom, completed in 1940 and soon the recipient of a purpose designed 2-litre four-cylinder pushrod engine.

Since 1932 the firm had been owned by Newcastle shipping magnate Sir Arthur Sutherland Bt, and managed by his son Gordon. In 1944, for the nominal sum of £5, the ownership of Aston Martin was transferred from father to son and, whilst the Atom

clearly represented the way ahead, Gordon Sutherland was realistic enough to recognize that it would require 'much more money than I personally could risk' to put it into production.[67] So, in the autumn of 1946, he took the unusual but, as it transpired, prudent step of placing an advertisement in *The Times* offering, under a box number, a car company for sale. One of those who responded was David Brown of David Brown and Sons Ltd, the gear manufacturers of Huddersfield, Yorkshire. 'I replied, and you can imagine my surprise when I learned that it was Aston Martin. After all, that was a very famous name.'[68]

Brown initially offered £14,000, but after some haggling Aston Martin was his for £20,500. The news was broken in February 1947. When he later viewed the prototype Lagonda saloon, Brown immediately recognized the performance potential of its twin cam

six and to him goes the credit for the concept of uniting Bentley's engine with the chassis of the Atom. A casualty of this union was Hill's projected power unit, a six-cylinder version of the existing four, and he left the company in 1949.

The business was established at new premises in the Hanworth Air Park, near to Aston Martin's original factory. Yet despite Brown's long term plans, the first post war Aston Martin was, in effect, a rebodied Atom fitted with a touring body by Lagonda's Frank Feeley. Unveiled at the 1948 London Motor Show, and titled the 2-litre Sports, the retrospectively titled DB1 attracted little interest and only 16 examples of this £2,331 car were built. The DB2 of 1950 was, however, a very different concept. Not only was Hill's chassis combined with the Lagonda 2.6-litre 105 bhp engine, but the superbly styled bodywork, once again by Feeley, was closed in the manner of

The Jowett Javelin was the most advanced British family saloon of the 1940s, with its flat-four engine, all-torsion bar suspension and aerodynamic styling. On the debit side, in the words of the late Michael Sedgwick, 'the engine was inaccessible and drowns in wet weather'. This first production model is seen outside the company's London showrooms with C. Calcott Reilly, Sales Director, who is about to take the car on a tour of Switzerland, Belgium, and Holland. (NB)

The first Rolls-Royce product to have an all-steel body was the Bentley Mark VI. It and its successor the R-type outsold the coachbuilt Bentleys by 83 to 17 per cent. The bodies were made to Rolls-Royce design by Pressed Steel of Cowley. (NMM)

the latest Italian *Gran Turismos*. In its original form the car was capable of 110 mph but early in 1951 came the more raucous 125 bhp Vantage version, which pushed the top speed up to over 115 mph. Demand for all versions was strong and 410 examples were built before the model was uprated in DB2/4 form in 1953. This differed from the original in having two occasional rear seats so as to appeal to the family man and, progressively, there was an opening tail gate to provide access for luggage. Later, in 1954, the engine's capacity was enlarged to 3 litres. A Mark II version

The most advanced post-war Armstrong Siddeley, the Sapphire was made from 1953 to 1960. This is the 4-litre Star Sapphire, made in the last two years only. It had a twin-carburettor engine giving 165 bhp, and disc brakes on the front wheels. A rival to the Jaguar Mark IX, it was significantly less powerful and the Jaguar had disc brakes all round. At £2,499 the Star Sapphire was £615 more expensive. (NB)

followed in 1955 but demand for the model was slowing and only 190 had been produced by 1957. The majority of DB2s were sold to British customers, although a small but dedi-

cated following began to build up in America, Canada and the Antipodes.

The Aston Martin road car line was being run in tandem with an ambitious sports racing programme which, since 1950, had been in the capable hands of John Wyer, who had the unenviable task – in view of the firm's limited resources – of carrying out David Brown's desire to win the Le Mans 24 hour race. This was finally achieved with the Ted Cutting-designed DBR1 in 1959, when the firm also won the World Sportscar Championship; but in the meantime much effort and resources had been expended to the detriment of the road cars.

In 1955 came a change in the way in which Aston Martin and Lagonda cars were built. Labour disputes had begun to interrupt body production at Feltham with the result that the contract for the 2/4 body was awarded to Mulliners of Birmingham. Then, in June 1954, Mulliner came to an agreement with Standard Triumph for the exclusive allocation of its output, which presented Aston Martin, amongst others, with a supply problem. David Brown resolved this at the end of 1954 by buying Tickford Bodies of Newport Pagnell, Buckinghamshire,

and body production began there in 1955. By 1957, all car assembly had been transferred to the former Tickford works, having first been briefly moved to a David Brown factory at Meltham, Yorkshire. However, the drawing offices, and racing and service departments remained at Feltham.

In 1956 John Wyer was made Aston Martin's general manager. The 2/4's DB4 replacement had been under way since 1954 and he was only too aware that, by 1957, 'for the first time since 1950 we were in the position of having a product which had largely ceased to appeal to the buying public . . . the losses were mounting to the point where even David Brown was looking at them askance.'[69] Serious consideration was even given to closing down the business and putting it on a care and maintenance basis but the risk of dispersing the highly skilled workforce put paid to that idea. Instead Wyer decided on a world tour of Aston Martin dealers. Before doing so, 'we cobbled together the Mark III (2/4 of 1957). This was really nothing more than a cosmetic operation, with some minor improvements, but it at least gave me something to talk about.'[70]

The message Aston Martin's general manager received, if it had been needed, was that a replacement for the 2/4 was urgently required. However, work on what was titled the DB4 (the DB3 of 1951 was a sports racer) had been proceeding apace since 1954, but such was the need for Aston Martin to have a new car to market that it was unveiled well before all the necessary development work had been completed. Wyer's verdict was that it was 'potentially a great sports car . . . completely lacking in detail refinement.'[71]

Prematurely announced at the 1958 Paris and London motor shows, the DB4's engineering was the responsibility of Harold Beach, who had joined the company in 1950. Wyer was insistent that, rather than having it styled in-house, like its predecessor, the work should be undertaken by an Italian *carrozzeria*, and Touring of Milan essayed the superlative lines although the body was built by Aston Martin. An all-new car with no carry-overs from earlier Aston Martins, it was powered by a 3.7-litre six-cylinder twin overhead camshaft aluminium engine, and top speed was approaching 140 mph, which made it one of the world's fastest Grand Tourers. Selling for £3,976 – around £1,000 more than the DB Mark III it replaced – the DB4 was the most expensive model in the company's history, as well as being the best-selling Aston Martin of its day; a record 1,110 examples were built.

Bristols were built to the high standards of the aircraft industry

Production proper did not begin until 1959 but, sadly, the DB4 soon reflected its hectic gestation. It suffered from a variety of problems of which the most serious related to the engine, which succumbed to bearing failure, and thus broken connecting rods, during sustained high speed runs. In due course this shortcoming was resolved, although troubles with the David Brown-built gearbox were never wholly cured and only finally overcome when it was dispensed with altogether: the DB5 was equipped with a German ZF unit. There was also a short-wheelbase GT version of 1959, outwardly similar to the mainstream model, and also its delectable and rare sports racing Zagato-bodied derivative of 1960. The DB4 series survived until 1963 when it was replaced by the greatly improved DB5, which was what the DB4 should have been in the first place.

Aston Martin was not the only British manufacturer to take up the *Gran Turismo* theme in these early post war years. In 1947 the Bristol Aeroplane Company unveiled its first ever car, the 400, a product of the spoils of war in that it was based on designs created in the 1930s by the German BMW company. Its uncon-ventional antecedents came about following an agreement made between Bristol's George White and H. J. Aldington, whose AFN company had built the Frazer Nash car pre-war and, since 1934, had imported the BMW into Britain.

During 1945 Aldington made a number of visits to BMW's bomb-damaged Munich headquarters. On the first of these sorties he returned with one of the six special 328 BMWs that the company had run in the 1940 Mille Miglia, as he believed it could form the basis of the post-war Frazer Nash. This car was later circulated within the British industry and, as already indicated, its lines were reflected in Jaguar's XK120. In July, Bristol took a majority shareholding in Aldington's AFN business and, on a second trip to Germany, undertaken in October at Bristol's behest, he returned with more prizes. These consisted of the drawings and other relevant information relating to the 326, 327 and 328 BMW models. It was on these that the new car was to be based. This was to have been called the Frazer Nash-Bristol but, in April 1947, there was a falling out between White and Aldington; the deal was unscrambled, the Frazer Nash prefix dropped, and the cars became plain Bristol. 'Aldy' then proceeded to revive the Frazer Nash, built in limited numbers between 1948 and 1957, for which Bristol supplied engines and gearboxes.

The Bristols were hand-built to the demanding standards of the aircraft industry, so as much as possible of the car was made at Filton. The 400 represented a heady cocktail of BMW ingredients and was based on the chassis of its best-selling 326 model and the potent 328's six-cylinder cross pushrod 2-litre engine, whilst the 400's bodywork was inspired by that of the 327 Autenrieth coupé, even down to BMW's distinctive radiator grille. The resulting 400 sold for £1,853. Its proven engineering ensured that roadholding was impressive and this 90 mph car was built until 1950, by which

The Jaguar Mark VII was the first of the company's saloons to have completely fresh styling and to use the twin-ohc engine which had been intended for it. This one dates from 1954, the first year for optional overdrive which should have given some improvement to the 16 mpg fuel consumption. (Nick Georgano)

time 700 examples had been completed. Of these, and despite the export orientated climate, only 69 cars were sold abroad, of which 49, or 71 per cent, went to Australia. Belgium came next with four cars and America third with just three.[72] These proportions similarly applied to the 400's successor.

This was the 401, introduced in 1948 and initially sold in tandem with the 400. Mechanically similar to it, the 401's body differed radically and was a modern coupé, which had started life as a Touring design and was skilfully refined by chief engineer Dudley Hobbs and his team into an aerodynamically efficient 100 mph model. Acceleration was also improved and the 401 set the design philosophy for subsequent Bristols. It sold 608 examples and was built until 1953, when it was replaced by the outwardly similar 100 bhp 403 which remained available until 1955 and found 281 customers.

Also announced in 1953 was the two-seater short chassis 404, which was more in the Italian Grand Touring idiom. This was the first Bristol to dispense with the BMW-derived radi-

ator grille and subsequent cars featured its revised air intake. But at £3,542 the market was a limited one and only 51 were built. More successful numerically was the cheaper 404-based Bertone-bodied Arnolt Bristol, created by Chicago car dealer, Stanley 'Wacky' Arnolt, for the American market. At $3,995 the basic open car undercut the standard 404 by a substantial $2,755 and decisively outsold it by nearly three to one: 142 examples were built in 1953 and 1954. Of these, the overwhelming majority (139 cars) were roadsters,[73] the balance being made up of a trio of coupés which were much more expensive. The Arnolt-Bristol was therefore the only representative of the breed to have sold in significant numbers in America.

The 405 of 1954 was a four-door 404 derivative and a less happy visual confection, although 308 had been produced by 1958. The 406 coupé of 1958–61 with all-round disc brakes was more in the 403 idiom but sales were down appreciably, to 182. This was no doubt a reflection of its £4,493 price tag and the fact that the BMW-

derived six, although enlarged to 2.2 litres, dated back to 1936 and was beginning to show its years.

It was in this knowledge that, in the early 1950s, respected Bristol engineer Stuart Tresilian began work on a purpose-designed 2.9-litre twin overhead camshaft six-cylinder alloy engine, which was intended to replace the BMW unit. Designated Type 160, it was to power a new Bristol 220 and, by early 1956, had grown to 3.6 litres.[74] Sadly, its development coincided with a downturn in the affairs of the British aircraft industry, of which Bristol represented a significant part. The company therefore had to reappraise all its activities and, sadly, the all-important Type 160 engine intended for the next generation of Bristols was a casualty. If the car line was to continue, the only alternative for the firm was to adopt a proprietary engine, although at the price of some dilution of personality. However, the 2.2-litre six continued to power the 406 model until 1961, but since then all Bristols have used a Chrysler V8 engine and its attendant automatic transmission. A secondary impact of this more stringent fiscal climate was a change in corporate status. Hitherto, the vehicles had been built by the Car Division of the Bristol Aeroplane Company, but in January 1956 Bristol Cars was established as its separate, though wholly-owned, subsidiary.

In addition to powering its own cars, Bristol also sold the potent and versatile six-cylinder engine to other manufacturers. The Cooper-Bristol showed its worth on the race track from 1952, whilst its best-known application in a road car was as an alternative power unit in the AC Ace roadster and its Aceca coupé derivative. These models

The second of the 'Docker Daimlers', a two-door coupé by Hooper on the straight-eight DE36 chassis, at the 1952 Earls Court Show. The paintwork was in two tones of powder blue and grey, the lighter panels being covered with hand-painted four-leaf clovers. The lizard-skin trimmed interior was double glazed and thermal insulation was fitted to the roof. (NMM)

were, however, a world away from AC Cars's first post-war product, in the shape of the elegant but dated 2-litre Saloon which appeared in 1947. This seemed an appropriate product from a firm with a factory located in Thames Ditton, Surrey, and it was powered by AC's long-running six-cylinder single overhead camshaft engine. But as time went on it became increasingly expensive and, by 1952, cost £1,899. This was for a two-door car which lacked independent front suspension. Nevertheless, it lingered on until 1958, by which time some 1,300 had been built.

By then the Ace had been in production for five years. It revived a pre-war model name and had appeared in 1953, though it was not an AC design. Based on a Bristol-engined sports racer, created by John Tojeiro and campaigned with great success by Vincent Davidson, it featured a ladder type chassis with all independent transverse leaf suspension, and the open two-seater body resembled Ferrari's famous *barchetta*. AC's Charles Hurlock and his nephew Derek liked what they saw, took over the design, and agreed to pay Tojeiro a royalty of £5 per car. Power came from the faithful AC six, in which form the car was capable of a little over 100 mph. Early in 1956 the Bristol engine became available as a desirable option, which pushed the Ace's top speed to beyond 115 mph with acceleration to match. It was also the most popular of the two units and accounted for 466 cars, compared with 226 fitted with AC's own engine.

From mid-1961, when Bristol decided to discontinue its six, the 2.6-litre Ford Zephyr engine was offered but only fitted to 38 cars. The Ace survived until 1963 to form the basis of the formidable Ford V8-powered Cobra. Initiated by American racing driver Carroll Shelby, this was yet another reminder of AC's membership of the serendipity school of marketing, which proved to be successful in the short-term, but in the longer term could not be considered as a substitute for a coherent product strategy.

The coupé version of the Ace was the Aceca of 1955. It was similarly offered with both engines but was less popular: 320 were built. There was also the four-seater Greyhound of 1959 which was usually Bristol-powered, but only 80 had been completed by the time that production ceased in 1963.

One of the reasons that AC lasted longer than many of its contemporaries in the specialist sector (it survived until 1984) was that it built its own coachwork. This all-important degree of self-sufficiency meant that it was not dependent on an outside supplier for its bodies, which were, in any event, the products of a dwindling industry. By contrast, as befitted its elevated position in the market place, the Coventry-based Alvis company never possessed a body shop. Like Rolls-Royce, it only produced its cars in chassis form and they were then bodied by a specialist coachbuilder. This inheritance was to haunt Alvis in the post-war years and was a major factor in the firm ceasing car production in 1967.

A further all-important factor to the demise of the Alvis car was rooted in a decision taken in 1933, when the firm decided to diversify into the aero engine business. A prototype unit, the compact nine-cylinder Leonides radial, was built in 1936, but the outbreak of the Second World War interrupted production, which did not begin until 1947. However, the firm gained invaluable experience during the hostilities when it undertook the demanding task of manufacturing and overhauling Rolls-Royce aero engines. It was thus well-equipped, in every sense, to begin the production of its own, and the Leonides was soon in demand for use in helicopters and light aircraft.

Despite these developments, in July 1945 the firm decided to remain in the car business even though it lacked a bodyshop. A range of six-cylinder cars produced before the war was discontinued and it was reduced to a single model in the form of the TA14, marketed as the Fourteen, in 1946. Essentially an updated version of the 12/70 introduced for the 1938 season, its manufacture only became possible when, following a tip-off in a local pub, the tooling was found by an employee in the bottom of a water tank![75] Still retaining a separate chassis, the Fourteen's saloon body was by Mulliners of Birmingham. Powered by a 1.9-litre four-cylinder overhead valve engine, it was well engineered and built in the best Alvis traditions, and capable of a brisk 75 mph. Made until 1950, production in a seller's market amounted to 3,311 units, which was a record for the marque.

The Fourteen was a traditionally British offering and Alvis needed a car more suitable for export markets. The outcome, in 1948, was a sporting version in the shape of the TB14 with an extravagantly styled open two-seater body built by Panelcraft, its lines apparently the work of a Belgian coachbuilder. The traditional Alvis radiator was dispensed with and replaced by a chromium grille, completing a package which the English Midlands imagined the Americans wanted. But demand was limited: just 100 were built.

In 1946 Alvis had a new chairman in the shape of John Parkes, who had a background in the aircraft rather than the motor industry, having been general manager of de Havilland's airscrew and engine division. He approved the creation of the first all-new Alvis car of the post-war years, in the shape of the TC 21, which appeared at the 1950 Geneva Motor Show. Like its predecessor, this was a rather upright, old-fashioned Mulliner-built saloon, still with separate front wings and running boards, which concealed a new 3-litre six-cylinder engine. It was capable of a smooth, flexible 85 mph, despite weighing over a ton and a half. Alvis made efforts to pep up the car's rather dowdy image by announcing, at the 1953 London Motor Show, the 108 bhp Grey Lady version which was capable of 100 mph, although at the expense of an excessive amount of wind noise.

Then, in 1954, Alvis literally experienced a body blow when Standard Triumph obtained its commitment from Mulliner for its entire output. This move struck at the very heart of Alvis's car manufacturing programme, a dilemma which, as we have seen, it shared with Aston Martin. Matters were made worse at the end of the year when Tickford, which built a drop-head coupé version of the TC 21, was sold to David Brown as part of his strategy to keep Aston Martin in the car business. Thankfully, the loss of its body supplier had little impact on Alvis's financial position. Despite only building a handful of cars in the 1954–5 financial year, it attained a record net profit of £150,000.[76] This was on account of a strong demand for its aero engines at home and abroad, the existing unit having been joined by the larger Leonides Major in 1951. The firm had also successfully diversified into the military vehicle market and, in 1952, had launched the Rolls-Royce-engined Saracen armoured car.

The Alvis motor car therefore seemed destined for extinction by the end of 1954, had it not been for the activities of the Swiss-based Graber coachbuilding concern. At the 1955 Paris motor show it unveiled a lovely coupé body on the TC 21 chassis, the lines of which were as elegant and assured as the Mulliner saloon had been archaic. The Graber-bodied car, powered by the more potent Grey Lady engine, was also exhibited at the London show on the Alvis stand; otherwise the firm would have had little to display. What was designated the TC/108/G (the 'G' being for Graber) was thus elevated to the status of a factory model. At £2,621, it was a

The Aston Martin DB2 combined an exciting 2.6-litre twin-ohc engine with the Frank Feeley-styled coupé body reminiscent of an Italian Gran Turismo. *This one is competing in an Aston Martin Owners' Club event at Silverstone in 1954.* (NMM)

*Colin Chapman, seen here in 1972, was the only builder of kit cars who went on to make successful complete cars and Formula One winners. He spurred countless others to emulate him, most of whom fell out one by one, lacking his 'inimitable combination of determination, engineering knowledge, business acumen and luck' (*Complete Encyclopaedia of Motorcars*). (NMM)*

substantial £800 more than the Mulliner built saloon. A Graber styled car was again displayed at the 1956 show but its coachwork hailed not from Berne, but from Loughborough. There Willowbrook, which built bus and coach bodies, took over the coachbuilding contract under a licensing agreement, but the arrangement proved to be an unhappy one. The 3-litre's price soared to £3,452 and only 16 examples were built.

In March 1958 Alvis announced that Rolls-Royce's Park Ward subsidiary was taking over its body construction and the resultant car, the TD21, appeared at the 1958 Motor Show. Significantly, the price was reduced to £2,993 and the improved aerodynamics of the Graber design ensured that it was capable of a civilized 110 mph. Produced in this form until 1963, by which time 1,098 had been built, the model survived in its ultimate TF guise until manufacture

ceased in 1967. And with it went the Alvis car line.

This was because, in 1955, John Parkes had cancelled what would have been its successor and, once again, bodywork was a factor in the project's undoing. In 1952 he had secured the services of Alec Issigonis, already a rising star within the industry for his best-selling Morris Minor. He produced a characteristically distinctive offering in the form of an outwardly conventional four-door saloon with an interconnected suspension system of the type which ultimately appeared on the 1962 Morris 1100. Power came from a 3½-litre alloy V8 engine, and it was also available in 1.7-litre four-cylinder form. These were respectively designated TA 350 and TA175 and the intention was to produce a combined total of 5,000 cars a year. However, Pressed Steel quoted an unacceptable £900 per hull and Alvis would have needed to build a new factory in which to produce the car. The project was therefore scrapped after £76,000 had been expended on it.[77] Issigonis returned to BMC and was soon at work on the design of the Mini. But the cancellation of this fascinating Alvis sealed the company's fate as a car manufacturer.

Back in 1933 Alvis was in the vanguard of British car makers in offering the refinement of independent front suspension. However, many miles from the industry's epicentre, in the Worcestershire town of Malvern, the Morgan Motor Company had been producing its cars with such a system since 1910. It had been applied to the firm's famous three-wheelers and subsequently to its first conventional car, the much needed 4/4 (indicating its four wheels and four cylinders), which had appeared in 1936. Initially Coventry Climax engined, since 1939 the model had been powered by a 1.3-litre Standard Ten based overhead valve unit.

With the coming of the post-war years, like many of its contemporaries Morgan continued to produce its existing models but, unlike other

manufacturers who subsequently updated their products, Morgan made no apparent attempt to do the same. Its cars thus remained visually wedded to the 1930s, a policy that it has consistently applied ever since. Today the Morgan has acquired so-called classic status, but for the first 15 years or so after the war the firm would surely have gone out of business had it not been for the government-led export drive.

It was for this reason that, in 1948, Morgan established agencies abroad, in France and America.[78] Whilst the 4/4's traditional styling was welcomed, particularly across the Atlantic, the 1,172 cc Ford-engined three-wheeler was virtually ignored, probably because it did not benefit from the tax advantage it enjoyed in Britain. The firm had no alternative but to discontinue the model, and this occurred in 1952. Post-war production, which began in 1946, stood at a mere 252 cars.

Manufacture of the 4/4 continued, with the car's specification remaining essentially unchanged, until 1950; by this time a respectable 1,084 examples had been built. The model was discontinued because, in 1948, Standard had dropped all its other cars to produce just one, the export-conscious 2-litre Vanguard. This meant supplies of the 1.8-litre four would soon dry up and, whilst the larger capacity engine was also made available to Morgan, the 4/4 would require some modification to accommodate it. The model was therefore replaced by the Vanguard-powered Plus 4.

Outwardly similar to its predecessor, the Plus 4's wheelbase was four inches longer than the 4/4's and, whilst it could be wound up to over 80 mph, the suspension – despite its forward independence – could be unforgiving. Listed until 1958, from 1954 it was overshadowed by the more potent alternative Vanguard-based 1.9-litre TR2 engine, and the car's appearance was simultaneously improved by the introduction of a new, cowled radiator which replaced the long established flat-fronted one. The Plus 4 benefited from TR engine updates until the arrival, in 1967, of the six-cylinder TR5. By 1961 TR-engined Plus 4 production amounted to 2,237 cars.

The no frills 4/4 line was revived for 1956 after a five year hiatus and, at £698, it was the cheapest sports car on the British market until the arrival in 1958 of the Austin Healey Sprite, which undercut it by £80. This Series II car used Ford's 1,172 cc side valve four from the 100E, although its three-speed gearbox was a less desirable inheritance, and the model remained engined thus until 1960. But demand was weak; only 386 cars were built in the five years to 1960.

The firm's founder, H. F. S. Morgan, died in 1959, so missing the firm's 50th anniversary, but his son Peter had taken over as deputy governing director in 1951. In truth, the decade proved to be a difficult one for the company as the British public seemed to have deserted the Morgan's outdated styling and basic specifications. Peter Morgan has recalled some disappointing motor shows at this time, when he was 'left all alone on his stand for hours at a time',[79] although interest began to revive at the end of the decade. The only bright prospect was provided by overseas sales: in 1960, no less than 85 per cent of output went to American buyers.[80] But when, in 1954, Peter Morgan was approached by Sir John Black with a view to Standard buying the company, he wisely declined, and Morgan survives intact and independent to this day.

The London-based Allard company was less lucky in that it built its last car in 1955. Hill climb and trials enthusiast Sydney Allard had begun small-scale production of Ford-based specials in 1937 but only 12 were built before the war ended this activity. With the coming of peace, in 1945 the Allard Motor Company was duly registered and car production began near Clapham Common in South London early in 1946. From the outset the company's cars possessed the distinctive 'Allard look', which meant full-width front wings with integral headlamps and an oblong, heavily slatted waterfall grille. Power units were courtesy of Ford, mainly its 3.6-litre V8 engine, and the transverse leaf suspension came from the same source although, at the front, an LMB divided beam was employed. Allard's first model was the open two-seater K1, capable of an unrefined but exhilarating 85 mph plus, and a total of 151 examples were built by 1948. It was followed by the M1, which accounted for 500 units and remained available until 1950.

Colin Chapman (19) was deciding what to do with a 1930 Austin Seven

These and a handful of other models are little remembered today outside the enthusiastic confines of the Allard Owners' Club but the exception was the charismatic J2 of 1950, which was intended for use on both road and track. It resulted from a visit by the company's general manager, Reg Canham, to America where he was able to witness the growing popularity of sports car racing. In 1946 the company had produced a J1 competition car and its J2 successor had a new, lower, open two-seater body with a cowled nose that was expressly created for the transatlantic market. It was mechanically similar to its predecessors, apart from being coil sprung at the front and having a de Dion rear axle. The engine was still a Ford V8 although it was the 4.3-litre Mercury overhead valve conversion. The reality was that the model demanded a modern American V8 but currency restrictions prevented Allard from importing it in quantity.

The J2 was expensive. It sold for £1,050 in Britain, which reflected its hand-built status, and was £62 more than the Jaguar XK120, so exposing the vulnerability of the concept. Nevertheless, the car was in instant demand and Allard found itself in the situation of producing a popular model with limited facilities that prevented the manufacture of more than one a week.

American J2 owners were better off, the cars being exported less engines, and then fitted with one of the current range of new overhead valve V8s, usually by Cadillac and Oldsmobile though Chrysler and Lincoln units also featured. In 1951 the J2 was followed by the J2X which, for American customers, was powered by Chrysler's famous 5.4-litre 'hemi', the most powerful V8 of its day.

Despite its impact, there were only 173 examples of the J2 series family. The best-selling Allard was, by contrast, a closed car. The 3.6-litre P1 of 1949 was a two-door saloon which sold 559 units. Sydney Allard drove one in the 1952 Monte Carlo Rally, which he won, this being the first occasion a manufacturer driving his own car had triumphed in the event. Ironically, by this time Allard was in decline; it only survived for a further three years and the final model, the Ford Zephyr/Consul-engined Palm Beach of 1953, accounted for just 76 cars. By 1955 Allard, and many of its low-production sporting contemporaries that had flowered in the seller's market of the early post-war years, wilted in the wake of sure-footed opposition from, in particular, William Lyons's potent, value-for-money Jaguars.

There were, however, exceptions. In 1947, on the other side of the Thames in the London borough of Hornsey, 19-year-old Colin Chapman was deciding what to do with the 1930 Austin Seven fabric saloon left on his hands following an ill-fated sortie into the second-hand car business. He decided to convert it into a Special and, once the original upright body was dispensed with, it was replaced by a carefully-engineered open four-seater one of alloy-bonded plywood mounted on a stressed framework, with triple bulkheads, designed on aircraft principles to reinforce the Austin's flexible frame. After completion in 1948, what was now OX 9292 was registered as a Lotus,[81] so called because Colin called his girlfriend, Hazel Williams, 'my little Lotus blossom'.

Anthony Colin Bruce Chapman, who in 1948 left University College, London, with a B.Sc. engineering degree, was a supremely talented, restless ruthless, demanding engineer who drove himself to the limit and expected a similar commitment from his employees. With fellow enthusiast Michael Allen, in 1952 he established Lotus Engineering in the stables of Hornsey's Railway Hotel (run by his father). From these unlikely surroundings there emerged, in 1953, the first production Lotus in the form of the Mark VI, although it was sold mostly in kit form. But Allen soon departed and, in February 1953, aided by a £25 loan from Hazel – who in 1954 became Mrs Colin Chapman – the business was reformed as the Lotus Engineering Company *Limited*.

The Mark VI was mostly powered by engines of the owner's choice and it soon made a considerable impact on the club racing scene. In 1955 Chapman left his full-time job – as a constructional engineer with British Aluminium – to fully devote himself to Lotus. He had, in 1954, also set up Team Lotus to produce his sports racing Formula 2 and, ultimately, Formula 1 cars. After decades in the doldrums, in the late 1950s Cooper spearheaded the revival of Britain's grand prix fortunes and provided a momentum which was triumphantly maintained by Lotus in the following decade.

Most of the vehicles that Lotus built were intended for the circuit – and the one exception – the stark Seven of 1957, usually powered by the 948 cc BMC A Series engine was for the fearless. Its first significant road car was the Elite, announced at the 1957 London Motor Show. This was a model that began life in 1955 as the Mark 14 and provisionally titled the Lynx. Chapman ambitiously decreed that this was to be the world's first fibreglass monocoque. Styled by his

chartered accountant friend, Peter Kirwan-Taylor, it had to be a coupé rather than a roadster as it was to possess wind-cheating properties, and the shape was further refined by aerodynamicist Frank Costin and Ford stylist John Frayling. Power came from a 1.2-litre Coventry Climax engine and suspension was all independent, by coil springs and wishbones with Chapman struts at the rear.

Weighing only 1,484 lbs, the Elite proved to be a sensational if raucous performer capable of 115 mph and possessed of the leech-like handling qualities for which the marque was already renowned. However, it was 14 months before the first example was delivered, in December 1958, to band leader Chris Barber. Soon afterwards, in mid-1959, Lotus moved from its cramped north London premises to a larger factory in Cheshunt, Hertfordshire. The Elite, which was available in kit form from late in 1961, lasted until 1962, but by then Chapman calculated that he was losing £100 on every one he built . . .[82]

Some 988 Elites were produced and the Mark VI Lotus, that had survived until 1956, accounted for about 100 examples. Owners invariably opted for Ford's robust 1,172 cc side valve engine which, in essence, dated back to 1932. However, the new Consul and Zephyr models that Ford introduced in 1950 were, by contrast, some of the most advanced popular cars in the world.

Ford focused on finance, model planning and marketing

Because of Ford Britain's limited engineering resources, these cars were designed by its American parent, and represented a significant number of 'firsts' for the Dagenham company. Not only did they feature unitary hulls, but the abolition of the horsepower tax meant that manufacturers were no longer restricted from using oversquare engines and the 1950 Ford

featured them. In addition overhead rather than side valves were employed. The cars also used, for the first time, the now universal, cost-conscious MacPherson strut suspension at the front, the work of Earle S. MacPherson, Ford's vice president of engineering. On the debit side were three-speed column change gearboxes and, despite the modern specifications, the perpetuation of vacuum-operated windscreen wipers although, thankfully, the long running six-volt electrics were replaced by a 12-volt system.

The Consul and Zephyr were bodily and mechanically related, which saved costs and production time. The four-cylinder 1.5-litre Consul was the best-seller, with 231,481 built, and the slightly longer 2.3-litre Zephyr was, in effect, the Consul with two extra cylinders. In 1954 this six-cylinder car was joined by its more expensive Zodiac stable-mate. These popular models were updated in Mark II forms in 1956, with the capacity of the Consul enlarged to 1.7 litres and the Zephyr/Zodiac family to 2.5 litres which made them 90 mph cars. All survived until 1962.

The original Consul line was echoed in the smaller 100E two-door Anglia of 1954, although this used a side valve engine rather than an overhead valve one, which retained the 1,172 cc capacity of the earlier four and was extensively redesigned. This car, along with the four-door Prefect, was Dagenham's really big seller of the 1950s and accounted for a total of 449,395 units built between 1954 and 1959. It will be remembered that Ford had also kept the elderly Popular in production and this was made until 1959, by which time 155,350 cars had been completed. The Popular name was then transferred to the 100E model and a further 126,115 examples manufactured until Ford finally bade farewell to side valve power in 1962.

Whilst production was running at record levels during the 1950s Ford Britain was gradually gaining its engineering independence, and a significant step along this road came in 1956 when it established a research and development centre in Birmingham. Located as it was in Thames-side Essex, Ford was many miles away from the industry's heartland. This new facility, located in a former glass works, was sited so that the company could tap engineering talent in the Midlands.

In 1954 Ford initiated its first five-year development plan and the £75 million investment was intended to increase Dagenham's floor space by half as much again. Its principal feature was a new Paint, Trim and Assembly shop, opened in 1959. Significantly, this was financed by reinvesting profits of which, between 1947 and 1956, Ford retained 79 per cent, compared with BMC's 68 per cent.[83]

In addition to updating its products, Ford also began to change its management structure, with greater emphasis being placed on finance, model planning, and marketing. In the 1950s many of the staff had been with the company since its days in Manchester, a fact which was noted by John Barber, who in 1955 joined Ford from the

Ministry of Supply where he had been Principal of the Central Finance Department. Destined to become the firm's finance director in 1962, he remembers that 'when I joined Ford it was a fairly old-fashioned company and the finance department was full of little men in green eyeshades.'[84] Although a policy of graduate recruitment had been introduced, Barber recalls that by the mid-1950s there were still very few of them, 'about five or six; Terry Beckett, who was Patrick Hennessy's personal assistant, was one.' Following input from America, Barber 'decided we needed to move from having little more than a recording function to making a positive contribution to running the company. I set up the analytical functions at Ford and we hired a lot of high calibre people . . . Then we set up a formal graduate training scheme. They were the young financial analysts in their twenties who formed the new philosophy in Ford.'[85]

But whilst Ford changed, the British Motor Corporation chose not to. Like much of British industry at this time, BMC was a company run by engineers

who were preoccupied with product and possessed of a barely disguised dislike of accountants and marketing. Little wonder that one of chairman Leonard Lord's oft repeated aphorisms was 'build bloody good cars and they'll sell themselves.' During the inter-war years, Lord had gained the reputation of being one of the country's outstanding production engineers, but his management style was abrasive and, although he was capable of individual acts of kindness, he was fearful of rivals. In 1956 he summarily dismissed Joe Edwards, one of the Corporation's most able managers, accusing him of wanting his job. Edwards had served 28 years with Austin, and Lord peremptorily sacked him whilst they were having a pre-lunch drink. As Edwards later reflected, the ensuing meal was a quiet one,[86] but within months he became managing director of Pressed Steel with BMC as his most important customer.

Such a corporate environment was hardly conducive to good management and, significantly, George Harriman, Lord's long-standing heir apparent, owed his entire career to his friend and mentor. One of Harriman's contemporaries has recalled that: 'George was one of the nicest men you could wish to meet but he did what he was told. That was why Len Lord liked him.'[87] Following Lord's retirement in 1961, it would fall to Harriman to run the British Motor Corporation throughout that more turbulent decade when the perception grew within the industry and, more significantly, governmental circles, that he was not up to the job.

But following his own angry departure from Cowley in 1936, Leonard Lord would never have countenanced a Morris executive running BMC, if indeed there had been one of sufficient

The Lotus Elite was the world's first car with monocoque fibreglass construction. It was also the first closed Lotus. The price of weather protection was a very noisy interior. This one is competing at Silverstone in 1961. (NMM)

calibre to do so. The reality was that the so-called 'merger' of 1952 that brought the Corporation into existence was nothing of the sort. It was a take-over by Austin of Morris and although Lord Nuffield was, ostensibly, chairman, he retired at the end of the year, became honorary president, and took no further part in BMC's affairs. This allowed Leonard Lord (knighted 1954) to take over with Harriman, who had joined Austin in 1923, as his deputy. As if this was not enough, Lord was particularly hostile to those Morris directors who had opposed the merger. He sought to humiliate former vice chairman of the Nuffield Organisation, Reginald Hanks, and even used public occasions to criticize Morris Motors and all its works.[88]

This antipathy to Morris – 'those buggers in the country,' Lord used to bark from BMC's Longbridge head-quarters – reached new heights in 1952 when, in addition to BMC's existing five marques, he added yet another: that of Austin-Healey. The make was destined to win friends aplenty on both sides of the Atlantic but it does not detract from the fact that BMC already possessed a marque with an enviable racing and sporting pedigree in the shape of MG, the initials of which stand for Morris Garages.

Nevertheless, in 1952 Lord held an unofficial design competition for a corporate sports car to cater for the growing demand for open two-seaters in America. He commissioned proto-types from Healey, in-house MG, and Jensen, which did work for Austin. The winner was the Austin-engined Healey 100 which appeared at the 1952 London Motor Show and, overnight, became the *Austin*-Healey. MG's entry was thus sidelined; it was left with the ageing TF model, but its 1952 proto-type EX 175 finally appeared three years later, in 1955, as the MGA. Powered for the first time by an Austin, as opposed to a Morris engine, the 1½-litre A was essayed by MG's talented newly-appointed chief engineer Sydney Enever, although he had been unofficially doing the job for

years. This was because, in 1954, BMC gave permission for MG's Abingdon drawing office to be reopened. Hitherto MG design had been vested in Cowley but, for the first time since 1935, MG was once again responsible for creating its own cars. This corporate confidence was not misplaced. Under the impressive leadership of general manager John Thornley, the MGA endured until 1962 and, with over 100,000 built, it was the world's best-selling sports car, with 80 per cent of output crossing the Atlantic.

89% of the new Austin-Healeys were sold in America

Although this first generation of Austin-Healeys was built in smaller numbers, a slightly higher proportion, close to 89 per cent, was sold in America. The cars took their name from Donald Healey, a tough-minded Cornishman and outstanding competition driver, who had won the 1931 Monte Carlo Rally in an Invicta. He joined Riley in 1933, subsequently became technical director of Triumph and, after the war, decided to build cars under his own name at a factory he established at Warwick which was within easy reach of the industrial Midlands. He insisted that, like the Invicta, the Healey should be a 100 mph car, which is why it was powered by a 104 bhp 2½-litre Riley engine. For a time it was the world's fastest closed car, an example having attained 104 mph on the Milan to Como autostrada in 1946.

Initially produced in open Westland and closed Elliot forms, the Healey's hand-built status ensured that it was expensive. The Elliot, for instance, sold for £1,597 on the marque's 1946 arrival, when car production was running at five a week. Healey was badly hit in 1947 when purchase tax doubled on those models costing over £1,000 and such legislation, coupled with the regulations and form-filling of these years, made it a difficult time

for any car maker, let alone a small, newly-established one. Further designs in a similar vein followed but, by the early 1950s, Donald Healey recognised that he 'required a faster, lighter, cheaper car. Money was always tight and I could see us folding up if we did not produce a new model.'[89] The outcome was the Healey 100 which not only met these criteria, but also had the virtue of using Austin's redundant 2.6-litre engine from the ill-conceived Atlantic.

When the 100 was chosen as BMC's corporate sports car, there was some compensation for the West Bromwich-based Jensen Motors because it was awarded the contract to build the bodies. Richard and Alan Jensen had established their coachbuilding busi-ness in 1934 and began limited car production in 1936 using mostly American engines in the form of the Ford V8, Nash straight-eight, and Lincoln V12 units.

After the war Jensen produced the curious heavy-weight PW saloon of 1946, with a 3.9-litre Meadows eight-cylinder engine, although this was quickly sidelined to be replaced by the Nash one. Ultimately the PW was powered by Austin's 4-litre A135 six and, in all, about 15 were sold. This model was followed by the Interceptor of 1950 with a body which was, effec-tively, a scaled up version of the follow-ing year's Austin A40 Sports hull, which Jensen also built. It was this car that formed the basis of the distinctive fibreglass-bodied 541 grand tourer which was the best-selling Jensen of its day – by the time that production ceased in 1963, a total of 533 had been produced. The original 541 was followed, in 1957, by the greatly-improved 541R, which was longer and roomier than the original and provided comfortable 120 mph motor-ing. But these cars were a sideline when compared with some 72,000 Austin-Healey bodies which Jensen produced for BMC. For this work it assembled steel panels, pressed by Dowty Boulton Paul at nearby Wolverhampton, with the completed shells being then dispatched to Austin's Longbridge factory for final assembly.

The Austin-Healey 100 sold in relatively modest numbers, with 14,012 built between 1953 and 1956. As its name indicated, top speed was around 100 mph or perhaps a little more. No doubt to present a greater challenge to the likes of Jaguar, in 1956 the four-cylinder engine was replaced by BMC's 2.6-litre six and the model renamed the 100/6. Unfortunately its acceleration and top speed proved to be inferior to that of the car it replaced. However, the model came of age in 1959 when the engine was enlarged to 3 litres, so giving birth to the long-legged 3000, on a good day capable of over 110 mph.

Donald Healey had established a good rapport with Leonard Lord who used to quip: 'Here comes Healey – better sew up your pockets.'[90] Consequently in 1956, at BMC's request, the Healey company designed the Sprite, created in the spirit of the pre-war Austin Seven Nippy. Its cheeky, protruding 'frog-eye' head-lamps imbued it with plenty of personality and there was no shortage of buyers when this spartan two-seater was unveiled in 1958. Well priced at £678, the 948 cc Sprite could achieve 85 mph. Despite its basic specification, this Mark I car was destined to be the best-seller of the breed, 38,999 having been sold by the time it was succeeded, in 1961, by its more outwardly conventional Mark II successor.

Prior to 1957 all Austin-Healeys were assembled at Longbridge but, at the end of that year, this work was transferred to the MG factory at Abingdon, where, initially, they were built alongside MG's own MGA. This meant that the completion of some BMC saloons was moved to Cowley and Longbridge.

By their very nature, and despite being popular sports cars, these Austin-Healeys and MGs were essentially low production models, dependent on BMC's saloon car line for most of their mechanical components.

At the time of the Corporation's 1952 creation, saloons inevitably accounted for the overwhelming majority of the 14 models listed – nine Nuffield and five Austin – that, collectively, were powered by nine different engines. Leonard Lord, with his production engineering background, wasted little time in phasing out the older units, which happened to be the Morris ones. The 803 cc overhead valve four used in the 1950 Austin A30 was designated the A Series engine, while the four cylinder 1,200 cc unit, first used in the Austin A40 of 1948, became the B Series. However, the 2.6-litre six of 1956 was purpose-designed and the work of Morris Engines. Gearboxes and axles were similarly reduced to a core number.

Demand was such that the millionth Morris Minor was built in 1960

In 1952 BMC's A Series engine found its way under the bonnet of the Morris Minor when it replaced the existing side valve unit. The pre-war four had been a weak point and the transplanted engine greatly improved the car. The Minor was destined to be the Corporation's best-selling model of the 1950s and, in the first instance, 269,838 examples of this Series II version were built. This total includes a Traveller estate car, introduced for 1954, with a distinctive composite wood-framed and metal body. In 1957 the Minor, along with other BMC products, benefited from an enlarged 948 cc engine, becoming the Minor 1000, and a further 544,048 were produced by 1962. Demand was such that the millionth Morris Minor was built in December 1960, although this total took account of a van version, announced in 1953. It was the first British car to achieve this figure despite Leonard Lord and Austin stylist Dick Burzi having created a replacement in the mid-1950s. But the public kept on buying the Minor, its successor instead emerging in 1957 as

the Riley 1.5 and Wolseley 1500, so saving these two ailing marques from extinction. These models only lasted until 1965 although, for its part, the Minor survived until 1971.

This all-important rationalization of components was not, alas, extended to BMC's myriad of factories. These were mostly in the Nuffield sector and the inheritance of a business that had grown up piecemeal fashion during the inter-war years. The operational inefficiencies of such a scatter of facilities speak for themselves and dramatically contrasted with Ford which, in the 1950s, possessed a single car manufacturing plant in the form of the highly-integrated Dagenham works.

What was easier to achieve was for BMC to standardize its model range, once existing designs had been seen through. So it was not until 1958, six years after the merger, that the first true corporate car appeared. This was the new A40 with its novel body styled by the Italian Pinin Farina concern. At the time practically all cars were distinguished by a protruding rear boot but the A40 was one of the first instances of the so called 'two box' look which anticipated the modern hatch-back. This A Series-engined model survived until 1967, by which time some 340,000 had been built. There was no Morris version but the second Pinin Farina body, which appeared in late 1959, was a larger conventional four-door saloon, distinguished by fashionable rear fins, and carrying all the BMC marque names. The era of badge engineering had arrived.

Rather than drastically rationalize the BMC range to Austin and Morris core models, the Corporation had decided to maintain customer and dealer loyalty by retaining the Riley, MG, and Wolseley names. All were variously powered by the Corporation's B and C Series engines and the Austin and Morris versions, in particular, established a loyal following. There were, in all, about 296,000 Morris Oxfords and some 371,000 Austin Cambridges built but the other models were, by contrast, poor sellers.

Only 29,414 MG Magnettes were made, and there were just 25,091 cars in the Riley 4/68 and 4/72 family, but 87,841 examples of Wolseley's well equipped 15/60 and 16/60. These comfortable but heavy and increasingly uncompetitive saloons began to lose their appeal from the mid-1960s, although they lingered on until 1971.

Like Ford, in 1954 BMC announced an expansion programme but, once again, it was Longbridge which benefited from the £10 million investment. Yet Cowley's manufacturing facilities dated back, in essence, to the 1930s and had been installed by Leonard Lord himself when he was running Morris Motors. This was just one of the factors in BMC averaging a profit of £44 per vehicle in 1959, which compared unfavourably with Ford's £102.

In 1960 BMC built over half a million cars for the first time and pre-tax profits were also a record at £26.9 million. But impressive as these figures were, the Corporation's share of British car production fell from Austin and Morris's combined 43.4 per cent in 1946 to 36.5 per cent in 1960. What BMC clearly required, the Morris Minor excepted, was a really big seller. For its part, Ford's proportion had more than doubled from 14.4 to 30 per cent over the same period. Its profits, of £33.7 million, were the highest in the industry and £6.8 million greater than BMC's for building some 182,000 less cars.

Ford's 1953 purchase of Briggs Motor Bodies produced its own response at Longbridge, BMC promptly buying the Midlands firm of Fisher and Ludlow which built many of its bodies. This caused problems for Standard Triumph, another of Fisher and Ludlow's customers, which was told in no uncertain terms by the Corporation's chairman that, once existing contracts were seen through, BMC could no longer supply bodies to a competitor. This was just one of the many problems facing 37-year old Alick Dick who, early in 1954, had been appointed

The Austin-Healey 100 with the two men who made it into a success, its creator Donald Healey (right) and Leonard Lord, Chairman of Austin. The 100 provided a worthy home for the big four engine, previously seen in the less than successful Atlantic. (BMIHT/Rover)

Standard's new managing director.

Dick had been made deputy managing director in 1951, and was personal assistant for eight years to Sir John Black, whose departure had not been voluntary. Black's increasingly dictatorial management style, coupled with extravagant mood swings, came to a head at his house on New Year's Day 1954. There Sir John was confronted by the entire Standard Triumph board which presented him with a typed letter which stated that he was retiring on grounds of ill health. Faced with this unanimous ultimatum, 58-year old Black had little choice but to sign.[91]

Alick Dick was faced with a difficult job. Standard was the smallest of the 'big five' car makers. In 1946 it had an 11.6 per cent share of British car production but this had slumped to 8.6 by 1953. Then it built a mere 44,400 cars, and a significant contribution to its £1.6 million pre-tax profits had come from its Ferguson tractor production. This was to stand at 750,000 units built between 1948 and

1960. Dick was the first to recognize that, such was Standard's size, its future was dependent on it finding a partner to expand its manufacturing facilities and model base. After his appointment he wasted little time in contacting Spencer Wilks, his opposite number at Rover, to discuss such an association. United Motors Corporation or Consolidated Motors were contemplated as suitable names for the joint company, but Rover was fearful of Standard's profits forecast and, by July 1954, the discussions had foundered. The other obvious candidate was Rootes. Talks between the two firms began in the spring of 1955 and continued for the next 18 months but stalled, in April 1958, when Dick realised that the proposed board of directors was skewed in Rootes's favour.[92]

Soon afterwards, Standard's managing director became embroiled in discussions with Massey-Ferguson, the business which had been formed following the take-over, in 1953, of

The Pinin Farina-styled Austin A40 was hailed as a new design when it appeared in 1958, but few realized its significance. By getting away from the 'three-box' layout of traditional saloons and incorporating an opening door at the back, it was a precursor of the ubiquitous hatchback of today. 340,000 were made between 1958 and 1967. (Nick Georgano)

various locations could come together like pieces of a jigsaw. This model, which eventually appeared in 1959 as the Triumph Herald, did not arrive a moment too soon.

Sir John Black's one-model policy for Standard had come to an end with the arrival, in 1953, of the 803 cc Eight, which was aimed at Austin A30/Morris Minor territory. This was a no-frills model – it originally lacked hub caps and an opening boot – that kept the price down to a bargain basement £481. Over the next seven years it sold 136,317 examples. A Ten derivative arrived in 1955 and was destined, in the short term, to be even more popular: it found 172,500 owners and also lasted until 1960. By this time the Vanguard had become increasingly uncompetitive although it lingered on, in revised six-cylinder form, until 1963.

In addition the Standard name was becoming a victim of semantics and, in 1959, the business's name was changed to Standard Triumph International. Triumph thereafter became a name to watch, although it got off to an uncertain start. Its small, 1.3-litre razor-edged Mayflower saloon was only produced between 1950 and 1953, although the larger 2-litre Vanguard-engined Renown survived, in limited numbers, until 1954. By then the Triumph sports car line which had began with the unusual Roadster of 1946–49, was becoming established. This was one of the last British production cars to retain a dickey seat.

The versatile Vanguard engine also powered the TR sports car line, aimed like its other open two-seater contemporaries, at the American market. The breed began in 1953 with the TR2,

Harry Ferguson by the Canadian Massey-Harris company. In October that year Sir John Black had signed a new 12-year agreement with the firm which meant that Standard would continue to build tractors until 1965. But this contract was set aside because the eventual outcome of Alick Dick's dialogue, in August 1959, was that Massey-Ferguson bought Standard's Banner Lane tractor factory for £12 million. By this time Rover had reappeared on the scene and these funds would have helped to create Allied Motors; but, once again, the two parties could not reach an agreement.

Yet another of Dick's preoccupations was how to achieve corporate independence in body building following BMC's purchase of Fisher and Ludlow. Pressed Steel, the industry's largest independent body maker, was fully committed, so he had little choice but to turn to Mulliners of Birmingham, largest of the second division body specialists, with whom Standard had built up a close association. In June 1954 Alick Dick secured an agreement from Mulliners for its entire body output once existing contracts had been honoured, which,

as we have seen, caused considerable problems for the likes of Aston Martin and Alvis. Later, in May 1958, this liaison was consolidated by Standard's outright purchase of Mulliners.

In addition, the car company was building up its manufacturing base by buying a group of complementary but geographically unrelated companies. The first of these, Beans Engineering of Tipton, Staffordshire, was bought in 1956 for its foundry facilities and was followed in 1959 by the former Fisher and Ludlow body plant at Tile Hill, Coventry. In 1960 they were joined by Alford and Alder of Hemel Hempstead, Hertfordshire, and the Dunstable, Bedfordshire-based Auto Body Dies. Halls Engineering of Liverpool, which built body parts for Standard, was a more ambitious purchase, bought that year for £2 million.

These body supply problems were to have a direct bearing on the way in which the company's new family car, coded Zobo, was designed. Work under the direction of chief engineer Harry Webster had begun in 1956 and, unfashionably, it retained a separate chassis frame so that body parts from which only accounted for 8,628 cars, although the outwardly similar TR3 of 1955 was an improvement on the original. However, its TR3A successor, an unofficial designation, was the firm's first really successful model in America. No less than 58,236 were built between 1957 and 1968, with a mere 1,896 examples having British owners.

If Standard had been unable to find a partner in the 1950s, the same could also be said of Rootes which, although a larger company, was still small in national terms. In the 1956–7 financial year, which was a difficult one for the industry, Rootes built only 75,000 cars and alone recorded a loss, of £600,000, so exposing its vulnerability. However,

the Group had already expanded its product line in 1955 by buying Singer and proceeding to relaunch the marque, with limited success, as a more expensive version of the Hillman Minx.

In truth, the Birmingham-based Singer company had been living on borrowed time since its 1937 reconstruction. Saved by war-time contracts, with the coming of peace, and despite the car-hunger of the early post-war years, its cars had made virtually no impact on the market. The Super Ten of pre-war origin sold just 10,497 examples and the Super Twelve a mere 1,098. A flicker of individuality that these cars offered was the use of a single overhead camshaft engine, a

feature of the marque since 1927.

The 1½-litre SM1500 of 1949 was Singer's first new design of the post-war period and was slab sided, dull, expensive at £799, and retained a separate chassis. A total of 17,382 was built, which made it the best-selling post-war Singer of the pre-Rootes era. The SM1500 was followed in 1954 by its more attractive Hunter derivative but it came too late to stop the rot and, by August 1955, production was down to 40 cars a week. Talks with Rootes began in September and the sale came in December after Singer made a loss of £140,177 in the 1954–5 financial year. The price paid by Rootes was £235,000.

The creation of a new Rootes

The Triumph TR2 used a twin-carb 90 bhp version of the Standard Vanguard engine. This one, competing in a Tulip Rally, was assembled by Imperia in Belgium and has a hard-top not seen on British-made examples. (NMM)

marque to fill the yawning gap between Hillman and Humber made sound marketing sense and there were historical associations, because Billy Rootes had begun his motor industry career as a Singer apprentice in 1910. An indictment of that company's poor reinvestment record was underlined when he was surprised to find the lathe he had once used still in operation. Production at the firm's Birmingham factory ceased in 1956 and the plant became a Group parts depot. The Hunter survived there until 1956, although just 4,772 were built. It was replaced by the Ryton-built Minx-derived Gazelle with wood grained dashboard, still powered by Singer's single camshaft four. That too went with the Gazelle IIA of 1958, when the Rootes 1½-litre pushrod unit took over. The model evolved in Mark III form and survived until 1961, by which time a total of 43,545 had been produced.

Rootes' mainstay was, of course, the Minx, and when the new Series model arrived in 1956 it featured an attractive body which was destined, with minor revisions, to survive until 1966. This Series I car was a great improvement on past practice, being both roomier and faster than hitherto, although its 1.4-litre overhead valve unit was carried over from its Phase VIII predecessor. A respectable 202,264 examples were built and the Series III cars of 1959–61 received the 1,490 cc engine already fitted to the Singer Gazelle and the Sunbeam Rapier sports coupé. The latter, announced in late 1955 to replace the ageing Sunbeam 90 line, was the first glimpse that the public got of the body destined for the new Minx, although it was in two-door hardtop guise. The stylish Rapier soon developed a reputation for rapid, reliable motoring and survived until 1967. More sedate was the low-production Humber line. The 2.3-litre four-cylinder Hawk VI was discontinued in 1957 and replaced by the Hawk 1 with a new unitary body. For 1959 this hull was extended to the 2.6-litre six-cylinder Super Snipe and both models were built in these forms until 1964.

The Group unveiled its corporate sports car, in the shape of the 1½-litre 83 bhp Sunbeam Alpine, at the 1959 London Motor Show. Yet it was saloons that drew the crowds at Earls Court. Standard was displaying its Michelotti-styled 948 cc Triumph Herald with all independent suspension, whilst Ford's completely new 105E Anglia, distinguished by its inclined rear window, generated plenty of interest. But few would argue that the star of the event was the British Motor Corporation's revolutionary front-wheel drive Mini, the work of the Morris Minor's creator, Alec Issigonis. Here at last, perhaps, was BMC's much needed big seller.

This trio of family cars was an outward expression of a buoyant and healthy motor industry although, in retrospect – or to readers of *The Economist* at the time – it was one which contained serious fault lines. However, in 1959 Britain exported a record 539,268 cars. Conversely, imports were also running at an unprecedented level, but at 27,066 units they were largely disregarded. These came almost exclusively from Europe and were headed by the Renault Dauphine and Volkswagen Beetle. And just three cars entered the country from the Far East . . .

From a base in October 1959 of 100, the retail price index had risen to 143.2 points in October 1969. By comparison, the price of the cheapest Mini – *including* Purchase Tax – had only increased from £497 in October 1959 to £596 ten years later, an overall increase of less than 20 per cent, and in the period of low Purchase Tax from 1962 to 1966 a Mini had actually cost *less* than when introduced in 1959.[3] A car manufacturer such as BMC found it necessary to implement major increases on its basic ex-factory prices only in 1968 and later: the basic Mini price of £350 of 1959 had only gone up to £387 by 1967.

The net effect of the Labour government's policies was to curtail any further expansion of the British home market after 1964. In the circumstances the best hope for continued expansion of the motor industry lay in the export markets. However, unlike the early post-war period where a combination of factors, including strong government intervention, had channelled the majority of British car production towards overseas markets, there was by the 1960s seemingly less of a commitment to the export business. While, arguably, the late 1940s export figures of up to 70 per cent of total production was in the longer term detrimental to the British motor industry, it would have been desirable if the industry could have consistently exported some 40 per cent of production. Disregarding the 1960–1 'blip' caused by the collapse of the US market, and equally the devaluation-induced boost of 1968–9, the key figures from 1962 to 1967 saw exports drop from 43.6 per cent to 32.4 per cent of total production.

Since the war, the importance of Britain's traditional Empire market had declined somewhat. This was accelerated by Australia's determination to build up her own car industry which was protected by tariff barriers, and by New Zealand's import restrictions dictated by her balance of payments. The American experience had been rewarding for Britain's motor industry – in 1959, the USA took 209,333 British cars, which amounted to 36.8 per cent of the total exports of 568,971 cars. In 1960, however, the new car market in the USA collapsed, especially for the smaller type of imported car, and Britain sold only 132,492 cars there, which also sharply reduced Britain's overall production. In 1961 the figure crashed further, to a mere 30,519 cars, or 8.2 per cent of the total. Export sales to the USA would revive, although the annual figure only recovered to the level of 100,000 in the post-devaluation years of 1968 and 1969. While the USA in most years remained the largest single export market for British cars, its relative importance declined dramatically, besides which after 1959 most British cars exported to

Bearing a superficial resemblance to an MGB GT, the Elva Courier coupé was offered with MG or Ford Cortina engines. Fewer than 100 were made of this model, compared with about 400 open sports cars. (NMM)

the USA were of specialized sports and luxury types which were less important in other export markets or even in the home market.

The inevitable conclusion was that Britain's best possibility for remaining a large-scale car exporter lay on her doorstep: in Europe. Here, Britain had found some good markets for her car exports already before the Second World War, typically in the smaller non-car producing countries, with some of which Britain had traditional trading links: Eire, Denmark and Portugal were examples. At the end of the 1950s, Europe was becoming polarised in two groups in terms of trading – the Common Market (EEC) and the European Free Trade Area (EFTA). Of the major car producers, Germany, France and Italy all belonged to the EEC, while Britain

with the exception of Sweden was the only car manufacturing country within EFTA. In theory, Britain should have had excellent opportunities for exporting cars to the EFTA countries, even allowing for the fact that most of these markets were rather small (the countries in question were, apart from the UK, originally Austria, Denmark, Norway, Portugal, Sweden, and Switzerland; later Finland and Iceland also joined). Unfortunately, this did not entirely materialize. One contributory reason was that the supposed preference given to goods from other EFTA countries was quite modest: in 1961 the rates of import duty on cars in Sweden, Denmark and Switzerland were eight per cent, nine per cent and 14 per cent respectively on cars from other EFTA countries, and ten per cent, 12 per cent and 18 per cent on

cars from non-member countries. At the same time, most EEC countries still charged considerably higher rates of import duty even on cars from other EEC states, ranging from 36 per cent in Italy to 56 per cent in France; Germany was the exception, levying only ten per cent on EEC-sourced cars.[4]

Britain also started in a rather weak position. In 1960, 44,208 British cars were exported to EFTA countries (including Finland and Iceland), only 12.7 per cent of the total German, French and Italian exports to the same countries, which amounted to 347,546 cars. In that year, the total figure for British exports to all EFTA countries was exceeded by German exports alone to each of the following individual countries: Austria, Denmark, Sweden, and Switzerland. Things did improve tremendously over the decade. By 1969, British exports to the EFTA partners amounted to a record 161,557 cars, while the total from Germany, France and Italy had increased only to 512,167 cars – yet Germany alone sold more than twice as many cars in EFTA as did Britain.

For Europe as a whole, British exports improved from 127,054 cars in 1960 to 361,350 in 1969, by then almost 47 per cent of all British exports. In the same year, exports to the EEC had risen to 152,189 cars, not far short of the EFTA figure, with Belgium and Italy being the two largest European markets for British cars – Standard-Triumph and BMC had long since had CKD (Completely Knocked Down) assembly operations in these two countries. By contrast, the joint exports by Germany, France and Italy to each other and other countries

The Turner was quite an attractive little sports car, but with its 948 cc BMC A-type engine it was very close to the Austin-Healey Sprite in concept, yet more expensive. Coventry Climax-powered versions were faster, but not big sellers. Only 160 of this model were sold altogether, of which the majority had the 948 cc engine. (Nick Georgano)

within the EEC had reached a staggering figure of over 1.3 million cars by 1969 – the comparable figure in 1960 had been 338,059 cars. (In actual fact the precise figures for inter-EEC sales of cars will have been higher, but export statistics from Belgium and The Netherlands were not published in the SMM&T annual handbook.)

Little wonder, therefore, that the British motor industry was largely in favour of Britain becoming a member of the EEC when the application was first made in 1962. Their optimism about British prospects within the EEC may have been a little wary at first (see, for instance, interviews conducted by Nigel Lawson for *The Sunday Telegraph*).[5] In September 1961, the National Institute Economic Review forecast British car exports of around 1.1 million per year by 1970 – *if* Britain joined the EEC.[6] (The actual figure achieved in 1970 was less than 700,000 cars exported.) On 27 October 1961, Harry Mundy as Technical Editor of *The Autocar* wrote that, in case of Britain becoming a member of the EEC, 'increasing competition seems to indicate further mergers, possibly even between firms from different countries'. He may have been thinking of the missed opportunity for BMC to take over the bankrupt German Borgward company, as he could not possibly have foreseen BMW's take-over of Rover.

Walter Hitzinger, the general director of Daimler-Benz AG, when interviewed by *Der Spiegel* on 29 November 1961,[7] saw no danger from British competition in an extended Common Market and was downright disparaging of Jaguar, Rolls-Royce and Bentley when compared to his own products. *The Motor* pointed out that in 1960 Germany had sold more than 255,000 cars in the EFTA countries (not including the UK) compared to less than 42,000 British cars, while the number of German cars sold in Britain was three times the number of British cars sold in Germany. The tendency was to blame the high level of British

Two into one. The heads of BMC and Leyland, Sir George Harriman (left) and Sir Donald Stokes (right) whose companies merged in May 1968 to form the British Leyland Motor Corporation. Because of Leyland's stronger financial position, Stokes took charge and became Chairman, a post he held until 1975. He became Lord Stokes in 1969. Harriman became President but took no part in the day-to-day running of the Corporation. (Harriman BMIHT/Rover, Stokes NMM)

Purchase Tax on new cars for the perceived British inability to compete in a greater Europe. Until the cut in November 1962, tax accounted for some 38 per cent of the retail price of a new car in Britain, compared to 24 per cent in France, 13 per cent in Germany and ten per cent in Italy.

The Hon Brian Rootes stated that 'we have enough confidence in our products and in our ability to be certain that the increase in sales we shall gain on the Continent (when Britain joins the Common Market) will more than compensate for . . . tougher competition at home'.[8] He saw a greater European market as offering the biggest potential in terms of increased car production and sales of all the then accepted important world markets – Japan, as yet, did not enter the equation. There is therefore little doubt that the French veto against Britain's membership in early 1963 was a blow to the hopes and aspirations of the British motor industry. *Autocar* put a brave face on it, stating in a leading article on 8 February 1963 that 'so far as we can discover, the

British motor industry as a whole has not been overwhelmingly enthusiastic about Britain's entry into the Common Market; rather it has been a case of "On balance it is probably the best course to take."' *The Motor* on 13 February 1963 declared that 'one of the most disappointed men when negotiations between the UK and the Six broke down was Dr Ludwig Erhard, the German vice-chancellor, and it is interesting to discover that so far as business is concerned his regrets are expressed also by members of the German automobile industry.'

Although 1964 was a record year for both production and home market sales, it also marked the end of the five-year period of technical exuberance on the part of the British motor industry; the Austin 1800 was virtually the last outstanding British mass-production design. It was also the year when the American Chrysler company bought into Rootes. As the home market stagnated in the following years, and as BMC faltered, the American companies – especially Ford – became more and more able to set the pace for the

British Industry: for BMC and later BL, it became more a question of responding to the American challenge. In consequence, new British car designs became again more pedestrian and more dictated simply by home market demands. Therefore Britain's motor industry was generally in a much weaker position in the late 1960s and early 1970s when, once again, the road to Europe was opened. Another symptom was that with the general reduction of import tariffs, and British car buyers searching for the variety which was increasingly no longer available from domestic producers, the number of imported cars had grown steadily from an estimated two per cent of all new car sales at the beginning of the decade to five per cent in 1965, over ten per cent in 1969 and over 14 per cent in 1970 – more than the market share of either Vauxhall or Rootes/Chrysler.

When, in 1973, Britain did belatedly join the EEC, Britain's motor industry was scarcely competitive on the European scene any more, whether in terms of production figures or the product offered. The net effect of Britain becoming a member was that

the British home market was swamped by imports from Europe while British exports to other EEC members actually declined.

It could have been very different, if Britain had been admitted to the EEC ten years before, when her motor industry was in so much better shape. It is not too fanciful a theory that, as much as any other factor, it was the French veto against British EEC membership in 1963 which was responsible for the long-term decline of Britain's motor industry.

Summing up, the 1960s can be neatly split into two periods. The first half began actually in 1959, with the introduction of such cars as BMC's Mini, the Ford Anglia and the Triumph Herald: no excuse needs to be made for dealing with these important new models in a chapter devoted to the 1960s. It largely ended in 1964. This five-year period saw most of the excitement in terms of new product introduction, it saw both home and export markets expand, and the record year of 1964 probably led many to believe that Britain would be all right even

if not a member of the EEC. Then followed the lean years from 1965 to 1969, even into the early 1970s. This was a period of stagnation, of resting on laurels; a period when Britain's failing economy and the interventionist mood of the Government combined to create further difficulties for an already beleaguered industry. The twin nadirs for the British motor industry during this period were that Chrysler took total control of Rootes in 1967, and that BMC was forced to merge with Leyland in 1968. Another important structural change which went almost unnoticed at the time was that Ford of Britain's individual identity was submerged in the new corporate structure of Ford of *Europe* – an alliance whose centre of gravity turned out to lie in Cologne rather than Dagenham. The writing was now clearly on the wall, and as portents for the coming decade the two most important new car introductions of 1969 were the Austin Maxi from British Leyland – a final fling with the Issigonis school of advanced engineering; and the Capri from Ford – the very antithesis of the Maxi in every respect, but equally

British motor industry – key performance figures 1959-1969

	Production	Index of production	Exports*	Index of exports	Exports as percentage of production	Imports	Index of imports	Registrations (new/first) in the UK**	Index of registrations	Percentage of change in registrations compared to previous year
1959	1,189,943	100	568,971	100	47.8%	26,998	100	657,315	100	–
1960	1,352,728	114	569,889	100	42.1%	57,309	212	820,088	125	+24.8%
1961	1,003,967	84	370,744	65	36.9%	22,759	84	756,054	115	−7.8%
1962	1,249,426	105	544,924	96	43.6%	28,610	106	800,239	122	+5.8%
1963	1,607,939	135	615,827	108	38.3%	48,163	178	1,030,694	157	+28.8%
1964	1,867,640	157	679,383	119	36.4%	65,725	243	1,215,929	185	+18.0%
1965	1,772,045	149	627,567	110	35.4%	55,558	206	1,148,718	175	−5.5%
1966	1,603,679	135	556,044	98	34.7%	66,793	247	1,091,217	166	−5.0%
1967	1,552,013	130	502,596	88	32.4%	92,731	343	1,143,015	174	+4.7%
1968	1,815,936	153	676,571	119	37.3%	102,276	378	1,144,770	174	+0.2%
1969	1,717,073	144	771,634	136	44.9%	101,914	377	1,012,811	154	−11.5%

General note: All figures relate to cars only.

*Actual exports, not manufacturers' allocation for export; some CKD kits may be excluded.

**Great Britain and Northern Ireland, excluding Isle of Man and Channel Islands. Figures include Personal Export Delivery cars (Home Delivery Exports), and include first registrations of some used vehicles, such as imported second-hand cars, ex-WD vehicles etc; figures exclude hackneys, and exempt vehicles (such as Government-owned or disabled drivers' cars).

Source: *The Motor Industry of Great Britain*, annual handbook published by The Society of Motor Manufacturers and Traders.

long-lived and commercially far more successful, in Britain and internationally.

So, how swinging were the sixties? For Britain's motor industry, it seemed that it was a matter of losing more on the swings than was gained on the roundabouts. . .

In 1960, Britain still had the 'big five' mass producers, two leading independents (Jaguar, Rover) and a host of smaller specialists. Ten years later, the picture would have altered drastically. By 1969, there were only four big companies, three rather than two of which were in American ownership, Jaguar and Rover were no longer independent, quite a few of the small specialists had disappeared (although this group had also seen some newcomers) and the number of British makes on offer, whether from the big companies or from the specialists, had begun to decline.

The biggest individual company throughout was BMC (which after the BMC-Leyland merger in 1968 became the Austin-Morris division of BLMC). In 1960, the merger between Austin and Morris was eight years old and had begun to produce serious results. The basic range of passenger car engine designs had been reduced to three, and latterly the Corporation had intensified its policy of 'badge-engineering', using the same bodyshell design for up to five (later six) different marques. BMC in its own right was still one of the world's leading car manufacturers, at the time the fifth-largest in the world and Europe's number two (after General Motors, Ford, Chrysler, and Volkswagen). Disposing of something like seven different brand names and covering the spectrum from £500-worth of basic Mini to the gargantuan Princess limousine, BMC offered a greater variety than any other motor manufacturer in the world. And thanks to the genius of Alec Issigonis, BMC had suddenly also become a constructor of exceedingly advanced, indeed revolutionary motor cars. That the giant had feet of clay only became obvious in the second half of the decade.

Ford, although largely American-owned and controlled, had a 30-year history of catering to the tastes of British (and European) motorists. Their range was far smaller and more logical than that of BMC, Ford effectively competing only in the three main market sectors with only two basic bodyshells and three different engines (disregarding their practice of keeping an out-of-date small car with its own body and engine designs in production so as to offer a model at a particularly low cost). Their engineering and styling approach was, naturally enough, influenced by the parent company in Detroit, but especially with the new Anglia of 1959 they had become more attuned to European practice. As number two in the market-place and with a steadily widening product programme, Ford would become an increasingly credible challenger to BMC throughout the 1960s. (For a detailed discussion of UK market developments, see the following section.)

The TR3A sold well in the US until this market collapsed

In many ways resembling a smaller version of BMC, Rootes was still a family-controlled business. They disposed of four different makes of car, most of which in 1960 used one of two basic bodyshells and one of three different engines. Unlike BMC and Ford they did not contest the small-car class which they entered belatedly in 1963. As this product – the Hillman Imp – was wrong, and not the hoped-for success in the market-place, this weakened the Rootes company to the point where financial assistance was sought outside Britain, and was forthcoming from Chrysler in the USA, which bought into the company in 1964. Three years later, Chrysler took total control of the company, which in 1970 became Chrysler UK Limited.

Vauxhall was in a similar position to Rootes in the market-place, having no small car at the beginning of the decade – later rectified with rather more success than Rootes. Owned by the American General Motors company, like Ford their products were often inspired by Detroit. They had two basic models with different bodyshells, using four- and six-cylinder engines of similar dimensions and design. They were rather less export-orientated than most other British motor companies, GM giving preference to other makes in the USA, in Europe (Opel) and in Australia (Holden).

Smallest of the 'big five' was Standard-Triumph. This company was labouring for most of the 1950s under a misguided product policy which it only took steps to rectify with the new Herald car in 1959, by when it was almost too late. In the meantime their best car was the Triumph TR3A sports car, which sold strongly in the USA until this market collapsed in 1960–1. This was one of the main reasons why Standard was pleased to merge with the commercial vehicle manufacturer Leyland in 1961, first of the important mergers which happened in the industry in the 1960s. Under the new management, Triumph was rejuvenated over a period of years with a strong new product range and marque identity.

Jaguar and Rover were the most significant among the independent producers. Jaguar's product line consisted of sports and luxury cars which commanded an international following and were particularly successful in the USA. Rover cars had less international appeal but they were comfortably bolstered by the Land Rover, a highly successful light four-wheel drive utility vehicle which was and continued to be in great demand around the world. Both these companies, while still independent, would prove to be capable of producing cars of world-leading design.

Among the smaller specialists, Rolls-Royce and Bentley stood, as ever,

Though it retained the name Anglia, the 105E for 1960 was a completely new car. The oversquare engine gave a peppy performance, and the reverse-angle rear window made it instantly recognizable. Production of this and the larger-engined Super Anglia reached over a million before it gave way to the Escort in 1968. These three Anglias are displayed at the 1959 Paris Salon. (NMM)

at the top of the Industry's hierarchy, but, each in their own way, many other companies made important contributions to the progress of Britain's motor industry. Some, like AC or Morgan, were among the oldest in the industry, and while it was in the specialist group that most of the fatalities occurred in the 1960s, it was also in this group that new makes appeared, or sprung to increased prominence, such as Lotus or Reliant.

Of those companies that failed to make it through the decade, Alvis had not introduced a new model since the mid-1950s. Admirable though their 3-litre car was, it was getting old-fashioned and the company relied on armoured fighting vehicles for most of its business. Their merger with Rover in 1965 was synergistic in as much as both companies had strong interests in military vehicles. In 1966, Rover became part of the growing Leyland group. Some proposals were considered for new cars that might bear the Alvis name, including a Rover 2000-based coupé and a mid-engined sports car, but production of Alvis private cars ceased in 1967 and the company

concentrated thereafter on AFVs.

Armstrong-Siddeley had sadly backed the wrong horse in the shape of the 234/236 series in 1955, an ugly car which failed to compete against the Rovers or the small Jaguars. After 1958 they only made the ageing Sapphire model in small numbers. When the parent Hawker-Siddeley group merged with Bristol it was decided to concentrate on the aircraft and aero engine business, and the last Armstrong-Siddeley was made in the summer of 1960.

Bond of Preston in Lancashire was a post-war creation and had enjoyed some success in the three-wheeler business. During the 1960s they acquired a second string in the shape of a range of GT coupés and convertibles, with fibreglass bodies mounted on Triumph Herald and Vitesse chassis. The recipe was promising but the ground was cut from under their feet when the Ford Capri appeared in 1969. In that year, Bond was taken over by the other maker of three-wheelers, Reliant, the Preston factory was closed, and all existing Bond models discontinued. The 1970 Bond Bug

three-wheeler was a Reliant in all but name and its novelty value lasted only four years.

Elva was but one of many small sports car makers but, with an eleven-year run, more successful than some. They pioneered a mid-engined GT coupé in 1964 but this model never went into production. Their staple model relied on BMC or Ford engines and was usually sold in kit form. Production was down to a trickle after 1965 and a Ford V6-engined 3000 model was stillborn. The last cars were made in 1968.

The Gordon-Keeble was loosely based on the defunct Peerless/ Warwick, but instead of a Triumph TR3A engine featured American Chevrolet V8 power in a handsome Bertone-styled body. With strong overtones of the Alfa Romeo 2600 it was, in fact, an early work of the young Giugiaro. It was inevitably made from fibreglass when it went into production in 1964. The specification was attractive but the selling price was too low to impress. When the original company failed and was reconstructed, the price of the car was increased by 50 per cent. In 1968, Gordon-Keeble was taken over by an American businessman who intended to apply his own name, de Bruyne, to a revised model, but this project never got off the ground.

The age-old, revered name of Lagonda has suffered many misfortunes. Effectively merged with Aston Martin under the auspices of David Brown in 1947, small-scale production of expensive luxury saloons and convertibles petered out in 1958, but a new Rapide saloon was launched in 1961. This was based on the Aston Martin DB4 and created a good deal of interest but there were few takers at £5,000 – more than twice the cost of the Jaguar Mark X introduced in the following year. Little more than 50 Rapides had been made when the model was discontinued in 1964. Lagonda would be revived again in the 1970s, after David Brown had sold out, but by 1990 the make was once again in abeyance.

Lea-Francis was almost as well-established as Lagonda but had only existed on paper after 1953. A surprise of the 1960 Motor Show was the Lea-Francis Lynx, a monstrous-looking sports car with a Ford Zephyr engine. Only three were made. Subsequently the company became involved in an equally ill-starred attempt at building the German Fuldamobil bubble car in Britain under the name of Nobel, but it was taken over by Quinton Hazell in 1962 and car manufacturing rights were sold to A. B. Price Ltd of Studley in Warwickshire. A further comeback attempt was made in the 1980s, with Motor Show prototypes almost as grotesque as the 1960 Lynx.

Tornado was yet another of the myriad of specialist sports car manufacturers, typically based in the home counties (Rickmansworth in this case), utilising Ford (or BMC, or Standard Triumph) power plants, and fibreglass bodywork, often sold in kit form. Styling was as awkward as the early Marcos but the 1962 Talisman was prettier, and had the first-ever Cosworth-tuned engine. Cash-flow problems forced a reconstruction in 1963, but even so Tornado disappeared in the following year.

Turner, of Wolverhampton, survived longer than most, from 1951 to 1966. The recipe was like Elva or Tornado – simple chassis, bought-out engine, fibreglass body, and most home market cars sold in kit form. Turner, however, made the mistake of concentrating on small sports cars with the BMC A-series engine and so lost much of its *raison d'être* when the much cheaper Sprite and Midget series appeared. Later Turners sensibly moved on to more powerful Ford or Coventry-Climax engines, but the company went into voluntary liquidation after its founder Jack Turner fell seriously ill and chose to pull out of car manufacture.

Even among the bigger battalions there were casualties. These were typically rationalization moves made after mergers, a trend that would be greatly increased as British Leyland and Chrysler cleared out their stables in the early 1970s. All of the makes briefly obituarized below did in fact belong to one of these two groups:

Austin-Healey, backed by BMC, had been a tremendous success in the American sports car market ever since 1953, but their main model, the 3000, fell foul of the new American legislation introduced in 1968. After the 3000 was dropped only the Sprite remained in production, only to be withdrawn from the US market in 1969 in favour of its MG Midget cousin. Sales were then restricted to the home market and were negligible. Donald Stokes, chairman of the new British Leyland combine, decided in 1970 to cancel the agreement to use the Healey name – thereby saving the company the modest royalty paid to Donald Healey – and the marque disappeared at the end of that year.

Riley died from an overdose of badge-engineering. Taken over originally by Nuffield in 1938, the company became part of BMC in 1952 and the last trace of original Riley design vanished with the Pathfinder model in 1957. The most successful model was the One-Point-Five sports saloon but this was discontinued in 1965. Subsequently the name was found only on uninspired derivatives of basic Austin-Morris models, and production dropped to a few thousand cars sold mostly in the home market. In 1969 Riley became the first casualty of the BMC-Leyland merger.

The fate of Singer was very similar to that of Riley. Once one of Britain's largest car makers, they had led an increasingly precarious existence since 1930 but managed to hold out until 1956, when taken over by Rootes. For a couple of years the original Singer ohc engine was continued in a modified Hillman Minx bodyshell but all subsequent models were blatant examples of badge engineering. After Chrysler had gained total control of Rootes in 1967, Singer was the first casualty for euthanasia, administered in April

Several companies built cars with relatively large four-cylinder engines in the early post-war years. Standard had the Vanguard, Humber the Hawk, and Austin the A70. This is an A70 Hampshire whose 2,199 cc engine was basically that of the Sixteen first seen in 1945. This one is competing in the 1952 Eastbourne Rally, in company with an Austin A40 sports and an MG TC Midget. (NMM)

1970. Two months later Rootes ceased to exist and became Chrysler United Kingdom Limited.

Standard had made a number of fatal mistakes in the post-war period and by 1958 was down to a very low market share. More attention was now being given to the company's second-string marque, Triumph, which had been acquired in 1944. After Standard-Triumph was taken over by Leyland in 1961, a final Standard model was introduced, the make's belated entry in the six-cylinder market, unfortunately still featuring a seven-year old bodyshell. Its admirable 2-litre engine found a much better home in the Triumph 2000 of 1963, all other new models also being badged as Triumphs. After 1963, only a few light commercials continued to carry the name Standard which by then had come to mean the opposite of 'de-luxe' to most car buyers.

Above all, the 1960s was the decade of merger mania. Arguably the trend to merge individual companies together into larger, supposedly more viable units, had begun in the 1920s when, for instance, Hillman and Humber were fused to become the Rootes Group, and every decade since had seen its share of take-overs or mergers. But the trend was to accelerate during the 1960s, finding its culmination in the BMC-Leyland merger of 1968. Things started out modestly enough in 1960 when Jaguar bought the old-established Daimler company from the BSA group. Undoubtedly the main reason for this was that William Lyons of Jaguar wanted to expand production and, being refused permission to extend his own factory, found the large and under-utilized Daimler factory much to his liking. Although one of Daimler's existing V8 engines continued to be used in a Jaguar-based model until 1969, all subsequent cars were in truth badge-engineered Jaguars and remain so to this day. It was also part of a general policy of diversification on behalf of Jaguar; part of the Daimler dowry was a still thriving bus manufacturing operation. In the 1960s Jaguar also took over the Guy commercial vehicle company of Wolverhampton, and the Coventry-Climax engine, fork lift truck, and fire-pump manufacturing company.

The next step was Leyland's acquisition of Standard-Triumph in 1961. Standard's managing director Alick Dick had for some time been anxious to find a partner, negotiating from time to time with Rootes, Rover and American Motors in the USA. The reason for Standard's need to merge have already been briefly outlined. Leyland was at this time Britain's most successful heavy commercial vehicle manufacturer and had largely exhausted the possibilities of growth by acquisition in this sector – their stable now included also AEC, Albion, Crossley, Maudslay, and Thornycroft. They were anxious to gain an entry into the car market from which they had been absent since the 1920s. The result was largely beneficial for Triumph, which entered upon their most fertile period after the merger.

Less heralded but of even greater long-term importance was the merger in 1965 between BMC and the body manufacturer Pressed Steel. Of the other independent body manufacturers, Fisher & Ludlow had already been taken over by BMC in 1953, the same year that Ford took over Briggs. Pressed Steel, although co-founded by William Morris and with its main factory across the road from the Morris factory at Cowley, had been independent since 1930 and was an important supplier not only to BMC but also to Jaguar, Rolls-Royce, Rootes, and Rover, among others. BMC's desire was as much to control their own source of body supply, as it was to deny their competitors theirs; in fact Pressed Steel happily went on supplying, for instance, Rootes for many years after 1965. However, the BMC-Pressed Steel merger did concentrate the minds of the independent manufacturers.

In 1966, both Jaguar and Rover lost their independence. In the case of Jaguar, William Lyons controlled the majority of voting shares but at 65, without a male heir, wanted to surrender his company on his own terms,

The first fore runner of the Mini, XC 9001, was much closer to the subsequent BMC 1100 and 1800. It had Hydrolastic suspension but the engine had a single overhead camshaft, and drive was to the rear wheels. (BMIHT/Rover)

rather than be forced to do so. He was anxious to secure future body supply, and the BMC-Pressed Steel merger caused him some concern. Jaguar was also a little stretched by the considerable development costs of their next new model, the XJ6, which appeared in 1968. Logically enough, it was BMC that Lyons turned to. In the summer of 1966, BMC and Jaguar agreed to merge, the joint company becoming known as British Motor Holdings (BMH).

With Jaguar absorbed by BMC, it was the opposition that Rover turned to. The question of body supply was also of concern to them. To Leyland the Land-Rover provided much of the motivation for wishing to acquire Rover – as it has for all subsequent Rover bidders – and they most certainly did not wish to see Rover merged with BMC-Jaguar. An agreement was reached in December 1966, also including the Alvis company which Rover had taken over in 1965.

By the end of 1966, seven companies (if we include Pressed Steel and Alvis) had become two. The stage was almost set for the final act of the drama – the only ingredient missing was a catalyst to start the process. This was handily supplied when, in 1967, Chrysler took over full ownership of Rootes, in which it had held a minority stake since 1964. This did not go down well with Harold Wilson's Labour government, which was politically committed to further the interests of the British Worker, and which in any case was in an interventionist mood as far as the motor industry was concerned. It was the redoubtable Tony Benn who, as Minister of State for Technology, set the wheels in motion, originally by trying to persuade either BMC or Leyland to snatch Rootes from the predatory grip of Chrysler, subsequently by expressing his hope that BMC and Leyland 'would seek out ways of working together'.[9]

Talks between the two companies had actually, in a desultory fashion, preceded the Benn intervention by

An early production Austin Se7en, as Austin's version of the Mini was called, with the 1925 Seven with which John Coleman had recently made an epic 11,467 mile journey from Buenos Aires to New York. They are seen outside Palace House, Beaulieu. (NMM)

some time, but no doubt the high-level political interest now shown in the matter was a spur to both Donald Stokes of Leyland and George Harriman of BMC. Before a closer rapproachment was reached, the annual results of BMH to the year ending 31 July 1967 saw a drastic slump in after-tax profits to less than £4 million, from the previous year's result (for BMC alone) of more than £15 million.[10] It is likely that BMC then and subsequently traded at a loss. The reason for the poor performance was that from 1966 to 1967, BMC's share of the home market fell drastically from 35 per cent to 29 per cent (see also the following section), the largest up-or-down movement by far recorded for any UK car manufacturer from one year to the next in the 1960s.

The on-going discussions between BMC and Leyland were boosted when Harold Wilson invited Donald Stokes and George Harriman to dinner at Chequers in October 1967.[11] Here he elicited the information from both company directors that they felt a merger 'would be in the national inter-

est'. From then on the process became irrevocable, and it was only a matter of negotiating for specific terms. This in effect amounted to Leyland being able to squeeze BMC, the more apparent the deterioration of BMC's sales and financial position became. The official announcement of the merger was made in January 1968, to become effective at the end of May.

Because of the worsening state of affairs in BMC, what had at the outset been viewed as an equitable merger ended up as the effective take-over of BMC by Leyland. In the new British Leyland Motor Corporation, Donald Stokes ended up being completely in charge. In spite of the impressive turnaround he and his team had achieved at Triumph in the 1961–7 period, history will record that they were defeated by the problems facing them in the new, much bigger company; despite some pruning of the overgrown model range over the next few years, little was done in the way of rationalizing factories or reducing the overmanning. The first new model programme instituted after the merger resulted in the 1971 Morris

Marina – an uninspired knee-jerk response to the double challenge of Ford's Escort and Cortina models, rather than the result of the company's own evaluation of market trends. It was also one of those cars which were designed exclusively with the home market in mind, rather than being built for Europe or the USA. In consequence it was less than competitive in export markets, even at the dumping prices it was sold for in North America.

Much of the underlying malaise within British Leyland, however, only became apparent in the next decade, and the story of this company's misfortunes properly belongs in a subsequent chapter. While still in the 1960s, the merger had been greeted with a degree of optimism, a feeling that Britain could still present a motor manufacturing company able to compete on the world stage, although the position in 1968 of British Leyland as the fifth-largest car maker in the world, and the second-largest in Europe, was quite simply exactly where BMC had been at the beginning of the decade. Nor did the combined market share of British Leyland, at best 40 per cent in the UK, ever rise above the highest figure originally achieved by BMC on its own. So what had been gained? At best, respite: by closing ranks, the remains of Britain's motor industry attempted for a few more years to stave off the threat of take-over by a foreign company. Essentially, the BMC-Leyland merger was a defensive operation, and without all of the necessary surgery being carried out, it was doomed to fail.

By contrast, the story of Chrysler's take-over of Rootes is simplicity itself. The Chrysler Corporation, a slightly uneasy third in the US market, had eyed the successful European operations of GM and Ford for some time before finally taking the plunge. As a first stage they acquired a stake in the French Simca company (sold to them by Ford, who had obtained the Simca shareholding in exchange for the French Ford operation in 1955). Having thus a base in the EEC, it was logical also to seek an entry in the still-booming British, non-EEC market. On their part, Rootes was fast becoming a plum almost as ripe for picking as Standard-Triumph had been. Always with a smaller market share than the competition due to their lack of a small car, Rootes had been weakened by a prolonged strike in 1961 (discussed in detail in Chapter eight of the present volume). They declared pre-tax losses in both 1962 and 1963,[12] and made a number of wrong guesses in product planning, culminating in the unsuccessful Imp small car belatedly introduced in 1963, this project also absorbing large amounts of capital. Lord Rootes was approaching 70 and there were signs that his, and his family's management of the company was failing. The approach from Chrysler to buy a minority stake in the company in 1964 was in the circumstances warmly welcomed by the Rootes board.

Ford's first pan-European project was the Transit van

Apart from a modest pre-tax profit in 1964, Rootes continued to lose money. Chrysler by 1966 had invested £27 million in Rootes and held 62 per cent of the equity but only 45 per cent of the voting shares.[13] It cost them a further £20 million – and incurred the displeasure of the British government – to take control, which they did in early 1967. Remaining members of the Rootes family gradually retired from the board, and in 1970 the company was formally renamed Chrysler UK Limited. Apart from the fact that the cars since 1965 had born the Chrysler pentastar badge, there was – as far as the buying public was concerned – little to be noticed in the way of difference: since before the war, Rootes Group cars had had an American flavour to their styling. While Singer was dropped in 1970, the Humber and Sunbeam badges lived on to 1976, Hillman a little longer, then everything was re-badged Chrysler. In 1978 Chrysler's European interests, which by that time made losses which threatened the survival of the American parent company, were sold to Peugeot, and for a time the old Anglo-French Talbot name was revived. Again, the story of misfortunes of Chrysler UK belongs in the chapter dealing with the 1970s.

The transformation of Ford of Britain into an integrated part of Ford's multi-national operation began in 1961 when Ford of America spent £150 million to buy out the remaining British shareholders.[14] An American chief executive was appointed for the first time in 1965. While the continued independence of Ford's British and German subsidiaries had manifested itself clearly in 1962 when they brought out the Consul Cortina and Taunus 12M models respectively – two very different cars competing in the same class, and in many European export markets, against each other – the time had come for closer links to be forged across the North Sea as well as across the Atlantic. The first pan-European Ford project was the Transit van, which went into production in both Britain and Germany in 1965. This was such an outstanding success in its market that it was decided that the new small car intended as a replacement for Ford's British Anglia should also be produced in both countries. By the time the Escort was introduced in early 1968, Ford of Britain and Ford-Werke AG of Cologne had been formally merged into Ford of Europe, which came into being in 1967, quietly and without fuss. It is worth noting that in 1967, Ford still produced twice as many cars in Britain as in Germany, but the lamentable lack of success of the last all-British Ford car, the 1966 Zephyr/Zodiac Mark IV range, coupled with the greater growth in Continental markets and the fact that Britain was not yet in the EEC, made it inevitable that in the longer run, Ford's car making operations in Continental Europe (Spain and Belgium, apart from Germany) should

One of three innovative small British cars of 1959, the Triumph Herald had all-independent suspension and a remarkable 25 ft turning circle. Styling by Michelotti was more attractive than that of the Mini or Anglia. Convertibles and coupés (shown here) had twin-carb engines. (NMM)

assume far greater importance than their British factories.

Similarly, Chrysler's British and French operations were integrated in the 1970s, as were eventually Vauxhall with Opel in Germany, although in both cases this only occurred after Britain had joined the EEC in 1973. Again, one must reflect that if Britain had joined the Common Market ten years earlier than it happened, and if the British home market had continued its natural growth in the second half of the 1960s, the incentive would have been for the American multinationals to expand their operations in Britain, rather than develop additional manufacturing sites and generally extend their Continental European bases. By 1973, the British branches of Ford, General Motors and Chrysler were so much weaker than their step-siblings in Europe that the outcome was inevitable. Already by 1970, Opel in Germany on its own produced more

cars than all of British Leyland together, and more than four times the number of Vauxhall cars; Chrysler France produced almost twice the number of Chrysler UK; and Ford in Germany was only 40,000 cars behind Ford in Britain, which was more than offset by the extra 234,000 cars produced by Ford's German directed factory in Belgium. (It must be added that in all cases mentioned, the British companies produced far

more commercial vehicles than their Continental counterparts.)

The final important change that must be mentioned with regard to the structure of the industry is that the geographical spread of the industry was somewhat altered during the 1960s. This was owing to the government policy of encouraging motor car manufacturers to expand by setting up new factories in development areas. A carrot of financial assistance was combined with the stick of refusing planning permission for new factories in the Midlands. The response was mixed. Jaguar refused to move and instead bought the Daimler factory locally in Coventry. Reliant gave up expansion plans altogether. Rover only

The Farina-styled BMC saloon of 1959 eventually appeared with five badges (Austin, MG, Morris, Riley and Wolseley) and two engines, 1,489 and 1,622 cc. Critics may have called it a cynical exercise in badge engineering, but it paid off in the showrooms – more than 750,000 were sold between 1959 and 1969. Estate cars were offered in the Austin and Morris lines, but not in the more up-market marques. This is an Austin A55 Cambridge of 1959. (NMM)

A Jaguar E-type at Expo '67 in Toronto. Under the watchful eye of British Bulldogs, the Jaguar parades with mini-skirted dolly birds, accompanied by a Triumph GT6, a Mini, an unidentified bus and a David Brown tractor. (NMM)

There were already then strong indications of the cyclical nature of the market, rapid growth resulting in a new peak being followed by a period of stagnating or falling sales. This became particularly apparent in the 1960s. 1961 and 1962 were poor years, followed by another spurt of growth in 1963 and 1964 (induced by the cut in Purchase Tax in late 1962), then for the remainder of the decade sales stayed very flat and the next cycle of growth – followed by stagnation – would not follow until the early 1970s (see table for figures 1959–70).

The total registrations in the UK for the decade from 1960 to 1969 amounted to over ten million cars – 10,163,535, to be exact. Much the same total result over the period would have been achieved if the market had grown steadily for the ten years at a constant rate of 7.8 per cent per annum. There is little doubt that the often dramatic swings from year to year, from growth of almost 29 per cent

set up a fairly modest operation as their parts division headquarters in South Wales. By contrast, BMC began a new commercial vehicle and tractor factory in Bathgate in Lothian; Rootes also moved to Scotland, establishing the Hillman Imp factory at Linwood near Glasgow; Pressed Steel set up a factory on an adjoining site, originally manufacturing railway rolling stock, later supplying the Imp bodies, and eventually sold the complete factory to Rootes. The rest went to Merseyside – Standard-Triumph built a body and later an assembly plant at Speke, Vauxhall went to Ellsmere Port, and Ford to Halewood. In addition, Ford built an engine factory at Bridgend in South Wales, and a dedicated Transit commercial vehicle factory at Southampton. Of all these, only the Vauxhall and Ford factories are still operating; the rest were closed down when the British motor industry began to contract in the late 1970s.

The MGB was the company's first unitary construction sports car, and was to become their biggest seller, with more than half a million delivered between 1962 and 1980. This is a US specification model of 1962, with left hand drive. (NMM)

Despite the occasional set-back the development in the new car market in the UK has largely been one of growth. The best pre-war year had been 1937 with just over 318,000 new cars registered, a figure that was not to be improved upon after the war until 1954, when more than 394,000 new cars found buyers. The first half-million year came in 1955, then came the Suez crisis set-back of 1956–7, but further growth occurred in 1958–60.

in 1963 to the drop of 11.5 per cent in 1969, contributed to make life difficult for British car manufacturers when it came to planning future production. The problem was naturally exacerbated when one takes the widely varying export figures into account.

In the early post-war period distinct new trends had emerged in the car market. The necessity for export had encouraged car manufacturers to produce cars with larger engines than hitherto, and the government supported this by the introduction of the flat-rate tax (vehicle excise duty) in 1948, irrespective of engine size or other factors – a unique system compared to other European countries. The result was that by 1958, the 'over 2-litres' class accounted for almost 15 per cent of new registrations, an unheard-of figure by European standards – West Germany had at most five per cent of registrations in this class, France no more than two to three per cent, while in Italy it was negligible. All of the 'big five' car manufacturers in Britain of the late '50s contested the 2–3-litre class, and there were a dozen different models with engines over 3 litres – territory as yet uncontested by European manufacturers, apart from a single BMW model, the French Facel-Vega, and a couple of Italian luxury sports car makers. However, during the 1960s the relative importance of the large car class would decline in Britain, so that by 1969 only seven per cent of new cars registered had engines over 2 litres. (During the same decade, the German market for large cars, by contrast, increased substantially: by 1969 an estimated ten per cent of new German cars had engines of more than 2 litres.)

The smaller capacity classes were naturally more important. Taking again 1958 as the base year (in other words, before the introduction of the Mini), the 'below 1.2 litres' class accounted for 45 per cent of all registrations, and the '1.2 to 2 litres' class for 40 per cent. For a British manufacturer who wished to retain market share, it was necessary to offer at least one basic model in all three market sectors, although as yet only the two biggest makers, BMC and Ford, had complete market coverage. The three-model approach would come to dominate the thinking of British car makers in the 1960s, with Rootes and Vauxhall both entering the 'below 1.2 litres' class.

The typical model range that had become established at the end of the 1950s was as follows:

(1) A small four-cylinder car, with an engine between 800 cc and 1,200 cc, usually available in both two- and four-door saloon forms, and often also with an estate car derivative.
(2) A medium-sized four-door family saloon, with a four-cylinder engine between 1,400 cc and 1,700 cc, estate cars being slightly less common in this class.
(3) A six-cylinder four-door saloon with an engine between 2,200 cc and 2,700 cc. There were just a few estate cars available in this class.

Some of the independent specialists were active in the third class, but such specialized cars as were offered in the medium class were almost invariably products of big groups (BMC, Rootes) and were to a degree badge-engineered already before 1960, using at least mechanical components common to mass-production cousins (MG, Riley and Wolseley models based on Austin or Morris parts, or Singer and Sunbeam models based on the Hillman Minx).

One type of car which had emerged in the late 1940s was the 2-litre four-cylinder family saloon (typified by the Standard Vanguard; there was also the Austin A70 and the Humber Hawk). Such cars were originally designed for export and indeed did quite well for a time, until the locally-manufactured Holden was introduced in Australia, whereupon the Australian government introduced tariff barriers to protect the local industry. By the end of the 1950s, these cars had largely been overtaken by events, and were gradually being replaced by six-cylinder models, although both the Vanguard and Hawk remained in production in updated form.

In the 'over 3 litres' class, the specialists predominated. Of the 'big five' manufacturers, only BMC had a 4-litre car, the limited production Princess limousine. The leading manufacturer in this bracket was Jaguar, which comfortably outsold all other makers together.

Before 1965, the SMM&T did not collate and publish new vehicle registrations by make or model, but only by engine capacity, in steps of 100 cc. However, it is possible to judge the relative performance of various manufacturers, at least before 1959 when the Ford Anglia (997 cc) and the Triumph Herald (948 cc) both arrived to upset a virtual BMC monopoly in the 900–1,000 cc group. The figures for new car registrations in the UK in 1958 suggest that the individual car manufacturers had the following approximate market shares, estimated to nearest whole percentage point and split where appropriate into small cars (below 1,200 cc), medium cars (1,200–2,000 cc) and large cars (over 2,000 cc):

	BMC	Ford	Rootes	Vauxhall	Standard	Rover	Jaguar	Other UK	Imports
Small	23%	16%	–	–	4%	–	–		
Medium	17%	7%	9%	5%	1%	–	–		
Large	2%	3%	2%	3%	1%	2%	2%		
Total	42%	26%	11%	8%	6%	2%	2%	1%	1%

It will be seen that at this time, the 'big five' had a combined market share of 93 per cent. Without totally dominating the British market, BMC had the biggest market share by far, although it is likely that this had declined somewhat compared to the combined market share of Austin and Morris before 1952, which has been assessed as over 50% per cent. BMC could muster two popular family car makes, as well as three important specialist makes. They were able to offer buyers a choice of three or more cars in all the important market sectors, and had an unrivalled dealer network with more than 2,000 outlets. They were

Britain's largest producer of sports cars and had a number of other interesting niche models. BMC's capacity, had it been entirely devoted to home market production, could easily have met all requirements for new cars in the UK; however, they were also the nation's leading exporter. BMC's market share would decline during the 1960s, at home as well as abroad. The market share of the combined BL companies in 1968 and later would never equal that attained by BMC on its own in earlier years.

Ford, as described earlier, had a much simpler and more effective range. They had steadily been building

up their position in the UK since the 1930s, and although they introduced an increasing number of highly popular new cars in the 1960s – notably the Cortina – they would only substantially increase their market share and overtake BL in the 1970s. The other three big companies would not greatly alter their relative positions in the market-place during the 1960s, although Vauxhall would put on a few points to more closely equal Rootes, and Standard-Triumph also registered gains. The table below outlines the UK market shares of individual companies in the years from 1965 to 1970:

	1965	1966	1967	1968	1969	1970
BMC	35.65%	35.13%	29.22%	29.68%	29.91%	28.70%
Triumph	5.90%	6.77%	7.83%	7.30%	6.70%	5.95%
Rover	1.70%	2.24%	2.41%	2.43%	2.42%	2.35%
Jaguar	1.21%	1.09%	1.25%	1.15%	1.22%	1.12%
Total 'BL'	44.6%	45.23%	40.71%	40.56%	40.25%	38.12%
Ford	26.33%	25.06%	25.25%	27.28%	27.35%	26.53%
Rootes	11.92%	11.76%	12.16%	10.19%	9.67%	10.46%
Vauxhall	11.81%	11.17%	13.15%	13.15%	11.67%	9.99%
Other UK	0.35%	0.36%	0.42%	0.54%	0.63%	0.62%
Imports	5.13%	6.42%	8.31%	8.28%	10.43%	14.28%
Total	100.00%	100.00%	100.00%	100.00%	100.00%	100.00%

The Lotus Elan was described by Motor Sport's *editor William Boddy as 'one of the finest road clingers of all time'. Its 1,558 cc twin-ohc engine gave 105 bhp. These are S4 versions, made from 1969 to 1971, identifiable by the wide wheel arches to take low profile tyres.* (NMM)

It will be seen that the most dramatic movement within this table is the extraordinary drop in BMC's market share from 1966 to 1967, amounting to some 17 per cent of the 1966 share. The main beneficiaries of this seem to have been Vauxhall, and the imports. There is also a trend for both Rootes and Vauxhall to lose market share towards the end of the decade; this would in fact continue into the 1970s. Otherwise, the most striking feature is the relentless march of the imports, another trend which would be reinforced in the next decade. It may be added that at this time the import share of the UK market was still considerably lower than that of the main EEC countries – Germany, France and Italy in 1969 70 had an average share of some 24 per cent imports, about twice the UK figure. What happened was, of course, that the three large EEC member states were, by and large, selling cars to each other. Another way of looking at the figures is that if the imports are excluded, for instance, from the 1970 figure, the result is that in this year BL sold 44.47 per cent of all British cars in Britain. This still represents a drop from the late 1950s, where the combined share of the 'BL' makes was over 50 per cent of a market with hardly any import penetration.

Although the three-model pattern was to a degree still adhered to throughout the 1960s, a number of mould breaking new models appeared, and these would in the longer term alter our perceptions of the car market. The first was the BMC Mini of 1959 which brought the 'smaller than small' class to Britain, a type long favoured in France and Italy due to the different taxation structures of these countries but never able to make much impact in Germany owing to the leading market position of the Volkswagen. The Mini soon caught on and it is likely that in the period 1961–3 this model alone accounted for around 15 per cent of the UK home market. Some of the Mini's sales were genuinely 'new' sales in an expanding market; it is less likely that they represented conquest sales at

the cost of other manufacturers. Instead the Mini took sales away from other older BMC small car designs such as the Morris Minor. The Mini was followed by the much less successful Hillman Imp in 1963. Ford reputedly carried out a detailed cost analysis of an early Mini and concluded that BMC made a loss on each car; in consequence they decided not to enter this sector, and neither did Vauxhall. In the longer run, however, the existence of the Mini led directly to the new European 'supermini' class which was introduced after 1970, starting with the Fiat 127 and the Renault 5, and belatedly entered by Ford with the Fiesta in 1975.

The original British small car inevitably grew up over the years, notably with the introduction of the BMC 1100 in 1962, the Ford Escort in 1968, and also later generations of the Vauxhall Viva. By the 1980s, the direct successors to these cars would merge seamlessly into the other modern pan-European car class, the 1.3-litre hatchback typified by the VW Golf.

The second-mould breaker of the 1960s was the Ford Cortina of 1962, a 1.2-litre family saloon (soon also offered with a 1.5-litre engine). In terms of roominess and performance this was more than a match for the established 1.5-litre class, but it could be sold rather more cheaply thanks to Ford's painstaking weight saving, value engineering, and cost control. In the Cortina, the historian might to a degree see a revival of the old 10 hp class, spear-headed by the Hillman Minx in 1932. Where the original British tens had mostly grown into full-size 1.5-litre cars during the 1950s, the Cortina-size car also grew, by stages arriving at the typical 1.6-litre four/five-door family saloon of the 1980s. Thirty years later, this type of car also had a pan-European following.

By contrast, the original 1.5-litre class of the 1950s and 1960s lost out, except in those cases where later replacement models merged into the new executive class (for example: Ford Consul – Zephyr 4 – Granada – Scorpio; or Vauxhall Victor – Carlton – Omega). The emergence of the executive class as such was owing to the appearance in 1963 of a pair of new British cars, the third important mould-breakers of the period – the Rover 2000 and the Triumph 2000. Significantly both were products of smaller manufacturers, eager to extend market share by exploring new niches in the established car market hierarchy.

'The only rear-engined car to be made in any numbers in Britain', the Hillman Imp arrived too late and its production suffered from many teething problems. It was the last car to be built in quantity in Scotland, and was also badged as the Singer Chamois and Sunbeam Imp Sport. (NMM)

Two competitors for the burgeoning executive car class were announced within weeks of each other. The Rover 2000 (above) was the more advanced design with a unitary construction frame to which skin panels were bolted, a new four-cylinder single ohc engine, disc brakes all round, and totally fresh styling by David Bache. The Triumph 2000 (below) had an existing engine, the 2-litre six from the last Vanguard, and discs at the front only, but it was £170 cheaper. A fuel-injected 2½-litre engine arrived in 1969. (Both photos NMM)

Both were up-to-date in engineering and styling, they offered luxury and high performance in compact packages, and although they were more expensive than the Ford Zephyr/Vauxhall Velox type of car, their up-market image and cachet ensured them a ready following. Their success paralleled that of the BMW 'new class' in Germany.

Of the traditional British car classes of 30 years ago, only the original large family car has largely disappeared. Towards the end of the 1960s there was a marked swing away from the old-fashioned 3-litre six-cylinder car in favour of the new smaller executive models. The big Humbers were discontinued in 1967, the Austin 3-litre and Ford Zephyr/Zodiac in 1971, the Vauxhall Cresta/Viscount in 1972 and the Rover 3.5-litre in 1973. None of these cars had direct replacements in their makers' ranges, although often the same size engine would continue to be offered in a smaller bodyshell (Ford Granada, Rover 3500, and Vauxhall Ventora).

The specialist sectors of the 1960s have survived, more or less, although in the luxury sector the number of makes has been drastically reduced and Jaguar is now the only numerically significant such producer in Britain. The once-flourishing sports car sector gradually went into decline, and was almost deserted during the 1980s, although it was being rejuvenated in the early and mid-1990s. The Ford Capri, launched in 1969, was the first successful example of the non-sporting saloon-derived coupé in Britain. Another new type of vehicle, launched just after the 1960s were officially over, was the Range Rover, which began the trend towards luxurious leisure-type four-wheel-drive vehicles.

It will be clear from this brief outline how the traditional British three-car range of the 1950s developed into the four-car range which is now the European norm – for instance, Ford's Fiesta/Escort/Mondeo/Scorpio – offered with slight variations by all the European mass producers of today.

In terms of the number of different makes and models on offer, as late as 1960 there were some 40 different makes of car in regular production in Britain although only half had any status in the general market, and fifteen were brands manufactured by the 'big five' producers. This was still a significantly higher number than was available in Germany, France or Italy, and it could be argued that rationalization of the British motor industry was long overdue. Predictably, by 1970 the number of British makes had fallen below 30 – the more important of those which had gone are individually obituarized in the preceding section. About two dozen small specialist manufacturers also flitted across the stage during the 1960s but none had any lasting impact, nor was there any newcomer to the British industry during this period which would achieve any permanence.

In a previous table, the market shares of individual companies year by year from 1965 to 1970 were listed, but in the tables for the same years which appear at the end of this section, the ten best-selling models (or model ranges) have been quoted individually, with their actual annual sales figures, and their market shares in percentages. The ten best-selling models typically held almost 70 per cent of the market between them, while it was unusual for any one car to command 15 per cent of the market – the Cortina came nearest in 1967. This one year apart, it was the BMC 1100/1300 which was the best-seller of the period. The problems of Rootes are also high-lighted by the absence of any of their cars in the 1965 list, and the poor performance of the Imp throughout; on the other hand the new Arrow range (Hillman Hunter, etc) made an impressive debut performance, going straight into fifth place in its first full year of 1967.

It must be noted that there are consistent discrepancies between the 'total market' figures quoted in these tables, and the overall figures for registrations in the UK which are found elsewhere; the reason being that overall registration figures include certain types of vehicles which are excluded from the make/model statistics, such as first registrations of used vehicles (for instance, second-hand imports or ex-WD stock), and also tax-free Personal Export Delivery vehicles supplied under the Home Delivery Export Scheme which were temporarily registered in the UK. Hence the 'total market' figures for new car sales by make and model are lower than the overall registration figures.

1965

BMC 1100	157,679	14.35%
Ford Cortina	116,985	10.65%
BMC Mini	104,477	9.51%
Ford Anglia	84,589	7.70%
Vauxhall Victor	60,854	5.54%
Vauxhall Viva	58,884	5.36%
BMC 1.6 Farina	52,503	4.78%
Triumph Herald/ Vitesse	46,626	4.24%
Morris Minor	44,905	4.09%
Ford Corsair	44,463	4.05%
Total of above	771,965	70.25%
Total market	1,098,887	

1966

BMC 1100	151,946	14.51%
Ford Cortina	127,037	12.13%
BMC Mini	91,624	8.75%
Ford Anglia	68,209	6.51%
Vauxhall Viva	59,731	5.70%
BMC 1.6 Farina	48,077	4.59%
Vauxhall Victor	46,537	4.44%
Rootes Imp range	38,870	3.71%
Ford Corsair	38,412	3.67%
Triumph Herald/ Vitesse	38,076	3.63%
Total of above	708,519	67.64%
Total market	1,047,522	

1967

Ford Cortina	165,300	14.89%
BMC 1100/1300	131,382	11.89%
Vauxhall Viva	100,220	9.03%
BMC Mini	82,436	7.42%
Rootes 'Arrow' range	79,376	7.15%
Ford Anglia	55,735	5.02%
Rootes Imp range	40,858	3.68%
Vauxhall Victor	38,517	3.47%
Ford Corsair	35,993	3.24%
Morris Minor	34,565	3.11%
Total of above	764,382	68.85%
Total market	1,110,266	

1968

BMC 1100/1300	151,146	13.69%
Ford Cortina	137,873	12.49%
Vauxhall Viva	101,067	9.16%
Ford Escort	98,218	8.90%
BMC Mini	86,190	7.81%
Rootes 'Arrow' range	76,375	6.92%
Vauxhall Victor/ Ventora	40,128	3.64%
Rootes Imp range	35,295	3.20%
Ford Corsair	31,014	2.81%
BMC 1.6 Farina	30,284	2.74%
Total of above	787,590	71.35%
Total market	1,103,862	

1969

BMC 1100/1300	133,455	13.82%
Ford Cortina	116,185	12.03%
Ford Escort	85,156	8.82%
Vauxhall Viva	75,354	7.81%
BMC Mini	68,320	7.08%
Rootes 'Arrow' range	65,165	6.75%
Vauxhall Victor/ Ventora	33,582	3.48%
Ford Capri	33,047	3.42%
Rootes Imp range	28,161	2.92%
BMC 1800 range (est)	25,000	2.59%
Total of above	663,425	68.72%
Total market	965,410	

1970

BMC 1100/1300	132,965	12.35%
Ford Cortina	123,025	11.42%
Ford Escort	95,782	8.89%
BMC Mini	80,740	7.50%
Vauxhall Viva	76,838	7.14%
Hillman Avenger	50,133	4.66%
Rootes 'Arrow' range	43,111	4.00%
Ford Capri	38,340	3.56%
BMC 1800 range (est)	29,000	2.69%
Vauxhall Victor/ Ventora	27,930	2.59%
Total of above	697,864	64.81%
Total market	1,076,865	

The 1960s began a year early. In the words of the October 1959 edition of *The Times Survey of the British Motor Car Industry*, 1959 had been a 'vintage year for new models'. These ranged from BMC's new Mini, to a splendid new Rolls-Royce limousine reviving the Phantom name and introducing a remarkable all-aluminium V8 engine.

Of the new cars launched in 1959, the three small cars are of the greatest interest, firstly because they demonstrated a renewed interest in this sector of the market (which would be reinforced within a few years by the Hillman and Vauxhall small car contenders), and secondly because the BMC Mini, the new Ford Anglia, and the Triumph Herald all set the tone for subsequent developments from their respective manufacturers for the next decade.

Most revolutionary was the Mini. This Alec Issigonis design had originally been conceived in 1957 as a riposte to the bubble cars which had followed in the wake of the Suez crisis and petrol rationing. To obtain maximum space within the smallest possible bodyshell for four passengers and luggage, Issigonis turned the engine sideways to occupy a transverse position between the front wheels which were driven through a gearbox and final drive cleverly concealed in the engine sump. Other important features were all-independent suspension with rubber elements, and ten-inch diameter wheels. It was a mould-breaker in engineering as well as marketing terms. It created, in effect, an altogether new class of car, smaller although not a great deal cheaper than the accepted norm.

The basic design proved to be extremely versatile. Not only was the Mini acceptable across the board of all social classes – literally, it was bought by dustmen as well as duchesses – but a variety of Minis coped well with anything from winning major rallies to providing acceptable load-carrying in light commercial vehicle form. It is a tribute to the Mini and its designer that the original model lives on in production after more than 35 years, and that the vast majority of the world's motor cars now have transverse engines and front wheel drive.

The Triumph Herald featured Italian styling by Michelotti but, unusually by 1959, a separate chassis in place of the now accepted norm of the unitary construction body. The reason was that its sponsors could not afford the substantial investment required for unitary body tooling, nor did Standard-Triumph have the capacity to make such bodies on their own, and found it difficult to find an outside supplier to do it for them. So Herald bodies came in sections from a variety of suppliers to be assembled, Meccano-fashion, in Standard-Triumph's Coventry factory. The suppliers included Triumph Body Plant (formerly Fisher & Ludlow), Coventry; Mulliners, Birmingham; Hall Engineering (later Triumph body plant), Speke, Liverpool; Forward Radiator (part of Mulliners), Birmingham; Pressed Steel, Cowley; and Auto Body Dies, Dunstable (subsidiary of Hall Engineering). This expediency was put to good effect when Triumph offered the Herald with alternative body styles at little extra cost, including a convertible. There would also be other models built on the same basic chassis, including the Vitesse, an unusually small six-cylinder sports saloon, and the Spitfire and GT6 sports cars.

The Herald had a turning circle to rival London taxis

Other features of the Herald included an all-independent suspension system, although the rear suspension featured rather basic swing axles and a transverse leaf spring. The car also had a turning circle small enough to rival London taxis, and it was one of the first cars to be designed with fewer than normal greasepoints, which helped to cut down the need for regular servicing and maintenance. In pricing and marketing terms the model was pitched a little upwards of cars of the same size, although in its original form the car was singularly devoid of luxury features. It was obviously felt that the Triumph name was worth paying over the odds for.

By contrast to the Mini and the Herald, Ford's new Anglia was, in mechanical terms, largely conventional. Its engine was, however, of oversquare, ultra shortstroke type; cylinder dimensions of 81 mm by 48 mm would, a generation earlier, have rated the engine at 16 RAC hp, twice the norm for 1-litre cars. Its four-speed gearbox was Ford's first, but this was progress only by Dagenham's conservative standards. In true Ford tradition it was excellent value for money, with smart styling and a reverse-angle rear window which gave it a valuable instant-recognition factor. The combination of independent front suspension with McPherson struts and simple semi-elliptic leaf springs for the live rear axle was well-established Ford practice.

Most of the other new models of 1959 were down to BMC. Their medium and large car offerings were largely rationalized into two new basic bodyshells, both styled by Pinin Farina – a generously-proportioned 1.5-litre saloon under any of five badges, and a rather handsome six-cylinder car with a 3-litre engine, carrying three different nameplates. Technically, the bigger car was more interesting, with servo-assisted front disc brakes and a fully-synchronised three-speed gearbox with dual overdrive as standard, while an automatic gearbox was optional. With the Farina range, BMC went in for badge-engineering with a vengeance. The smaller car was remarkably successful in anybody's terms, about 750,000 being made until 1971, but the willy-nilly application of MG and Riley badges on what was very visibly an Austin Cambridge (with uninspired chassis design) hastened the demise respectively of MG saloons, and of the Riley marque altogether. The original rather extravagant tailfins were slightly cut back in a 1961 facelift which also saw engine sizes increased to 1.6 litres and the introduction of an optional automatic gearbox, the first in Britain on a medium-sized car. Another pioneering effort was the introduction of diesel-engined versions. The cars continued in some models until 1971 without much further in the way of updating and still sold remarkably well at the end of the decade.

Rootes's 1959 contribution was the Sunbeam Alpine, an interesting contender in the sports car market from which the company had been absent for some six seasons. The body styling was to a degree influenced by contemporary American themes, but Rootes cars normally had an American flavour and British sports cars were built with the American market in mind anyway. The platform for the unitary body came from the Hillman Husky, in effect a short-wheelbase version of the Hillman Minx saloon. Where the Alpine scored was in its roomy cabin and notable creature comforts by sports car standards, such as wind-down windows. Its most serious handicap in the long term was always its engine size, which constantly lagged behind the better-established competition from MG and Triumph.

The specialist car makers excelled themselves in engine design. Not only was there a V8 from Rolls-Royce (which, as some critics have alleged, may have been based on an existing Chrysler design, but was surely none the worse for it) but Daimler outshone them with *two* V8s, a 2.5-litre and a 4.5-litre, both designed by Edward Turner and both of them excellent engines. Where Rolls-Royce cast their engine in aluminium alloy, both the Daimler engines were of cast iron.

The Rolls-Royce V8 was installed in the current Rolls-Royce and Bentley saloons, and also in a new long wheelbase limousine reviving the Phantom name as the fifth incarnation of this model. The generous proportions of this chassis in terms of length devoted to passenger accommodation dictated bodies that were impressive rather than elegant. Phantom V cars, were, however, brought into use as official state cars for Her Majesty the Queen, thereby ending Daimler's long monopoly of this select business.

Daimler by this time could not produce a car to match the excellence of their new engines. The 2.5-litre engine was installed in a most un-Daimler-like car, the SP.250 sports model, with a chassis copied from the Triumph TR3A and a fibreglass body of dubious aesthetics. The bigger engine simply replaced the existing six-cylinder unit in Daimler's rather dowagerish saloon and limousine models. Neither were best-seller material. The V8 engines were Daimler's last gasp and the company was soon taken over by Jaguar.

In 1961 the accent was on medium-sized family cars

This new crop of models introduced at the threshold of a new decade offered contemporary observers as well as motoring historians a great deal of interest. The variety of new designs and the engineering ingenuity that had made them possible were encouraging pointers at the start of a new period in the history of the British motor industry. Almost every year from now on saw the introduction of a major new model from either a mass producer or a specialist manufacturer, and many of these new cars made substantial contributions to the progress of the industry and the state of British car design in general.

If everyone took a bit of breathing space in 1960, full activity was resumed in 1961. This year the accent seemed to be on the medium-sized family cars. As previously mentioned, these were face-lifted and modified versions of BMC's popular Farina saloons – all five of them. Ford brought out the Consul Classic (or 315) model which was, broadly speaking, a bigger Anglia, sharing the smaller car's over-square engine if with a longer stroke for 1,340 cc, and also featuring the Anglia's reverse-angle rear window. Unusually for this class, a two-door version was available. It was the first popular family saloon in Britain to feature front disc brakes and double

round headlamps but, despite the addition of an eye-catching Capri coupé version, was ultimately not successful in the market-place and was withdrawn after a short production run of two years.

To counter Ford, Vauxhall introduced a new Victor which was little changed from the original model in mechanical terms but which had much more restrained styling, and therefore found greater acceptance in the market. Vauxhall began a trend by offering the VX4-90 version, which apart from stylistic differences had a tuned engine, a floor-mounted gear-lever for its four-speed box, and a rev counter on the instrument panel. The third new medium-sized car had been intended as a straight replacement for the ageing Hillman Minx but turned out to be too large, heavy and expensive; it was instead launched as the Super Minx, with the inevitable attendant badge-engineered luxury models in tow: Singer Vogue and Humber Sceptre. (The earlier Minx and its derivatives were kept in production alongside the new cars.) Styling was a little heavy-handed, especially in Singer and Humber versions, and there was little of interest in the mechanical specification. It was one of the last new cars which was also offered in a convertible version, though this variant did not last long.

There was even more interest on the sports car front, with no less than three major new designs. Smallest and simplest was a restyled Austin-Healey Sprite which soon also spawned an MG Midget derivative, selling at a slightly higher price. The major improvements over the original Sprite were that the new car had an external opening bootlid, and a more conventional headlamp position. The Triumph TR4 was also in mechanical terms based on the superseded TR3A model, but had an all-new Michelotti-styled body which followed the example of the Sunbeam Alpine by offering improved comfort with wind-down windows and the option of an integrated hard top, with the unusual removable targa-type 'surrey' top. The later TR4A version adopted independent rear suspension.

Infinitely more spectacular was the Jaguar E-type, which made its debut in the Geneva show in March 1961. Here was the long-awaited successor to the famed XK-range, incorporating all the lessons which Jaguar had learned from their successful career in racing with the C- and D-types. The heart of the car was still the XK engine, in three carburettor 3.8-litre form giving 265 bhp, and assuring the car of a top speed of nearly 150 mph – measured at least by the motoring magazines, if rarely attained in practice by ordinary owners with standard cars. Most sensational was the price, which was £2,036 for the open two-seater, about £100 more for the fastback fixed-head coupé: only four times the cost of a Mini. The E-type styling was unmistakably Jaguar, and Jaguar at its best. What was not readily apparent at first was that the car also represented a major step forward for the company, with its part-unitary construction and sophisticated all-independent suspension, setting the pattern for all following new models.

By the time the London Motor Show came round in October, Jaguar had a further sensation – the new Mark X saloon, which adapted the E-type suspension arrangements and engine to a large new luxury saloon. It attracted notice as Britain's biggest car so far with unitary body construction, and while the styling at first drew favourable comment in comparison with the Mark IX model which it replaced, the Mark X has worn rather less well than most Jaguars and to most subsequent observers appears rather too bulky. Like the E-type it was remarkable value for money, at £2,256 undercutting its nearest rival, the similarly-specified Lagonda Rapide, by more than half.

The ball was firmly back in BMC's court in 1962. The year's two most important newcomers were both from Britain's biggest company. First came the Morris 1100, first of the ADO 16 models which it is simpler to refer to by the common designation of BMC 1100; an MG version was available from the start, Austin followed in 1963, Vanden Plas in 1964, and Riley and Wolseley in 1965. It was to some extent a scaled-up Mini, now with four-door saloon bodywork and interior space which would rival the 1.6-litre Farina models which were a good 30 in longer overall. The engine was yet another variety of the well-proven A-series, of 1,098 cc. Like the Mini, suspension was all-independent, but now using the clever Moulton-designed Hydrolastic system which used fluid as the suspension medium and was interconnected front to rear on either side of the car. It gave an at the time unrivalled combination of road holding and comfort. Styling was by Pinin Farina, an unusually neat two-box saloon whose proportions did not betray the tight packaging imposed by the Issigonis principles. Destined to become Britain's best-seller, the new model was hailed by *The Autocar* as a 'world car'.

BMC's other new contender was the MGB, replacement for the seven-year old MGA and a valuable up-date of a traditional design. It featured unitary construction bodywork, of mildly Italianate design although it was in fact designed in-house at Abingdon. Suspension and braking systems were little changed in principle, but the MGA's BMC B-series engine was bored out for a capacity of 1,798 cc. The MGB followed Sunbeam's and Triumph's example by improving cabin comfort, and new to the marque was the optional overdrive which was made available a few months after introduction. Although nobody at the time realised it, the MGB was destined for an 18-year lifespan and, with a total production exceeding 500,000, would become Britain's all-time most successful and best-loved sports car.

Another new sports model was offered by Triumph, the Spitfire 4, which was based on the Herald chassis but with a Michelotti-styled open two-seater body. This was a rival for BMC's Sprite and Midget series and threw down the gauntlet by offering a larger engine and a roomier, more comfort-

The Triumph 1300, of which 113,000 were made from 1965 to 1970, used the engine of the Herald 13/60, with the gearbox beneath it in Mini fashion, driving the front wheels. Unlike the Mini, the engine was longitudinal. Apart from the BMC models, it was Britain's only front-drive car at the time. The same body was later used for the rear-drive Toledo and the more exciting Dolomite. (Nick Georgano).

able cockpit. Remarkably, the Spitfire too would have an 18-year run, gradually acquiring engines of increased size. Also Herald-derived was the Triumph Vitesse, an interesting sports saloon with a 1.6-litre six-cylinder engine in an otherwise little modified Herald chassis and body. This was the smallest six to be offered in Britain since the 1930s and offered excellent performance coupled with refinement.

Ford and Vauxhall both had new contenders in the large saloon car class. The Ford Zephyr/Zodiac Mark III range was available with either four- or six-cylinder engines in time-honoured Ford tradition. The styling was brought up-to-date and these were the first production cars with curved side windows. The new Vauxhall Velox/Cresta range was only available in six-cylinder form, and was chiefly notable for its restrained styling, like the 1961 Victor a welcome change from the excesses of the previous Vauxhall generation.

There was, however, another new car from Ford, the first of the famous Cortina models. This was a particularly large and roomy saloon for its 1,200 cc engine. At 14 ft it was, for instance, 2 in longer than the Hillman Super Minx, yet it weighed only 15 cwt against the 21 cwt of the Hillman; even the Morris 1100, which was almost 2 ft shorter than the Cortina, weighed 16 cwt. The new Ford was the first car with a scientifically-designed lightweight bodyshell, which also enabled Ford to make important cost savings – the Cortina, model by model, cost less than the Morris 1100 equivalents. The styling was plain and much less fussy than other recent Fords, but appealed to most people. Interior accommodation was ample for four, and the boot was cavernous. In mechanical terms, the short-stroke engine, four-speed gearbox and McPherson strut front suspension followed established Ford practice. In 1963, 1,500 cc versions followed, also a tuned GT model, while eventually there would also be a desirable Lotus-Cortina with the Lotus-developed – but Ford-based – twin

overhead cam engine. Although it took almost ten years for the Cortina to become decisively established as Britain's best-selling car, by which time it had gone into its third manifestation, this new Ford was undoubtedly from the start Dagenham's hitherto strongest challenge to the British competition.

The final important new model of 1962 was proof of the continuing vitality of the specialist car builders, in this case Lotus. The first Elan featured the twin ohc 1.5-litre engine based on the Ford short-stroke design, mounted in a backbone chassis with all-independent suspension based on Lotus racing car practice. Other features were rack-and-pinion steering and four-wheel disc brakes. The lithe open two-seater body featured retractable headlamps and was constructed from fibreglass. The result was extremely impressive, but in broad terms the Elan cost 50 per cent more than an MGB and was therefore not entirely viable unless sold in Purchase Tax-saving kit form. It was destined to remain a limited-production machine, appealing mainly to the *cognoscenti*.

Rover and Triumph tapped the executive market with their 2000 models

---

The following year saw increased activity on the small car front. Of the new 1963 cars, in many ways the most remarkable was the Hillman Imp, Rootes's belated entry in the small car class. This was the only rear-engined car ever to be made in any numbers in Britain and arrived at a time when this configuration was losing popularity elsewhere. The engine itself was an aluminium four-in-line of 875 cc, based on a Coventry Climax design with an overhead camshaft, and tilted over on its side. Suspension was all-independent. Some effort was made to overcome the traditional packaging deficiencies of the rear engine layout, and the Imp had an opening rear window which gave access to a deep

luggage shelf behind the rear seat. The seat back folded forward to extend luggage space, and there was also a small 'boot' under the front 'bonnet'. The neat styling was clearly inspired by the Chevrolet Corvair. Built in an all-new factory at Linwood in Scotland, the Imp was plagued by numerous teething troubles and would never constitute a threat to the dominant position of the Mini in the small car class. The cost of the Imp project, and the relative failure of the model, contributed to drive Rootes into the arms of Chrysler.

A very different approach was followed by Vauxhall, whose new Viva was as conventional as could be. Not apparent to the casual observer, nor made much of at the time, was the fact that its salient features were largely shared with the Opel Kadett, introduced in the previous year by GM's German subsidiary. Unusual for the time was the transverse leaf spring for the independent front suspension. The styling was box-like but the car was fully competitive with the Ford Anglia and enabled Vauxhall to extend their market coverage and market share. There would later be a tuned Brabham version, while the Viva estate car turned out to be, literally, a van with windows. The van itself was badged as the Bedford HA.

In the medium range of family cars, the Ford Corsair was the only newcomer. This replaced the unloved Classic model and was positioned rather further up-market from the Cortina. The Corsair was chiefly remarkable for its styling, clearly paying homage to the American Ford Thunderbird with its pointed, dart-like profile. It was the largest British saloon and the only 1.5-litre model to be offered with the option of a two-door saloon body. In 1965, the Corsair became the first British Ford car to receive the new German-inspired V4 engine, in 1,700 and 2,000 cc forms, and Ford started a fashion in the luxury-saloon market with the 2000E model – E for executive – in early 1967, complete with vinyl-covered roof.

The 'executive' business had arguably started in the year the first Corsair was born, as 1963 also saw the appearance of two trend-setting new models from Rover and Triumph, both called 2000. Although clearly aimed at the same market sector, the two cars were very different. The Rover was the more exciting, especially as one had not expected one of Britain's stuffier car makers to come up with anything like this. The unitary construction body was built as a 'base unit' with non-structural bolt-on skin panels. Styling, by Rover's David Bache, had started out with strong Citroën DS19 overtones, although the end result was more conventional, an elegant semi-Italian three-box saloon with a hint of a wedge shape and a totally un-Rover like full-width radiator grille incorporating quad headlamps.

The engine was a single ohc square (85 mm by 85 mm) four which had the so-called Heron cylinder head with a flat face and the combustion chambers in the piston crowns. The engine bay it sat in had been designed with a view to accommodating a gas turbine engine, which also meant that the front suspension layout was unusual, bell cranks operating coil springs attached horizontally to the bulkhead. At the rear, there was a De Dion axle. Disc brakes were fitted all round, inboard at the back, and the Rover 2000 was the first British car to be fitted exclusively with radial tyres as standard. The interior was rather stark by Rover standards but had several notable safety and ergonomic features. The rear seat was shaped as two individual seats. The whole design was so notable and incorporated so many brilliant features that the Rover 2000 was chosen as the first international Car of the Year, as well as receiving other awards.

The Triumph 2000 was more conventional, but still held a lot of interest. Its handsome Michelotti-designed bodyshell was one of the first to reintroduce the quarterlight in the rear pillar. The engine was Triumph's well-proven straight six, first seen three years earlier in the last Vanguard.

All independent suspension was part of Triumph's stock repertoire but, unlike the swing axles of the Herald family, the 2000 had proper diagonal trailing arms, rather similar to, for instance, the German BMW 1500, and the Triumph likewise adopted McPherson struts at the front. The adoption of rack-and-pinion steering on such a large car caused a few raised eyebrows among contemporary commentators.

Both the new 2000s sold at premium prices compared to the larger six-cylinder family cars from Ford and Vauxhall – the Zephyr 6 and Velox both cost around £840, the Triumph 2000 £1,094 and the Rover £1,264, which took it almost into Jaguar territory; a Mark II 2.4-litre cost £1,348. As compact luxury cars offering excellent performance, both found a ready market, and both lived on side by side until 1976, long after their makers had been merged. There was also an additional Jaguar model in 1963, the S-type, which was an updated Mark II featuring the independent rear suspension from the E-type and Mark X and a restyled rear end.

After the spate of new cars in 1963, 1964 was a much quieter year. Vauxhall restyled the Victor, which became the 101 model, roomier but not as elegant as its predecessor. Vauxhall was now well into an almost American-like cycle of replacing or at least restyling their models every three years. The small specialist maker of three-wheelers and sports cars, Reliant, brought out the Scimitar GT which had an Ogle-styled fibreglass body fitted on the existing Sabre chassis with its Ford Zephyr engine. The body design had originally been intended for the Daimler SP250. It was the first of several Ogle-styled Reliant cars and would gain particular fame when later developed into the GTE sports estate model.

The most important new car during the year was the Austin 1800, third and largest of the Issigonis designs. Like the Mini and 1100, it had the transverse engine formula, and also featured

Hydrolastic suspension. The original body styling was by Pinin Farina, but in this case had been unsubtly changed by BMC's own designers. The most remarkable feature of the 1800 was the incredible amount of interior room it offered, with more comfortable accommodation than most 3-litre cars. Unusually for an Issigonis-designed BMC car, even the boot was capacious. The engine was a new derivative of the B-series, like the MGB of 1,798 cc but now with a five main bearing crankshaft. Much was made of the remarkable torsional stiffness of the bodyshell, and although at 22 cwt the car was heavy for its small overall dimensions (less than 14 ft long), performance was reasonable. While attracting a great deal of admiration, the 1800 was a little too expensive to become a straight replacement for the 1.6 Farina series (which was kept in production and which outsold the new model), and was seemingly not quite the car that the British family motorist wanted. It was plagued by numerous teething troubles which did not, however, prevent it from being 1964's Car of the Year.

The years from 1965 to 1969 saw perhaps rather less in the way of outstanding new designs than had appeared in the first half of the decade, but there were still many interesting new cars to come. The most outstanding of the 1965 crop was undoubtedly the Rolls-Royce Silver Shadow and its Bentley sister. These replaced the outdated ten-year old Silver Cloud models, although the relatively new 6.2-litre aluminium V8 engine was carried over unchanged. The Silver Shadow was the first Rolls-Royce to adopt unitary construction. Styling was restrained. The most commented-on feature was that the famous radiator was so much lower that it almost reverted to the original pre-First World War proportions. Fully independent suspension was featured, with trailing arms and coil springs at the rear, and there was a hydraulic self-levelling system. There were disc brakes all round, with triple hydraulic circuits and vacuum servo assistance. The hydraulic systems for self-levelling, brakes and power steering were based on those of the French Citroën. As befitted a Rolls-Royce, enormous care had been lavished on the design to ensure traditional standards of refinement, but with its more compact dimensions, lower stance and lighter weight than its predecessor, the new model also had improved performance and an almost sporting character.

Also of technical interest was the Triumph 1300, a compact saloon with some luxury touches which was the only front-wheel drive car in Britain apart from the BMC models. It had an in-line engine mounted above the gearbox. The engine was derived from the existing Herald unit while the styling was a shrunken version of the Triumph 2000. Rear suspension was naturally independent and the car had several interesting comfort and convenience features, like multi-adjustable steering wheel and driver's seat. Too expensive to become a Herald replacement, the 1300 was in its original form a brave effort, but the basic design would later be mutilated and ended up as the uninspired rear-wheel drive Toledo.

More simple and straightforward was the next generation Vauxhall Cresta model (the Velox name was dropped), with a 3.3-litre engine now Britain's largest capacity family saloon in the under £1,000 bracket, and bringing to Britain the latest American styling fad – the Coke-bottle shape of dubious merit. Still to come was a new luxury version labelled as the Viscount. In the sports car field, the new GT version of the MGB deserves a mention. Conceived as 'the poor man's Aston Martin', this model was a car that 'no managing director need be ashamed of turning up at the office in' and it became as successful as the roadster. More intriguing was the Jensen FF, at this time still sharing the awkwardly-styled fibreglass body of the CV8 model as well as the Chrysler V8 engine. This was the first production car to feature the Ferguson four-

Made in England and Germany, the Ford Capri was aimed at a variety of markets. Adopting the strategy of the American Ford Mustang, it was available from the start with four sizes of engine, 1300 and 1600 in-line fours, a 2-litre V4 and 3-litre V6, with power ranging from 61 to 140 bhp. This is a 1970 1600GT XLR with a top speed of 100 mph. (NMM)

wheel drive system and Dunlop's Maxaret anti-skid braking system. The FF would have a greater impact when it was re-launched using the new Vignale-designed all-steel Interceptor body which Jensen introduced a year later.

Apart from the new Jensen, 1966 was largely a year for new family cars. There was a restyled version of the Vauxhall Viva, abandoning the box-like Mark 1 shape for a reduced version of the Cresta's Coke-bottle styling, and incidentally the first British car to adopt rectangular headlamps. Ford had a new Cortina, largely following the successful recipe of the original model. Of greater interest was the all-new Zephyr/Zodiac Mark IV range. The extravagantly long bonnet was a legacy of American styling but was partly justified by the Citroën-like fitting of the spare wheel in front of the radiator. Further back in the engine bay you would come across either the Corsair 2-litre V4, or the first British Ford V6 engine – of 2.5 litres in the Zephyr and 3 litres in the Zodiac. This was the first Ford car to feature independent rear suspension, with trailing arms and coil springs similar to the systems adopted by Triumph and

Rolls-Royce.

Rootes introduced a new Hillman saloon, first under the name of Hunter with a 1.7-litre engine, a little later also as a Minx with a 1.5-litre engine, as well as Singer Vogue/Gazelle derivatives, followed by a Humber Sceptre and a fastback coupé under the Sunbeam name. Such badge-engineering was still the accepted norm. Collectively known as the 'Arrow' range, these cars quickly replaced the previous Rootes mid-range saloons and restored the company's popularity in this important sector of the market. The design was simple but effective, with a lightweight body and McPherson struts taking a leaf out of Ford's book, and the Arrow may indeed be seen as the first of several British cars designed in response to the Cortina. Among other new 1966 cars was the Triumph GT6, a fastback coupé version of the Spitfire fitted with the 2000 six-cylinder engine, and yet another variation on existing themes from Jaguar in the shape of the 420 saloon with a Daimler counterpart under the Sovereign name. BMC had nothing to offer beyond an estate car version of the 1100 and a Morris-badged 1800.

There was still little in the way of new models from BMC in 1967. The Mini and 1100 ranges were offered with larger engines – 998 cc and 1,275 cc respectively – in that autumn's Motor Show, and also had modest stylistic facelifts. There was also the inevitable Wolseley version of the 1800, offering power steering as standard and with an optional automatic gearbox where the primary drive from engine to gearbox was by roller chain. Shown in prototype form at Earls Court in 1967 was the new Austin 3-litre, the replacement for the ageing Farina range. This was a disappointment. The centre body section was from the 1800 but longer front and rear ends had been grafted on. The 3-litre engine was fitted with a seven main bearing crank. The car had rear-wheel drive, and the all-independent suspension was a developed Hydrolastic system to which self-levelling had been added. The same engine went into the MGC, a supplementary model to the MGB which was modified in detail.

The most important new model of the year was an all-new Vauxhall Victor. Styling was similar to the latest Viva and Cresta models but the engine

was a brand-new 1.6/2-litre unit which was Britain's first to have a single overhead camshaft driven by cogged belt. It was canted over at 45° to allow a lower bonnet line. While Vauxhall still eschewed independent rear suspension, there were now coil springs and a Panhard rod for the rear axle. Oddly, a three-speed gearbox was still listed as standard. While Ford had no major new model on offer, the Cortina benefited from being fitted with a revised engine with a cross-flow cylinder head where the combustion chambers, Rover 2000-like, were in the pistons.

Among the specialists, Lotus had a developed GT version of the Elan known as the '+2' model, as well as the Europa, which was Britain's first mid-engined sports car to go into production. Of exceptionally low build, the Europa originally used the French Renault 16 engine and was at first only available for export. It later received Lotus's normal Ford-based twin ohc engine. Another significant development in the sports car sector was that the first British car with petrol injection went on sale – this was an updated version of Triumph's classic TR4 design, with a 2.5-litre version of the

2000's six-cylinder engine, and a Lucas mechanical injection system. Oddly enough the North American export version, the TR250, stuck with traditional carburettors. The PI engine would later go into Triumph's large saloon model as well.

This was also the year when Rover adopted V8 power. The 3.5-litre aluminium engine was a design which Rover bought from GM's Buick division in the USA, and its extra power transformed the existing P.5 model. Subsequently, the same engine was fitted in the P.6 2000 model, as well as in the Range Rover of 1970 and other later Rover and Land-Rover models. It was also adopted by a multitude of small specialist car makers led by Morgan, and the engine survives in production to this day, notably in 4- and 4.6-litre forms in the current Range Rover.

The most elegant debutante of 1967 was undoubtedly the Aston Martin DBS, replacing the ten-year old basic design of the DB4/5/6 range. The styling was the work of ex-Rover designer William Towns. Built on the existing DB6 platform, the new car had alloy body panels over a tubular structure on the Superleggera principles. There was a De Dion rear axle in place of the superseded car's live axle. The engine was the classic Aston Martin twin ohc 4-litre straight six, but the DBS would soon receive an all-new four ohc V8 engine of 5.3 litres, installed in the DBS V8 of 1969, and still around in the 1990s to power a later generation of Aston Martin cars.

In January 1968, Ford broke the established custom of introducing new models in the run-up period to the Motor Show by introducing the Escort, a replacement for the Anglia. Apart from the Transit van of 1965, this was the first European Ford, going into production in Germany a few months later. The base model had

The Lotus Elan chassis, showing the box-section backbone frame branched out at front and rear to hold the engine and strut suspension. (NMM)

grown to 1,100 cc, and at the top of the range was a version with the Lotus-developed 1.6 litre twin cam engine. It was the first Ford to feature rack-and-pinion steering. Suspension was conventional and the car, of course, still had rear wheel drive. Styling was perhaps more anonymous than the Anglia with a normal rear window but the new model was roomier. A four-door saloon version was added later.

The trend away from the six-seater family barges towards the smaller 'executive' type of car was marked not only by the Rover 3500, extending V8 power to the smaller P.6 range, but also by the Vauxhall Ventora, a Victor into which the big 3.3-litre straight six from the Cresta had been shoe-horned. (Opel in Germany had performed a similar trick with the Rekord-6 in 1964.) Of the large family cars, the big Humbers had already disappeared without replacement, and the new Austin 3-litre was proving to be a lame duck in the market-place.

The most important British newcomer of 1968 was the Jaguar XJ6, launched in September to international acclaim. Its superb styling was the last – and greatest – of the William Lyons design. While the car still relied on the well-proven XK engine, it was designed so that it would accept Jaguar's new V12 engine which was well ahead in design and would be unveiled in 1971. Meanwhile, the XJ6 in 4.2-litre form offered superb performance and refinement; the new smaller 2.8-litre engine was mainly intended as a tax-beater for certain export markets and has left behind a mixed reputation for reliability. Where the XJ6 mainly impressed was by its extraordinary refinement, coupled to impeccable road holding and handling. The well-established all-independent suspension was modified and refined, with anti-dive geometry for the front suspension, and specially developed rubber mountings for the front and rear suspension subframes. Jaguar now also adopted rack-and-pinion steering, with power assistance, and there were dual circuits for the disc brakes.

Dunlop developed special low-profile radial tyres for the car. The only slight criticism of the XJ6 was that interior room, especially in the back, was limited, partly due to the low build of the car – something which in due course would be addressed by a long wheelbase version – but there was little doubt that Jaguar now had its finest-ever saloon car, able to challenge the best in the world, including Rolls-Royce.

The Maxi's seating would convert into a double bed

The last year of the decade was dominated by two vastly different new designs from Britain's two greatest manufacturers. If the long-awaited Austin Maxi was the motoring equivalent of the Proverbs, then the Ford Capri was more like the Psalms. The Capri came first, in January 1969, and like the year-old Escort was a European car. It had only the name and its general coupé configuration in common with the previous Classic-based model. While not a sports car, its styling and, in larger-engined models, its performance were sufficient for it to become a potential rival to some MG and Triumph models, not least because of its attractive price. It was based on a combination of Escort and Cortina mechanical components but offered an unusually wide variety of engines, from 1.3- and 1.6-litre straight fours, through the 2-litre V4 to the 3-litre V6. Its appeal was further enhanced by Ford's cleverly packaged option scheme which enabled you to all but personalise your Capri. It was touted as 'the car you have always promised yourself' and went straight into the best-seller list.

Where the Capri was conventional and pretty, the Maxi was completely the opposite. Despite some last-minute styling retouches, it was an uncompromisingly functional car, the final product of the Issigonis school of thought. The transverse engine, front-wheel

drive and Hydrolastic suspension were standard BMC practice, but there was a new engine, the 1.5-litre E-series with a single overhead camshaft, and the sump-mounted gearbox was a fully-synchronized five-speeder – Britain's first – sadly marred by an 1800-like cable activated gearchange. The Maxi was the first properly-designed five-door hatchback saloon in Britain and had an incredibly versatile interior with seating that would convert into a double bed for those that were that way inclined. The car was let down by poor performance, the styling, the gearchange, and by the usual BMC teething troubles; it did not sell in anything like the hoped-for numbers.

Apart from a few styling touches, the Maxi was still really a BMC car and less influenced by the new management of British Leyland. The same could not be said for the new Mini versions which appeared before the end of 1969, with a rather pointless front end restyling job for the Clubman and 1275GT models. It was also a year of restyling for Triumph, face-lifted versions of the 2000 and 2500 PI saloon models appearing, as well as the TR6 sports car, a reskinned version of the TR5/250 models.

So the decade ended, with Britain's other manufacturers having little to offer. In fact there would be more excitement in store for 1970, with new models such as the Triumph Stag and the Range Rover, apart from the Hillman Avenger and an oddity such as the Bond Bug – yet most of the new designs of the next decade would prove unable to match the high standards of innovation set by British car makers throughout most of the 1960s.

Consider this: At the beginning of 1959, all British cars had front engines and rear-wheel drive (barring a few left-over microcars or bubble cars). Only the AC Ace and the Lotus Elite sports cars had independent rear suspension. They were also the only cars to have single overhead camshaft engines, while twin overhead cam engines were found only in Aston

Martins, Jaguars and the MGA Twin Cam. Outside the luxury class, disc brakes were found only on a handful of sports cars. Rack-and-pinion steering was used on some sports cars, but its main exponent in the family car class was the Morris Minor. Ford and Vauxhall all still had three-speed gearboxes, column changes were common, and no all-synchromesh gearbox was available. Automatic gearboxes were optional on most larger-engined cars but no car with an engine of less than 2 litres could be so equipped, although some 1.5-litre saloons had various semi-automatic shift devices.

On the plus side, unitary construction bodies had become the accepted norm, and virtually all cars had independent front suspension, usually with coil springs; torsion bars were less common. The only truly antiquated car was the authentic pre-war style Ford Popular with its side-valve engine, mechanical brakes, and transverse leaf springs for its front and rear beam axles; it would be discontinued in 1959, although its engine lived on for another couple of years, as the last production side-valve engine. While most British cars were up to the average standard of popular Continental designs, there was as yet no British design which could be compared with the best of advanced European practice. The balance would be redressed before the year was out, and new British cars over the next few years not only caught up with Continental designs but were often more advanced.

Of the engineers who had made these changes possible, the foremost was Alec Issigonis of BMC, who became a media star and received the ultimate accolade of a knighthood. Several of his colleagues in the motor industry were also moved into the limelight, including Peter Ware of Rootes, Harry Webster of Triumph, and Spen King of Rover. It became quite the fashion for motor manufacturers to demonstrate their awareness of current and future trends in engineering design. By contrast, the emerging motor industry folk heroes

of the 1970s were mostly stylists.

At the end of the 1960s, Britain had five different front-wheel drive cars and one rear-engined model in production. Overhead camshafts and in particular independent rear suspension were becoming commonplace, and front disc brakes were near-universal. Fully-synchronized four-speed gearboxes had automatic alternatives even on as small a car as the Mini, and all the leading manufacturers had adopted rack-and-pinion steering on at least some of their models. While in the previous section the most important new models of the decade were outlined in chronological order, the purpose of the following is to look in detail at the engineering developments which occurred during the 1960s.

Of basic configurations, four- and six-cylinder in-line engines continued to dominate. There was, however, increased interest in V-engines; Rolls-Royce and Daimler had V8s in 1959, Rover the bought-in Buick V8 in 1967, Aston Martin their own design in 1969, to be followed by Triumph in 1970. BMC experimented with a V4 for the Austin 1800 and MGB, and were rumoured to have a V8 version of the E-series under development by 1969. Ford of Britain followed the lead of Ford of Germany by introducing a V4 as well as a V6; the V4 did not last long but the Ford V6 – with the exception of Lancia the first mass-production engine of this configuration – was the start of a revolution. Jaguar had their V12 under development from the mid-1960s onwards and were considering a V8 version as well. Among the in-line engines, there were several which were canted over to save height, seen on the Hillman Imp, the 1967 Vauxhall Victor, and literally to a lesser degree, on the Hillman Hunter.

Pushrod-operated overhead valves remained the norm but there was quite a spate of ohc engines, starting with the Hillman Imp and Rover 2000 in 1963. Cogged belt drive was adopted for the Vauxhall Victor in 1967. By then Triumph also had a single ohc

engine but built this only for use in the Swedish SAAB company's 99 model. The first new BMC engine for 15 years was the E-series of the 1969 Austin Maxi, also with a single ohc. Lotus developed a twin overhead cam conversion of the Ford pushrod engine, fitted not only in their own cars but also used in sporting versions of Ford saloon cars.

Even those makers who did not at first adopt overhead camshafts became increasingly preoccupied with greater efficiency. Valves in V-formation and a hemispherical combustion chamber were used on the big Humber six-cylinder engine, a design actually supplied by Armstrong-Siddeley. In 1959, Ford began a range of super-oversquare engines using a common 81 mm bore, and some years later gave it a cross-flow cylinder head. Many other new engines also used oversquare or square cylinder dimensions. Compression ratios were gradually increased to take advantage of improved fuels; the highest ratio adopted as standard on a popular car was the 10.0:1 found on the Hillman Imp. More efficient cylinder head design made it desirable also to ensure bottom-end robustness, Ford leading the way with a five-main bearing crankshaft for the 1,500 cc version of the Classic in 1962, followed by the 1,798 cc BMC B-series engine in 1964.

Only a few engines as yet had their cylinder blocks cast in aluminium but notable were the Rolls-Royce V8 of 1959 and the Hillman Imp of 1963. The ex-Buick Rover V8 of 1967 was in the same material. Apart from the disappearance early in the decade of the last side-valve engine, another lost cause was the F-head with overhead inlet but side exhaust valves, abandoned by Rolls-Royce in 1959 (except for the engine supplied to BMC for the Vanden Plas Princess 4-litre R from 1964 to 1968), and by Rover in 1967. Fuel injection appeared on the Triumph TR5 PI in 1967, some years after Mercedes-Benz and Peugeot had introduced their systems. Superchargers were available only as after-market tuning 'goodies' and turbochargers were as yet virtually unknown.

Of alternative powerplants, only one diesel-engined car made its appearance, the Austin Cambridge/Morris Oxford fitted with a 1.5-litre engine normally used in BMC light commercials. Rover continued to develop gas turbine engines, but although the Rover-BRM racing car with this type of engine ran at Le Mans in 1963 and 1965 it was still an unrealistic proposition for road cars. Nobody showed much interest in the new German Wankel rotary engine although Rolls-Royce took out a licence.

The big breakthrough was the front-wheel drive system devised by Alec Issigonis for the Mini and other BMC models, with the gearbox and final drive built into the sump of a transversely-mounted engine. The only other front-wheel drive car introduced by a British manufacturer was the Triumph 1300 of 1965, with an in-line engine, the combined gearbox and final drive mounted below it. While the Hillman Imp was the only rear-engined design, several small specialist manufacturers began to design mid-engined sports or racing cars of which the 1966 Lotus Europa was the most important production model. The tireless – and, by all accounts, sometimes tiresome – inventor Harry Ferguson built prototypes of four-wheel drive cars but only managed to persuade Jensen to adopt his system for a production car.

Three-speed gearboxes were still generally accepted by the public and Ford's first four-speeder was found on the 1959 Anglia, while Vauxhall waited until 1961 to introduce a four-speed box on the new Victor – which then however set a new standard by having synchromesh on all forward ratios, something Ford could only match a year later. The Hillman Imp in 1963 also had an all-synchro four-speed box, so did the Austin 1800 in 1964. In 1969, the Austin Maxi became the first British car to offer a five-speed box, while in the same year, the basic Vauxhall Victor still had only three forward gears.

Steering column gearchanges had been introduced on most British medium and large family cars soon after the Second World War and still had their adherents throughout the 1960s, being especially well-suited to the Ford or Vauxhall three-speed gearboxes; but there was a general trend back towards the central floor-mounted gearlever, usually now also with remote control. Makers of front-wheel drive cars faced particular problems. The original 1959 Mini had a long willowy things protruding from the toeboards, BMC later tried cable actuation on the 1800 and Maxi (with unhappy results), and the Triumph 1300 had a gearlever coming out from

By the 1960s the craft of the bespoke coachbuilder was almost dead. After the introduction of the integral Rolls-Royce Silver Shadow in 1965, the only chassis available to the coachbuilder was the Phantom V. Most of these were bodied by Mulliner, Park Ward, the amalgamation of two well-known firms. This is a very rare type, a State Landaulette on a 1964 Phantom V chassis. (NMM)

somewhere under the parcels shelf.

Overdrive remained a popular option and would continue to be so until ousted by the universal adoption of front-wheel drive and five-speed gearboxes. It was particularly common on Jaguars and Triumphs but was even found on some models of Ford and Vauxhall. Not many makers fitted it as standard, with the exception of a few Rovers and early examples of the big BMC Farina saloons introduced in 1959, which had a three-speed all-synchromesh gearbox with dual over-drive as standard. The possibilities of five forward speeds were largely ignored by drivers who found the under-parcels shelf overdrive switch awkward to operate. More logical was Triumph's overdrive switch mounted in the gearlever knob. Overdrive was also popular on many sports car, including the Austin-Healey 3000 and the MGB.

From the mid-1950s onwards, most British car makers had introduced automatic transmission as an option on their bigger models, usually with a three-speed Borg Warner gearbox although the Vauxhall Velox/Cresta models had two-speed Powerglide. Rolls-Royce, Bentley, and the Austin Princess used four-speed Hydramatic. Some 1.5-litre family cars were offered with semi-automatic devices such as the Manumatic system favoured by BMC or Easidrive on certain Rootes models, which were in effect automatic clutch systems mated to conventional gearboxes. Only when Borg Warner developed the type 35 automatic gearbox, which was suitable also for cars with engines of less than 2 litres, did automatics become more widespread. In 1961 the revised BMC 1.6-litre Farina range become the smallest British cars so far to be offered with this type of gearbox but by the end of the decade it was commonly available on all cars of similar size. Apart from Rolls-Royce and Bentley, not many cars were fitted exclusively with automatic boxes, but there were examples such as the Vanden Plas Princess 4-litre R, the Rover 3.5-litre

from 1967 onwards, and most of the Daimler V8 2.5-litre saloons.

A more important development was the new Automotive Products four-speed automatic gearbox, designed especially for the BMC Mini and 1100 ranges and unveiled in 1964, although it took a good year before serious production got under way. Not only was this unique for an automatic gear-box by being built into the sump of a transverse engine but it even managed to subsist only on the engine's oil supply. It also gave drivers the choice of proceeding more or less normally through the four gears, or simply staying in drive. By contrast the BMC 1800 models used a 'conventional' Borg Warner box but, to ease transverse installation, adopted primary drive by chain.

In 1959 disc brakes were mainly used in luxury cars

The breakthrough towards independent rear suspension began in 1959, with the Triumph Herald and the BMC Mini. The former had fairly simple and not wholly satisfactory swing axles and a transverse leaf spring, while the Mini used trailing arms and rubber cone elements which were also used for the front suspension. Later BMC front-wheel drive cars adopted the Hydrolastic system, with fluid-filled suspension elements which were interconnected front to rear.

Most other makers adopted semi-trailing arms and coil springs, led by the Triumph 2000 of 1963, followed by Rolls-Royce in 1965 and the Ford Zephyr range in 1966. The rear-engined Hillman Imp on which independent rear suspension was a necessity had a similar layout. Jaguar introduced their famous double-jointed parallelogram on the E-type in 1961, also fitted on all subsequent models in increasingly refined form. Rover adopted a De Dion axle for the 2000 in 1963, and Aston Martin also

preferred this system for the DBS of 1967. Lotus sports cars used the strut suspension pioneered on their racing cars. Of the major manufacturers only Vauxhall did not introduce some form of independent rear suspension but at least the 1967 Victor had a better-located live axle and coil springs at the rear. Self-levelling was adopted only by Rolls-Royce and by the Austin 3-litre of 1967.

The most common system of front suspension was wishbones and coil springs, but the elegantly simple McPherson struts pioneered by Ford were adopted by Triumph for the 2000 in 1963 and Rootes for the Hillman Hunter in 1966. Torsion bars were less common and would not feature on many new models; although still used by the Jaguar E-type, on the same maker's Mark X they were replaced by coil springs. The only car to have a transverse leaf spring for its independent front suspension was the first-generation Vauxhall Viva.

Britain, Dunlop, and Jaguar had led the world in the development of disc brakes in the 1950s, but in 1959 they were still mostly confined to a few luxury cars and sports models apart from Jaguar. They would become increasingly common in the following decade and by 1970 it was unusual to find a new model which still had drum brakes on the front wheels. Front disc brakes were adopted by the Humber Super Snipe, the Rovers, and the new BMC Farina six-cylinder saloons in 1959. In 1961, the Ford Classic was the first popular family car to have them as standard, and in that year Lockheed developed a special miniature disc brake to fit inside the ten-inch wheel rim of the Mini Cooper. All BMC 1100 cars had front disc brakes from 1962 onwards, and they became optional on many other small-capacity cars. Fewer makers adopted them for rear brakes as well but the Rover 2000 was an exception; on this car they were mounted inboard by the differential, to save unsprung weight, being found also in this location on Jaguars with independent rear suspension from the 1961 E-type onwards. Rolls-Royce had an all-disc system on the Silver Shadow in 1965.

Servo assistance was already fairly common, at least on bigger-engined cars, at the beginning of the decade. Dual circuits became mandatory on export models for the USA from the start of 1968, but apart from Rolls-Royce and the Jaguar XJ6 no-one bothered with them for the home market as yet. Only the four-wheel drive Jensen FF had the Dunlop Maxaret anti-skid system.

Rack-and-pinion steering had been introduced in Britain on several Nuffield cars in the 1940s, notably the Morris Minor and the MG sports car, but was slow to make headway; at the beginning of 1959, apart from the Nuffield/BMC designs, it was found only on some sports models such as the Jaguar XK, the Aston Martin, and the Bristol, which were also the largest cars at this time to use this type of steering. Then the Triumph Herald arrived, while of course all BMC's front-wheel drive models used rack-and-pinion steering. Rack-and-pinion was still considered by many as mostly suitable for small cars, and the other manufacturers all at first introduced the system on smaller cars – the Hillman Imp and Vauxhall Viva in 1963, the Ford Escort in 1968. The bigger steering effort typically required, especially on a front-heavy car, was countered by BMC whose 1967 Wolseley 18/85 became the smallest car so far to have power steering fitted as standard.

Collapsible safely steering columns were another mandatory requirement in the USA from 1 January 1968. This was another feature which most makers were slow to adopt across the board including home market cars, although already the Rover 2000 had a steering column which would compress under impact, aided by the position of the steering box on the scuttle. The front-wheel drive BMC cars enjoyed a similar safety benefit from having their steering racks placed behind the engine, even if the resulting

'Oddly shaped speedometers enjoyed a vogue.' This is the strip speedo on the 1961 Vauxhall Victor Super. It was new for that year. (NMM)

bus-like driving position was the subject of frequent and adverse comment.

The biggest single development in tyres during the 1960s was that radials became commonplace. Britain was slow to follow the example set by Michelin and Pirelli, and Dunlop's first effort, the late 1950s Duraband tyre, was only short-lived. Most British cars which were available with radial tyres specified Michelin. The first car on which radial tyres were fitted exclusively was the 1963 Rover 2000, with a choice of Pirelli Cinturatos or the new Dunlop SP.41. In the following year, the Austin 1800 had Dunlop SP.41 tyres as standard. While gradually more and more cars became available with radial tyres as an option, high-speed cross-ply tyres (such as Dunlop's RS-series) became less common, although Avon continued to offer their Turbospeed series. The 1968 Jaguar XJ6 had specially developed low-profile Dunlop radials of very high speed rating. By the end of the decade radials were beginning to oust cross-plies altogether.

The wire wheel had already largely disappeared on saloon cars, only Jaguar continued to offer a regular wire wheel option on some saloons until 1968. They were, however, still popular on many sports cars, although legislation forced the replacement of traditional knock-ons with hexagonal or (in the case of MG, naturally) octagonal nuts. Centre-lock disc wheels enjoyed a brief vogue, seen on the MGA Twin Cam, the Gordon Keeble, and some Lotus models. Cast-alloy wheels were as yet largely only available as after-market accessories, the most famous types being offered by Minilite and Wolfrace, but were homologated for and fitted to, for instance, many of BMC's works rally cars. The first mainstream production car to have them was the Triumph Dolomite Sprint of 1973.

More important was the general tendency for wheels to become smaller. This trend was started by the ten-inch wheels of the Mini in 1959; the BMC 1100 and other small cars mostly had 12-inch wheels, while 13-inch turned out to be the smallest practical size for medium-sized cars – they were found on the BMC 1800 and the Triumph 2000, apart from all Fords from 1961 onwards. By 1965, precisely four cars still featured 16-inch wheels: the Bristol, the Daimler Majestic, the Vanden Plas limousine, and the Austin taxi.

There was a tendency towards more 'styled' wheel designs, often imitating the early cast-alloy wheels; thus the Ford Capri of 1969 sported Rubery Owen's new 'Rostyle' wheel which was also adopted for MG sports cars before the year was out. There was also a move towards greater variety in hub cap design, and several makers adopted full-width wheel trims, such as the Ford Zodiac in 1966. By contrast the once-popular wheel trim rings – so-called 'Rimbellishers' – which had enjoyed a brief popularity in the late 1950s and early 1960s soon disappeared altogether.

The 1959 Triumph Herald was the most important new design not to have unitary body construction, using instead a perimeter-type chassis frame. Otherwise the unitary body was the norm, most mass manufacturers having introduced them in the period between 1948 and 1955, and the specialists following suit, until even Rolls-Royce adopted this method of construction in 1965. There was a degree of variation, such as the BMC Mini and 1100 with their separate subframes, the base-unit construction of the Rover 2000, and the front subframe of the Jaguar E-type. Even open sports cars went unitary, from the Austin-Healey Sprite of 1958 and the Sunbeam Alpine of 1959 to the MGB of 1962.

With the disappearance of separate chassis, the few remaining exponents of specialized coachbuilding went into rapid decline. Only the Rolls-Royce Phantom V continued to be available in chassis form and most bodies for this were constructed in-house by the Rolls-Royce subsidiary Mulliner Park Ward, although James Young also built some Phantom V bodies. Barker and Hooper had been taken over by

Daimler, and Hooper's last effort was a coupé on the Daimler SP250 chassis shown in the 1959 Earls Court Motor Show. Thrupp & Maberley had long been part of the Rootes Group, and BMC owned Vanden Plas, whose Kingsbury factory continued to produce Princess limousines. While this and the largest Daimler limousine continued to be made in chassis form this was largely to the benefit of the undertaking trade.

Ford and Vauxhall built the first professional styling studios

Outside the small car class, four-door saloon bodies were the norm; only Ford essayed mid-range family cars with two-door bodies (Classic and Corsair models) and they sold mostly in export markets. Estate cars would grow tremendously in popularity during the 1960s, with more and more versions becoming available. On the other hand, the tourer or convertible styles became quite scarce. Only the Morris Minor and the Triumph Herald/Vitesse remained available throughout the decade; the last Ford convertibles were discontinued in 1961, and Hillman dropped their open cars in 1964. Some specialists such as Bond tried to fill the niche, and roof-choppers such as Crayford did good business, their Mini convertible being especially popular.

The Austin A40 Farina Countryman had in effect pioneered the three-door hatchback, although nobody in 1959 realised it. There were other small estates of the 1960s which a later generation would also have called hatchbacks, such as the Ford Anglia and the BMC 1100. The Hillman Imp went a step further, to minimalise the inconvenience of its rear engine layout, while sports coupés such as the Jaguar E-type and the MGB GT also had rear hatches. However, the first true hatchback in Britain was the Austin Maxi of 1969, and this was to remain the only such

model from a British manufacturer for a few more years.

Until 1959, most British cars had rather uninspired styling. The first generation of post-war models had aped American themes of various vintages, Ford and Vauxhall naturally continued to draw inspiration from Detroit, and Rootes cars were likewise clearly influenced by American themes, not least as they employed the famous Raymond Loewy as a consultant. Sometimes the American styling was taken to excess, the first Vauxhall Victor being a particularly grisly example. The best British styling of the 1950s was that of Jaguar, usually owing to the mastery of Sir William Lyons.

Little wonder that several British makers turned to Italy for renewed inspiration. First and foremost there was the liaison between BMC and Pinin Farina, whose first result was the Austin A40 of 1958 and whose most outstanding work was the BMC 1100 of 1962. Standard-Triumph likewise beat the path to Turin, securing the services of Michelotti, whose first job became the Triumph Herald. Smaller manufacturers did likewise, including Aston Martin who went to Touring, AC to Frua, and Jensen to Vignale, Ford consulted Frua for the design of the 1961 Zephyr/Zodiac.

The first professional styling studios in the modern sense were built up by Ford and Vauxhall, followed by Rootes, while most other car makers had at least a semblance of a styling department. At BMC, technical director Alec Issigonis had a legendary aversion to styling and stylists, and he usually got his way. When BMC merged with Pressed Steel they inherited the nucleus of a styling studio which was later moved to Longbridge, merging with their modest existing studio. As the 1960s wore on, while most British designers continued to draw on Italian themes for inspiration, the trend was once again back towards in-house styling. A small number of designers branched out and set up consultancies. An early pioneer was Ogle, whose original car-making efforts failed: instead they became a design firm with credits including the influential Reliant Scimitar GTE. Another was William Towns with the Aston Martin DBS. Tom Karen of Ogle was one of the original tutors when the Royal College of Art in London set up an industry-sponsored post-graduate course in automotive design in 1967. One of their first students was Peter Stevens, whose portfolio in the 1980s and 1990s came to include the Lotus Elan and the McLaren F1. The RCA course greatly contributed to raising awareness of design among British manufacturers, their graduates finding ready employment in Britain and abroad, and an impressive list of designs could be attributed to RCA graduates by the mid-1990s.

In the 1950s, one of the most frequently predicted major changes in automotive design had been the conversion to plastic bodywork. In fact this did not occur, although fibreglass became the mainstay of many small specialist producers, among them Jensen, Reliant, and Lotus. Only the last would essay a unitary construction plastic body for the original Elite. For mass production, steel reigned supreme. Apart from a few expensive hand-built cars such as Aston Martin and AC, only Land-Rover featured aluminium bodywork, and nobody tried a unitary aluminium structure. Some new materials did gain ground, for instance bright trim of brushed aluminium or stainless steel rather than chrome-plating, and an increasing number of interior trim parts were moulded in plastic.

Styling fads came – and mostly went. Two-tone colour schemes had come back on a grand scale in the second half of the 1950s but had largely disappeared again ten years later; hooded headlamps did not last even that long. Vinyl-covered roofs were a novelty in 1967. Tailfins, in one form or another, were with us for most of the decade after 1959. Double round headlamps were introduced in Britain on the Humber Super Snipe in 1959

and were at one time or another used by almost all car manufacturers, gaining the ultimate seal of approval when they were adopted by Rolls-Royce. The second-generation Vauxhall Viva of 1966 was the first British car with rectangular headlamps. The panoramic windscreen with dog's leg pillars did not go beyond the large Humbers and the 1957–8 generation of Vauxhalls, and nobody bothered to imitate the reverse angle rear window of the Ford Anglia and Classic models. Aerodynamics remained an unapplied science. Only the Jaguar E-type looked as if it had ever been in a wind tunnel, while one of the lowest-drag British designs was the Hillman Imp – a fortuitous coincidence brought about largely by its rear-engine design.

As late as the early 1960s, the heater was still an option on most British family cars, and the first modern convenience accessory – the humble windscreen washer – was sometimes not offered at all. However, on one front at least progress was being made from an early date: maintenance requirements were quickly being reduced. In 1959, the Triumph Herald offered a chassis free of grease nipples, and the first semi-sealed cooling system with an expansion tank arrived with the BMC 1100 in 1962. Thanks to new self-cleansing multigrade oils manufacturers were able to extend the recommended intervals for oil changes, and the tiresome business of using different oils summer and winter was gradually abolished. Longer-life batteries requiring less frequent topping-up were being introduced.

The DB5 was the first British car to have an alternator as standard

---

Car interiors changed relatively little during the 1960s. A few manufacturers still mounted instrument panels centrally – so convenient for British manufacturers who were obliged to offer left-hand drive on most export models – but most new cars had the

instruments in front of the driver. The Mini was the most important hold-out. Upper-class makers still offered full instrumentation, but the requirement for an oil pressure gauge was being reduced with better oils and more robust engines, able to withstand even high-speed motorway driving. With the introduction of high-output alternators and better batteries, ammeters disappeared or were replaced by voltmeters. There was a general tendency to introduce more and more warning lamps, some makers such as Triumph placing them logically together in a cluster. Rev. counters were uncommon on saloon cars – even Mini Coopers never had them – and in the BMC saloon hierarchy they were fitted only to Rileys, not to MGs; but they did appear on the new generation of sporting Fords and Vauxhalls.

Oddly-shaped speedometers enjoyed a vogue, Ford and Vauxhall perpetrated some shapes which must have greatly taxed the ingenuity of Messrs Smiths, while BMC went in for austere strip-type speedometers, seen on the Rover 2000 as well. The upper crust and some sporting fanatics could still insist on instruments marked British Jaeger – by now Smiths under another name. The 1963 Ford Corsair had the first printed circuit for the instrument panel. Controls were slow to migrate from facias to steering columns. Jaguar for a long time had eight identical switches in a row, while the typical Rolls-Royce switch panel was imitated on the Vanden Plas Princess. Rover and Triumph went some way towards meeting ergonomic requirements, with differently-shaped switches which gradually acquired internationally recognised symbols.

Switchgear multiplied and became more complicated as new conveniences came into favour, such as the Triplex Hotline electrically-heated rear window which appeared as optional equipment on some cars in the early 1960s and eventually became universal standard equipment. On the other hand the number of cars offering front fog lamps as standard gradually decreased – no doubt thanks to the clean air act – while long-range driving lamps were rendered superfluous by the general improvements in headlamp design, including sealed beam lamps and lamps with asymmetric beam pattern. Halogen headlamps were available as after-market accessories but were controversial and contributed to BMC's disqualification in the 1966 Monte Carlo Rally. With the general proliferation of electrical fittings, the introduction of the higher-output alternator was a welcome step forward; the first British car to have an alternator as standard was the Aston Martin DB5 in 1962, by 1966 new family saloons from Ford and Hillman were also equipped with alternators, and they had become universal by the early 1970s.

One control that largely disappeared was the conventional starter button or pull, replaced by key-operated starters. Steering locks were found only on

some export models and did not become universal in the home market until 1971. Chokes were still mostly manual except on cars such as Jaguar, which used the SU thermo-electric choke device. Early Hillman Imps had an automatic choke but most of these were recalled and converted to manual. The return of the gearlever from steering column to floor has been mentioned; similarly during the 1960s more and more makers abandoned the under-facia mounted pistol-grip handbrake in favour of a handbrake mounted between two separate front seats.

This return to central controls was coupled with a return from the bench front seat to individual seats. The front bench had always been a questionable asset on narrow British cars which, unlike their American patterns, could not comfortably seat three adults in the front (nor, for that matter, in the back). Some makers evolved the split-bench

front seat which permitted individual adjustment for driver and front seat passenger, yet would allow a third person to be carried on occasion. But generally, the movement was back towards individual seats. Rover was one of few makes which, logically enough, fitted individual rear seats.

Leather upholstery was mainly fitted on luxury and some sports models, although it remained an option on many family cars. A few cars, notably from Ford and Vauxhall, had woven nylon cloth trim but in general cloth trim was considered cheap: witness the original Mini, where the rare standard model had cloth trim while the de-luxe had vinyl trim, in two-tone colour schemes of course. Two-tone or patterned trim had a brief vogue in the early 1960s but was rejected by the British motorist who still liked trim to look like leather, even if it was not. Many of the problems associated with early plastic trim materials such as Vynide were banished when the 'breathing' Ambla material became available in the mid-1960s. By 1968 Ambla was found instead of leather even on some Jaguars. Towards the end of the decade there was a depressing tendency for trim to be uniformly black, this colour having supposedly a sporting image. Floor rubber mats, however practical, were associated with foreign cars and were also considered cheap and nasty. They were again found on early standard Minis but were soon replaced by traditional carpets, and were thereafter found only on some open sports cars, apart from cars supplied to the Police.

During the 1960s, the safety issue began to be taken seriously. Seat-belt mounting points, at least for the front seats, were found on most cars from around 1961 onwards, and in 1965 became the subject of one of the first

Numerous safety features were included on the Rover 2000, among them, visible here, the padding on the facia in front of driver and passenger, and the collapsible steering wheel. (NMM)

whether operating in Britain or not.

The reason for discussing the unions' report on BL in some detail is that this is a particularly interesting historical example of the interest and insight shown by the workers' organizations in the company that employed their members. It was not by any means a selfish or narrow-minded interest either – the nearest the report came to promote the workers' traditional interest was by outlining the social costs of the closure of BL, while in the introduction it was stated that 'for the industrial relations climate to improve there has to be trust and some sort of guarantee for the future. This report is part of the trade union input to achieving those objectives.'[1] Indeed it could be argued that the report showed a genuine concern for the welfare of the company, and – by implication – for the nation.

There is no reason to believe that the report had much impact on the management of BL when it was published. It is not referred to in Sir Michael Edwardes's autobiography *Back From the Brink* (1983), although in this volume Sir Michael deals extensively both with the Robinson dismissal, and with BL's own various plans for joining forces with another foreign car manufacturer. This apparently muted reaction from the company is in a way quite interesting, as it may be considered a symptom of the state of industrial relations in the British motor industry around 1980. To examine how this state of affairs was arrived at, it is necessary to go back almost two centuries to the start of the industrial revolution and almost 100 years before the birth of the motor industry.

That Britain became the cradle of the industrial revolution in the years around 1800 was due to the fortuitous

The Napier work-force in 1906 numbered about 1,200 – a good proportion of whom must be in this photograph – probably not a single union man among them at this date. Note that, with very few exceptions, every man and boy wears some form of headgear, mostly traditional cloth caps, though a few bowler hats and stylish straw boaters can be seen. (NMM)

combination of relatively easily available raw materials such as iron and coal, together with the presence of ingenious inventors, engineers and manufacturers. The technological changes wrought within a generation were enormous. The impact on society was equally great, for instance in terms of the shift of the majority of the population from rural areas to the quickly-growing manufacturing towns and cities. It is, however, obvious that British institutions took much longer to come to terms with the new developments and their social impact. British institutions and socio-political systems are extremely resilient, and the nation as a whole is particularly resistant to change, while the population, by and large, tends to be of a stoic and phlegmatic disposition. There has not been any drastic change to the system of government since 1689, nor has Britain experienced civil war since 1745. We may compare this to Germany which in the twentieth century alone has experienced no less than four sweeping changes to its fundamental systems. The net result is that Britain at the end of the twentieth century retains a surprising number of features in its systems and institutions which have been in place for two centuries, in some cases for much longer.

Britain as a nation and as a society has therefore been much more stable than most others. It is undeniable that this stability was an important factor which encouraged industry and trade in the nineteenth century and the early part of the twentieth. However, this stability has been accompanied by an innate conservatism and a perhaps at times exaggerated respect for the sanctity of traditions, heritage and not least privilege. The consequence is that Britain, arguably more than any other Western nation, remains a class society. It is against this background that the development of the organized labour movement since around 1800 must be seen, both in terms of the history of the trade unions, and its political dimension. While the trade unions came before the Labour Party, the close links forged through more than a hundred years remain strong today. These links, and the occasional links between the trade union movement and those political factions which are to the left of the Labour party, have undoubtedly contributed to deny the trade unions political respectability in the eyes of many who are at the opposite end of the political spectrum. The polarization which has often occurred in British political life as a result of what is effectively a two-party system, and which in itself may be said to reflect a traditional class structure, has in turn often been reflected in the environment of the workplace. Not surprisingly, until comparatively recently the climate of industrial relations at times remained unnecessarily and fruitlessly confrontational. In modern times, the miners' strike of 1984–5 remains the most frightening example of such confrontation, in this instance not aided by the personalities on either side of the conflict, but some of the episodes which occurred during this strike would seem to be only slightly modernized versions of events that took place some 140 years earlier during the Chartists' riots.

By the 1900s trade union membership was over two million

The history of the British labour and trade union movement is well covered in many publications, such as C. P. Hill's *British Economic and Social History 1700–1982* (fifth edition, 1985). The origins of trade unions can be traced back to the latter part of the eighteenth century. While the French Revolution from 1789 onwards does not seem to have inspired the British working class, undoubtedly the reaction of the British ruling class to events across the Channel contributed to Parliament passing the Combination Act of 1799. Under this act workmen were forbidden to form any 'combination' – or trade union – in their efforts to obtain better working conditions or more pay. This first piece of trade union legislation was repealed in 1824 but a new law in 1825, while making trade unions legal, in effect forbade strikes. Thus began a remarkable sequence of changing trade union legislation which has continued to the present day, depending on the political philosophy and allegiance of whatever government was temporarily in charge.

A number of trade unions were nevertheless formed in the early part of the nineteenth century. In 1833 the first concerted attempt at forming an all-embracing union movement followed in the shape of the Grand National Consolidated Trades Union, the brainchild of Robert Owen, a manufacturer who had already made his name as a model employer in his mill at New Lanark in the early years of the century. Although the GNCTU quickly reached a membership in excess of 500,000, it folded almost as quickly, not least after the case of the Tolpuddle martyrs who were charged with administration of an illegal oath when planning to join the union and who were sentenced to transportation in 1834.

A forerunner of the trade union in its modern form was the Amalgamated Society of Engineers, founded in 1851, drawing its membership from skilled employees in the engineering industries. Probably under the influence of the failure of the Chartist movement, this union did not have an overt political agenda. It had a moderate outlook and undoubtedly a restraining influence. It offered its members a range of benefits in the way that a friendly society might.[2] The ASE at the turn of the century became one of the first unions to be active in the motor industry.[3] Other unions were formed and in 1868 the Trade Union Congress held its first meeting. The Trade Union Act of 1871 gave protection to union funds, although the Criminal Law Amendment Act of the same year forbade peaceful picketing. This act was repealed in 1875, by which time the TUC represented over one million members. By the turn of the century, trade union membership had risen to over two million.

Particularly after the successful dockers' strike of 1889, the strike weapon was becoming increasingly frequently used. This and many other early conflicts were over the rates of pay. In 1901 a railway strike in Wales led to the railway company suing the union concerned and being awarded damages, a decision that was reversed in 1906 when the Trade Disputes Act protected union funds from actions for civil damages. Another legal matter, regarding the practice of trade unions making a political levy whereby a part of their members' subscriptions was paid to the Labour Party, was finally resolved in 1913 when such a levy was made legal by the Trade Union Act, providing that individual members could contract out, in other words opt for not paying the political levy. In 1927 this was changed so that trade union members had specifically to

contract in. The law on the political levy was changed again in 1946, and in the 1980s.

In its early years, the trade union movement was strongest in mining; in heavy industry, typically concentrated in the North of England and the lowlands of Scotland, such as shipbuilding; and in the transport sector, such as railways and docks. By contrast the fledgling motor industry in the years before 1914 did not appear to provide much in the way of an opportunity for the organized labour movement. There were several reasons for this, not least the fact that the motor industry was still insignificant in terms of size and number of employees. In 1913, total trade union membership stood at around four million[4] while it may be estimated that in the same year, the total labour force in the motor industry was around 50,000 – compared to more than 1.2 million employees in the coal industry.[5]

Furthermore, only a handful of motor manufacturers employed more than 2,000 people in one company.

Most motor manufacturers were in the Midlands, somewhat removed from the traditional strong centres of union activity (London, South Wales, North of England, and Southern Scotland). The metal-working industries of Coventry, Birmingham, and the Black Country towns were based on a tradition of skilled workmen employed in a large number of small firms. This was typical also of the early motor industry where the majority of employees were mechanics or other skilled workers who enjoyed higher rates of pay and better conditions than workers in other, more highly unionized industries. There was a strong pride in the craft tradition in the motor industry, shared by employers and employees alike. This pride would not begin to be eroded until the larger manufacturers

The body shop at the Sunbeam works, c.1910. Coachbuilders in particular had a strong pride in the craft tradition. This and relatively good rates of pay made them resistant to unionization. (NB)

began the change to mass-production in the 1920s, and survived long after in the case of many small specialist manufacturers – even, in a few instances, to this day.

Such unions as did cater for workers in the infant motor industry were small and fragmented, and still often had the character of craft associations.[6] This would only change under the impact of the First World War. As mentioned, the Amalgamated Society of Engineers was active in the motor industry. One particular source of conflict was the introduction of the piecework system which in the period between 1905 and 1910 gradually came to replace the original method of payment where a fixed rate was paid per hour.[7] There were many examples of disagreement over rate-fixing for individual jobs, and another contentious issue was the bonus scheme which sometimes supplemented the piecework system. A common complaint was that piecework rates were usually imposed, rather than subject to negotiation between management and workers. While individual unions were too small and had not been able to attract the membership of the majority of workmen in the motor industry, there is at least one example of joint union efforts: the 1910 agreement between five engineering unions and the Coventry Engineering Employers' Federation to limit overtime in an effort to overcome the problem of seasonal employment as demand for motor vehicles rose and fell at different times of the year.[8] Interestingly enough the limit for overtime was set at 15 hours per week when a standard working week in the motor industry was 54 hours per week – which may be contrasted with the fact that in 1908, the Coal Mines Act introduced the eight-hour day for miners.[9]

Many of the improvements in actual working conditions in the nineteenth and early twentieth centuries were introduced by legislation, often brought about by social reformers who, by campaigning were able to change public opinion, which in turn exerted an influence on parliament and government. These reformers included some employers whose social conscience was often based on Christian beliefs, as many of them were connected with the Society of Friends (the Quaker Movement). Such employers saw it as their duty not only to provide improvements in working conditions but often did much to improve the living conditions of their workers. An early pioneer was Robert Owen, whose New Lanark model village took shape in 1817, followed from around 1850 by Sir Titus Salt's Saltaire estate at Leeds. Further impetus came from the teachings of John Ruskin and William Morris, as well as the novels of Charles Dickens and Benjamin Disraeli, all of whom highlighted the social problems which had been created by the industrial revolution. These concerns about the living conditions of the working class merged with new ideas in architecture and town planning, demonstrated by Norman Shaw at Bedford Park in London in 1875, later codified by Ebenezer Howard in *Garden Cities of Tomorrow* (1898–9). Among industrialists who put these theories into practice was Lever with Port Sunlight at Liverpool in 1888, and notably the Cadbury family, Quaker cocoa and chocolate makers, who built their 'factory in a garden' with its adjacent Bournville housing estate on the south side of Birmingham from 1895 onwards.

By the time individual motor manufacturers became large enough to undertake similar schemes, the time for the paternalistic gesture had perhaps largely passed, and there were few examples of similar benevolence in the early motor industry. It is, however, worth mentioning that the most splendid of the early car factories, the Argyll company's factory at Alexandria near Glasgow, at the time of its opening in 1906 boasted not only the infamous 'marble halls' but also unheard-of facilities for the workmen – 'each section of the works was equipped with lavatories with hot and cold water and lockers and uniforms were provided by the company for all workers'.[10] *The Autocar* in April 1906 observed that: 'Nothing has been omitted that can tend to add to the comfort of the workpeople. The sanitary arrangements are above criticism, and the space devoted to lavatory and cloakroom accommodation for the workpeople occupies as much ground, and must have cost as much money, as many a factory complete.'[11] The cost of the factory was quoted as £220,000. Whether the marble halls or the generous facilities contributed more to the speedy decline of the Argyll company is now difficult to determine but it is certain that the sheer scale and lavishness of the Alexandria factory for many years remained a warning to more prudent and parsimonious motor manufacturers; thus William Morris (Lord Nuffield) was famously quoted as saying 'there will be no marble halls at Cowley' – and indeed there were not.

Perhaps the only example of a motor manufacturer trying to create a Bournville, if on a much smaller scale, came from an almost neighbouring concern in Birmingham, the Austin company. Between 1914 and 1918, war production at Longbridge swelled the work-force from around 2,000 to no less than 20,000 – a figure comparable to the number employed in the same factory at any later date. Many workers were recruited from areas outside the West Midlands, many were single, a considerable proportion were women. A convent near the factory was taken over and converted to a hostel, another hostel was opened at Bromsgrove some miles to the south. Then in 1917–18, the Longbridge estate was built on a 123-acre site.[12] This consisted of 252 houses, mostly pre-fabricated wooden bungalows imported from Canada, laid out on garden suburb lines, with a village hall, a laundry, and a Church of England mission room.[13] R. J. Wyatt claims that the estate housed 7,000 people which, if true, must have represented serious overcrowding – in all likelihood his figure includes work people living in the company's various hostels. The individual houses had indoor toilets and even bathrooms, which was considered very advanced for the time.[14] The estate still exists, although the Austin company has long since divested itself of any interest in it.

In Coventry, the engine makers White & Poppe were given a government grant to build barracks which housed some 3,200 women workers. Inadequate and expensive housing was a contributive factor to industrial unrest in the Coventry motor industry in 1917.[15] Yet after the First World War, when motor industry employment was reduced to more normal peace-time levels, the responsibility of providing accommodation for its work-force was largely removed from the motor industry. The general housing shortage of the war and immediate post-war years was gradually alleviated as local authorities began constructing massive estates of council houses, offering adequate accommodation at low rents to the working class. Thus when Ford decided to build what was at the time Europe's largest car factory at Dagenham, one of the factors that made the company choose this particular location was that the London County Council was constructing the equally massive Dagenham estate of 25,000 houses nearby.[16] Thereafter most manufacturers' efforts at improving the conditions of their work-force were limited to providing better facilities in the factories, for welfare purposes such as medical centres, or recreational facilities such as sports grounds. Many companies also actively encouraged the formation and to a degree subsidised a variety of clubs and societies for their work-force, ranging from sporting bodies devoted classically to pastimes such as golf or angling, to friendly or charitable societies, aimed at supporting members in need, or helping to meet hospital or medical bills.

Some motor manufacturers operated apprenticeship schemes and had done so since the beginning of the industry. In Coventry, Daimler 'had begun to attract pupils from public schools with such success that shortly before the First World War there was a hostel full of them in a pleasant house in St Nicholas Street, near the Coventry works'.[17] One of the best known of these apprentices was the racing driver and journalist S. C. H. (Sammy) Davis. Many attended part-time day classes in the Coventry Municipal Technical Institute.[18] Their example was later followed by other companies which adopted more formalized and improved training schemes in the years between the wars. The Austin company took a particularly enlightened approach,[19] establishing the Austin Technical Society as early as 1917, offering technical instruction to employees, and teaching apprentices mathematics and engineering drawing. One of the war-time workers' hostels was eventually converted into an engineering college with accommodation for 75 premium pupils, providing 'all the usual advantages of a public school life'.[20] Similar, if less elaborate, schemes were operated, for instance, by Wolseley. Many of these apprentices who received a sound education in engineering or commerce later rose to leading positions inside or outside the motor industry.

Other manufacturers were less concerned with the provision of facilities for the work-force, taking instead the route of offering comparatively high rates of pay – one factor which also made it difficult for a long time for the trade unions to recruit on any large scale in the car factories. An early leader in this field was the British Ford company, established at Trafford Park in Manchester in 1911. In the company's own magazine, *Ford Times*, it was declared in 1914 that the company's employees were 'the highest paid labour known to factory industry'.[21] This meant a minimum income for all male employees over the age of 22, who were the bread-winners of a family, of £3 for a 48-hour week. (Ford did not employ the piecework system but paid a fixed day rate.) This was an extremely good rate in Britain at this time, although not as generous as the much publicized $5-day introduced in Ford's factories in Detroit in the same year. It

A Vauxhall OD 23/60 with partially completed body at coachbuilders Martin & Young. The body is of an unusual kind, with only a single door on the near side. (NB)

did, however, mean that a British Ford worker's annual wages were comfortably in excess of the price of a new Ford Model T car, at that time between £125 and £135. No other manufacturer in Britain could produce a similar comparison until the 1920s or even 1930s.

William Morris at Cowley adopted a similar policy, claiming that 'no factory can turn out a cheap car on low wages'.[22] Morris's wages were, in fact, paid on a combination of a basic piece-work rate with a bonus calculated on the number of units produced over and above the standard number. It was calculated that the bonus system could increase the average unskilled worker's weekly pay packet from a basic 54s to 89s, while average wages rose from 59s in 1919 to 86s in 1925. If this could be maintained throughout the year, it means that the annual wages rose from around £150 to well over £200 over this period while at the same time the price of the cheapest Morris car was halved from £330 to £162 10s.[23] While it must be added that, in 1926, the SMMT calculated that an annual income of £450 was required to maintain a car[24], in 1928 the *Morris Owner* claimed that a Morris Minor could be maintained by 'any steady-going work-ing-man in regular employment'.[25] That car then cost £125 in its cheapest form.

While it may be suggested that the greatest social reform brought about in the twentieth century is the very spread of car ownership, with all its implications, few of the early manufacturers other than Henry Ford or William Morris had the vision of mass-motorization in mind from the start. Morris's intention was to produce cars that were cheap enough for the worker to go to his factory by car.[26]

The years between the wars therefore saw tangible progress towards the situation where a worker in the motor industry could reasonably aspire to afford one of the cars he helped to manufacture. There were also at least two schemes promoted by car manufacturers where employees were encouraged to take a share in the business itself. They were, however, both limited in scope. In 1932, the Austin company encouraged employees to buy shares in the company on favourable terms but restricted the offer to employees with a record of 20 years' continuous employment, and most of the shares allocated under the scheme were bought by white-collar salaried staff.[27] Lord Nuffield (as he had by

then become) in 1937 established the Nuffield Benefaction for Employees to which he donated one million ordinary shares in Morris Motors, then worth £2,125,000. The stock was held in trust for the benefit of hourly-paid employees who would receive the annual dividend as a bonus on top of their wages. For the first year, the bonus amounted to almost £112,000 which equated to over 3.5% of the total wage bill of £3.1 million, and by 1954 the total amount paid out was more than £2 million.[28] In practice it meant that a worker with an average pay packet would receive some £12–£15 round about June or July, as a help for his summer holiday.[29] These figures, incidentally, suggest that typical annual wages within the Morris companies by 1937–8 had risen to £350–£400. Yet by that time the price of the cheapest Morris car was around £120.

If we sum up the situation in the British motor industry before 1914, with the prevailing factors of a multitude of small companies each with a low number of employees, most being skilled workers enjoying relatively high rates of pay, and the lack of organized labour in most factories, industrial relations in the infant motor industry were comparatively tranquil. With the expansion of many factories during the war, the situation would alter drastically. The war years produced the first examples of a large-scale industrial conflict in the industry. Sometimes industrial unrest was caused not by actual conflict in the workplace but by the workers' frustration over the prevailing difficult living conditions in war-time, including housing difficulties and food shortages, which led to widespread strikes in Coventry in November 1917.[30] Unrest in the

The Morris production system before the £500,000 investment in new facilities at Cowley. Here Minor (left) and Oxford chassis are at the end of the line in the erecting shop (C block), prior to being towed to the body mounting shop (G block). (BMIHT/Rover)

factories was also often caused by employers' refusal to recognize workers' representatives in the form of shop stewards or trade union officials. In at least one well-documented case, a strike was called because of the alleged victimization of a workers' representative – the Peacock strike in Austin's Longbridge factory in January 1918.[31] To some extent this episode has fascinating parallels with the much later McHugh strike at Austin in 1953, and even with the Robinson dismissal in the same factory in 1979 (both discussed below).

Arthur Peacock was an East Anglian who had volunteered for munitions work. Employed as a fitter at Longbridge, he became chairman of the works committee, a body which was recognized neither by Austin nor by the Ministry of Munitions. In this capacity he became the leader of a campaign to have a contentious bonus system replaced by a guaranteed higher weekly wage. Peacock had applied for a transfer to work nearer his home, but when in the middle of the wages conflict he was transferred by the Ministry to a position at Lincoln, this was seen by the workers as victimization. Some 10,000 workers went on strike. Although initially Austin and the Ministry refused to negotiate until work had been resumed, after some days they gave in and allowed Peacock to be reinstated, pending an enquiry. There is no evidence as to the outcome of this enquiry, nor is there any suggestion that Peacock was otherwise active in the organized labour movement as represented by the trade unions.

The transition from war work and the resumption of peace-time activities presented the car manufacturers with a considerable challenge. Some companies which had expanded considerably in the 1914–18 period laid ambitious plans for the mass-production of popular cars on American (ie, Ford) lines.[32] Many of these were, however, relative newcomers to the industry, with Austin the main established manufacturer among them.

Encouragement was offered by the short-lived post-war boom of 1919–20 when four years' pent-up demand for new cars could be satisfied by any manufacturer with sufficient capacity. The British economy as a whole was, however, in a poor state, and there was considerable unemployment not only among demobilized soldiers but also among munitions workers who were being made redundant as the factories scaled down their operations. It obviously also took time for the industry to produce new models; several new designs were displayed in the first post-war London Motor Show in 1919, but in many cases deliveries of these new cars could only be effected on any scale in 1920 or even 1921.

The unions' problems were compounded by the 1921 depression

In the middle of this difficult period the first large-scale strike affecting more than one company in the motor industry occurred. This was the iron moulders' strike from September 1919 to January 1920, directly involving 50,000 men but – in a subsequently oft-repeated pattern – leading to twice that number being laid off as the motor industry was deprived of castings. Opinions differ as to its effects – Richardson says that 'its seriousness for the motor industry has been overestimated by some', yet others claim that 'Austin barely survived the effects of the 1919 moulders' strike'[33] and that the strike led directly to Napier's decision to pull out of the motor car business altogether. Research by D. G. Jones[34] has secured correspondence from the Ford archives in the USA demonstrating that at the time of the strike and soon after, Sir Herbert Austin negotiated with General Motors for the sale of his company, and in July 1920 unsuccessfully offered the Austin company to Henry Ford – behind the backs of his directors, incidentally, never mind the shareholders.

As is well known, by April 1921 the Austin company's affairs were in such a state that an official receiver was appointed.[35] However, there were other reasons apart from the moulders' strike which led to Austin's difficulties, notably the relative failure of the company's product policy and the slump which affected the motor industry from late 1920. It may also be speculated that some companies in 1920 used the moulders' strike as a convenient excuse to cover up their other difficulties in gearing up for full-scale post-war production. Another theme which would recur again and again for many years was that labour difficulties were blamed for the general problems of the industry.

Certainly the bare statistics seem to bear out the theory that the slump of 1920–1 had more serious effects on the industry than the earlier strike. Overall car production in Britain had been 24,000 in 1919, had risen dramatically to 50,000 in 1920, but then declined to 32,000 in 1921 (SMMT statistics; approximate figures). For the first time, the engineering trade in the West Midlands was hard hit by unemployment – the percentage of unemployed was 21.9 in February 1921, rising to 33.1 in June.[36] From the low point of 1921, conditions rapidly improved, with substantial increases in British car production being recorded every year until 1929. And as the market for new cars increased, so also did employment in the industry. By 1924, the British motor industry accounted for the employment of some 200,000 workers.[37]

One effect of the war was that with the enormous increase in the number of industrial workers, trade union membership also greatly increased, from four million in 1913 to double that number in 1919.[38] Shop stewards, who were more or less informally elected by their workmates to act as workers' representatives when dealing with management, for the first time began to play an important role in industrial relations. Many trade unions were amalgamated or reorganized:

thus the National Union of Vehicle Builders, for many years one of the most prominent unions in the industry, was formed in 1919 through the merger of four smaller unions.[39] The Amalgamated Engineering Union came into existence in 1920, the Transport and General Workers' Union in 1921.[40] However, throughout the inter-war period the motor industry remained by and large un-unionized. The unions' problems, particularly in Coventry, were compounded by the 1921 depression with many firms cutting back or going bankrupt. The Workers' Union almost ceased to exist and the AEU also suffered, the more so when it was defeated in the general lock-out in the engineering industries in 1922.[41] Some firms like Ford simply did not recognize the unions until forced to do so during the Second World War.[42] Almost invariably, the motor industry could afford to and did pay its workers well above the 'going rate' in the engineering industry, and even more in excess of the minimum wage demanded by the unions, average earnings in the motor industry in 1927 being some

27 per cent higher than in the general engineering industry.[43] No wonder that, in 1927, William Morris could claim 'I never allow trade unions to interfere with me'.[44]

One of the important features of employment in the motor industry between the wars was that it was highly seasonal. New models for the coming year were typically introduced in the period between August and October and were then displayed to the public in the annual London Motor Show held in October. This was the occasion when manufacturers would take the orders which dictated their production plans for the following months. Quite often, a manufacturer would display what was in reality only a prototype car at the show, and the resulting orders – or their absence – would determine whether or not the car actually went into production. A famous example was the Rover Scarab, a rear-engined small car displayed in the Olympia Motor Show in 1931 and almost immediately withdrawn.

With a full order-book from the Motor Show, manufacturers would

gear up production throughout the winter and spring, in readiness for the main selling season which began around Easter and lasted into the early part of the summer.[45] When this was over, most factories went on short time, laying off the majority of workers until the annual cycle began again at the end of the autumn. Such evidence as is available in the form of personal memoirs and contemporary accounts show that this was the accepted pattern – the generally high wages of the motor industry, coupled with bonus or overtime payments at the busy periods, were considered as a trade-off against short-time working and periods of being laid off altogether. Some workers found other employment during the summer months – necessary at a time when the dole was 10s. per week – and some took the opportunity of moving to a new job with another firm when the busy season began again.[46]

One possibility which might have helped the British motor industry to overcome this stop-go cycle forced upon them by the seasonal variations in demand in the home market, would have been to increase their export sales. A few British manufacturers did make efforts to introduce special export models in the 1920s and 1930s but they were mostly uncompetitive against cheaper and more robust American cars, even in Empire markets such as Australia, South Africa, or New Zealand. A classic example is the ill-fated Morris Empire Oxford of 1927. Before the Second World War, the best figures achieved for export sales were around 20 per cent of total production.[47] In 1934, an admittedly small specialist manufacturer such as Cecil Kimber of MG could afford to state that: 'The overseas market we do not look upon very seriously ... [we] look upon ... overseas sales as being helpful in carrying a certain proportion of the general factory overheads'.[48]

Only with the substantial investments made in the industry in the early 1930s did it become necessary for car

Body drop procedure in G block at Cowley, with a body being lowered by electric crane. The car is a Morris Ten Six Special coupé of 1934. (BMIHT/Rover).

manufacturers to try to overcome the seasonal variations in output. The increasing demand for new cars in Britain made it viable for companies such as Morris and Austin to reorganize their factories, introducing true mass-production techniques with powered moving assembly lines – some 20 years after Ford. With the considerable investment made in new production facilities, car manufacturers simply could no longer afford to have their factories standing idle for extended periods. Between 1933 and 1936, Morris invested £500,000 in new production facilities at Cowley.[49] This created one of the most modern assembly plants in Britain, with an annual capacity of around 100,000 cars. Concomitant with this, Morris introduced a new range of cars starting with the Morris Eight in August 1934, followed by other 'Series' models which were introduced unseasonably in May and June 1935.

At the introduction of the new models, Morris's managing director L. P. Lord stated specifically that 'in future there were to be no more dated [sic] Morris models, they were to become known by Series numbers and the new versions were to be brought out as and when desirable.'[50] Deliveries from Cowley in August 1935 showed a three-fold increase over the previous best August, and in 1938 Morris Motors published figures which showed that in the previous three years, the months of June, July and August had been the second best-selling quarter of the year, whereas previously the summer months had been the slackest period. The benefit to the work-force was that it became less necessary to lay off workers during the summer, as production and deliveries were evened out over all 12 months of the year. Although other manufacturers did not take as drastic or well-publicized steps as Morris to overcome the seasonal buying pattern, no doubt their own investments in new plant was a factor in the annual model change being gradually abandoned during the 1930s,

with major changes to popular cars only occurring at less frequent intervals. The Morris Eight, for instance, was produced in largely unchanged form for four years.

Whether seasonal or not, increased demand in the British home market meant that car production rose sharply in the years between the wars, reaching the pre-war highest figure of 389,633 in 1937,[51] with some 312,000 new cars being registered in the UK in the same year.[52] Employment rose likewise. By 1939 the Ministry of Labour figures revealed that over 500,000 people were employed in the motor industry and motor trade combined,[53] the figure for those employed directly in the production of complete vehicles probably being around 152,000.[54] The motor industry was thus still very much a growth industry, yet had only begun to tap a fraction of its ultimate market potential. While not by any means free from industrial unrest, the motor industry between 1919 and 1939 was significantly less affected by disputes than coal-mining, heavy industry, or the transport sector.

Thus the most famous example

of industrial conflict in inter-war Britain, the general strike of May 1926, started with a dispute in the coal-mining industry and, with the support of the TUC, spread to the transport sector as well as many industries. While some stoppages occurred in Coventry car manufacturing firms, others such as Austin worked more or less unaffected throughout.[55] Only small and isolated groups such as wood machinists and toolmakers went on strike at Longbridge, while the NUVB actually instructed striking members to return to work, and 400 volunteers were recruited from among Austin's workers to safeguard the company's electricity and gas supplies during the strike or to serve as special constables. In actual fact, the general strike gave a longer-term boost to the motor industry by demonstrating the value of motorization, as private cars took over many of the transport tasks normally carried out by the railways and other forms of public transport.

While unemployment was a serious problem in Britain for most of the inter-war period, especially in the

Even before the General Motors take-over, Vauxhall had a flowline system. This 1926 photo shows on the left 14/40, and on the right 25/70 sleeve valve models, on the final chassis assembly lines. Ten separate crafts were involved in the making of 26 vehicles a week. (NB)

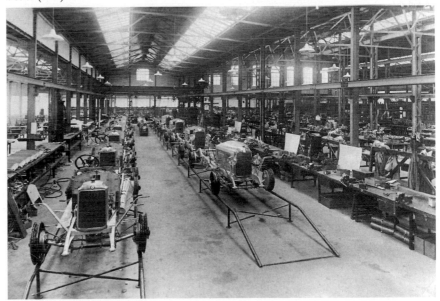

Ernest Bevin was effectively the founder of the TGWU and one of the leading trade unionists in the country during and after the Second World War. As Minister of Labour he arbitrated on any disputes which could not be settled at local level. Here he is addressing the Labour Party Conference at Blackpool in 1945. (Hulton Deutsch Collection Ltd)

depression years from 1929 to 1934, the evidence that is available shows that since the high levels of unemployment in the Midlands engineering industry in 1921 referred to above, unemployment in this area stayed well below the national average. In 1934, 67 per cent of workers in Jarrow – the worst affected area – were out of a job, while the figure for Birmingham was six per cent, and for Coventry and Oxford five per cent.[56] In Coventry in particular, by 1939 the motor industry accounted for 38 per cent of the total labour force of just over 100,000 workers in this city.[57] The figures for vehicle production showed only a relatively small set-back in the years 1930 to 1932, in the order of less than five per cent from 1929 to 1931 when commercial vehicles and private cars are counted together; 1929 had seen total production of 238,805 vehicles, the lowest figure in the depression being 226,307 vehicles in 1931.[58] While the fall-off in private car production was somewhat steeper, this was partially off-set by an increase in the production of commercial vehicles. The reason was undoubtedly that, at the time, most sales of new cars were made to the relatively affluent middle classes whose employment and income were less affected by the depression.

The industry was not strike-free, however. The most important study in the field, *Labour Relations in the Motor Industry* quotes the following statistics for major motor industry strikes between the wars:[59]

Years	Number of Strikes	Workers involved (thousands)	Working days lost (thousands)
1921–30	27	22	84
1931–9	37	56	226

In 1964 Graham Turner reported that the average basic rate for a skilled worker at Vauxhall was around £18 per week. Three years later they were still campaigning for £20, as here at Pope's Meadow, Luton, in September 1967. (Hulton Deutsch Collection Ltd)

– and then, in the case of Austin, goes on to list the following major strikes which occurred in this company between the wars: 1921, over an employment issue; two strikes in 1929, in protest over wage reductions, one of which involved 11,000 men (at a time when the total work-force was around 13,500); and in 1938, among workers engaged in aircraft manufacture in the Austin shadow factory. The authors also enumerate the reasons for strikes, of which claims for wage increases or other wage disputes accounted for 15 of the 27 strikes in the 1920s and 23 of the 37 strikes in the 1930s, in other words an average of some 60 per cent of disputes.

More detailed information on strikes at Austin is available from other sources.[60] When in 1923 the company's management endeavoured to introduce new piece rates without consulting shop-floor representatives, the workers protested. The company then asked officials of the National Union of Vehicle Builders to settle the matter. According to the Journal of the NUVB, the company 'gracefully gave way and promised not to offend in the future'. This amounted to a *de facto* recognition of organized labour and this union by Austin, occurring well in advance of almost anywhere else in the British motor industry. Although Austin continued to operate an open shop and union membership at Longbridge stayed very low, the prestige of the NUVB was greatly enhanced, and, as Adeney puts it, 'Austin's technique was to use the NUVB in particular as a kind of policeman to get workers back, refusing to negotiate except with the union, even though most workers did not belong to it'.[61]

Another short-lived conflict at Austin in 1924 had at its root the problem of work being transferred from skilled workers, in this case body makers who belonged to the NUVB, to semi-skilled workers. Such problems would increasingly occur as the motor industry gradually made the transition from batch production, to flow pro-

duction, to mass production – the 1924 dispute at Austin may be seen as a forerunner of the many disputes over demarcation in post-war years, also of the frequent examples of a small skilled group of workers (such as toolmakers) going on strike and thereby bringing an entire factory to a halt.

Good personal relations contributed greatly to industrial peace

The more important of the 1929 disputes occurred when, as part of Austin's transition to flow production, works manager Engelbach reorganized production methods and introduced a new grading system. A strike committee was formed under the leadership of a Welsh ex-miner, with the intention of staging a 'stay-in' but refusing to work – an early example of what later became known as the 'sit-down' strike. Although this was frustrated when the management closed the factory, some 5,000 workers – mostly non-union members – stayed out on strike. After five days, agreement was reached through union officials for a meeting between management, union and non-union representatives to discuss the new working arrangements, and the strikers returned. The result was seen as a victory for the organized labour, and one important result of the negotiations which followed the strike was that Austin's management agreed to recognize shop stewards, even providing a room for the weekly meetings of the shop stewards' committee.

Another far-reaching effect of this dispute was that it was agreed that all future changes in rates had to be mutually agreed between management and workers – a principle that was not abandoned at Longbridge until 1980. On the whole there was justified optimism in trade union circles that this strike would lead to greatly increased unionization in car factories, and that even management would come to appreciate the benefit of being able to negotiate with a disciplined and

responsible labour force, although within a few years the relative importance of the shop stewards' committee at Austin declined – especially with the influx of a greater number of unskilled and unorganized workers in the 1930s.

A 1936 strike at Longbridge occurred over a dispute with regard to the reduction of piece-work rates, while in 1938 workers in the new aero factory (a shadow factory built at Cofton Hackett adjacent to Longbridge) went on strike over their claim to be re-graded and to receive wages on a par with workers in the aircraft industry proper – which was eventually conceded with a wage increase of 15 per cent. Both of these strikes were unofficial, but both were eventually settled by negotiations between management and the recognized union representatives.

These examples of inter-war strikes in the motor industry show that already some classic causes for industrial unrest can be identified, such as rate fixing, grading, parity, and demarcation, apart from the issue of pay itself. The issues of consultation between management and work-force, and of the recognition of unions and shop stewards, have also made their appearance. Although on at least one occasion (the 1936 strike over piecework rates) the Austin company threatened to sack all workers who failed to resume work, this ultimatum was quickly withdrawn, and Church notes that the comparatively good industrial relations at Longbridge in the inter-war period may have been attributable to 'a sound negotiating relationship between Engelbach (the works manager), who was responsible for devising the wages system at Longbridge, and the shop committees'.[62] In fact good personal relationships between workers' representatives and managers may have contributed more to keeping the industrial peace than is generally realized. It is interesting that such relationships in some cases continued into the rather more confrontational post-war period, regardless of differences over work-related matters or in political opinion, such as in the cordiality shared between Dick Etheridge, the Communist who became senior shop steward and plant conveyor at Longbridge, and George Harriman, BMC's managing director and chairman in the 1960s.[63] In at least one case long-term good industrial relations have been credited to the personality of the company's chairman, that of Sir Charles Bartlett of Vauxhall.[64]

In absolute terms, the unions made only little headway in the motor industry before the Second World War. The most obvious reason was that the motor industry continued to provide better wages and conditions than almost any other branch of manufacturing industry at the time. Even at Austin where, as we have seen, the unions gained more in recognition and standing than anywhere else in the industry, actual membership was and remained quite low. From the Morris factory at Cowley, a despondent NUVB branch secretary in 1927 pointed out 'the futility at any attempt at organization in this district'.[65] Similarly, Jack Jones, who became district organizer for the Transport and General Workers' Union in Coventry in 1939, could only point to 2,000 local members – 'the overwhelming majority of workers in the area belonged to no union at all'.[66]

Those unions which, like the Amalgamated Engineering Union (AEU) and the NUVB, had a background as craft unions and therefore a history of recruiting mainly skilled workers, were not at first particularly active in recruiting the new semi-skilled or unskilled workers who came to the motor industry, particularly with the introduction of assembly lines in most companies in the 1930s.[67] Into this apparent void stepped the originally Midlands-based Workers' Union which, with others, in 1928 was amalgamated into the Transport and General Workers' Union. In the 1930s, the TGWU assumed a more active role in recruiting assembly line workers in the motor industry. This in turn

led the AEU and NUVB to intensify their membership drives, and the National Union of General and Municipal Workers also began to take an interest in the motor industry.

While some firms apart from Austin recognized trade unions, others remained implacably opposed, including Morris but also Ford and Vauxhall, which both followed the policy established by their American parent organizations. Jaguar, under the autocratic leadership of William Lyons, also refused to acknowledge the unions. Some companies had a reputation for sacking union activists, usually during the slack period in the summer.[68]

The turning point, not only for the position of trade unions in the motor industry but for the role of organized labour in British society over the next forty years, came with the Second World War when Winston Churchill formed his national government in May 1940 and appointed Labour MP Ernest Bevin as Minister of Labour. Bevin (1881–1951) was effectively the founder of the TGWU, having been the secretary of this union from 1922, and had become chairman of the TUC general council in 1937. He was one of the leading trade unionists in the country. With the passing of the Emergency Powers (Defence) Bill by Parliament in May 1940 and the issue in July 1940 of order no. 1305. Conditions of Employment and National Arbitration, companies as well as labour were put under government control. On the subject of industrial relations, collective bargaining continued but employers who had not previously recognized unions were now obliged to accept such conditions and terms as had been agreed between the unions and other employers in a particular trade or district. Any dispute which could not be settled by local negotiation had to be referred to the Minister and through him, to a newly-formed National Arbitration Council, with strikes and lock-outs being illegal until a period of 21 days had expired without a settlement having been agreed.

There were other far-reaching innovations implemented during the war. Unions agreed to allow greater numbers of unskilled workers to perform jobs which previously had been the preserve of skilled men. Bevin intervened personally to get employers and unions to agree on extending the number of women employees in the engineering industry. Then there was the Coventry toolroom agreement whereby skilled toolroom workers would be paid at least the average earnings of skilled production workers not only in their own factory but throughout the district – 'a momentous deal which would echo down the car industry's industrial relation nightmares, famous to the unions, infamous to the employers'.[69] Its long-term effect was to create a never-ending wages spiral.

Gradually, the unions gained acceptance throughout the industry – though often only grudgingly, as a necessary evil. In 1942, Vauxhall agreed to recognize the AEU and the NUVB, and set up its famous Management Advisory Council which, long into the post-war period, continued to exert a beneficial influence on industrial relations in the Luton factory.[70] The MAC consisted of 22 workers' representatives elected in individual factory 'wards' by secret ballot for a three-year period. In practice most MAC members were shop stewards. Vauxhall continued the practice of negotiating only with these two unions, which therefore became the most influential unions in the company. Although, curiously, by 1965 Vauxhall had a lower level of unionization than any other British car manufacturer – 85 per cent of manual workers organized, instead of the 100 per cent that was by then customary – two-thirds of these were AEU members, almost twice the average of AEU penetration in major car companies, 29 per cent were NUVB members and only five per cent belonged to other unions.[71] G. Turner, writing around the same time, describes the – mostly friendly – rivalry between these two unions at Vauxhall.

At Ford, unions did not become recognized until 1944, and even then this only happened after a damaging sit-in strike.[72] Ford's agreement with the unions was reached through the TUC, partly under pressure from the Ministry of Labour. It involved some 20 unions, and negotiations were conducted primarily with the national officers of the unions. Arrangements were formalized in 1946 with a procedure agreement which called for shop-floor grievances to be referred to a joint committee of management representatives and national trade union officials.[73] In 1955 Ford set up a National Joint Negotiating Committee for collective bargaining on a national level with all of the unions involved. While this avoided the fragmentary plant-by-plant approach which dictated – and soured – industrial relations in BMC and later BL, the machinery created by the Ford procedural agreements was quite cumbersome and arguably left too much power in the hands of local shop stewards.[74] Ford's industrial relations problems were compounded by the number of different unions involved and their relative strengths, which varied greatly, and – more than in most other car factories – by the presence of militant left-wing or Communist shop stewards. These factors gave plenty of scope for inter-union rivalry, although the fact that shop stewards elected on a geographical or departmental basis often had to represent workers from trade unions other than their own, in practice caused relatively few problems.

Despite the 1940 order, there was an increasing incidence of industrial unrest in the industry during the war years. Figures quoted by Adeney show that from the low number of 79,000 working days lost in the engineering industry in 1940, it then rose inexorably to a peak of 600,000 in 1944.[75] Often the unions had to take the blame for these problems. A works superintendent at Jaguar later said: 'We didn't know anything about unions until 1943, but then we had to be affiliated. We had troubles then, stoppages.'[76]

This was perhaps not entirely surprising in view of the fact that this company had continued its policy of victimizing trade union activists, even during war-time – thus nine activists were dismissed from Jaguar in March 1940.[77] It was realized by many that the war had brought about fundamental changes to the industrial relations climate, and some felt that the Labour victory in the 1945 election would make these changes immutable – thus Miles Thomas, vice-chairman of the Nuffield Organization from 1940 to 1947, felt that the 1945 election was 'the point of no return in the economic affairs of Great Britain'[78] and that 'militant trade unionism and the whole shop steward system was henceforth in control'. Thomas, a self-confessed and unrepentant Tory, was apparently unchallenged when at the annual general meeting of Morris Motors Limited in 1947 he reported that

'extravagant expansions' had been cancelled because of labour difficulties,[79] when he might more justifiably have blamed Lord Nuffield's indifference to the introduction of new post-war products.

The war-time period which should have given motor industry managers on the one side, and unions and shop stewards on the other, their first chance to work together and find common ground in their joint efforts to boost industrial output, thereby helping to gain victory for Britain, thus often only served to reinforce ancient prejudice and antagonism. Many motor industry leaders found it difficult to adjust to the new situation where they were forced to work in harness with the unions, and it was not only Thomas who openly expressed his distaste for the growing influence of the unions. Another example was the works manager of Austin who

Ford had a mixed record on industrial relations in the 1970s; an 11-week strike in 1971 and a four-week one in October 1978 which, among other things, resulted in no new cars on display at the Motor Show that year, but a rejection of a strike call and the end of an overtime ban in February 1973 restored Henry Ford's faith in the British Ford workers. Here a group of workers comment ruefully on a reported 80 per cent pay rise for Chairman Sir Terence Beckett, during the 1978 dispute. (Hulton Deutsch Collection Ltd)

stormed out of a meeting between the employers' federation and the unions, having delivered the following salvo to union leaders: 'You are enemies of our company; you are enemies of our country; you are enemies of God. Goodday.'[80] His choice of words suggests that in his mind at least, the unions had already become associated with the Communist menace. On this point Miles Thomas had a more level-headed approach: 'Russia, our Ally during the war, became a potential enemy. That saddened me. Every attempt of British labour to obtain more wages for a reduced effort was dubbed Communist.'[81] Whether or not there was much reality behind the perception of the Communist bogey as the root of all evil in British industrial relations post-1945, it is certainly true that many prominent union leaders or, perhaps more correctly, leading shop stewards (Dick Etheridge and Derek Robinson, to name but two) were Communists, although only a fraction of the rank-and-file membership in their unions shared their political views. It is, however, also true that Communism became an only too convenient scapegoat for many industry leaders and managers.

In the immediate post-war period, under the Labour government of Clement Attlee from 1945 to 1951, government involvement in the motor industry continued, although not to the extent that it had during the war. The Minister of Supply in 1946 set up the National Advisory Council for the Motor Manufacturing Industry, composed of eight representatives of the manufacturers, two trade unionists and one independent member. This was not a policy-making body but was intended as an organ for communication. It was instrumental in effecting, for instance, the change in the road fund licensing system from being

Marching Ford workers show less than enthusiastic loyalty to their company. Hundreds marched from Tower Hill to Central Hall, Westminster, in October 1978. (Hulton Deutsch Collection Ltd)

based on the RAC horsepower of an engine to the flat-rate tax which still prevails, and also discussed issues relating to the export trade and standardization. It does not appear to have concerned itself directly with industrial relations although the minority representation of the trade unions was an interesting step.

While the Labour government was politically committed to full employment, to be achieved – as far as the motor industry was concerned – chiefly through expansion of the export trade (to which end the Government introduced a series of other measures), in industrial relations terms it followed largely a hands-off policy. In 1947 the motor industry in general changed from a five-and-a-half day week to a five-day week. The TUC moved that a 40-hour week should be introduced generally in the industry, but the Government refused to legislate on this, stating that it was a matter for negotiation.[82]

Officially the Government operated a policy of wage restraint, and this seems to have received the general support of the trade union movement. It did not, however, prevent wages in the motor industry from continuing to run ahead of general wage levels in the engineering industry. The wage increases in the motor industry seem to have been more instigated by employers than demanded by the workers. As war-time restrictions on the movement of labour were lifted and as industry in general expanded, workers who wanted to improve their pay could easily find better-paid jobs elsewhere, and undoubtedly the manufacturers saw still-higher wage offers as being the best way to retain workers. The following figures taken from *Labour Relations in the Motor Industry*, [83] clearly demonstrate that the question of wages itself was a diminishing cause for industrial unrest in the post-war period:

Years	Number of strikes	Caused by wage claims or wage disputes	Percentage caused by wage claims/disputes
1940–4	121	87	72%
1945–9	78	38	49%
1950–4	59	22	37%

– which may be compared to the figure of some 60 per cent of strikes caused by wage claims or wage disputes in the pre-war period, as noted above. After 1954, however, the question of remuneration would again rise high on the strikers' agenda.

The mould-breaker in the industry was the Standard Motor Company Limited in Coventry. As noted in the PEP Report,[84] in 1945 this company took the unusual step of leaving the Engineering and Allied Employers' Federation as a result of a disagreement over the company's system of paying its workers by results. In 1948 Standard introduced a new wage system, agreed by negotiation with the Confederation of Shipbuilding and Engineering Unions to which most of the important motor industry unions belonged, including the AEU, the NUVB, and the TGWU. Under the new system, piecework – traditional in the Midlands at least since the 1920s – was abolished, and 92 basic rates formerly in operation for male workers were reduced to eight. The agreement guaranteed a minimum wage of £5 per week to male adult workers, this being supplemented by a bonus system where bonuses were paid to all members of designated teams, and where the upper limit of the bonus was 100 per cent of the guaranteed basic wage. In fact, from 1948 to 1949 the average male earnings at Standard rose from around £9 to £11 per week.[85] Pay rates at Standard would stay ahead of the rest of the industry until the 1960s, and their rates had a considerable knock-on effect at least in the Coventry area. Standard's chairman and managing director Sir John Black was said to have 'bought' industrial peace, and H. A. Turner speculates that this policy 'may well have contributed to the commercially unfortunate later history of the firm', although other factors also played their part in Standard's ultimate failure. It may be noted that the Standard company eventually did rejoin the employers' federation, and also that the company reintroduced the piecework system in the 1950s under union pressure.[86]

One post-war innovation was that the Government would now set up a court of inquiry to investigate cases where labour relations had broken down. The first time such a court was set up to examine a motor industry strike was in 1953, following the McHugh strike at Austin, until then the biggest strike to have affected a single firm in the industry, involving 2,200 members of the NUVB directly, with another 7,000 workers being laid off, lasting three months and resulting in a loss of 239,000 working days. This strike is described in detail by H. A. Turner.[87] At the root of the strike lay one of the early rationalization plans put into effect after the Austin-Morris merger in April 1952. This led to the discontinuation of the not very successful Austin A90 Atlantic model which went out of production in August 1952 at apparently very short notice, leading to some 700 hourly-paid workers and 100 staff being made immediately redundant. One of the men laid off was John McHugh who was president of the local NUVB branch and secretary of the joint shop stewards' committee at Austin.

BMC's 6,000 lay-offs affronted people's belief in the dignity of man

The NUVB maintained that McHugh had been victimised for his union activities. The company claimed that the NUVB was trying to secure preferential treatment for a shop steward. Although Austin had undertaken to give preference to redundant workers when engaging new Labour, when McHugh twice applied in the autumn of 1952 he was not re-employed, and Austin's works manager is alleged to have ordered that McHugh was not to be re-engaged without the matter being referred to him. When vacancies arose and the union pressed for McHugh's re-employment, the response was that he must take his chance with everybody else.

After some five months of inconclusive negotiations, the strike was finally called for 7 February 1953. The Confederation of Shipbuilding and Engineering Unions suggested that the strike should be referred to a court of enquiry but this was only put to the strikers by the local district committee of the NUVB at a mass meeting six weeks later. The meeting endorsed the recommendation for a court of enquiry. On the same day as the meeting was held, Austin issued a notice that strikers who had not resumed work by the end of the week would be regarded as having left the company's employ. The NUVB declared itself willing to call a meeting for the following Monday to recommend a return to work, but Austin rejected this. Some 1,600 strikers who did not return by the stipulated day were dismissed.

The Court of Inquiry sat during April and found that McHugh's dismissal was 'neither vindictive nor irregular in form and cannot be attributed to victimization on account of . . . trade union activities. Furthermore [the strike] was not based upon any real grievance as to [McHugh's] dismissal or the form which it had taken, but was designed by [the area organizer of the NUVB] to secure the principle of preferential treatment for shop stewards, a principle which formed no part of the official policy of his own union, nor . . . of any other union with membership in the company's works.'[88] McHugh was not re-employed.

Although the number of strikes in the motor industry remained at a fairly low, constant level for the first ten years after the war – typically with less than 20 recorded major disputes per year – the number of working days lost fluctuated quite wildly, depending on the size of individual disputes. In 1952 as a result of a month-long stoppage affecting Ford and the still-independent Briggs body plant at Dagenham, with the loss of 247,000 working days, and again in 1953 with the McHugh strike at Austin, for the first time the annual number of days lost in the motor industry reached the level of

250,000, whereas the worst pre-war figure had been 70,000 working days lost in 1937.[89] (In 1959, in *The Times Survey of the British Motor Car Industry*, the figures given for working days lost through disputes in the motor industry were: 1951, 266,000; 1952, 468,000; 1953, 589,000. There is no obvious explanation for this fairly remarkable discrepancy in published statistics.)

While individual firms lost considerable production because of strikes, it is more difficult to determine whether the industry as a whole was set back by industrial unrest at this time. It is correct that there was a set-back from the first post-war high production of 783,672 in 1950 to figures some 50–100,000 less in 1951 and 1952, but by 1953 production was back up again to a new record of 834,775 (SMMT statistics for cars and commercial vehicles). It should be noted that there was a drop in exports to the USA in 1951 as small British saloon cars met increasing sales resistance in this market, and this was followed in 1952 by the disastrous set-back in sales to Australia as the Australian government sharply increased import tariffs in order to protect their domestic industry.[90] Nor was there much comfort to be gained from the home market, where government policies intervened to restrict demand: thus the rate of Purchase Tax payable on a new car was doubled from 33.3 per cent to 66.6 per cent in April 1951, and in February 1952 the first restrictions on hire purchase were introduced.

It is arguable that another decline in export sales in 1956 – where, for instance, BMC's sales to Australia were halved – combined with home market restrictions, including an increase in Purchase Tax, led directly to the 200,000 drop in production from 1955 to 1956, which in turn was to lead to the next important episode in the history of motor industry industrial relations: for the first time since the war, large-scale redundancies were imposed by manufacturers in 1956–7. Ford, for instance, cut their work-force

by 4,000 and Standard laid off some 3,000 workers. Both figures were overshadowed by BMC's drastic cut which affected over 6,000 workers or 12.5 per cent of the company's work-force, of which some 5,000 were in the Birmingham area.[91]

BMC announced the redundancies on Wednesday 27 June 1956. They would be effective from Friday 29 June. According to Kahn, the scale of the dismissals 'was unprecedented as far as post-war Britain was concerned, and it came as a rude shock to the nation.' *The Times* called BMC's action 'unjustified provocation' and printed a letter from a Conservative MP who wrote that the redundancies 'affronted everyone who has a fundamental belief in the decencies and dignity of man.' *The Economist* (28 July 1956) reported that the Prime Minister, Sir Anthony Eden, 'nodded vigorously' when Labour MPs criticized BMC's action in parliamentary debate. The Minister of Labour strongly criticized BMC in a statement to the House of Commons in which he described the company's action as 'profoundly disturbing'.[92]

Lay-offs raised doubts about BMC's own management skills

There had been no form of consultation with shop stewards or union officials prior to the issue of redundancy notices. This, and the suddenness of the action, caused deep resentment among BMC workers. Threats of strike action, or actual strikes, followed in many of the plants affected. At a meeting between trade union leaders and BMC representatives, the unions pressed for redundant workers to be compensated, which was rejected, and a strike in all BMC factories was subsequently called from 23 July. Only about half of BMC's workers went on strike and, in any case, the works summer holiday of two weeks began soon after. The Engineering Employers' Federation now took the initiative to

renew discussions with the unions, these taking place under the auspices of the Ministry of Labour, and a settlement was reached on 10 August, under which BMC would pay compensation to workers with at least three years' service, at the rate of one week's pay for those with from three to ten years' service, two weeks' pay for those with more than ten years' service (hardly generous by those standards which, years later, were dictated by law). The strike was then called off and work was resumed on 13 August.

The effect of the redundancies was to create a 'blip' in the local unemployment statistics for the Midlands region. While in 1956, the national unemployment rate averaged 1.2 per cent, it had been less than half that in the Midlands region until it went up to around two per cent in July–August 1956. As at the time the nation enjoyed a condition of almost full employment it may be noted that an estimated 95 per cent of the redundant BMC workers had in fact found other employment within a period of six months from redundancy, and about half were eventually re-employed by BMC, although mostly only between six and 12 months after being made redundant from the company (figures based on the sample of 447 workers interviewed by Kahn in 1958; of these 417 were BMC workers at the time of their redundancy). The importance of the 1956 episode lies in the fact that for the first time, the employer agreed to pay redundant workers compensation. The other important effect of the BMC redundancies in 1956 is that they greatly contributed to increasing the feeling of distrust that workers had in their employers' competence in managing their businesses: the large-scale redundancies in 1956 could be seen simply as a panic reaction to a short-term problem, in view of the fact that already by 1957 British car production was back up to the 1955 level and thereafter increased steadily for the remainder of the decade. The events of 1956 thus had unforeseen long-term repercussions for the whole industrial relations climate in the motor industry.

That the problems were growing towards the end of the 1950s and into the 1960s is evident from the statistics as well as from individual episodes. The annual survey of the British motor car industry, published by *The Times*, became a lamentable catalogue of industrial disputes. While the 1957 issue, under the headline 'Peace With Labour?', expressed guarded optimism that 'the labour battles in the motor industry in the past 18 months have cleared away a good many misconceptions ... there appear to be prospects of a more peaceful and co-operative spirit than in the past ... By and large labour relations in the industry are brighter than they have been for many years'; but in the 1959 issue the subject attracted the headline of 'Lost Time – A Bad Year – But Strikes Are Unevenly Spread', and it was recorded that 'there were 84 strikes in the vehicle building industry in the first half of [1959], which was the same number as in the whole of [1958], and more than in any other of the past ten years. The number of working days lost was 290,000, which was more than in any other industry, except paper and printing'. The writer reported that Rootes and Vauxhall had been almost free from trouble, that Standard had shown great improvement, and that most of the disputes were concentrated in BMC and Ford. The 1960 issue listed the following events as recorded in the column of *The Times* from November 1959 onwards:

3 November – Production of Austin cars halted by token strike.

4 November – Work resumed at Austin but sit-down strike at Rover because shop steward refused permission to take his private car to be serviced in firm's time.

6 November – Rover strike ends.

11 November – Production of Ford Anglia affected by token stoppages.

17 November – BMC output dislocated by unofficial strike at Nuffield Metal Products (where the Morris Minor bodies were made).

18 November – Jaguar send home 300 men because of piecework dispute.

20 November – BMC men return to work.

9 December – Strike at Rootes Group factory at Acton (British Light Steel Pressings, body panels and bodies).

10 December – Strike at Mulliners (body factory) threatens employment of 10,000 workers at Standard. 4,000 out of work at Jaguar because of stoppage by 64 men.

14 December – Mulliner strike over.

15 December – Jaguar strike over.

30 December – Production at stand still at Rootes because of sit-down strike by clerks. 2,000 laid off at Rover because of paint shop stoppage.

31 December – More out at Rover factory, but work resumed at Rootes.

1960

1 January – Brief stoppage at Vauxhall because men were 'too hot'. Paint shop strike at Rover ended.

7 January – Rover strike over.

17 January – Strike at Hardy-Spicer (leading supplier of components including universal joints and prop shafts) because foreman swore at man who arrived late.

19 January – Unofficial strike makes 5,000 idle at Morris.

20 January – Strike threatens 13,000 jobs at Rootes, Acton (presumably a strike at Acton threatened 13,000 jobs at Rootes). Morris men return.

21 January – More workers laid off at Rootes.

25 January – 8,600 laid off at Rootes, Coventry assembly lines at standstill.

26 January – Complete BMC stoppage threatened by strike of 55 maintenance men.

28 January – Rootes strike ended.

29 January – More than 24,000 idle at BMC while new strikes threaten Standard Triumph and Rover.

(NB: author's explanatory notes in parentheses)

– and so on. These excerpts for a period of only three months show a wide cross section of stoppages, mostly unofficial, some of them called over what seems in retrospect the most trivial reasons, others amply illustrating how a strike by a disproportionately small group of key workers could bring an enormous company to a virtual standstill – the strike by the 55 electricians at BMC recorded under 26 January eventually led to 31,000 workers being idle in Birmingham, Coventry, and Oxford, only one model of car remained in production, and by the time the strike was over on 5 February, BMC reported a loss of 25,000 vehicles and £12 million turnover.

The causes for major strikes were now increasingly questions of pay. H. A. Turner[93] records that of 197 strikes from 1955 to 1959, 108 were caused by wage claims or disputes, while of 401 strikes from 1960 to 1964, 224 had these causes – at around 55 per cent an increase from the 1945–54 period (cp.

Sir Don Ryder holding a copy of his report, British Leyland: The Next Decade, *just before it was delivered to the Prime Minister in March 1975.* (Hulton Deutsch Collection Ltd)

above). This contrasted with the fact that in April 1959, motor industry workers were reported to be the best paid workers in British industry, with average earnings for men in the motor and cycle industries of £17 12s 3d (weekly), compared to the average figure for industry in general of £13 2s 11d (*The Times Survey of the British Motor Car Industry* October 1959, p. 56). According to H. A. Turner by this date wages (as expressed by average hourly earnings for adult males) were highest in the Coventry firms of Standard and Rootes, which both paid more than 9s per hour; Austin paid a shilling less; and Ford and Morris were both well below 8s an hour. The average working week in the motor industry was reported as 47.5 hours, which must have included some overtime.[94] The difference in pay levels between Birmingham-based Austin and Oxford-based Morris within the same BMC company some seven years after the merger is in itself interesting, and this was a factor which probably caused a great deal of additional labour unrest in the Morris and other Nuffield factories in the south Midlands.

The effects of the high levels of pay in the motor industry are well dis-cussed by Graham Turner in *The Car Makers*,[95] who took Vauxhall as his example. While the basic rate for a top skilled man was around £18 per week, with nightwork and overtime it was possible to boost this to £23–24. Turner's interviews with Vauxhall workers, union representatives and shop stewards revealed that the majority had joined the company simply for the money and that many kept up remarkably affluent life-styles for manual workers in the early 1960s, buying their own houses on mortgages, as well as cars and other consumer durables which were bought on hire purchase, while Continental holidays were becoming commonplace. Turner sums up: 'This, then, is a slice of Vauxhall, with its gadgets, its status symbols, its restless, tireless pursuit of money. The old working class patterns are fast disappearing . . . The signs of a new middle class on the American pattern are plain to see'. Thirty-five years later we may reflect that this was never quite achieved in Britain, but such an American-style, blue-collar middle class did most certainly emerge in West Germany.

Apart from pay-related strikes, there were major stoppages over such questions as redundancies and dismissals, especially if these involved union activists or shop stewards; over a variety of questions regarding work practices – almost inevitably so if a change was proposed or implemented by management without consultation with the work-force; and increasingly, over the matter of the closed shop, with union members at times refusing to work with non-union members. The unions were largely successful in their drive for increased membership in the late 1950s and early 1960s, and a variety of sources agree that by the mid-1960s, many firms had a 100 per cent membership among their manual workers.[96] By then the AEU had become the largest union in the motor industry, with some 35 per cent of union members belonging to this union; the TGWU had 31 per cent and the NUVB (which was eventually to be diminished with falling member-ship, experience financial difficulties and living largely off its investments) 20 per cent. Five per cent belonged to the NUGMW, which had its strongest position at Ford, and the final nine per cent belonged to a multitude of other smaller unions, such as the National Sheet Metal Workers' Union which was particularly strong at BMC and Jaguar.

The sharp drop in British car pro-duction in the second half of 1960 and 1961 – largely caused by the dramatic decline in the still-vital export market of the USA, coupled with less favourable trading conditions in the home market – led to widespread short-time working and redundancies in the motor industry, one of the hard-est hit firms at this time being Standard Triumph. The almost inevitable result was a fresh wave of industrial unrest. 1960 saw new records set, both in the number of strikes and in the number of working days lost. Employers were becoming increasingly concerned, particularly over the level of unofficial stoppages. The Government was by now suffi-ciently concerned for the Minister of Labour to call together leading repre-sentatives of the employers as well as the trade unions – but excluding the shop stewards. After the talks, a joint statement was issued on 19 April 1961. An important point of agreement was that there should be stricter adherence to established procedures for the handling of disputes, thus: 'We have fully and candidly considered the various procedures for handling disputes and we have satisfied ourselves that these procedures are generally adequate if operated in the right spirit . . . Accordingly both sides will act in accordance with their respective constitutions to secure observance of those procedures by employers and union members.'[97]

This led for a time to the so-called 'firm line' being implemented. The most spectacular example of this was the damaging strike at British Light Steel Pressings at Acton in London, a subsidiary of the Rootes Group which made complete bodies for certain models and panels for others.[98] The immediate cause for the strike was that the shop stewards' combine feared the possibility of redundancies and attempted to raise this with management but was rebuffed. A mass meeting of workers resolved to remain on strike until the management declared a policy of no redundancies. The Engineering Employers' Federation denounced the strike, and the unions involved ordered their members to return to work. Although the EEF and the unions reached agreement on a formula to return to work this was rejected by the strikers. Rootes sent each of the 1,000 strikers a letter threatening dismissal if they did not return to work, and subsequently gave notice to 8,000 workers in Coventry who were laid off owing to the lack of supplies from Acton. A drift back to work started, with Rootes declaring that some 150 of the strikers would not be re-employed. After three months, the strike finally ended on 30 November 1961, and almost all of the original members of the shop stewards' combine lost their jobs.

While, ostensibly, the end of the strike had vindicated the firm line

taken by the Ministry of Labour and by the management of Rootes, victory had been bought at a high price. Production of Rootes vehicles slumped from 149,000 in 1960 to 100,000 in 1961,[99] and for the year ending 31 July 1962 the firm recorded the then substantial loss of £2 million. It is generally estimated that the BLSP strike cost Rootes some £3 million, and the hypothesis has been convincingly advanced that this strike contributed to Rootes' decline which eventually led to the company being taken over by the American Chrysler firm.

An almost identical pattern was seen in a strike at Pressed Steel's body factory at Swindon in 1961, the issue in question here being the workers' demand for wage parity with the same company's employees at Cowley. In October 1962, an AEU shop steward in Ford's Dagenham factory called a meeting (which eventually took place during the dinner break) without the required management permission and was dismissed, leading to unofficial action which lasted a fortnight. Ford then appeared to use this action as an excuse for dismissing a number of alleged trouble-makers (mostly militant left-wingers or Communists), which in turn led to the threat of an official strike in early 1963. The Ministry of Labour set up an official Court of Inquiry under Professor Jack. The eventual recommendations of this court – which, incidentally, remained unimplemented – were interesting. The court criticized the firm line approach followed by Ford, and felt that the strict adherence to procedure had led to discontent (possibly exacerbated by Ford's cumbersome National Joint Negotiating Committee system described above). The recommendations were that a full-time union official be appointed to oversee the activities of shop stewards; that a six-man negotiating committee replace the current committee which had one member from each of the 22 unions on it; that secret balloting be introduced; and that education programmes be established for shop stewards.[100]

It is thus evident that as the 1960s progressed, there was growing concern about the level of industrial unrest in the motor industry, both from the employers and the Government, as well as from the unions which were often put in a difficult position when shop stewards acted against union policies or instructions. An attempt at bringing about some form of reconciliation came after a Labour government had come to power again under Harold Wilson in 1964. In September 1965, leading employers and national union officials were called to 10 Downing Street – where, presumably, they were offered beer and sandwiches – to be presented by the Minister of Labour with a virtual ultimatum:[101] either the industry 'put its own house in order' or the Government would intervene, possibly by instituting compulsory arbitration. As Dunnett points out, shop stewards were again excluded. No immediate results came from this meeting, nor from the setting up of a Motor Industry Joint Labour Council under Jack Scamp. Scamp, in a report of motor industry labour relations, was particularly damning of the unions, finding that 'the major cause of poor labour relations was the total and general incompetence of the trade unions . . . The lack of internal structure of the many unions . . . made it impossible to enforce collective agreements, and so created a situation of "anarchy".'[102]

Strike activity continued unabated. By the late 1960s, the number of working days lost each year had reached well over a million. In October 1968 Barbara Castle as Secretary of State for Employment and Productivity called the 'cards on the table' meeting, again of employers and top union officials, again with the exclusion of shop stewards – which arguably meant that the workers were not fully represented, or at least had cause to feel unrepresented. Mrs Castle and the Labour government were determined to introduce labour reform and in 1969 published the paper 'In Place of Strife'. Among the ideas put forward in this were a proposal to make collective agreements binding; the introduction of compulsory conciliation pauses; secret ballots over strike; and that unofficial strikers be dismissed. As Dunnett puts it, 'this aroused very considerable union hostility'. Not surprisingly, the proposals were quickly watered down.

In 1966, the Government had established a Prices and Incomes Board, in an effort to limit inflationary wage and price increases. In February 1969, shop stewards' conveners from all British Ford plants voted to reject a pay deal which had been agreed by union negotiators. The Ford factory at Halewood near Liverpool (one of the new 1960s greenfield factories built with government assistance in development areas, with a 'fresh' work-force which often seemed more volatile than workers in the established factories) came out on strike in support of the shop stewards, although this action was unofficial. The strike led to a split between the more moderate Electricians' Union and the more militant TGWU/AUEW. There was a general feeling that the dispute was as much aimed at the Government, as at Ford's management, and the Electricians' Union were reluctant to take on what was after all a Labour government, but the TGWU eventually got its way, and Barbara Castle had to agree to a ten per cent wage increase, in excess of what the Prices and Incomes Board would normally have accepted. Thus the Labour government's attempt at maintaining an incomes policy was overturned by the unions in the motor industry. The 1969 Ford strike heralded a new era, lasting for the next decade, where openly political issues became more frequent as causes for industrial unrest. It is likely that the failure of Labour's attempts at tackling industrial relations against the might of the unions, for which the Labour party was largely dependent on funding, led to the electorate bringing back a Conservative government under Edward Heath in the 1970 election.

The new government had as one of its priorities the matter of improving industrial relations, and passed a new Industrial Relations Act in 1971. This introduced legally binding contracts and banned closed shops, aiming to bring an end to the unofficial disputes by transferring power from the shop stewards to union officials. Shop-floor opposition to the act was such that 1971 became the hitherto worst year for industrial unrest in the motor industry, with over three million working days lost.[103] Ford was strike-bound for 11 weeks, with an estimated loss of 150,000 vehicles and £100 million. The American parent company scrapped plans for a new engine factory in Britain. In *The Times* for 24 February, Henry Ford II commented that 'the labour situation has got to be cleaned up otherwise our customers will go elsewhere'.[104] On the other hand, when in February 1973 Ford workers rejected a strike call and voted to call off an overtime ban at Dagenham, Henry Ford announced that his confidence had been restored in the British Ford workers.[105]

When in 1974 Labour came back into power, the Industrial Relations Act of 1971 was repealed. The Conservative government's incomes policy was also scrapped, in favour of a 'social contract' between the Government and the unions, according to which wage claims should only keep pace with the cost of living – which in any case was escalating rapidly, with steep inflation in the wake of the 1973 oil crisis. This guideline was almost immediately exceeded by a wage claim at Ford. On behalf of the Government, Michael Foot, as Secretary of State for Employment, attempted to paper over the cracks by blaming the problem on the previous government: 'one of the difficulties of Fords and elsewhere are the injustices and anomalies left over by that statutory incomes policy'.[106] What was increasingly clear was that the motor industry, in particular Ford, was becoming a battle ground for workers, whether represented by shop stewards or unions, against the policies of the government of the day, whether Conservative or Labour. Ford in particular was also becoming a pace-setter, not only within the motor industry but for the labour market as a whole. The annual pay settlement at Ford was guaranteed to have wide-ranging repercussions.

By 1974, Britain's motor industry was in severe decline, and nowhere was this as apparent as in British Leyland, the unwieldy conglomerate formed in 1968 as a result of the government-inspired merger between BMH (itself formed two years before by a merger between BMC and Jaguar, and also comprising Pressed Steel) and Leyland, which by then included Standard Triumph and Rover. In the early 1970s, British Leyland was as plagued by industrial unrest as was Ford – while most disputes within Leyland were probably smaller and of shorter duration than the regular mammoth strikes at Ford, their cumulative effect was just as devastating. In 1974, Leyland ran out of money and approached the Government for assistance. In December 1974 Tony Benn, then Secretary of State for Industry, called upon a team of inquiry led by Sir Don Ryder (afterwards Lord Ryder) to report on the company and its prospects for the next decade. The report was delivered on 26 March 1975, and was subsequently published by HMSO in abbreviated form (deleting certain passages for reasons of commercial security). As part of their report, the Ryder team devoted considerable attention to the matter of industrial relations.[107]

Interestingly, the report stated that 'we do not subscribe to the view that all the ills of BL can be laid at the door of a strike-prone and work-shy labour force', but then went on to acknowledge the scale of the problem. From 1971 to 1974, the number of man-hours lost through industrial action trebled from 8.3 million to 23.8 million, or around 3 million working days: as BL at the time had some 170,000 employees in the UK, in round figures every single one of these was either on strike, or laid off, for more than 17 days in 1973–4. Of the lost man-hours, some 9.6 million – or only around 40 per cent – were attributable to disputes within BL, demonstrating the by now frequent problems of suppliers' strikes paralysing the car manufacturing plants. In October–November 1974, BL lost 37 per cent of scheduled production, of which half was due to industrial disputes and most of this (15 per cent of scheduled production) due to internal BL disputes.

The report went on to identify three specific areas – payment systems, collective bargaining, and industrial democracy – where it was felt that action was desirable to improve industrial relations. On these points, the Ryder committee was advised by representatives of the executive council of the Confederation of Shipbuilding and Engineering Unions, as well as an elected group of BL shop stewards and staff representatives, and elected representatives of BL's middle management.[108]

On the question of payment systems, the Ryder report endorsed the transition to measured day work which BL had introduced for the majority of manual employees between 1970 and 1974, in place of the old piecework system, but at the suggestion of the unions left the door open for the introduction of an additional, incentive pay element, such as a bonus system tied to output (which was, in fact, introduced at BL in the 1980s). As regards collective bargaining, the Ryder report noted that BL's then 170,000 employees were divided among 60 plants, eight divisions and 17 different unions, resulting in a total of no less than 246 separate bargaining units, despite some recent success in reducing the number of such units. These efforts had to some extent been hampered by the suspicions of the trade unions although, for instance, centralized bargaining over pension arrangements had been introduced. In discussion with the Ryder committee, the trade unions acknowledged that there would be scope for a gradual reduction in the number of bargaining units, also that a common

renewal date for different agreements could be introduced. The Committee's recommendation for the future of collective bargaining was based on these points and also suggested maximum use of the then-new Advisory, Conciliation and Arbitration Service (ACAS, only established in 1975). It was also recommended that greater authority to conduct bargaining should be vested directly in BL's line management, rather than be conducted remotely through the Engineering Employers' Federation negotiating with the unions on a national level on BL's behalf as had been the custom.

The Ryder recommendations with regard to industrial democracy were much wider in scope and implications. The committee recognized the power and influence of the shop stewards at plant level but pointed out that the British Leyland Shop Stewards' Committee was an unofficial body, recognized neither by BL nor by the unions, and that there was thus no single body which could be said specifically to represent BL's workers. On the assumption that BL would be nationalized – as the trade unions had recommended – the unions put forward a

plan for a range of joint management/union committees on all levels, from departments through individual factories or areas, to divisions of the corporation. These committees were to consist of voting representatives elected by union members and non-voting (!) ex-officio management, and would operate under an overall group board of management, which in turn would be composed half of union nominees and half of government nominees – the latter appointed on a basis of consultation with the unions – and again, non-voting ex-officio management representatives. The responsibilities of this board of management would include appointment of the actual management team, and the board would need to sanction all new policy decisions by the management team.

While the trade union proposals 'seemed to [the Ryder committee] to go further than is practicable',[109] the committee in the report nevertheless recommended that a new structure of joint management/union committees should be worked out in consultation with the trade unions. In recognizing that the company's management must not be hamstrung by committees, the

Derek Robinson (left), 'Red Robbo' to the press, senior shop steward and convenor at Longbridge, at the demonstration after his dismissal on 27 November 1979. Next to him, from the left, are retired shop steward Jack Neill, Labour MP Leslie Huckfield, and Robinson's partner Phyllis Davis. They have chosen to be photographed in front of a poster for one of BL's least successful cars, the Austin Allegro. (Hulton Deutsch Collection Ltd)

Ryder report therefore recommended that there should be no joint management/union committee at corporate level, but proposed the introduction of two joint management councils (for BL Cars, and for Truck and Bus respectively), with two tiers of joint management committees operating below them. It was recognized that this scheme gave a major role to the shop stewards, but it was thought essential that the new structure, in order to be successful, had to 'recognize the realities of power and influence within the existing employee organizations'.[110]

Even had the recommendations of the Ryder report been implemented in full – which they were not – it is questionable whether they would have effected any great improvement in industrial relations within the company. There was undoubtedly a great deal of idealism reflected in the outline for industrial democracy recommended by Ryder, but little regard for the practicalities of running a motor manufacturing company. The implementation in full of the Ryder proposals would have required an overnight complete change of outlook on behalf of management as well as the workers' representatives, and it could be argued that after two decades of confrontation nei-

ther side was inclined to be particularly co-operative. Sir Michael Edwardes is typically forthright by stating that the 'Ryder remedy . . . only produced a bureaucratic paperchase dissipating management resource and effort.'[111]

While, in 1975, the Government did acquire the majority of British Leyland shares through the National Enterprise Board (they were later transferred to the Secretary of State for Industry) and the company therefore became *de facto* nationalized, it took less than two years for the Ryder report to become totally discarded. As chairman of the NEB until 1977, Lord Ryder was able to exercise considerable influence over the day-to-day running of the company. While the unions should have been pleased that their recommendations to nationalize BL had been put into effect, this did not bring about any reduction in the level of industrial unrest affecting the company – if anything, matters became rather worse. The worst case was the tool-room strike of February–March 1977. The background was that the unofficial tool-room committee, anxious to secure separate bargaining rights contrary to the policy of their union (the AEUW), called the strike in order to secure official recognition. At

the height of the strike, 40,000 employees were on strike or laid off.[112] The strikers only returned to work when the BL board threatened to dismiss them for striking unofficially and unconstitutionally. The strike is estimated to have cost BL £150 million [113] and it also stated that the total of over 700 strikes at BL in 1977 cost the company over 250,000 vehicles in lost production (around a quarter of the potential annual output).

The Ryder report recommendations on industrial democracy would have gone too far, too fast. A similar approach was taken by the Bullock report which was published in January 1977 under an order of the House of Commons and which proposed workers' directors and greater worker participation – it proved unacceptable to management as well as workers and was quickly shelved. The only tangible result of government commitment to industrial democracy during this period was the reorganization, with enthusiastic backing from Tony Benn, of the all-but defunct Triumph motor cycle company as a co-operative, an ambitious scheme which would eventually fail for commercial reasons. It is not irrelevant to contrast the half-hearted attempts at introducing some form of industrial democracy in Britain in the 1970s with the German system where a workers' representative, usually a senior national official of the appropriate trade union, has a seat on the supervisory board of every industrial company over a certain size. This has been the practice ever since the birth of the modern German Federal Republic. German workers are also represented by elected works councils, set up under German law, which, to a far greater extent than in Britain, regulates matters pertaining to industrial relations and conditions of work and employment. (For a comparison of labour relations in Britain and other countries see, for instance, Kujawa, *International Labor Relations Management in the Automotive Industry*, 1971.)

On 1 November 1977, Michael

Japanese companies brought new working practices with greater equality between blue- and white-collar workers, even to the same (optional) uniform. This is the engine plant at Nissan's Sunderland factory in 1994. (Nissan Motor (GB) Ltd)

Edwardes (later Sir Michael) began his five-year stint as executive chairman of British Leyland. He only accepted this post on the understanding that he would be given a free hand by the Government to run the company as he found necessary. Of the many changes he and his team implemented, those that mainly concern us here are the down-sizing of the company, and the way in which he handled industrial relations. It was immediately obvious that BL, apart from still having a too-large and illogical model range, had substantial overcapacity and far too many employees – reckoned to be around 198,000 (including employees overseas) at the beginning of 1978. Edwardes's initial estimates suggested that at least 12,500 and possibly up to 17,000 jobs would be lost, with a cut in production capacity from 1.2 million to just over 800,000 vehicles.[114] He took an early opportunity to present his ideas to a meeting of 720 employee representatives, shop stewards and union officials, and was rewarded by a vote of confidence of 715 in favour and only five against.

The first plant to be closed was the Triumph assembly factory at Speke near Liverpool, like neighbouring Halewood (Ford) and Ellesmere Port (Vauxhall) one of the new factories of the 1960s with their history of volatile industrial relations. In 1978 Speke's staple product was the Triumph TR7 sports car. Although there was a body factory adjoining the assembly plant, TR7 production was dependent on most other components being transported from Triumph factories in Coventry and suppliers also based in the Midlands. The TR7, launched in 1975, had not been the hoped-for success in the important US market, and it was calculated that each vehicle was sold at a loss to BL. At the end of 1977, the Speke work-force was actually on strike over a manning dispute. This was still going on when the closure was announced on 15 February 1978, when it was also stated that redundancy terms would be offered only on the understanding that the workers

returned and offered no opposition to the move of production to Coventry which was scheduled for May.[115] The work-force did eventually go back, and did vote to accept the company's terms.

The Speke episode was important in several respects. It was the first time after the Second World War that a British car manufacturer had completely closed a major factory. It was the first time since the Rootes strike in 1961 that the workers' 'bluff had been called'.[116] And as it turned out, it was but the first of several plant closures that Edwardes was to see through during his time at BL, the Speke assembly plant being followed by the Speke body plant; the MG factory at Abingdon; the Park Royal and Vanden Plas factories in London; partial closures of the Triumph factory at Canley, Coventry, and of the Bathgate commercial vehicle factory in Scotland (both later completely closed); moth-balling of the almost brand-new Rover SD1 assembly hall at Solihull (later re-commissioned for expanding Land-Rover production); and several other smaller factories mostly involved in components manufacture.

In tandem with the plant closures, Edwardes began tackling the task of winning over the workers remaining with the company to his policies, and of curbing the power of the often militant shop stewards. A company-wide poll in 1977 had already found in favour of introducing centralized collective bargaining. Much progress was made in the first two years, including a five per cent pay rise in line with the Government's Social Contract being accepted by the manual workers in December 1978 – unlike Ford, where after a four-week strike the management agreed to negotiate a pay settlement in excess of government guidelines. At BL in February 1979, a company-wide strike over non-implementation of additional productivity-related payments was only narrowly averted, while a renewed strike by tool-room workers in April quickly fizzled out. In May 1979, the Conservative party won the election

and Margaret Thatcher became Prime Minister. This election victory followed what has been called 'the winter of discontent' where a number of strikes had occurred largely in defiance of the Labour government's wages restraint policy, and was held against a background of the then unprecedented figure of one million people being unemployed, similar figures not having been recorded since the depression of the early 1930s. The Conservative election slogan of 1979, 'Labour isn't working', subsequently backfired when unemployment levels under the new government quickly trebled. This, however, did not prevent the Conservative party from also winning the next three elections, among other legislation introducing several measures designed to curb the power of the unions and altering the ground rules for industrial conflict.

At BL, Edwardes formulated his philosophy – that the managers must be allowed to manage – and in September 1979, on the day that at least in MG lore has been enshrined as 'Black Monday', presented his recovery plan which called for the complete or partial closure of 13 factories, including the MG plant at Abingdon. He also forecast job losses of at least 15,000, possibly up to 50,000. When the plan was rejected by the TGWU, BL arranged for a postal ballot of the work-force through the Electoral Reform Society. The result of this, declared on 1 November 1979, was that 80 per cent of employees had voted, and of those 87.2 per cent – over 106,000 – had voted in favour of the Edwardes plan.[117] These figures indicate that there were at the time around 152,000 employees in the UK, and around 70 per cent of the total work-force had endorsed the recovery plan. This at least was an unequivocal result, and the ballot could be described as an example of industrial democracy put into practice, even if by 1979 few BL workers could have had any illusions about the future, and if a man knows he is to be made redundant in a fortnight, it concentrates his mind wonderfully.

While the unions were prepared to accept the result of the ballot, some of the shop stewards were not. Soon after the ballot result had been published, a pamphlet was found circulating among BL workers, urging resistance to the recovery plan. Whether or not the pamphlet was part of a Communist party conspiracy – as Edwardes seems to suggest – is now a moot point; it is a fact that the main signatory to it, the senior shop steward and conveyor at Longbridge, Derek Robinson, was a Communist. When Robinson, in the presence of the AUEW district secretary, was invited to withdraw his name from the pamphlet by the Longbridge plant director and refused to do so, he was instantly dismissed.

This led to a partial walk-out at Longbridge. Although Robinson was a member of the AUEW, this strike was declared official by the TGWU. Following negotiations between BL management and the AUEW, it was agreed that the AUEW would set up a formal inquiry into the Robinson affair, and the TGWU called off the strike. While the eventual AUEW report was critical of Robinson, speaking of his 'serious failings and lack of responsibility', it nevertheless concluded that he should be reinstated as the company had not followed the correct procedure in his dismissal, and strike action was threatened. It was now February 1980, and talks about BL's pay offer for 1979–80 had finally broken down after a majority of workers had voted against the company's offer. On the other hand, a vote at a mass meeting at Longbridge overwhelmingly rejected the move to strike over the demand for Robinson to be reinstated. (These meetings were traditionally held in the pleasant Cofton Hackett park immediately to the south of the factory, a location which became familiar to millions of television viewers and where the present author himself has stood on at least one occasion, listening to Derek Robinson and his colleagues.)

According to Edwardes, Robinson – who was given the media nickname of 'Red Robbo' – 'had kept Longbridge in ferment and upheaval for 30 months [and] 523 disputes, with the loss of 62,000 cars and 113,000 engines, worth £200 million.'[118] In the wake of the Robinson dismissal, and regardless of the ballot in which the pay offer had been rejected, in April 1980 BL unilaterally imposed the pay deal as well as new working conditions – 'arguably the most important industrial relations move since the war.'[119] The new working conditions abolished the long-cherished concept of 'mutuality', going back to the 1929 dispute at Longbridge (compare above) and considered established practice since the Second World War, which meant that every small change had to be agreed between management and workers' representatives before it could be implemented. The practice of 'buying out' – in other words, offering cash inducements for 'customs and practices' to be changed – was abolished, and greater flexibility for management to allocate workers was introduced. There was no concerted long-term effort at resistance to the implementation of the new practices which undoubtedly – together with the introduction of the commercially successful new Metro model in October 1980 – greatly helped to bring about a dramatic improvement in productivity, especially at Longbridge but also in other BL plants.

In the early 1980s the number of strikes dropped sharply

It is to a large extent this so-called 'Blue Newspaper' of April 1980 which still forms the basis for industrial relations of the Rover Group.[120] BL was also in April 1980 finally able to implement centralized bargaining on a company-wide scale, to reduce some 500 classifications of hourly-paid employees into five company-wide grades, and to establish a bonus incentive system which put earnings in all plants on a similar output-related basis.[121] In the following months, however, there were some disputes over detailed issues contained in the 'Blue Newspaper', notably over rest period allowances at Longbridge in late 1981 when the company implemented a 39-hour week without any reduction in production targets, and a month-long dispute at Cowley over similar issues in April 1983, just as the new Maestro model was going into full-scale production in this factory.

The statistics clearly demonstrate that while strikes still occurred, over pay-related as well as non-pay related issues, the number of working days lost declined steeply in the early 1980s: in 1977, BL had lost more than 3.3 million working days, but by 1983 this figure was down to 187,500. The number of vehicles lost through industrial action declined similarly, from 250,000 to 28,000.[122] While observers are careful to point out that these reductions must be viewed against the falling numbers of employees in the company, the number of employees was not similarly reduced by more than 90 per cent in this period! The company's annual pay offers had been accepted in both 1980 and 1981; although the 3.8 per cent offer in 1981 was not recommended by the unions, it was accepted by the work-force at mass meetings in the individual factories. The 1982 negotiations resulted in the first two-year pay deal, a practice which has since become more widespread in the motor industry, and which has become acceptable to the unions in the climate of low inflation of the late 1980s and early 1990s.

Sir Michael Edwardes's management style has been called 'macho'.[123] There was certainly a degree of brinkmanship involved, and he was never afraid of confrontation. Nor was he shy of publicity and he put his, and the company's, points of view across most effectively through the media. But on the other hand he was no uncritical union-basher either, he and his team happily conducted the often protracted – but always civil – negotiations with union officials that were necessary to hammer out the annual pay agreements. He has largely become a symbol of the turn-around in Britain's motor industry in the period around 1980, although other companies also introduced new working practices and conditions, notably Ford with the 'After Japan' programme. These events all took place against the background of growing unemployment during the 1980s, and the Thatcher adminstration's introduction of new trade union legislation on issues such as compulsory secret ballots, secondary pickcting, the political levy and the closed shop.

There was also the establishment of Japanese car manufacturers on new greenfield sites in Britain. These companies brought with them elements of Japanese industrial relations and management philosophy, including greater equality between blue-collar and white-collar workers, breaking down the ancient and established barriers by offering both groups the same facilities and benefits. There was also the principle of the single union deal, with all workers in the company belonging to the same union (if any). There was the introduction of same-style work attire – or company uniform – for everybody, from managing director downwards, although not necessarily on a compulsory basis. Above all, there was the Japanese philosophy of the employer accepting a commitment to giving employees greater job security, in return for the employees' long-term loyalty to their company.

Many of these ideas were also adopted by what, since 1986, had been called Rover Group, in some measure perhaps due to the influence of Honda, the company's partner in product development and some time part-owner (until the BMW takeover in 1994 and the dissolution of the cross-shareholdings). Also within Rover, the principle of direct communication between management and employees has been maintained and extended since Michael Edwardes first began this in 1978. There have been successful efforts at involving employees – who are now, perhaps symbolically but

also tellingly, all called 'associates' – in fundamental issues which are crucial to the company. A good example is quality control where 'quality circles' have been set up, to ensure that everyone involved has a chance to discuss the issues and help to bring about improvements, and associates are encouraged to put forward suggestions on all work-related matters. The company is to a far greater extent than hitherto people-motivated. The accent is now on teamwork, and at the same time flexibility. In 1992 Rover introduced its 'New Deal' where in return for the work-force agreeing to greater flexibility, the company undertook a commitment to job security. While not quite the 'jobs for life' deal that it was described as in certain sections of the media, the principle was that the company would not again impose compulsory redundancics. The company also embarked on training programmes, some directly job-related, others simply offering financial assistance to employees who wanted to learn new skills by taking courses in their spare time.

The industrial relations climate in Britain's new motor industry has improved out of all recognition since the 1970s. While industrial unrest still occurs, strikes – whether unofficial or official – have become much more infrequent. The atmosphere is now much less confrontational, and hand-in-hand with the lessening of workplace tensions have come great strides forward in terms of productivity, as well as the quality of the product. As an example of how far confrontation has been replaced by consultation and communication, it is worth mentioning that when, in February 1994, the BMW take-over of Rover was announced, one of the priorities of the BMW chairman was to meet with the British trade unions, to explain his company's plans and intentions for Rover. On this occasion, Bernd Pischetsrieder was given a unanimous endorsement by the unions, and although he may well have given out what in the past would have been

considered confidential information, there was no hint of any of this being leaked to the media by union representatives. Nor was there any suggestion of any form of protest action on behalf of the Rover Group work-force against the take-over – something which could well have happened if Rover had merged with a foreign company ten or 15 years earlier, notwithstanding the realistic attitude shown in the union report of 1980 discussed in the introduction to this chapter.

While, therefore, Britain's motor industry had contracted drastically in terms of size, work-force and annual output by the mid-1990s, and while all of the major manufacturers, as well as several of the small specialist producers, were now in foreign ownership, there was very real hope that the remarkable improvements in industrial relations achieved over the last 15 years would help to form a stable foundation for the future.

The production line at Toyota UK's Deeside engine plant. In October 1991 Toyota UK signed an agreement with the Amalgamated Electrical & Engineering Union giving the union exclusive representation at the Deeside and Burnaston plants. Toyota and the AEEU have agreed a shared commitment to flexible working practices and non-adversarial techniques for solving disputes. (Toyota (UK) Ltd)

CHAPTER NINE

Decline, then Revival

Jonathan Wood

As the indigenous motor industry's foremost company, the affairs of British Leyland and its successors have, inevitably, dominated the years since 1970. This era has proved to be the most traumatic in the history of car making in Britain, when its very survival seemed imperilled. Yet what today is the Rover Group has impressively rebuilt itself and its corporate image to the extent that in 1993 such an avowedly Conservative and middle class newspaper as *The Daily Telegraph* voted Rover the 'most improved car maker of the decade'; an accolade that, even in the late 1980s, would have been unthinkable.

It has been a long haul back. In 1974 many of the industry's deep-rooted weaknesses and frailties were fatally exposed by the world recession, triggered by the previous year's oil price-rise, and the British Leyland Motor Corporation collapse. The Labour administration of the day had little choice, in 1975, other than to nationalize the business. For two years Leyland Cars drifted as it fruitlessly endeavoured to implement the Government's flawed Ryder Report and labour disputes reached a level which began to threaten the company's very existence. A turning point came in 1977 with the appointment of Michael Edwardes as Leyland's chairman. He decisively re-jected Ryder, restructured the management, introduced much needed rationalization, rebuilt the model range, and successfully tackled the militants, aided by the labour legislation of Margaret Thatcher's Conservative government. Edwardes also recognized

that the future of what was now BL Cars was dependent on it co-operating with another car maker and, in 1979, a fruitful association was begun with the Japanese Honda concern.

When Sir Michael, as he became, retired from the post in 1982 he handed over a greatly slimmed down company but one which, in the public's perception, was emerging from years of chaos. Later, in 1986, when Graham Day took over as chairman he changed the firm's name to the Rover Group, to reflect a move up-market which was a tacit recognition that the volume car side of the business was no longer a viable force. By this time some of Britain's famous marque names had disappeared. Wolseley went in 1975 and was followed in turn by Morris, Triumph and, in the wake of the corporate move up-market, Austin, whose last car was built in 1987. Today, of the bevy of makes once produced by British Leyland, only two, those of Rover and MG, are destined to reach the twenty-first century. The Rover Group returned to the private sector in 1988 when it was bought from a grateful government by British Aerospace, which retained it until early in 1994. Then, to almost universal surprise, BAe announced that it was to sell the car business to BMW of Germany, with the result that Britain's last surviving major car company is now in foreign ownership.

So if Rover is no longer a competitor in volume car manufacture, what of Ford, which is the country's most successful practitioner of the craft? During these years Ford of Britain

continued an ever closer integration with its German counterparts, following the creation, in 1967, of Ford of Europe. The first model sharing a common body and engines to be built in both countries, as well as in a new Spanish plant, came in 1976 in the form of the Fiesta, which was the European company's first front-wheel drive car. Ford's British operations are now an ingredient, albeit an important one, of its European operations, but its role is one within the American company's global activities. The Dunton technical centre, working in close co-operation with its Merkenich counterpart, plays a pivotal function in the creation of Ford's European products. However, more recently it has been deeply involved in the design of the Mondeo of 1993, which is Ford's first world car since the Model T. This is despite the fact that this model is not built here but is exclusively manufactured in Ford Germany's plant at Genk, Belgium. Having said that, the international jigsaw that is the modern motor industry means that Ford's engine factory in Bridgend, Wales, also produces the Mondeo's twin cam Zeta power units.

The integration of Ford's European operations was subsequently followed by its General Motors rival but to the detriment of Vauxhall, which continued its unspectacular post-war performance into the 1970s. Invariably, only a single model, the Viva, reached the ranks of Britain's top ten best-sellers; but since 1979, although the cars continue to be built here – at Luton and Ellesmere Port – all Vauxhalls have been rebadged, German-designed Opels. With the arrival in 1981 of a new generation of front-wheel drive models spearheaded by the Cavalier, the sales graph has been in the ascendancy, mostly at the expense of Ford. In 1993 a duo of Vauxhalls occupied the places just behind the two top-selling Fords in the year's British sales league. And like Ford, General Motors also imports cars from its European plants in Germany, Belgium and Spain.

Chrysler, the smallest of the American 'big three' car makers, had a less than happy experience in Britain. Troubles with its home market, compounded by the effects of the world recession, saw it withdraw ignominiously from Britain, having in 1978 sold the former Rootes operation to Peugeot. By then the Singer, Sunbeam, Humber and Hillman marque names had been consigned to oblivion and today Ryton produces only Peugeots. However, unlike Chrysler, which conceived models for its European operations in Coventry, the French company manufactures cars which are no longer designed here.

If American influence receded with Chrysler's departure, it has increased with Ford's inroads into the specialist sector. In 1987 Ford bought Aston Martin, so underpinning a company with years of financial uncertainty behind it, and has demonstrated its future commitment to the famous name by creating the universally acclaimed DB7 of 1993. This is the first Aston Martin to have a Jaguar engine for, in 1988, Ford was able to purchase the latter company for a substantial £1.6 billion, in the face of a challenge by General Motors. One of the few remaining jewels in the British automotive crown, Jaguar, nearly annihilated during the Ryder years, was rebuilt from 1980 under Sir John Egan's formidable chairmanship, was privatized in 1984, and fell to Ford five years later.

General Motors's further British expansion has a less happy history. In

1982 Colin Chapman, founder and driving force of Lotus, died unexpectedly and four years later, in 1986, the road car business was sold to GM for £22.7 million. The Corporation financed a much needed new model but, despite a promising specification, the Elan proved to be an expensive failure. In 1993 Lotus was bought by the Italian-based, Luxembourg-registered Bugatti concern and nobody knows who owns that . . .

Lotus was a contributory factor in the demise of Jensen, having supplied the West Bromwich company with its then untried 2-litre engine for the Jensen-Healey of 1972, intended to fill the gap caused by the end of the Austin-Healey 3000 in America. The unreliability of this Lotus unit did little to help the company's image; the car lacked charisma, and the 1974 world recession did the rest. Jensen closed its doors in 1976, was revived in 1983, succumbed in 1992 as the world economy took yet another nosedive, only to be saved once again.

Of all the corporate bankruptcies that occurred during these years, it was the collapse of Rolls-Royce in 1971

that most caught the public imagination. This seemingly invincible symbol of British excellence proved itself vulnerable to the realities of the marketplace although, ironically, this was not the fault of the Car Division, which by then was profitably producing the Silver Shadow, in that regard the most successful Rolls-Royce since the Silver Ghost. The root of the problem lay in the creation of the RB211, the first of a new generation of so called 'big fan' aero engines, the development costs of which had soared out of control. In February 1971 the seemingly impossible happened when, after a 65-year life, Rolls-Royce declared itself bankrupt. It fell to Edward Heath's Conservative government to nationalize the business, which returned to the public sector in 1977 having divested itself of its car making activities, which in 1973 had been publicly floated as Rolls-Royce Motors. Later, in 1980, it merged with the Vickers engineering group, which still owns the business. In 1992 news broke that it was undertaking talks with BMW about the development of a much-needed new generation of cars, but although the

The BMC 1100/1300 was made from 1962 to 1973, and was the best-selling car on the UK market from 1965 to 1970, apart from 1967 when it was beaten into second place by the Cortina. It carried the badges of all five BMC marques. This is a 1968 Morris 1300 Super. (NMM)

market has taken an upturn, the long-term future of Rolls-Royce, and its revived Bentley marque, remains open to question.

These respected makes, along with the seemingly evergreen Morgan, the reinvigorated TVR sports car compa-ny, and Bristol remain the sole British-owned survivors of the myriad of companies which once constituted the country's motor industry. In 1993 it built no less than 1.3 million cars, which was the highest figure since 1974 and represented a significant advance on the 887,679 cars built in 1982, produced at the nadir of the world recession.

A significant factor in this impressive revival of the industry's fortunes has been the presence in Britain of Japan's three principal car makers which were, in part, drawn here by the industrial peace that had broken out in the country's car factories. Nissan, the first to arrive, opened its plant at Washington, Sunderland, in 1986, and was followed in turn by Honda and Toyota. They build cars not only for the British market but, from their position inside the European Economic Community, for customers in Continental Europe.

Harry Webster's policy for BMC in the 1970s was that the advanced, Issigonis-inspired front drive cars would carry Austin names, and the conventional rear-drive cars would be Morrises. Austin had several models – Allegro, Maxi, 1800, and 2200 – while Morris had only the Marina. (Above) is the largest-engined Maxi, a 1750 of 1978–9, while (below) are saloon and coupé versions of the Marina in its original 1972 form. With sales of 1.2 million (including the Ital), the Marina outsold any of the front-drive Austins. (Both NMM)

Back in 1970 Japanese exports to Britain stood at a mere 4,291 cars and the two-year old British Leyland Motor Corporation, which that year built 788,737 was far and away the country's largest car maker with 38 per cent of the market. The majority of these were produced by the Corporation's Austin Morris division, headed by George Turnbull, who, arguably, had the most difficult job in British Leyland after Lord Stokes. In 1970 he had overall responsibility for the building of Britain's best-selling car in the shape of the Issigonis-designed 1100/1300 model which, 1967 excepted, was still outselling the rival Ford Cortina, which had been revised in Mark II form in 1966.

However, although the 1100/1300 model continued to dominate the British market, on a worldwide basis the Mini was the company's best-selling model, for, in addition to its British production, the car was also built in Australia, at Seneffe in Belgium, and by Innocenti in Italy. The two-millionth example had been produced in 1969, and in 1971 world-wide production stood at an all-time record of 318,475 cars. Despite this upbeat performance, the model was hardly making any contribution to the Corporation's coffers. Finance director, John Barber, recalls: 'we jacked the Mini's price up quite a bit, but it wasn't making any money, apart from the spare parts.'[1] The 1970 model year cars, announced at the 1969 London Motor Show, had for the first time dispensed with the Austin and Morris marque names and were thereafter badged as plain Minis. But the end of Alec Issigonis's reign as Longbridge's technical supremo was reflected by the introduction of a supplementary Clubman version, with its distinctive squared off front end, which was to endure until 1980. Even the Mini itself was now bereft of sliding windows, a typical Issigonis touch, and they were replaced by conventional winding ones although, in the process, the handy and commodious door pockets were lost.

However, British Leyland was having less luck with the Maxi hatchback, another Issigonis design. Following its unhappy launch in 1969, at the 1970 London Motor Show Leyland unveiled the greatly improved 1,750 cc version with a revised camshaft and its much criticized gearchange now featured rods in place of the original cables. The interior was also improved, its rather stark dashboard being replaced by a handsome wood veneered one. The 1500 version remained in production and, thus reinvigorated, the Maxi remained a steady if unspectacular seller until it was a discontinued in 1981, after 472,098 had been built. Incredibly, when BMC conceived the model in the 1960s it had contemplated building no less than 250,000 a year.

It was not until April 1971 that British Leyland unveiled the Morris Marina, the first design it had initiated as opposed to inherited from BMC. As befitted Harry Webster's corporate plan in which Austins were technically advanced and Morrises would follow a more conventional approach, this was a front-engined, rear-wheel drive car intended to challenge Ford's formidable Cortina. It was, in effect, a rebodied Morris Minor, in that it retained its A series engine and torsion bar independent front suspension although it could also accommodate the larger B Series Four. However, as

the car would need to feature – like the Cortina – synchromesh on bottom gear, the gearbox was a Triumph unit and, as it transpired, the Marina's Achilles Heel. What was destined to be the last Morris car was available in two-door coupé and four-door saloon forms. Their lines were the work of former Ford stylist Roy Haynes, who had been responsible for the Mark II Cortina amongst other models. Whilst the Marina's bodies were less inspired they did not, unlike some later Leyland cars, offend the eye.

The Allegro's failure marked the start of the industry's decline

The Marina was to be built at Cowley, which Lord Stokes was acutely aware was in drastic need of modernization following years of neglect by BMC. The state of the plant was, he recalls, 'deplorable'.[2] Consequently the factory was partially gutted, a new production line introduced, and a quarter-mile long weatherproof conveyor was built from Pressed Steel on one side of Oxford's Eastern Bypass to the assembly line on the other. British Leyland hoped to build 5,000 Marinas a week and even though it did not approach this figure, in 1972 and 1973 it became the Corporation's best-selling model until being intermittently overtaken, from 1974 onwards, by the Mini. Marina sales peaked in 1973 and the model survived, latterly in revised Ital form, until 1983. With 1.2 million sold, it is sobering to reflect that this thoroughly conventional model, conceived in some haste between 1968 and 1970, was the best-selling car to be created during the British Leyland years.

What was destined to be the last BMC design to be seen through to fruition by British Leyland was unveiled in 1972. The evolution of the 2200 graphically illustrates the problems experienced by Harry Webster's team in having to design a car using components inherited from its prede-

cessors. It was a cocktail of parts: the body and suspension were related to the ageing Mark III 1800 model, fitted with a newly developed six-cylinder 2.2-litre version of the E Series Maxi engine. This evolved from the 1500 Maxi unit and, as such, could not benefit from the 1750's improved cylinder head. A 2.6-litre six on these lines suffered from excessive torsional vibrations and, because of the narrowness of the cylinder block with no water jacketing between the bores, a new crankshaft was not a practicality. So a 2.2 it had to be, and the car's under-bonnet area was radically restructured; otherwise it would have too great a turning circle. As a result, the radiator was transferred from its usual side location to the front of the engine compartment, which was the first occasion that a British Leyland transverse-engined car had been so equipped. It also had the virtue of keeping rain off the power unit, which was a much publicized problem on BMC front-wheel drive models.

If the Webster plan had been applied, this would have only been an Austin, but because Morris dealers just had the Marina to sell, the 2200 was also so badged, and there was a more expensive version marketed as the Wolseley Six. Sadly, sales had echoes of the bad old days of BMC. This expensive, dated, thirsty though roomy model attracted few buyers and only 20,865 examples of the Austin and Morris versions were sold, whilst the better-equipped Wolseley found 25,214 buyers. Sales were hit by the 1973 oil price hike, although the model lingered on until 1975.

The next British Leyland car was, unquestionably, the most important, not only in corporate terms but, on a broader canvas, to the future of volume car making in Britain. In 1971 the Issigonis-designed 1100/1300 series, which dated back to 1962, was still the country's best-selling car, but in 1972 it was at long last overtaken by the Ford Cortina. Yet unlike the rapidly conceived Marina, Leyland had a full five years in which to develop the

Austin Allegro that not only turned out to be a lemon but also looked like one. Work on the project, coded ADO 27, had begun in 1968, the year of British Leyland's creation, but whilst the 1100/1300 series had been impressively styled by the Italian Pininfarina concern, this model, like the Marina, was to be undertaken in-house. The Longbridge styling facilities were undergoing enlargement, which is why the Allegro's lines were conceived at Cowley by a youthful Harris Mann, his design being chosen in preference to one undertaken by his colleague, Paul Hughes. A clay model was duly produced and, in December 1968, Austin Morris managing director George Turnbull and British Leyland's technical director Harry Webster, who had overall responsibility for the model, liking what they saw, gave the project the green light.

The Allegro was finally unveiled in May 1973, but a few months before its launch the dumpy-looking model was discreetly shown to a small group of motoring journalists and their reaction was anything but favourable. It was 'lukewarm', to say the least. About the best compliment that they could pay the car was that at least it looked different enough not to be confused with anything else. They entered several strong pleas, not least that the nose should be given more character.[3] British Leyland's idea was to produce a model with so-called 'durable' styling that would enjoy a long production run whilst simultaneously disposing of the shortcomings of its predecessor. What, alas, occurred was that the Allegro was manifestly inferior to the model that it replaced and its sales never began to approach those of the BMC car. And the Cortina, having moved into the number one British sales slot, stayed there. For its part, the Austin Allegro was even outsold by the in-house Morris Marina, itself no great trail-blazer. Destined to endure until 1982, total Allegro production stood at 642,350 cars, compared with 2.1 million 1100/1300s built worldwide. Thus the Allegro's failure marks

the beginning of the end of the British-owned motor industry as a volume car producer.

The design passed through a number of evolutionary phases. The original intention was for it to have a solid front end with the air intake located beneath the front bumper, to alleviate the bugbear of the transversely mounted engine, of rain reaching the ignition system, so causing it to cut out. The radiator was similarly left in its side location but noise levels from that part of the car rose to such a pitch that they would have breached the Common Market's decibel limits. Therefore a feature which was intended as a very real improvement on past experience had to be dispensed with and, instead, the radiator was moved to the front of the car, where it required an electric fan, but also helped to keep the elements at bay. This, in turn, meant lengthening the Allegro's nose.

'Longbridge-designed cars were always mediocre' – Stokes

In addition to the model retaining the 1100 and 1300 engines, it was also designed to accommodate the 1,500 and 1,750 cc E Series Maxi units because that model's sluggish sales meant that its £20 million purpose-built Longbridge manufacturing facility was under utilized. The interconnected Hydrolastic suspension of the 1100/1300 family was dispensed with and replaced by a less bulky Hydragas system. It retained similar fluid chambers but nitrogen-filled spheres were introduced which doubled as shock absorbers. These had the advantage of not requiring subframes, which saved cost and weight, particularly as the rear one on the 1100/1300 had been susceptible to corrosion. But the absence of self-levelling meant that a well laden Allegro would appear tail heavy.

When it came to the car's overall dimensions, it was 5.6 in longer and 3 in wider than its predecessor and,

similarly, produced in two- and four-door forms. Another criticism of the BMC model was its small boot, so the petrol tank was moved forward in the Allegro and the tail extended by 6 in. But in practice, the car proved to be difficult to load. Despite the wheelbase being over an inch more than the model it was replacing, at an early stage in the ADO 67's creation the interior had 4 in less room than the 1100/1300. Although this was subsequently rectified, finance director John Barber was horrified by the car: 'Even then it was a bit of a problem to get into the rear seat and we had to cut off a bit of the corner of the cushion; it was very much a bodged job.'[4] Another of the Allegro's more controversial features was the gimmicky quartic steering wheel, shaped 'like a television screen'. It was, however, almost universally condemned and only survived for two years before being replaced by a conventional circular one.

If the Allegro looked inferior to its predecessor, would it perform any better? The answer was, alas, that it did not. When *Autocar* magazine came to test the Allegro 1300, its 0–60 mph figure of 18 seconds was one second greater than that of the BMC 1300, whilst the 82 mph speed was also inferior. It was also slower than the Morris Marina, which was powered by the same 1,275 cc engine.

This was the car which British Leyland hoped would not only challenge and overtake what Ford was producing in Britain but would also be able to take on the best of the European imports which would enter the country in increasingly large numbers following Britain joining the EEC. Coincidentally this occurred in 1973, which was the same year as the Allegro's arrival. Sadly the model proved to be no match for such cars as the Volkswagen Golf, Renault 5, and Fiat 127, all of which were hatchbacks – yet another design feature that the Allegro did not possess.

Little wonder that the new Austin never attained the sales figures of its predecessor. Just 28,713 found British owners in the introductory year of 1973, its most popular 12 months being in 1975, when 60,619 were sold. By contrast, sales of the 1100/1300 family never fell below the 100,000 mark between 1963 and 1972. Amazingly there was still worse to come because, in 1974, the four-door 1.5- and 1.7-litre versions were offered under the Vanden Plas name with a revised front end which was, if anything, visually even worse than the original. Inevitably, sales were modest and only 11,842 found buyers, despite it being listed until 1980. As if that was not enough, in 1975 came a curious-looking three-door estate car version. The Allegro 2, outwardly similar to its predecessor, appeared at the same time and survived until the arrival of the Allegro 3 – identifiable by a new radiator, bonnet and boot lid in 1979. Ray Horrocks, who ran Austin Morris at this time and inherited the model, remembers that it 'looked like an egg and was expensive to make'[5] which should, perhaps, be its epitaph.

In later years Lord Stokes candidly admitted to the writer that the Longbridge-designed British Leyland cars were 'always sort of mediocre, really'.[6] But by transferring George Turnbull and Harry Webster from Triumph to Austin Morris, he had believed that they would do for Longbridge what had been achieved for Leyland at Canley in the 1960s.

In many respects the Triumph Stag of 1970, hailed as the corporate flagship, possessed all the strengths and weaknesses of the marque during the British Leyland years and beyond. This generation of the marque suffered from a combination of designs that were rushed into production before they were fully developed, and

Larger than the 1300 but less attractive, less reliable and with an inferior performance, the Allegro lost out to the imported hatchbacks and the native Marina and Cortina. The quartic steering wheel (right) was a particularly infelicitous design which was dropped after two years. (Both NMM)

poor build quality; the Canley assembly line had the reputation of being the most anarchic in the Corporation. Nevertheless, the Stag's Michelotti-styled open four-seater body was well received, this 115 mph car with all independent suspension, which sold for £1,995, being over-ambitiously intended to take Triumph into Mercedes-Benz territory. The 145 bhp 3-litre single over camshaft V8 engine looked promising but, somehow, the model never lived up to expectations. Triumph intended to produce 10,000 Stags per annum but in reality the

model survived for just seven years and production stood at a mere 25,877. So what went wrong?

Despite its good looks, the Stag soon acquired a reputation for unreliability which mostly centred around the V8 engine, which proved troublesome. It blew cylinder head gaskets and, in time, the single as opposed to the customary double link timing chain stretched, so that in extreme cases it would jump its sprockets and wreck the engine. Manufacturing quality also left something to be desired; the car was, as ever, completed at Canley but

began life at Triumph's two Liverpool plants, both of which suffered from poor labour problems. Because of the Stag's poor reputation, a hoped-for export market never materialized and a mere 6,780 cars found overseas customers. When it was discontinued by the post-British Leyland management in 1977, one of those who mourned its passing was Lord Stokes, the model being one of his favourite cars. 'I think that the Triumph Stag was beginning to become good but they went and scrapped it', he reflected.[7] Ironically, some 20 years on, with the model's mechanical problems largely identified and resolved, the Stag enjoys a dedicated following amongst classic car enthusiasts.

Triumph's move up-market had begun with the 2000 model of 1963. This popular and respected car had been uprated in 2.5-litre Mark 2 form in 1969, was successfully facelifted and survived until 1977, by which time 104,580 had been built. But even that model could not escape the marque's increasingly tarnished image, because too many examples of the simultaneously announced 2.5PI version – Britain's first fuel injected family car – suffered from intermittent misfiring and instances of under-bonnet blazes. Not surprisingly, and despite the fact that on a good day it was capable of 105 mph, less than 50,000 were built by 1975.

At the other end of the range was the Herald, which had served Triumph well since 1959 but ceased production as the 13/60 in 1970, when it was replaced by the Toledo, which was available with 1.3- and 1.5-litre engines. In 1967 Harry Webster, still at Triumph, had decided to use the Michelotti-styled 1300 front-wheel drive model of 1965 as the building block for a new generation of medium-sized saloons. One outcome was the rear-wheel drive Toledo, which sold some 120,000 cars until its departure in 1976, and the other was the front-wheel drive 1500, a more powerful version of the 1300, outwardly similar to the Toledo but distinguished by four

headlamps. An 85 mph car, it was only moderately successful and lasted for just three years during which just 66,353 had been built. With its demise, Triumph built no more front-wheel drive cars. Its replacement, which lasted until 1976, was the outwardly similar 1500TC but the public stayed away; only 25,549 were made.

In 1973 Triumph adventurously announced the Dolomite Sprint which was a brave attempt to create a sports saloon in the BMW image and, once again, the specification was ambitious but the model failed to come up to expectations. The engine was a 2-litre single overhead camshaft slant four, related to the Stag's V8 but fitted with an ingenious 16-valve cylinder head. The outcome was a 127 bhp 115 mph car but only 22,941 had been sold by its 1980 demise. Despite the engine having great potential, it was powering an ageing body and substructure, and the Sprint's reliability record did nothing to inspire confidence in the Triumph name. John Barber ran an example for a time but found it was a car which could not be depended on and had to be continually returned to Triumph for rectification. He remembers that 'I used it fairly hard . . . The

head castings were made so badly that water flow would be impeded, the heads used to distort and the head gaskets would go. They never got it right.'[8]

Of Canley's sports cars, the well-established Spitfire appeared as the 1500 in 1970 and was destined to survive the decade as the last separate chassis Triumph. However, its 2-litre six-cylinder GT6 first cousin survived in Mark 3 form until 1973, American exports having collapsed. Just 13,042 were produced. Much more successful was the 120 mph 2.5-litre six-cylinder TR6 of 1969 although it was, in truth, a TR5 with a Karmann face-lifted body. Early fuel injection problems were experienced with the TR5, so those cars sold in America – over 90 per cent of the 94,619 built, a record for the series – had carburettored engines, with injection confined to the home market and European exports. The TR6 survived until 1976 and had been replaced in the previous year by the TR7, which was conceived as British Leyland's corporate sports car. Once again, it seemed that the revered MG name had been passed over.

In 1970 a then record of 36,106 MGBs left the Abingdon factory. But

With better reliability the Triumph Stag would have been an excellent car, but the 3-litre V8 engine, exclusive to this model, was plagued with problems, especially with gaskets. 25,877 were made from 1970 to 1977. (BMIHT/Rover)

general manager John Thornley, whose inspired management had overseen the creation of the highly successful MGA and its MGB successor, had departed in 1969 on grounds of ill health. There had been clashes with his new masters and he was certain the MG's fate was sealed with British Leyland's creation, as its top management hailed from the rival Triumph company. This was despite the fact that, at the time, the MGB was the world's most successful sports car and the MG name was held in the highest esteem on both sides of the Atlantic.

But that an anti-MG bias existed at Longbridge, which revived the hostility of the BMC years, was widely perceived at Abingdon and was also the view of the motoring press, though hotly denied by the company. In reality it was perfectly true and was witnessed, at first hand, by John Barber. He recalls: 'There was often conflict between Triumph and MG. Donald Stokes and George Turnbull were Triumph people and they were quite ruthless about it: Triumph was going to have the sports car market – I think it was completely the wrong decision.'[9]

Having said that, there is some irony in the fact that MG was destined to play a part in its own demise. At British Leyland's request, in 1969, Abingdon began work on the design of a car to replace the MGB which could also double as British Leyland's corporate sports car. What was coded ADO 21 was an advanced mid-engined two-seater wedge-shaped coupé, powered by the under-used 1750 Maxi unit. The car's styling was the responsibility of British Leyland's Harris Mann and it is a paradox that one of his most successful creations for the Corporation never entered production. Triumph had, in the meantime, produced its own more conventional front-engined design, coded Bullet. Both concepts were viewed by the higher echelons of British Leyland in November 1970 and they opted for the Triumph. But what emerged in 1975 as the TR7 was, in fact, an unhappy amalgam of the two cars, which may go some way to explaining why the finished product proved to be visually so unsatisfactory.

Sadly, this decision meant that there would be no new car at Abingdon to replace the MGB when it eventually ceased production. Roy Brocklehurst, who in 1971 took over from Syd Enever as MG's chief engineer, puts the demise of this projected MG into perspective: 'I wouldn't be arrogant enough to say that the Leyland management took the wrong decision when ADO 21 was cancelled . . . Ours was an advanced vehicle and, apart from the engine/gearbox unit, it was completely new from stem to stern and would have required enormous investment to produce. But it was *our* decision to go mid-engined. We sealed *our* own fate but we couldn't have known it at the time.'[10]

In the circumstances, Abingdon had little choice but to continue with the MGB in its roadster and GT forms although, thankfully, demand was running at record levels. The 1970 model year cars reflected MG's new British Leyland parentage in that, on Longbridge's instructions, the car's traditional slatted radiator grille was dispensed with and replaced by a corporate styled recessed device, the only effect of which was to visually unsettle the front of the car. However, this change prompted such a storm of protest from the American market that Leyland was forced to backtrack and an MG grille, albeit in modified form, was reinstated in the 1973 season. Despite these cosmetic alterations, MGB production hit an all time high in 1972, when 39,366 cars were built, and its says much for the soundness of the design that the model was by then in its tenth year of manufacture. As ever, over 80 per cent of MGBs were exported to America and, from the 1975 model year, the cars were to some extent disfigured by the fitment of energy absorbing 'rubber' bumpers to meet the increasingly stringent transatlantic safety regulations. As this accounted for the overwhelming majority of MGBs, production needs

One of the most promising designs of the 1960s, the Rover P6B coupé with mid-mounted 3½-litre Buick-derived V8 engine. Production was originally planned for the Alvis factory, but it aroused jealousy from both Triumph and Jaguar. Sir William Lyons was adamantly opposed to a car which could have undercut the E-type by £500. This is the first prototype of 1966, which survives in the Heritage Motor Centre at Gaydon. A later version of 1969 had smoother lines. (BMIHT/Rover).

dictated that those cars destined for the home and European markets had to be similarly modified.

Although the sands were running out for the MGB, in 1971 British Leyland initiated the introduction of a supplementary model in the form of the MGB GT V8. As its name implied, this was the closed car which was fitted with Rover's 3½-litre V8 engine. In 1970 enthusiast Ken Costello began to offer such V8-powered MGBs, an exercise which came to British Leyland's attention.

It responded by suggesting that Abingdon produce its own version, which duly appeared in August 1973, but the model was expensive at £2,294 – a good £500 more than Ford's V6-powered Capri 3000 GXL and although capable of about 120 mph, the car's elderly lines produced a considerable amount of wind noise. Soon after its arrival came spiralling petrol prices in the wake of the 1973 oil price-rise, which saw sales of large-engined cars slump. The MGB GT V8 survived until 1976 with a total of 2,591 having been built over a three year period.

The ex-Buick 3½-litre V8 was already more than proving its worth at Solihull, where Rover was using it in the 3500 saloon and a revitalized big 3½-litre saloon, which began life as the 3-litre model back in 1958. Yet more significantly, this versatile engine provided power for the company's new Range Rover which triumphantly combined the cross-country attributes of a Land-Rover with the comfort of a saloon. Still greatly in demand today and widely imitated by manufacturers the world over, this model is one of the few British success stories in an otherwise bleak period of the industry's history. Significantly, it was a Rover design, as opposed to a British Leyland one.

The Land-Rover was, of course, the well-established mainstay of the company and work on its larger capacity stable-mate, created by Rover engineers, Spen King and Gordon Bashford, had begun in 1966. Unlike

its predecessor, the Range-Rover's four-wheel drive system was permanently engaged and this, coupled with its purposeful, well-proportioned two-door body – refined by Rover's accomplished stylist, David Bache – made it an instant success. Capable of 100 mph on the straight, few owners seemed concerned that petrol was consumed at the rate of 12 to 15 mpg. Although outstripped, in production terms, by the longer established and cheaper Land-Rover, over 100,000 Range Rovers were built by 1982, the model's appeal having been greatly extended by the replacement of the original body by a more practical four-door one in 1981. This had been waiting in the wings since 1972 but the financial problems of British Leyland and its successors ensured that it was an unforgivable nine years before it entered production.

Rover sports car shelved as could challenge E-type market

From his position at the time as finance director, John Barber also recognized that 'Rover was easily the best controlled company in British Leyland. It had much more information about its costs than any other.' He also had a high regard for its management and engineering teams; the Wilks brothers had left behind an impressive legacy. In particular, Barber had considerable respect for Spen King: 'He was a super engineer and marvellous at development. One of his great strengths was that he could visualise a total motor car and not all engineers can do that.'[11]

When Harry Webster retired as British Leyland's technical director in 1974, John Barber replaced him with King, who had previously been moved by Stokes to Triumph as Webster's successor there. Initially, however, he declined Barber's offer, modestly declaring, as a reference to his administrative rather than his technical abilities: 'I couldn't run a sweet shop'.

Sadly, he was unable to make any tangible contribution to corporate engineering because 1974 proved to be a crisis year when the Government stepped in to prevent British Leyland's collapse. Yet if Spen King had been able to exercise a greater influence earlier on, the story might have been different. In any event, he continued to play an important engineering role within British Leyland and its successor until retirement in the 1980s.

But one of King's other projects was already causing the British Leyland board problems. This was the exciting P6BS mid-engined V8-powered sports car, created in prototype form in 1966 prior to the Leyland take-over. It would have done wonders for the firm's image, in the wake of a bevy of mediocre designs from Longbridge. The only trouble was it would have represented a formidable challenge to Jaguar's ageing E-type and that was something that Sir William Lyons could not countenance. Barber says that 'he was afraid that Rover would damage Jaguar. He kept on and on about it, so it was dropped.'[12]

In the meantime, work was proceeding at Solihull on Rover's big, expensive so-called Mercedes-eater, but it was destined to suffer the same fate as the sports car. This was a long term project, work having begun on the P8 as a successor to the P5 3½-litre saloon in 1963. Scheduled for the 1972 model year, once again there was a conflict of interests with Jaguar and the car was cancelled in March 1971, just six months before it was due to enter production. But by then many millions of pounds had been expended on the project.

A year later, in March 1972, four years after British Leyland's creation, the Rover and Triumph companies were merged to avoid the inevitable duplication of models encapsulated by both firms having produced rival 2200 saloons that were now in need of replacement. In the early days of the Corporation, Lord Stokes, who was devoting much of his energies to Austin Morris, decided to leave those parts of the empire which were profitable to their own devices and both businesses, along with Jaguar, had been part of Leyland's Specialist Car Division. Inevitably, Rover dominated this new alliance, which was run by Sir George Farmer, and seven out of the key 12 executive appointments went to Solihull men.

The belated creation of this Rover-Triumph Division considerably strengthened Rover's position within the combine, which also reflected the conflict taking place behind the scenes at British Leyland to determine a successor for Lord Stokes when he finally stepped down as chairman. On the one hand was Austin Morris's George Turnbull, who believed that the Corporation's future was as a volume producer; on the other was John Barber, who advocated that the route should be a more up-market one which, by its nature, meant a reduction in output. For him such cars as the Morris Marina should never have been built, 'because they competed with Ford which was a very strong company. My advice, all the way through, was that we ought to go a bit up market of Ford.'[13] And this is where Rover came in.

Although it had lost the P8, in 1969 Solihull had begun work on Gordon Bashford's P10 which was intended as a successor to the revised 2200 range, and in 1971 had been chosen in preference to a Triumph design and would thus also serve as a replacement to that company's 2200. This was a commodious four-door hatchback saloon once again competently styled by Bache. In 1971, with this new model in the offing, Rover proposed that a new factory be established at Solihull to increase production to 1,500 cars a week. But as Barber's approach began to hold sway, the British Leyland board advocated a doubling of its size to the 3,000 a week mark. This new Rover was the car intended to haul the Corporation up-market into Mercedes-Benz and BMW territory and long-term profitability, although in doing so Rover was once again moving

into Jaguar's traditional territory.

As will have already become apparent, Sir William Lyons continued to keep a watchful eye on Jaguar's interests within British Leyland until his retirement, at the age of 70, in March 1972. As such, Stokes was happy that Jaguar should continue to proceed with its own highly successful brand of styling, engineering, and marketing, although with the E-type sports car coming to the end of its production life – its manufacture ceased in 1974 – Jaguar was briefly left with a single model line in the shape of the highly acclaimed XJ6 saloon. In this car the company possessed what was, arguably, one of the finest models in its class in the world even though, sadly, complaints of poor build quality were being heard with increasing frequency. Production had begun in 1968 and the model was revised in Series II form, identifiable by a squatter radiator grille and higher bumper line, in 1972. The same year came the long awaited V12-engined version, using the 5.3-litre engine that had first appeared in the Series III E-type of 1971.

Robinson was new type of manager from outside industry

With Sir William's retirement, the position of chairman lapsed and 60-year old 'Lofty' England was made Jaguar's chief executive but, inevitably, his could only be a short term appointment. Soon after Lyons's departure, in June 1972 Jaguar suffered a ten-week strike that was the worst stoppage it had experienced since 1965. But in September 1973 there was a new managing director in the shape of 34-year old Geoffrey Robinson. His appointment was a recognition by British Leyland that, whilst Rover was a senior partner in the alliance with Triumph, Jaguar was to continue as an all-important separate entity.

Geoffrey Robinson had been in the motor industry for a mere two years when he took up his appointment at

Browns Lane, although he undoubtedly represented a new breed of manager, with a background which contrasted starkly with those of his contemporaries at Jaguar. He had read French and German at Cambridge prior to joining the Labour Party as a research assistant. Lord Stokes had recruited him to the board of the Industrial Reorganisation Corporation. On its disbandment in 1971 by the incoming Conservative administration he joined British Leyland as financial controller, and in 1972 was running its Milan-based Innocenti subsidiary.

Robinson was the first to recognize that, in global terms, Jaguar was now a small company. In 1971, the year prior to his appointment, 32,589 cars had left the Allesley plant which then represented a record output for the company. However, the labour problems of 1972 saw the figure plummet to 22,988. Output rose some 7,000 in 1973, which saw Robinson's first full year in office and, at the end of the year, he spoke publicly of an ambitious £60 million development programme for Jaguar. This would contribute to increasing the company's annual output to the 60,000 mark with the possibility of a further extension to 90,000 at a later date. But even this latter projection was overshadowed by the rival BMW concern, with its three model line, that in 1973 built 196,075 cars.

It was also in the same 12 months that the matter of the Corporation's succession was finally resolved, with the appointment in May 1973 of John Barber as deputy chairman and managing director, as such becoming Lord Stoke's heir apparent. This represented a triumph for his finance director's oft-stated creed of shifting the emphasis of the business away from the volume side of manufacture, up-market into the higher profits of the specialist sector. Lord Stokes coupled this promotion with news of a £500 million expansion programme which was intended to boost British Leyland's output to 1.5 million vehicles a year. In a key passage of his statement, the Leyland chairman declared: 'Although

Another project to suffer through competition with Jaguar was the Rover P8 'Mercedes eater', which exuded money yet had none of the lithe grace of the Jaguar XJ6. Prototypes had the 3½-litre V8, but for the production car it was hoped to use the long-stroke 4.4-litre version which powered the Australian-built Leyland P76. (BMIHT/Rover)

Austin Morris will continue to expand and develop, there will be a major swing of investment into the highly profitable Jaguar and Rover-Triumph divisions.'[14] This was in accord with Barber's view that Jaguar and Rover produced the only cars of world-class quality in the Corporation. Triumph would cease to compete with Rover but would also move up-market to produce sports saloons in the BMW idiom.

The resolution of this boardroom battle clearly spelt the end of George Turnbull's ambitions for running British Leyland and soon afterwards, in September 1973, he resigned from his position as managing director of the Austin Morris division. This champion of volume production would direct his undoubted abilities to the burgeoning motor industry of the Far East, taking up an appointment with the Hyundai Motor Corporation the following year to create South Korea's first maker of international standing. He later reflected that his time at Longbridge was 'five years of extremely hard work . . . I will never work so hard again, nor wish to.' An able communicator, much of his energy had inevitably been expended on the labour problems that plagued British Leyland throughout its seven-year existence. Turnbull estimated that during 1970 he 'had a period of two weeks without any industrial action – which was quite exceptional when the norm was several strikes per *day*.'[15]

One of the many troubles that Stokes and his team had originally inherited was that BMC had never been rationalized, which meant there was a multiplicity of plants and the inefficiencies that went with them. Acutely aware of the need to rationalize, he was prevented from doing so because of 'a core resistance within the trade unions to any job losses whatsoever and we just couldn't face a strike because it would have resulted in an all out one.'[16] Rather than initiate redundancies, he optimistically hoped that production would expand to take up the extra numbers. Another inheritance was a piecework pay system whereby, instead of receiving a day rate for the job, as at Ford or Vauxhall, British Leyland employees were paid on results and each process was the subject of a separate negotiation. Piecework had originally been introduced to induce traditional craftsmen to work as fast as they were able but the arrival of highly automated production lines, in which machines rather than individuals dictated the rate of production, meant that what had once been a motivation to work was now obsolete. But the trade unions remained wedded to the system, which meant that the company was particularly vulnerable when it introduced a new model as each stage of production came up for reappraisal, a dialogue that could last for anything up to six months.

Lord Stokes recalls that 'there were different rates of pay and different rewards, and you couldn't cost anything. Once the piecework rate was agreed, you couldn't change anything, it was custom and practice, and if you did you had to retime the whole car.'[17] As a result, each year there were 246 separate pay negotiations spread over British Leyland's many plants. The need to streamline this cumbersome, archaic mechanism was therefore overwhelming.

It was against such a background that, in 1970, the company appointed its first director of industrial relations in the form of Pat Lowry, who had 25 years of experience with the Engineering Employers Federation. He proposed that piecework should be replaced by measured daywork to bring British Leyland into line with the rest of the international motoring community. Lowry did not attempt to disguise the difficulties that would ensue but the nettle had to be grasped and, in 1971, the Corporation began to phase out piecework, over a three-year period, for those of its 134,000 employees who were so remunerated. In turn this new system presented its own problems, because the number of individuals required to complete a particular task had to be agreed with the shop stewards and often agreement could only be reached by the management accepting a level of overmanning which played havoc with productivity.

By 1974 the company had a total of 211,000 employees on its payroll of which 176,000 were based in Britain and 35,000 overseas. However, paying workers by the day did ultimately reduce the number of disputes but, less happily, without the spur of piecework it also slowed the production process.

In its strong opposition to daywork, trade unions were reflecting the antipathy of their membership. Jack Bellinger, then a foreman at Pressed Steel, provides some perspective to this hostility. The Corporation had hoped to introduce daywork in 1969 on the Austin Maxi body, the first new model of the Leyland era, but 'there was a lot of opposition from the unions and, after much negotiation, the management pulled back and allowed piecework payments.' This resistance to change, says Bellinger, was rooted in the fact that, in the short term, an employee would be financially worse off under the new system, and 'would not work so hard, initially for less money. But year on year an individual would be as well and, eventually, better off.'[18] With an agreement finally reached between the two sides in 1971, the Cowley-built Morris Marina was the first Leyland model to be produced under the daywork programme.

Unfortunately, the introductory year of 1971 coincided with the labour related upheavals which followed the implementation of the Conservative government's Industrial Relations Act. The reduction of damaging strikes had been one of the key planks of Edward Heath's manifesto but, initially, the legislation resulted in British industry suffering from the worst year of labour stoppages since the General Strike. In the 1969–70 financial year British Leyland lost 5 million man hours through such action, which doubled to 10 million in 1971–2. Stoppages fell back to 7.4 million in 1972–3 though, sadly, rose again to 9.6 million hours in 1973–4.

Yet another factor in measured daywork not having more impact on British Leyland's strike record was the emphasis it placed on foremen. John Barber points out that 'under daywork a foreman is absolutely crucial because he's the one who keeps the men at work for, without the incentive of piecework, you've got to have your manager on the spot. In British Leyland, for the first time, the foremen became front line managers . . . So, for the first few years, we operated measured daywork with inadequate managers and it took some time to catch up. It was this deficiency that was probably the biggest single factor in making our productivity so low.'[19] And low it was. The figure of 5.6 vehicles per employee applied on the Corporation's creation in 1968; this dropped to 4.9 in 1974, which placed it at the bottom on the international motor manufacturing league. The Marina, for instance, took 1.4 times as many man hours to build as the Ford Cortina, and 2.7 times as many as the Taunus, produced at the company's German facility. Similarly, a Mini took 2.3 times as many hours to assemble at Longbridge than at British Leyland's plant at Seneffe, Belgium.[20] Managing director Barber placed an immediate ban on recruitment, and by 1975 the number of individuals employed by the company was reduced by some 30,000 to 180,000, of which, 155,000 were in Britain and 25,000 overseas. But by then British Leyland was a nationalized company.

The midway point of the Heath adminstration marked the beginning of the 'Barber Boom', so named after his chancellor Anthony Barber's reflationary 1972 budget that aimed at a five per cent growth rate, which many of the Prime Minister's critics subsequently blamed for the rampant inflation experienced later in the decade. But in the short term the economy expanded and helped British Leyland to achieve its highest ever pre-tax profits, of £51.5 million, in the 1972–3 financial year. These would, in fact, have been considerably higher had it not been for the failure of the Marina and Allegro to attain their anticipated market shares. The company had never, in fact, made a loss, though it had come close to one in 1970 when it achieved a surplus of a mere £4 million.

Nevertheless, the 1973 figure was a move in the right direction; but in

Chairman of Ford of Britain, Sir Terence Beckett, with three generations of the Cortina, the car with which he is most associated. Left to right, a Mark I of 1965, a Mark II of 1968, and a Mark III of 1975. The Cortina was Britain's best-selling car throughout the 1970s. (NMM)

October of that year the boom came to an abrupt halt when the Arab-Israeli war broke out. The ramifications were soon felt the world over because, for the first time, the Arab oil-exporting states used the commodity as a political weapon. Those countries which were viewed as supporting Israel in some instances had their quotas cancelled whilst others suffered cutbacks, which in Britain's case amounted to a 15 per cent reduction. In addition, oil prices rose five-fold, from $2.50 a barrel in January 1973 to $11.65 the following year. The United Kingdom's own supplies were not to come on stream until 1976, and it was dependent on oil for 50 per cent of its energy needs.

The Government was also in trouble with its Stage Three counter inflationary policy – which, coincidentally, was announced the same October – which prompted a miner's overtime ban. A state of emergency was declared, a three day working week was instigated on 1 January 1974 to conserve coal supplies at the power stations, and a 50 mph speed limit was introduced to save fuel. Garage queues for petrol became commonplace and such scenes were repeated throughout the indus-

trialized world. The economic downturn triggered a global depression and the automobile manufacturers, volume producers and specialists alike, were particularly vulnerable as car sales slumped. Those models in demand were invariably of the cheaper, more economical variety.

In the short term, therefore, John Barber's strategy for moving British Leyland's products up-market, into larger more expensive cars, appeared fatally flawed; as Lord Stokes so graphically put it, everyone started buying 'the ruddy Mini again'.[21] This was, of course, only marginally profitable, but its miserly 40 mpg fuel consumption proved irresistible to the public, and between 1974 and 1976 this 15-year old model overtook the Morris Marina as Leyland's best-selling car.

The political climate had also changed, the Conservatives losing a general election called by Heath in February. Harold Wilson was back as Prime Minister of a minority Labour government with Tony Benn returning as Secretary for Industry, which had been his brief in opposition. As Minister of Technology in Wilson's first administration he had been close-

ly involved with British Leyland's creation, and British Leyland's problems were soon the subject of ministerial concern. Benn noted in his diary for 6 March, the day after he took office, that he and his colleagues were having discussions on 'how we would use public ownership as an ambulance for failed firms because British Leyland and one or two other firms are in serious difficulties.'[22] The economic sand storm from the east had swept aside the Corporation's fragile recovery. A projected £68 million profit in the 1973–4 financial year was replaced by a £16.6 million loss in the six months to the end of March. By the summer of 1974 the Corporation recognized that it had little hope of implementing the expansion plans it had announced the previous year and, in July, met with its bankers to modify the programme.

By this time Stokes had visited Benn to discuss rumours that he was going to intervene and nationalize the company. The industry secretary noted in his diary for 2 July that he had told Stokes: 'Do let me know if you get into trouble because I really wouldn't like to know at the last minute. "Oh no, we are all right," he said, "we might need a bit of money in the spring of next year but we are managing. But we can't sustain our investment programme".'[23] In these circumstances, Benn asked Stokes to prepare a shadow investment programme for him to consider. A cash conservation scheme was instituted in September when British Leyland was predicting a £9.9 million loss which, when taken in conjunction with a £11.5 million deficit following the closure of its Australian subsidiary, took the anticipated figure to £21.7 million. In the event it proved to be £23.9 million. Lord Stokes recalls: 'We were stretched financially, and were on a pretty tight rope. With the oil crisis, export and domestic markets collapsed; it was a disastrous situation.'[24]

The end came, quite dramatically, on Wednesday 4 December and is recalled by company secretary Ron Lucas, who was the sole member of the

The Fiesta cost Ford close on a billion dollars, but it has repaid the investment by being in the top three UK best-sellers for most of the past 18 years, and in the top slot in 1990 and 1991. This is the Kingfisher, a limited edition special of 1978–9, with two-tone paintwork. (NMM)

British Leyland board to have survived from the previous BMC administration. Lucas and his colleagues were based at Leyland House, the Corporation's new headquarters in London's Marylebone Road, and he remembers the arrival in his room of finance director Alex Park, who had replaced John Barber on the latter's promotion in 1973. Park presented Lucas with the stark message: 'We're broke.' He had brought the news to him first because of his knowledge of corporate law and for his advice on the liability of the directors in such circumstances. 'I said that we should go and see Stokes which is what we did. When we told him, he went white and then recounted to us his July conversation with Benn.'

A meeting was immediately arranged with the industry secretary for that evening and Lucas recalls that the British Leyland party, of which he was a member, arrived at the industry department's office at 1 Victoria Street at about eight o'clock in the evening 'We were let in by a side door and I remember that Tony Benn had this enormous purple banner with gold lettering, presented to him by the mining union, behind his desk. We outlined the situation and he said that he was glad we had come to see him and made it clear that the Government could not possibly allow a company that employed some 200,000 people worldwide to go broke. He said, "What I'd like to do."' and, says Lucas, 'these are the precise words he used, "is to send one of my chaps to see your people tomorrow and check through the figures you've given me."'[25]

The following day the individual duly arrived with a number of colleagues who, remembers Lucas, 'spent most of their time with Alex Park and John Barber. They then went back to Victoria Street. We rather expected to hear something that night or the following morning but then, after lunch, Tony Benn made a statement to the House of Commons.' This was on Friday 6 December. He announced that because of the company's impor-

tance to the economy and as a leading exporter, parliamentary approval would be sought to guarantee its working capital. This spelt the end of British Leyland as a private sector company and the business was effectively nationalized the following year. The bulk of Britain's indigenous motor industry would remain in public ownership for the next 13 years, during which time it would consume £2.9 billion of public funds and be guaranteed a further £1.6 billion. Benn also announced that the Government has appointed a team, headed by its industrial adviser, Sir Don Ryder, 'to advise on the company's situation and prospects and the team will consult with the company and the trade unions in the course of its work.'[26]

Ford was the only major British car maker to stay profitable

On 19 December, just 13 days after his Commons statement, Tony Benn had lunch with Stokes and the British Leyland board, 'all of whom seem very relaxed about the collapse', he recorded in his diary. 'They were pretty angry that they had been caught by the Government because although Donald himself has been very cordial all along, it is a very *private* enterprise company.'[27] Benn also confided: 'But I wasn't very impressed with them except Pat Lowry's not bad. John Barber, the deputy chairman, is the old financial guy from AEI who came to them via Ford'.[28]

This is an appropriate point at which to remember that the country's motor industry involved companies other than British Leyland. How had they fared since 1970 and, in particular, to what degree were they affected by the calamitous effects of the oil price increase? The reality was that Ford was the only British front line car maker to remain profitable and, in the crucial year of 1974, achieved a respectable profit of £48.8 million. It had remained consistently in surplus

throughout the decade, with the exception of 1971, when it made a loss of £30.7 million. This was the outcome of a disastrous ten-week strike that shut down all its British facilities.

It will be recalled that since the creation in 1967 of Ford of Europe, the American company's British business was progressively integrated with its German arm, a process that, in corporate terms, was completed by 1972, even though the product lines took rather longer to commonize. However, Ford of Britain continues to exist within the European company and retains its own chairman. Sir Leonard Crossland filled the void left on Sir Patrick Hennessy's retirement in 1968, and, like him, came to the job via the demanding environment of the firm's purchasing department. He was replaced in turn in 1972 by Sir William Batty, who came to the post from the company's tractor division. In 1976 he was succeeded by Sir Terence Beckett, whose career with Ford had been built on the creation of the top-selling Cortina family, which contributed approximately half Ford of Britain's car line profits until coming to an end in 1982, still with a front located engine driving the rear wheels, just as the Mark I Cortina had done 20 years before.

The Cortina had emerged in Mark III form in 1970. The Dagenham-built car looked much more American than its predecessors, with its so called 'Coke-bottle' kickover over the rear wheels, and was masterminded by Harley Copp, Ford of Europe's American vice president in charge of engineering. The German version, named Taunus, essentially shared the Cortina's engineering but with crisper body lines which dated less quickly. Despite a rather cheap-looking interior, the Cortina name had by then acquired an unstoppable momentum, and in 1971 it overtook British Leyland's ageing Issigonis-designed 1100/1300 range to become Britain's most popular car. The Mark III sold 187,159 cars on the home market in 1972 which was a new record for a

Ford model and, with the exception of 1976, it continued as the country's top selling car until 1981, after which production began to run down. Even in 1976, when there was a model change over, it was in second place behind Ford's smaller Escort. The millionth Mark III was built in October 1975, and it ceased production in July 1976, by which time 1.1 million had been completed.

The Mark IV Cortina was little more than an ingenious reskinning of the Mark III floorpan by Uwe Bahnsen, vice president in charge of design, with the German Taunus's body thus integrating the two model lines. Like its predecessor, it was destined for a six-year production life. A face-lift for 1980 resulted in the unofficially titled Mark V and the last example was driven off the Dagenham production line, in July 1982, by Ford Britain's chairman, Sam Toy, who had replaced Beckett in 1980 and whose career with Ford had begun in 1948 when he joined the firm as one of its first graduate recruits.

The nine-year old 105E Anglia was replaced early in 1968 by the Escort produced in 1.1- and 1.3-litre forms. Work had begun on the project in 1964, prior to the creation of Ford of Europe, and it was subsequently decided, in addition to building the car at Halewood, to also put it into production at Ford Germany's Belgian plant at Genk, opened in 1964, and from 1970 at a new assembly facility at Saarlouis in the south-west of Germany. Although British-designed, the car's excellent four-speed all synchromesh gearbox was contributed by Ford Germany, so introducing an appropriately European element to the model. There were German fears that the traditional front engine/rear drive configuration was not sufficiently radical, but the Escort proved to be a great success on both sides of the North Sea. Its base version proved popular with fleet buyers and the two- and four-door saloons made plenty of friends amongst family motorists. From 1972 the model was firmly established as Britain's second-best selling car behind the Cortina, where it remained until 1974 when it ceased production. By this time 2.2 million Escorts had been produced, of which a million were British built.

Its replacement of 1975, also named Escort, was in essence a reskinning of its predecessor's floorpan with crisper body lines and 23 per cent more glass area. In 1972 work had begun on Project Brenda, named after a secretary in Ford Britain's Essex-based product development division, and, unlike the Mark I Escort which, belatedly, was given a European profile, the Mark II was an unalloyed Ford of Europe project. Once again built at Halewood and Saarlouis, production lasted until 1980 and the car proved to be no less successful than the original. It was built for a rather shorter time – five as opposed to six years – with British output just outstripping German, which stood at 960,007 and 848,388 units respectively.

Both the Cortina and Escort were available in a variety of engine and trim options. The car which introduced this proven, American approach to Europe was the Capri, in which the concept of the Mustang was successfully transferred across the Atlantic. Though created by Ford of Britain there was, inevitably, input from America, and it was developed under the appropriate Colt coding. As in the case of the Mark I Escort, at a late stage in the model's evolution it was decided to manufacture the Capri in Germany in addition to building it at Halewood, and the design had to be reworked to accommodate Cologne's V4 and V6 engines. Announced in 1969, the British version ran to no less than 26 derivatives, with engine options varying from a 1.3-litre four to a 3-litre V6. The Capri proved to be far more successful than Ford's product planners had ever dreamt and it was destined to remain available for 18 years. The last example left Ford's Cologne assembly line, where it had been exclusively built since 1976, late in 1986, by which time a total of 1.8 million had been produced.

Although the basic specification of the two-plus-two coupé remained unchanged, it had passed through a number of evolutionary stages, having been first revised for 1974 in Mark II hatchback form. Dubbed Project Diana after an inspirational product planning secretary of that name, its

The Vauxhall Chevette was GM's first 'world car', also made in the US and Brazil as the Chevrolet Chevette, and in Germany as the Opel Kadett. Hatchbacks, saloons and estates were made, and the HS2300 was a successful rally car. This is a Special four-door saloon of 1980, a limited edition model with tinted glass all round and sports-type wheels. (NMM)

creation echoed a slump in German sales, unlike those on the home market which remained fairly constant. The Mark II was therefore aimed more specifically at the British motorist, which resulted in a rather bland product. In its ultimate Capri III form, coded Carla, British demand was maintained to the end; but after its demise, the Capri was not immediately replaced.

All these cars followed the familiar front engine/rear drive design, but in 1976 Ford of Europe unveiled its first front-wheel drive car in the shape of the Fiesta two-door hatchback, which also marked its entry into the supermini class. Not only built at Dagenham and Saarlouis, it was also manufactured at a new Spanish facility Ford established at Valencia, which was its first factory in the country since the civil war had forced the closure of a Barcelona plant 40 years before. Coded Bobcat and created with input from Ford's design facilities on both sides of the Atlantic, the car's all-important body lines hailed from the Turin-based Ghia styling house, acquired by the multinational company in 1970.

After close on a billion dollars had been expended on the project, the Fiesta was initially available in 957, 1,100 and 1,300 cc forms. The half-millionth car was produced in 1977, making it the fastest-selling model by any European car maker, and the millionth was built in 1979. The Fiesta was face-lifted in 1984 and revised in 1989. It remains a strong seller and in 1993 was only outsold in the British market by the Escort, itself in the number one slot.

All these models had reflected a sure-footed approach to design and marketing, but the last of the British-created big Fords represented an exception to this rule. Ford of Britain's American engineering supremo, Harley Copp, was insistent that the Mark III's successor be an even larger car and the outcome was the massive and very American Mark IV Zephyr/Zodiac of 1966, the first British Ford to employ independent

In contrast to the advanced Imp, the Hillman Avenger was as conventional as you could get, despite being a completely new design when it appeared in 1970. Engine options were 1250, 1300, 1500, and 1600. 638,631 were sold under the Hillman name up to 1976, then it became a Chrysler until 1979 (150,413 made) and finally a Talbot to 1981. This is a 1972 1500 DL. (Nick Georgano)

rear suspension. It ceased production in 1971 after output had fallen every year since its announcement. A respectable 50,593 were built in 1966 but this had progressively dropped, to a mere 18,925 in 1971. A total of 122,597 Mark IV's were produced.

Its Granada successor, which also replaced the German 17/20M family, with the Consul name revived for the cheaper versions, was, thankfully, considerably smaller than its predecessor. It was designated the MH range by Ford, standing for Medium Hummer (the latter name, curiously, means lobster in German). Built at Dagenham and Cologne, its sales were badly hit by the oil crisis, only 16,786 Granadas being registered in Britain in 1976, the year that production was transferred to Cologne. Manufacture ceased the following year and, despite its latter-day problems, no less than 846,609 had been produced. Its successor, also named Granada, was only built in Germany and was a reskinning of its predecessor's sub-structure. Destined for a nine-year production life, this

Cologne-built model endured until 1985, the manufacture of 639,440 cars reflecting that it spanned the recession prompted by the second, post-1979, oil crisis.

By the end of the 1970s the British and German design teams were working together without much of the apprehension that had been an inevitable feature of Ford of Europe's early years. Its British activities were concentrated on a new £10 million research and development centre at Dunton, Essex. On its opening in 1967, it was the largest facility of its type in Europe and in the first instance concentrated on engine design whilst its German opposite number at Merkenich made a complementary speciality of body and chassis engineering. In addition to Ford's existing British factories, in 1978 it opened an engine plant at Bridgend, South Wales. Costing £150 million, of which the British government contributed £30 million, it was capable of producing 500,000 engines a year, and this greatly expanded plant continues to service the company's world-wide needs.

Ford's story was one of steady progress. In July 1974, it outsold British Leyland in the British marketplace for the first time ever with 20,031 registrations compared to its ailing rival's 18,603. In 1975 Ford pulled ahead and, by the end of the decade led the British market with a 28.2 per cent share (1979) which compared with Leyland's 19.6 per cent. Yet of the 485,559 Fords registered in Britain that year, no less than 49 per cent were imported, mostly from the Continent, a trend that continues to this day. So in indigenous terms, British Leyland was still ahead.

If Ford emerged as the strongest and most potent force within the British motor industry in the 1970s then the reverse was true of Vauxhall, its General Motors-owned rival. By contrast, it experienced its worst ever decade for sales which further undermined its position as the smallest of Britain's volume car producers. It lost money for an unprecedented four years between 1972 and 1975, not even benefiting from the brief boom of 1972–3 and, when it was back in the black in 1976, profits were a mere £7.6 million. Sadly, these years also marked the end of the British-designed Vauxhall. Between 1975 and 1979 these were phased out and replaced by cars which continued to be Vauxhall-badged and built at Luton and Ellesmere Port, but were designed in Russelsheim, Germany by General Motor's Opel subsidiary.

Unlike Ford, General Motors had kept a tight rein on its British business with the result that Vauxhalls tended to look far more American than their Ford contemporaries. Mechanically, there was greater common ground between the two and, whilst European manufacturers were switching to front-wheel drive, the Americans remained faithful to the traditional, and cheaper, front engine/rear drive configuration. Vauxhall's transatlantic looks damaged its sales and the debacle of the swiftly rusting F-type Victor of the 1950s cast a long shadow. Paradoxically, Luton's best-seller was the Viva, initiated by Vauxhall itself. However, Opel's position was far stronger than Vauxhall's, as it was Germany's second-largest car maker

A specialist car par excellence, Bristol has followed the same theme – a large, relatively slow-revving Chrysler V8 engine with restrained British styling – from 1961 to the present day. The 411 was in production from 1970 to 1976 with minor styling changes, then gave way to the Zagato-styled 412 convertible and 603 saloon. (NMM)

'Very much the poor relation of the Interceptor'. The Jensen-Healey took the West Bromwich company into new territory, that of the MGB or the old Austin-Healey 3000. It failed to establish itself in a very competitive field, and was hit by teething problems and the fuel crisis. Production ended in 1976. (NMM)

behind Volkswagen. But change was in the air, although not 'until Detroit realized that the corporation had lost substantial ground to foreign competition did the board of directors scuttle the paternalistic policies of old.'[29] In corporate terms this meant that the head of the overseas companies were promoted to vice presidents, which gave them the same status as general managers of the domestic divisions. And as far as its European operations were concerned, there could be no doubt which was the senior partner; in 1970 Opel built 820,852 cars compared with Vauxhall's 178,089.

The deciding factor was Opel's creation of General Motors's first so-called 'world car'. This was a small model, to be sold by all the Corporation's overseas subsidiaries and, in 1976, even by Detroit in the wake of the oil price hike. Initiated in 1970, it featured a unitary hull that was ingeniously designed to accept locally-produced engines and transmissions. Coded Project 1865, in Europe it emerged as the Opel Kadett C in 1973 and the Vauxhall Chevette in 1975. This work proved to be a turning point for the German company, for the 'difficult task was brilliantly handled by the Russelsheim engineers and undoubtedly led to the decision to place the European passenger car design and engineering centre with

Opel.'[30] This occurred in 1974 and, as far as Vauxhall was concerned, the decision did not come a moment too soon, because whereas the 1950s had seen a highly rationalized range of products, two decades on, the model scene appeared to be one of excessive and, apparently, fruitless diversification.

The FD Victor of 1968, Vauxhall's rival to the Ford Cortina, never began to match its sales. This was despite the fact that it was an all-new car with a slant-mounted four-cylinder engine, of 1.6- and 2-litre capacity, with a single overhead camshaft driven by a toothed belt. This was the first occasion that such a now commonplace design feature had appeared on a British car. But the public stayed away; the model appeared too big and ungainly and the interior excessively 'plasticky'. Only 24,337 Victors were bought in Britain in 1970, which was the same year in which Ford sold 123,256 Cortinas. The Victor's more powerful VX 4/90 derivatives found a mere 14,277 owners.

Its FE type replacement of 1972, the fifth generation Victor, pointed the way to future trends, in that its floor-pan was shared with the Opel Rekord, but it was another flop, with sales of 44,078 in four years' production. In 1976 it was renamed the VX1800 and 2300, to reflect its optional engine capacities, but only survived until 1978. Just 25,185 were built. Luton's answer to the Ford Capri, the visually unhappy Firenza sold a mere 18,352 examples between 1971 and 1973.

The six-cylinder line was no less happy. The American-looking 3.3-litre Cresta of 1965 was a 100 mph car but accounted for 53,912 units built until 1972, while the up-market Viscount version of 1966 sold 7,025 examples. The Victor-related Ventora of 1968, which also used the Cresta's engine, was only bought in penny numbers. Its best year was the first, when 5,356 found British owners, though sales slumped to only 2,366 in 1973, by which time the model was out of production.

The Viva, Vauxhall's small car line, introduced in 1963, was very much more successful. The HC version of 1970 was offered, in the American tradition, with a wide range of engines from 1.1 to 2.3 litres, and trim options. In 1973 those Vivas of over 1.7-litre capacity were renamed Magnum and survived until 1977 but never sold in appreciable numbers. The Viva, for its part, was built until 1979, with 549,288 being produced.

The Viva's demise marked the last of the British-designed Vauxhalls but by this time the re-badged Opels were already selling strongly. The 1.2-litre Viva-engined Chevette, Luton's version of Project 1865, arrived in 1975

and this three-door hatchback progressively replaced Vauxhall's long-running small car and, in the process, became the company's best-selling car. Production of 415,608 cars spelt out the success of the theme, and the model endured until 1984. It also spawned the Chevette HS homologation which often successfully challenged the Ford Escort on the rally field. The Cavalier of 1975, still with rear-wheel drive, was a rebadged Opel Ascona imported from GM's Belgian plant before being taken over by Luton. The larger Carlton of 1978 was related to the Opel Rekord and endured until 1986 although it was not a strong seller – around 80,000 were produced in all. But the Cavalier accounted for 238,980 units, which paved the way for greater successes in the 1980s.

As Chrysler raised its profile, Rootes names disappeared

Paradoxically, in 1968 General Motors had begun work on a 700-acre proving ground at Millbrook to the north of Luton, which was completed in 1970. This was a mere four years before Vauxhall lost its engineering self-sufficiency and later, in 1987, GM put the facility up for sale.

While General Motors and Ford had a long-established European presence, Chrysler – the smallest of America's 'big three' – was a comparatively new arrival in the Old World and, in particular, in Britain. In 1967, it took a majority shareholding in the ailing Rootes Group which, together with the French Simca concern and a Spanish subsidiary, subsequently constituted Chrysler Europe. But unlike its contemporaries, a lacklustre performance on its home market resulted in Chrysler spending substantially less on its European operations than its rivals. By the end of 1971 it had invested $626 million in them compared with Ford's $1,556 and GM's $1,097 *billion*.[31]

Where the former Rootes business differed from those of Chrysler's

Continental companies was that they performed well. Simca was consistently profitable, apart from the depression years of 1974 and 1975, and had suffered no labour disputes for 30 years. It was much the same picture in Spain. John Bullock, Chrysler's UK's Director of Public Affairs at the time, recalls: 'the executives of the Simca and the Spanish company were very fed up with the continuing industrial relations problems and the frequent strikes taking place at Rootes which affected the overall profits of Chrysler in Europe . . . It was only in Britain that strikes occurred.'[32] In these circumstances, the British company was a continual drain on the Corporation, having generated accumulated debts of £23.3 million in the 1960s, and recording a £10.6 million deficit in 1970, its second-biggest loss. If strikes were an ongoing problem, in Rootes Chrysler had also inherited a business that was urgently in need of reinvestment, a fact underlined in a 1975 survey of its manufacturing facilities, which revealed that the majority of the machine tools were between 14 and 25 years old. Chrysler United Kingdom, as Rootes Motors became in 1970, had a mere $2,300 in fixed assets per employee compared with France's $4,550 and Spain's $5,700.[33]

Despite the disappearance of the Rootes name, the second Lord Rootes continued as chairman, to look after the interests of the minority shareholders until 1973 when he retired. His place was taken by Gilbert Hunt, formerly of Massey-Ferguson, who had become managing director in 1968, and his deputy, the American Don Lander, moved up into his vacated position.

Chrysler had decided to underline the corporate identity of its European operations and its five-pointed blue pentastar began to appear on former Rootes outlets in Britain and throughout Europe. This was the first stage of an operation that would see the disappearance of the old Rootes marque names. Singer was the first to go in 1970, and the last Hillmans and

Humbers were built in 1976. Thereafter all the cars were badged Chrysler.

In 1970 Chrysler UK built 216,995 cars, well ahead of Vauxhall's 178,089; and it remained ahead throughout the decade. But the car range did require updating. On the one hand there was the slow-selling rear-engined Imp, which dated back to 1963, and on the other the Hillman Minx, which had been revised under the Arrow coding in 1966 and was also available in better-equipped Hunter form from 1967. Inevitably, the long-running Minx was the mainstay of the range but Rootes had obtained a lucrative contract with Iran and had designed the largest British car plant in the Middle East in the shape of the National Manufacturing Company facility on the outskirts of Tehran. From 1967 it assembled Hunter kits produced at Ryton, although the car was badged as the Paykaan, which is Arabic for Arrow. In October 1968 this contract was underpinned when the Shah decreed that only three types of cars, small, medium and large, were to be produced, the Hunter representing the medium category.

By this time the once-prestigious Humber had been reduced to a single model, in the shape of the Hunter-based Sceptre, whilst Sunbeam was represented by the Imp-related Stiletto and Sport. The range was completed by the Roy Axe-styled Sunbeam Rapier, which resembled a scaled down in-house Plymouth Barracuda, even though its Hunter floorpan and engineering rather diluted the mixture. But sales virtually ceased after 1973, although the Rapier

The DeLorean was an ill-starred attempt to build a sports car for export to the USA in an area of high unemployment in Northern Ireland. Power came from a 2.8-litre PRV V6 engine, as used by Peugeot, Renault, and Volvo, and the body was made of unpainted stainless steel. About 8,400 were made before financial collapse in 1982, which cost 2,500 jobs. (NMM)

continued to be listed until 1976.

In 1970 came what was destined to be the last Rootes-created model in the shape of the Ryton-built Hillman Avenger, intended to slot in between the Imp and Minx. This was the last model planned by the Rootes brothers, when it was known as the B Car Project, and was completely new, although its front engine/rear drive layout was as conventional as the Imp had been advanced. In its most basic form the Avenger was a 1.2-litre car, with an alternative 1500 engine, later replaced by 1300/1600 options, and was intended to take Chrysler into the highly competitive market sector dominated by the Ford Escort, Morris Marina, and Vauxhall Viva. The Avenger was also sold as a Sunbeam on some foreign markets and as the Plymouth Cricket by Chrysler in America. It proved to be a reasonable success for Chrysler although until 1973 was always outsold by its rivals in the British market. But sales began to fall away from 1975 onwards, Chrysler's well-publicized financial problems undoubtedly being a factor.

Between 1971 and 1973 the company had, for the first time, enjoyed an uninterrupted three years of profitability and the £3.7 million surplus attained in 1973 was the highest achieved in Chrysler UK's short life.

This was despite the fact the business suffered its worst ever year for industrial disputes when it lost a record 91,129 vehicles as a result of internal and external stoppages. However, the fiscal pendulum swung dramatically back in 1974, when it recorded a record loss of £17.7 million. The world depression triggered by the oil price-rise was beginning to bite and Chrysler was caught in a pincer movement as, across the Atlantic, its home market contracted, which resulted in substantial losses that were also sustained by its European operations and, in particular, the United Kingdom subsidiary.

In 1974 British banks began to refuse loans to Chrysler UK without guarantees from the parent company. At the end of the year a $12 million cash injection came from America, and in the first few months of 1975 the British business was maintained by monthly cash contributions of $13 million. The British government had, in the meantime, begun to express its concern. Early in 1975 industry secretary Tony Benn wrote to Chrysler to request its intentions as far as the British subsidiary was concerned. Although the American company's response was essentially non-committal, Prime Minister Harold Wilson took this as an indication that it would continue to maintain a British pres-

The Aston Martin V8 Vantage Zagato was a limited edition coupé using a lightened version of the existing V8's floorpan, a developed version of the 5.3-litre engine, and a body both styled and built by the Italian company. Rarity (52 coupés and 25 convertibles) made it an instant collector's car. (Nick Georgano)

ence. However, Wilson asked Sir Don Ryder, then in the midst of his investigation of British Leyland, to widen his brief to include Chrysler's British operations.

In March 1975 Chrysler made a formal request for £35 million from the government-supported Finance for Industry programme to restructure its debts, an application that was ultimately rejected. In May came a further request to the Department of Industry for £25 million to develop a Linwood-built replacement for the ageing Arrow range. But in July, the Chrysler Corporation recorded a six-month loss of $153 million. By this time Ryder's Department of Industry report was nearing completion; but the company ominously requested that it be deferred and, on 30 October, Gilbert Hunt and Don Lander left Britain for a Chrysler board meeting in America.

In fact events were to overtake them, because on the previous day, Chrysler's new chairman, John Riccardo, declared that the disposal of its British subsidiary was the Corporation's 'biggest single problem.' This was the first public recognition of its intentions. But the remark was made without prior consultation with the British government, which then demanded Riccardo's presence in Britain. At a meeting with Wilson at Chequers in November (at one stage the proceedings were blacked out by a local power strike) the Chrysler chairman presented the Prime Minister with three options: that the business be liquidated; that it be given to the Government; or that 80 per cent be transferred to the state while Chrysler retained a 20 per cent interest.

There followed much governmental agonizing; consideration was given to integrating the business with British Leyland and approaches were also made to Ford and Vauxhall, but none of these options proved viable. But it was decided that Chrysler UK could not be allowed to cease trading. This decision was taken against the background of a rising tide of unemployment. In addition there was the valuable Iranian contract to be considered, which accounted for around 30 per cent of the company's output, as well as the impact of liquidation on Britain's balance of payments. A further factor was the potential effect of Linwood's closure on the Scottish economy and its impact on the rise of the Scottish Nationalist party when the Government had a majority of just five seats in the House of Commons.

Matters were even further muddied by various changes of posture by Chrysler but, in December 1975, a settlement was finally reached. The Corporation agreed that it would continue to operate its British company but the Government would bear the first £50 million of an anticipated 1976 loss. It was likewise committed to bear the cost of up to £10 million of losses in 1977, to a maximum of £12.5 million losses in 1978 and 1979, and there would also be a £35 million loan. The grand total of this governmental support stood at £162.5 million. Chrysler agreed to contribute £10 million to its 1976 and 1977 losses, £12.5 million to its anticipated 1978 and 1979 losses, and also waived £19.7 million interest payments on loans to Chrysler UK. In these circumstances, the Chrysler Corporation was forbidden to make 'any substantial alterations to the nature of its business . . . and from disposing of any subsidiary companies without the agreement of the secretary of state.'[34] The Hillman Imp was nearing the end of its life, and so that Linwood would have something to build, Avenger production would be transferred there while Ryton would produce Chrysler's new Coventry-designed, medium-sized front-wheel drive Alpine hatchback, which became Car of the Year in 1976. It was then only being built in France as the Simca 1307/1308. The firm also agreed to contribute £10 to £12 million for its British manufacture.

The settlement was signed on 5 January 1976, but an all-party report of the affair declared: 'By no stretch of the imagination can the events leading up to this agreement with Chrysler be said to form a glorious chapter in the history of the Government's industrial relations.'[35] As expected, the 1975 losses of Chrysler UK were substantial and the largest in the industry, having reached a record £35.5 million. The following year's deficit, at £31.9 million, was nearly as bad. However, the company's situation greatly improved in 1977 when it was only £8.2 million in the red.

The last Hillman Imp was built in 1976 and, as scheduled, its place at Linwood was taken by the Avenger in the summer of that year. In 1977 it was joined by the hastily conceived Chrysler Sunbeam, where an old Rootes marque name became a model one. This was a three-door hatchback based on a shortened Avenger floorpan and engineering and, in addition to the existing engines, it was available with an enlarged 928 cc Imp unit.

Chrysler UK's production slumped to 144,586 cars in 1975, its lowest figure since 1965. Output rose by some 25,000 in 1977, when its share of the British market stood at 6.02 per cent, which increased to 7.07 in 1978 when production rose to 196,481. But by then the Americans had sold their business to the French Peugeot Talbot group.

News of the sale broke on 10 August 1978 and, despite Chrysler's assurances of January 1975, came as a complete surprise to the British government. It was not, however, news to the French administration which, in October 1976, had begun to covertly broker such a deal. Its motivation was that Chrysler's Simca business should revert to a French manufacturer so that the Gallic motor industry would, once again, be under wholly national ownership. The state-funded Renault company was the original candidate but it was then decided that private, as opposed to public, money would be required and this meant Peugeot Talbot, then being dynamically revived by Jean-Paul Payrare. But Chrysler

wanted £1 billion for its European business which was more than Peugeot was prepared to pay and, in any event, the prize was Simca, not the loss-making Chrysler UK with its labour problems and troubled Linwood facility. There the matter rested until January 1978, when talks began again. However it was August before agreement was finally reached in Paris after an all-night negotiating session.

There were considerable tax advantages to Peugeot for the sale to be signed on British soil, so the team immediately flew to London in Payrare's executive jet, and the signing took place in the very un-businesslike surroundings of Heathrow Airport. Peugeot's lawyer, Peter Paine, produced a table and, with the backdrop of a crowded arrivals and departures terminal, the documents were signed. The deal made Peugeot Talbot the world's third-largest car maker in unit terms, and Chrysler lost approximately 25 per cent of its capacity. Chrysler received 15 per cent of Peugeot stock, worth some £200 million, but the deal ended the dream of Lynn Townsend, Chrysler's president in the 1960s, that the Corporation would be a true multinational company, like its Ford and General Motors rivals.

'Bristol hardly have to sell their cars – people just come and buy them'

In more parochial terms, Peugeot became France's largest car maker and its industry, just as its government had intended, became wholly French-owned. Peugeot paid £230 million cash for the business and inherited £400 million worth of debts and Chrysler UK. Its labour problems were underlined by the fact that in the weeks prior to the agreement, the Linwood work-force had gone on strike and losses were running at £1.2 million a week. Of the £165.5 million allotted by the British government in 1975, just £7.5 million remained. Nevertheless, this assistance had

helped the business to survive the severest recession since the war. In the longer term, a sector of the British motor industry had switched from American to French control. However, unlike Chrysler, which had designed all its European cars in Britain, those to be produced there by Peugeot Talbot would, ultimately, have been engineered on the other side of the English Channel.

When Chrysler disposed of its European operations in 1978, it was effectively left with two foreign subsidiaries in the form of corporate presences in Mexico and Canada. The latter facility had, for some years, provided V8 engines for two British manufacturers of grand tourers, namely Bristol, which survived the rigours of the world depression, and Jensen, that succumbed to them.

Bristol Cars continued in its own enigmatic way, directed with unruffled efficiency by its proprietor: Anthony Crook. As that great authority on the marque, L. J. K. Setright, has observed: 'They are a curious firm. They scarcely ever advertise or publicise. They hardly have to sell their cars; people just come and buy them.'[36] In such circumstances, it is only possible to speculate on how Bristol fared during the 1973 recession, but as the firm is still very much in existence it is safe to assume that it weathered these difficult years without production at its Filton factory dropping much from its three cars a week maximum.

For 1970 Bristol had introduced the 411 which was destined to remain in production until 1976, during which time it was built in five different series which was more than any other Bristol. Outwardly similar to its 410 predecessor and still retaining a chassis rooted in the 1940s, it was destined to be the last of the second generation of Bristols, which had begun in 1961 with the first of the Chrysler-powered models, the 407. As such, the 411 was the heaviest of the range but performance was maintained by the presence of a 6,277 cc V8 that was a full litre more in capacity than its 410 predecessor. Top speed was an effortless 130 mph although the Series 4 car for 1974 saw an increase in capacity to 6.5 litres. So much for the oil crisis! By the time that production had ceased in 1976, a total of 600 had been completed.

The 411 and its predecessors were all coupés but in 1975 Bristol unveiled the 412, its first convertible since the demise of the 405 drophead in 1958. The body was a brutally angular offering by Zagato which evolved into a so-called convertible/saloon, with a detachable roof panel, in 1976. A Series 2 version of 1977 was powered by a smaller 5.9-litre V8. In 1980 the 412 was renamed the Beaufighter in memory of a famous Bristol aircraft and, although it resembled its predecessor, it differed in being turbocharged and was destined to enjoy a production run of an unprecedented – for a Bristol –13 years, this 5.9-litre car remaining available until 1993. A drophead coupé version with similar engineering, the Beaufort, which lacked the Beaufighters's distinctive rollover bar, was also available.

For 1977 Bristol replaced the 411 with a new model designated the 603.

Perhaps a 413 was not for the superstitiously inclined and Bristol historian Charles Oxley-Sidley says that the model number was chosen 'to commemorate the 603 years that had passed since the City of Bristol received its first royal charter from King Edward III.'[37] The chassis was essentially carried over from the 411 but there were two engine options, an 'economy' 5.2-litre which was discontinued in 1977 and a mainstream 5.9-litre. With air-conditioning and automatic transmission as standard, the 603 sold for £19,666 which was just £4 more than the price of a Rolls-Royce Silver Shadow.

The 603 was built until 1982, in which year the car followed 412 precedent when the company dispensed with the numerals and replaced them with the names of illustrious Bristol aircraft. Like the open Beaufighter and Beaufort, the Brigand coupé, as one version of the 603 became, was turbocharged, while the outwardly similar Britannia continued in normally aspired form. Spiralling development costs meant that, like the convertible, these had to soldier on until 1993.

If these magnificently engineered

Bristols survived the turbulent 1970s, the same, alas, could not be said of West Bromwich-based Jensen Motors, which went into liquidation in 1976 after a decade of corporate upheavals. In 1959 Jensen was bought from its founders by the Norcross group and although the company built low-production cars under its own name, the real money came from the BMC contract to manufacture bodies for the Austin-Healey 3000, which ceased in 1968. The firm had also, since 1964, produced the Ford V8-engined Sunbeam Tiger, but when Chrysler took over the Rootes Group in 1967 that model was similarly discontinued. Thus, for the first time since 1952, Jensen had to rely on its own resources. This meant a single model in the form of the costly but well received Chrysler V8-powered 6.2-litre Interceptor of 1967 that was destined to be the best-selling model in the company's history. But its existence could not prevent Jensen's 1966 turnover of £3 million, which produced a profit of £183,000, becoming a £52,000 loss in 1968. By this time the work-force had been reduced from 1,400 to around 400. Norcross brought in 'company doctor' Carl Duerr, who aimed to increase Interceptor production to 14 or 15 a week; but in June 1968 Norcross sold out to merchant bankers William Brandt, which passed on 40 per cent of the equity to Duerr and Jensen's other directors.

By 1969 Jensen had lost £360,000 in 18 months. Now losing £40,000 each month it was flirting with insolvency, despite having that year delivered the 1,000th Interceptor. Brandt wasted little time in bringing in its own consultant, Alfred Vickers, who recognized that whilst the company's overheads were geared to building 15 cars a week, it was only producing 11 and selling eight.[38] The business had suffered from a lack of investment that was reflected by the use of old equipment, which resulted in inefficient production methods. When Vickers returned to Jensen as general manager in 1970, Duerr departed.

Rolls-Royce has never had its own body department. When the coachbuilding era waned, bodies were built by Pressed Steel at Cowley, later Pressed Steel Fisher. Here a Silver Spirit body is being checked for accuracy at Cowley, prior to transfer to Crewe for the fitting of engine and transmission. (Pressed Steel Fisher)

The Reliant Scimitar began as a Ford-powered coupé styled by David Ogle. The GTE sports estate version which appeared in 1968 combined performance and load-carrying capacity, and set a fashion later copied by Volvo, Lancia and Honda. It was made until 1986, the last example going to HRH the Princess Royal. It was her seventh GTE, and her first with power steering. The design was taken over by Middlebridge Engineering, who made them for a further four years.
(Nick Georgano)

The thread of the story now passes to Donald Healey. He still retained his Warwick-based design facility and was the first to recognize the vacuum that existed following the demise of the Austin-Healey 3000 in America. On one of his regular visits to the United States, he had met up with Norwegian-born Kjell Qvale (pronounced Shell Cavarley), who owned San-Francisco-based British Motor Car Distributors, America's largest importer of British cars. According to Healey's son, Brian, 'the demise of the Austin-Healey 3000 had left Kjell looking for a replacement, so he suggested to DMH that Warwick should design something suitable.'[39] News of this dialogue reached Alfred Vickers at Jensen and 'I suddenly realised that Jensen Motors Ltd was possibly the only company in the UK with the capacity and resources to make the new sports car at the rate Qvale required which was between 150 and 200 units a week.'[40] Vickers wasted little time in contacting Qvale in America. A series of meetings between all the interested parties ensued and the outcome, in April 1970, was that Qvale took over the shares held by Duerr, together with some owned by Brandt. This gave him 84 per cent of Jensen Motors and he became president, Donald Healey chairman, and Alfred Vickers managing director. Qvale initiated redundancies, but improvements in build quality and a steady demand for the Interceptor saw the firm back in the black in the 1970–1 financial year with profits of £100,000. However, the

slow selling, thirsty, four wheel drive FF version was discontinued after only 320 had been built.

In the meantime work was proceeding apace on what was to be called the Jensen-Healey and this two-seater roadster was unveiled at the 1972 Geneva Motor Show. But there was little doubt that, visually, the new car lacked the charisma that the Austin-Healey 3000 had possessed in abundance. The Austin-Healey stylist, Gerry Coker, had long since departed for pastures new in America and the Jensen-Healey's lines were the work of former Chrysler stylist Hugo Poole. However, Qvale had been dissatisfied by the car's appearance, which had been altered following difficulties in finding a suitable engine, and had brought in William Towns who reworked the front end.

The matter of the right power unit also took time to resolve. The Healey's original choice of the Vauxhall Victor's new 2.3-litre single overhead camshaft four had to be abandoned because it adversely responded to the detoxing required by the new American emissions regulations. Ford Germany's V6 and a BMW unit were also contem-

plated but without success. Then in 1971 Kjell Qvale met up with Colin Chapman of Lotus who was developing a new Type 907 2-litre 16-valve twin-overhead camshaft four-cylinder aluminium engine for his own cars. According to Brian Healey, Chapman 'offered this promising unit . . . to Qvale for the new Healey.' It had the advantage of sharing the Vauxhall's dimensions and he 'agreed to buy the Lotus engine – accepting it without warranty, and completely lacking in development.'[41]

The net result of all these factors was that, from the outset, the Jensen-Healey was plagued by unreliability and, in the first instance, the cars were badly built and paint quality was poor. Lotus was never able to deliver the quantity of engines it had promised and, if the cars were parked with a full tank of petrol, the fuel would find its way into the engine's sump. The Healeys brought in Jaguar's former respected chief engineer, William Heynes, for advice and Syd Enever, latterly of MG, similarly gave of his expertise. Gradually, the cars became more reliable. Only 705 Jensen-Healeys were built in 1972, but by mid-1973 production was running at about 100 a week – still far short of the intended 200 target. Output for that year stood at 3,846 units. For its part, the Healey family believed that Jensen looked upon the car as very much the poor relation of the Interceptor. Each Jensen-Healey took around ten days to build compared with seven weeks for the larger model, which was by then being produced at the rate of 25 to 30 a week.[42]

Donald Healey relinquished the Jensen chairmanship in 1972 and, in the following year, the respected Alfred Vickers left for Cosworth Engineering and his place as managing director was taken by chief engineer Kevin Beattie. By 1974 output was reaching 150 cars a week and production peaked at 4,550 that year. But then along came the world recession, to which Jensen was particularly vulnerable. In an era of spiralling petrol prices it was producing the Interceptor, by then enlarged to 7.2 litres and returning an unhealthy 11 mpg, while the Jensen-Healey had yet to establish itself in a market that was more fragile than most.

The sands were running out. In July the closed two-plus-two seater version of the Jensen-Healey, as required by the American market and pointedly named the *Jensen* GT, was announced. But three months later, in September 1975, the Bank of America appointed John A. Griffiths as receiver and manager. Production continued for a time and a further 51 sports cars were built in 1976, but in May that year the business closed its doors. After 40 years of building cars under its own name, Jensen was no more. However, this was not quite the end, for the business survived as a parts and service company and, in 1983, it revived the Interceptor, which was produced at the limited rate of 12 cars a year. In 1992 this operation also ceased, though Jensen has once again been saved since then.

By the time that the Jensen-Healey ceased production, Lotus, headed by Colin Chapman, had introduced the new models for which the 2-litre Type 907 power unit had been conceived. The firm had decided to move its products up-market – prompted, to some extent, by the imposition of VAT, which effectively killed the kit car – and so embraced a philosophy which would see output volume fall somewhat and, in theory, profits rise.

After 40 years of building cars, Jensen was no more

In 1970 Lotus was building the last of its second generation cars in the shape of the Elan, Elan +2, and mid-engined Europa. These were replaced in turn by a larger, more expensive trio of models of which the first, the four-seater Elite hatchback, appeared in 1974, just as the world recession began to bite. Not only was this model well behind schedule, but Lotus's finance director Fred Bushell, subsequently revealed that 'almost the night before the new car was launched, the costings were checked and it was found that the price would have to be around the £5,000 mark, whereas it had always been intended that it should be no more than £3,500. And this was after we had already committed ourselves to launch it with a production volume of 50 cars a week based on the intended price.'[43] Lotus had no choice but to adhere to the higher price, which was £5,857, but, says Bushell, it 'exposed the company to selling a product with inadequate marketing and also, to some extent, inadequate quality control.'

The Elite was followed in 1975 by the related but cheaper two-door Eclat, and the flagship of the range in the shape of the Ital Design-styled, mid-engined Esprit. Yet, as Chapman's biographer has pointed out, the Esprit 'was no quicker than the Elite, it did not handle as well and it was noisier . . . it did not become ready for sale until June 1976 because there was just not sufficient money available for the tooling required!'[44]

In 1969 Lotus had built 4,506 cars, which stands as an all-time production

record for the firm. Although output dropped to 2,822 in 1973, profits hit an unprecedented high of £1.15 million. But as the recession began to bite, Lotus plummeted to a loss of £488,000 in 1975, a year in which just 536 cars left the factory at Hethel, Norwich. In 1976 output rose to 926, but the firm was only marginally back in the black, to the tune of £17,000. This year saw the engine supply contract with Jensen cease. Production increased to 1,070 cars in 1977 and there was a surplus of £557,000. Despite this improvement, however, Lotus clearly needed to broaden its product base and to end its sole reliance on specialist car sales, which were so vulnerable to variations in the economic climate. In 1977 Chapman therefore decided to follow the example of Porsche and establish an engineering consultancy business for the use of manufacturers throughout the motor industry. The finance required to generate this expansion was supplied by American Express, which in October 1977 provided a £2.2 million loan, repayable over five years, and a £600,000 overdraft facility. The consultancy service was subsequently formalized, in 1980, as Lotus Engineering.

It was at about this time that Chapman distanced himself from his road cars and, disenchanted with his factory, turned to his first love: that of motor racing and, in particular, his 'ground effect' Formula 1 car. The production side of the business was placed in the hands of Mike Kimberley, who had joined Lotus from Jaguar in 1969, and had become chief engineer in 1974.

The consultancy business attracted many clients, the vast majority of whom remained anonymous, but one very public commission came from the DeLorean Motor Company, headed by former General Motors vice president John Z. DeLorean who, in 1979, had succeeded in obtaining British government funding, to the tune of £35.9 million, to build a rear-engined gull-wing-bodied sports car. The aim was to sell it in America. For the Labour administration, the attraction – and hence the finance – was that the car was to be produced at a purpose-built factory established in an area of high unemployment at Dunmuray, to the south of Belfast. In November 1978 Lotus was awarded the $17.5 million (£9.4 million) contract to undertake all important development work on the car; but what was to have been a ten month commission was only completed at the end of 1980, 25 months later. During this time the DeLorean was completely re-engineered and the resulting 2.8-litre car was, in effect, a V6 Renault-engined Lotus.

Then in 1979 along came the second and even more severe oil price induced recession. Lotus's output slumped to 383 cars in 1980 and although it made a profit of £461,000, Bushell stated in October 1981 that a significant proportion of this had come from the De-Lorean contract. Trading conditions also worsened, particularly abroad, and between 1979 and 1983 the company's American sales collapsed.

In 1980 the car range was updated. This particularly applied to the new, extensively refined Esprit Turbo. A Series 2 Esprit followed in 1981, and the Elite and Eclat were similarly improved. All models benefited from an enlarged 2.2-litre engine. It was also in 1980 that Lotus recognized it had made a serious error in not pursuing the Elan concept and work began on a replacement in the shape of the M90 project, intended to drive production targets up to 5,000 cars a year. But the only way that the car could be economically developed was for it to have a Japanese power unit. For this reason an approach was made to the Toyota company which resulted in it awarding Lotus a research and development contract, and the creation of a non-running Toyota-engined M90 prototype. A further benefit to Lotus from the association with Toyota was the use of its components – namely gearbox, final drive, and disc brakes – in the Excel, which replaced the Eclat for the 1983 season. Only 18 Elites were built between 1981 and 1983 and it ceased

production in the latter year, by which time 2,535 had been completed. Lotus's road car line now consisted of the Excel and Esprit models.

Across the Irish Sea in Belfast, the DeLorean had entered production in December 1980, but in November 1981 news broke that payment for the work to Lotus had been made via the Panama-registered, Geneva-located General Product Development Services Inc (GPD). The unwelcome publicity increased pressure on Chapman, who had always had a reputation within the industry for sailing close to the financial wind. Involvement with DeLorean continued to haunt Lotus thereafter. Despite up to 40 DeLorean cars being built per day at one stage, the anticipated American sales failed to materialize in this time of deep recession. A receiver was appointed in February 1982, and production ceased in October. The exercise had ultimately cost the British taxpayer £77 million and 2,500 people lost their jobs.

Lotus rejected Toyota's first bid, fearing loss of control

Despite its problems DeLorean had nevertheless built more cars than Lotus in 1982, when just 541 were produced. And now trouble was looming on the financial horizon as only £900,000 of the American Express loan had been repaid by the agreed September 1982 expiry date. Lotus urgently required a new backer. Clearly the coming year of 1983 was going to be a particularly difficult one, but Fred Bushell had begun to notice a difference in Colin Chapman's response to his troubles. 'He did not seem to show the same concern as he had on previous occasions when the company had been having financial problems. It now seemed as though he had said to himself, "I have done all I can to keep this small car company in business, but now it doesn't really interest me any more and, in fact, if it

does go down it could be a big relief!"'[45]

Then, on December 1982, 54-year old Chapman died suddenly of a heart attack. With Lotus and the motoring world stunned, Bushell took over the chairmanship at this crucial time and was joined by Alan Curtis, joint chairman of Aston Martin in 1978–80, and Mike Kimberley. With a refinancing package now a priority, an approach was made to Toyota, who sent a team to the Hethel factory and talked to the firm's bankers. March 1983 represented the nadir of the firm's fortunes and director Peter Kirwan-Taylor recalls that Lotus Cars came within 'a couple of weeks' of closure. Toyota was by then contemplating a response to its appraisal of the business, an exercise that was destined to take some months. But, says Kirwan-Taylor, 'around the middle of March, we said "we're going to be running out of time at the end of the month, and we need £500,000." They [Toyota] sent us the sum of money we asked for within two weeks, as an advance payment on engineering contracts. There were no strings attached to it . . . which was a very good gesture of good faith.'[46] Toyota subsequently came up with definite proposals to invest in the business but since, in the longer term, these would have meant a loss of control the board of the Group Lotus parent company felt that it had no alternative but to reject them.

Meanwhile, Alan Curtis had been talking with David Wickins, founder of British Car Auctions, and in June 1983 BCA – which was attracted to the potential of Lotus Engineering – took a 25 per cent share in the company. Toyota came in with 22 per cent and merchant bankers J. Henry Schroder Wagg had 10 per cent. Wickins became chairman of Lotus. In 1984 two members of the old guard retired as directors: they were international financier and stylist of the original Lotus Elite, Peter Kirwan-Taylor; and Fred Bushell, who then concentrated on running Team Lotus racing which, as always, was separate from the road car business. That year, as trading conditions improved, the company was back in the black, with profits of £476,000 and production up to 837 cars.

The JCB excavator company subsequently took a 12 per cent holding in Lotus, but what the firm really required was a major backer, as Toyota had declined to increase its share in the company. This would allow Lotus to improve its product range and develop the Elan replacement, the project having evolved from the M90 and an X100 coding. It was General Motors – attracted, as BCA had been, by the potential of Lotus Engineering – which eventually bought the company, in January 1986, for $31.9 million (£22.7 million). It acquired a controlling 58 per cent holding which comprised the Schroder Wagg/BCA and JCB stakes. Then, in May, Toyota sold its own 22 per cent of Lotus to GM which, by October 1986, held 91 per cent of the company. With Mike Kimberley as chief executive and managing director of Group Lotus, the firm now possessed the funds and confidence to face the future and, above all, to put the X100 into production.

As a postscript to this traumatic period in Lotus's history, the simmering DeLorean affair finally boiled over and, in 1992, a decade after that company's collapse, Fred Bushell was sentenced by the Belfast Crown Court to three years imprisonment for his part in conspiring to defraud the DeLorean company of up to £9.49 million. He was also fined £2.5 million. What the judge, Lord Justice Murray, described as a 'barefaced, outrageous and massive fraud' followed the DeLorean Motor Company having been talked into paying all of the $17.5 million (£9.49 million) development costs for the car in advance. These funds were then channelled through GPD Services, set up by Chapman and Bushell the previous year.[47] The money had been shared between John DeLorean, Chapman and Bushell. DeLorean had $8.5 million (£4.72 million) for his personal use whilst the two Lotus executives had opened secret numbered Swiss bank accounts and shared the $8.39 million (£4.66 million) balance between them. Chapman took a 90 per cent lion's share, which amounted to $7.5 million (£4.16 million), and Bushell the balance of $848,000 (£471,000), for what the prosecuting counsel described as 'their personal benefit.'

In happier times, in the early 1970s when Lotus's fortunes were riding high, Chapman had contemplated buying Aston Martin and had approached Sir David Brown, the company's owner. Chapman was concerned that the M50 Lotus then under development, which emerged as the Elite, differed so significantly from the firm's previous products that it would be better received if it were marketed under a name more closely associated with costly, high performance cars, such as Aston Martin. He felt that its Newport Pagnell factory, within close reach of the M1, was an ideal location for an Aston Martin and Lotus maintenance department. But following a visit to the works – which, in Chapman's opinion, was somewhat disorganized and involved a high degree of hand-work – the idea was taken no further. This episode does, however, underline Aston Martin's very exposed position at the time.

In 1970 the last of the Aston Martin DB6s were being built, and in April that year came the firm's long-awaited 5.3-litre DBS V8 model. This William Towns-styled coupé had entered production in six-cylinder DBS guise in 1967 but tooling costs had amounted to £500,000. In addition to this burden, the firm had never really recovered from the government-induced credit squeeze of 1966 when it had been building 18 cars a week and was aiming for a profitable 20. By contrast, in the early 1970s six V8s a week were being produced, although the figure could have been much higher had engines been available in larger numbers. All these factors resulted in Aston Martin recording a £1.1 million loss in 1970 on a turnover of £2.8 million.

Various options were contemplated on how to increase output. The aim was to double production to 12 cars a week, which was the profitability

The Rover SD1 (Specialist Division No. 1) used the familiar 3½-litre V8 engine in an all-new five-door hatchback body. This photograph of the final finish and valeting area at the new Solihull factory was released at the car's launch in July 1976. Early examples were poorly finished, but the SD1 became Car of the Year for 1977. (NMM)

threshold. In a bid to reduce overheads, in June 1971 30 per cent of the Aston Martin work-force, 230 employees, were made redundant. But the 1971 loss was even worse than the previous year's, with turnover having dropped to £2.3 million and losses having increased to £1.2 million. Aston Martin's difficulties were compounded when the David Brown organization began to experience liquidity problems. To remain competitive in the tractor market, it had invested heavily to increase production from 600 to the 1,000 a week mark, but there followed a world wide slump in sales. In this combination of circumstances, Sir David Brown had little choice but to sell the car company that he had owned since 1947, and the business was bought in February 1972, for a token £100, by the Solihull-based Company Developments Ltd. The deal was made on the condition that Aston Martin would not be encumbered by £5 million worth of debts and bank overdrafts incurred via inter company loans accounts.

Sir David Brown later ruefully reflected that 'naturally it was a wrench losing Aston Martin, but it was pretty obvious at the time that it would be difficult to produce a motor car of this kind and make a profit out of it.'[48] In the early days of his stewardship this had not been his concern but the harsher realities of the 1970s meant that he had no choice. He simultaneously disposed of his tractor division, which had been a feature of the David Brown business since 1939.

On the face of it, William Willson's Company Developments Ltd appeared to be an unlikely saviour for Aston Martin as it had no experience of the motor manufacturing industry and was involved in building development and secondary banking. Widely voiced fears of asset stripping were confirmed when the company's collection of old models were sold off and ten acres of land adjoining the factory, which constituted the firm's playing field, was disposed of for £425,000.

In April 1972, four months after the new owners had taken control of Aston Martin Lagonda Ltd, the V8 appeared in revised form, this Series 2 car being identifiable by its greatly improved front end with two large headlamps in place of the four small ones which had featured hitherto. The car was named the V8, with the DB initials (for David Brown) absent for the first time since 1950. Yet, once again, the company's prospects were adversely affected by international events, with a downturn in the world economy in the autumn of 1973. Not only did it affect Aston Martin's sales – suddenly there was little demand for a £7,031 car which returned 12 mpg – but it also jeopardized Company Developments's own activities as the property market took a nosedive. In consequence the car business was, yet again, plunged into a deep financial trough. In January 1974, Company Developments applied to the Department of Industry for a £500,000 loan but, despite two applications, the request was rejected.

Aston Martin had received a life-saving order for 200 cars from America, its largest export market. But first the V8 needed to meet the stringent US emissions regulations, which required that an appropriately modified car had to cover no less than 50,000 miles. This was finally achieved in October 1974, but by then it was too late. Willson, meanwhile, had been the first to recognize that Aston Martin urgently needed a second string to its V8 coupé line and decided to put the Aston Martin Lagonda, the four-door version of the model, into production. A prototype had been built in 1969 for Sir David Brown but the design had been in abeyance since then. Listed at £14,040, the car sadly attracted few buyers and only seven examples were built. The end of Company Developments's stewardship of Aston Martin was not far off. On 30 December 1974 it declared the business insolvent, owing the parent £750,000, and car production ceased the following day. A creditors' meeting took place in January and the receiver and manager was given six months to dispose of the business as a going concern.

Such events have regularly punctuated Aston Martin's history and, in June 1975, the firm's salvation came from a consortium, which bought the business for £1.05 million. Its two formative members came, independently, from across the Atlantic and both were in their thirties. They were Peter Sprague, an American, who ran the National Semi conductors electronics company and had made something of a speciality of salvaging ailing companies, and George Minden, a Canadian engineer who operated his country's Rolls-Royce dealership from Toronto, sold Aston Martins, and was also a restaurateur. Sprague became chairman and Fred Hartley, previously sales manager, was made managing director. Subsequently, early in 1976, the board of the restructured Aston Martin Lagonda (1975) Ltd was joined by two British businessmen, both of whom had previously put in bids for the business, in the shape of Alan Curtis, who had property and aviation interests, and Denis Flather, recently retired as chairman of his family's Sheffield-based steel company. The engineering team was rebuilt and former experimental department chief Mike Loasby returned to Newport Pagnell as chief engineer. It took nine months to get production restarted, but by the middle of 1976 it was running at six cars a week, which was the same level as three years before.

Like previous incumbents, the new management team recognized that Aston Martin desperately needed a new model to be built alongside the already ageing V8 coupé. The intention was to display the car at the 1976 Motor Show for, above all, it was intended to make a statement to the world that the new regime at Newport Pagnell was deeply committed to the firm's long-term future. Peter Sprague and Alan Curtis found it in the Aston Martin Lagonda which had so fruitlessly appeared at the 1974 Motor Show. It was decided to retain its substructure, and stylist William Towns was commissioned to produce sketches for a new body. Early in 1976, he daringly came up with a futuristic four-door saloon with crisply angular lines. The car had to be ready for that year's Motor Show, then a mere nine months away and, in February 1976, Towns began work on the design. By working 12 hours a day for a month, he completed it by 1 March. Despite being a non-runner the Lagonda made it to the Show.

This 140 mph luxury saloon, which took Aston Martin decisively into Rolls-Royce and Mercedes-Benz territory generated considerable interest. This was not only in response to the car's appearance but to its revolutionary solid state electronic instrumentation. Here the influence of Sprague was apparent, for the read-outs were displayed on what appeared to be a glass screen, just as on an electronic calculator. With a projected price of £20,000, Aston Martin immediately took orders for some 100 cars. But it was not until over two years later, early in 1979, that Lagonda deliveries began in earnest, by which time the car's price had soared to £50,000. The delays had been mostly caused by the car's sophisticated electronics and Alan Curtis, who replaced Hartley as managing director in 1977, was to candidly acknowledge the seriousness of these difficulties. 'All our planning was thrown into total disarray. Suddenly I realized that the way things were going, Aston could go broke again. And it was Peter [Sprague] and myself who were basically responsible: we had to stand up and admit it.'[49]

However, once in production the Lagonda made a very real contribution to Aston Martin's survival and, in 1982 and 1983, the company built more saloons than coupés (76 and 94 Lagondas, compared with 58 and 61 V8s). The model survived until 1990, by which time some 650 had been completed. Curtis had originally hoped that, in the long term, the Lagonda might replace the V8 altogether, but the latter was not neglected. In 1977 the company revived the

concept of the top-line Vantage version which, with a top speed of 170 mph, was one of the world's fastest cars. By the end of that year, Aston Martin was back in profit. In 1978 came the Volante (open) version, as demanded by America, which was the last assignment to be undertaken by Harold Beach, who had so skilfully engineered the road car line of the 1958 to 1974 era.

In 1978 Alan Curtis joined Peter Sprague as joint chairman although, in the autumn of 1979, he became involved in a bid to save the MGB sports car. This followed the announcement by BL Cars, in September, that it was going to discontinue the model (see page 248). Just a month after the decision Curtis had put together a consortium, which had pledged £30 million to rescue the car. There followed lengthy negotiations between the two parties and in April 1980 came the news that agreement had been reached with BL for the Curtis alliance to buy MG's Abingdon factory and that it was to be given a 'licence for the building and sale of MG cars.'

It was with the impending MGB purchase in the offing that the Aston Martin board acquired some new recruits. In January 1980, Peter Cadbury, a consortium member and chairman of Westward Television, became a director, to be followed in May by Tim Hearley, chairman of CH Industrials, descendant of the old Coventry Hood Company, who had a particular interest in the MGB project as it would have required his company's products. He was at the same time joined by old car enthusiast Victor Gauntlett, chairman – and founder in 1972 – of Pace Petroleum, the fortunes of which, in the wake of upwardly spiralling oil prices, were riding high. But then the MG plan began to unravel. The effects of depression were felt throughout the industry and Aston Martin itself was, once again, particularly vulnerable with a profitable 1978 having been followed by a loss in 1979. Despite a last minute attempt by

Curtis to include Toyota in the rescue package, by the summer of 1980 the offer could no longer be sustained. In July 1980, BL stated that the MGB was to cease production later in the year and its Abingdon factory close.

With trading conditions still poor, in mid-1980 Aston Martin decided to adopt a policy to end its total reliance on luxury car sales. Following the example of Lotus, it was to establish a wholly-owned subsidiary as an engineering services company for the industry, under the Aston Martin Tickford name. It was so called because, in 1955, David Brown had bought the old established Tickford coachbuilding company and had then transferred Aston Martin to its Newport Pagnell premises.

By the end of 1980 Aston Martin had built 195 cars, 76 less than in 1979, and Alan Curtis came to believe that the answer to riding out the recession was to reduce production to one vehicle a week. In this proposition he found himself at odds with Gauntlett and Hearley. George Minden had already departed in 1978 and the remaining members of the 1975–6 intake, including Curtis, now left. Gauntlett and Hearley took over as joint chairmen in January 1981, which reflected their respective companies taking on equal 48 per cent share in the business. The four per cent balance was owned by Peter Cadbury, who subsequently sold it to the new owners. Gauntlett also became managing director and the company's name reverted to that of Aston Martin Lagonda Ltd. The new team turned its attention to adapting the Lagonda for sale in America, and the Middle East proved to be a useful growth area which Gauntlett wasted little time in exploiting.

In 1981 Aston Martin Tickford was established at Milton Keynes and the parent company's engineering department was transferred there. Its work for Aston Martin was undertaken on a preferential hourly rate but, in practice, was found to take longer than at Newport Pagnell, on account of the fact that it had never been so scrupulously costed.

Just as it had been for Lotus, 1983 proved to be a crucial year for Aston Martin. The volatile oil market began to exercise an impact on Pace Petroleum as prices fell. This meant that Gauntlett had to spend an increasing amount of time at his oil company's headquarters in Farnham, Surrey. Control of Aston Martin therefore tilted towards CH Industrials, which promoted Bill Archer to the position of managing director. He was to be faced with a discontented work-force and unrest prompted by disagreements over a bonus scheme. Michael Bowler, at the time Pace's public relations manager and Gauntlett's personal assistant, recounts that Archer's 'response to a prolonged period of confrontation was to dismiss the panel beaters. This all but brought the company to the ground.'[50] Simultaneously, Pace began to receive overtures from a suitor which were probably conditional to the oil company divesting itself of the Aston Martin holding. Archer resigned in mid-1983, Gauntlett returned to the factory and, by the end of the year, production had risen, marginally, to 155 cars.

Thankfully salvation was at hand and it came, once again, from America. There Peter Livanos, of the Greek shipping family, had taken a share in Aston Martin Lagonda Inc, the firm's US subsidiary. Along with his fellow countrymen, the brothers Nicholas and John Papanicolaou of the Titan Shipping Brokerage, they created Automotive Investments Inc, which in 1983 took a majority share in the Aston Martin importers. Later that year Automotive Investments went on to buy all of Pace's shareholding in Aston Martin Lagonda, increased to 55 per cent. However, this was conditional on Gauntlett running the business full time and he was able to do so because,

The Jaguar XJ12 of the type which so impressed Sir Don Ryder, made in this upgraded Series II form from 1973 to 1979 with a 285 bhp V12 engine.

with Pace no longer having a stake in the car company, in September 1983 it was brought by the Kuwaiti-backed Hays Group.

Automotive Investments soon exercised its option to buy all the remaining shares in Aston Martin Lagonda, which it did in April 1984. This was in exchange for control of Aston Martin Tickford passing to CH Industrials which, from the outset, had been uneasy about the AII involvement. Hearley accordingly renamed the business Tickford Ltd, and the car company subsequently relinquished all its interests. In the process Aston Martin lost its entire engineering department, both equipment and personnel. Therefore, late in 1983, a new facility was established at Newport Pagnell, under the direction of graduate engineer Bowler and staffed, in part, by former employees.

Just as Aston Martin appeared to be getting back on an even keel, a further crisis arose when the mercurial oil market began to present problems for Titan's tanker business. The result, says Michael Bowler, was that in 1984 Aston Martin Lagonda found itself in the invidious position 'of funding its parent's problems . . . and trading was very tight in the summer of 1984 with cars for America unable to be shipped.'[51] In consequence Peter

Livanos took over the Papanicolaou's holding, giving him 75 per cent of the company, with Gauntlett taking the 25 per cent balance. By the end of 1984, annual production was up 49 to 204 cars built.

The Aston Martin management needed little reminder that the V8 coupé was urgently in need of replacement. Its chassis dated back to the DB4 of 1958 and the lines had first appeared in 1967. For the time being a new car could not be contemplated but Gauntlett came up with the idea of reviving the concept of the legendary two-seater sports racing DB4 Zagato of the 1960s. An approach was made to the Italian styling house and, at the 1985 Geneva Motor Show, the firm displayed an alluring sketch of what was to be called the V8 Vantage Zagato. There it was stated that the model would be capable of 187 mph and cost £70,000, some £25,000 more than the production model. Manufacture would be limited to 50 cars. A £15,000 deposit was required to secure an order, and by August 1985 all of the projected output had been allocated. The first car was completed in 1986, but by this time the price had risen to £87,000.

Nevertheless, the concept was so successful – eventually 52 were built – that a Volante version followed in 1987

and Victor Gauntlett believes that the Vantage Zagato, an exercise in ingenuity on limited resources, was an important factor in Aston Martin being bought that year by Ford. The initiative came from Henry Ford himself and the announcement, made at the 1987 Frankfurt Motor Show, stated that the company had purchased, for an undisclosed sum, a 75 per cent holding in Aston Martin, the 25 per cent balance being shared equally between Gauntlett and Livanos. With no less than six changes of ownership in the 15 years since Sir David Brown had disposed of the business in 1972, the Newport Pagnell team was looking forward to a period of much-needed stability.

Aston Martin's history had been regularly punctuated by receivership, but the same could never be said of Rolls-Royce which had been consistently profitable since its formation in 1905. However, in 1970 the firm recorded its first ever deficit, an interim £3 million, and, on 4 February 1971, the seemingly impossible occurred when Rolls-Royce Ltd declared itself insolvent. Overnight, Edward Heath's Conservative government nationalized the company. A receiver was appointed and, 19 days later, the business was renamed Rolls-Royce (1971) Ltd. Ironically, this extraordinary event was unrelated to the company's Motor Car Division but rooted in the seemingly buoyant Derby-based aero engine business. For Rolls-Royce cars, after years of unprofitability, had since 1968 consistently returned a surplus following the arrival in 1965 of the Silver Shadow, destined to be the best-selling Rolls-Royce car since the Silver Ghost.

As such, the reasons behind the collapse of what was little short of a national institution fall outside of this study. It is sufficient to say that it was the result of the company's decision to develop the RB211, the first of a new generation of so called 'big fan' jet engines. A key element in the specification was that the 25 massive fan blades were to be made of carbon fibre

but, after signing a fixed price contract in 1968 for the RB211 to power Lockheed's TriStar wide-bodied airliner, Rolls-Royce found that these Hyfil blades proved susceptible to bird strikes. They were redesigned in titanium but this put up weight and, in addition, the engine's predicted 40,600 lb thrust failed to materialize.

Rolls-Royce's 3,000 production mark was exceeded in 1975

Development costs soared out of control and the company turned to the Government for support. As a result, in 1970 Sir Denning Pearson was replaced as chairman by Lord Cole but by then it was too late and bankruptcy followed in 1971. It was a tragic vindication of Lord Hives's famous axiom that 'if the engineers are wrong, then we are all wrong.' Thankfully, in 1970 Rolls-Royce had recalled Dr Stanley Hooker, former chief engineer of its jet engines division and recently retired technical director of Bristol, to redesign the RB211. This he successfully accomplished and the TriStar entered service in 1972 but only remained in production until 1984 and never made a profit for its builders.

When Rolls-Royce was nationalized in 1971 it did not include the car, diesel, or light aero engine businesses, which continued trading under the direction of the receiver, E. Rupert Nicholson. The same year the Car Division had a new managing director in the shape of David Plastow, formerly marketing director, who had joined the company in 1956 from Vauxhall where he had served an engineering apprenticeship. Subsequently, in 1973, Rolls-Royce Motors Ltd was offered on the stock exchange for public subscription, so separating the company's car and aviation business after 58 years.

In 1970 Crewe had built 2,009 cars which almost exclusively consisted of the Shadow, to a lesser extent its T Series Bentley equivalent, and the two-door Rolls-Royce Corniche.

Mention should also be made of the low production Phantom VI which was produced at the firm's North London-located Mulliner, Park Ward subsidiary. All models benefited from an enlarged 6.7-litre engine in 1970 and the greatly improved Silver Shadow II with a new split level air-conditioning system followed in 1977. It remained in production until 1980 by which time 27,915 examples of the mainstream saloon had been built since 1965. Its Silver Spirit replacement was, in effect, a rebodied Shadow with revised independent rear suspension.

In 1975 these cars had been joined by the two-door Camargue, based on the Shadow's engineering. At £29,250 it was nearly £6,500 more than the Corniche and only produced in Rolls-Royce form. The model had been a long time coming: work on the project had begun in the late 1960s and the original intention was to market a coachbuilt version of the Shadow. Instead Rolls-Royce commissioned Pinin Farina to design the body, which was to incorporate a new split level air-conditioning system, the design of which had begun in 1968. A prototype was completed at the company's Mulliner, Park Ward works in 1971 but the corporate bankruptcy, subsequent hiving off of the Car Division in 1973, and a damaging strike at Mulliner, all conspired to delay its introduction until 1975. But by then the world was reeling from the effects of the recession.

The Camargue's Pininfarina body lines received a mixed reception, but building the model proved to be a lengthy and unwieldy business. The hull began life at Pressed Steel's Cowley plant, whereupon it went to Mulliner, Park Ward for completion, then to Crewe for rust proofing and engineering. Next it was returned to the London facility for trimming and road test. This took about six months to complete. However, from late 1978 the process was simplified with Cowley's hulls being dispatched to Motor Panels in Coventry and from there on to Crewe and a newly created trimming facility. The Camargue survived until 1986. Just 531 examples had been built, its potential perhaps unrealized.

Despite this modest output, overall demand for Rolls-Royce products grew throughout the 1970s. The 3,000 production mark was broken for the first time in 1975, when 3,134 cars were built, and the 1978 figure of 3,347 stands as an all-time record for the company. But the Rolls-Royce's vulnerability to fluctuations in the financial climate was underlined when output slumped to 2,489 cars in 1982 and 1,568 in 1983. By this time the firm had a new owner in the Vickers engineering group, which bought Rolls-Royce in 1980. David Plastow had been a non-executive director since 1975; he became Vicker's chief executive and his place at Rolls-Royce was taken by George Fenn, formerly materials director of the Car Division.

Since 1933 Rolls-Royce had also built Bentley cars but by the 1970s this marque was in serious danger of being extinguished, a process that was exacerbated by the 1971 bankruptcy, after which corporate efforts were concentrated on the promotion of the Rolls-Royce name. Between 1977 and 1980, sales of the Series T2, the Bentley equivalent of the Silver Shadow II, accounted for a mere 58 cars compared with 10,566 examples of the latter. However, the Bentley version of its Silver Spirit successor, rather than having a designating letter, was given the Mulsanne model name. This was in memory of the famous straight at Le Mans, which had witnessed five Bentley victories between 1924 and 1930. Despite this initiative, by 1982 Bentley sales fell to around five per cent of the total and, unbelievably, Rolls-Royce later acknowledged that it had 'thought seriously about dropping the name.'[52] But market research showed the firm that the 'Bentley appeals to an audience of younger owner drivers who want a comfortable, classically styled car with sporting performance.'

The outcome was the arrival, in 1982, of the Mulsanne Turbo, which marked the beginning of a turnabout in the marque's fortunes because it was only available in Bentley form. This turbocharged model pushed top speed up from around 120 to a limited 135 mph. Despite this improved performance the model's suspension went unchanged until Rolls-Royce rectified the deficiency with the arrival, in 1985, of the Turbo R, in which the 'R' stood for roadholding. Demand for the make began to rise and by 1987 almost half of Rolls-Royce products sold in Britain were Bentleys, an extraordinary transformation in the fortunes of one of Britain's most famous motoring names.

In 1970 a Rolls-Royce Silver Shadow cost £9,272 while, at the other extreme, Britain's cheapest car was the 700 cc Reliant Regal, a fibreglass-bodied three-wheeler that cost £593 and was taxed as a motor cycle. The Reliant Motor Company of Tamworth, Staffordshire, had first begun to exploit this loophole in the law in 1935 when it took over the manufacture of the Raleigh three-wheeled van. The Regal of 1952 was its first car, fibreglass bodywork followed four years later, and the firm's own aluminium 600 cc four-cylinder engine arrived in 1963. The Regal was enlarged to 748 cc in 1973, by which time sales were running at around 14,000 units a year. It was replaced for 1974 by the Ogle-styled Robin, still powered by the faithful four and able to return a respectable 45 mpg. In 1982 the model was joined by the face-lifted Rialto.

In 1969 the Tamworth company took over its Bond rival which had built three-wheelers at Preston, Lancashire, since 1949. This gave Reliant an output of 20,000 vehicles a year, which made it the country's second-largest wholly British-owned car maker behind British Leyland; but this production level was not, alas, maintained. The Bond plant was closed, manufacture transferred to Tamworth and, in 1970, Reliant introduced the wedge shaped 700 cc Reliant-engined Bond Bug three-wheeler, which at least one commentator described as 'looking like a slice of cake on a roller skate.'[53] Despite its price including a

Michael Edwardes addressing BL's 700 union officials and shop stewards in February 1978, when he set out the firm's parlous state and his future plans. On his right is Austin-Morris managing director Ray Horrocks, and on his left, BL International managing director David Andrews. Pat Lowry, industrial relations director, is next to Andrews. (Jonathan Wood Collection)

year's tax, the Bug did not catch on and was discontinued in 1974, taking with it the Bond name.

In 1964 the firm had expanded into the four-wheeled market and the Rebel, which shared the Regal's engine, survived until 1973 although it lacked the appeal of its relative and only around 700 were produced. It was replaced, after a three year gap, by the Kitten of 1975, also Ogle-styled but with its engine enlarged to 845 cc. A total of 4,072 were built by the time production ceased in 1982 but the model was not replaced. Far more successful was the 120 mph GTE of 1968 which combined the carrying capacity of an estate with the performance of a GT. Widely imitated by the Big Battalions, the Ford 3-litre V6 engined, Ogle-styled model took Reliant decisively up-market. If this three-door car had a limitation it was a lack of interior space and, in 1975, after 5,127 had been built, the model was enlarged. Outwardly similar, its successor was both longer and wider than the original and remained in production until 1986.

Since 1964 Reliant had been owned by the Hodge Group of Cardiff and Sir Julian Hodge became its chairman. But the 1970s was a decade of switch-back fortunes for the firm; in 1972–3 Reliant made a profit of £350,000, but in 1973–4 it lost £780,000 as sales of

three-wheelers slumped in the wake of adverse publicity which questioned their stability. By 1976 annual production had dropped to 3,247 cars and, in May 1977, Hodge's Standard and Chartered Bank parent disposed of Reliant to the J. F. Nash Securities financial holding company of Kettering, Northants. Then along came the post-1979 world recession, and Reliant was badly hit. In 1980 it built 582 cars but in 1981 and 1982 production slumped to 89 and 87 respectively. The company urgently needed a new model line which arrived for 1985 in the form of the 1.3-litre Ford-engined Scimitar SS1 sports car. The concept of an open two-seater was a welcome one, as was the entry level price of around £7,000, but the car was let down by its styling, the work of Edgardo Michelotti, son of Giovanni who had so successfully transformed Triumph's visual image in the 1960s.

Reliant's output crept up to 738 cars in the SS1's introductory year of 1985 when the company recorded an interim £600,000 loss and, before long, the world economy took a further nose-dive. The slow-selling sports car was visually face-lifted by William Towns and renamed the SST for 1990 but, in October, Reliant went into receivership. It remained in abeyance for nine months, until August 1991, when the business was bought by Beans

Engineering of Tipton, Staffordshire, a long time subcontractor. This company was a descendant of the firm which had built the Bean car in the 1920s and was purchased by Standard Triumph in 1956. Beans was thus drawn into the creation, in 1968, of the British Leyland Motor Corporation, a body which officially ceased to exist in June 1975 following the Labour government's acceptance of the Ryder report.

This document had been delivered by its author to Industry Secretary, Tony Benn, on 27 March 1975, 14 weeks after it had been commissioned. Benn recorded in his diary. 'Don Ryder came at 9 with his report on British Leyland. He said there would be no redundancies; the company would be turned into four divisions . . . [it] will have to produce a new Mini by 1980'.[54] Benn also noted: 'He's going to sack Barber and Stokes and put in Alex Park who is the finance director. He was obviously very pleased with it and we promised to consider it very quickly after Easter.'[55]

The Ryder Report was then passed to a cabinet committee and, subsequently, on 22 April, debated by the full cabinet. Chancellor of the Exchequer Denis Healey, spoke on behalf of the committee and said that the investment would be £1,500 million, which was equivalent to £2,800 million with inflation over seven years, and would determine the Government's policy for its lifetime. It would be 'a tricky gamble' but the alternative was nearly a million unemployed and the end of the British motor industry. The following day, 23 April, Lord Stokes arrived at the Department of Industry and saw Tony Benn at 8.40 a.m. who recalled that: 'I talked to him alone for about 15 min-

The Austin Metro was launched as a three-door hatchback in October 1980 in 1- and 1.3-litre forms. A five-door version followed in 1984, and it has had two changes of name, to Rover Metro in 1990 and to Rover 100 in 1994. (Austin Rover)

utes. I didn't tell him the details [of Ryder] but I said that the Government had decided that an enormous programme to make British Leyland one of the great motor companies of the world had been agreed, and we wanted him to be associated with it as president of the company, not on the board, and Don Ryder would come in and discuss it in a minute. Well, he took this very well, he is a nice chap . . . I stressed that it would mean a majority Government holding because of the amount of money involved. Well, on hearing this, Donald Stokes was very relaxed about it though he had been tense.'[56]

Later that day Harold Wilson made a lengthy statement to the House of Commons in which he gave details of the Report's findings. In essence, Ryder proposed that British Leyland should continue in both volume and specialist market sectors and the business would, as Benn had noted earlier, be split into four divisions of Cars, Trucks and Buses, International, and Special Products. On the radical creation of a single car Division, Ryder had stated that he and his team recognized there was a need to preserve the distinctive identity of the products, but maintained that 'BL cannot, however, compete successfully as a producer of cars unless it can make the most effective use of all its design, engineering, manufacturing and marketing resources.' Ryder therefore concluded that 'a single integrated car business . . . would serve the best interests of BL in the future.'[57]

At a stroke, John Barber's strategy for moving British Leyland's products up into the more profitable specialist sector was set aside. Ryder predicted that Leyland's share of the home market would be maintained at 33 per cent which took no account of the fact that its penetration had slumped, from 40.6 per cent in 1968 to 32.7 per cent in 1974, and was still falling. During this period Ford had taken over as the country's market leader and imports had tripled from 102,276 to 375,421 cars over the same period.

In addition to the £1,500 million investment programme, the company would also require a further £500 million between 1976 and 1978. The majority of these funds were required, Sir Don explained at the press conference to launch his Report, because 'we found that British Leyland had been suffering from years of under investment. A large proportion of the plant and machinery is old, outdated and inefficient. A massive programme of modernization must be put in hand immediately.'[58] The document stated that the new capital expenditure programme 'should be staged and each new stage should depend on evidence of a contribution, both by the work force and the management, to the reduction of industrial disputes and improved productivity.'[59]

Unless BL raised both output and sales, it must shed labour

On the all-important matter of industrial relations, Sir Don declared: 'We do not subscribe to the view that all the ills of British Leyland can be laid at the door of a strike prone and work shy labour force. But there must be a reduction in the man hours lost through industrial disputes. More productive use must be made of plant and machinery. This must mean more realistic manning levels and more mobility and interchangeability of labour. We have therefore proposed a new structure of joint union management councils, committees and conferences to take advantage of the ideas, the enthusiasms, and the energy of British Leyland's workers in planning the future of the business on which their livelihood depends and to reach agreement on the action required.'[60]

Not only was Ryder's plan thought to be unworkable by the retiring British Leyland management, which might have been expected, but an all-party parliamentary committee, set up after the Corporation's collapse, felt the same way. Chaired by Labour MP

Patrick Duffy, the committee published its findings in a report called 'The Motor Vehicle Industry' in August 1975, three month's after Ryder's. It was highly critical of the Report on a number of key issues. In particular, it questioned how Ryder had costed his programme, and his over optimistic forecast for the British Leyland share of the home market. The committee also believed that he had placed more onus on personalities than structure, which 'could have been avoided by organizing mass produced and quality cars in separate divisions.'[61] The nine-strong committee also censored the plan to gear tranches of cash to industrial relations, maintaining that this was not 'a practical proposition.' Ryder had not recommended any plant closures or redundancies and the committee pointedly concluded: 'Unless the Corporation achieves a very much higher level of output, and related sales than Ryder forecasts, it must shed labour.'[62] At this time British Leyland was at the bottom of the international productivity league in that each of its 191,000 employees was producing 4.9 vehicles, which compared with a European average of 13.

The government body responsible for implementing the Ryder recommendations was the National Enterprise Board, which came into being in November 1975. Its role was similar to that of the Industrial Reorganisation Corporation of the 1964–70 Labour administration, which was to encourage industrial efficiency and profitability. But its first chairman was none other than Ryder himself, who had just been made a life peer, with a brief to see through his own recommendations . . .

By this time the British Leyland Motor Corporation was no more. John Barber had departed although Lord Stokes remained as corporate president. The business had, in June 1975, been renamed British Leyland Ltd, but despite being government funded, it was not a nationalized industry in the accepted sense of the word. This

John Egan, Chairman and Chief Executive at Jaguar from 1980 to 1990, restored morale to the work-force and rebuilt the shattered reputation of the car. He was knighted in 1986. (NMM)

was because of the delay that would have ensued in putting such a bill through parliament, so further clouding the company's already tarnished image in the eyes of the buying public. The Government therefore decided to offer British Leyland stock holders 10p a share and all but a handful responded, with the result that the government's holding in the Corporation stood at an overwhelming 99.8 per cent.

Leyland's non-executive chairman was Sir Ronald Edwards, president of the Beecham Group, but he only held office for four months; he died suddenly in January 1976, and his was place taken by Sir Richard Dobson, former chairman of British American Tobacco. The chief executive, much to his surprise, was British Leyland's former finance director, Alex Park, whilst the individual with the unenviable task of making Ryder's recommendations work was Derrick Whittaker, former head of the Corporation's body and assembly division, who became managing director of Leyland Cars.

Despite the upheavals of 1975, models created during the Stokes era continued to appear and the first of these to reflect its engine options, the 18-22 series, arrived in March. Offered in Austin and Morris forms, with the E Series 1.8-litre four and 2.2-litre six, it

was also available in Wolseley Six form. Replacing the ageing but reliable 1800 and 2200 range, these were distinctive wedge-shaped, roomy, front-wheel drive models. Yet somehow the formula did not work, particularly when a car was empty, because its looks improved when the tail was well down,[63] which was almost an inducement for an owner to drive around with a boot full of luggage. However, within six months of its announcement, in September 1975 the three marque names allocated to the model were dispensed with and replaced with that of Princess. A by-product was the disappearance, after 79 years, of Wolseley, but since Six production had only accounted for some 3,800 cars there were few mourners.

The arrival of a new Leyland make could not disguise the fact that the model suffered from the poor build quality which was continuing to plague the company's cars. In consequence, examples proved to be difficult to sell second-hand and their poor reputation was not enhanced when it emerged that luckless owners of the manual gearbox version of the six were experiencing drive-shaft problems after the car had covered 9,000 or so miles. In consequence, the car was taken out of production for some months during 1978 at which point the automatic version was offered as a 'limited edition' Special Six.[64] Little wonder that, at about this time, Leyland had around 900 vacancies in its engineering design office.

The next new Leyland model, which arrived in May 1975, was visually related to the Princess and, like it, the Triumph TR7 proved to be an inferior product to the TR6 it replaced. This was the company's long-awaited sports car aimed foursquare at the American market and intended to ultimately succeed the ageing but respected MGB. In any event, the MGB GT was discontinued in the US so as not to clash with the new model. The wedge-shaped coupé body was stylistically uneasy although, in theory, there was more potential in the

2-litre slant-mounted single overhead camshaft four-cylinder engine. This 92 bhp unit was related to that of the Triumph Dolomite Sprint but with eight rather than 16 valves, and endowed the TR7 with a top speed approaching 110 mph.

The model was produced in Liverpool, at Leyland's Number 2 plant at Speke, from pressings produced at the Number 1 facility but, sadly, the model entered production before a number of inherent design faults had been rectified. It was also badly built. David Andrews was running Leyland Cars' International Division at this time and recalls his problems with the TR7. A fundamental flaw was that it had been 'originally designed with a four speed derivative of the Marina "55 mm" gearbox but it wasn't up to the job. In a hilly place like San Francisco it just couldn't cope and it reached the stage when I refused to take TR7s with the four speed unit and insisted on a five speed one which was fitted from 1976. But the whole car was unreliable and we were getting terrible warranty problems.'[65]

If 1975 had produced a pair of duds, surely the Solihull designed Rover SD1, which appeared in July 1976,

Norman Tebbit, as Industry Secretary, supported the idea of a new engine for BL, which emerged in 1989 as the twin-ohc aluminium K-Series unit. In this he opposed Prime Minister Margaret Thatcher, who favoured more buying-in of engines from Honda. (Hulton Deutsch Collection Ltd)

offered better prospects? This was a model which encapsulated the Barber approach for moving British Leyland's products up-market and, in theory, a big model meant big profits. Here was a stylish, roomy, 3½-litre V8-powered car with a big opening tailgate from a brand new factory ready to take on the BMW and Mercedes-Benz opposition. Happily, the Rover was well received and became Car of the Year in 1977 but, from the outset, it was in short supply; only 6,816 SD1s were sold in Britain in 1976 while in 1977, the first full year of production, just 12,374 found buyers.

These early examples were poorly finished, an unforgivable shortcoming on any car, let alone a corporate flagship which cost £4,958. Like the TR7, such was the need for the model that it was rushed into production before it was ready, which made it particularly vulnerable because not only was the manufacturing facility untried, but the bodies were produced at Castle Bromwich, which had been equipped with a new paintshop. Solihull's protests to this effect were overruled by Leyland executives and one Rover director subsequently recalled: 'It was a nightmare of a debut for a car which had received so many rave reviews and for which we had so many high hopes. It was two years before it recovered.'[66] Body and paint problems meant that the new Rover soon began to suffer from front end rusting and even worse corrosion developed around the rear wheel arches. Inside the car, the electric windows and central locking mechanism presented problems and the ends of the instrument binnacle had a habit of detaching themselves.

Thankfully, the original SD1 relied on the mechanically proven V8 unit but when the smaller capacity versions arrived in 1977, with Triumph-designed 2.3- and 2.6-litre six-cylinder engines, they were initially plagued with the unreliability to which that marque was notoriously prone. At this point the long-running Triumph 2200 was discontinued. This left Rover as Leyland's principal marque, but its

hitherto almost unblemished reputation had received a serious setback.

The situation at Jaguar was no less happy. It had lost its managing director, Geoffrey Robinson, who resigned in May 1975, officially because of his opposition to the Ryder Report. The truth was rather different. Three months before, Tony Benn had recorded in his diary for 19 February that Robinson had 'twice asked the Board of British Leyland to approve a new paintshop for Jaguar at the cost of £25 million and it had been turned down by the Board and Geoffrey had been quietly ordering the steel . . . It is obviously a very serious piece of industrial ill discipline. On the other hand, to find an industrialist who is secretly investing is so attractive that I couldn't avoid a smile.'[67] Tony Thompson from Cowley replaced Robinson to chair not, alas, a board but the Jaguar operating committee which helped to keep the flame alive. But it had very real problems because, whilst the works was at Browns Lane Plant Large/Special Vehicle Operations, its engines were produced by the separate Radford Engines and Transmissions Plant. Even the reputation of Jaguar's XJ6 mainstay was suffering because 'quality control at Browns Lane was probably worse than it had ever been in the company's history.'[68]

Knight's cunning plan helped save Jaguar Engineering

With the arrival of Leyland Cars, Jaguar was faced with the disbandment of its formidable engineering team which Jim Randle, at the time chief engineer, has rightly maintained 'would have meant the annihilation of the product.'[69] But in June 1975 Leyland unexpectedly announced that the 'Jaguar engineering division is to preserve its autonomy,'[70] which proved to be the one recommendation of Ryder not to be implemented. So how had this all-important reversal come about? Randle is unequivocal

that credit be accorded to engineering director Bob Knight. It was 'through his efforts that we remained free.' For his part, Knight is convinced it was an incident which occurred in the spring of 1975, when Sir Don Ryder's Rolls-Royce burnt out, that played a pivotal role in ensuring that Jaguar Engineering remained independent. Ryder considered a Jaguar XJ6 as a more appropriate replacement and ordered a six-cylinder 4.2-litre model from Browns Lane. But, cannily, Knight prepared a pre-production fuel-injected V12 version which was due to be launched later in the year. It was, he says, 'a very good car, even by the standards of the day.'[71]

The XJ12 saloon was duly dispatched to London but, initially, Ryder's chauffeur refused to take delivery although eventually he did so because Sir Don had a long trip the following day. The morning afterwards, Knight recalls, Ryder rang Geoffrey Robinson at 9 o'clock and 'purred into the telephone about this incredible motor car . . . It was really this experience which caused Ryder to keep Jaguar Engineering as an entity.' Once this had been confirmed Knight also made a point of reporting directly to Leyland's managing director, Derrick Whittaker.

At the beginning of 1975, Jaguar announced that its E-type sports car would cease production that year, but the XJ-S coupé, which arrived in September, could not be regarded as its successor. At £8,900, it was a 155 mph grand tourer. Its lines were more unusual than distinctive, and its arrival could not have been worse timed, as the world was still reeling from the effects of the oil price-rise. The 5.3-litre V12 engine, with automatic transmission, consumed petrol at the rate of around 12 mpg. All of these circumstances together ensured that the XJ-S got off to an uncertain start.

It was not surprising that Jaguar's production fell to 23,688 cars in 1977, which was its lowest figure since 1967. In addition, the Allesley factory suffered strikes during 1976, a microcosm of the industrial unrest felt throughout British Leyland. During the same year there were stoppages at SU Carburettors, Triumph at Canley, Rover's Solihull and Llanelli plants, Longbridge, and Drews Lane, Birmingham. At the end of 1976 Eric Varley, who had succeeded Tony Benn as Industry Secretary the previous year, warned that the Government's commitment to the car company was 'not, of course, open ended.'[72]

The following year was the nadir of the firm's fortunes. A particularly damaging tool makers strike began in February, and *The Economist* reported that 'for the first time since the rescue operation, the Government, the National Enterprise Board and the company management are seriously considering the possibility of eventually shutting part of the troubled car division.'[73] The tool makers remained out for a month, during which time the same magazine spoke for many when it bluntly declared: 'The Ryder plan to save and reconstruct British Leyland is now officially a lame duck. The company is next to being a dying one.'[74] Then, in August, Lord Ryder suddenly resigned from the chairmanship of the National Enterprise Board. His mentor, Harold Wilson, had also stepped down as Prime Minister the previous year and was replaced by James Callaghan. Ryder's place was taken by Leslie Murphy, deputy chairman of Schroder's merchant bank. During the two years of his chairmanship, bizarrely, Ryder had refused to countenance suggestions and comments from members on British Leyland's problems, on the grounds that his position as the Government's industrial adviser insulated him from his NEB role. But with a new chairman, the Board could now candidly discuss the car maker's all too obvious difficulties. If Murphy had any apprehensions of the scale of the crisis, he could not have been reassured by his first meeting with Leyland's chief executive, Alex Park. When he enquired about which BL models made money and which did not, Park

responded: 'I can't find out. The accounting system at BL is such as not to produce an answer.'[75]

As British Leyland drifted, its fortunes appeared fated when, in October 1977, it suddenly lost its chairman, Sir Richard Dobson. He resigned following an incautious remark made at a private dinner party, where he made reference to 'the respectable fact' that BL 'was bribing wogs', comments which were surreptitiously tape-recorded by a guest. His place was taken by the diminutive 47-year-old South African-born Michael Edwardes, who also took over as managing director. An NEB member and chairman of the Chloride Corporation, he was on a three-year secondment from his employers. On 1 November 1977 Edwardes took over what, arguably, was the most difficult job in British industry.

What was the state of the business he was to manage? In 1974, Leyland's share of the British market had stood at 32.7 per cent, but by 1977 this had sunk to a new low of 24.2. Its best-selling model was the Morris Marina, a poor third behind the Ford Cortina and Escort, and followed in turn by the Mini and Allegro, with the Princess and Maxi bringing up the rear with sales of around 30,000 cars a year. The Rover SD1 had experienced a disastrous launch and the situation at Jaguar was no less happy. The company had just suffered its worst-ever year for industrial stoppages; staff morale, to quote Edwardes, 'was at rock bottom' and the cars were probably as badly built as they ever had been. Nevertheless, in 1976 British Leyland had exported over 45 per cent of its output. Conversely, car imports into Britain were running at record levels and had broken the 500,000 unit mark for the first time.

Despite all these difficulties, the car company was just profitable. A loss of £75 million in 1975 had been replaced by a surplus of £112 million in 1976. The following year, when Edwardes arrived, witnessed a pre-tax profit of £77 million, but the post-tax figure was a £5 million loss and the company

was on the point of running out of money again. The number of its factories stood at 55, which was precisely the same figure as in 1975 when Ryder presented his report, whilst the workforce had risen some 4,000 to 195,000 in 1977 and productivity had sunk to four vehicles per employee. Since 1975, such was the industrial turmoil at British Leyland, it had only drawn on £150 million of government funds.

On his arrival, Edwardes recounts that there was considerable support within the company to retain the Ryder-imposed centralized organization. For his part the new chairman believed that 'the Cars structure was claustrophobic . . . Great names like Rover, Austin, Morris, Jaguar and Land-Rover, were being subordinated to a Leyland uniformity that was stifling enthusiasm and local pride . . . Cars operation was split [as at Jaguar] by function and geography . . . In short, the worst type of corporate centralism was at work; I found it stifling.'[76] He was all too aware that British Leyland possessed too many plants and was hopelessly overmanned. But he differed from his predecessors, having a brief from the NEB to reform the company's management. Once installed, he recognized that Leyland had 'a classic case, on a massive scale, of faulty executive appointments – the wrong people in simply hundreds of key jobs.'[77] He used psychological assessment with success at Chloride and now did so at Leyland, as a result of which many managers were asked to resign. Of the company's top 300 executives, 60 replacements were recruited externally and, of the other 240, some 150 found themselves in new positions.

It took Edwardes three years to effect all these changes but at stake was the very future of the company. In February 1978 he unveiled the essence of his Corporate Plan to the trade unions. The Ryder-initiated centralized approach would be disbanded and Leyland Cars split into three roughly equal sized divisions which echoed, in some respects, the approach of the

Stokes era. Where it differed was that, instead of tilting the business towards specialist car production, it would perpetuate the Ryder recommendations of maintaining presences in all market sectors. Volume cars would be produced by Austin Morris, while specialist and sports cars came within the remit of Jaguar Rover Triumph; Land-Rover, which had been perpetually starved of funds, was established as a separate business. Bodies and parts were to be produced by BL Components. Edwardes also began to tackle overmanning and informed the unions that 12,500 jobs would have to go that year, mostly through natural wastage. He also wanted to downgrade the Leyland name and in July 1978 British Leyland Ltd disappeared, to be replaced by a more anonymous BL Ltd with the automobile division being named BL Cars, so allowing the marque names to flourish.

As ever, the head of Austin Morris was a key appointment and it went to Ray Horrocks, ex-Ford and previously head of its Advanced Vehicle Operations. It was Horrocks and David Andrews, also formerly from Ford, who emerged with Edwardes as the management team responsible for the day to day running of the company.

The same day that the chairman was delivering his address, Leyland announced that it was going to close Speke Number 2, the Triumph TR7 plant on Merseyside. It had been on strike at the time of Edwardes's appointment, was still so in February, and the announcement was made with the full knowledge of Prime Minister James Callaghan. Despite strong union opposition, it was shut in May 1978, although the Speke Number 1 pressings facility was unaffected. TR7 production was transferred to Canley and restarted in October. In the intervening five months some 2,000 modifications were made to the sports car with the intention of improving its sales prospects.

Another problem that Edwardes had to address was that British Leyland's ageing and uncompetitive model range was urgently in need of replacement. Where practical, cars would be updated, but new models were desperately needed. When he arrived at Leyland, the one project that was in a well-advanced state was a Mini replacement, coded ADO88, on which over £300 million had been expended. This had suffered badly at consumer clinics and the new chairman decided that it looked 'like turning into a national disaster.'[78] Eight weeks after Edwardes took over, ADO88 was scrapped and replaced with LC8, which retained the previous model's substructure, reskinned to take it into the Super Mini class. The trouble was, this was the market sector that generated some of the lowest profits. A replacement for the ailing Allegro was the priority project but, says Edwardes, 'no amount of juggling could advance the all important LC10 [the Maestro] from its 1983

Launched in 1982, the Ford Sierra had very different lines from the conventional Cortina, and took some time to be accepted by the British public. Six different engine sizes were offered. This is a 2.0GL of 1983. (Nick Georgano)

launch date . . . we didn't have the engineering resources to alter the order . . . switching it would have meant that *neither* could have been launched in 1980.'[79]

Another of Edwardes's briefs from the National Enterprise Board was that British Leyland had been so mortally weakened by this time that its survival was dependent on a collaborative venture with another manufacturer. A dialogue began with a variety of European car makers as well as those in the Far East with the outcome that, in May 1979, an agreement was signed with the Japanese Honda company. One of the attractions was that Honda produced approximately the same quantity of cars as Leyland so would not dominate it. David Andrews, who played a key role in the negotiations, says that 'the attraction for them was a way through into Europe, later an exposure of the executive car market and it provided for us a good challenge for our people and gave them an insight on how things worked in Japan and the foundation of what they were achieving, which up until then had been a bit of a closed book.'[80] As a result, Honda's new Ballade model, then under development, would also be badged a Triumph, with what was coded Bounty due to enter production at Canley in 1981.

By this time Britain had a new government, Margaret Thatcher's Conservatives having won the general election of May 1979. Markedly less interventionist than her predecessor, Thatcher's attitude to BL was that, whilst she applauded Edwardes's firmhanded approach to the trade unions, she deplored the ongoing drain on the exchequer but recognized the calamitous effects on employment and the balance of trade if BL went to the wall. Her choice as Industry Secretary was the 'bone dry' Sir Keith Joseph.

The financial markets liked what they saw. Sterling had begun to rise in January and this, coupled with the recognition that Britain's oil reserves could only improve the country's economic prospects, maintained the upward trend so that by January 1981 the currency was worth 20 per cent more than it had been on election day.[81] For a company such as Leyland, which in 1978 had exported over 40 per cent of its production, this was little short of calamitous. By the summer of 1979 it was losing £900 on every MGB it sold in America. Though BL had made a £75 million profit in 1978 the strengthening of the currency was a major factor in its losses soaring to some £500 million in 1980 and 1981. A further ingredient was that, in January 1979, the Shah of

Iran had fled his country and oil prices had trebled overnight, so triggering the second world recession of the decade.

With such a bleak economic outlook and the fact that while corporate revenue had grown by 3.5 times, fixed expenses had increased by 4.5, Edwardes and his team responded by drastically reducing the company's excess capacity. The diplomatically titled Recovery Plan, announced in September, declared that a further 25,000 jobs would go, the Speke Number 1 and Castle Bromwich pressings facilities would be shut, Triumph production at Canley would cease, and the MG factory at Abingdon would close. This last decision meant the end of the much-loved MGB sports car and produced a public outcry. For a time it seemed as though Aston Martin would take over the marque (see page 238) but the plan collapsed the following summer.

Edwardes decided that the Plan should be put before the entire Leyland work-force in a postal ballot and, of the 80 per cent who did vote, over 106,000 employees, or 87 per cent, approved. In adopting such tactics the BL management was appealing directly to its employees over the heads of their trade union representatives, the plan being consequently fiercely opposed by Derek Robinson ('Red Robbo'), the Communist chairman of the Leyland Combined Trade Union Committee and senior convenor at Longbridge. The Committee produced a pamphlet in response to the projected closures, entitled *The Edwardes Plan and Your Job* which referred to the fact that 'in other industries . . . work-ins and occupations have been necessary to prevent closure. If necessary we shall have to do the same.' In November, Robinson

Badged Aston Martin, the DB7 is Jaguar-powered and made in the Jaguar/Walkinshaw factory rather than at Newport Pagnell. With 335 bhp it is more powerful than the 5.3-litre Virage, yet costs little over half the price. (Aston Martin Lagonda)

was asked to withdraw his name from the pamphlet. He refused and was dismissed, and although this prompted a strike and walk-out, a subsequent mass meeting of the Longbridge work-force, in February 1980, overwhelmingly rejected his reinstatement. (See Chapter Eight). There would be further confrontations between management and the trade unions but, in the public's perception, 'Red Robbo's' dismissal was a significant step along the road to industrial peace.

It was against this background that, in November 1979, Edwardes submitted his 1980 Corporate Plan, which required a £300 million funding, to the National Enterprise Board that was being retained for a time by the Tories. The request received qualified governmental approval, but as the recession deepened output slumped throughout the motor industry and, in 1980, British car production fell below the million mark for the first time since the Suez crisis of 1956. BL built 395,820 cars in 1980, over 100,000 less than in 1979 and, in the meantime, the effects of the Recovery Plan were being felt. Triumph production ceased at Canley in August, which marked the end of the Spitfire sports car and the Dolomite saloon; the origins of both, significantly, were rooted in the 1960s. In the meantime, TR7 production had been transferred, for the second time, to Solihull. The Canley plant was retained by BL but the company's Abingdon factory was sold after the last MGBs had been built there in October 1980. And that, it seemed, was the end of the MG sports car.

As the market contracted the firm continued to reduce its work-force, and in August 1980 it was reported that 'BL is now shedding workers by the thousand. Its hourly paid workers now number fewer than 77,000 (against 89,000 a year ago) and 5,000 of them are on short time.'[82] By then Edwardes and his team had formalized BL's 1981 Corporate Plan. It had become all too apparent that the 1979 Recovery Plan had not been sufficiently radical and further reductions in

capacity would have to be made to reduce the company's annual output to 600,000 cars while still leaving room for some surplus. The most radical decision was that Rover SD1 production would have to cease at the four-year-old Solihull factory and be transferred to Cowley. However, the plant could be used for burgeoning Land- and Range Rover manufacture. This also spelt the end of the TR7 which was prematurely discontinued in 1981, the last mass-produced British sports car of its generation. It had been the best-selling TR ever, with 112,368 examples built, but, conversely, it was also the most unreliable.

Metro was best received corporate car since Morris 1100

1980 was not just a year of cutback and retrenchment. It saw the arrival of the updated Marina, essayed by Ital Design and accordingly named the Morris Ital, and the Allegro appeared in Mark III form; but there could be little doubt that the big event was the culmination of the LC8 project, by then named the Austin Mini Metro, which appeared at the 1980 British Motor Show. Built at a new, robot-infested assembly plant at Longbridge, it was unquestionably the best-received corporate car since the arrival in 1962 of the Morris 1100, no less than 18 years before. *Motor* magazine's correspondent spoke for many when he wrote: 'Like the Mini before it, I can see it becoming a cult car. It looks chic but, above all, it is very good.'[83] Ideally suited for the bleak economic climate, the Mini had taken over as BL's top-selling model in 1979 and, two years later, the Metro took over this pole position. The half millionth example was built in 1984. Updated in 1990, the Metro continues as one of the company's most popular cars at the time of writing (1994). For 1995 it was rebadged as the Rover 100.

The Metro's reception greatly strengthened the hand of the newly

knighted Sir Michael Edwardes when he came to submit BL's 1981 and 1982 Corporate Plans to the Government in November 1980. The requirement was for £1.14 billion, £620 million for 1981–2 and £370 million for 1982–3, which received initial support from Industry Secretary Sir Keith Joseph, who produced a paper in this vein. But after Christmas, in January 1981, when the Plans came to be considered by a cabinet committee, employment secretary Jim Prior recalls: 'He changed his mind completely . . . Against his own paper's advice and against his own Department officials' advice, he was proposing that the state funding of BL should cease and the company put into receivership.' Prior suspected that Sir Keith had allowed 'his more out of touch and extreme friends to persuade him' and the employment secretary found the Prime Minister's response 'fascinating. She was in favour of saving BL . . . But Margaret knew that these decisions did not fit her rhetoric or her image . . . She would therefore conduct a very penetrating cross examination in cabinet and cabinet committee. poor Keith used to have sweat all over his face as he contorted himself and his conscience.'[84]

Mrs Thatcher was all too aware that the Treasury estimated it would cost £3 billion to wind up BL and also add a further 150,000 to the already growing unemployment register. So Edwardes got most of his money, to the tune of £990 million, and the Government also approved of his plan to split the business up into four divisions so that the profitable, healthy parts would not affect the loss making ones, and therefore make them more attractive for privatization. From there on, BL consisted of: BL Cars, Land-Rover, Unipart, and Leyland Group commercial vehicles. Responsibility was also transferred from the National Enterprise Board to Sir Keith's industry department. The creation of Land-Rover as a separate business was an indication that it represented one of the few bright spots, along with Unipart, in an otherwise dark corporate outlook. It had made a profit of some £30 million in 1980 (despite output sinking to a 9,684 unit low), a V8-powered Land-Rover had appeared in 1979, and a much-needed four-door version of the Range Rover arrived in 1981, after waiting in the wings for a decade. But the recession meant that there was little demand for the big SD1 Rover, the production of which had slumped from 37,128 cars in 1979 to 14,732 in 1980, at a factory intended to manufacture it at the rate of 3,000 a week.

Jaguar was, if anything, in an even worse plight. Annual production had been bumping along at around the 13,000 mark in 1979 and 1980 and, when 40-year-old John Egan arrived at Browns Lane in April 1980 the workforce was on strike. Significantly, he was the first chairman of the newly-created Jaguar Cars – which marked the end of the Jaguar Rover Triumph division – since Sir William Lyons's retirement in 1970. But first the dispute, which was over a recognition of skills, had to be resolved. Egan recalls that the unions were 'in the middle of a shoot out with Michael Edwardes. He said that, unless they accepted the standard terms and conditions of BL, then he would definitely close Jaguar down. The work-force said: "Well, you've done everything else to us, you might as well do that" so I thought that I was going to be the only chairman of a car company who never made a single car.' Egan spent the next three days doing some 'very, very hard talking. I had nothing to offer except myself. I said "Well, I'm new. I'm going to do my best." Strangely enough, they agreed that they would have a go.'[85]

Egan had immediately recognized the importance of rebuilding shattered morale and, once the employees were back at work, one of his first actions was to place the famous Jaguar mascot outside the factory gate. But he also wasted little time in turning his attention to the product; the XJ6 had arrived in greatly improved Series III form in 1979, but build quality was still poor. Work had begun in 1976 on a new car coded XJ40 but, says Egan, 'some woolly thinking began to emerge that the XJ40, in some sense, could be the saviour of the company. I always thought it would be far too late. I believed that we always had to turn ourselves around with our existing products.[86] So a customer research programme was put in hand to see how Jaguar compared with its BMW and Mercedes-Benz rivals. This identified

1990 Lotus Elan SE, a potentially good sports car whose chances were damaged by poor build quality and too high a price. (NMM)

150 key areas for improvement which revealed that 60 per cent of complaints related to bought-in components. These findings were conveyed to the component suppliers, which were then made liable for warranty claims. Not surprisingly, these began to lessen in number.

Jaguar made a loss of £47 million in 1980, which was cut back to £32 million in 1981, and production rose slightly to 14,677 cars. The improved 1982 model year cars appeared in August 1981 and, says Egan, 'registrations began to pick up . . . By the following January we were actually making our first profits.'[87] Sales of the thirsty, V12-powered XJ-S coupé had virtually ceased by this time but, thankfully, an HE (for 'high efficiency') version was in the offing and it appeared in 1982. Its arrival was coupled with an improvement in quality and, as the economy began to revive, so did XJ-S sales, thus giving Jaguar the semblance of a two-product line.

Even more significantly, in the public perception John Egan was becoming personally identified with Jaguar's revival, just as Michael Edwardes was with BL's. As this became more apparent, the company became a prime candidate for early privatization. However, once floated on the stock market, it could fall prey to take-over by a foreign car maker. This danger was concerning Norman Tebbit, a self-confessed car enthusiast, appointed Trade and Industry Secretary in 1983, who had received approaches from General Motors and BMW with regard to Jaguar. The response was the government-initiated take-over blocking 'Golden Share', although Tebbit reveals that he 'fought for a very long term "Golden Share" arrangement to frustrate such bids. Unhappily, I could secure only a golden share lasting until 1990.'[88] Jaguar was duly privatized in 1984, and in the following year recorded profits of £120 million. The highly acclaimed new XJ6 appeared in 1986, and in 1988 no less than 51,939 cars left Browns Lane

which represented an all-time production record for the company. Despite this, in international terms it was still a relatively small business. The same year saw BMW and Mercedes-Benz produce 463,651 and 553,772 cars respectively.

Whilst Jaguar was being so impressively revitalized, had Michael Edwardes's 1979 Recovery Plan been adopted a new Triumph would have been being built at Canley, on the other side of Coventry, in 1981. But the disappearance of that production facility in 1980 meant that the car, the first fruit of BL's association with Honda, was produced at Cowley. Announced in October 1980, the Acclaim was, in effect, a rebadged Honda Ballade and although the 1.3-litre front-wheel drive saloon may have been stylistically anonymous, it was destined to be more popular than any Canley built Triumph of the late 1970s. This was an indication, if one had been needed, that, as far as the public was concerned, provided that a car was reliable it mattered little from where the design originated. The Acclaim survived until 1984, by which time 160,157 examples had been built. After an existence of 51 years, the Triumph name disappeared with it.

The next model, the Austin Ambassador, appeared in March 1982 and was clearly derived from the Princess range. In fact, every body panel had been replaced and it incorporated the fifth door which should have featured in the first place. The Princess had received BL's new overhead camshaft O Series engine in 1978 and this was perpetuated in 1.6- and 2-litre forms. Destined to survive until 1984, the model was replaced by the Austin Maestro hatchback which arrived in March 1983.

This all important car, coded LM10, was initially available in 1.3- and 1.6-litre guises. Drivers of the more expensive versions received instructions from a synthesised voice which echoed the gimmickry of the Allegro's quartic steering wheel and the feature was soon dropped. But

whilst the Maestro looked distinctive, it lacked the flair of a Renault R16 and build quality still left something to be desired. One company employee candidly 'described his early Maestro as a "rattling good car", with the stress on rattling.'[89] Whilst the model was to sell reasonably well, the best position it attained in the British sales charts was sixth in 1983–4, but thereafter demand gradually declined although the Maestro remains available at the time of writing (1994).

Its Montego saloon stable-mate arrived in April 1984. Better-looking and better built, it consistently outsold the hatchback and had the distinction of being the last model to be badged an Austin. Like the rest of the corporate range, it lost the 81-year-old name in 1987. The Montego saloon ceased production in 1993, but the model continued in its commodious estate car form until 1994. The Austin marque was not the decade's only casualty, the Montego's appearance in 1984 having marked the end of the Marina-based Morris Ital, which was not replaced. After 71 years, Morris – Britain's most successful make of the inter-war years was no more.

The Maestro and Montego had been conceived under Sir Michael Edwardes's stewardship of BL. He finally stepped down as chairman in September 1982, having extended his original three-year secondment by a further two at the Prime Minister's request. Edwardes left a very different company from the one that he had joined in 1977; car production had dropped by 37 per cent, from 651,067 units that year to 405,116 in 1982, and BL's share of the British market had contracted, from 24.3 to 17.8 per cent, over the same period. Losses stood at £497 million in 1982 although the outgoing chairman predicted that the car business would be back in the black in 1983. The British work-force, of 87,000, was about half that of 1977. On a more positive front, labour disputes had been dramatically reduced and the management was seen to be in control of the business. Strikes had been reduced from 5.9 per cent of working man hours in 1977 to 1.6 in 1982. Factory closures meant that Longbridge and Cowley were now BL's sole car manufacturing facilities but they had undergone much needed modernization and the efficiency of the new Metro line was rivalling some of the best European plants. The model range had been rebuilt, although exports during the Edwardes years had contracted, from 45 to 33 per cent of production, this reflecting the end of the British sports car in America. But Jaguar, still within the BL corral, was fast rebuilding its tarnished reputation there and overseas sales of the Land- and Range Rovers remained buoyant.

With Edwardes's departure, the post of chairman became a non-executive one and went to the low-profile Sir Austen Bide, chairman of Glaxo. BL was thereafter run by two executives, Ray Horrocks, who was responsible for Cars and Unipart, and David Andrews, whose brief was Land-Rover and Leyland commercial vehicles. As Edwardes had predicted, the car business made a small operating profit of £2.7 million in 1983 but, as Ford and General Motors pursued an aggressive price war, it was back in the red in 1984. The reality was that although the Maestro and Montego models were a considerable improvement on their immediate predecessors, neither model was able to repeat the sales success of the less-profitable Metro. The Montego made an impact on the lucrative fleet market, but not a sufficiently large one, and by 1985 was being outsold two to one in Britain by the Vauxhall Cavalier. By maintaining presences in both market sectors, BL combined the model range of a volume producer with the output of a specialist one.

Its share of British sales averaged 17.8 per cent in 1984 and 1985 but the company was still cash hungry. It was also having to bear the burden of a depressed truck market and the privatization, in 1984, of Jaguar. BL recorded a further loss in 1985, of £138 million, greatly to the displea-sure of the Prime Minister. Whilst Margaret Thatcher recognized that considerable progress had been made since the dark days of Leyland Cars, she considered that BL's 'management was still poor. Moreover, the same old bromides were used to justify failure. Next year or the year after was always the time when losses would be turned to profit as long as new investment was provided by the British taxpayer today.'[90]

BL leaked US takeover news when Tories 'most vulnerable'

In her view of BL, she was not always in accord with that of Industry Secretary Norman Tebbit, who supported the firm's need to replace part of its ageing engine range, at a cost of £200 million, with its own purpose-designed power unit. However, Mrs Thatcher believed that the company should 'buy in engines from Honda.'[91] Had this occurred, BL would have been relegated internationally to the role of 'tin basher' but, early in 1985, Tebbit's view held sway and he records that he was able to gain approval for 'the production of a new small engine which, for some time, had been in doubt.'[92] The four-cylinder, twin overhead camshaft unit emerged in 1989 as the universally praised and innovative aluminium K-Series engine.

In 1986, BL's British market share dropped a full two points, to 15.8 per cent, and net losses plummeted to a record £892 million. An undoubted factor in this decline was the turmoil created by the revelations, which broke in February, that the Government was secretly negotiating to sell BL to the Americans. First came news that General Motors wanted to take over Leyland Trucks and Land-Rover, to be followed by the disclosure that similar confidential discussions were taking place with Ford with a view to it absorbing BL Cars. Paul Channon was the newly-appointed Trade and Industry Secretary, but the latter dialogue had begun during Norman Tebbit's occupancy of that office. He has recalled that they followed exchanges, in November 1983, between himself and Ford of Britain's chairman, Sam Toy, of merging Ford and BL's commercial vehicle operations, which led on 'to talks on a takeover of the BL Cars business.'

Interestingly, by this time Tebbit had noticed 'how Ford's view of BL changed as the American company realised that, in some aspects of industrial relations and labour productivity, BL was already ahead of Ford and technical respect grew to the stage of serious discussions of a Ford proposal for the two companies to buy engines from each other, and eventually in 1986 to an interest in a purchase of the whole BL Cars group.'[93] BL was requested to provide Ford with detailed financial information of its car operations and, when the news broke, the Prime Minister considered that 'BL had almost certainly leaked it when we were at our most vulnerable as a result of the Westland affair.'[94] But such was the public outcry, led by MPs of both parties with motoring constituencies who were fearful of the threat to jobs, that on 6 February, after chairing what Mrs Thatcher described as an 'extremely difficult' cabinet meeting, it was decided that the talks should end, a decision that was announced to the House of Commons that afternoon. The General Motors discussions lingered on but had ended by March.

Mrs Thatcher already believed that 'there must . . . be a new management and new chairman at BL, tighter financial disciplines and, above all, a renewed drive for privatization.'[95] A new chairman arrived on 1 May 1986, in the shape of the lanky, bearded Canadian lawyer Graham Day, who had just completed three years of running the nationalized British Shipbuilders. He was destined, in the Prime Minister's eyes, to be a 'superb' chairman of BL. A new, crucial phase in the history of Britain's last significant car maker was about to begin.

The last occasion that the British-owned sector had occupied the number one sales slot was in 1971 when Leyland's 1100/1300 was the country's most popular car, but since then this accolade has been retained by Ford. However, by the 1980s Ford's British registered cars were not necessarily the product of indigenous manufacture, but might have been imported from any one of Ford of Europe's plants in Germany, Belgium, or Spain. Their long-running and highly successful Cortina line, having come to an end in 1982, was replaced by the Sierra, visually a very different concept from its ultra-conventional predecessor. The aerodynamically honed lines represented something of a gamble for the conservative Ford company and the first example left the production line, at Genk, Belgium, in June 1982. Also built in Germany, in 1983 manufacture was extended to Britain. Engines ranged from 1.3 to 3 litres but the Sierra did not succeed in repeating the Cortina's sales success. In 1983 it was in second place in the British sales league but by 1984 had dropped to fifth, having been decisively outsold by the Vauxhall Cavalier, and Ford spoke of its sales forecast having been 'wildly optimistic'. Changes to the car's front end for 1985, and a greater acceptance by the public of its lines, helped to put the Sierra back as Britain's second-best selling car in 1989 and it maintained a strong presence until production ceased in 1993.

The Ford that did take the number one sales slot from the Cortina in 1982 was project Erika, which had emerged as the front-wheel drive Escort of 1980 and replaced the popular rear drive model of the same name. Like all models of this generation, allocation of design responsibility within Ford of Europe is far from clear cut but, very approximately, Britain's Dunton plant was assigned the Escort's engine development, suspension, steering, brakes, and interior, with Merkenich in Germany being allotted styling, engine structure, transmission, and final

proving.[96] Endowed by Ford's styling director Uwe Bahnsen – who, perversely, was Essex-based – with what he described as a 'rear end bustle' intended to suggest the presence of a boot, the car was actually a hatchback. Engine options varied from 1.1 to 1.6 litres in Britain, where the car was built at Halewood, and there were hopes of it being a true world car, being produced in both Europe and America, but in practice it was modified in accordance with local requirements. The Escort remained Britain's top-selling car until 1990, when it was replaced by a Mark II version which did not attain the number one slot until 1992 (this having been occupied, in the meantime, by Ford's Fiesta).

The company's first true world car since the demise of the Model T in 1927 was the Mondeo, which replaced the Sierra in 1993. Once again the work of Ford of Europe, it followed much of the advanced and pre-planning work being undertaken in America which, in 1987, was transferred across the Atlantic. Widely acclaimed, it is once again difficult to disengage the creative responsibility between Britain and Germany although vice president Richard Parry-Jones is credited with being the driving force behind the model. But despite a strong British input, the Mondeo is produced exclusively at Ford's Genk plant. Those intended for the European market are powered by the Zeta engines of 1.6- to 2-litre capacity, manufactured at Bridgend, South Wales, and Cologne, Germany. From 1994 American Mondeos have been powered by a US-designed and built 2.5-litre V6 engine which is also available in Europe. As these are shipped across the Atlantic, they pass *en route* batches of the Mondeo's five-speed manual gearbox destined for the New World, all part of the international jigsaw that is Ford.

Following the successful launch of the Mondeo came news, in 1994, that the company's global operations were to be restructured under the Ford 2000 umbrella. Since 1995 the company's

hitherto autonomous European and North American operations have been merged under a single new organization of Ford Automotive Operations (FAO). In this realignment, Europe has taken over responsibility for the world's front-wheel drive cars with America allocated the larger rear drive models. So whilst Dunton is now involved in creating cars for a global market, the same progression, alas, cannot be accorded to Ford's British manufacturing operation that now produces only two models, the UK-built Sierra not having been replaced. Today Halewood is responsible for the Escort, and Dagenham the Fiesta, whilst German Ford output, of some 600,000 cars a year, is about double that of Britain's. This is a reversal of roles, for in the 1950s Dagenham decisively outstripped the production of the then separate Cologne plant to the tune of nearly four to one.

Although BL had ceased to be a serious rival to Ford, a significant challenge to its dominance of the British market has come from its General Motors rival in the form of the German-designed, British-built Vauxhalls, and is a momentum that continues to this day. The assault was spearheaded by the 1.3/1.6-litre Cavalier – the Opel Ascona in Germany – which, as GM's international J-Car, was impressively revised in front-wheel drive form for 1982. By 1984 it was Britain's second-best selling model, sandwiched between the Ford Escort and Ford Fiesta. Two other Vauxhalls, the Spanish-built 993 cc 1.3-litre Nova small car, and the medium-sized Astra – otherwise the Opel Kadett – produced at Ellesmere Port after a £50 million refit, also featured in that year's top ten. General Motors kept up the pressure with its J'89 project, which appeared as the revised Cavalier for 1989, and by 1993 the make was mainly responsible for eroding Ford's best ever 31 per cent penetration of the British market, attained in 1981, to 21.4. This put it second in the market with a 17.09 per cent share, and in July 1993 Vauxhall

The arrival of the Japanese is, unquestionably, the most significant change to the constitution of the British motor industry since Ford set up their Manchester plant before the First World War. The first Japanese-designed car to be assembled in Britain was the Nissan Bluebird. Assembly began in 1986 and full-scale manufacture in 1988. This is a Bluebird 2.0 GLX hatchback, which gave way to the Primera in 1990. (Nissan Motor (GB) Ltd)

topped the British sales figures for the first time ever.

It will be recalled that Chrysler, the third of the American 'big three', had disposed of its British operations to Peugeot in 1978. As chairman and managing director the French company appointed George Turnbull, who had completed his South Korean assignment and returned to Britain in 1978, and the business was renamed Talbot UK in 1979. Turnbull could not have arrived at a worse time, as the effects of the oil price-rise were soon beginning to bite and Talbot's share of the British market slumped from 7.7 per cent in 1978 to a record low of 3.6 per cent in 1982. The company's best-seller was the Chrysler Alpine, as it was initially badged, to be followed in 1979 by the Simca 1100-based Talbot Horizon which from 1982 was built at Ryton.

It was in the depths of the recession that, in 1981, Peugeot decided to shut its troubled Linwood factory, opened by Rootes in 1962, and with the closure went any hopes of expanding the motor industry into Scotland. This left Talbot with just two plants, one at

Stoke in Coventry the other – the principal facility – at Ryton, just outside the city. Losses soared, amounting to £61.9 million in 1981 alone, but in 1984 came a return to profitability, at which point George Turnbull completed his five-year contract with Peugeot.

His replacement as managing director was Geoffrey Whalen, who had joined Talbot in 1980 as personnel and industrial relations director. In 1985 the Horizon was replaced by the Peugeot 309 saloon, and in the following year the French firm completed a £30 million refit of the Ryton plant in the wake of impressive improvements in productivity and build quality. Whalen had frankly declared in 1985: 'Four years ago, we weren't really very good. We had all the faults of car makers of the 1970s, bad industrial relations, production volumes were inconsistent, production was inadequate and quality was indifferent. The French wouldn't have invested in the UK if our attitude hadn't changed.'[97] Tough talking had taken place with the unions over manning levels and 'we have put responsibility back in the

hands of managers and supervisors.' As a result, the Ryton-built cars equalled any produced within the Peugeot Group.

The Talbot name disappeared from Britain in 1987. Thereafter all cars were badged Peugeot, despite the company still being named Peugeot Talbot Ltd. By this time Stoke had ceased operating as a production facility although the company's headquarters are still based there. Manufacture of the 1.1/1.9-litre 309 ceased in 1989 but, two years previously, it had been joined by the 1.6/1.9-litre 405. In 1993 the British subsidiary lost £8.7 million in a depressed market, but the following year Peugeot announced that it was going to invest a further £150 million in Ryton, with the aim of increasing output by 25 per cent from 1,600 to 2,000 cars a week. The former Rootes facility has become Peugeot's sole manufacturer of right-hand-drive models for the quality-conscious Japanese market and, in addition, production of the popular 306 range has begun there. Productivity has also been increasing in recent years, with Ryton's 3,000 employees achieving, in 1992, a 12 per cent improvement on the previous year and a further six per cent in 1993.

That year Peugeot was fourth in the British sales league, behind Ford, Vauxhall, and Rover, although the majority of its products are imported from France and, to a lesser extent, Spain. For the French company, the purchase of Chrysler UK has worked well but the reality is that its products are designed on the other side of the English Channel and not in Britain. This transition became all too obvious when, in 1986, Peugeot sold to Jaguar the former Chrysler design centre at Whitley, Coventry, once coveted by BL.

Despite the newly privatized company recording profits of £120 million in 1986, by the middle of the following year the weakness of the dollar was beginning to adversely affect Jaguar, dependent as it was on transatlantic sales for over half its revenue. However, in 1988 corporate morale received a fillip when, after 31 years, Jaguar was once again victorious in the Le Mans 24 hour race although, unlike its C- and D-type predecessors, the winning XJR-9 was built not at Browns Lane, but by Tom Walkinshaw Racing, based at Bloxham near Banbury, Oxfordshire.

Jaguar's chairman Sir John Egan (knighted 1986) was all too aware that his company's future prospects were overshadowed by the Government's take-over blocking 'Golden Share' that was destined to expire at the end of 1990. But in September 1989 news broke that General Motors had been engaged in a nine-month dialogue with Jaguar and, as its preferred partner, was intending to take a minority 29.9 per cent shareholding in the business, which would continue to remain independent. Interestingly, though, nearly a year earlier Ford had been showing interest, as Alan Clark recorded in his

diary entry for 17 October 1988: 'I took the opportunity to warn her [Mrs Thatcher] about Jaguar being in jeopardy, which she didn't like.' In a footnote he expands: 'Sir John Egan had told AC that Ford of America were buying Jaguar shares systematically and threatening a take-over.'[98]

Within days of the GM announcement, Ford responded with a declaration that it proposed to take a 15 per cent stake in Jaguar – the maximum permitted under the Government's 'Golden Share' scheme – with a view to becoming the company's owner. The pace quickened when, on 31 October, free market principles prevailed and the Government lifted its 'Golden Share' restriction, which still had 14 months to run. This inevitably spelt the end of Jaguar as a British-owned car company and there was little surprise when it subsequently emerged that the decision had been

taken in the face of strong opposition from Egan and his board. Ford offered 850p a share, which amounted to a £1.6 billion bid; there was no comparable response from GM and on 1 November 1989 it was overwhelmingly approved by Jaguar's shareholders. This compared with £238 million that the company raised when it had been floated on the stock market only four years before. Board, governmental and formal shareholder approval rapidly followed and, after 58 years as a car maker, Jaguar was in American hands.

Sir John Egan departed in mid-1990, but not before he witnessed a second Jaguar triumph at Le Mans, with another XJR-12 in second place. Egan was replaced by Ford's Bill Hayden but the company had few illusions about Jaguar's manufacturing facilities which were suffering from years of under-investment. After his first tour of the factory, Hayden

The British-built Nissan Micra was voted Best Small Hatchback by Autocar *in 1993. By 1991 Nissan was Britain's most efficient car factory.* (Nissan Motor (GB) Ltd)

remarked: 'I've been to car plants all around the world. Apart from some Russian factories, Jaguar's was the worst I'd ever seen.'[99] Earlier, in a celebrated exchange with a group of city analysts, Ford's British-born Alex Trotman, today company chairman, had quipped: 'There's nothing wrong with Jaguar that a bulldozer through Browns Lane would not put right.'[100]

Ford inherited the XJ6 saloon and XJS coupé model lines, scrapping a projected F-type sports car, but was soon feeling the effects of the world recession. Jaguar's losses accelerated and by 1992 annual production had slumped to 20,601 cars. Thankfully the corner was turned in the first half of 1993, when sales leapt by 46 per cent, and in 1994 Jaguar unveiled an acclaimed revised version of the XJ6. This retains the centre section of its predecessor with new front and tail sections and there is a top of the range, headline grabbing 150 mph XJR, powered by a 321 bhp supercharged 4-litre version of the twin cam six. The model has been developed in tandem with a £100 million investment programme which has updated Jaguar's body building facilities at Castle Bromwich, its Radford engine plant, and Browns Lane final assembly line. With a new sports car and smaller model in the Mark II idiom of the 1960s in the offing, a reinvigorated Jaguar looks set to take on the best that Germany and Japan can offer.

When Ford bought Jaguar in 1989 it meant that, within a little over two years, this American company had acquired two of Britain's most respected sporting marques. The other, it will be remembered, was its 1987 purchase of Aston Martin, and this dual ownership has made possible the creation of the 3.2-litre DB7 coupé, which is the first Jaguar-engined model in Aston Martin's history. Based on Browns Lane's aborted F-type project and announced in 1993, it has been superbly styled by Ian Callum and seems destined to become numerically the most successful Aston Martin since the 1960s when the DB4/5 and 6

models were at the height of their popularity.

DB7 production began at the Jaguar/Walkinshaw facility near Banbury in 1994, whilst the costly, low-volume Virage continues to be built at Aston Martin's Newport Pagnell factory. This long-awaited replacement for the ageing V8 model appeared at the 1988 British Motor Show, a year after the Ford take-over, work on the project having only begun in 1986. With a new coupé body, essayed by the Heffernan/Greenley partnership, it retains the 5.3-litre capacity of the V8 but incorporates new four valve cylinder heads. However, a top speed of 155 mph meant that the Virage was only marginally faster than the V8 model it was due to replace. This was discontinued, after a 20-year run, in 1989 and Virage production began in earnest in 1990. In the usual Aston Martin tradition there was a Volante (open) version of the model which became available early in 1992.

Victor Gauntlett had remained as chairman at the new owner's request, but he departed in 1991 and was replaced by Walter Hayes, an old Ford hand. In 1992 came a tacit recognition by the factory that the Virage needed to be faster and, for £50,000, customers could have their existing cars uprated to 6.3 litres, with a 40 per cent increase in power to 465 bhp. This endowed it with a top speed of 174 mph, some 20 mph more than the original. Vulnerable as ever to the effects of recession, however, Aston Martin saw production drop in 1992 to two cars a week, consisting exclusively of the Virage Volante as demand for the coupé had all but evaporated. For 1993 the company unveiled the more muscular Vantage Virage, outwardly only the doors and roof panel of the original having been retained. The 5.3-litre engine was extensively modified and boosted by the presence of twin Eaton superchargers. Selling for £177,600, the company claims that it has a top speed of 185 mph.

Although output had slumped, from

167 cars built in 1991 to a mere 60 in 1992, Hayes, as a vice president of Ford of Europe, possessed the corporate clout to initiate the creation of the DB7, Sir David Brown having given permission for his initials to reappear on the model before his death in 1993. The new car, selling for £78,500, did not come a moment too soon. Ford is also contemplating reviving the concept of the Lagonda saloon, appropriately powered by a V12 engine, using, in essence, two V6 Mondeo units mounted in tandem.

Whilst Ford's ownership of Aston Martin has underpinned its long term future, mention should be made of AC, the second British sports car company which Ford bought in 1987. With the demise in 1973 of the Cobra-based 428 model, AC announced its 3-litre Ford V6 mid-engined ME 3000 coupé, although there was a six-year hiatus before it entered production in 1979. Only 71 were built by 1984. The car was then licensed to a Scottish company but a mere 18 examples were produced in Glasgow before that business went into receivership in 1985. In the meantime, Brian Angliss's AC Autokraft had begun building replica Cobras and had a 40 per cent holding in AC Cars. He initiated a Len Bailey-designed, Ford-engined, four-wheel drive AC Ace convertible and a prototype appeared on the Ford stand at the 1986 London Motor Show. In October 1987, four weeks after it had taken over Aston Martin, Ford announced the purchase of a controlling interest in AC Cars – the balance was retained by Angliss – with the intention of putting the Ace into production. But subsequently, in 1990, the deal was unscrambled; the AC name and the Ace thereafter reverted to Autokraft and the revised 5-litre Ford V8-powered rear drive car entered limited production at its factory, located within the old Brooklands motor course, in 1994.

So AC survives in much slimmed-down form, which status similarly applies to Lotus that had also been owned by an American car company

– General Motors – which subsequently disposed of its ownership. However, this was not before GM had invested £100 million in a business which saw its losses rise from £2.1 to £12.7 million between 1988 and 1990. At the time of GM's 1987 take-over, Lotus was producing the Excel and mid-engined Esprit and Esprit Turbo. For 1988 the Esprit range was revised with new, softer body lines although the Excel continued in its original form and survived until 1992, by which time 1,327 examples had been completed.

The long-awaited Elan replacement finally appeared, nine years after the concept had been first mooted, at the 1989 London Motor Show. Appropriately reviving the name of its famous predecessor, on paper the concept looked impressive; a fibre glass-bodied front-wheel drive open two-seater powered by a 1.6-litre twin overhead camshaft four-cylinder engine – also available in turbocharged form – from the Japanese Isuzu concern, in which GM has an interest. Top speed was in excess of 120 mph. Production began in earnest early in 1990 but a mere two and half years later, in June 1992, Lotus announced that it was discontinuing the car's manufacture, and did so the following month, after 3,885 examples had been built.

So what killed what was, arguably, the most significant British sports car of its generation? One factor was timing; the Elan's arrival coincided with the onset of the world recession which played havoc with sales not only in Britain but also in America – just 250 were sold there in 1991 – and the old Lotus bugbear of poor build quality also reared its head. A contemporary opinion was articulately voiced by Lotus specialist and enthusiast Miles Wilkins, when he declared that: 'The Elan was too long in gestation, fiercely difficult to build, even more difficult to repair and far too expensive. By the time it got to the market, the Japanese were already there. Of course it goes like hell but costing £25,000 it ought to.'[101] The Japanese car in question

was Mazda's front engine/rear drive, no frills MX-5 roadster which undercut the Lotus by a substantial £7,700 and, paradoxically, was inspired by British sports cars of the 1960s which included the original Elan.

The new model's arrival had seen Lotus's annual production soar to 2,241 cars in 1992 but it fell back again to 688 in 1993 and, in February that year, General Motors announced that both the car and the engineering business were for sale. They were bought six months later, in August, by the revived, Italian-based Bugatti company which has declared its intention that the Lotus sports car will continue. In the meantime, the Esprit models remain in production and, in 1994, the balance of 800 Elans were completed from spare parts.

If there is a question mark over Lotus's future, the prospects for another British sports car company appear, against all the odds, rather brighter. TVR Engineering is one of the handful of firms which today constitute the British-owned motor industry. The origins of the Blackpool-based company go back to 1947 when Trevor

Wilkinson established the Trevcar Motors garage business in the city. Soon afterwards, Wilkinson imbued TVR Engineering with the bones of his Christian name (TreVoR) and proceeded, in 1949, to build the first of a number of specials with a multi tubular chassis which later, in 1956, were fitted with fibreglass bodywork. They were followed by the Grantura coupé of 1958, the first recognizable TVR model, and some 500 were produced between then and 1962. But financial problems were commonplace. Layton Sports Cars took over in 1958, a Grantura Engineering subsidiary was formed in the following year, and Wilkinson departed. In 1961 the business was refinanced by Aitchinson-Hopton of Chester and TVR Cars established. Yet by the autumn of 1965 the company had once again collapsed and, in November, the assets of Grantura Engineering were bought by TVR dealer Arthur Lilley and his son Martin, who was responsible for the day to day running of the factory.

The arrival of the Lilleys heralded an uncharacteristic period of stability for the firm with the establishment of

The first British-built Honda Accord leaving the production line at the £70 million factory at Swindon on 8 October 1992. (Honda (UK) Ltd)

TVR Engineering, which is the company that builds TVR cars today. Existing models had to be seen through but the really significant car of the Lilley stewardship came with the 1980 arrival of the Tasmin, named after a girlfriend of Martin Lilley's, which had no carry-overs from previous models. Styled by Oliver Winterbottom, who had the lines of the Lotus Eclat and Excel to his credit, power came from a 2.8-litre Ford V6 engine.

It was a Tasmin owner, 38-year-old Martin Wheeler, who ended the Lilleys' 16-year ownership of TVR when he bought the company in December 1981. A graduate chemical engineer, he had run a successful business selling specialist equipment to the fast-growing North Sea oil industry. Wheeler's arrival saw the Tasmin name progressively phased out following the appearance, in 1983, of a 3½-litre Rover-powered version of the model, titled 350i to indicate its engine capacity. The V6 model accordingly became, from 1985, the 280i and continued in production until 1988. Inevitably, it was overshadowed by the bigger-engined car which, with a top speed of over 135 mph, was around 5 mph faster than the V6. In 1984 the 350i was offered with an optional 3.9-litre engine which was subsequently available in TVR modified 4-, 4.2- and, ultimately, 4.5-litre forms. The final example of the Tasmin family was built in the autumn of 1991.

By this time TVR had introduced its S-type two-seater convertible, competitively priced on its 1986 introduction at £12,995 and powered by 2.8-litre Ford V6 engine. The styling, though not the chassis, was reminiscent of TVR's popular 3000S model of the 1970s and a 2.9-litre S2 version followed in 1988. Destined to be the company's best-seller of its day, some 2,200 examples were built before production ceased in 1993. But by this time, the fabulous Griffith was occupying centre stage.

The prototype Griffith two-seater roadster was unveiled at the 1990 British Motor Show and employed an S-type chassis and 3.9-litre Rover V8 engine. But it was the magnificently contoured body, a complete departure from the Tasmin's angular look, that really drew the crowds. At one point during the show, TVR staff were taking orders at the rate of one every eight minutes. By the end of the event, over 350 individuals had committed themselves to the new car. It subsequently emerged that the sensational lines were the work of Wheeler himself and his new stylist, John Ravenscroft, who had sculpted the shape from blocks of plastic foam.

Despite this overnight success, it would be about 18 months before the first cars were delivered, early in 1992. In the meantime the chassis had been redesigned and the engine enlarged to 4.2 litres. By the middle of the year 15 cars a week were leaving TVR's Bristol Avenue factory.[102] At over £27,000 apiece, the Griffith was capable of over 160 mph, but production for the home market ceased at the end of 1992. However, in the middle of the following year the car emerged as the 5-litre Griffith 500 for the 1994 season.

That model's arrival did not prevent TVR from producing yet another new car in the form of the visually and mechanically similar Chimaera which entered production in 1993. Rumour has it that the distinctive front turn indicator recesses were the work of Wheeler's gundog, Ned, who had taken a bite out of the foam body master . . . The model is tamer than the Griffith but cheaper and more popular. It is offered with a range of 4- and 4.3-litre Rover V8-based engines, but TVR is also planning its own V8.

The net result of all this frenetic activity is that, at a time when many other companies were making cutbacks in production, TVR was building the highest number of cars in its history. In 1993 it manufactured over 900, of which some 90 per cent were intended for the home market that Peter Wheeler prefers to serve. This contrasts with 1978 when 45 per cent of production was exported, mostly to America.

If TVR had experienced multiple changes of ownership during its initially turbulent post-war history, then the reverse is true of Morgan, established in 1910 and still in the hands of its founder's family. The cars are still built in their traditional way, despite the fact that, in 1990, Morgan was featured by former ICI chairman Sir John Harvey-Jones in his BBC Television *Troubleshooters* series. He suggested that the firm double production with a view to reducing its long waiting list, increase its prices, and streamline the manufacturing process. Morgan responded by continuing to build its cars just as it had done for decades, and today the cars are still as popular as ever. British customers will have to wait five or six years before they are able to take delivery of a new Morgan . . .

So it is very much the mixture as before, with the current Morgan range consisting of the 4/4, revived in 1955; the Plus 8, which dates from 1968; and the Plus 4 of the 1951–62 era, that reappeared in 1985. Externally, the 4/4 looks much the same as it did in the 1950s and the 4/4 1600 of 1968 was powered by the 1.6-litre Ford ohv Kent engine. With its replacement in 1982 came a choice of 1.6-litre fours: Ford's XR3 Escort overhead camshaft CVH series, or the fuel-injected twin cam Fiat 131 Supermirafiori unit, the first occasion that Morgan has used an engine from an overseas manufacturer. In 1985 it was extended, in 2-litre form, to the 4/4-based revived Plus 4.

Fiat's decision to switch its model range exclusively to front-wheel drive made these engines unsuitable for use by Morgan and in 1987 both models reverted to the Ford four. But in 1988 came a switch to Rover's 2-litre M16 16-valve engine, although for 1994 the 4/4 once again became Ford-powered by Morgan's adoption of the 2-litre twin cam Zeta unit. However, the Plus 4, now with a Plus 8 style body, has Rover's T16 2-litre four under its louvred bonnet. By contrast, the Plus

8 has been Rover-powered from the outset although it has benefited from updates as the unit has been enlarged and refined by its makers. Beneath the surface, the dated separate Moss gearbox was dispensed with, to be replaced in 1972 by Rover's four-speed unit, and a five-speed all-synchromesh followed in 1977. The current 120 mph car has a fuel-injected 3.9-litre V8 and there is a 4.2 option.

Morgan is currently producing around 480 cars a year, of which no less than 52 per cent are exported, with Germany as the principal overseas market. Some ten cars a week leave the Malvern factory, with the Plus 8 currently in the greatest demand. The Morgan work-force numbers some 198 individuals and, such is the state of the ever-lengthening waiting list, Morgan is in the enviable position of having already sold sufficient cars to take it into the twenty-first century.

Between 1910 and 1935 Morgan only built three-wheelers but today the revived Reliant concern remains the industry's sole manufacturer of that breed. Currently, some 80 employees build around 20 examples of the 850 cc Robin and the Rialto estate each week. The low production Reliant Scimitar Sabre sports car accounts for a further five units with the entry-level model now using the 1.4-litre Rover K Series engine. The faster version employs the 1.8-litre turbocharged Nissan four, courtesy of the Silvia Turbo ZX of 1984–9 vintage.

At the other end of the automotive spectrum, the switchback fortunes of Rolls-Royce have underlined the vulnerability of a specialist manufacturer with an ageing product range and a 2,000 cars a year break-even threshold. Output rose every year from the 1,568 unit low of 1983 and there came a return to profitability in 1984 as production jumped to 2,201, reaching an 11-year high in 1990 when 3,274 cars left Crewe. Thereafter Rolls-Royce tumbled back into deficit in 1991. In the following year output sunk to 1,258 cars and losses rose to some £20 million. But the business was back in the

black in the second half of 1994. Little wonder that, in early 1992, Rolls-Royce closed its North London-based Mulliner, Park Ward subsidiary, and with it went a relic of another age the form of the commodious Phantom VI limousine. However, the current Silver Spirit has a substructure dating back to 1965 whilst its V8 engine first appeared in 1959 and, in these circumstances, new models are urgently needed. Alas, in 1991 Rolls-Royce's Vickers parent was unable to finance such a project and the car company was discreetly put up for sale.

In 1992 came news of technical co-operation with BMW but, with a return to profitability in the offing,

Carina E bodies on the final weld line at Toyota's Burnaston factory. Engines are made at a separate plant at Deeside, North Wales. Components come from several European countries including France, Belgium, Germany, Austria, Spain and Italy. Less than five per cent of these suppliers have Japanese parentage. (Toyota (UK) Ltd)

early in 1994 Vickers announced that Rolls-Royce was a core business and, as such, was one which it no longer wished to sell. Of the £200 to £300 million required to build a new car, it was prepared to contribute £100 million, with the balance coming from co-operation with a partner.[103] Subsequently it was revealed that talks were taking place to this end with BMW, Mercedes-Benz, and Ford. These took concrete form at the end of 1994, when it was announced that future Rolls-Royce and Bentley cars would use V8 and V12 engines from BMW. These would be modified to Rolls's own specification, with development split between RR, BMW, and Cosworth, which is also owned by the Vickers group. The Bentley Java convertible, planned to go on sale in 1999, would make use of the BMW 5 Series floorpan and turbocharged V8 engine.

On the marketing front, Bentley has continued to maintain the progress begun in the 1980s and the production, in 1990, of 1,744 cars outstripped the 1,530 Rolls-Royces built, so rekindling a dominance that had been dormant since the 1950s; and Bentley, with its formidable sporting pedigree, having once overtaken Rolls-Royce has stayed in front. The marque's revival was given an added impetus when, in 1991, Rolls-Royce announced the Continental R coupé, which is the first Bentley to have a purpose-designed body since the demise of its S-type namesake in 1959. Styling was the work of John Heffernan and Kenneth Greenley and the 6.7-litre turbocharged engine is closely related to that of the Turbo R saloon, which continues in production. For its part the luxurious 145 mph coupé is being built at the rate of 70 examples a year.

Like Rolls-Royce, Bristol is also seeking a partner to develop its next generation of cars; the current model's BMW-related chassis is even older than the Silver Spirit's and dates back to the marque's origins in 1947. This became all too apparent when, in mid-1993, Bristol announced its new Blenheim model for 1994 which is, in effect, the Britannia/Beaufort line enhanced by the presence of new front and rear ends. Priced at £109,980, the Blenheim retains its predecessor's 5.9-litre Chrysler V8 engine and is fitted with a new four-speed automatic gearbox. Bristol's owner, 70-year-old Anthony Crook, has cautioned that the Blenheim is likely to be the last model he could develop single-handed, informing *Autocar & Motor*: 'I can't go on financing Bristol forever; I'm not indestructible, even if the cars are.' With a 'completely new car' in the off-

The Honda Ballade-based Triumph Acclaim gave way in 1984 to the Rover 200 series, somewhat misleadingly described in advertising as 'Born to be Rover'. With the 1300 engine it was pure Honda apart from its individual front end. The later 1600, such as this 1988 216SE, used the Austin-Rover S-Series engine. In its fuel-injected form it gave 104 bhp. (Nick Georgano)

ing, 'the time has come to share the burden, but I'd like Bristol to go on as an independent British company.'[104]

The hand-built Bristol is, literally, a world away from the Japanese motor industry which, since 1980, has been the global leader. However, today Britain has first-hand experience of Japanese production methods because, between 1986 and 1992, three of that country's principal car companies established manufacturing presences in the UK. These plants do not merely supply the local market but also the massive European one, greatly to the benefit of Britain's balance of payments.

The first of these, the Nissan factory at Washington, Sunderland, began assembling the Bluebird model in 1986 and, two years later, was manufacturing it. The arrival of Japan's second-largest car maker in Britain was the culmination of months of tough negotiations with the British government and these were only concluded a few days before industry minister Norman Tebbit announced the decision to the House of Commons in January 1981. Crucially, Nissan's choice of Britain to build its cars was a recognition that the motor industry's labour problems were largely behind it; the result, in the short term, of lengthening dole queues and, in the longer one, the Thatcher government's trade union legislation. Established in an area of high unemployment, with state aid totalling £100 million, the plant's work-force initially numbered 1,800. Further jobs were created by component suppliers, which were encouraged to establish 'just-in-time' facilities nearby, in return for single-source, long-term contracts. The Bluebird was succeeded in 1990 by the Primera, which helped Nissan to attain sixth place and gain a 5.02 per cent share of the British market in 1993.

Although Nissan was the first Japanese car maker to establish a British plant, Honda's links with BL dated from 1979 and the British company began building its partner's Legend and Ballade models in 1986, to be followed in 1989 by the Concerto. In the meantime Honda was establishing its own factory, that began production in 1992, at Swindon in Wiltshire, located conveniently near to what is now the Rover company's body pressing facility which, in addition to its own requirements, also supplies Honda's needs.

At the end of 1992, Toyota, the world's largest automobile manufacturer, began production at its own plant at Burnaston, Derbyshire, and in the first instance employed 1,700 people to build 50,000 cars. As in Britain's other Japanese factories, the work-force belongs to a single trade union and, similarly, around 70 per cent of the cars it produces are exported to Europe.

The arrival of the Japanese is, unquestionably, the most significant change to the constitution of the British motor industry since Ford established a plant in Manchester before the First World War to mass produce the Model T. Like the Ford, the Japanese cars are not designed in Britain but each factory has the capacity to produce some 200,000 vehicles a year. They have also helped to reinvigorate the country's components industry as EEC regulations require that their products contain a minimum of 60 per cent local content (in fact they contain closer to 80 per cent). But, above all, the trio of Japanese car makers are practitioners of what has become known as 'lean production' (see Appendix Five). This has permitted them to achieve unparalleled levels of productivity which has acted as a competitive spur to the rest of the British motor industry.

By 1991, Nissan was far and away Britain's most efficient car factory, producing 21.7 cars per employee, although Toyota was looking to surpass this by aiming at a figure of 29.4. This compared with Vauxhall's 13, Rover's 6.4, and Ford's 4.5.[105] Ford responded, in 1992, by cutting its work-force by 2,100 to 38,000, from a peak in early 1980 of 72,000. It was a move that would also help Ford to bridge the pro-

ductivity gap between its British and European plants. In 1991 it took 40 hours to build a Fiesta at Dagenham compared with 28.5 at Cologne. Similarly, a Halewood Escort was completed in 43 hours whilst Saarlouis assembled the same model in 30.5.[106] Employment levels may fall even more as the Japanese, in particular, strive for ever greater efficiency. In 1994 Nissan UK declared that it was aiming to be the world's most efficient car maker by 1996, aided by the fact that the proportion of its 'just-in-time' component deliveries had reached 96 per cent, which compared with 99.98 in Japan.[107]

Japanese influence was all too apparent when, in June 1984, BL unveiled the 200 Series saloon, its replacement for the Honda-based Triumph Acclaim and effectively a new generation Ballade. If precedent had been followed, this 1.3/1.6-litre car would have been badged an Austin but it was given the Rover name, which boded ill for the Austin one. The 200 proved to be a steady seller and, by 1987, was being produced in larger numbers than the indigenous Maestro and Montego.

BL's next model, which appeared in July 1986, was arguably its most important because the new front-wheel drive 800 Series replaced the Solihull-designed Rover SD1 and, in theory, big executive cars meant big profits. Coded Project XX, it also differed from the 200 Series in being a joint venture between the British and Japanese companies. But whilst the resulting cars shared the same substructure and 2½-litre Honda V6 engine, the Rover 800 also had its own 2-litre twin overhead camshaft M16 unit, and each had a different body. Both had been engineered at Austin Rover's new £5 million Canley styling studio. The lines of Gordon Sked's 800 saloon quite deliberately echoed those of its SD1 predecessor, although they were considered by many commentators as being excessively bland. This first generation 800 proved to be a moderate success for the company.

Output peaked at 54,354 in 1987, the first full year of production, but fell away somewhat thereafter, with demand inevitably affected by the recession. In 1991 it dropped to a 12,652 car low.

Honda's version, the Legend, was its first executive car and had appeared the previous year. The 800 was also badged Sterling, created exclusively for sale in America. But whilst build quality was a considerable improvement on what had passed before, it still did not match that of Honda, and the Legend decisively outsold the Sterling on the other side of the Atlantic. Sales were poor anyway. A mere 4,015 cars found buyers in 1990 and when, in August 1991, the company announced that it was withdrawing from the market, for the third time in 20 years, just 1,878 Sterlings had been sold in the preceeding seven months.

The new chairman, Graham Day, had taken over in May 1986, and in July, just prior to the 800's launch, he changed the business's name from BL Ltd to the Rover Group. This marked a fundamental shift in corporate objectives which were underlined in September, when Day declared: 'Market share is not a God I worship'.[108] This was the clearest possible indication that he recognized the company's future resided in the profitable specialist sector. By overtly signalling the end of Rover as a volume car maker he was reviving a policy – first advocated by John Barber during his days at British Leyland – implemented in 1973 but disregarded by the Ryder Report and similarly bypassed during the Edwardes era. Rover was moving into BMW and Mercedes-Benz territory, a message further underlined when, in 1987, the Austin name was discontinued, leaving the business with just two marques: those of Rover and MG

Ray Horrocks and David Andrews left within months of Day's appointment and he wasted little time in disposing of corporate assets regarded as being suitable for privatization. The Unipart spares business was the sub-ject of a management buy-out early in 1987, Leyland Buses followed a similar route and, later in the same year, Leyland Trucks and Freight Rover were merged with the Dutch DAF Trucks. These moves delighted the Prime Minister but, recounts Mrs Thatcher, 'that did not mean that I was happy with the sort of figures the company's Corporate Plans contained. It retained an apparently insatiable appetite for cash – it had absorbed £2.9 billion of public money in total since we came to office in 1979.'[109]

Rover would provide BAe with more regular cash flow

In 1987 Rover's share of the British market stood at 14.7 per cent and it recorded a pre-tax and interest profit of £27.9 million, which was clearly a move in the right direction, but the company was not yet ready for privatization. Lord Young had taken over as Trade and Industry Secretary in 1987 and his worst fears were confirmed when Graham Day submitted his 1988 Corporate Plan. This, says Young, 'required about £1 billion reinvested during the five year plan period and the profits forecast was just too fragile to support any kind of flotation.'[110]

But then, 'when the prospects appeared the darkest there was a startling development.' Earlier in the year, British Aerospace had acquired a new chairman in the form of Professor Roland Smith, who, in November 1987, had mentioned to Graham Day that BAe 'could be interested in Land-Rover', which was conveyed to Young via his permanent secretary, Sir Brian Hayes. Subsequently, just as the Industry Secretary was preparing to leave his office for the Christmas break, he heard that Smith 'could be interested in the whole group but he would not be sure until some time in February. What a marvellous Christmas present I thought. I did not put too much store in it.'[111] Smith duly confirmed Aerospace's interest and, after some extremely robust negotiations that nearly faltered at the eleventh hour, on 1 March 1988 the Government announced that British Aerospace was negotiating to buy the Rover Group. The price was subsequently agreed at £150 million which was confirmed by BAe shareholders. But approval for the deal also had to be sought from the European Commission and although this was obtained, BAe was later required by the European Court to repay £48 million of illegal 'sweeteners'.

British Aerospace's purchase of Rover was the first of a spate of diversifications by Smith with the intention of providing a more regular cash flow to a group which received substantial civil and military contracts but at irregular intervals. BAe agreed not to dispose of Rover within five years from its August 1988 purchase date and so, after 13 years in the public sector, what was left of the country's largest car maker reverted to the private one whilst also remaining in British ownership.

In October 1989 the increasingly popular 200 Series line was updated and, like its predecessor, this two- and four-door hatchback closely resembled its Honda Concerto sister, which had appeared the previous year. It retained the Japanese car's 1.6-litre single overhead camshaft 16-valve engine, but also heralded the arrival of Rover's new alloy twin overhead camshaft 1.4-litre K Series four. Costing, in its entry level form, around £1,800 more than the comparable Ford Escort, in 1990 the 200 became the second-best selling model in the Rover range behind the Metro and, in 1991, took over pole position. The Rover 400 series, which arrived in 1990, was effectively a four-door, booted version of the 200, although it has not enjoyed the same popularity as its stable-mate.

If the 200 family was the latest fruit of the Rover/Honda partnership, the Land-Rover Discovery that also appeared in 1989 was an all-British effort. Positioned between the basic Land-Rover and the Range Rover, the

Discovery was Solihull's contribution to the burgeoning four-wheel drive leisure market dominated by the Mitsubishi Shogun. The model has proved to be a great success and helped Land-Rover to build a record 47,261 vehicles in 1990. That year the Honda association with Rover was further underpinned when the Japanese company took a 20 per cent share in Rover's £520 million equity. For its part Rover had a reciprocal holding in the newly-formed Honda UK Manufacturing.

In mid-1991 Rover unveiled a revised version of the 800 Series. Following market research, the company had decided to make its cars outwardly different from Honda's and the 800 was the first model to benefit from this new approach. Gordon Sked's amendments revived visual memories of the Rover P4 range of the 1950s, incorporated in a new front end that was underlined by the presence of the traditional radiator grille. The formula has proved to be immensely successful, and considerable improvements in build quality helped the 800 to be voted Britain's best-selling executive car of 1992.

This change in the public's perception of Rover cars was a reflection of the fact that a quiet revolution had taken place behind the scenes at the Group's factories. Previously, reinvestment had intended to concentrate on Longbridge, but in 1990 Rover launched a two-year £200 million investment programme at Cowley that involved the demolition of Morris Motors's old North and South works on the north side of the Oxford Eastern Bypass. The site has now been redeveloped as a business park by Arlington Securities, a British Aerospace subsidiary.

New production facilities have been concentrated on the site of the former Pressed Steel works on the opposite side of the road. On their completion in 1992, this Large Car plant, which had been capable of manufacturing 50,000 vehicles per annum, was able to produce 110,000 in considerably less space. In addition, Honda's association with Rover has also extended to the way that the company builds its cars, and in 1992 a new agreement was reached with the 32,000 strong workforce. The outcome of this Japanese-style agreement is that employees are guaranteed jobs for life, they no longer clock in, they work in teams, and take responsibility for many of their own tasks. Graham Day had meanwhile stepped down as Rover's chairman in 1991. He was replaced by George Simpson, who had begun his motor industry career in 1969 as an accountant in British Leyland's finance department and had subsequently become managing director of Leyland Trucks.

With Rover riding high as a marque

The MGF with mid-mounted 1.8-litre K Series engine marks a return to quantity production of the MG sports car, and a serious challenge to the Mazda MX5 and Fiat Barchetta. (Rover).

name, what of MG? Following the demise of the MGB in 1980 the name was in temporary abeyance until 1982, when it appeared as a successful variant of the Metro and then on faster versions of the Maestro and Montego. All these models were discontinued in 1991 so as not to dilute the impact of the arrival of the MGB's spiritual successor, the MG RV8 roadster, which appeared in 1992. Based on British Motor Heritage's revived MGB bodyshell and fitted with the company's current 3.9-litre V8, the RV8 echoed the MGB GT V8 of the 1973–6 era although that model had never been built in open form. It was originally intended for sale on the American market where the MG name still held sway, but Rover's decision to withdraw from the US meant that the car would only be produced in right-hand drive form for sale in Britain, although it could be exported to – and has found favour in – Japan. Production began in 1993 and was limited to 2,000 cars, that were completed in 1995 to pave the way for the new, all-British mid-engined MG sports car, using a turbocharged K Series engine.

In April 1993 came yet another new Rover in the shape of the much praised 2/2.2-litre 600 Series which, although it shares a substructure with the Honda Accord, has its own impressive body, complete with the now obligatory Rover radiator grille. It is built at Cowley on Rover's first wholly 'lean production' line and, although more expensive than its Japanese counterpart, is outselling the Accord at the rate of two to one.

Despite a chilly economic climate, Rover had performed well in 1992, when it made a modest loss of £49 million; but the following year came an operating profit of £56 million, transformed into a £9 million deficit after the payment of £65 million interest charges. However, the corporate land-

scape at Rover's British Aerospace parent had by then changed significantly, for in 1991 Roland Smith was ousted in a boardroom coup. Despite the turnabout in the car company's fortunes, while it generated £4 billion of turnover it remained cash hungry to the tune of some £250 million a year and had yet to produce significant profits. Arlington Securities, which specialized in business parks, was another Smith purchase that suffered badly in the recession, and likewise contributed to British Aerospace experiencing a £430 million cash crisis. Smith's replacement was John Cahill, who believed that BAe should revert to its core business of manufacturing aircraft; and, at any time after August 1993, it was free to dispose of Rover.

Britain has one of Europe's smallest motor industries today

Against a backdrop of such manoeuvring and to the astonishment of the industry, on 31 January 1994 the news broke that British Aerospace was selling Rover to the BMW company for £800 million. The German firm was clearly attracted by the complementary four-wheel drive expertise of Land-Rover, the front-wheel drive car technology, and the acclaimed K Series engine which has many years of development ahead of it. BMW has also removed its principal competitor from the British market. Bernd Pischetsrieder, who had only became BMW's chairman in May the previous year, spoke of the combined business – which has a potential output of a million vehicles a year – as being 'the world's largest specialist car maker.' He wasted little time in dispelling fears of job losses. In a letter to the President of the Board of Trade, Michael Heseltine, he declared: 'The distinctiveness of products and brands is in

both cases one of their most valuable assets. We want to protect that asset and therefore intend to maintain BMW and Rover as separate enterprises, each with their own manufacturing plants and their own design and development capabilities.'[112] Having said that, there is an overlap of models; the Rover 600 Series, for instance, was targeted four-square at the BMW 3 Series and the use of rationalized platforms in the future appears both logical and inevitable.

Not surprisingly, Honda, which had played such a significant role in Rover's revival, was understandably miffed that the deal had been struck. However, it had been offered the company by British Aerospace but chose not to extend its 20 per cent share to beyond the 47.5 mark and favoured placing the balance for stock market flotation. It subsequently disposed of its 20 per cent holding in Rover – which BMW bought for £200 million – but in September 1994 announced a £350 million investment at its Swindon plant, and that it would continue to co-operate with Rover until at least the end of the century.

In international terms, Britain has one of Europe's smallest motor industries today, having in 1955 ceded pole position to Germany, which has held it ever since. In the past 20 years Germany has also emerged as the pre-eminent force in the British motor industry in both volume and specialist markets, for in addition to BMW's ownership of Rover and its involvement with Rolls-Royce, Ford cars sold in the UK have a strong German engineering input and the revived Vauxhall range exclusively so. This is the culmination of an influence that reaches back to the birth of Britain's motor industry in 1896, which began with the exploitation of a German invention. One hundred years on, the historical wheel has turned full circle.

The Government's Views on the British Motor Industry, 1945

Jonathan Wood

On 5 April 1945, a month before VE Day, the reconstruction committee of the war cabinet met to consider a report prepared by its official sub-committee entitled *Post War Resettlement of the Motor Industry*. The meeting was chaired by the Minister of Reconstruction, Lord Woolton, who had been charged with the task of evaluating the export potential of British industry, as overseas sales in the post-war years were to be crucial in restoring the country's currency reserves which had been a victim of the conflict.

The committee recognized that 'the motor car industry was rapidly expanding before the war and can be regarded as one of the most prosperous and successful industries.' Nevertheless, it identified the fact that overseas car sales, having risen from a figure of 47,000 in 1927 to 108,000 a decade later, 'are not, however, as satisfactory as they appear, as exports from this country were almost wholly in small cars, and the important trade in larger cars was mainly in the hands of the United States and Canada. Further, 80 per cent of our exports of private cars went to the British Empire, under specially favourable conditions, some of which may not continue.' On the subject of foreign cars sold on the British market, it pointed out that: 'During the same period [1927–37], imports varied considerably from year to year. In 1937 they amounted to 18,500 private cars . . . this was a substantial increase on the figures in preceding years and was mainly caused by a sudden increase in imports from Germany.'

As for the all-important export market in the post-war years, it was 'suggested that the industry should be invited to plan for expansion and exports'. The committee was only too aware that the horsepow-er tax 'favoured the home market', with the result that 'little attempt was made by British manufacturers to capture a share of the world market in the larger class of car. The manufactruers argued that the market in this country is chiefly for a small car and, that without a greater home demand for large cars, they could not be expected to put these into production for the export market.' In view of this, the committee questioned whether 'an attempt be made to secure a *reduction in the large number of different models* [original italics] produced, on the grounds that this would facilitate mass production methods.'

In a far more interventionist stance, compared with the *laissez-faire* approach of pre-war governments, it also considered whether, if this was not an economic proposition, 'an attempt [should] be made to get all manufacturers – or a group of them – *to combine in the mass production of one high powered model*'. If this was not possible, 'should not *special governmental assistance* be given, to induce them to embark on projects which they now regard as too risky?'

Although large cars had a considerable export potential, the committee also identified that 'a large proportion of the 100,000 cars exported annually from the Continent were small cars; and after the war a cheap car, with low running costs, should find a ready market in countries with good roads and high taxation.'

However, export prospects were 'gravely affected by the division of the industry into *too many, often small scale, units*, each producing too many different models. Manufacturers should be urged to collaborate more closely to improve sales, servicing and spares facilities for British cars overseas. The arrangements made before the war, both in the dominions and in exports countries generally were very poor, and compared disadvantageously with those of the Americans.'

Having identified the British motor industry's shortcomings, the committee was pessimistic as far as the future was concerned. This was because 'the motor car industry has developed under conditions tending to give it a monopoly in a home market,' and had 'no strong incentive . . . to embark upon large scale mass production (of either high or low powered cars), reduction of the number of models and standardisation of components and accessories – all of which are needed if costs are to be lowered far enough to allow us to compete fully in the world market. Manufacturers at present show little sign that they intend, after the war, to produce one or two models on a large scale, in the expectation that demand will mature great enough to absorb them; nor does it seem that they propose to treat the export market as more than an accessory to their assured home market.'

The committee cautioned that 'unless the Government intervene, however, it seems that there is little prospect that any manufacturer or group will undertake the large scale manufacture of a car or cars of types likely to produce a substantial expansion of our export trade; and unless such action is taken, employment in the industry will decline towards the levels prevailing before the war.'

In the event, when Labour came to power in July 1945 these radical proposals were watered down and the industry left to its own devices to continue to produce wholly unsuitable cars for a government-directed export drive. The rest, as Henry Ford might not have said, is history.

Austin in Canada

Jonathan Wood

Ron Lucas had joined Austin's accounts department in 1927 and qualified as a chartered secretary before being called up, in 1943, for war service in the army. On his return to Longbridge in 1947, he went back to his old job but remembers that the 'number of financially qualified people there was not great'.[1] At this time Austin was concentrating its efforts on the export market. This was because chairman Leonard Lord could see that the only way for the firm to obtain the steel it required was to dramatically increase the number of vehicles it sold abroad, as steel allocation was entirely dependent on export performance. 'So in 1947, he took the Devon and the big Sheerline over to the 'States and then on to Canada and decided that there was no point in solely having agents to sell the cars; Austin would have to establish its own subsidiaries there. First came an American one and it was soon followed by The Austin Motor Company (Canada) Ltd. To run it, he dug out from retirement a man named Crane Williams who had been the Austin representative in Australia and was then living in Edmonton, Alberta. Crane said to Lord, "I want a good finance man," to which he agreed but insisted the rest of the team would have to be recruited locally. That is how I got to be sent to Canada.

'At the time there were three Austin distributors in Canada and if they had sold ten cars a year apiece, they were doing very well. One was Austin Sales and Service in Montreal, which was responsible for the East Coast. Another company was Fred Deeley Ltd of Vancouver, who had started a motor

cycle business and imported Nortons and had a franchise for Austin cars. The third was based on Vancouver Island and named Thomas Plimley Motors Ltd. Crane Williams got himself an office in the premises of Austin Sales and Service in Mountain Street, Montreal, and used its facilities to get started.

'I was scheduled to go out in October 1947 but there was a serious seamen's strike in Canada and I did not arrive until March 1948. I took over what little paperwork there was. We soon appointed more distributors and had the basis of a sales organization. There was great enthusiasm for the Austins because, at the time, you could not buy a car for love or money. There were left-hand drive Devons, Dorsets, and Sheerlines which were collectively imported at the rate of around 20,000 a year. The only trouble was, we had no facilities for pre-servicing them. Then someone in England had the idea that, if the cars were assembled in Canada, substantial financial savings could be made. So without a word to us, Austin went and bought a former glass-making factory in Hamilton, Ontario, and chaps came out from England to turn it into an assembly plant.

'But Clarence Howe, who was the minister of trade in the Ottawa administration, had done a deal with the English government, whereby certain commodities could be imported into Canada at a substantial discount and so avoid the tax that would otherwise have arisen. So we brought our cars in on very favourable terms; there were no import duties whatsoever. We also levied a tax on the cars, known as the

Sales and Excise Tax, not on the selling price of the vehicle but the imported one. Had we begun to assemble cars in Canada, we would have lost all of those advantages Also unskilled labour rates were particularly high. Thankfully, it didn't happen because Joe Graves, who was the head of engineering at Longbridge, paid us a visit. I told hm all this, to which he asked, "why don't we know?" and I said, "nobody asked us, you've just gone on and done it." Anyway I was asked to write a report and, early in 1949, Longbridge stopped it immediately. But some good came out of the purchase because our service facilities were completely inadequate and Austin kept on the factory and established what, in its day, were very good premises for servicing.

'It was just as well because, at that point, we began to experience problems with the A40's chassis frame as the suspension mounting points began to fracture and break off. They weren't strong enough for the Canadian roads and Longbridge sent out a team of welders that went all over the country putting right the trouble. But as soon as domestic production began to pick up, our sales began to fall away.'

However, demand for sports cars in North America began to rise and, by the 1960s, what had become BMC's operation was contributing £1 million to the Corporation's coffers. However, in 1965 Lucas returned to Britain to become BMC's deputy managing director with special responsibility for financial matters and he subsequently became company secretary of the British Leyland Motor Corporation.

Benn on the Motor Industry

Jonathan Wood

Tony Benn was the politician most closely associated with the creation, in 1968, of British Leyland, as the government of the day 'did not want the British Motor Corporation destroyed by Ford and General Motors. If we had done nothing, BMC would have collapsed completely'. Benn believes that it was a company that was symptomatic of much of British industry. 'On the whole, the people who ran it were old-fashioned and inadequate and it was easy for them to blame the workers. As a nation we have found this a scapegoat without ever looking at the real cause of decline which was, what was happening to the profits? The answer is that when a company was profitable it didn't bother to invest [BMC's neglect of Cowley immediately comes to mind] and when it wasn't it couldn't afford to. Bit by bit production was ratcheted down.'

The answer, he believes, is state intervention. 'You're not talking about subsidizing failure. We wanted the motor industry to make a contribution to exports with the capacity to remain strong in world markets.' Benn had proposed nationalization when, in 1966, he suggested that Leyland take over the ailing Rootes Group, in addition to BMC, but 'the Government wouldn't agree.'

'Of course, the Japanese intervene continuously in their industry. The Ministry of International Trade and Industry was the war time planning ministry that they kept in peace-time and treated civil manufacture as they had military production. It was something that you planned and the banks supported the government.'

As far as British Leyland itself was concerned, 'the management problem was a formidable one. By the time I had come back as industry minister in 1974, Stokes was saying that it was going alright but, at the end of that very year, it could have gone into receivership.'

But where Benn, as the leading voice of the left in British politics, found himself most at odds with industrialists, the Tory press, and even with some of his parliamentary colleagues, was his attitude to the role of the trade unions, who in the eyes of many were largely responsible for Leyland's woes. 'I don't blame the unions. Productivity is the product of investment and, where you have proper spending on modern plant and equipment, you have a high increase in productivity.' Part of the management's shortcomings was its 'failure to recognize that you can't run any industry without the goodwill of those who worked in it. The workers never had power anyway, were never able to decide anything, only to withdraw their labour when things got bad. Take Derek Robinson, they called "Red Robbo", who was sacked. He'd worked at Longbridge all his life and knew more about it than Michael Edwardes who'd been brought in as a management expert and told to slash it back. This generation of new managers was not interested in expanding the industry's volume; you can make anything profitable if you make it on a small enough scale. In the end they sold it off to a widow in Bavaria.

'I have no doubt whatever that, if we had adopted as a national policy, a view I took then and take now, that British manufacturing industry is a national interest, like farming, you would have done what was necessary to see that it was properly re-equipped and reinvested. Instead it was left to a capitalist market system which did not re-equip industry with its own profits. We've lost out by simply turning ourselves from a Victorian manufacturing industry to a nation of heritage museums.'

The Think Tank's Views on the British Motor Industry, 1975

Jonathan Wood

When British Leyland collapsed in 1974, the Labour government of the day initiated a tripartite investigative response. First came the Ryder Report, to be followed by the House of Commons's Trade and Industry subcommittee's deliberations on the Motor Industry, whilst the third inquiry came in the form of a 141-page document published in 1975, entitled *The Future of the British Car Industry*, and prepared by the Central Policy Review Staff, better known as the Think Tank.

The Staff's 'five main conclusions were:

'1. The prospect is one of very tough competition in the Western European car industry for at least the next decade.

'2. The British car industry has serious competitive weaknesses. There are too many manufacturers with too many models, too many plants and too much capacity. These are the responsibilities of management.

'3. Other severe weaknesses are poor quality, bad labour relations, unsatisfactory delivery record, low productivity and too much manpower. With the same power at his elbow and doing the same job as his Continental counterpart, a British car assembly worker produces only half as much output per shift. It is not too late to correct these weaknesses. They basically arise on the shopfloor and it is on the shopfloor that they must be corrected.

'4. If the weaknesses are not corrected, employment could fall by 275,000 by 1985 and the balance of trade in cars deteriorate by over £1 billion a year at 1975 prices. The most optimistic prospect is a United Kingdom industry volume of 1.9 million in 1985 [the actual figure was very much lower, at 1 million]. The volume is bound to be lower in the years between. 1.9 million in 1985 will only be reached if, in the years immediately ahead, productivity sharply improves (and therefore manning levels are reduced). Without a reduction in the labour force in the short term there is no prospect of large scale employment long term.

'5. To improve productivity investment alone is not enough. The basic problem is attitudes – attitudes of both management and labour. The future of the industry lies in its own hands and in no one else's, but the Government now owns half the industry and cannot avoid the responsibility of leadership. The Government must:

'(a) Declare its determination to do all in its power to achieve a viable, substantial, internationally competitive and unsubsidised car industry in the 1980s.

'(b) Sponsor a programme designed to achieve the fundamental changes in attitude throughout the industry required for improving productivity, quality and continuity of production.

'(c) Recognise the need to rationalise plants and reduce assembly capacity and to ensure that this reduction takes place with the least possible adverse effects on the general level of employment.

'(d) Stabilise the domestic market for cars in particular by stabilising fiscal policy towards the industry. Study alternative means of restraining Japanese imports against the possibility that the coming talks with the Japanese should not prove satisfactory.

'(e) Take action in British Leyland to bring about the changes the Central Policy Review Staff has shown necessary throughout the industry. Make the provision of capital to BL dependent on achieving *specified* improvements in productivity, quality and continuity of production. Consider future requests for financial assistance from other car manufacturing firms in the light of the CPRS Report.'

Lean Production

Jonathan Wood

In 1913 Henry Ford introduced a moving track assembly line to his factory at Highland Park, Detroit, and bequeathed the world the concept, in the automotive sense, of mass production. It was a system conceived to build the Model T and was destined to be employed by the world's leading car makers for the next 70 or so years. But today, Ford's legacy is in retreat and is in the process of being replaced by the 'lean production' concept which hails from Japan and, in particular, Toyota, which is today the world's largest car maker.

So what is lean production? I can do no better than quote from *The Machine that Changed the World*,[2] an influential book based on a Massachusetts Institute of Technology $5 million world-wide study into the process. It also coined the name 'lean production', so called because 'it uses less of everything compared with mass production – half the human effort in the factory, half the manufacturing space,

half the investment in tools, half the engineering hours to develop a new product in half the time. Also, it requires keeping far less than half the needed inventory on site, results in many fewer defects and produces a greater and ever growing variety of products.' Because of all these advantages, lean production is twice or even three times more efficient than the Ford system.

Lean production was conceived at Toyota in the days after the Second World War by Eiji Toyoda, who rose to become chairman, and his chief engineer, Taiichi Ohno. One of the factors in its introduction was that the company lacked the capital investment to buy Western automotive technology. Part of the philosophy is that a car company plans in the long term; its work-force has jobs for life and, in return, agrees to undertake flexible manufacturing practices. This involves employees working in teams which are charged with a much higher degree of respon-

sibility than was previously the case with the more repetitive mass production process. It is an approach that extends to suppliers, which are fewer in number, and is crucial to the success of the 'just-in-time' system, also invented by Ohno. This requires that components are delivered to the factory a mere three hours before they are fitted to the car rather than weeks before, as had been the norm. Not only is storage space reduced and the expense of carrying stock saved, it also means that mistakes on the line can be speedily corrected.

In America, the home of mass production, Ford has been in the vanguard of the lean production process since the early 1980s, via the Japanese Mazda company in which it has a financial interest. In Britain, Rover, in particular, has greatly benefited from the technique, which it has learnt from its association with Honda which, in turn, acquired it from Toyota.

References

Prologue

1. *Illustrated London News*, 15 September 1860, p.260 (Quoted in T. R. Nicholson, *The Birth of the British Motorcar* Volume 2, p.212.
2. *Banffshire Journal*, 4 October 1860 (Quoted in T. R. Nicholson, op.cit. p.213.
3. R. Tangye, *The Rise of a Great Industry*, quoted in T. R. Nicholson, op. cit. p.226.
4. *The Autocar*, 30 November 1895, p.53.
5. T. R. Nicholson, op.cit. Volume 3, p.378.
6. *National Motor Museum Trust Friends Newsletter*, December 1994, article by Andrea Bishop.
7. G. Rose, *A Record of Motor Racing 1894–1908*, pp3–5.
8. *Veteran Car*, October 1993, p.83.
9. *The Autocar*, 30 November 1895.
10. *Guernsey Evening Press*, 9 May 1958, reminiscences of Ernest Henry, family friend of Major Thom.
11. T. R. Nicholson, op. cit p.360.

Chapter One

1. J. McMillan, *The Dunlop Story*, p.15.
2. D. Cannandine, *Aspects of Aristocracy*, p.65.

Chapter Two

1. T. R. Nicholson, *The Birth of the British Motorcar* Volume 3, p.365.
2. *The Autocar*, 21 November 1896, p.670.
3. *The Automotor Journal*, November 1896, p.70.
4. *The Autocar*, 9 May 1896.

5. T. R. Nicholson, op.cit. p.471.
6. *The Autocar*, 23 January 1897, p.59.
7. Interestingly, when the prospectus inviting purchase was issued on 15 February, Lawson's name was not used. In the intervening months the financial press had been far from complimentary about what they saw as yet another Lawson promotion.
8. *The Autocar*, 11 July 1896, p.434.
9. T. R. Nicholson, op.cit. p.433.
10. *The Autocar*, 6 March 1897, p.153.
11. Ibid. 14 November 1896.
12. G. N. Georgano, *History of the London Taxicab*, pp41-2.
13. *The Autocar*, 23 January 1897, p.61.
14. Ibid. 20 November 1897, p.739.
15. Letter from A. C. Brown to John Pollitt, 1945, in the Pollitt Papers.
16. Tim Moore, who has restored examples of both Panhard and Daimler cars, says that the metallurgy of the French car was inferior, many of the castings being full of blowholes. Also the valves were on different sides, so one cannot say that the Daimler was an exact copy of the Panhard.
17. B. R. Kimes and H. A. Clark, *Standard Catalog of American Cars*, p.1431.
18. G. N. Georgano (ed), *The Complete Encyclopaedia of Motorcars*, p.594.
19. *The Autocar*, 3 July 1897, pp421–4.
20. Ibid. 20 November 1897, p.739.
21. C. Jarrott, *Ten Years of Motors and Motor Racing*, p.5.
22. *Automotor Journal*, December 1896, p.109.
23. T. R. Nicholson, op.cit. p.497.
24. P. Tritton, *John Montagu of Beaulieu*, p.47.

Chapter Three

1. *The Autocar*, 2 June 1900, p.535.
2. D. Thoms and T. Donnelly, *The Motor Car Industry in Coventry Since the 1890s*, p.16.
3. *The Autocar*, 25 November 1899, p.1077.
4. P. Collins and M. Stratton, *British Car Factories from 1896*, p.218.
5. S. B. Saul, *The Motor Industry in Britain to 1914*, p.25.
6. I. Nichols and K. Karslake, *Motoring Entente*, pp9–10.
7. *The Autocar*, 16 February 1901, p.149.
8. S. B. Saul, op.cit. p.28.
9. Ibid. p.31
10. J. Davy, *The Standard Motor Car 1903–1963*, pp12–13.
11. *History of AC Cars Ltd*, p.26.
12. *The Automobile*, September 1994, pp30–3.
13. Thoms and Donelly, op.cit. p.57.
14. Ibid. pp57–8.
15. D. Cannandine, *Aspects of Aristocracy*, p.65.
16. H. Edwards, *The Morris Motor Car*, p.112.
17. Letter dated 11 October 1906, quoted in Montagu, *Rolls of Rolls-Royce*, p.135.
18. G. N. Georgano, *The Classic Rolls-Royce*, p.22.
19. D. Cannandine, op.cit. p.62.
20. *The Times*, 6 September 1901, quoted in Plowden, *The Motor Car and Politics*, p.43.
21. W. Plowden, op.cit. p52.
22. Ibid. p.56.
23. Quoted in D. Noble, *Milestones in a Motoring Life*, p.3.

24. L. Lee, *Cider with Rosie*, p.216.
25. Quoted in H. G. Castle, *Britain's Motor Industry*, p.65.
26. G. Hunt, foreword to 1973 facsimile edition of 1903 Show catalogue.
27. G. N. Georgano, *History of the London Taxicab*, p.60.
28. Montagu, *Lost Causes of Motoring*, p.29.
29. P. Collins and M. Stratton, op. cit. p.255.
30. M. Adeney, *The Motor Makers*, p.59.
31. Montagu, op. cit. p.33.
32. Ibid. p.37.
33. St. J. Nixon, *Daimler 1896–1946*, p.57.
34. Ibid. pp106–7.
35. A. Bird and F. Hutton Stott, *Lanchester Motor Cars*, p.180.
36. St. John Nixon, op.cit. p.130.
37. *Financial Times*, 27 September 1910.
38. Collins and Stratton, op.cit. p.215.
39. Montagu, op.cit. p.203.
40. Collins and Stratton, op.cit. p.203.
41. From works delivery books, provided by Derek Grossmark.
42. Montagu, op.cit. p.211.
43. *The Autocar*, 27 April 1907, p.622.
44. H. Nockolds, *The Magic of a Name*, p.61.
45. A. Clark, *Diaries*, p.165.
46. A. Bird and F. Hutton-Stott, op.cit. p.22.
47. *The Autocar*, 1 November 1913, pp856–65.
48. A. Bird, *The Horizontal-Engined Wolseleys*, p.3.
49. St. J. Nixon, *Wolseley*, p.43.
50. Collins and Stratton, op.cit. p.199.
51. S. B. Saul, op.cit. pp37–8.
52. *The Cyclecar*, 12 March 1913, pp413–4.
53. L. Jarman and R. Barraclough, *The Bullnose Morris*, p.30.
54. S. B. Saul, op.cit. p.36.
55. H. Nockolds, *Lucas, the First Hundred Years*, p.116.
56. Ibid. p.131.
57. J. McMillan, *The Dunlop Story*, p.27.
58. P. Jennings, *Dunlopera*, p.131.
59. B. Laban (ed), *The World Guide to Automobiles*, p.410.
60. S. B. Saul, op.cit. p.36.
61. Ibid. p.37.
62. G. Turner, *The Car Makers*, p.56.
63. *Toyota Factfile, 1994*.
64. UK figure from Saul, op.cit. p.24; USA from *Automobiles of America*, p.104. French from W. Laux, *In First Gear*, p.210.
65. S. B. Saul, op.cit. p.25.
66. Ibid. p.44.
67. Prices quoted in *Autocar*, 14/21 December 1994.
68. *The Cyclecar*, 27 November 1912, p.11.
69. *The Motor*, 8 October 1907, p.255.
70. *The Cyclecar*, 12 March 1913, pp413–4.
71. S. B. Saul, op.cit. p.23.
72. Montagu, op.cit. pp19–20.
73. N. Baldwin, *A–Z of Cars of the 1920s*, p.77.

Chapter Four

1. *Automobile Engineer*, 1913.
2. Ibid. February 1930.

Chapter Five

1. M. Sedgwick, *The Motor Car 1946–1956*, p.189.
2. M. Sedgwick, *Cars of the 1930s*, p.300.
3. P. Collins and M. Stratton, *British Car Factories from 1896*, pp93–6.
4. Quoted in a letter by Nick Georgano to *The Daily Telegraph*, 24 August 1989.
5. J. Stanford, *The 30-98 Vauxhall*, Profile No. 32, p.3.
6. W. O. Bentley, *W. O., an Autobiography*, pp153–4; 178–9.
7. K. Day, *Alvis, the Story of the Red Triangle*, p.35.
8. G. Robson, *The Rover Story*, p.33.
9. Proceedings of I.A.E., Volume 28, session 1933–4.
10. Information from MG accounts 1930–9 held in BMIHT deposit, Modern Records Centre, University of Warwick Library. See also article, *Who Owned MG?* in MG Magazine (USA), Nos. 40 and 41, 1992.
11. I.A.E. proceedings, op.cit.

Chapter Six

1. *The Economist*, 16 April 1938, pp131–2.
2. Public Records Office reference number CAB 87/15.
3. C. Barnett, *The Audit of War*, p.275.
4. A. J. P. Taylor, *English History 1914–1945*, p.559.
5. *The Autocar*, 23 November 1945, p.859.
6. Ibid. p.852.
7. M. Platt, *An Addiction to Automobiles*, p.162–3.
8. C. Edwards, A. Fogg, *Motor Industry Management*, p.27.
9. Sir M. Thomas, *Out on a Wing*, p.239.
10. C. Fraser, *Harry Ferguson*, p.167.
11. Ibid. p.169.
12. Ibid.
13. D. Noble, *Milestones in a Motoring Life*, p.195.
14. *The Story of the Vanguard*, p.17.
15. Ibid. p.9.
16. M. Sedgwick, *The Motor Car 1945–1956*, p.213.
17. M. Adeney, *The Motor Makers*, pp206–7.
18. *The Story of the Vanguard*, p.11.
19. P. Pagnamenta and R. Overy, *All Our Working Lives*, p.229.
20. Adeney, op. cit. p.207.
21. K. and J. Slavin and G. N. Mackie, *Land-Rover*, p.11.
22. G. Robson, *The Rover Story*, p.86.
23. Slavin and Mackie, op.cit. p.13.
24. P. Addison, *Now the War is Over*, pp190–1.
25. *The Economist*, 9 June 1945, p.782.
26. Thomas, op.cit. p.237.
27. P. Skilleter, *Morris Minor*, p.30.
28. Thomas, op.cit. p.250.
29. Skilleter, op.cit. pp44–5.
30. Ibid. p.30.
31. J. Rae, *Nissan/Datsun, a History of Nissan Motor Corporation in the USA*, p.27.
32. Skilleter, op. cit. Appendix Four, *Minors in America* by J. Voelcker and R. Feibusch, p.208.
33. Quoted in *Automobile Quarterly*, Vol 10, No 1.
34. Letter to *Autoweek*, 5 April 1993.
35. J. R. Bond, *Sports Cars in Action*, p.108.
36. Letter from Keith Marvin to Jonathan Wood, 1994.
37. G. Turner, *The Leyland Papers*, pp92–3.

38. P. W. S. Andrews and E. Brunner, *The Life of Lord Nuffield*, p.218.
39. Adeney, op. cit. p.206.
40. D. G. Rhys, *The Motor Industry, an Economic Survey*, p.363.
41. Platt, op. cit. p.172.
42. M. Wilkins and F. Hill, *American Business Abroad*, p.364.
43. J. Wood, 'Birth of the Ford Cortina', *Thoroughbred and Classic Cars, July 1983*, p.44.
44. *Wilkins and Hill*, p.366.
45. Ibid.
46. Ibid. p.387.
47. J. Wood, 'Jowett, the Inside Story', *Thoroughbred and Classic Cars, February 1980*, p.34.
48. P. Clark and E. Nankivell, *The Complete Jowett History*, p.179.
49. J. Wood, 'Jowett R4', *Thoroughbred and Classic Cars*, November 1979, p.56.
50. I. Lloyd, *Rolls-Royce, the Years of Endeavour*, Appendix XI.
51. W. Robotham, *Silver Ghosts and Silver Dawn*, p.199.
52. Ibid. p.200.
53. G. Robson, *The Rolls-Royce and Bentley, Volume 3, A Collector's Guide*, p.37.
54. Sedgwick, *Twenty Years of Crewe Bentleys 1946–1965*, p.27.
55. Ibid. p.24–56.
56. R. P. Bradly, *Armstrong-Siddeley*, p.185.
57. Sir W. Lyons, *The History of the Jaguar and the future of the Specialist car in the British motor industry*, Lord Wakefield Golden Memorial Paper, 28 April 1969, p.5.
58. P. King, *The Motor Men*, p.131.
59. P. Skilleter, *Jaguar Sports Cars*, p.7.
60. Lyons, op.cit. p.6.
61. Ibid.
62. Ibid. p.7.
63. Ibid.
64. A. Whyte, *Jaguar*, p.145.
65. *The Times*, 12 December 1983.
66. R. P. T. Davenport-Hines, *Dudley Docker*, pp231–2.
67. G. Courtney, *The Power Behind Aston Martin*, p.40.
68. J. Wyer, *The Certain Sound, Automobile Year*, 1981, p.87.
69. Ibid.

70. Ibid.
71. Ibid. p.109.
72. C. Oxley, *Bristol, the Illustrated History*, p.66.
73. Ibid. p.128.
74. Ibid. pp100
75. K. Day, *Alvis, the Story of the Red Triangle*, p.91.
76. Ibid. p.100.
77. Ibid. pp100–1.
78. G. H. Bowden, *Morgan, the First and Last of the True Sports Cars*, p.167.
79. Ibid. p.168.
80. Ibid.
81. I. Smith, *The Story of Lotus*, p.11.
82. D. Nye, *The Story of Lotus*, p.13.
83. J. Wood, *Wheels of Misfortune*, p.116.
84. Ibid. p.115.
85. Ibid.
86. Turner, op. cit. p.98.
87. Wood, op. cit. p.141.
88. Turner, op. cit. p.96.
89. J. Wood, 'Healey', *Thoroughbred and Classic Cars*, August 1983, p.xi.
90. Ibid.
91. Turner, p. cit. pp40–1.
92. Ibid. p.48.

Chapter Seven

1. P. J. S. Dunnett, *The Decline of the British Motor Industry*, p.89.
2. Ibid. p.88.
3. R. Golding, *Mini*, p.60.
4. *The Motor*, 29 November 1961.
5. *The Autocar*, 23 June 1961.
6. *The Motor*, 18 October 1961.
7. Ibid. 21 February 1962.
8. *The Times Survey of the British Motor Industry*, October 1962.
9. G. Turner, *The Leyland Papers*, pp83–6 and 112.
10. Figures from annual reports quoted in G. Robson, *The Cars of BMC*, p.294.
11. G. Turner, op. cit. pp120–2.
12. G. Robson, *Cars of the Rootes Group*, p.192.
13. G. Robson, op. cit. pp142–3.
14. J. Wood, *Wheels of Misfortune*, pp150–2.

Chapter Eight

1. TGWU/AUEW-TASS, *British Leyland, the Next Decade*, p.5.

2. C. P. Hill, *British Economic and Social History 1700–1982*, pp. 155–6.
3. Minute Books of the ASE Coventry branch, quoted in D. Thoms and T. Donnelly, *The Motor Car Industry in Coventry Since the 1890s*, pp. 61–2.
4. Hill, op. cit. p.239.
5. Ibid. p.247.
6. K. Richardson, *The British Motor Industry, 1896–1939*, p.81.
7. Thoms & Donnelly, op. cit. p.61.
8. Ibid. p.62.
9. Hill, op. cit. p.124.
10. P. Collins and M. Stratton, *British Car Factories from 1896*, p.255.
11. Quoted in Lord Montagu, *Lost Causes of Motoring*, p.32.
12. R. Church, *Herbert Austin*, p.43.
13. R. J. Wyatt, *The Austin, 1905–1952*, p.38.
14. Z. Lambert and R. J. Wyatt, *Lord Austin, the Man*, p.110.
15. Thoms and Donelly, op. cit. p.80–1.
16. Collins and Stratton, op. cit. p.118.
17. Richardson, op. cit. p.32.
18. Thoms and Donnelly, op. cit. p.60
19. Church, op. cit. pp46–7
20. Wyatt, op. cit. p.60.
21. Quoted in M. Adeney, *The Motor Makers*, p.162.
22. R. J. Overy, *William Morris, Lord Nuffield*, p.113.
23. L. P. Jarman and R. P. Barraclough, *The Bullnose and Flatnose Morris*, p.228.
24. Richardson, op. cit. p.103.
25. Quoted in Overy, op. cit. p.112.
26. W. R. Morris, *Policies that Built the Morris Motor Business*, quoted in Overy, op. cit. p.112.
27. Church, op. cit. pp155.
28. P. W. S. Andrews and E. Brunner, *The Life of Lord Nuffield*, p.275.
29. M. Thomas, *Out On a Wing*, p.188.
30. Thoms and Donnelly, op. cit. pp80–1.
31. Church, op. cit. p.45; and Wyatt, op. cit. pp 39–40.
32. T. R. Nicholson, *The Vintage Car, 1919–1930*, p.244.
33. Adeney, op. cit. p.171.
34. *The Automobile*, July 1994.
35. Wyatt, op. cit. p.62.
36. Richardson, op. cit. pp81–2.
37. Adeney, op. cit. p.160.

38. Hill, op. cit. p.239.
39. Richardson, op. cit. p.81.
40. Hill, op. cit. p.257.
41. Thoms and Donnelly, op. cit. p.108.
42. Adeney, op. cit. p.161.
43. Ibid. p.162.
44. Ibid. p.165.
45. PEP Report, *Motor Vehicles*, p.67.
46. G. Bardsley, *Vintage Style*, pp45–7.
47. Morris Industries Exports Ltd, annual statistics to 1940, BMIHT archives.
48. C. Kimber, *Making Modest Production Pay in Motor-car Manufacture*, IAE Proceedings Vol. 28, Session 1933–4, p.445.
49. H. Edwards, *The Morris Motor Car, 1913–1983*, pp208–9.
50. Ibid. p.212.
51. SMMT statistic, quoted in PEP report, op. cit. p.10.
52. Ibid. p.59.
53. Adeney, op. cit. p.160.
54. PEP Report, op. cit. p.15.
55. Church, op. cit. pp149–50.
56. Hill, op. cit. p.261.
57. Thoms and Donnelly, op. cit. p106.
58. SMMT statistics, op. cit. p.10.
59. H. A. Turner, *Labour Relations in the Motor Industry*, p.59.
60. Church, op. cit. pp147–56; Adeney, op. cit. pp171–2.
61. Adeney, op. cit. p.171.
62. Church, op. cit. p.149.
63. G. Turner, *The Car Makers*, pp81–2.
64. Ibid. p.117.
65. Adeney, op. cit. p.172.
66. Ibid. p.170.
67. H. A. Turner, op. cit. pp192–3.
68. Ibid. p.194.
69. Adeney, op. cit. p.187.
70. G. Turner, op. cit. pp116–23.
71. H. A. Turner, op. cit. p.195.
72. J. J. Flink, *The Automobile Age*, p.261; also H. A. Turner, op. cit. p.194.
73. H. A. Turner, op. cit. p.275.
74. E. Wigham, *What's Wrong with the Unions?*, pp93–5.
75. Adeney, op. cit. p.190.
76. Ibid. p.191.
77. Thoms and Donnelly, op. cit. p.143.
78. Thomas, op. cit. p.234.
79. P. J. S. Dunnett, *The Decline of the British Motor Industry*, p.54.
80. Adeney, op. cit. p.191.

81. Thomas, op. cit. p.235.
82. Dunnett, op. cit. p.53.
83. H. A. Turner, op. cit. table p.59.
84. PEP Report, op. cit. pp47–50.
85. H. A. Turner, op. cit. pp139, 141–2.
86. Dunnett, op. cit. p.55.
87. H. A. Turner, op. cit., pp139, 271–5.
88. Ibid. p.273, and Dunnett, op. cit. p.53.
89. H. A. Turner, op. cit., tables pp108 and 110.
90. G. Turner, op. cit. tables p.37.
91. For a detailed study, see H. R. Kahn, *Repercussions of Redundancy*, especially pp 21–24.
92. Ibid. p.23.
93. H. A. Turner, op. cit. table p.59.
94. Ibid. tables p.139.
95. G. Turner, op. cit. pp101–15.
96. H. A. Turner, op. cit. table p.195.
97. Ministry of Labour Gazette, May 1961, quoted in H. A. Turner, op. cit. pp35–36.
98. H. A. Turner, ibid. pp284–6.
99. G. Robson, *Cars of the Rootes Group*, pp191–2.
100. Dunnett, op. cit. pp108–10; also H. A. Turner, op. cit. pp281–2.
101. H. A. Turner, op. cit. p.37.
102. Dunnett, op. cit. p.111.
103. Dunnett, op. cit. p.140.
104. Quoted in Dunnett, op. cit. p.142.
105. *The Times*, 22 February 1973, quoted in Dunnett, op. cit. p.144.
106. *The Listener*, September 1974, quoted in Dunnett, op. cit. p.141.
107. Ryder report, summary pp7–9 and chapter 9, pp31, 43.
108. Ryder, op. cit. p.34.
109. Ibid. p.40.
110. Ibid. p.42.
111. M. Edwardes, *Back from the Brink*, p.39.
112. Ibid. pp37–8.
113. Dunnett, op. cit. p.173.
114. M. Edwardes, op. cit. pp60 and 65.
115. G. Robson and R. Langworth, *Triumph Cars*, p.282.
116. Ibid. p.282.
117. Edwardes, op. cit. p.106.
118. Ibid. pp109 and 117.
119. Ibid. p.125.
120. For a detailed study, see Marsden, Morris, Willman and Wood, *The Car Industry*, especially chapters 2, 5 and 6.
121. Ibid. p.101.
122. Ibid. table p.131.
123. Ibid. p.10.

Chapter Nine

1. J. Wood, *Wheels of Misfortune*, p.139.
2. Ibid. p.173.
3. J. Daniels, *British Leyland, the Truth about the Cars*, p.122.
4. Wood, op. cit. p.192.
5. Ibid. p.222.
6. Ibid. p.250.
7. Ibid.
8. Ibid. p.187.
9. J. Wood and L. Burrell, *MGB, the Illustrated History*, p.110.
10. Ibid. p.111.
11. Wood, op. cit. p.182.
12. Ibid. p.182.
13. Ibid. p.176.
14. *Autocar*, 17 May 1973, p.20.
15. M. Taylor, 'Troubled Times', *Classic Cars*, May 1987, p.70.
16. Wood, op. cit. pp 173–4.
17. Ibid. p.249.
18. Interview with Jack Bellinger.
19. Wood, op. cit. pp179–80.
20. P. Williams and G. Winch, *Innovation and Management Control: Labour Relations at BL Cars*, p.28.
21. Wood, op. cit. p.250.
22. Tony Benn, *Against the Tide*, p.115.
23. Ibid. pp191–2.
24. Wood, op. cit. p.197.
25. Interview with Ron Lucas.
26. *British Leyland: The Next Decade*, pp12–13.
27. Benn, op. cit. p.287.
28. Ibid. unpublished diary entry.
29. E. Cray, *Chrome Colossus, General Motors and its Times*, p.519.
30. 'Opel Wheels to the World', *Automobile Quarterly*, 1984, p.106.
31. M. Moritz and B. Seaman, *Going for Broke*, p.186.
32. J. Bullock, *The Rootes Brothers*, p.235.
33. Moritz and Seaman, op. cit. p.187.
34. S. Young and N. Hood, *Chrysler UK, a Corporation in Transition*, p.290.
35. Moritz and Seaman, op. cit. p.188.
36. L. J. K. Setright, *Bristol Cars and Engines*, p.143.

37. C. Oxley, *Bristol, the Illustrated History*, p.266.
38. M. Taylor, *Jensen Interceptor*, p.131.
39. P. Garnier, *Donald Healey*, p.178.
40. Taylor, op. cit. p.132.
41. Garnier, op. cit. p.180.
42. Ibid. p.181.
43. G. Crombac, *Colin Chapman*, p.267.
44. Ibid. p.272.
45. Ibid. p.330.
46. 'Lotus Back from the Brink', *Lotus Remarque*, July 1983, p.1.
47. *The Independent*, 20 July 1992.
48. G. Courtney, *The Power Behind Aston Martin*, p.47.
49. F. McComb, *Aston Martin V8s*, p.91.
50. M. Bowler, *Aston Martin V8*, pp193–4.
51. Ibid. pp223–4.
52. Bentley Press Release, 20 July 1984.
53. *Car Mechanics*, July 1970.
54. Benn, op. cit. p.358.
55. Ibid. unpublished diary entry.
56. Ibid.
57. *British Leyland. The Next Decade*, p.47.
58. *Transcript of Press Conference by Mr Tony Benn and Sir Don Ryder on the British Leyland Motor Corporation*, 24 April 1975, courtesy Tony Benn.
59. *British Leyland: The Next Decade*, p.42.
60. Transcript op. cit.
61. *The Motor Vehicle Industry*, paragraph 238.

62. Ibid. paragraph 227.
63. A. Clausager, *Complete Catalogue of Austin Cars*, p.93.
64. Ibid. p.94.
65. Wood, op. cit. p.220.
66. *The Times*, 10 July 1986.
67. Benn, op. cit. p.320 and unpublished diary entry. Also see *The Economist*, 17 May 1975, p.220.
68. P. Skilleter, *The XJ-Series Jaguars, A Collector's Guide*, p.58.
69. P. Porter, *Jaguar Project XJ40*, p.46.
70. *Autocar*, 28 June 1975, p.22.
71. Porter, op. cit. p.47.
72. *The Economist*, 12 February 1977, p.107.
73. Ibid. 26 February 1977, p.101.
74. Ibid. 5 March 1977, p.88.
75. P. Whitehead, *The Writing on the Wall: Britain in the Seventies*, p.264.
76. M. Edwardes, *Back from the Brink*, p.54.
77. Ibid. p.54.
78. Ibid. p.175.
79. Ibid. p.174.
80. Wood, op. cit. p.226.
81. N. Lawson, *The View from No 11*, p.59.
82. *The Economist*, 23 August 1980, p.53.
83. *Motor*, 11 October 1980.
84. J. Prior, *A Balance of Power*, pp127–8.
85. Wood, op. cit. pp230–1.
86. Ibid. p.232.
87. Ibid.
88. N. Tebbit, *Upwardly Mobile*, p.278.

89. Clausager, op. cit. p.100.
90. M. Thatcher, *The Downing Street Years*, p.437–8.
91. Ibid. p.438.
92. Tebbit, op. cit. p.304.
93. Ibid.
94. Thatcher, op. cit. p.440.
95. Ibid. p.438.
96. J. Walton, *Escort, Mk 1, 2 & 3*, pp217–18.
97. *Autocar*, 6 November 1985, p.6.
98. A. Clark, *Diaries*, p.232.
99. *The Sunday Times*, 18 November 1990.
100. *The Sunday Times*, 24 September 1989.
101. *The Independent*, 18 June 1992.
102. G. Robson, *TVR, a Collector's Guide*, p.88.
103. *The Times*, 3 March 1992.
104. *Autocar & Motor*, 28 July 1993.
105. *The Independent*, 8 February 1992.
106. *Daily Telegraph*, 8 February 1992.
107. *The Times*, 21 April 1994.
108. *The Times*, 26 September 1986.
109. Thatcher, op. cit. p.679.
110. Lord Young, *The Enterprise Years*, p.289.
111. Ibid.
112. *The Times*, 2 February 1994.

Appendices

1. Interview with Ron Lucas.
2. Rawson Associates, 1990.

Bibliography

Addison, Paul, *Now the War is Over*, BBC, 1985.

Adeney, Martin, *The Motor Makers*, Collins, 1989.

Andrews, P. W. S. and Brunner, E., *The Life of Lord Nuffield*, Blackwell, 1955.

Baldwin, Nick, *A-Z of Cars of the 1920s*, Bay View Books, 1994.

Bardsley, Gillian, *Vintage Style*, Brewin Brooks, 1993.

Barnett, Corelli, *The Audit of War*, Macmillan, 1986.

Benn, Tony, *Against the Tide, Diaries 1973–76*, Hutchinson, 1989.

Bentley, W. O., *W. O., An Autobiography*, Hutchinson, 1958.

Bird, Anthony, *The Horizontal-Engined Wolseleys, 1900–1905*, Profile Publications, 1966.
The Motor Car 1765–1914, Batsford, 1960.
and Hutton-Stott, Francis, *Lanchester Motor Cars*, Cassell, 1965.

Bond, John R., *Sports Cars in Action*, Holt, 1954.

Bowden, Gregory Houston, *Morgan, the First and Last of the True Sports Cars*, Gentry Books, 1972.

Bowler, Michael, *Aston Martin V8*, Cadogan, 1985.

Bradly, Robert Penn, *Armstrong-Siddeley*, Motor Racing Publications, 1989.

Bullock, John, *The Rootes Brothers*, Patrick Stephens, 1993.

Burgess-Wise, David, *Complete Catalogue of Ford Cars in Britain*, Bay View Books, 1991.

Cannandine, David, *Aspects of Aristocracy*, Yale University Press, 1994.

Castle. H. G., *Britain's Motor Industry*, Clark & Cockeran, 1950.

Church, R., *Herbert Austin*, Europa, 1979.

Clark, Alan, *Diaries*, Weidenfeld & Nicolson, 1993.

Clark, Paul, and Nankivell, Edmund, *The Complete Jowett History*, Haynes, 1991.

Clausager, Anders, *Complete Catalogue of Austin Cars since 1945*, Bay View Books, 1992.
Essential MG T-types and Midgets, Bay View Books, 1995.
Jaguar, a Living Legend, Brian Trodd, 1990.
Original MG T-series, Bay View Books, 1989.

Collins, Paul, and Stratton, Michael, *British Car Factories from 1896*, Veloce, 1993.

Courtney, Geoff, *The Power Behind Aston Martin*, Oxford Illustrated Press, 1978.

Cray, Ed, *Chrome Colossus, General Motors and its Times*, McGraw-Hill, 1980.

Crombac, Gerard, *Colin Chapman*, Patrick Stephens, 1986.

Culshaw, D., and Horrobin, P., *The Complete Catalogue of British Cars*, Macmillan, 1974.

Daniels, Jeff, *British Leyland, the Truth about the Cars*, Osprey, 1980.

Davenport-Hines, R. P. T., *Dudley Docker*, Cambridge University Press, 1984.

Davy, John, *The Standard Motor Car, 1903–1963*, J. R. Davy, 1967.

Day, Kenneth, *Alvis, the Story of the Red Triangle*, Gentry Books, 1981.

Demaus, Brian, and Tarring, John, *The Humber Story, 1868–1932*, Alan Sutton, 1989.

Dunnett, P. J. S., *The Decline of the British Motor Industry*, Croom Helm, 1980.

Edwards, Courtney, Albert Fogg, *Motor Industry Management* (Institute of the Motor Industry), September 1986.

Edwards, Harry, *The Morris Motor Car 1913–1983*, Morland, 1983.

Edwardes, Michael, *Back from the Brink*, Collins, 1983.

Flink, J. J., *The Automobile Age*, M.I.T. Press, 1988.

Fraser, Colin, *Harry Ferguson*, John Murray, 1972.

Frostick, Michael, *The Cars that Got Away*, Cassell, 1968.

Garnier, Peter, *Donald Healey, My World of Cars*, Patrick Stephens, 1989.

Georgano, G. N., *History of the London Taxicab*, David & Charles, 1972.
The Classic Rolls-Royce, Bison Books, 1982.
(editor), *The Encyclopaedia of Motor Sport*, Ebury Press, 1971.
(editor), *The Complete Encyclopaedia of Motor Cars*, Ebury Press, 1982.

Golding, Bob, *Mini – Thirty Five Years On*, Osprey, 1994.

Hackett, Dennis, *The Big Idea, the Story of Ford in Europe*, Ford Motor Company, 1978.

Hill, C. P., *British Economic and Social History, 1700–1982*, Arnold, 1985.

Hubner, Johannes, *The Big Mini Book*, Bay View Books, 1992.

Jarman, Lytton, and Barraclough, Robin, *The Bullnose and Flatnose Morris*, Macdonald, 1965.

Jarrott, Charles, *Ten Years of Motors and Motor Racing*, E. Grant Richards, 1906.

Jennings, Paul, *Dunlopera*, Dunlop, 1961.

Kahn, H. R., *Repercussions of Redundancy*, Allen & Unwin, 1964.

Kimes, Beverly, and Clark, Henry Austin, *The Standard Catalog of American Cars 1805–1942*, Krause Publications, 1989.

King, Peter, *The Motor Men*, Quiller Press, 1989.

Kujawa, D., *International Labor Relations Management in the Automotive Industry*, Praeger, 1971.

Laban, Brian (editor), *The World Guide to Automobiles*, Macdonald Orbis, 1987.

Lambert, Zoe, and Wyatt, R. J., Lord *Austin, the Man*, Sidgwick & Jackson, 1968.

Lawrence, Mike, *A-Z of Sports Cars since 1945*, Bay View Books, 1991.

Lawson, Nigel, *The View from No 11*, Bantam Press, 1992.

Lloyd, Ian, *Rolls-Royce, the Years of Endeavour*, Macmillan, 1978.

Marsden, D., Morris, T., Willman, P. and Wood, S., *The Car Industry*, Tavistock, 1985.

McComb, F. Wilson, *Aston Martin V8s*, Osprey, 1984.
MG by McComb, Osprey, 1984.

McMillan, James, *The Dunlop Story*, Weidenfeld & Nicolson, 1989.

Minns, P. J. (editor), *Wealth Well Given*, Alan Sutton, 1994.

Montagu of Beaulieu, Lord, *The Brighton Run*, Shire Publications, 1990.
The British Motorist, Macdonald, 1987.
Lost Causes of Motoring, Cassell, 1960.
Rolls of Rolls Royce, Cassell, 1966.

Morewood, Steven, *Pioneers and Inheritors, Top Management in the Coventry Motor Industry*, Coventry Polytechnic, 1990.

Morgan, Bryan, *Acceleration, the Simms Story*, Newman Neame, 1965.

Moritz, Michael, and Seaman, Barrett, *Going for Broke, the Chrysler Story*, Doubleday, 1981.

Morton, C. W., *A History of Rolls-Royce Motor Cars, 1903-1907*, Foulis, 1964.

Nichols, Ian, and Karslake, Kent, *Motoring Entente*, Cassell, 1956.

Nicholson, T. R., *The Birth of the British Motor Car*, Macmillan, 1982.
The Vintage Car, 1919–30, Batsford, 1966.

Nixon, St. John, *Daimler, 1896–1946*, Foulis, 1946.
Wolseley, Foulis, 1949.

Noble, Dudley, *Milestones in a Motoring Life*, Queen Anne Press, 1969.

Nockolds, Harold, *Lucas, the First Hundred Years*, David & Charles, 1976.
The Magic of a Name, Foulis, 1950.

Nye, Doug, *British Cars of the 1960s*, Nelson, 1970.
The Story of Lotus, Motor Racing Publications, 1972.

Oliver, George, *The Rover*, Cassell, 1971.

Oswald, Werner, *Deutsche Autos 1945–1975*, Motorbuch Verlag, 1976.

Overy, R. J., *William Morris, Lord Nuffield*, Europa, 1976.

Oxley, Charles, *Bristol, the Illustrated History*, Crowood Press, 1990.

Pagnamenta, Peter, and Overy, Richard, *All Our Working Lives*, BBC, 1984.

Pevsner, Nikolas, *The Sources of Modern Architecture and Design*, Thames & Hudson, 1968.

Pimlott, Ben, and Cook, C. (editors), *Trade Unions in British Politics*, Longman, 1991.

Pither, Don, *The Scimitar and its Forebears*, Court Publishing, 1987.

Platt, Maurice, *An Addiction to Automobiles*, Warne, 1980.

Plowden, William, *The Motorcar and Politics 1896–1970*, Bodley Head, 1971.

Porter, Philip, *Jaguar Project XJ40*, Haynes, 1987.

Prior, Jim, *A Balance of Power*, Hamish Hamilton, 1986.

Rae, John, *Nissan/Datsun, a History of Nissan Motor Corporation in the USA*, McGraw Hill, 1982.

Rhys, D. G., *The Motor Industry, an Economic Survey*, Butterworth, 1972.

Richardson, Kenneth, *The British Motor Industry 1896 1939*, Macmillan, 1977.
Twentieth Century Coventry, City of Coventry, 1972.

Robotham, William, *Silver Ghosts and Silver Dawn*, Constable, 1970.

Robson, Graham, *A-Z of Cars of the 1970s*, Bay View Brooks, 1990.
The Cars of BMC, Motor Racing Publications, 1987
Cars of the Rootes Group, Motor Racing Publications, 1987.
The Rolls-Royce and Bentley, Motor Racing Publications, 1985.
The Rover Story, Patrick Stephens, 1988.
TVR, a Collector's Guide, Motor Racing Publications, 1993.
and Langworth, Richard, *Triumph Cars*, Motor Racing Publications, 1988.

Rose, Gerald, *A Record of Motor Racing, 1894–1908*, Motor Racing Publications, 1949.

Ryder, Sir Don, *British Leyland, the Next Decade* (abridged edition of the Ryder report), HMSO, 1975.

Saul, S. B., *The Motor Industry in Britain to 1914*, Business History V, 1962.

Sedgwick, Michael, *Cars of the 1930s*, Batsford, 1970.
The Motor Car 1945-1956, Batsford, 1979.
and Gillies, Mark, *A-Z of Cars, 1945–1970*, Bay View Books, 1986.

Sedgwick, Stanley, *Twenty Years of Crewe Bentleys 1946–1965*, Bentley Drivers Club, 1973.

Seherr-Thoss, H.C. Graf von, *Die Deutsche Automobilindustrie*, Deutsche Verlags-Anstalt, 1974.

Setright, L. J. K., *Bristol Cars and Engines*, Motor Racing Publications, 1974.

Skilleter, Paul, *Jaguar Saloons*, Haynes, 1980.
Jaguar Sports Cars, Haynes, 1975.
Morris Minor, Osprey, 1989.
The XJ-Series Jaguars, a Collector's Guide, Motor Racing Publications, 1984.

Slavin, K., Slavin, J., and Mackie, G.N., *Land-Rover*, Haynes, 1986.

Smith, Ian, *The Story of Lotus*, Motor Racing Publications, 1970.

Stanford, J., *The 30-98 Vauxhall*, Profile Publications, 1966.

Sutton, Dr Alan, *Malvernia*, Michael Sedgwick Memorial Trust, 1987.

Taylor, A. J. P., *English History 1914-1945*, Oxford University Press, 1965.

Taylor, Mike, *Jensen Interceptor*

Tebbit, Norman, *Upwardly Mobile*, Weidenfeld & Nicolson, 1989.

Thatcher, Margaret, *The Downing Street Years*, Harper/Collins, 1993.

Thomas, Sir Miles, *Out on a Wing*, Michael Joseph, 1964.

Thomas, David, and Donnelly, Tom, *The Motor Industry in Coventry since the 1890s*, Croom Helm, 1985.

Tritton, Paul, *John Montagu of Beaulieu*, Montagu Ventures, 1985.

Turner, Graham, *The Car Makers*, Eyre & Spottiswoode, 1963.
The Leyland Papers, Eyre & Spottiswoode, 1971.

Turner, H. A., Clack, G., and Roberts, G.,

Labour Relations in the Motor Industry,
Allen & Unwin, 1967.

Walton, Jeremy, *Escort Mk1, 2 & 3*,
Haynes, 1985.

Whitehead, Philip, *The Writing on the
Wall: Britain in the Seventies*, Michael
Joseph, 1984.

Whyte, Andrew, *Jaguar, the History of a
Great British Car*, Patrick Stephens,
1980.

Wigham, E., *What's Wrong with the
Unions?*, Penguin, 1961.

Wilkins, Mira, and Hill, Ernest, *American
Business Abroad – Ford on Six
Continents*, Wayne State University
Press, 1964.

Williams, Paul, and Winch, Graham,
*Innovation and Management Control:
Labour Relations at BL Cars*,
Cambridge University Press, 1985.

Williamson, Geoffrey, *Wheels within
Wheels*, Bles, 1966.

Womack, James, Jones, Daniel T., and
Roos, Daniel, *The Machine that Changed
the World*, Rawson Associates, 1990.

Wood, Jonathan, *Wheels of Misfortune*,
Sidgwick & Jackson, 1988.
and Burrell, Lionel, *MGB, the
Illustrated History*, Haynes, 1993.

Wyatt, R. J., *The Austin, 1905-1952*, David
& Charles, 1981.

Wyer, John, *That Certain Sound*,
Automobile Year, 1981.

Young, Lord, *The Enterprise Years*,
Headline, 1990.

Young, Stephen, and Hood, Neil, *Chrysler
UK, a Corporation in Transition*,
Praeger, 1977.

**Government Publications and
Annuals**

*Fourteenth Report from the Expenditure
Committee*, HMSO, 1975.

The Future of the British Motor Industry,
report by the Central Policy Review
Staff, HMSO, 1975.

*The Motor Industry of Great Britain
1945–1993*, SMMT.

Other Publications

British Leyland, The Next Decade, a report
by the TGWU with AUEW-TASS, c1980.

Newspapers and Periodicals

The Autocar (now *Autocar*); *Autocar &
Motor*; *Automotor Journal*; *The
Automobile*; *Automobile Quarterly*;
Business History, especially Volume 22,
1962, S. B. Saul, '*The Motor Industry in
Britain to 1914*'; *Car*; *Classic Cars*; *Classic
& Sports Car*; *The Cyclecar*; *The Daily
Telegraph*; *The Economist*; *The Financial
Times*; *The Independent*; *Institute of
Automobile Engineeers Proceedings*,
especially Volume 28, 1933–4, Cecil
Kimber, '*Making Modest Production Pay
in Motor Car Manufacturing*'; *MG
Magazine (USA)*, especially 1992, A. D.
Clausager, '*Who Owned MG?*'; *The Motor*
(later *Motor*); *Motor Car Journal*; *National
Motor Museum Trust Newsletter*; *The
Sunday Times*; *The Times*; *Veteran Car*.

Index